terra australis 21

Terra Australis reports the results of archaeological and related research within the south and east of Asia, though mainly Australia, New Guinea and island Melanesia — lands that remained *terra australis incognita* to generations of prehistorians. Its subject is the settlement of the diverse environments in this isolated quarter of the globe by peoples who have maintained their discrete and traditional ways of life into the recent recorded or remembered past and at times into the observable present.

Since the beginning of the series, the basic colour on the spine and cover has distinguished the regional distribution of topics as follows: ochre for Australia, green for New Guinea, red for South-East Asia and blue for the Pacific Islands. From 2001, issues with a gold spine will include conference proceedings, edited papers and monographs which in topic or desired format do not fit easily within the original arrangements. All volumes are numbered within the same series.

List of volumes in *Terra Australis*

Volume 1: Burrill Lake and Currarong: coastal sites in southern New South Wales. R.J. Lampert (1971)

Volume 2: Ol Tumbuna: archaeological excavations in the eastern central Highlands, Papua New Guinea. J.P. White (1972)

Volume 3: New Guinea Stone Age Trade: the geography and ecology of traffic in the interior. I. Hughes (1977)

Volume 4: Recent Prehistory in Southeast Papua. B. Egloff (1979)

Volume 5: The Great Kartan Mystery. R. Lampert (1981)

Volume 6: Early Man in North Queensland: art and archaeology in the Laura area. A. Rosenfeld, D. Horton and
        J. Winter (1981)

Volume 7: The Alligator Rivers: prehistory and ecology in western Arnhem Land. C. Schrire (1982)

Volume 8: Hunter Hill, Hunter Island: archaeological investigations of a prehistoric Tasmanian site. S. Bowdler (1984)

Volume 9: Coastal South-west Tasmania: the prehistory of Louisa Bay and Maatsuyker Island. R. Vanderwal and D.
        Horton (1984)

Volume 10: The Emergence of Mailu. G. Irwin (1985)

Volume 11: Archaeology in Eastern Timor, 1966–67. I. Glover (1986)

Volume 12: Early Tongan Prehistory: the Lapita period on Tongatapu and its relationships. J. Poulsen (1987)

Volume 13: Coobool Creek. P. Brown (1989)

Volume 14: 30,000 Years of Aboriginal Occupation: Kimberley, North-west Australia. S. O'Connor (1999)

Volume 15: Lapita Interaction. G. Summerhayes (2000)

Volume 16: The Prehistory of Buka: a stepping stone island in the northern Solomons. S. Wickler (2001)

Volume 17: The Archaeology of Lapita Dispersal in Oceania. G.R. Clark, A.J. Anderson and T. Vunidilo (2001)

Volume 18: An Archaeology of West Polynesian prehistory. A. Smith (2002)

Volume 19: Phytolith and starch research in the Australian-Pacific-Asian regions: the state of the art.
        D. Hart and L. Wallis (2003)

Volume 20: The Sea People: late-Holocene maritime specialisation in the Whitsunday Islands, central Queensland.
        B. Barker (2004)

Volume 21: What's changing: population size or land-use patterns? The archaeology of Upper Mangrove Creek,
        Sydney Basin. V. Attenbrow (2004)

terra australis 21

What's Changing: Population Size or Land-Use Patterns? The archaeology of Upper Mangrove Creek, Sydney Basin

Val Attenbrow

ANU
THE AUSTRALIAN NATIONAL UNIVERSITY

E PRESS

ANU
E PRESS

This edition © 2006 ANU E Press

The Australian National University
Canberra ACT 0200 Australia
Email: anuepress@anu.edu.au
Web: http://epress.anu.edu.au

National Library of Australia Cataloguing-in-Publication entry

Attenbrow, Valerie, 1942-.

What's changing: population size or land-use patterns? The archaeology of Upper Mangrove Creek, Sydney Basin.

Bibliography.

ISBN 978 1 74076 116 1 (pbk).
ISBN 978 1 921313 05 9 (web).

1. Aboriginal Australians — New South Wales — Mangrove Creek — Antiquities. 2. Excavations (Archaeology) — New South Wales — Mangrove Creek. 3. Mangrove Creek (N.S.W.) — Antiquities. I. Title. II. Title : Archaeology of Upper Mangrove Creek, Sydney Basin. (Series : Terra Australis ; 21).

994.4201

Cover: Upper Mangrove Creek between Loggers and Black Hands Shelters, August 1979. (Photographer Val Attenbrow).
Back cover map: *Hollandia Nova*. Thevenot 1663 by courtesy of the National Library of Australia.
Reprinted with permission of the National Library of Australia.

Series Editor: Sue O'Connor

Typesetting and design: Emily Brissenden

To Patricia Vinnicombe

Foreword

One of the most common problems in archaeology is the publication of excavations — a problem because it is done cursorily, or by someone else decades later, or not at all. The thrill of fieldwork past dulls as the enormity of necessary analytical tasks become apparent and the romance of further fieldwork calls. Those who do produce the results in a timely fashion should thus be honoured in the profession. Even more praiseworthy is when these results move beyond a dry catalogue to be presented in the frameworks not only of the original investigations but also of those which have arisen and developed during the years of analysis. This monograph is one such publication.

Val Attenbrow's archaeology in Upper Mangrove Creek was among the first pieces of research aimed at the scientifically rigorous understanding of an environmentally defined area. It attempted to sample the area and the sites in a theoretically justifiable way. These data, the original block of which was from a salvage program carried out by a public utility, were then enlarged and transformed by Val's perspicacity and persistence into a larger-scale, research-oriented PhD thesis. The core problem of the thesis in 1987 was whether a proposed 'intensification' of Aboriginal occupation during the later Holocene could be substantiated in a close-grained analysis of excavated data. The 17 years between thesis and publication have seen continuing research by consultants and academics. The original proposals concerning 'intensification' have been modified and new views and approaches raised. The question is no longer as simple as it first seemed. Environmental changes, better dating, more sophisticated technological understanding and a wider range of possible subsistence and land-use patterns can all now be seen as parts of a larger, more complex prehistory. This monograph not only discusses all of these aspects, but remains, in my view, Australia's best data-driven analysis of this proposal. Val's results demonstrate how complicated the archaeological record is and how apparently simple propositions wilt under careful scrutiny.

Val Attenbrow's archaeological career has been marked, in particular, by a commitment to regional archaeology. Her Honours and PhD theses were both concerned with areas of New South Wales. Her earlier employment, as a consultant and then with the National Parks and Wildlife Service (NSW), continued this focus. Her research since 1989, based at the Australian Museum, has seen the completion of the large-scale and successful Port Jackson (aka Sydney Harbour) Project and the beautiful and comprehensive publication, *Sydney's Aboriginal Past* (UNSW Press 2002). These, along with this monograph on Upper Mangrove Creek, establish her as a profound interpreter of the Sydney region's archaeological past and as someone who can contribute substantially to the wider understanding of Australia's Aboriginal past.

J. Peter White

Contents

Appendices

List of Figures

terra australis 21

List of Tables

Tables: Appendix 1

Tables: Appendix 2

Acknowledgements

Since the beginning of my research into the archaeology and prehistory of the Upper Mangrove Creek catchment in 1979, many people have helped in a variety of ways and at different times — during the initial salvage program for the Mangrove Creek Dam, during my PhD research project and, finally, during the transformation of the thesis into a published monograph. Fieldwork and analyses were carried out during the salvage program as a consultant to the NSW National Parks and Wildlife Service and as a PhD student in the Department of Anthropology, University of Sydney. Revision of the text and production of the monograph have been completed during my employment with the Australian Museum.

At the NSW National Parks and Wildlife Service (NPWS), I wish to thank the staff of the (then) Cultural Resources Division — in particular, Helen Clemens, Kate Sullivan and Sharon Sullivan. I also wish to thank staff in the NPWS Hawkesbury District Office: Brian Vile, Dave Lambert, Tony Williams and Ian Webb for their interest, help and advice on local matters.

The NSW Department of Public Works gave permission for me to have access to the Mangrove Creek Dam catchment so I could continue with my research work once the salvage project was completed. I wish to thank Alan Griffiths, John Palmer, Kevin Carter, Paul Gilbertson, Barry Hunt and John Madden for their assistance.

At the University of Sydney, I wish to acknowledge the support, help and assistance of the members of staff and students of the (then) Department of Anthropology throughout the course of my research — in particular, I wish to thank J. Peter White for acting as my supervisor, providing advice on all aspects of my thesis as well as looking after the administrative side of things; Richard Wright for providing advice on statistical matters; Roland Fletcher for discussions on theoretical issues and acting as supervisor when Peter White was away; Roland Fletcher, in association with Helen Clemens of NSW NPWS, for providing advice on sampling strategies for the catchment site survey; John Clegg for discussions on matters pertaining to all manner of things, and Ed Roper for equipping me with knowledge and skills about computers and computer programs.

At the Australian Museum, I particularly wish to thank Betty Meehan, Jim Specht and other members of the Anthropology Division for their encouragement and assistance in bringing this monograph to publication stage. In addition, I wish to thank the Museum's Photography Department, in particular Carl Bento and James King, for their expert and invaluable assistance in producing photographs and digitised versions of photographic figures.

The Australian National University's Department of Archaeology and Natural History provided a place for me to work in peace during 1996 and 1997 when I was updating the text at that time. Particular thanks to Ann Andrews, then of the Publications Department, who organised these facilities as well as providing an encouraging and positive welcome during my visits to the department.

During the many site survey and excavation fieldwork periods, many people helped. I wish to thank them not only for their hard labour, working long hours under sometimes difficult conditions, but also for the many useful and lively discussions which took place. In particular, I wish to thank Tessa Corkill, Kathy Perrin and Edna Turvey, who were constant members of the fieldwork teams. At the time of fieldwork between 1979 and 1982, there were no Aboriginal organisations or land councils established in the Gosford–Wyong region. However, several Aboriginal people assisted in the fieldwork at various times; they included local residents and NPWS site officers: Lindsay Bostock, Wayne Cook, Dallas Donnelly, Jenny Fraser, Peter Ivanoff, Glen Morris and Aden Ridgeway, as well as Phil Gordon from the Australian Museum.

Local residents provided advice on the existence of archaeological sites in the catchment and the general locality, and on many aspects of the local environment — in this regard I wish to thank Robert Thompson and family, Mark Swinton and Lionel Young.

Reference materials were provided by many people and advice was received during discussions held with numerous others. I wish to thank these people for the time they spent and the assistance provided: Peter Hiscock, Eugene Stockton and Dan Witter on stone artefacts; Robin Torrence and Todd Whitelaw on risk; Harry Lourandos on intensification; Tim Murray on theoretical issues; Philip Hughes and Marjorie Sullivan on geomorphology; Mike Barbetti on radiocarbon dating; Dan Lunney and Peter Smith of the NSW NPWS on animal behaviour; Pat Vinnicombe on potential habitation shelters and information deriving from the North Hawkesbury study; Mike Williams, then of NSW NPWS, on identification of stone materials; Ken Aplin and Su Solomon on the origin of faunal remains in archaeological deposits; Mrs J. Thompson and Doug Benson of the NSW Herbarium on the identification of plant remains; Brian O'Toole of the University of Sydney Sample Survey Centre on sampling methods; Anthony and Christopher George (my nephews) on calculating the average annual growth rates and writing a small computer program for this purpose; and Frank Sinn for mathematical advice. John Edgar more recently calculated the revised K-means employed in the final chapter. I wish to thank Roger Luebbers, Richard Robins and Mike Morwood for their timely responses to my requests for copies of unpublished documents. Peter Roy of the Coastal Studies Unit, Department of Geography, at the University of Sydney for advice on changing sea-levels and coastal morphology. Scott Mooney of the School of Biological, Earth and Environmental Sciences, University of New South Wales for advice on climatic change. For Chapter 7, data from some excavated sites were reanalysed to produce depth/age curves so that I could calculate artefact accumulation rates. In doing this, I did not consult with individual researchers to obtain information beyond that which was available in publications or public documents because of the number of sites involved. Lack of certain data about the deposit and stratigraphy in sites may well have led to some incorrect artefact accumulation rates, and I apologise to researchers who may feel I have misrepresented their data.

Fiona Roberts reproduced line drawings from my revised originals, and I thank her for her thoroughness and patience in providing the digitised versions.

I would like to give special thanks the late Patricia Vinnicombe, Kate Sullivan, Philip Hughes and Marjorie Sullivan, who provided much encouragement, stimulation and good advice, particularly during the formative stages of the project, but also through to the end. My thanks also to Phillip Hughes and Marjorie Sullivan for providing accommodation and a stimulating environment in which to retire during visits to Canberra when revising this monograph.

During the production of the monograph, several people read drafts of the chapters and provided useful comments and discussions. For their helpful comments and advice, which helped change my thesis into the present monograph, I wish to thank Sarah Colley, Richard Fullagar, Phillip Hughes, Margrit Koettig, Ian McNiven, Scott Mooney, Peter Roy, Jim Specht, Marjorie Sullivan and Robin Torrence.

Funds were provided by several organisations: NSW NPWS for fieldwork and photographic expenses and for radiocarbon dates; Carlyle Greenwell Bequest (Anthropology Department, University of Sydney) for radiocarbon dates and fieldwork expenses; the Australian Museum awarded me grant-in-aid funds for Ken Aplin to undertake the faunal analysis and, more recently, has paid for additional radiocarbon dates, as well as photographs and illustrations for the monograph. The last two years of the PhD research in the Department of Anthropology at the University of Sydney were carried out under a Commonwealth postgraduate award. NSW NPWS also gave permission for me to use their camping and excavation equipment as well as a 4WD vehicle during fieldwork periods, and use of their laboratory for the analysis of materials.

In acknowledging the help of the above people, I hold none responsible for any faults or omissions in the final product — these are my responsibility alone.

Finally, I wish to thank my husband, Barry Higgins, as well as my family and friends for their continued support and encouragement in my research endeavours.

1

Introduction

Often-used indicators of cultural and demographic change include changes over time in numbers of sites and stone artefacts. They have often been interpreted as indicators of population increase in continent-wide and regional prehistories in Australia. At a regional or local scale, variations in numbers of sites and artefacts over space and time have been used as the basis for proposing changes in land and resource-use patterns which include the redistribution of populations. In addition, changes in artefact numbers in individual sites have been used as evidence for the extent to which the use of specific locations varied over time — often referred to as changes in 'the intensity of site use'. Unprecedented large-scale increases in numbers of sites and artefacts were said by some researchers to have occurred about 4000 BP and to have been associated with the introduction of the 'Small Tool Tradition'. Furthermore, these quantitative changes have been part of the archaeological evidence used since 1980 in theories for late Holocene intensification and/or increased sociopolitical complexity in south-eastern Australia — a theme which became a major focus in Australian archaeological research.

In this context, the study of quantitative changes in the archaeological record of the Upper Mangrove Creek catchment has much to contribute. Of particular interest in the catchment data is the lack of correlation in the timing and direction of dramatic late Holocene changes in numbers of sites and artefacts. Most conspicuous are the differences in timing in the dramatic increases in sites and artefacts which occurred in the second and third millennia BP respectively, and a decrease in artefact accumulation rates in the last 1000 years, which contrasts strongly with the continuing increase in site numbers. Such trends and patterning throw doubt on claims that chronological changes in numbers of sites and artefacts reflect population changes. This study of the catchment data also clearly demonstrates that dramatic changes in numbers of sites and artefacts do not necessarily coincide in time with the introduction of the 'Small Tool Tradition', or other changes in the stone artefact assemblages, such as the appearance of backed artefacts, the increasing use of bipolar technology for core reduction, and variations in the abundance of certain raw materials. Other behavioural explanations may account for these dramatic changes in sites and artefacts and the ways in which they can be interpreted and explained depend on the assumptions that are made. For example, they could be the result of the reorganisation of habitation patterns and subsistence strategies, which included the adoption of different mobility patterns and other risk minimization strategies in the face of environmental change. If so, it is likely that such processes involved the restructuring of social relationships as well as technological systems.

Research aims and context — past and present

The aim of this study is to investigate ways in which chronological and spatial changes in numbers of archaeological sites and stone artefacts can be interpreted and explained in terms of demography and human behaviour, using the Upper Mangrove Creek catchment as a case study. The original research aim of my doctoral thesis, however, was to investigate pre-colonial land-use and subsistence strategies in the coastal regions of south-eastern New South Wales, that is, the land between the Great Dividing Range and its associated ranges and the ocean shoreline. This strip of land can be divided into two geographical/environmental zones: the coastal plain associated with the shoreline or maritime zone, and the coastal hinterland. The central NSW coastal hinterland, except for areas such as the Cumberland Plain and Hunter Valley lowlands (respectively, to the south and north of the Upper Mangrove Creek catchment), is predominantly forested hills, ranges and dissected sandstone plateaux, which is often very rugged country. The Upper Mangrove Creek catchment lies within the coastal hinterland (Fig. 1.1).

Field-based coastal studies in south-eastern NSW of the 1960s and 1970s focused principally on the excavation of shell middens in close proximity to the shoreline (e.g., Megaw 1968a, 1968b, 1974; Lampert 1966, 1971a, 1971b; Bowdler 1970, 1971, 1976). The coastal bias in this excavation work in conjunction with the interpretation of local historical sources led researchers to the viewpoint that the hinterland (usually referred to as 'inland') was used to a much lesser extent than the ocean and estuarine shoreline zones (Lawrence 1968, 1971; Poiner 1971, 1976; Lampert and Hughes 1974). Poiner and Lawrence proposed that most of the population was concentrated along the coastal shoreline and subsisted predominantly on marine resources. They claimed the hinterland regions were used only in times of hardship; that is, in winter and/or stormy weather when fish and shellfish were difficult to obtain. Lampert (1971a: 63–4) concluded that the upper deposits at Burrill Lake and Currarong represented the activities of people with wide-ranging economic interests (land, estuary and seashore), but with a strong orientation towards seashore resources. Later regional studies for the NSW far south coast and central coast by Attenbrow (1976) and Ross (1976) respectively led to models for site distribution and subsistence patterns in which the coastal hinterlands were occupied to a greater degree than proposed by some of the earlier researchers. These two literature reviews showed that inhabitants of the coastal hinterlands of these regions belonged to different clans who spoke different dialects (or, for the Sydney region, Ross claimed a different language — see also Ross 1988) from the people who lived along the adjacent ocean coastline. The Upper Mangrove Creek catchment was most likely part of the country of a hinterland group — a clan of the Darginung (Capell 1970: Map 1; Attenbrow 1981: 16–22).

In 1979, initial results from the Mangrove Creek Dam salvage project indicated that the catchment was an ideal locality in which to undertake a field investigation into Aboriginal use of the coastal hinterland. There were numerous sites with various types of archaeological evidence (e.g., archaeological deposits, pigment and engraved images, grinding grooves and scarred trees); there were stratified sites with chronological depth to the archaeological record going back ca 11,000 years; and the length of habitation recorded at individual sites with archaeological deposits varied (Furey 1978; Attenbrow 1980; Vinnicombe 1980 IX C: 6–11). It was also known that within the observed time depth, temporal changes occurred in various aspects of the archaeological record — in the stone artefact types and assemblages, in the technology, and in the raw materials from which stone artefacts were produced. It was thus with some knowledge of the catchment's archaeological record from the salvage excavations and within the above research context that I began my research project in the Upper Mangrove Creek catchment.

However, I considered the data obtained from the salvage project, which was restricted principally to the storage area (i.e., the valley bottom), were a biased sample and unlikely to be representative of the evidence for Aboriginal use of the total catchment. Additional fieldwork was therefore undertaken in that part of the catchment which lies above the storage area. An intensive survey of the upper part of the catchment in a manner similar to

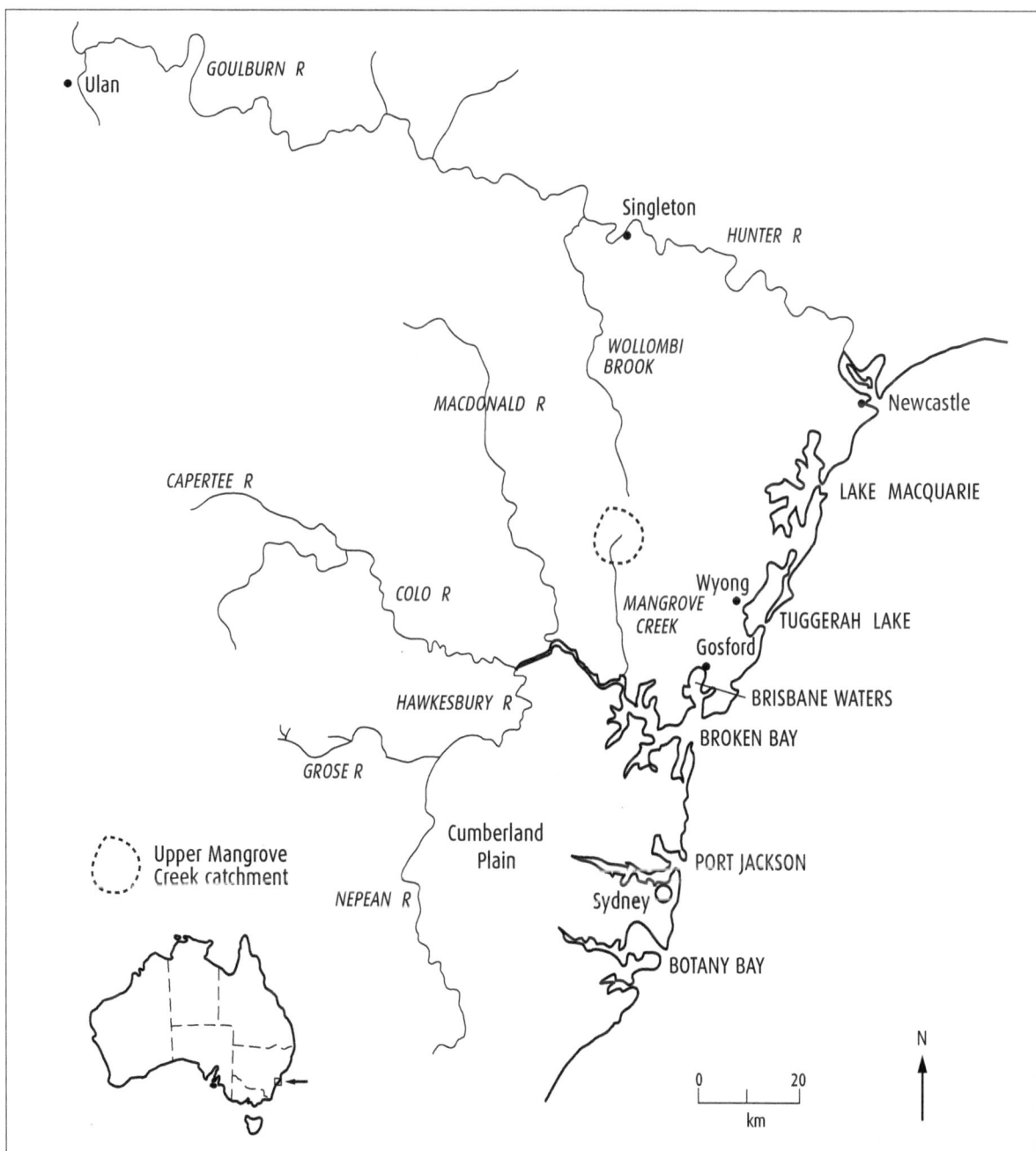

Figure 1.1   Location of Upper Mangrove Creek catchment, NSW central coast.

that undertaken for the storage area was not practicable in terms of the finances available and time constraints, so I designed a survey program to sample the catchment.

During the course of the research project it became clear to me that the nature of the archaeological evidence available from the catchment would be far more detailed than anything that was yet recorded for the coastal/maritime zone in the NSW central or south coasts. Thus comparisons between the two zones (coast and hinterland) could not be made at the same level. Such comparative work will have to wait until a study comparable to that undertaken in the Upper Mangrove Creek catchment is carried out in the coastal zone.

It also became apparent during analyses of the data that certain quantitative changes in the catchment's archaeological record were relevant to and had consequential implications for then current research issues relating to the interpretation and explanation of the mid- to late Holocene archaeological record in Australia (Attenbrow 1982b). These issues involved a perceived continuing increase in the numbers of sites and artefacts through time in many regions in eastern Australia, and the belief that dramatic increases in sites and artefacts were the product of dramatic population increases (e.g., Lampert and Hughes 1974; Hughes and Lampert 1982; Ross 1981, 1984; Beaton 1983, 1985). These changes also were argued to be associated with the introduction of the Small Tool Tradition, and were a principal line of evidence for advocates of intensification and/or increased sociopolitical complexity in the late Holocene (Lourandos 1983a, 1985a; Ross 1984; Williams 1985, 1987, 1988).

I considered that the chronological changes in the number of habitations established, the number of habitations used and the numbers of artefacts accumulated which I had documented in the Upper Mangrove Creek catchment were relevant to the then current models and hypotheses which incorporated population increase. Of particular relevance was the late Holocene decrease in the artefact accumulation rates which occurred in the first millennium BP in the catchment as a whole and in some individual sites. These decreases occurred during the same period as the numbers of sites inhabited and the numbers of sites established continued to increase. Changes in numbers of artefacts and sites could thus not both be indicators of population change. Also of significance was the fact that the documented quantitative changes did not necessarily all occur at the same time — dramatic increases in artefact numbers occurred in the third millennium BP, whereas they occurred in site numbers in the second and first millennia BP. In addition, the timing of these quantitative changes did not correlate with the timing of qualitative changes in the stone artefact assemblages.

Early in 1985, I altered the focus of my research. Rather than focusing on the interpretation of site/artefact distribution patterns across the catchment in a regional context, I began investigating temporal changes in quantitative aspects of the catchment's archaeological record and the factors that may have produced such changes. Broader issues which I began to investigate at this time included how quantitative changes, particularly those pertaining to numbers of sites and artefacts, had been identified in the past in other regions of eastern Australia, as well as problems involved in interpreting and explaining the changes. These investigations highlighted the limited nature of both the data that were then available and our understanding of the ways in which changes in population numbers and different aspects of human behaviour are manifested in the archaeological record.

This monograph is based on my doctoral thesis submitted in 1987, however, some changes have been made. In addition to restructuring the presentation of some information and discussions, certain sections of the thesis as well as some tables and figures are excluded as they are not directly relevant to the monograph's main theme. Thesis Chapter 2, in which I reviewed previous site and/or artefact distribution studies, is excluded. This chapter illustrated the type of studies that were based on spatial patterning of sites and artefacts across the land, the type of investigations that had included or had been based on site and artefact distribution studies in

Australia, and the way in which my study was similar to and/or differed from other Australian distribution studies. A review of sampling theory and the use of sampling in archaeological surveys in Australia is also excluded (in thesis Chapter 4), as well as discussions on spatial distribution patterns within the Upper Mangrove Creek catchment (in thesis Chapter 5).

Additional information has been included in the monograph to acknowledge the numerous studies that have taken place since 1987. In addition, a further four radiocarbon dates for sites in the catchment are included in the analyses (Chapter 6), and more recent dates from studies carried out in regions adjacent to the catchment are referred to (Chapter 7). These additional studies and radiocarbon dates support the findings of the thesis. The last four thesis chapters (8 to 11) have been reordered so that the chapter about climatic and environmental changes, which has been revised to incorporate the findings of current palaeo-ecological studies, is now Chapter 9. Thesis Chapters 9, 10 and 11 have been rewritten as Chapters 8 and 10. The final chapter (10) now presents behavioural interpretations of the catchment habitation and artefact indices in terms of changes over time in subsistence and mobility patterns and risk minimisation strategies — themes that were introduced but not explored in the thesis.

Research methods — an outline

The following lines of investigation were undertaken as part of the research project and have been presented in subsequent chapters in the following order.

- A review of interpretations and explanations proposed by other researchers during the 1970s and 1980s for quantitative changes in the archaeological record (Chapter 2).
- Archaeological site survey and excavation in the Upper Mangrove Creek catchment. The aim of the fieldwork program was to retrieve evidence of the length, nature, extent and intensity of Aboriginal use of the catchment. The fieldwork was designed to obtain an unbiased (and hopefully representative) set of quantified data relating to spatial and temporal changes in the archaeological record. The survey was carried out under a probability sampling scheme — a stratified random sample. All excavatable sites with archaeological deposits and a purposefully selected sample of potential archaeological deposits in rockshelters in the random sampling units were excavated (Chapters 3 and 4).
- An examination of factors likely to have affected the archaeological record and the data sets which form the basis of the analyses. This examination was undertaken to establish whether the documented spatial and temporal changes were likely to have been biased by natural (e.g., geomorphological), methodological and/or analytical processes. It was included so that I would be aware of, and perhaps could control for, at least some of the biases which may have skewed the results and subsequent conclusions (Chapter 5).
- Analyses of field data from the Upper Mangrove Creek catchment. The analyses were designed to obtain information on the spatial distribution of archaeological sites and potential habitation sites in the catchment, as well as the timing of initial habitation and temporal changes in the contents of each excavated habitation site. To quantify temporal changes in the numbers of sites inhabited and the numbers of artefacts accumulated, I calculated three indices: the rate of habitation establishment, the number of habitations used and the rate of artefact accumulation. The latter was calculated not only for each of the habitations, but also for the catchment as a whole and for each topographic zone. When applied to the combined data for the whole catchment, this index is called the local rate of artefact accumulation (Chapter 6).

- Examination of the data from several regions in eastern Australia on which explanations for quantitative changes have been and/or can be based. The reason for this examination was twofold: firstly, to examine the data on which researchers of the 1970s and 1980s had based their conclusions and, secondly, to establish whether the temporal trends documented for the Upper Mangrove Creek catchment were anomalous (Chapter 7).

- A re-examination of population-change and behavioural explanations of the 1970s and 1980s against the archaeological evidence on which they were based. This comparison indicates that simplistic relationships between numbers of sites/artefacts and numbers of people, or between artefact numbers and introduction of the 'Small Tool Tradition' or Bondaian assemblages, are unlikely to describe the full complexity of a region's prehistory (Chapter 8).

- A review of the evidence for climatic and environmental change during the Holocene and late Pleistocene in eastern Australia. Climatic and environmental change may have influenced human behaviour and thus may have been an indirect factor in producing the observed changes in the archaeological record. These discussions concentrate on the period during which the Upper Mangrove Creek catchment is known, from the archaeological evidence, to have been inhabited; that is, the last 11,000 years (Chapter 9).

- Interpretation of the Upper Mangrove Creek habitation and artefact indices based on prior models and theories relating to habitation, subsistence and mobility patterns and risk minimisation strategies (Chapter 10).

Research area

Mangrove Creek is a southerly flowing creek draining into the Hawkesbury River on the NSW central coast. The research area is the catchment of Mangrove Creek Dam, which was constructed between 1978 and 1982 to supply water for the Gosford–Wyong area. The catchment, which is 101 sq km in area, is about 80km north of Sydney Harbour (Fig. 1.1). It is north-west of Wyong, approximately 33km from the ocean shoreline and 28km north of the Hawkesbury River. Geologically, the area is part of the Hornsby Plateau of the Sydney Basin. It is heavily dissected sandstone country with a maximum elevation of about 200m. The valley floor at the dam wall has an elevation of about 25m above sea-level. Valleys are steep-sided with clifflines and small outcrops of sandstone on the ridgesides and along most of the creeks. Cliffs range up to 8m high.

The catchment was part of McPherson State Forest, except for small cleared areas of freehold along the wider parts of the valley bottoms and on the northern and eastern ridgetops adjacent to George Downes Drive. It was thus principally undeveloped land covered with eucalypt forest and woodland with rainforest species growing along the banks of less open and steep-sided gullies (Figs 1.2 to 1.4). Except for the area inundated by the dam waters, the area remains the same today.

Mangrove Creek is estuarine in its lower reaches, but within the dam catchment it is all fresh water. Estuarine conditions extend almost 10km (as the crow flies) up Mangrove Creek, i.e., about 18km from the southern end of the catchment. Tributaries in the upper parts of the catchment have been known to dry up in extremely hot weather, but even in these rare times water is available from small springs scattered throughout the catchment (pers. comm., Robert Thompson, Kulnura 1980). (For a fuller description of the catchment environment and general region see NSW Department of Public Works 1977; Benson 1978; Vinnicombe 1980; Attenbrow 1981, 1982a).

Figure 1.2 Forested land in valley bottom, looking north along Wattle Creek. Easter 1980. Photographer Val Attenbrow.

Figure 1.3 Lower slopes of forested ridgeside with Black Hands Shelter in large boulder in middle distance. Easter 1978. Photographer Val Attenbrow.

Figure 1.4 Periphery ridgetop on eastern side of catchment with Sunny Shelter. August 1982. Photographer Val Attenbrow.

Previous fieldwork in the Upper Mangrove Creek catchment

The first archaeological work in the Upper Mangrove Creek catchment was undertaken in the 1960s by N. W. G. Macintosh, who recorded the art and excavated the deposit in a rockshelter known as Dingo and Horned Anthropomorph. The drawings in one part of this rockshelter are spectacular and in some respects unique (as the site's name implies). The most interesting find in the deposit was some dark red ochre, which was said to match the colour of the drawings and which came from levels dated to 581±120 BP (GX-0070) (Macintosh 1965: 85, 96–7).

The catchment, however, became the focus of major archaeological work in the late 1970s when a dam was being built across the upper reaches of Mangrove Creek. An initial survey (Collier 1976) confirmed to the NSW NPWS the presence of Aboriginal sites in the storage area. A salvage program, to record archaeological evidence of the Aboriginal use of the area to be inundated — an area of 12 sq km — was subsequently implemented under the management of the NPWS on behalf of the NSW Department of Public Works. The salvage program included an intensive site survey of the storage (inundation) area directed by Kate Sullivan, then of the NPWS, and Louise Furey, consulting archaeologist (Furey 1978; Sullivan 1983: 7–9); detailed recording of pigment and engraved images by Ben Gunn (1979) and Leo Rivett (1980); an inspection of selected shelters with pigment images by Alan Watchman (1982); and test excavation and excavation of sites with deposits by Pat Vinnicombe and myself (Vinnicombe 1980: Chap. IX; Attenbrow 1981, 1982a, 1982b, 1982c). Geomorphological studies were undertaken by Phillip Hughes and Marjorie Sullivan (Hughes and Sullivan 1979; Hughes 1982), analyses of faunal remains by Ken Aplin and Klim Gollan (Aplin 1981; Aplin and Gollan 1982), and analyses of stone artefacts from Loggers and Deep Creek by Nicola Stern (1981, 1982). Subsequent site survey of a small area above the storage area and salvage excavation of an open archaeological deposit were undertaken by Theresa Bonhomme (1984, 1985) for additional works associated with the dam. Recently, information about all recorded open archaeological deposits in the catchment has been collated in a single report (Attenbrow 1997 [1998]).

I first became involved in the salvage excavation program in January 1978 as assistant archaeologist to Patricia Vinnicombe, who was then undertaking the North Hawkesbury Archaeological Project for NSW NPWS (Vinnicombe 1980). After the initial 1978 fieldwork seasons, it was realised that the salvage work would exceed that originally envisaged. This realisation and her existing commitment to the North Hawkesbury Archaeological Project, led Pat Vinnicombe to relinquish her position as project archaeologist for the excavation component of the salvage program and I undertook that role from mid-1978.

The salvage program, which was completed in 1982, revealed a wealth of archaeological data. Thirty-four sites were recorded: nine rockshelters with art and archaeological deposits, 17 rockshelters with archaeological deposits, two rockshelters with art, four axe grinding grooves, one open campsite and one scarred tree. For the salvage program, major excavations (between 2 sq m and 13 sq m) were carried out at four sites (Loggers, Black Hands, Mussel and Wattle Creek). Smaller areas (between 0.25 sq m and 1 sq m) were test excavated in 21 locations, 10 of which were initially recorded as potential habitation shelters; only four of the rockshelters proved to have sterile deposits.

The salvage excavations showed that use of Loggers Shelter began about 11,000 years ago. At the other sites with radiocarbon age determinations in the storage area, the age of initial habitation varies from about 8500 years to 1365 years ago. The type and amount of archaeological material in the sites also varies. Stone artefacts were present in all sites, but the number retrieved varied widely, the smallest number being five (from a test pit 0.25 sq m in area and 60cm deep). The largest number of artefacts was recovered from Loggers, where the greatest area and volume was excavated. The highest density of artefacts (number/kilo or number/cu m of deposit), however, came from Mussel, where an area of 1 sq m with a depth of 140cm produced 14,191 artefacts (Attenbrow 1981: Tables 6.6 and 6.8). Further excavation at Mussel after submission of the 1981 salvage report showed that the cultural deposit has a total depth of 180cm and provided an earlier radiocarbon age of 8730±70 BP (SUA-2410).

The research potential of the catchment was realised not long after the salvage program began and I registered as a part-time postgraduate student at the University of Sydney in 1979. This was well before the salvage program was finished and, for the next four years, both the salvage program and the research project were carried out simultaneously within similar research frameworks. The study area for my postgraduate work, however, consisted of the total catchment — that is, the land above the storage area as well as the storage area. To differentiate between the two studies in this monograph, I refer to them as the 'salvage program' and the 'research project'. The study area for the research project is referred to as 'the Upper Mangrove Creek catchment' or 'the catchment', and the area inundated by the Mangrove Creek Dam as the 'storage area'.

For the salvage excavation reports (Attenbrow 1981, 1982b), data from the storage area only were presented and conclusions relating to use of the area were drawn on the basis of those data. In my doctoral thesis (Attenbrow 1987) and this monograph, I concentrate and base conclusions on the results of a sampling program of the total catchment, which includes land within as well as above the storage area. Some sites in the storage area also occur in the catchment sampling units and thus the 'storage area' and 'catchment' data sets are not mutually exclusive.

2

Increases and decreases in numbers of sites and artefacts: a review of interpretations and explanations of the 1970s and 1980s

The archaeological record indicates that many aspects of Aboriginal life and culture — tool kits, technology, use of raw materials, and modes of subsistence — changed throughout the period of Australian prehistory. In addition, although finding them archaeologically is difficult, it is acknowledged that changes occurred in the demographic, social, ideological and political aspects of life throughout this period. Stanner (1965: 4) believed Aboriginal society and culture were 'the end-products of millennia of non-linear development' and 'were made up of forms and values far removed and transformed from an adaptive plane'. White and O'Connell (1982: 133) stated that the many varied life-ways recorded during the 18th and 19th centuries were 'the end-result of a long history, but their final form was developed particularly during the last few thousand years'; and Lampert (1971a: 70) said that the archaeological record for the past 5000 years in south-eastern Australia shows the formation of 'culture-areas' within which similar changes seemed to have occurred.

It is thus accepted that changes in the archaeological record indicate significant social and cultural changes within hunter-gatherer societies (e.g., Mulvaney 1975: 120–2; McBryde 1977: 225; Bailey 1983a: 185–6; Lourandos 1985a: 385; David and Chant 1995: 513–6). However, the direct or indirect causal relationships between social and cultural changes and documented changes in the archaeological record are far from clear, and the nature of the cultural changes that may have occurred and the reason/s for them have been much debated. Are economic, technological or demographic shifts being reflected in the archaeological record, or social, political or ideological changes (e.g., Fletcher 1977a, 1977b: 49, 146–7; Conkey 1978, 1984; Gamble 1982, 1983; Bailey 1983d; Beaton 1983, 1985); or is it a combination of these various aspects of life which together represent a late Holocene intensification associated with increasing complexity in sociopolitical organisation, which was accompanied by population increase (Lourandos 1983a, 1984, 1985a, 1985b, 1987, 1988, 1993, 1997)? The 'intensification debate' (as it is often referred to) has become one of the most contentious debates in recent Australian archaeology, and has its proponents (e.g., Morwood 1984; Ross 1984; Williams

1985, 1988; Flood et al. 1987; Barker 1991; David and Chant 1995: 361–3, 437–8; David 1990: 90–1; Ross et al. 1992: 109; Lourandos and Ross 1994) as well as opponents and critics, especially in terms of the forms of evidence and sources used (e.g., Rowland 1983: 72–4, 1989: 40; Yoffee 1985: 177–80; Hall and Hiscock 1988b: 16–19; Davidson 1990; Bird and Frankel 1991a; Sutton 1990; Williamson 1998: 144–6; Mulvaney and Kamminga 1999: 270–2; Lilley 2000).

Changing numbers of sites and artefacts are often involved in the proposed explanatory and interpretive models at a continental, regional or site level. Climatic and/or environmental changes are often involved in explanations as well, and, in this regard, regionalisation, risk minimisation and changes in mobility patterns are now used increasingly as contexts in which alternative models and hypotheses are proposed for changing numbers of sites and artefacts in association with other archaeological evidence. This chapter focuses on studies of the 1970s and 1980s in which changing numbers of sites and artefacts were the principal lines of evidence for claims of dramatic increases in population size (at a continental, regional or site-specific level), as well as part of the archaeological evidence on which the concept of late Holocene intensification was formulated.

In analysing archaeological evidence from the Upper Mangrove Creek catchment, I calculated several indices that document temporal changes in numbers of sites and artefacts. These indices are referred to as:

1.   the rate of habitation establishment;
2.   the number of habitations used; and,
3.   the rate of artefact accumulation.

I refer to changes in these indices collectively as 'the quantitative changes in' or 'the quantitative aspects of' the archaeological record (for methods of calculation, see Chapter 6). These terms have not been employed by all researchers, and other terms used include changes in the number of sites occupied, increases through time in numbers of sites and artefacts, changes in the concentrations of artefacts, changes in discard rates, changes in the intensity of site use, and changes in intensity of occupation (with more sites, artefacts and people).

Many researchers proposed or accepted that in Australia there was a continuing increase over time in the number of archaeological sites (especially habitation sites) established and/or used in various regions, and/or in the number of artefacts accumulated in individual sites, particularly in the last 5000 years (Johnson 1979: 39; Bowdler 1981; Morwood 1984: 371, 1986, 1987; Ross 1984, 1985: 87; Beaton 1985: 16–18; Fletcher-Jones 1985: 282, 286; Lourandos 1985a: 393–411, 1985b: 38; White and Habgood 1985; see also discussion in Hiscock 1986). These late-Holocene increases were often relatively dramatic compared with earlier increases.

Many 1970s and 1980s explanations for these late-Holocene increases were based on the acceptance or assumption that, after an initial dramatic increase, the indices continued to increase until British colonisation. However, several researchers documented decreases in the rates of artefact accumulation at individual sites (e.g., Schrire 1972; Stockton and Holland 1974; Johnson 1979: 94, 111; Kohen et al. 1981; Moore 1981; Smith 1982; Ferguson 1985; Morwood 1986, 1987; Hiscock 1984, 1988b), while Hiscock (1986) claimed a decline in site numbers as well as in artefact discard rates. Hughes and Lampert (1982) acknowledged decreased implement accumulation rates in the last 1000 to 2000 years at some sites on the NSW south coast, but their conclusions suggest they assumed the general regional or continent-wide pattern was for implement accumulation rates, and thus population size, to continue increasing. Most researchers who identified a decrease in the indices put forward various interpretations and explanations, but general population decrease, as opposed to redistribution of populations at a local or regional level, was not advocated.

In studies of other parts of the world where examination of temporal changes in the quantitative aspects of the archaeological record were included, population increase, climatic/environmental change, intensification and increasing cultural and social complexity also featured in explanatory and interpretive models. Many overseas studies used quantitative data to describe processes involved in the change from a hunter-gatherer subsistence mode to a farming (agriculture/animal domestication) and usually more sedentary lifestyle, or change within post-hunter-gatherer periods (e.g., Willey 1953, 1956; Schwartz 1956; MacNeish 1964, 1973; Binford 1968; Barker 1975). Other studies investigated temporal change within the period of hunter-gatherer subsistence mode in Africa (Mazel 1989a, 1989b), Europe (Mellars 1973: 268–73; Conkey 1978: 75–80; Gamble 1982, 1983, 1984; Bahn 1983; Bailey 1983b, 1983c, 1983d; Bailey et al. 1983; Clark and Straus 1983; Davidson 1983; Straus and Clark 1983) and America (Streuver 1968; Bettinger 1977, 1981; M. Hall 1981), but the periods under study in Europe and Africa were at a much earlier time than in the Americas and Australia. In Europe, they concerned the transition from the Middle to the Upper Palaeolithic, and in Africa the periods from the time of 'early tool-using hominids' (ca two million years ago) to the late-Holocene.

The following review of Australian studies divides the interpretations and explanations of quantitative changes in the archaeological record into two main groups:

1.   those that are based on the acceptance and/or assumption that the number of sites and/or artefacts continued to increase until contact;

2.   those that are based on the acceptance that there was a decrease in the number of sites and/or artefacts in the late-Holocene.

Within each of these two groups, the interpretations and explanations proposed by previous researchers are discussed under three headings:

1.   *Population change*: this refers to changes in the number of people or size of the population;

2.   *Behavioural change*: changes in behaviour relating, for example, to tool manufacturing and subsistence practices, and use of space within a site (this excludes explanations that relate directly to demographic changes involving birth and death rates);

3.   *Natural processes*: including geomorphological and biological processes which may have affected the archaeological record. These processes have been proposed as explanations only for the increases in the habitation indices (or to explain the lack of or low numbers of early sites).

The evidence used by Lourandos for population increase in his model of late-Holocene intensification is discussed under 'Increases — population change'.

In the following review and discussions, I take a broad view of the term 'population change' and include not only explanations which proposed general or continent-wide population change, but also redistribution of regional and local populations, and changes in the number of people- or person-days spent in a site or region. The population-change explanations and most of those that come under behavioural change could be said to be based on two opposing assumptions.

1.   The population-change explanations are based on an assumption that the ratio between the number of people (or number of person-days) and the number of habitations and/or artefacts remained relatively constant over time, and therefore the magnitude of the quantitative changes in the archaeological record is indicative of the magnitude of the changes in population size (national, regional, or site specific).

2.   The assumption underlying many of the behavioural-change explanations is that the quantitative changes are the product of changes in behaviour associated with habitations and stone artefacts, while the population size remained relatively stable. That is, the ratio between the number of habitations and/or artefacts and the number of people changed.

Smith (1982: 114), in discussing temporal changes in the quantity of occupational debris within a site, referred to changes in the number of people per unit time (Assumption 1 above) as 'simple functional change', and to Assumption 2 as 'a change in the rate of discard', which he called 'complex functional change'.

The dichotomy is not as extreme as these two assumptions imply. Some of the population-change advocates said that the magnitude of the changes in the archaeological record is not necessarily equivalent to the magnitude of the change in the population size; that is, the ratio between numbers of people and numbers of habitations/artefacts did not necessarily remain constant over time (e.g., Ross 1984: 235, 1985: 83). If this is the case, changes in behaviour associated with the use of habitations and/or artefacts must have occurred at the same time as the number of people increased or decreased. Changes in behaviour were probably associated with many of the population-change explanations (particularly those relating to redistribution of populations and 'intensity of site use'), so the headings 'Population change' and 'Behavioural change' should not be taken too literally.

In some of the studies reviewed, data presented by the researcher do not necessarily support the trends perceived by the researcher and/or the conclusions they reached. However, in this chapter I am interested in how perceived trends were interpreted and explained, and the data used are examined later in Chapters 7 and 8.

'Increases' in the archaeological record

Most of the researchers who proposed interpretations and explanations for dramatic or substantial increases in the quantitative aspects of the archaeological record drew their conclusions from a specific set of regional data they had studied, although they often drew on data from other regions for support (e.g., Hughes and Lampert 1982; Lourandos 1983a, 1985a; 1987; Morwood 1984, 1986, 1987). The discussions under each of the following headings are therefore presented in terms of regions as much as being the conclusions of individual researchers.

Population change

Explanations involving changes in numbers of people at a continental or regional scale have been divided into General Population Increase, Redistribution of Populations, Increased Intensity of Site Use, and Intensification and Increasing Social Complexity.

General population increase

Some of the earliest explanations involving population increase were put forward to account for greater numbers of excavated sites with Bondaian assemblages than sites with pre-Bondaian assemblages in south-eastern NSW (Wade 1967; Megaw and Roberts 1974; Tracey 1974). (For terminology and dating of stone artefact assemblages in south-eastern NSW, see Table 3.6, and Chapter 3, Temporal sequences.) Other researchers postulated increasing population as the explanation, or part of the explanation, for increases in quantitative aspects of the archaeological record; the appearance of sites in less favourable and/or marginal areas in the latter half of the Holocene; and/or an increasing use of offshore islands (e.g., Hallam 1972: 15, 1979: 10–12, 34; Lampert and Hughes 1974; Flood 1976: 32, 1980: 281–2, 1999: 248–9; Lourandos 1980a, 1980b, 1983a, 1984, 1985a, 1985b, 1987; Ross 1981, 1982, 1984: 267, 1985; Blackwell 1982; Hall 1982; Hughes and Lampert 1982; Sullivan 1982b: 16; Beaton 1983, 1985; Morwood 1984: 369, 1987; Ferguson 1985: 453, 498; Williams 1985, 1988).

Wade (1967: 39) was one of the earliest to comment on an increase over time in the number of inhabited sites in the *NSW south coast and Sydney region* (I use the term 'Sydney region' to refer to land south of the Hawkesbury River, east of the Blue Mountains and north of Wollongong). Wade said that in the majority of sites excavated near Sydney, no evidence of habitation was found earlier than the Bondaian or 'microlithic phase'. He considered the increase in site numbers to be 'indicative of changes in settlement pattern probably due to an increase in population'. He discounted the argument that the patterning may be due to non-random selection of sites for excavation, and concluded that:

> ... the increased number of inhabited sites near Sydney indicates the exploitation of food resources near these new sites, due to the pressure of population increase. (Wade 1967: 39)

Megaw and Roberts (1974: 9) stated that the evidence tended to suggest that the Bondaian phase (which they called Phase II) was a key period for maximum population expansion.

Increasing implement and sediment accumulation rates at three sites on the NSW south and central coasts (Bass Point, Burrill Lake and Curracurrang 1CU5/-) were used by Lampert and Hughes (1974: 231–4) as a measure of 'the intensity of site occupation'. Increases in these two indices were used to support their view that the sites were used more intensively over time which, in turn, they said, supported their hypothesis of population increase during the last 7000 to 5000 years along coastal NSW. They argued that the increase in stone-working coincided with the arrival of the Small Tool Tradition, but at the same time there was an increase in the rate of human-induced sedimentation. The concurrence of the increase in sedimentation and stone-working was seen as evidence supporting their hypothesis that the sites were being used more frequently, rather than the view that the increase in stone-working was simply due to the introduction of the Small Tool Tradition, that is, to qualitative changes in the artefact assemblages.

Lampert and Hughes (1974: 231) considered that within the past 7000 to 5000 years, two factors led to increased availability of marine food resources, which in turn would have led to the increase in population:

1. changes in coastal morphology resulting from the sea remaining at more or less its present level throughout the past 7000–5000 years, which extended the inter-tidal and tidal zone; and,

2. the introduction of new fishing methods.

Lampert and Hughes (1974: 231) hypothesised that if, along the NSW coast, it was generally true that hunter-gatherer population size was adjusted to the available subsistence resources, then there was a significant increase in the population of this area within the past 7000–5000 years. They (1974: 233) acknowledged that the archaeological evidence is equivocal with regard to demographic change, but believed it was outweighed by their ecological evidence. They concluded, however, that it may have been a purely local rather than a large-scale demographic episode, or it may simply reflect the arrival of coastal people at the present shoreline.

In a later paper, Hughes and Lampert (1982: 19, 24–6) used accumulation rates for implements and sedimentation as measures of the intensity of site occupation for five NSW south coast sites: Burrill Lake, Bass Point, Currarong 1 and 2 and Sassafras 1. They noted that it was after the sea reached its present position that the most dramatic increase took place — a six- to tenfold increase on average in the last 5000 years. At the same time, they noted that there is variation in the archaeological record at individual sites after 2000 BP:

> ... all of these sites show a marked intensification of site occupation during Holocene times that continued at least up until 2000 BP. After that time the trends diverged in that at some sites the

> increase in intensity of site occupation continued but at others the intensity levelled off or there
> was a slight decline. (Hughes and Lampert 1982: 19)

In support of their argument for population increase, Hughes and Lampert argued, on the basis of 20 sites excavated in the Sydney area and on the NSW south coast, that there was an increase in the number of new shelters occupied over time. They stated that the increase in sites between 8000 BP and 6000 BP reflected 'the arrival of the sea at its present level' (1982: 20), and that the two- to threefold increase in the numbers of sites occupied in the last 5000 years does not simply reflect the destruction of earlier sites, or the establishment of sites on newly formed sandy landforms.

The two sets of evidence, they added, must represent population increase since increased accumulation rates also occur at sites away from the coast (e.g., Sassafras 1, which is 35km from the coast), and increasing site numbers are seen as far inland as Willandra Lakes in western NSW. After looking briefly at a series of alternative hypotheses to explain the numerical increases, they concluded that 'only a rise in population provides an acceptable explanation' and that the 'postulated' population increase 'after 3000 BP' cannot be explained in terms of environmental change as the coastline had essentially taken its present configuration by then (Hughes and Lampert 1982: 26). The decreases in artefact accumulation rates that occurred at some sites after 2000 BP does not appear to be taken into account in Hughes and Lampert's population-increase models. The quote above is the only point in the paper where they referred to population increase 'after 3000 BP', as opposed to 'in the last 5000 years'.

One of the explanations put forward by Flood (1976: 32–3, 1980: 281–2) for the archaeological evidence from the *NSW southern uplands-tablelands* built on Lampert and Hughes' conclusions. Flood stated that the present evidence (i.e., the basal dates from habitation sites and the type of artefacts found) suggests the main period of occupation in the NSW southern uplands was within the last 5000 years. She hypothesised that the late occupation of the southern uplands was the result of population pressure on resources on the NSW south coast. This pressure followed the considerable population increase on the south coast, which occurred after the resources increased about 7000 BP to 5000 BP, when the sea-level stabilised. Consequently, there was a move to the less-favourable environment of the uplands. She (1976: 33) proposed that occupation of the south-eastern 'highlands' of Australia began with seasonal occupation of rockshelters on top of the coastal ranges (e.g., Sassafras I, which has a basal date of 3770±150 BP, ANU-743). Seasonal hunting was then extended into the southern tablelands, the Canberra region and the Monaro; later still, the region was occupied all year round.

Subsequently, after the analysis of the materials from Birrigai, with its basal date of 21,000±220 BP (Beta-16886; Flood et al. 1987: 16, 22) and a fourfold increase in the rate of artefact accumulation ca 3000 BP, which was maintained until the present (1987: 18), Flood et al. concluded that in the NSW south-eastern highlands there is evidence for 'an increased usage of individual sites (Birrigai), increased usage of marginal environments (highlands), and the increased establishment of new sites after 3000 BP' (Flood et al. 1987: 23). They saw no evidence for a late-Holocene de-intensification period at Birrigai, but that 'the evidence strongly suggests a redistribution of people through the landscape during the late Holocene'. They added:

> For these predictions to hold true, two consequences should be visible after about 3000 years:
> (a) a decrease in site use and a decrease in the establishment of sites in favourable zones, and (b)
> an increase in site use and an increase in the establishment of sites in marginal environments.
>
> If these conditions are met, then it is possible that the 'intensification' events initially identified
> by Lourandos entailed a re-organisation of human groups, and consequently a re-organisation
> of economic networks, through the landscape. Such a phenomenon may also have involved
> changes in population numbers, an issue which will have to be examined independently.
> (Flood et al. 1987: 23)

Redistribution of populations at regional and local levels

Hughes and Lampert's arguments for general population increase on the NSW south coast (outlined in the previous section) relate more specifically to the changes after ca 5000 BP. However, they (Lampert and Hughes 1974: 233; Hughes and Lampert 1982: 20) say increases in implement and sediment accumulation rates that occur in sites before 5000 BP could be due to a purely local rather than a large-scale demographic event, or may simply reflect the inland movement of coastal people as the shoreline retreated to its present position. Ross' and Flood's models, which are outlined in the previous section, also include local shifts in populations.

Models proposed by two other researchers, Luebbers (1978, 1981, 1984) and Beaton (1985), differ from those above in that they explain temporal changes in the number of habitation sites in different environmental zones in terms of local shifts in population. General population increase was included by Beaton in his interpretations, whereas Luebbers (1984: 91–2) said population increases are inferred by the developments he proposed for the Coorong, but were not substantiated by available data.

Using changes in site distribution patterns and site numbers, Beaton (1985: 2) identified, described and dated changes in the local environment and associated changes in the occupation history of *Princess Charlotte Bay in northern Queensland*. Beaton (1985: 5, 9) considered the region was unoccupied until about 4700 BP, and that initial occupation of the area was in rockshelters near the coastal foreshore and was of a minor nature. Chenier-building associated with coastal progradation began about 4000 BP, but it was not until about 2000 years ago that occupation shifted to the chenier plain; the earliest evidence for occupation of the nearby islands dates to about the same time, 2500 BP. As consecutive cheniers formed, they too were camped on, but use of the older cheniers did not cease. Between 1200 BP and 800 BP, the shell mounds were more numerous and larger than in other periods. During the last 600 or 500 years, use of the mainland foreshore and islands continued; however, chenier formation virtually ceased and, though foraging continued in the mangroves, shell-mound deposition ceased on the chenier plain and it appears to have been abandoned as a significant camping location. He (1985: 5–11) considered abandonment of the camps on the cheniers to be due to the loss of *Anadara granosa* beds, which changed the human focus away from the chenier plains.

The changes in site distribution patterns in the last 2500 or 2000 years, which involve an initial increase and subsequent decrease in site numbers on the chenier ridges, are related by Beaton to changing coastal morphology and resource availability. Beaton placed the initial occupation of Princess Charlotte Bay in the context of a wider trend which saw increasingly dense coastal populations in the late-Holocene. He postulated that the coastal economy was a recent adaptation, similar to the widespread incursions into previously marginal zones which Lourandos (1980a: 259) saw as a geographical and ecological expansion of the hunter-gatherer niche. Thus Beaton viewed the increase in coastal populations as 'an expression of the incorporation of yet another class of resource community into the total foraging economy of Australia', which he suggested happens in the late Holocene rather than late Pleistocene and 'is due primarily to increasingly dense populations' (Beaton 1985: 18).

Three projects were undertaken by Luebbers (1978, 1981, 1984) in the coastal areas of *south-eastern South Australia*. One project involved an area referred to as the 'lower south-east' South Australia (1978) and the other two projects were on the Younghusband Peninsula (northern and southern Coorong) (1981, 1984).

In *lower south-east South Australia* (between Robe and Cape Banks), Luebbers (1978) documented change in the character of sites which is associated with a change in site distribution patterns. He (1978: 108) identified an Early and Late Cultural Horizon on the basis of site content, morphology and stratigraphy. The Early Horizon lasts from ca 10,000 BP to ca 6000 BP; the Late Horizon is divided into an Early and Late Phase. He (1978: 307–9) claimed that significant changes in population and economic organisation occurred during the Late Horizon, that is, the last 6000 years, and that the formation of the coastal economy was a relatively recent event. The population changes postulated by Luebbers did not necessarily involve a general population increase, but rather there was a local shift in population with increases in some geographic and/or environmental areas, and decreases in others.

The early-Holocene occupation was widespread across eastern South Australia — along the coast, the lower Murray River, and associated with swamps, such as Wyrie (Luebbers 1978: 108). Luebbers (1978: 209–11) maintained that the site distribution pattern changed during the Early Phase (ca 5800 BP to ca 1300 BP) and again during the Late Phase (ca 1300 BP to contact). During the Early Phase, there was a low level of occupation, which was predominantly in the coastal hind-dunes with small numbers of sites in the sandhills 2km inland. Occupation appears to have been transitory and to have consisted of short-duration visits by shellfish gatherers. In the Late Phase, the character of the coastal economy shifted towards more intensive occupation, which was concentrated on the cliff tops and sandhills, with a few visits as far as 12km inland, and near the lagoon. More intensive use of marine resources and a more diversified economic focus on the coastal margin itself were seen along with a recurrent use of sites, more sedentary settlement and establishment of a network of communications and trade. Whereas microliths are associated with the Early Phase sites, they are rare or absent from the Late Phase sites.

According to Luebbers (1978: 302–3, 307), the increased occupation of the coastal strip occurred at a time of severe disequilibrium — some lagoons and environments were deteriorating and becoming less productive, while in other areas swamps and lakes were forming and/or increasing. However, Luebbers (1978: 215–16) said the differences in the archaeological record of the two phases indicate that the change was not related entirely to environmental factors, but that the differences suggest that reorganisation of subsistence strategies occurred on a large scale, which may have involved an increase in population, a higher frequency of visitation, or both. He added that this may have been accomplished by seasonal visits of longer duration, or by intensifying exploitation by more effective organisation and procurement skills, which then allowed more resources to be included in the menu.

Luebbers (1978: 303) related the postulated changes in the coastal strip to the wider geographic area and to general environmental changes. He referred to inland swamp areas such as Wyrie Swamp, which have been documented as being important to early-Holocene economies. He postulated that when conditions became drier after 3000 BP, and particularly between 2000 BP and 500 BP when swamps were completely dry and biomass was drastically reduced, the traditional way of life around the swamps could no longer be maintained and people were forced to find an alternative food supply. He (1978: 306) added that the environmental change would have affected the total southern drainage — during wetter conditions and in the mid-Holocene, Aboriginal people could have inhabited a wide range of well-watered habitats and presumably occupation densities increased accordingly. With the emergence of the dry phase, populations would have been forced towards more productive areas along the rivers and the coast. For the lower south-east, this meant concentrating on the swamps along the Woakwine Range and in the coastal margin itself. Solutions also involved construction of eel traps and the large habitation mounds of western Victoria, and the extensive fish weirs in South Australia. He (1978: 308) concluded that marine economies emerged in south-eastern South Australia 2000 to 1300 years ago as a result of substantial changes in the regional demographic structure after a major reduction in inland swamp-side resources.

Head (1983: 78–9) was critical of Luebbers' interpretation on the grounds that the lesser number of Early Phase sites in the coastal zone may be due to their destruction by coastal erosion. Luebbers (1978: 215) accepted that some Early Phase shell middens had been lost, but said the patterns of campsite distribution characterising each phase were still detectable.

For the *Younghusband Peninsula/southern and northern Coorong* (which is north-west of the lower south-east), Luebbers (1981, 1984) proposed a different explanation for temporal variations in site distribution patterns, site characteristics (e.g., their morphology, size and contents) and the age of different site types. However, he still associated archaeological changes in different geographic zones with environmental changes. The latter are associated with the formation of the Coorong, a shallow relict estuary bounded by the mainland on one side and the Younghusband Peninsula on the other. Luebbers studied the area in terms of three zones: the mainland, the peninsula's estuarine shore and the peninsula's ocean shore.

Luebbers (1981: 3, 32–3) related changes in the archaeological evidence to the biological productivity of the Coorong, which he said decreased in the past 6000 years. During this period, geomorphological processes closed the estuarine exits to the sea and changed the Younghusband Peninsula from an island (or island chain) to an area of continuous land joined to the mainland. While this gave people greater access to ocean marine resources, closure of the tidal gaps caused the Coorong to gradually silt up and estuarine resources to decline in abundance.

By the end of his 1984 study, Luebbers (pp. 3–4, 91–3) identified four phases of Aboriginal settlement. The earliest phases of coastal occupation focused on the mainland shores of the estuary and inland swamps (Luebbers 1981: 32). The peninsula (islands, at that time) was initially occupied about 6000-5000 BP by groups based on the mainland who made short visits. Visitors swam or canoed across the Coorong. As the barrier formed and dunes developed, occupation of the peninsula increased and a more diverse range of resources was exploited, including marine shellfish (*Plebidonax* syn. *Donax* sp.), which were transported from the ocean shore to camps on the estuarine shore (Luebbers 1981: 3–4, 32–3, 43–5, 1984: 91–3). The use of *Plebidonax* continued to increase and, from about 2000 BP, very large middens (mounds) representing recurrent occupation of preferred locations, were formed, which Luebbers interpreted as signs of increased sedentism. Camps were occupied along both the ocean front and the Coorong shore.

Luebbers thus interpreted temporal changes in the character and distribution of habitation sites on the Younghusband Peninsula as local shifts in population between the mainland and the peninsula in response to environmental changes which affected the reliability and availability of food supplies in the Coorong. At the same time, the environmental changes enabled greater access to ocean resources and ultimately increased sedentism and more permanent occupation of the Younghusband Peninsula. Luebbers (1984: 91) believed the change in land-use patterns and the magnitude of the increase in the size of some sites (mounds) can not be explained by increased sedentism alone. He argued for a net increase in the resident population at the coast, due possibly to migration. The role of population increase, he said, is a matter for conjecture.

In a different explanatory context, Bowdler (1981: 108–10, 1993: 130) interpreted the increasing amounts of archaeological materials at individual sites in the NSW Blue Mountains, the New England tablelands (NSW) and the Queensland uplands, and the late date for the initial establishment of sites in the NSW southern uplands, all of which occurred after 5000 BP or 4000 BP, as the 'first successful highlands occupation'. She explained that the reason for this increased occupation was the result of an increase in ceremonial activities which were focused in the highland regions of eastern Australia. The 'highlands or higher regions' were the venue for the 'rituals of exclusion' to which the women and children were not allowed to go. These activities were associated with the adoption of what Beaton (1982: 57) called 'communion food' — in particular, *Macrozamia* sp., *Microseris scapigera* (daisy yam) and *Agrotis infusa* (bogong moths) — which enabled large rituals/ceremonial gatherings to be held.

Bowdler, along with Jones (1977: 201–2) and Beaton (1982: 57–8), linked increases in quantitative aspects of the archaeological record to the introduction of the Small Tool Tradition and to increased ritual and ceremonial activities. Bowdler (1981: 108–10) concluded that the first successful exploitation of the highland regions of eastern Australia was part of the transformation of Aboriginal society some 4000 years ago, for which the Small Tool Tradition could be used as an indicator.

Increased 'intensity of site use'

Many researchers interpreted increased rates of artefact (or implement) accumulation at individual sites as 'increased occupation', 'an increase in the intensity of occupation', 'an increase in the intensity of site use' or 'increased human activity on the site' (Lampert and Hughes 1974; Stockton and Holland 1974; Moore 1981; Hughes and Lampert 1982; Smith 1982; Flood et al. 1987). The increases in the artefact accumulation rates were seen to reflect changes in:

1.   the number of people using the site, that is, variation in group size; and/or,
2.   frequency of visits to the site; and/or,
3.   the length of time spent at the site during each visit

(e.g., Smith 1982: 114; Ross 1985: 83).

The net effect of any one of these circumstances is that more person-days were spent at an individual site. Smith (1982: 114) referred to this as Simple Functional Change.

As outlined above, some researchers have used changes in artefact (or implement) accumulation rates at individual sites as evidence for general population increase (e.g., Hughes and Lampert 1982; Lampert and Hughes 1974 — see above), or redistribution of populations at a local or regional level (e.g., Jones 1985: 296; Lampert and Hughes 1974 for the period before ca 5000 BP). Lourandos (1985b: 38) suggested that 'greater usage of individual sites in a restricted area may merely represent more intensive usage of the region by broadly similar numbers of people' or that local group sizes were larger. Lourandos' phrase 'more intensive usage' could mean the same number of people visited more often or stayed for longer periods on each visit, or that more activities were carried out or a greater effort was spent on the same activities by the same number of people in the same period of time. His explanation could be seen as 'redistribution of local populations' or some smaller-scale event/s, but one of the outcomes is that there was a change in the number of person-days spent in an area over a particular period of time.

Small-scale movements of people and social reasons were proposed as explanations for changes in artefact accumulation rates as well, rather than widespread general population increase or movement of the local population from one environmental zone to another. By 'small-scale movement of people', I mean people using one site in preference to another within the same locality or environmental zone. This includes changes either from one habitation site type to another type (say, from rockshelters to bark shelters in open settings) or from one habitation site to another of the same type because of either preference or local environmental changes.

At sites in the Hunter River and the Macdonald River valleys, Moore (1981: 414–15) noted that at three sites the 'maximum occurrence' of stone artefacts was in levels dating from ca 2300 to ca 1700 BP. He interpreted this as a 'period of maximum activity' or as 'apparent intensification of occupation in sites at both ends of the Boree Track about 2000 BP' (Moore 1981: 414–15, 423). He associated the 'intensification' to an apparent late occupation of the Hunter Valley and subsequent establishment of contact between the different tribes at both ends of the track.

In the NSW Blue Mountains, Stockton (1970a: 297) noted that the sites without Bondi points (an artefact he considered to be diagnostic of the Bondaian phase) were not as deep and large as the 'caves' with Bondi points. He initially considered that this indicated either that the Bondi point was a domestic rather than a hunting tool, or that the Bondaian flourished in a period when the climate was comparatively cold and wet and shelter was in greater demand. After more extensive excavations, Stockton and Holland (1974: 56, 60) described 'peak concentrations' in stone artefacts in the Middle Bondaian levels of several sites: 'increasing abundance of flaked material in rock shelters reaching a peak of concentration at about 1000 BP'. They proposed that:

> In the absence of factors likely to disrupt steady deposition at a site … such concentration seems to indicate increased human activity on the site. Where this is verified at a number of neighbouring sites at the same time, one is led to consider a peak population and/or a peak of preference for cave dwelling. (Stockton and Holland 1974: 56)

They concluded that the growing importance of the Bondaian industry and its subsequent regression in the last 1000 years may well be a response to climatic factors:

> The concentration at the middle Bondaian levels may denote weather conditions which either demand permanent shelter or render mountain dwelling more attractive; subsequent regression again may signify either worsening mountain climates or decreased dependence on permanent shelter. (1974: 60; see also Stockton 1977c: 343)

> Bark shelters may have come into more general use in the Late Bondaian corresponding with lessened dependence on rockshelters (hence greater mobility). (Stockton and Holland 1974: 58)

In his reanalysis of the Devon Downs stone artefact assemblage, Smith initially queried whether quantitative changes in stone artefact assemblages at Devon Downs were principally due to:

> … variation in the amount of stone working carried out on site. This affects the total amount of stone in a deposit and is related to the availability of suitable stone and the intensity of occupation. (Smith 1982: 110)

However, after analysis of all materials from the site (i.e., faunal remains and ochre, as well as stone artefacts), and looking at alternative explanations, he concluded:

> The increased quantities of a wide range of archaeological remains — stone, retouched artefacts, emu egg-shell, ochre and animal bone — as primary or de-facto refuse [Schiffer 1976: 30–4] at Devon Downs shelter, suggests an increase in the intensity of occupation between 2000 and 4000 years ago. (Smith 1982: 114)

> The types of changes likely to be associated with changes in the rate of discard (availability of stone, amount of on-site knapping, changes in reduction processes, changes in seasonality, economic changes) do not account for the observed changes in quantity of occupational debris at this site. We are justified therefore, in interpreting this as simple functional change. The shelter was used more intensively between 2000 and 4000 years ago. (Smith 1982: 114)

Smith considered that there was an increase in the number of person-days spent at the site. He (1982: 115) stated that changes in both group size and the frequency of visits may have been responsible for the observed variations, but 'the link between increased use of a site … and population increase is unclear'. (The decrease in archaeological materials in the last 2000 years at Devon Downs is discussed below under Decreases in the Archaeological Record, Behavioural Change.)

Intensification and increasing social complexity

Lourandos (1980a, 1980b, 1983a, 1984, 1985a, 1985b) included quantifiable temporal changes in the archaeological record as support for his hypothesis for *intensification* during the last 5000 to 4000 years. He included general population increase, redistribution of populations and increases in 'intensity of site use' as part of his arguments.

In his use of the term, Lourandos saw intensification as a broad concept that referred generally to increases in both productivity and production, but he followed Bender (1978) in allowing the concept to refer to social as well as economic factors (Lourandos 1983a: 81; 1985a: 389–90). Thus the definition of intensification used by Lourandos was broader than that accepted by some researchers (e.g., Beaton 1983: 95). In addition, while intensification is usually viewed as a relatively short-term process, Lourandos (1985a: 391) considered it justifiable to extend its usage to include any perceivable long-term increases in the frequency of selected variables in the archaeological record.

Lourandos (1984: 30) argued that social forces were the primary element or influence which brought about late-Holocene changes in economic and habitation behaviour — it was a restructuring of social relations at the inter-group level, specifically associated with ceremony and exchange, which placed continually increasing demands on economy and production (Lourandos 1983a: 81, 1985a: 386). He suggested these dynamic processes may have resulted in increases in the complexity of social relations and economic growth, semi-sedentism and, by inference, population sizes. In emphasising a 'social' mechanism to explain late-Holocene change in Australian prehistory, Lourandos' approach contrasts with those studies which emphasise environmental and demographic factors as agents of change. However, although Lourandos (1985a: 403, 412) argued that the development of increasingly more complex social networks and alliance systems lies closely behind these processes of intensification, he also saw them stimulated in some ways by environmental and climatic changes and perhaps influencing, as well as being influenced by, 'the more elusive factor of demography'. Even so, he said neither environmental nor demographic changes provide adequate explanations for the late-Holocene archaeological changes in Australia (1984: 32, 1985a: 403), and he believed demographic change was just as much a consequence of other factors as a causal agent itself, and could not be regarded as a prime mover or considered separately from cultural or environmental influences.

Lourandos (1985a: 411) proposed that during the last 5000 or 4000 years, mainland Australia experienced a period of cultural expansion which was characterised by:
1.   rearrangements in settlement and economic patterns (towards more sedentary and intensive economies);
2.   an expansion in exchange networks; and,
3.   significant changes in other variables such as art and stone artefacts.
In some regions in south-eastern Australia, he considered that the changes in 'the intensity of occupation' appeared to have become progressively more marked throughout the late-Holocene (1985a: 411).

The main archaeological variables which Lourandos (1983a: 82, 92, 1985a: 391, 400) claimed to be general indicators (direct or indirect) of intensification during the last 5000 or 4000 years — and to suggest expanding economies (in terms of land and resources), increasing sedentism as sites and locales became more intensively used (i.e., a trend towards the establishment of longer-term base camps) and more intensive inter-group relations (exchange, ceremonies) — are:
1.   intensity of site usage (measured by sediments and cultural remains);
2.   rate of establishment of new sites;
3.   usage of marginal environments (arid, montane, rainforest and swampland);

4.   complexity of site economy (resource management strategy and wide range of resources and activities represented);

5.   complexity of exchange systems and ceremonial events.

He pointed out that the above characteristics appeared not only on the coastal strip but inland as well, and, as support, quoted the evidence from the NSW south coast, the Mangrove Creek Dam storage area, the NSW southern highlands, central Queensland highlands, NSW Blue Mountains, the lower Murray Valley, south-eastern South Australia and the Victorian Mallee, as well as western NSW, Koonalda Cave, the Strzelecki Desert, south-western Western Australia, Arnhem Land and Tasmania (Lourandos 1985a: 392–401). At this time, he (1985a: 403) said his interpretation suggested a general (but not necessarily uniform) population increase over time in most environments.

Although his investigations began in order to explain the presence and development of Aboriginal drainage systems and the cultural complexity documented in the 19th-century historical records of south-western Victoria (1976, 1977, 1980a), Lourandos built up a hypothesis which he considered was applicable Australia-wide. He saw the strength of the intensification model lying 'in the general consistency of the independent results obtained by a large number of researchers from a wide set of archaeological variables and ranges of Australian environment' (1985a: 403). Given the breadth of the evidence, he found it difficult to explain these archaeological patterns in terms other than a general amplification of socioeconomic behaviour. In his later writings, Lourandos acknowledged more recent archaeological studies and developed his model, placing the broad series of cultural changes within the last 4000 years or so and especially the last 2000 years (Lourandos 1987: 157, 1988: 149, 158) or the last 3000 to 2000 years (Lourandos 1993: 79, 80). He admitted that 'while the more recent processes of socio-economic intensification are becoming increasingly evident, their genesis, presumably in the mid-Holocene and earlier, is less clear' (1988: 160). More recently, in *Continent of Hunter-Gatherers*, he proposes what he calls a 'socio-demographic model' of cultural change (1997: 243, 318–21, 327–30).

As a package along with other evidence, Lourandos (1983a: 92, 1984: 31–2, 1985a: 391) thus saw quantitative changes in the archaeological record as indicators of intensification, and suggested (1985a: 402) that it would not be implausible for there to be an association between the archaeological data and demographic patterns (though he said all interpretations must be inferential [1983a: 92]). In this sense, one can say he believed population increase was instrumental in bringing about the quantitative changes in the archaeological record, though social change was the prime mover for intensification.

Ross (1984: 199–201, 238) proposed population increase as the most probable explanation for a tenfold increase in sites in the *southern Mallee (western Victoria)* during the late-Holocene period. A decrease in, or less substantial use of, the *northern Mallee* (Raak Plains and Lake Tyrrell) is proposed in the late-Holocene (Ross 1984: 180–2). Changes in site numbers are the principal evidence Ross used for her interpretation of the archaeological record in the Mallee, where she (1984: 15–16, 177, 182–4, 238, 265–6) saw two phases of occupation:

1.   the first phase, dating from ca 12,000–10,000 to ca 6000 BP: occupation concentrated in the northern part of the Mallee, around Raak Plains and Lake Tyrrell; the southern Mallee was rarely visited prior to 4500 BP;

2.   the second phase, after 4500 BP: more widespread occupation occurred throughout the study area and a tenfold increase in sites occurred in the south; the evidence suggests only short-term, small-scale use of Raak Plains in the northern Mallee at this time.

Ross (1981: 153; 1984: 15–16, 198, 266) linked the first phase of occupation in the northern Mallee to the early-Holocene when, she stated, lake levels were high and freshwater availability was greater than at present, and people based on the Murray River expanded their range. The second phase of occupation, she said, occurred during a period of environmental decline — after ca 6000 BP, the northern Mallee became more arid and the water sources became saline. At this time, the population retreated back to the Murray River and occupation was less frequent (Ross 1984: 198, 265). The south also became drier and thus, according to Ross (1984: 227), the increase in sites in the southern Mallee must lie away from general ecological or environmental explanations. She stated (1984: 238, 267) that the most likely explanation for the late-Holocene increase in sites in the southern Mallee is general population increase associated with intensification and social change in south-western Victoria.

Ross (1984: 236) proposed that the evidence from the Mallee may be an initial test of Lourandos' model of alliance network growth in south-western Victoria since:

> Any increase in population density in the wetlands is likely to have provided a trigger for expansion into more northerly districts. It may therefore be suggested that population growth in south western Victoria led to population expansion into the southern Mallee. (Ross 1984: 236–7)

> … archaeological evidence from elsewhere in south eastern Australia is certainly *suggestive* of a general increase in numbers of people in the late Holocene, it is most likely that the principal factor involved in population increase in north western Victoria was population expansion from the better watered areas outside the region. (Ross 1984: 236; see also Ross 1981: 152–3)

Ross (1984: 234) did not consider population change 'as an independent variable or a prime mover causing change', rather it was 'one element of the wider subject of social change, possibly associated with the development of complex alliance networks'. In this respect, Ross as well as Williams and Morwood (see below) were influenced by Lourandos.

Population increase was seen by Williams (1985, 1988) to be associated with the formation of mound sites in the late-Holocene in *western Victoria*. Mounds first appear after 2500 BP, that is, in the late rather than the mid-Holocene (Williams 1985: 5, 311; 1987: 318–19; 1988: 2, 216). All but one mound site are dated to later than 2000 BP (Williams 1985: iii, 316; 1988: Fig. 10.1). Williams (1985: 310, 316; 1988: 218–21) concluded that the appearance of mounds about 2500 BP suggests their appearance was in part related to climatic changes, being an adaptation to a more waterlogged environment, and was not related to technological change (i.e., to the Small Tool Tradition).

In 1985 (iii, 5), Williams proposed that population increase, shifts in alliance networks leading to intensification, as well as an environmental shift to a wetter climate about 2000 years ago, contributed to the changes; that is, the changes involved complex interaction between climatic shifts, demographic pressure and social variables. Williams (1985: 325) also stated that, because the formation of mounds may have been related in part to a shift in climatic conditions, it is difficult to separate the relative contributions of environmental factors from social and economic ones. However, in subsequent publications, Williams (1987: 319; 1988: 221) argued that the formation of mounds was associated primarily with changes in social networks, that climatic and environmental shifts played only a minor role in triggering change, and population increase occurred only after other major changes had taken place. It was changes in alliance networks in the region after 3000 BP (associated with expanding redistribution and alterations in social relations) that triggered increases in production (intensification), which was achieved by shifts in organisation of labour and settlements, and a more sedentary occupation of sites. The archaeological evidence Williams associated with these changes was the appearance of mounds and an increase in the number of sites in the late-Holocene (Williams 1988: 220–1). Evidence for the increase in population was an 'increase in sites at this time' (Williams 1988: 221).

For his study of the *central Queensland highlands*, Morwood (1984) synthesised the archaeological work undertaken by himself and several other researchers (Clegg 1965, 1977; Mulvaney and Joyce 1965; Beaton 1977, 1982; Morwood 1979, 1981). The archaeological evidence for the central Queensland highlands spans a minimum of 22,000 years, and Morwood (1984: 371) considered substantial changes occurred ca 4300 BP in the technology and range of stone artefacts as well as the rock art of the region. At the same time, he (1984: 358, 369, 371) said there was an increase in the intensity of occupation in sites with long sequences, this being measured by rates of artefact, ochre and sediment deposition. The evidence suggested to him (1984: 371) that all the changes were sudden. Because change occurred in these several types of evidence, Morwood (1984: 369) said the 'more intensive occupation' cannot be explained just in terms of changes in knapping behaviour.

He (1984: 369–71) believed the evidence from the central Queensland highlands supports Lourandos' interpretations, and required fundamental changes in Aboriginal social relations and mechanisms for exchange of resources, knowledge and genes, as well as an associated increase in the scope of ceremonial gatherings. Morwood (1984: 358) said that if the increased number of sites containing artefacts belonging to the Small Tool Tradition is a guideline, then Aboriginal use of the central Queensland highlands appears to have become more extensive. After reviewing some of the evidence from other regions, he (1984: 369) argued that 'the evidence from all mainland areas indicates that the earliest occupation of any intensity only occurred with the elaboration of stone artefact assemblages circa 4500 to 3000 BP'. He saw an 'abrupt increase' in site numbers applying to both rockshelters and open sites in diverse environments (NSW coastal and sub-coastal areas, Blue Mountains and Darling River). Morwood (1984: 369) concluded that 'In some (perhaps all) regions the sudden increase in site numbers and occupation intensity is best explained in terms of population increase'.

Morwood (1987) considered that some aspects of the archaeological record in *south-eastern Queensland* are explicable in terms of a model for increases in population and social complexity, and saw environmental change leading to greater resource availability as part of the model. Morwood (1987: 343) proposed that in the past 6000 years changes in climate and sea-level 'allowed extensive estuarine and mangrove areas of concentrated biological productivity to develop', which 'provided scope for an accelerating increase in population in the region, especially after 4000 bp'. He suggested that population increases were triggered initially by the expanded resource base, but later increases resulted from the development of social and demographic mechanisms which increased the effective carrying capacity of regional resources. The archaeological criteria for identifying population increases, he said, could include:

(i)   increases in the rate of site formation;

(ii)   increases in occupational intensity at sites; and,

(iii)   more intensive economic exploitation as indicated by the use of new habitats, resource types, extractive technologies and management strategies, etc. (Morwood 1987: 343)

The archaeological criteria for development of social and demographic complexity which he included were:

(i)   increases in the number of sites concerned with symbolic activities (e.g., art sites, bora rings);

(ii)   changes in site content (e.g., the appearance of exotic materials and technologies); and,

(iii)   increased status differences and restrictions on access to knowledge and specific localities, as reflected in a reduction in occupational intensity at some sites, or developments in technological and organisational complexity. (Morwood 1987: 343)

Morwood (1987: 343–7, Fig. 4) considered that the results of his own fieldwork and archaeological data gained by other researchers (e.g., Hall 1982; Lilley 1984; Nolan 1986) showed increasing site numbers and increasing complexity in the archaeological record in south-eastern Queensland. He believed the evidence from Gatton, Maidenwell and Bishops Peak (rockshelters with art and deposits) supported his claims for increases in social complexity. Morwood (1987: 346) said these sites were 'first utilised at 4300±300 bp right at the point of inflection in the site frequency curve, and associated with the appearance of new technologies and artefact types of diverse origin', and that 'it seems that more people were interacting more intensively and in new ways'. From other regional studies, Morwood saw accelerating increases in site numbers from about 4300 BP, which were associated with an increase in artefact discard rates at sites with long occupational sequences, as well as other changes in technology, artefact assemblages and economic activities. On the basis of this evidence, Morwood (p. 347) argued that major changes in population density and the scale and intensity of social interaction throughout Australia are indicated.

In an earlier article presenting the evidence from Gatton and Maidenwell, Morwood (1986: 117) was more cautious in his conclusions. He stated: 'If the growth of site numbers over time provides a general measure of population increase, then more people were obviously interacting more intensively, and in new ways.' He added (1986: 118), 'The question still remains open as to whether these recent developments in S.E. Queensland were environmentally, demographically and/or socially determined.'

However, in 1987 Morwood (1987: 348) concluded that the available evidence indicates that significant demographic and social changes occurred in south-eastern Queensland from mid-Holocene times at the same time as marked changes in post-Pleistocene resource levels and character. He explained:

> The increased population potential resulted not only from the development of new maritime resources in Moreton Bay but also from the now complementary nature of seasonal food abundances. The occurrence of inland, summer bunya crops and coastal, winter fish runs must have promoted the development of finely-honed, demographic flexibility and the required reciprocity network. Such developments would have led to continuing increases in carrying capacity, while increases in population would have led to an increased potential for the development of more complex patterns of exchange, and so on.

> If this scenario is correct, then these social changes, involving more effective use of available resources, would have diffused into adjacent areas, even where there was no quantitative Holocene increase in resource base. It is possible that the social, demographic and technological changes that swept through mainland Australia c.4000 BP were triggered in 'key' areas by the post-Pleistocene emergence of new resources *and resource configurations*. South-east Queensland is likely to have been such a key area. (Morwood 1987: 348)

Further comments on explanations involving population increase

The above explanations, which involve increasing numbers of habitations being established or used over time, and increasing numbers of artefacts accumulating over time, concentrate on population increase, intensification, increasing sociopolitical organisation and increased ceremonial activities. Many of the researchers saw the archaeological evidence reflecting general population increase; others related the increases in archaeological evidence in particular environmental zones to redistribution of local or regional populations, though general population increase is still seen by some to be part of the local movements or as a matter for conjecture. A change in preference for particular habitation sites (i.e., increased or decreased use of a site of the same type or of a different type), environmental or climatic change as well as the introduction of new subsistence technology are also included as part of the explanations for the increases in archaeological evidence.

All the 'population-change' explanations were based on the assumption that an increase in the numbers of sites and/or artefacts reflects an increase in the numbers of people who were using a region, or an increase in the number of person-days spent in a site or region. Of the studies reviewed, only Lampert and Hughes (1974) and Hughes and Lampert (1982) used *implements* as the units of measurement rather than all *artefacts* in the total assemblage, and used the sites as well as the implements as evidence.

Another assumption made in many archaeological studies, and one which still requires investigation, is that there was a direct relationship between the location of artefact use and artefact discard (Binford 1973: 242–3; Foley 1981b: 165). Hiscock (1981: 31–2) queried whether the 'number of stone implements per unit time' adequately measures the 'intensity of site usage', saying it is unclear whether using implement counts is any better than using the entire assemblage. He also questioned what these indices measure:

> What is being measured in this intensity index (of the number of implements per unit time) is mainly a reflection of technology; it will not necessarily indicate the numbers of people who are knapping, eating, sleeping, or walking in the site, nor the duration of those activities. If we require a general measure of 'intensity', that is one which involves more than one type of behaviour, we will have to measure more than one type of archaeological debris ... Ultimately, however, the usefulness of the exercise will not be measured in the cleverness or skill with which we produce a measurement, but in the strength of arguments defining the concepts of usage, intensity and their causal relationships to chipped stone accumulation rates. (Hiscock 1981: 32)

The use of more than 'one measure of intensity' was increasingly adopted by researchers (e.g., Morwood 1984, 1986, 1987; Smith 1982; Hall and Hiscock 1988a; Hiscock 1984, 1988b). Smith (1982: 114), however, cautioned against accepting quantitative changes in archaeological deposits as changes in the 'intensity of site use' and then stating in turn that they reflect broader changes in population size or settlement patterns.

Behavioural change

Explanations which do not involve an increase in population size (general, regional/local or site specific) were proposed for the increasing rates of stone artefact accumulation and habitation establishment over time. Many of these interpretations and explanations were put forward simply as suggestions without much discussion. Most alternative explanations were proposed in opposition to the idea that the increases in the archaeological record were produced by increases in the size of the population. Many explanations, however, were of a general nature and can be used to explain decreases in archaeological evidence as well as increases; for example, Hiscock's (1986: 48) 'underlying changes in the structure of discard behaviour, settlement patterns and economy'.

Increases in site numbers
Explanations involving behavioural change that were proposed for dramatic increases in site numbers, that is, for the lack of early sites, included:
1. in the latter half of the Holocene, sites were located in different situations to those of earlier periods and in these new situations the sites are more likely to have survived and/or to be visible today (Hughes and Lampert 1982: 24);
2. increased mobility (Attenbrow 1982a: 76; Rowland 1983: 73); people inhabited more sites within the same area, spending less time at each site, and perhaps travelling

shorter distances between sites than in the previous period; that is, the number of movements within the locality increased. This may or may not have been associated with movements between other resource zones or over longer distances;

3.   changes in hunting and gathering techniques (Attenbrow 1982a: 76–7);

4.   greater site visibility due to an increase in the number of stone artefacts manufactured by each person, which meant more artefacts were discarded and thus evidence for Aboriginal occupation (in the form of stone artefacts) for some periods is more abundant (Attenbrow 1982a: 77). (This would have involved a change in the ratio of people to artefacts);

5.   'more sites … may merely represent more intensive use of the region by broadly similar numbers of people' (Lourandos 1985b: 38).

Increases in the number of stone artefacts accumulated

Alternative explanations for increases in the number of stone artefacts accumulated involve qualitative changes in the stone artefact assemblages, changes in discard behaviour and changes in as yet undefined behavioural processes. The explanations involving qualitative changes in the stone artefact assemblages relate to changes in the number and range of artefacts and/or implement types manufactured, changes in the stone technology and changes in the stone materials used (i.e., typological, technological and raw material changes). Except for changes in discard behaviour and post-depositional breakage patterns, these changes are assumed to increase the number of stone artefacts or implements (tools) per person, thereby producing a change in the ratio of numbers of artefacts to numbers of people.

1.   Technological changes which produced more manufacturing debris (Hiscock 1981; Ross 1984: 200);

2.   different technologies may produce different numbers of implements (Hiscock 1981: 32; Ross 1985: 83);

3.   changes in stone tool technology, that is, 'when the maintenance tools of the core tool and scraper tradition were joined by a mixture of maintenance and extractive tools of the small tool tradition' (Hughes and Lampert 1982: 24–5; see also Ross 1984: 200);

4.   the adoption of new stone-working processes or reduction processes (e.g., blade technology) (Smith 1982: 114);

5.   a change in the stone material available or preferred, which affected discard rates (Smith 1982: 110–11; Hiscock 1982b: 43; Ross 1985: 83);

6.   increased range of activities for which stone tools were used, for example, the barbing of spears (Ross 1984: 200);

7.   shifts in technology which occurred about 2000 years ago when backed artefacts tended to drop out of assemblages and were replaced by quartz artefacts which are mostly unretouched. Williams (1985: 327–8) proposed this as a reason for a continuing increase in artefact numbers and not for the postulated increase at the beginning of the Small Tool Tradition.

The above explanations assume that the typological, technological and raw material changes resulted in more implements and/or more manufacturing debris being left in habitations, and that the number of people visiting or the number of person-days spent in the habitations remained the same. That is, it was the amount or type of activity that changed (see discussions in Lampert and Hughes 1974; Hiscock 1981, 1986; Hughes and Lampert 1982: 24–5; Kefous 1982; Smith 1982; Ross 1984, 1985). The raw material changes include changes in the percentage frequency of certain raw materials as well as the introduction of different raw materials.

Lourandos' (1985b: 38) statement that there was 'greater usage of individual sites in a restricted area' (presumably referring to sites where a greater number of artefacts accumulated over time) may simply mean a region was being used more often by broadly similar numbers of people and not that the general population increased. In this context, it may mean that a greater range of activities was carried out, or a greater effort (greater amount of time) was spent on the same activities by the same number of people, but the period of time (i.e., the number of person-days) spent at the site/s was the same as in the previous period/s.

Documented changes in the artefact accumulation rates in individual sites may also represent changes in the *'location of discard'* (Smith 1982: 114; Hall and Hiscock 1988a: 54), changes in site use which increased *post-depositional breakage* through trampling (Hall and Hiscock 1988a: 58), or in the *'location and use of hearths'* which thermally fractured artefacts and thus affects artefact counts (Hall and Hiscock 1988a: 59; Hiscock and Hall 1988: 101). Smith included changes in discard location under Complex Functional Change, which he said occurred when the rate of discard or amount of debris per person varied (though I would regard changes in the location of discard as Simple Functional Change). To invoke a change in the location of discard suggests that one assumes there was little or no change over time in (1) the ratio of artefacts to people, (2) the number of person-days spent at the location, and (3) the range of activities undertaken at the site. That is, people were simply discarding their debris in different parts of the site in different periods because they altered the locations within the site at which particular activities were carried out.

Natural processes
Several natural processes were proposed as explanations for the increases in the number of sites over time. These include geomorphological processes, the decomposition and degradation of materials, and the formation of palimpsests, as well as environmental changes and the rise in sea-level associated with climatic changes.

Geomorphological processes
Geomorphological processes were proposed as an explanation for the lack of early sites. These processes are said to have operated in several ways, all of which directly affected the archaeological materials, in contrast with other explanations which involve indirect agents of change.
1.   Some early sites or early habitation levels in sites (in all situations, including the coast and inland, and rockshelter and open sites) were destroyed by erosional processes, and there will always be fewer sites the earlier ones goes back in time.
2.   The rate of site destruction decreased in recent times due to less erosion associated with climatic or other environmental change.
3.   Early sites have been buried by alluvial deposits or obscured by vegetation growth and are not visible today unless some form of disturbance occurs to the ground and/or vegetation.
(See Worrall 1980: 81–3; Attenbrow 1982a: 77; Blackwell 1982: 50; Hughes and Lampert 1982: 24–6; Head 1983: 78-9; Bonhomme 1985: 33).

The rise in sea-level, climatic changes and associated environmental changes
The low numbers of pre-8000-year-old coastal sites, shell middens in particular, were acknowledged by many as being due to the post-glacial rise in sea-level, which would have inundated many sites associated with the earlier shorelines (e.g., Hughes and Lampert 1982: 19; White and O'Connell 1982: 52, 99; Godfrey 1989). Rowland (1989: 38–9) considered that even after the sea-level stabilised ca 6000 BP, minor changes in sea-level and coastal erosion by storms and cyclones could have destroyed many shell middens and could account for the large difference in the number of sites pre- and post-2000 BP along parts of the Queensland

coast. He also argued, in contrast with Lourandos, that even if Holocene sea-level and climatic changes were relatively small-scale and local by comparison with those of the Pleistocene, they may nevertheless have had very significant effects on Aboriginal populations, resulting in dispersion and a great diversity of economic and social adaptations, as well as population increase (Rowland 1983: 63, 71–4). Rowland proposed that such movements could account for the marked increase in artefact numbers and numbers of sites after 4000 BP.

Decomposition and degradation of materials
In the case of the absence or lower numbers of earlier coastal shell middens, organic materials such as shell are unlikely to have survived, particularly at locations which were infrequently used or were single-occupation sites (Hughes and Lampert 1982: 19; Rowland 1983: 73; Hall and Hiscock 1988b: 11). Degradation of shell will have led to the total disappearance of sites which consisted solely of shell, or to lower visibility of sites where only stone artefacts remain. The end result is greater numbers of more recent shell middens.

The formation of palimpsests
The formation of palimpsests may also be the reason for an apparent lack of early sites, particularly in areas predominated by open surface artefact scatters. By palimpsests, I mean assemblages in which the elements or artefacts from one or more periods have been mixed (Foley 1981b: 172–3; Robins 1997: 23; Holdaway et al. 1998: 1–2, 16). Palimpsests may result from geomorphological processes (e.g., erosion, deflation or conflation) or lack of sediment accumulation. The problem in dating the materials in such contexts in most areas of Australia arises principally because there are no artefacts which are temporally diagnostic of the 'early' Australian assemblages (the erroneously called 'Core Tool and Scraper Tradition', Mulvaney and Kamminga 1999: 44–7; Hiscock and Allen 2000: 103; Bird and Frankel 2001). Early artefact forms continued to be made after the appearance of 'new' tools associated with Holocene assemblages. These 'new' tools, particularly backed artefacts, are often taken as indicators of the now challenged concept of the 'Small Tool Tradition' (Hiscock and Attenbrow 1998: 59) or, in eastern NSW, as indicating the Bondaian phase of McCarthy's Eastern Regional Sequence. On originally unstratified or deflated open deposits (i.e., surface artefact scatters), where artefacts of several periods are mixed, it usually is not possible to distinguish artefacts which may be Pleistocene in age from those of a Holocene assemblage. As a result, in the absence of datable material, a whole site or assemblage is likely to be classified as Holocene in age.

Similar circumstances may occur in the basal levels of stratified deposits in rockshelters. If few artefacts were discarded during an early phase of use with limited sediment accumulation, later assemblages could become indistinguishably mixed with the earlier materials (Hughes and Lampert 1982: 19–20; Schrire 1982: 152).

'Decreases' in the archaeological record

Most 1970s and 1980s explanations for 'decreases' in the archaeological record related to rates of artefact accumulation (often referred to as decreased densities of artefacts) rather than to numbers of sites, and concern decreases in the late Holocene rather than earlier periods. However, decreased numbers of sites and artefacts at the end of the Pleistocene and during the early-Holocene in some parts of Australia were discussed; for example, by Hallam (1977) for western NSW, and by Ferguson (1985) for south-western Western Australia.

Hiscock (1986: 40) was one of the few to acknowledge a decline in site numbers in the late-Holocene. Hiscock did not put forward any one interpretation or explanation for the decreases he documented in both site numbers and the artefact accumulation rate in the last 800 years BP in the NSW Hunter Valley. He believed that late-Holocene Australian prehistory cannot be explained by population change, and that changes in the structure of settlements and technology may be better descriptions of what happened.

Several other researchers put forward explanations for decreases in artefact accumulation rates in individual sites, which are outlined below. No natural processes were proposed as explanations for the decreases in the late-Holocene, or the early-Holocene decreases in the arid zones, and the examples below are discussed under the headings 'population change' and 'behavioural change'.

Population change

The population-change explanations for decreases in the archaeological record of eastern Australia related to redistribution of populations and changes in the 'intensity of site use'.

Redistribution of populations

In the NSW Blue Mountains, Stockton and Holland (1974: 55) pointed out that there is a sterile gap between the Capertian and Bondaian assemblages in all stratified sites, somewhere between 6050 BP and 3360 BP, though the dates for these sterile layers are not the same at all sites. In support of their views, they referred to disconformities at Kenniff Cave, Noola and Capertee, all of which are highland sites. They interpreted the 'hiatus' as a gap in occupation at those sites (1974: 55) and a 'vacation of the mountains' (1974: 60). They suggested this may signify a response to or a worsening of the climate or might merely reflect social factors as yet unknown (1974: 46). Epidemic and cultural upheaval are mentioned (1974: 55).

Stockton and Holland concluded that population decline may have occurred in the Blue Mountains during two periods — between ca 6000 BP and ca 3500 BP and within the last 1000 years. The earlier decline, they indicated, may have been more widespread in other highland areas of eastern Australia, but it is presented in terms of redistribution of the local population (movement out of the Blue Mountains) rather than general changes in population size. The hiatus in Blue Mountains sites was refuted by Johnson (1979: 10, 23, 111), who said such sterile or relatively sterile zones may relate purely to use of the specific site and not to the general area.

Hallam (1977: 10) proposed that the large number of Pleistocene sites and the few late sites in the Willandra Creek system (NSW) are evidence that increasingly arid regions could not maintain their high Pleistocene population levels. Ferguson (1985: 1, 3) argued that the early to mid-Holocene archaeological record in south-western Western Australia is evidence of a progressive abandonment by a formerly large population, and, that from about 6000 BP to about 4000 BP, the entire region was virtually depopulated; a process which he said began about 10,000 BP. Ferguson (1985: 490–1) based his argument on a 'drop in artefact numbers' during the mid-Holocene at some seven, possibly nine, sites across south-western Western Australia (an area of about 220,000 sq km). Ferguson (1985: 493–7) acknowledged that rising sea-levels must have enforced a pattern of relocation to the east and the north. However, since the pattern appears to have been maintained in areas not directly affected by the rising sea, he (1985: 4) postulated that an increase in the distribution of thick sclerophyll forest due to climatic change moved the focus of human exploitation into adjacent desert areas, which would have been made more productive by the increased rainfall of the period.

Decreased 'intensity of site use'

One of Morwood's (1987, see above) criteria for 'development of social and demographic complexity' was 'a reduction in occupational intensity at some sites reflecting increased status differences and restrictions on access to knowledge and specific localities'. Morwood (1986, 1987) documented a decrease in stone artefact deposition rates about 1000 BP at two sites in south-eastern Queensland: Maidenwell and Gatton. At Maidenwell, since there was very little bone, and the charcoal as well as stone decreased in the uppermost deposits, Morwood (1986: 96, 98) suggested there was 'a significant reduction in the intensity of site use' after 1000 BP, though he considered that artistic activities continued. For the decreases at Gatton, Morwood (1986: 117) proposed a different interpretation — see below under Behavioural Change, Qualitative Changes to Artefact Assemblages.

Stockton and Holland (1974: 56) (as stated previously) interpreted trends in the NSW Blue Mountains sites as either a 'peak population and/or a peak of preference for cave dwelling'. If one accepts the former, this implies that they saw a population decrease in the last 1000 years; if the latter, then there was a change in the type of location that people preferred to inhabit; for example, a change from rockshelters to bark huts in open locations (1974: 48, 58; Stockton 1981: 13). Stockton and Holland (1974: 48) suggested, in addition, that increased mobility must also be considered as an alternative to the foregoing proposal. Johnson (1979: 111) suggested the marked fall-off in artefact concentrations in the last 500 to 1000 years at Capertee 3 may reflect not so much 'a shift in Aboriginal exploitation of **the area** but simply in the sporadic occupation of **the site**' [my emphasis]. He added that such sterile or relatively sterile levels in sites may be the norm rather than the exception and that they need not be regarded 'as hiatuses of occupation ... dense concentrations of artefacts may reflect length of stay and group size/composition rather than intensity of occupation of the area as a whole' (see comments above as well).

At Devon Downs (on the lower Murray River, South Australia), Smith (1982: 114–15) argued for a decrease 'in intensity of site use' or a 'decline in use of the shelter', as well as for a 'change in site function' after 2000 BP. He (1982: 114) based this on the 'marked decline in quantity of occupational debris and the utilisation of proportionately more shellfish in units 1 and 2'. Smith suggested:

> The absence of a marked decrease in the amounts of stone and bone in the upper levels of
> Fromms Landing No. 2 suggests that the decrease noted at Devon Downs shelter is the result of
> local factors. (Smith 1982: 115)

This interpretation contrasts with Mulvaney's (1960) earlier more general explanation (see below). The local factors suggested by Smith were migrations of the main river channel, which changed the suitability of the shelter as a campsite. He suggested the function of the site therefore changed:

> ... the consumption of more shellfish and the use of less stone on-site are consistent with more
> ephemeral use of the shelter as a 'dinner-time' camp by people exploiting the resources
> available in the nearby river. (Smith 1982: 115)

In this interpretation of the decreased artefact accumulation rates, Smith provided a more complex set of reasons, in which decreased intensity of site use was associated with changes in the local environment as well as subsistence patterns (i.e., behavioural change).

Behavioural change

Explanations for decreases in the archaeological record involving behavioural changes relate to changes in:

1.   qualitative aspects of the artefact assemblages — artefact types and raw materials;
2.   subsistence strategies, methods and/or technologies; and,
3.   intra-site discard patterns.

Qualitative changes in artefact assemblages

Qualitative aspects of the artefact assemblages include the types of implements made as well as the types of raw materials used in making items of material culture, and the explanations incorporate changes in both raw materials and subsistence methods/technology.

Several researchers proposed that decreased artefact accumulation rates in the upper levels of sites were due to a change in the raw materials being used, but the change was not simply from one type of stone material to another, it was a change from stone to another type of raw material. Mulvaney (1960: 74) and Ross (1985: 83) proposed that a change from stone (a durable material) to organic materials (e.g., bone, shell or wood, which have not survived) would leave a record which suggests that there was a decrease in the implements/artefacts manufactured. In his explanation for the sequences at Devon Downs and Fromms Landing 2, Mulvaney (1960: 74–5) suggested that organic materials replaced stone. He suggested that a switch to a greater use of wood, reeds and fibre in manufacturing artefacts (as described in the objects used at contact) was part of adapting to a riverine environment and may have been the reason for the decline in stone- and bone-working and deterioration of stone-working in the upper levels at these sites. He (1975: 243, 1969: 91–2) later adopted a more universal explanation which related to south-eastern Australia generally: 'a move towards the use of local organic raw materials and a decline in both the quality and quantity of stone utilisation'.

Schrire (1972: 664–6) pointed out that in the upper level at Borngolo (Arnhem Land) there was an abrupt drop in the density of stone and bone tools, but that it was not associated with a decline in the overall density of faunal debris. She (1972: 665–6) interpreted this as foraging continuing, and explained that the decline in stone tools 'may have resulted from the introduction of iron, for use as spear tips and knives', which was introduced by Macassan traders. No iron was discovered in the upper levels of Borngolo, but Schrire explained its absence by saying it was probably a rare and valuable commodity that was seldom discarded or mislaid.

Changes in subsistence strategies/technology

In Morwood's (1986) explanation for decreased artefact accumulation rates at Gatton, qualitative changes in the artefact assemblages (i.e., disappearance of backed artefacts) were seen to be associated with changes in subsistence behaviour. At Gatton, faunal remains, charcoal and sediment deposition did not decrease at the same time as the number of stone artefacts decreased about 1000 BP (Morwood 1986: 117). Morwood said the decreases in stone artefact deposition rates and the disappearance of backed artefacts and barbs, if taken in isolation, suggest a late decrease in the activity range and occupational intensity. However, he argued that the increased rates of faunal, charcoal and sediment deposition in the upper levels indicate the site was being used more intensively, while late increases in faunal diversity show a broadening of the resource base. He (1986: 117) concluded that 'If changes in the artefactual and faunal sequences are functionally related, then general changes in the technology of predation are indicated'. Morwood suggested there was a change in emphasis from 'individual pursuit strategies … in which both spears and macropods featured prominently to use of both individual pursuit and co-operative hunting strategies using nets'.

Morwood's explanation contrasts with that of Smith (1982: 114), who also associated the 'decline in occupational debris in the upper levels' at Devon Downs with a change in subsistence. Smith believed that change in 'the type of food consumed' on site after 2000 BP (from mammals to shellfish, i.e., food in smaller packages), appears to reflect a significantly different use of the shelter after 2000 BP. For Devon Downs, Smith (1982: 114) concluded that, although the decrease in occupational debris in the upper levels was associated with a change in the type of food consumed, there was also a change in the occupational intensity of the site (see previous discussion under Decreased Intensity of Site Use).

Changes in intra-site discard behaviour

It has been proposed that changes in the location of discard within a site may have produced apparent decreases in artefact accumulation rates (Johnson 1979; Smith 1982: 114; Hiscock 1984: 134). For Capertee 3, Johnson (1979: 94–5) said, 'The presence of a relatively sterile zone between the last major Capertian horizon and the succeeding Bondaian occupation does not necessarily imply any out-of-the-ordinary abandonment of the area' (see above sections), but it may 'reflect shifting patterns of site usage, so that any one part of the shelter was only used sporadically as a dumping or knapping zone'; that is, the locations of discard changed at the intra-site level (i.e., Bailey's [1983d: 127] functional change).

Discussion

Many interpretations and explanations proposed in the 1970s and 1980s for changes over time in the number of sites inhabited and the number of artefacts accumulated in individual sites centred on population increase, or population increase associated with intensification and increasing social and political complexity. There was, however, an increasing awareness that factors other than demography accounted for or were involved in these quantitative changes in the archaeological record.

In the studies reviewed above, increases in populations were often seen as part of a general continent-wide event, but the redistribution of people from one environmental zone to another (without necessarily involving general population increase) was also given as an explanation for an increase in either the number of sites or the amount of material at individual sites in a particular zone. Changes in the amount of material in individual sites (often referred to as changes in the 'intensity of site use') were also interpreted as reflecting smaller-scale changes within the same environmental zone; for example, a change from the use of one habitation type to another (rockshelter to open), or from one site to another of the same type, although it was often not explicitly stated. More 'intensive' use of a region by similar numbers of people was proposed also as an explanation for increased numbers of sites and greater amounts of material in individual sites, as well as an expansion into the 'eastern highlands' associated with increased ceremonial activities.

Other interpretations and/or explanations for increasing archaeological evidence included changes in the typology, technology or raw materials in the stone artefact assemblages (which I refer to as qualitative changes), changes in hunting and gathering techniques/methods/strategies (including mobility), as well as environmental, geomorphological and other site formation processes. Climatic or environmental changes were frequently seen as contributing factors for a significant or dramatic increase in the number of sites at a particular time, though some researchers gave these changes a determining role. Climatic and/or environmental changes were seen as agents in arguments for general population increase (where they were seen as influential or contributing factors), redistribution of populations from one zone to another (where they played a more 'determining' role) and changes in the preference for one habitation type over another. Many researchers proposed that a combination of factors may have led to the present archaeological record. The population-change advocates usually include environmental and behavioural factors in their models, with variations between their models occurring because of the prominence given to different factors.

Decreases in site numbers and artefacts were less often acknowledged. Part of the reason for this may be the scale at which people viewed the archaeological record; that is, they were looking for differences between the pre-5000 and post-5000-year period or the pre-4000 and post-4000-year period (e.g., Bowdler 1981; Ross 1985). Such broad divisions are unable to reveal a decrease that occurred in the last 1000 or 2000 years BP. Most interpretations and explanations for 'decreases' were similar to those given for 'increases', although Stockton and Holland (1974: 46, 48, 55, 60) also suggested a changing preference for open campsites (bark huts) rather than rockshelters, 'social factors as yet unknown' and 'epidemic and cultural upheaval'. Morwood (1987: 343) proposed 'increased status differences and restrictions on access to knowledge and specific localities' and Mulvaney (1960, 1969, 1975) and Schrire (1972) suggested changes from one raw material (stone) to another which has not been preserved (organic) or one which was not left behind (iron). The presence of organic materials (shell or bone artefacts and food refuse) which survive in the upper levels of many sites has allowed more complex and/or plausible behavioural explanations to be proposed for decreases in stone artefacts in the late-Holocene (e.g., Mulvaney 1960, 1975; Smith 1982; Schrire 1972; Morwood 1986, 1987), than for low artefact numbers and accumulation rates in early-Holocene and late-Pleistocene levels. Most of the alternative explanations for population increase or 'increasing intensity of site use' were given as brief, relatively general statements which were not investigated in any detail.

Although the idea of population increase appears to have acquired prominence in the literature in the 1980s, the concept of population decrease, albeit usually regional, was not missing in earlier work; for example, Stockton and Holland (1974) in eastern Australia, and Hallam (1977) and Ferguson (1985) for other parts of Australia. The explanations put forward by Stockton and Holland (1974: 55, 60) for the excavated sequences in the NSW Blue Mountains included suggestions that there was an early-Holocene hiatus or population decline between ca 6000 BP and ca 3500 BP, a middle Bondaian peak in occupation between ca 3500 BP and ca 1000 BP, and that, after ca 1000 BP, there was a decline in the population of the Blue Mountains. Stockton and Holland interpreted their evidence as shifts in population from one area to another. Hiscock (1986: 47) said that while the decline in artefact accumulation rates could be interpreted as either a reversal of intensification or a decrease in population, it need not imply any devolution — it may simply reflect changes in nature and structure of settlement, technology or resource use. In most studies advocating population increase, the evidence was an increasing number of habitations established and/or used. In contrast, apart from Hiscock (1986), studies including population decrease based their interpretations on a decrease in the number of artefacts or in the artefact accumulation rates at sites.

In studies where continuing population increase was claimed, a long-term increase was usually implied — slow at first but with a more dramatic rate of increase in the mid- or late-Holocene; the population size at contact was assumed to be the maximum reached throughout the history of Aboriginal occupation of Australia (Lourandos 1980a: 245, 1985b; Morwood 1984; Ross 1984: 202–6; Beaton 1985: 16). Some (e.g., Birdsell 1977: 149; Ross 1985: 81) accepted that short-term fluctuations occurred, although they did not indicate the length of the period over which they assumed a short-term decrease would have extended. Beaton (1985: 17) acknowledged that population changes in Australia may have been different at different times in different places, but he (1983: 96) argued that something on a continental scale happened in the mid-Holocene. He claimed a simple population increase model would adequately account for all the archaeological expressions (increase in number of sites, increased use of some sites, increased use of marginal environments, and an apparent increase in communication) without reference to social transformations or restructured economies. He stated:

> If the gross volume and overall distribution of archaeological remains even roughly reflects the numbers and distribution of people then what we already know about the abundance of mid- to late-Holocene archaeological sites should be sufficient justification for us to hypothesise that the Australian population had its significant growth period beginning about 4000 or 5000 years ago. (Beaton 1983: 96)

Beaton's model for population increase contrasts with some of the models, such as Birdsell's (1957, 1977), which had the 'ceiling' being reached early in prehistory (ca 2000 years [1957] or ca 5000 years [1977] after colonisation) and then population size remaining stable for the greater part of Aboriginal occupation (see discussions in Lourandos 1980a: 256; Beaton 1983, 1985; Ross 1984: 202–7). Beaton's (1983: 96) conclusion that 'the Australian population had its significant growth period beginning about 4000 or 5000 years ago' could be right, but is too simplistic.

The 1970s and 1980s studies document both decreases and increases in artefact accumulation rates, habitation establishment rates, and the numbers of habitations used in the late-Pleistocene, early-Holocene and late-Holocene archaeological records of many regions, although they were documented more often for the latter half of the Holocene. If one assumes these quantitative changes in the archaeological record by themselves indicate variations in population size, then the evidence suggests that population levels in some regions may have altered quite significantly before 5000 BP as well as after 5000 BP, and that changes in both periods included population decreases as well as increases. The assertions of continuously increasing population sizes in some regions in the late-Holocene are not sustainable, and whether postulated redistributions in local and regional populations had any relationship to overall continental trends cannot be determined. Equally, if one assumes that the quantitative changes are indicative of changes in different behaviours, then the demographic trends of pre-colonial Australia are still open to debate, and the reasons for the increases and decreases in numbers of sites and artefacts require further investigation.

The foregoing studies were the context in which the archeological material from the Upper Mangrove Creek catchment was analysed. In the past decade or so, many regional studies have built on concepts introduced in the 1970s and 1980s — particularly those relating to technological systems, the reorganisation of subsistence strategies including mobility patterns, and the restructuring of social relations. These recent studies are incorporated into discussions in the final chapters.

3

Upper Mangrove Creek catchment: fieldwork and analysis: aims and methods

The fieldwork program was designed and implemented within the focus of the original research project, which was to study site and artefact distribution patterns across the catchment to investigate past land-use and subsistence strategies in the coastal regions of south-eastern NSW. Although these specific aims — to investigate relationships between coast and hinterland — were not pursued, the fieldwork framework and the data it produced proved ideal for the research directions ultimately taken: the interpretation and explanation of chronological changes in numbers of sites and artefacts.

Terminology and definitions

Terms commonly used by archaeologists to describe Aboriginal sites that occur in the Upper Mangrove Creek catchment are rockshelters with archaeological deposit; rockshelters with archaeological deposit and art; rockshelters with archaeological deposit, art and grinding grooves; rockshelters with archaeological deposit, art and burial; rockshelters with archaeological deposit and grinding grooves; rockshelters with art; open artefact scatters; rock engravings (on open rock platforms); axe grinding grooves (on open rock platforms).

Since many sites contain more than one set of archaeological evidence (particularly rockshelters), these terms were not only cumbersome but inappropriate for the analyses I undertook. It was also considered inappropriate to use the term 'site type' for the evidence at sites, since these categories (archaeological deposit, art and grinding grooves) are themselves not types of sites, but types of archaeological evidence at sites (or at different types of locations, e.g., in rockshelters or on rock platforms). I therefore use the words *location, archaeological trait and contents (assemblages or elements)* to describe and refer to places where archaeological fieldwork was carried out and in discussing and analysing the archaeological evidence recorded. Reasons for using these terms are outlined below, and abbreviations for various terms used in tables and figures are set out in Table 3.1.

The term 'site' is used and defined by researchers in different ways for recording and analytical purposes depending on the aims of their project. I use the term *site* (or

Table 3.1 Upper Mangrove Creek catchment: terminology and abbreviations used for archaeological evidence.

LOCATIONS: MICRO-TOPOGRAPHIC FEATURES ON/IN WHICH ARCHAEOLOGICAL TRAITS OCCUR

Location	*Abbreviation*
Rockshelter	SH
Open deposit	OD
Open rock	OR
Tree	T

ARCHAEOLOGICAL TRAITS: TYPES OF PHYSICAL EVIDENCE PRODUCED BY HUMAN BEHAVIOUR

Archaeological trait	*Abbreviation*
Archaeological deposit	AD
Image	IM
Grinding area	GA
Burial	BR
Scarred tree	ST

CONTENTS: ARCHAEOLOGICAL ASSEMBLAGES AND ELEMENTS CONTAINED WITHIN EACH TRAIT

Archaeological trait	*Assemblage/element*
Archaeological deposit	Stone artefacts
	Bone artefacts
	Faunal remains
	Plant remains
	Ochre
	Charcoal
Image	Figures (pigment [drawings, paintings, stencils] and engraved)
Grinding area	Grooves (of different shapes)

TYPES OF DEPOSIT:

Type of deposit	*Abbreviation*
Archaeological deposit	AD
Sterile deposit	SD
Potential archaeological deposit	PAD
No deposit	ND

archaeological site) only for places where there is archaeological evidence for Aboriginal use of the location. Definitions used during the field recording and analyses undertaken for this project are given below.

Location

The word 'location' was introduced since excavation was carried out not only at archaeological sites but also at places which proved not to be archaeological sites (i.e., potential habitation shelters — see below). Since the term 'site' by itself is usually used in archaeological literature to refer to archaeological sites, it became confusing to call places where there were no archaeological remains (or no proven archaeological remains) sites. I use the term 'location' when referring to all places at which excavation was undertaken. The term 'excavated location' covers rockshelters or open areas with or without archaeological evidence.

A location is a place in or on which an archaeological trait (defined below) exists or may exist. In this sense, locations are micro-topographic features, as distinct from macro-topographic ones such as ridgetops, ridgesides and valley bottoms. Locations in which archaeological traits occur are divided into sheltered and open. Sheltered locations are rockshelters; open locations are areas of open ground (deposit, sediment) and expanses of open sandstone (e.g., rock platforms). Trees are also included as a type of location. These four locations, referred to as *rockshelters* (SH), *open rock* (OR), *open deposit* (OD) and *trees* (T), are described below.

Rockshelters form in both the Narrabeen Group and Hawkesbury sandstone and occur in any size cliff face as well as in large isolated outliers and fallen boulders (Figs 1.3, 1.4, 3.1 and 3.2). They have formed by cavernous weathering and/or block-fall. The floor area and height of the shelters in the catchment vary greatly. Floors can be rock or sediment, flat or sloping, dry or wet. The non-cultural components of deposits forming shelter floors may derive from outside the shelters — for example, slopewash (depending on the configuration of the shelters and their position on the land) — or can be restricted to roof-fall and/or windblown sources.

Open rocks are expanses or exposures of sandstone (e.g., rock platforms), which vary in shape, size and slope. They occur in all topographic zones, and include creek bottoms where water runs over bedrock (Fig. 3.3).

Open deposit is sediment of any depth which can occur on alluvial or colluvial flats forming creek banks (Fig. 3.4), on structural benches on ridgesides, and on ridgetops. These areas vary in size and defining the boundaries in most cases was almost impossible, or relatively arbitrary. Structural benches are flat to low-gradient areas along ridgesides formed during the weathering of the underlying sandstone bedrock.

Archaeological traits

During the analyses, the different types of archaeological evidence at each site were considered as discrete units and I needed a general term which I could use to refer to these units. As stated above, the term 'site type' was considered inappropriate for these units and the term 'type of archaeological evidence' was cumbersome. The term 'archaeological component' already has an accepted use in archaeology, particularly in America (Willey and Phillips 1962: 21; Chang 1972: 7, 9–10; Thomas 1979: 231–4, 458). I initially used the word 'feature' (Attenbrow 1987: 93–5), but now use the term 'trait' as the term 'feature' is often used to refer to particular

Figure 3.1 Loggers: shelter with archaeological deposit dating back to ca 11,000 BP. June 1980. Photographer Val Attenbrow.

Figure 3.2 Emu Tracks 2: shelter with archaeological deposit. February 1980. Photographer Val Attenbrow.

Figure 3.3 Grinding grooves in headwater tributary of Bucketty Gully. Grooves are at bottom left extending beside deepest part of channel in the sandstone bedrock where water generally flows. June 1981. Photographer Val Attenbrow.

Figure 3.4 Black Hands open archaeological deposit. Cleared river flat and colluvial slope adjacent to Mangrove Creek, which is marked by the line of wattle trees behind the tents. January 1978.

phenomena, such as hearths or flaking floors, within sites (e.g., McManamon 1984: 229). I use the term archaeological trait to refer to the type/s of archaeological evidence at a site, each trait being the physical evidence of a distinct part of a past behavioural system, which took place in various parts of the countryside. One or more traits may exist at a site; for example, archaeological deposit, art and grinding grooves can all occur in one rockshelter. Because some sites have more than one trait (multi-trait sites), the total number of traits recorded in the catchment is greater than the total number of recorded sites.

Rather than the term 'art' or 'pictures' (Clegg 1984: 10–11; 1985: 44) or 'rock-art' (Chippindale 2001), I have used the term 'image/s'. I use the term 'open archaeological deposit' instead of 'open artefact scatter', 'open site' or 'open campsite', which are the terms often used by archaeologists to refer to surface concentrations of stone artefacts in the open. In using the term open archaeological deposit, I include locations where artefacts have been recorded on the ground surface only as well as locations where artefacts are known to occur at depth throughout sediment. I use the term 'open site' to distinguish sites which are in open locations from those which are in rockshelters; for example, grinding grooves and engravings are usually 'open sites', though they also occur in rockshelters.

The archaeological evidence in the catchment has been classified into five archaeological traits: **A**rchaeological **D**eposit (AD), **Im**age (IM), **G**rinding **A**rea (GA), **B**urial (BR) and **S**carred **T**ree (ST) (Table 3.1; Figs 3.5 to 3.11). These terms, as used in this monograph, are defined below.

Archaeological deposit is sediment which contains one or more of the following: stone artefacts, bone artefacts, faunal remains, plant remains, ochre and charcoal. In the case of plant and faunal remains, deposits were classified as archaeological only where the remains could be identified as being humanly derived and were not from natural deaths or animal predation. The status of charcoal is less clear and is discussed in a later section of this chapter. Archaeological deposits are assumed to be the remains of campsites or habitations (inhabited sites); no quarries were identified. Sites with deep deposit and large, rich stone and faunal assemblages — for example, Loggers Shelter (Fig. 3.5) — were places where people stayed overnight for one or more days, and in and from which they carried out a range of activities. Some archaeological deposits, especially those with small assemblages, may be places where people stopped during the day to rest or carry out a variety of tasks, such as tool and equipment maintenance by both men and women during hunting and gathering trips, as well as the eating and/or processing of food. Other deposits could represent transit camps where people stayed en route, for example, to ceremonies or to trade with other groups.

Archaeological deposits occur in open locations as well as rockshelters. In a few rockshelters (e.g., Axehead Shelter, Firestick Shelter), archaeological materials were found where there is virtually no deposit; that is, the deposit is a thin lens of unconsolidated sediment which was less than 3cm deep, with occasional pockets up to 10cm deep in small depressions or crevices in the rock floor. The archaeological materials were, in effect, lying on the rock floor. In these circumstances, the rockshelters were still classified as having 'an archaeological deposit'.

Images consist of drawings, paintings, stencils, engravings and/or scratched outlines (Figs 3.6 to 3.8). The first three are referred to as pigment images and the latter two as engraved images. All figures, whether their motif type was recognisable or indeterminate, are included in counts. The context in which images were made is not directly identifiable. Religious belief pervades most aspects of Aboriginal life and, while many images may have been made in a religious, spiritual or ceremonial context (Mathews 1896a, 1897; Morphy 1999), others would have been for secular purposes. By using the term 'image' to refer to all figures that occur at a single location, I am not implying that all figures were made at the same time, or that their makers saw them all as a single entity or necessarily as being associated with each other.

Figure 3.5 Loggers Shelter during excavation of Squares E and F. Squares A, B and C at right. August 1978. Photographer Val Attenbrow.

Figure 3.6 Charcoal images, including emu and other birds, macropod, people (male and female) and snakes (including death adders?) in Boat Cave. 1978. Photographer Val Attenbrow.

Most of the images are pigment figures. Engraved figures occur in only two open locations (rock platforms), each with a small number of figures (all macropods), and in two rockshelters where the only images recorded are emu tracks — Emu Tracks 1 has one engraved and possibly five red pigment tracks; Emu Tracks 2 has 15 engraved tracks (Fig. 3.8). Although Clegg (1984: 16) and McDonald (1994: 141, 150, 192–6, 334–6) refer to the engraved images in Emu Tracks 2 as 'Panaramitee', there is nothing to indicate their age or that they are of great antiquity. Emu Tracks 1 is a shallow cavernously weathered concavity with no floor deposits. The deposits in Emu Tracks 2 have not been radiocarbon-dated, but the nature of the excavated sediments and stone artefact assemblages suggest the shelter was inhabited no more than ca 4000 years ago.

Grinding areas are locations where grooves have been ground into the surface of sandstone bedrock or broad ground surfaces have been created by human activities. In the catchment, most grooves are of the size and shape that are interpreted as being locations where ground-edged implements (e.g., axes/hatchets) were shaped or sharpened (Figs 3.3 and 3.9; Attenbrow 1987: 139–40). Some grooves, however, may have been for other purposes (Vinnicombe 1980: XI: 6), for example, large deep ones and broad shallow areas may have been associated with plant processing, whereas narrow, deep grooves (Fig. 3.9) were probably for shaping wooden spears or bone tools (NSW NPWS 1979). A broad ground area (ca 25cm x 25cm) adjacent to a grinding groove was recorded on a low, floor-level sandstone shelf at the rear of White Figure (Fig. 3.10). Similar ground areas have been reported infrequently in the region — for example, locally in rockshelters in Hungry Creek (Koettig and Hughes 1983: 10, 22, Table 1, Fig. 5), slightly further away on Mt Yengo (McDonald 1994, Appendix 1, Fig. A1.5), and on an open rock platform with engravings and grinding grooves at Daleys Point overlooking Brisbane Waters (pers. obs.). Sub-incised grooves (i.e., a 'normal' groove with a narrower groove centred along its base) were found at two sites, Sharp Gully and Geebung Grooves. Some grinding grooves in the catchment were recorded in rockshelters (e.g., under driplines), but most were on open rock platforms. No portable grooves were found in association with archaeological deposits, and they are rarely found in the Sydney/Hawkesbury region except in coastal sand dunes (pers. obs. Australian Museum archaeological collection). No engraved/incised channels associated with rock pools were found in the catchment, although they occur at other sites in the region (Mathews 1896b, 1901; Vinnicombe 1980: XI: 6).

Burials are buried human skeletal remains.

Scarred trees usually have areas where sections of bark and often a piece of the underlying wood have been removed from the trunk and large branches of trees. Bark was often removed for shields, containers, canoes and shelters. The only scarred tree in the catchment which was accepted as being the result of Aboriginal activities has several footsteps cut up its trunk (Fig. 3.11). The steps, which appear to have been cut with a metal axe/hatchet and thus date to early colonial times, were probably cut in order to gain access to possums or honey. In deciding that other scarred trees were not of Aboriginal origin, the dimensions, shape and location of the scar/s on the tree as well as the age of the tree, and extent of regrowth around the scar, were considered. The occurrence of current and recent historical forestry activities in the catchment was also taken into account.

The contents

The materials or artefacts in an archaeological trait are referred to as its contents. They consist of various assemblages, e.g., assemblages of stone artefacts, faunal remains, figures and grinding grooves. Archaeological deposits may contain more than one type of assemblage or material, which is often a major analytical component (e.g., stone artefact assemblages and faunal assemblages); the images and grinding areas contain only one type of assemblage — that is, figures and grooves respectively (Table 3.1). Classification of the contents is discussed in more detail later in this chapter.

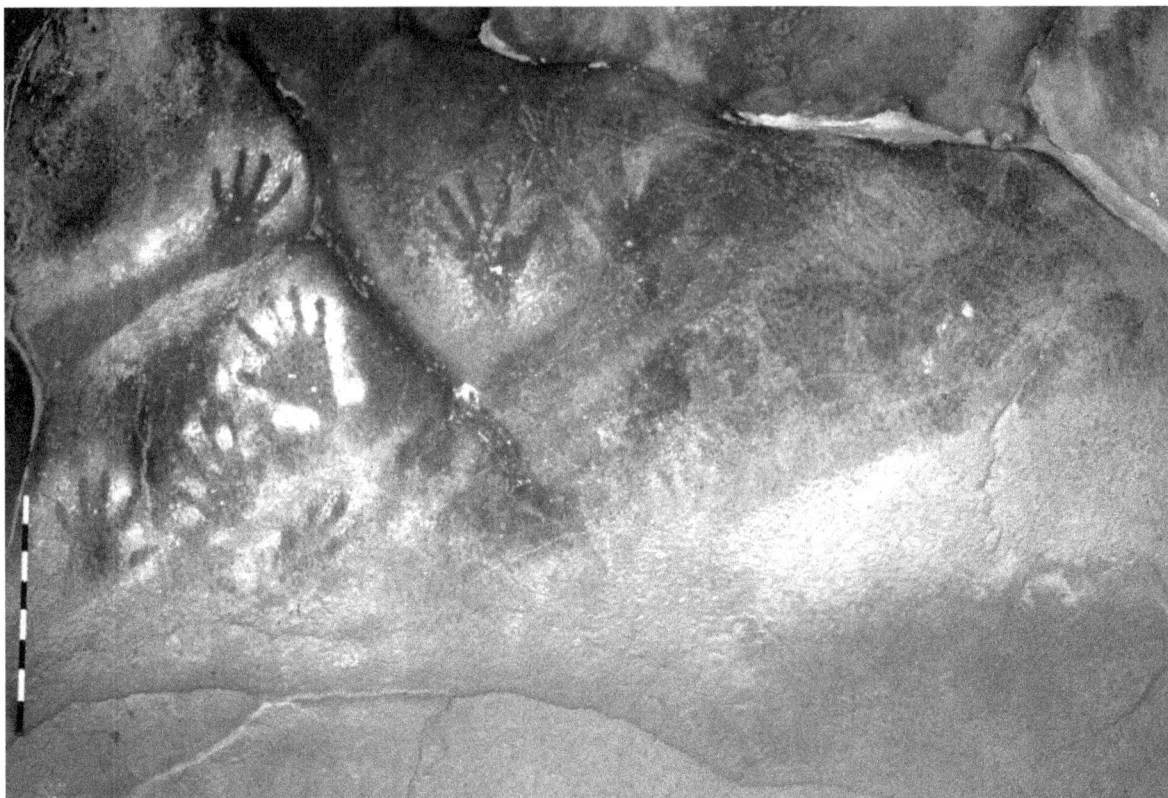

Figure 3.7 Hand stencils, including one with forearm, and black infilled kangaroo head in Black Hands Shelter. August 1978. Scale has 10cm divisions. Photographer Val Attenbrow.

Figure 3.8 Engraved images in Emu Tracks 2: emu tracks. August 1979. Scale has 10cm divisions. Photographer Val Attenbrow.

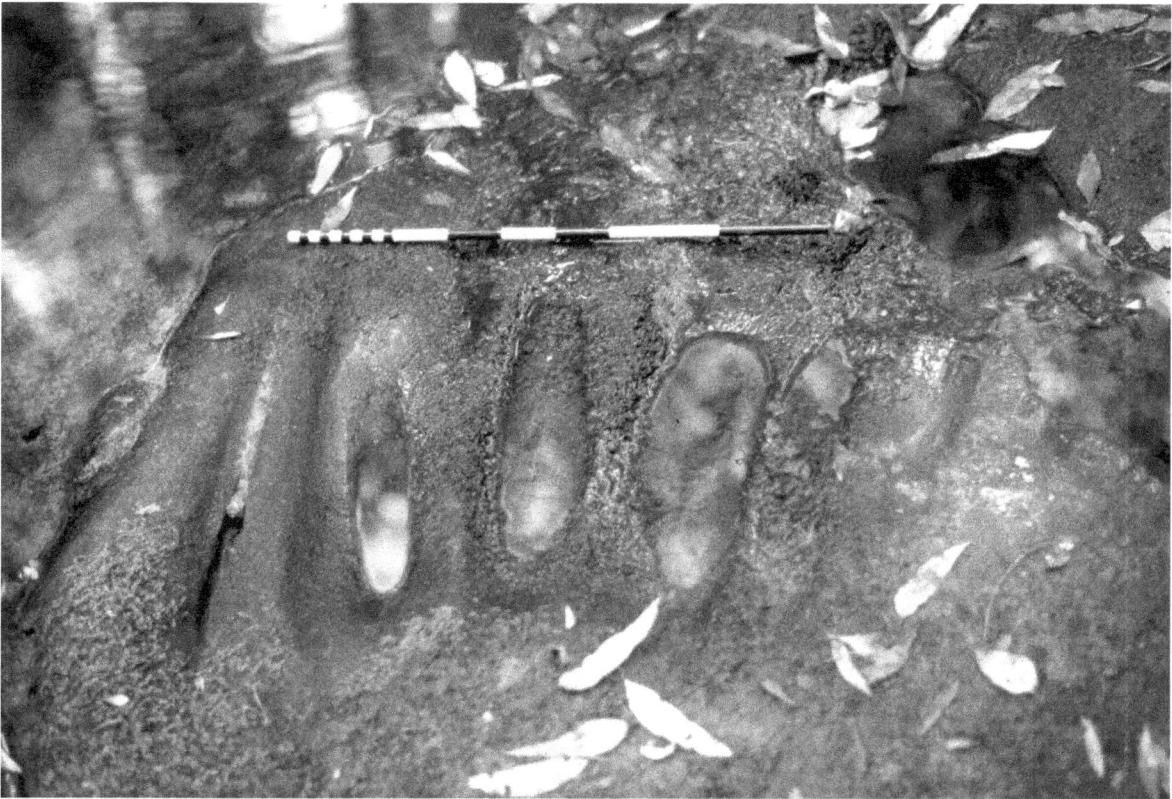

Figure 3.9 Grinding grooves at Sharp Gully: note narrow groove on left. Easter 1980. Scale has 1/5/10cm divisions. Photographer Val Attenbrow.

Figure 3.10 Ground area adjacent to grinding groove in White Figure Shelter. August 1982. Scale has 1/5/10cm divisions. Photographer Val Attenbrow.

Figure 3.11 Scarred tree: one of a series of footsteps made with a metal axe up the tree trunk. The tree was dead when found by loggers adjacent to Mangrove Creek below its junction with Boomerang Creek. October 1979. Scale has 10cm divisions. Photographer Val Attenbrow.

Sites

The term 'site' is used only when referring to *a location with one (or more) archaeological trait/s.* A site is any location where physical evidence of Aboriginal activity or activities is found, except for an 'isolated find' (see below). No locations are known that would be classified as 'natural mythological sites', that is, locations at which there is no archaeological evidence but which are or were of spiritual significance to Aboriginal people.

Isolated finds

When recording and classifying stone artefacts found in the open, a distinction was made between an 'isolated find' and a site. A single artefact found in the open by itself may have been an accidental loss or a chance discard when, for example, people were out hunting or en route from one habitation site to another. In contrast, since the same element of accident or chance cannot be applied to the presence of a single grinding groove or drawing, single items in these categories are considered traits and, if by themselves, sites. However, isolated stone artefacts in open contexts were recorded since even a single stone artefact indicates the presence of people in an area. The possibility that buried artefacts may be present at the same location as an isolated artefact, and that an isolated find is simply the only visible item of an open archaeological deposit, is discussed in the following chapter.

Defining Sites

The following criteria were taken into account when determining whether particular archaeological traits were at the same or different sites.

Open archaeological deposits are distinguished from isolated finds on the basis of the number of artefacts and the distance between artefacts and/or artefact clusters (Fig. 3.12). Two (or more) artefacts less than 50m from each other constitute a site. An individual artefact found more than 50m from any other artefact (single or clustered) is classified as an isolated find. Two or more clusters of artefacts with less than 50m between them are classified as one site, while if the distance between them is greater than 50m they are regarded as separate sites. In instances where a creek or gully exists between two clusters of artefacts, even if less than 50m apart, they are classified as two sites, as a conscious decision may have been made to sit on one side of the watercourse or the other; each side of the watercourse may have a different aspect and receive sunlight at different times of the day, or for varying lengths of time in different seasons. In these situations, the gully must have existed for a much longer period of time than the artefacts presently exposed on the ground surface — at a minimum, a gully that one could argue is not the result of European land-use and is not cutting through what was originally a large open archaeological deposit.

Artefacts which are in the open in front of a rockshelter with archaeological deposit and which could derive from activities within or immediately in front of the rockshelter are classified as part of the shelter deposit and thus part of that site. At none of the rockshelters in the random sampling units were visible artefacts found extending continuously for any great distance in front of the shelter (i.e., >20m), and thus the problem of having to decide whether the site should be classified as both a sheltered and an open location was not encountered. However, stone artefacts found in the open above a rockshelter are classified as a separate site, as a decision may have been made to undertake activities away from the rockshelter, that is, at a different type of location.

Traits in adjacent locations. Although single artefacts and/or artefact clusters have to be more than 50m apart before they are classified as separate sites, where each archaeological trait is in a different type of location or a separate physical location, the distance criterion is not used. For example, grinding grooves which occur in a creekbed below a rockshelter with archaeological deposit are classified as being at a separate site even if the distance between the creek and the rockshelter is less than 50m. Similarly, if two rockshelters with archaeological deposit and/or images are less than 50m apart, they are classified as separate sites (unless the archaeological deposit appears to be continuous between the two rockshelters — a situation which was not recorded in the catchment).

Open images (rock engravings, engraved images). A criterion similar to that used by McDonald (1986a) to define open images in the Maroota project was adopted:

> … all those artefacts occurring on/in a discrete platform … physically separated from other archaeological entities by either a distance of 100 metres <u>or</u> by the presence of vegetation separating sandstone platforms … each and every platform is potentially an individual site. (McDonald 1986a: 18; the term 'artefact' in this quote refers to engraved figures.)

Engraved figures on separate rock platforms are classified as separate sites, but I use a distance of 50m and not 100m as used by McDonald. For the open images recorded in the Upper Mangrove Creek catchment, this criterion did not conflict with the 50m distance criterion. However, according to both criteria (distance and separate rock platforms), some figures, which were originally recorded by Ian Sim as one site (Kyola Road/Nevertyre, NPWS Site card 45-3-528), are classified in my analyses as two sites (and thus two archaeological traits).

In practice, the above definitions and criteria mean that:

1.   Archaeological evidence/materials are classified as separate traits if they are of a different type (e.g., archaeological deposit, image or grinding groove) or if a distance >50m separates each assemblage of like elements (e.g., stone artefacts, figures and grooves). That is, two clusters of stone artefacts along the same creek bank (or two sets of grooves along the same creek) which are >50m apart are classified as two separate traits (and also separate sites). Exceptions to the distance criteria are:

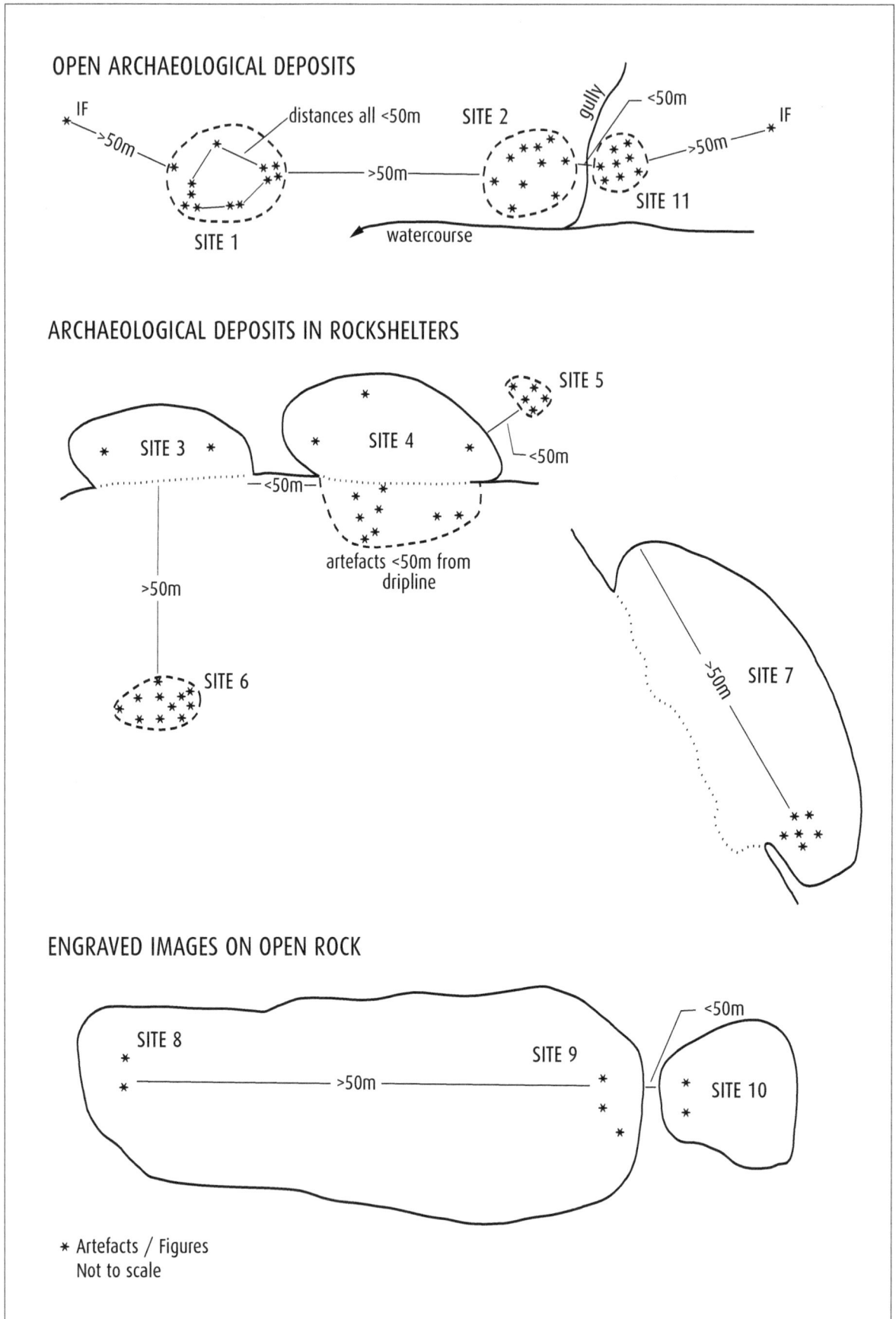

OPEN ARCHAEOLOGICAL DEPOSITS

ARCHAEOLOGICAL DEPOSITS IN ROCKSHELTERS

ENGRAVED IMAGES ON OPEN ROCK

* Artefacts / Figures
Not to scale

Figure 3.12 Distance criteria applied in defining sites.

(a)   where a rockshelter >50m in length has surface archaeological evidence at both ends but the deposit in between is unexcavated and could potentially contain archaeological materials; in these cases, the total deposit is classified as a single trait and the rockshelter and all the deposit within it is classified as one site; and,

(b)   where two (or more) locations can be classified as separate physical locations, for example, two rockshelters, two rock platforms or the opposite sides of a creek which are <50m apart. In these instances, the locations are classified as separate sites and thus the contents of each location are considered as a separate trait or traits.

2.   Traits of different types are classified as being at the same site if they are <50m apart as long as they are in or on the same type of location, for example, in the same rockshelter, on the same rock platform or on the same creek bank. This means that traits in the following situations are not classified as being at the same site, but as being at separate sites:

(a)   two open archaeological deposits which are <50m apart but each is on opposite sides of a small creek or gully (i.e., they are not on the **same** creek bank);

(b)   where traits are in separate rockshelters or on separate rock platforms which are <50m apart.

The implications of using these site definitions are discussed where relevant in future chapters. The distance of 50m adopted in defining sites is arbitrary, but did have a practical benefit. At a distance of 50m, two locations are sufficiently far apart that they can be mapped and given separate grid references on 1: 25K topographic maps.

Potential habitation shelters and potential archaeological deposits

Rockshelters without archaeological evidence, but with particular dimensions and characteristics, were also recorded during the survey. These rockshelters are called *potential habitation shelters* (PH shelters). A rockshelter was deemed to be a PH shelter if it had space for at least two people to gain 'adequate shelter'. The following criteria were used in the field:

1.   floor space: suitable for two people to sleep in a curled-up position, that is, flat and horizontal with a minimum area of 2m × 1m;

2.   height: sufficient for two people to stand or stoop in a comfortable working position, that is, at least 1.2m high;

3.   protection: the overhang is deep enough (from dripline to back wall) to protect the floor area from weather, that is, 1m minimum;

4.   dryness: the floor (or part of it), and inside the rockshelter generally, must be dry;

5.   accessibility: the rockshelter must be easily accessible.

(Furey 1978: 10; Vinnicombe 1980: VIII: 2–3, 1984: 109; Attenbrow 1981: 12, 1982b: 72.)

During the North Hawkesbury project, Vinnicombe (1980: VIII: 2–3) sought more reliable data on the reasons why particular rockshelters and particular locations were selected as habitation sites. She wished to assess rockshelters that were available for use against those shelters which were actually used by comparing the location, distribution and characteristics of the occupied rockshelters with those that were not occupied. For this, Vinnicombe required data on all rockshelters that were available for habitation, and rockshelters whose floors were either deposit or rock were recorded as potential habitation shelters. During the course of the Mangrove Creek Dam fieldwork, it was noted that many of these rockshelters had floor deposits but there was no visible evidence in the form of stone artefacts to indicate that they were 'archaeological deposits'. It was decided that such deposits should be considered as potential archaeological deposits, that is, a deposit which has no surface evidence such as stone artefacts to indicate it may contain buried archaeological materials (Attenbrow 2003–4). In addition, it was perceived that a *potential archaeological deposit* could also occur in a rockshelter that was already classified as an archaeological site on the basis of having images on the walls.

More recently, in environmental impact projects and many cultural heritage management projects, rockshelters without deposit or any other evidence for occupation are not necessarily recorded and the term Potential Habitation Shelter is seldom, if ever, used. The term *potential archaeological deposit* (PAD) has, however, been adopted to refer to a deposit that may contain archaeological materials and they are usually test excavated if threatened by proposed developments. Initially, it was used only in connection with deposits in rockshelters (e.g., Attenbrow 1981: 131–2; Attenbrow and Conyers 1983; Haglund and Stockton 1983; Greer 1985; Corkill 1995; Corkill and Edgar 1996; Haglund 1995), however, as in America (e.g., Wobst 1983; McManamon 1984; Shott 1989), use of the concept has been extended to include the recording and testing of PADs in open contexts. These include flat areas which would have been suitable for camping on; for example, alluvial river banks or terraces, structural benches on ridgesides, ridgetops and dunes. Investigation of these deposits has been incorporated into Australian cultural resource management projects with positive results (e.g., Koettig 1986: 5, 28, 1989: 2–3, Appendix I site POK6, 1991 Appendix 2, site B58; McDonald and Rich 1993; McDonald, Rich and Barton 1994; Jo McDonald CHM 1999; Baker and Martin 2001).

Use of the potential habitation concept and the test excavation of PADs in the catchment thus enabled the detection of otherwise 'invisible' sites and archaeological deposits. Recording and testing of potential open archaeological deposits was not, however, included in the Upper Mangrove Creek projects.

Fieldwork aims

The fieldwork was designed to retrieve the following sets of data in order to address questions relating to the nature of Aboriginal occupation in the catchment, and whether such occupation varied in different parts of the catchment and/or changed over time:

1. the type and nature of the traits at archaeological sites in the catchment; that is, the archaeological deposits, grinding areas, images, burials and scarred trees;
2. the contents or types of archaeological materials in the traits; for example, the type of stone artefacts and faunal remains in the archaeological deposits, the type of figures in images, and the type of grooves at grinding areas;
3. the frequency, distribution and location of sites, archaeological traits and selected assemblages/elements in relation to terrain variables such as topography, vegetation and geology; that is, the location and setting of the traits/sites on the land;
4. the on-site characteristics (attributes) of the site's location (e.g., of the rockshelter or rock platform): morphology, dimensions, aspect, slope, geology, nature of ground (rock or sediment);
5. temporal changes in the frequency, density and distribution of sites, archaeological traits and selected elements during the documented period of prehistoric/Aboriginal occupation (in particular, sites with archaeological deposit);
6. the date of initial use of individual sites (in particular sites with archaeological deposit);
7. the date at which quantitative and qualitative changes in the stone artefact assemblages at individual sites occurred.

In addition, it was necessary to have data about the contents of each archaeological trait in quantifiable terms — for example, the number of different types of artefacts, bones, grooves and figures. This was required to investigate whether there was variation in the assemblages at sites in different parts of the catchment, and to assess the rate of temporal changes that occurred within individual sites and in the number of sites in the catchment.

After the original research project was modified in mid-1985 (once the implications of the documented quantitative changes to 'the population increase/intensification debate' were apparent — see Chapter 2), analyses of the survey data within a spatial framework were taken to a preliminary stage only, and only part of the data outlined above was utilised. However, adopting probability sampling methods for the site survey to ensure that data retrieved were from an unbiased sample of sites, and the level of recording undertaken, proved most advantageous to the line of research ultimately undertaken. The procedures adopted during the research project for the survey, recording, excavation and classification of the archaeological evidence in the catchment are outlined in the remainder of this chapter.

Field Survey

Sampling design

The storage area of the proposed dam (12 sq km) was totally surveyed for sites (Furey 1978; Attenbrow 1981). The aim of the storage area survey was to record all Aboriginal sites that would be lost due to inundation or other works associated with the dam construction. However, to address my original research questions relating to site distribution patterns within the catchment (Attenbrow 1987: 63–6), information about the population parameters for the archaeological evidence in the total catchment was needed. This included data on the range of archaeological evidence in the catchment as well as the frequency and density in which sites and traits occurred in different areas of the catchment. The storage area, consisting only of the valley bottoms, was thus a biased sample of the catchment for my purposes, and it was necessary to gain data about the archaeological evidence from the area of the catchment above the storage area.

Neither time nor funding permitted an intensive survey of that part of the catchment above the storage area (about 89 sq km). Total survey was not necessary for my research purposes if I could gain an unbiased, and hopefully a representative, sample of the archaeological evidence in the catchment. Binford (1975: 253) considered:

> Sampling is a procedure which is concerned with providing a representative and unbiased view of the archaeological record as it exists at the time the archaeologists begin making observations.

One of the basic purposes of probability sampling is to reduce bias (Read 1975: 53). However, probability sampling can reduce bias only in the 'human' selection of the sample; it cannot assist in removing biases introduced by past and present environmental factors, for example, destruction due to erosion of sediments, and decreased visibility due to sediment accumulation or dense vegetation. In addition, Chenhall (1975: 20) points out that sampling is based on the premise that the sample adequately represents the total population, though he goes on to demonstrate that it may not be an adequate representation even where probability sampling is adopted. If selecting a 'representative' sample is taken to mean picking examples that exhibit the extremes in the ranges of variation, or picking at least some examples of all types, or all diagnostic types, then such samples are possible, but the result is most unlikely to be 'representative' in any other sense (Cowgill 1975: 261). If 'representativeness' is taken to mean that the sample statistics are virtually identical to the corresponding values for the population, then there is no way we can be positive that this is so without already knowing the population values. In archaeological field projects, this is usually not possible.

Probability sampling methods were adopted for the site survey in the Upper Mangrove Creek catchment in an attempt to obtain an unbiased and representative sample of the archaeological evidence in the catchment. The sample selected in the catchment can be considered unbiased only in terms of my site selection processes. Environmental factors which may have biased the record are discussed in Chapter 5. However, since the total population of archaeological evidence in the Upper Mangrove Creek catchment is not known, whether the sample gained is representative of the total catchment is not known.

The sampling design has been outlined previously (Attenbrow 1982b: 68–72), but some details were not included and some parts were not described in conventional sampling language. Details of the sampling design are therefore presented below.

The sample fraction or percentage of the catchment selected for site survey was 10%. There is no formula that can be used to calculate the optimal percentage that should be covered — the size of the appropriate sample fraction depends on many things. The figure of 10% was chosen somewhat arbitrarily but, on the basis of the previous surveys, I considered that a sample of this size (which included 10.1 sq km of the catchment) would provide a sufficient number of sites for statistical analyses.

When selecting the sample to be intensively surveyed for sites, the fact that the storage area had been surveyed previously was disregarded, and the total catchment was taken as the area to be sampled. Several ways of obtaining the 10% sample were considered:

1. *a 10.1 sq km block*: a single 10.1 sq km block which encompassed total small creek systems as used by Vinnicombe (1980: IX; 1984: 107–9) for her surveys of coastal and estuarine ecosystems;

2. *a simple random sample*: sampling units chosen under a simple random sampling scheme using:
   - quadrats (or grids) of 0.25, 0.5, 1 or 2 sq km in area,
   - transects across the catchment of varying widths;

3. *a stratified random sample*: sampling units chosen under a stratified random sampling scheme with the catchment stratified according to topographic zones, and with 10% of the units in each stratum selected randomly; sampling units to be 0.25 sq km in five of the zones and 1 sq km in the sixth.

The scheme used by Vinnicombe was included for consideration since the results of archaeological work for the Mangrove Creek Dam were to be integrated with her findings for the North Hawkesbury project (Vinnicombe 1980: IXC: 7). However, it was not possible to select a 10 sq km block equivalent to the survey areas in Vinnicombe's other ecosystems as none of the larger tributaries were short enough to be included as such a block. In addition, the possible areas that might have equated to Vinnicombe's survey areas did not provide the data required for my research purposes.

The use of transects within a simple random sample was considered impracticable given the dissected and rugged nature of the terrain. In initially considering a random sample by quadrat method, 1:25K topographic maps of the catchment were gridded and a series of samples, each using sampling units of a different size, were selected on the basis of random number tables. However, from the maps it became clear that these schemes would not fulfil my research aims. None of the schemes produced a sample which included units in all of the three topographic zones in which previous work indicated specific types of archaeological evidence may be associated — that is, ridgetops, valley bottoms and ridgesides. Schemes using the larger sized units (1 and 2 sq km) provided an even less adequate sampling of all parts of the catchment than did the 0.25 and 0.5 sq km units.

I finally decided that before selecting the sampling units, the catchment should be stratified according to the three topographic zones — ridgetops, valley bottoms and ridgesides — and scheme 3 (a stratified random sample — without replacement) was adopted. Stratification into these topographic zones was considered necessary to investigate questions about the relationship of particular Aboriginal activities to various topographic zones within the catchment. For example, are sites with the largest assemblages and/or richest archaeological deposits only in the 'main' valley bottoms; what is the distribution of grinding grooves; and are engravings sites more commonly found on the ridgetops?

Consideration of how the catchment may have been used in pre-contact times also influenced this choice — that is, if people had been visiting the catchment as part of their subsistence round to hunt and gather, the base camps (major habitations) may have been along the main section of Mangrove Creek and its larger tributaries creeks where water was more plentiful (i.e., the valley bottoms). The main section of the creek system is thus distinguished from the more minor tributary (subsidiary) creeks. If people had been only passing through the area, say en route between the Hunter Valley and Brisbane Waters (Gosford), then major habitations may have been on the ridgetops — in particular, the periphery ridgetops, since historical accounts indicate that some of the major ridge systems were used as travelling routes through the region. A report by Francis Barrallier (1801) refers to contact between people of the lower Hunter Valley and the Hawkesbury, crossing the mountains near Mt York, as well as Broken Bay. McCarthy (1936, 1939b: 407, 1939c: 100) reported contact between people of the Singleton area in the Hunter Valley and Gosford/Brisbane Waters. In a field report, McCarthy reported that Peter Howe, a resident of Somersby Falls, had informed him that there was a 'trade and travelling route from Gosford along the Mangrove Mountain which formed a great highway along the ridge as far north as Singleton, via Wollombi' (1936: 2–3; see also McCarthy 1939a: 1, where he refers to the Bulga Plains area). His published version (1939b: 407) states, 'they followed a track which traversed Cockfighter Creek [present-day Wollombi Brook] and the Macdonald River to Mangrove Mountain.' Such a route includes the ridges forming the northern and eastern, and possibly western, watersheds of the Mangrove Creek catchment. Groups from Lake Macquarie on the adjacent coast also went 'to the mountains with upwards of 60 spears to exchange for oppossum cord made of the fur' and also to participate in a ceremony (Threlkeld 1826 in Gunson 1974, Vol. 2: 206). Whether 'the mountains' included the catchment is not clear, but it is possible; the word 'mountains' is more likely to refer to the sandstone plateau of the coastal hinterland than the Blue Mountains/Great Dividing Range. Further to the west, the Boree Track is reported to have been used for travel between the territories of the Wonarua of the upper Hunter Valley and the Darginung of the Macdonald Valley (Moore 1981: 423). The possibility of periphery ridgetops being trade routes is one of the reasons why they are distinguished from peninsula ridgetops in the sampling strategy.

Another reason why periphery and peninsula ridgetops were distinguished is that the peninsula ridgetops are long narrow areas, usually without water, except for rock pools. In contrast, the periphery of the catchment has much broader, flattish areas with low relief where the upper reaches of the tributaries often contain springs which flow all year round, even in dry seasons (Robert Thompson, Kulnura, 1980, pers. comm.).

The geology of the catchment is predominantly sandstone with two small areas of highly weathered volcanic breccia. The valley bottoms and lower ridgesides are within a sequence of sandstones, siltstone, claystones and shales of the Gosford Formation of the Narrabeen Group, while the upper ridgesides and ridgetops are Hawkesbury sandstone (NSW Department of Public Works 1977, Vol. 2: 8). Any significant relationship between particular archaeological features and geology can still be detected within the topographic stratification of the catchment, and thus geological variation did not warrant special consideration in the sampling design. However, the existence of Hawkesbury sandstone in only the upper elevations of the catchment is a consideration when interpreting its site distribution and land-use patterns.

Vegetation was not used as the basis for stratification, since the whole catchment was covered with Eucalypt forest or woodland. Although there are some differences in the plant communities, depending on slope and aspect, none were known to be meaningful in terms of Aboriginal subsistence strategies which might be reflected in site locations (though this still requires testing). In addition, the distances within the catchment and between different plant communities are so small that it did not seem likely (at the time of survey design) that habitations would have been located within a specific vegetation zone in order to exploit resources which were available only therein. However, as discussed in Chapter 9, Aplin's subsequent (Aplin 1981: 33–4; Aplin and Gollan 1982: 20–6) interpretation of faunal changes in Mussel and Deep Creek Shelters suggests otherwise.

Each of the three topographic zones (valley bottoms, ridgetops and ridgesides) was further subdivided into two as outlined in Table 3.2 and shown in Figures 3.13 and 3.14. I considered 0.25 sq km to be the optimum area for sampling units in five of the topographic zones given the irregular shapes of the zones and the number of units (sample size) that would result: peninsula ridgetops, main valley bottoms, subsidiary valley bottoms, main ridgesides, subsidiary ridgesides. Periphery ridgetops are relatively larger and relatively flatter than the other zones and were divided into units of 1 sq km. Once these sampling units were marked on the map, several small areas <0.25 sq km remained at the upper ends of subsidiary creeks and several small peninsula ridgetops. These were treated as separate 'zones' when selecting the sampling units to be included in the survey, but in the analyses the small peninsulas were included with peninsula ridgetops and subsidiary creek ends with subsidiary creeks. The eight zones from which samples were selected were thus:

Ridgetop	Periphery (RT-PERI)	*periphery ridgetops*
	Peninsula (RT-PEN)	*peninsula ridgetops*
	Small Peninsulas (RT-SPEN)	*small peninsulas*
Valley Bottom	Main Creek (VB-MC)	*main valley bottoms*
	Subsidiary Creek (VB-SC)	*subsidiary valley bottoms*
	Subsidiary Creek Ends (VB-SCE)	*subsidiary creek ends*
Ridgeside	Main Creek (RS-MC)	*main ridgesides*
	Subsidiary Creek (RS-SC)	*subsidiary ridgesides*

For ease of reference during future discussions, the topographic zones are referred to by the terms listed in the third column. Abbreviations noted in brackets are used in tables and figures.

Each sampling unit was numbered and random number tables were used to select (without replacement) a 10% sample of the units in each of the eight zones. The total area of each of the topographic zones ranged between 0.7 and 31.1 sq km, so that the total number of units in each zone varied and ranged between nine and 110 (Table 3.3). Where the total number of sampling units in a topographic zone was not an even 'ten' (i.e., 10, 20, 30), the number of units selected was based on the figure being rounded up or down to the nearest 'ten' (e.g., 12 to 10, 28 to 30; thus 10% of 12 was taken as one unit and 10% of 28 as three units). The main ridgesides (RS-MC) are an exception to this rule due to a mathematical error and the number was incorrectly rounded up and not down. The units selected for surveying are called Random Sampling Units (RSUs). Selecting 10% of the units from each of the eight zones resulted in a total of 31 sampling units (Fig. 3.15), which represents a sampling fraction of 10.7% (Table 3.3). RSU.117 is in two sections because of the way the 0.25 sq km units were 'counted' out on the map. It is in the low relief upper reaches of a tributary where the periphery ridgetop adjoins the subsidiary valley bottom, and the land between the two sections of RSU.117 are parts of these zones (compare Figs 3.14 and 3.15).

Although the sampling design for the survey is stratified random sampling (without replacement), it would be classed as stratified random cluster sampling (without replacement) for analyses investigating the comparison of artefact assemblages at individual sites (see discussions in Mueller 1975 and Judge et al. 1975). Since the analyses undertaken to date for this project deal only with the frequency and density of sites and artefacts in particular zones, it has not been necessary to take these factors into account.

Table 3.2 Upper Mangrove Creek catchment: description of topographic zones into which catchment was stratified for sampling purposes. Figure 3.14 shows distribution and Figures 1.2 to 1.4 and cover show views.

---

1. RIDGETOPS

Flat to flattish land on the tops of ridges, plus 10m below the break of slope which distinguishes ridgetop from ridgeside. Where the ridgetop sloped down gradually from the top for a considerable distance, the boundary between ridgeside and ridgetop was not always easy to determine, and an arbitrary, but what seemed appropriate, line was drawn.

Ridgetops are divided into:

(a) Ridgetops — periphery (RT-PERI)

Flat to gently sloping land at the periphery/perimeter of the catchment, which contains the headwaters of the creeks before they become steep-sided gullies. In some places, this coincides with the boundary between the Hawkesbury sandstone and the underlying Narrabeen Group.

(b) Ridgetops — peninsula (RT-PEN)

Ridgetops that extend into the catchment from the periphery ridgetops and inter-finger between the major creeks and gullies. For sampling purposes, several small ridgetops running off the periphery ridgetops were treated as separate zones and were called small peninsula ridgetops (RT-SPEN).

2. VALLEY BOTTOMS

Land up to 40m above the creek bottom on either side of the creek (except in the upper reaches of the catchment where this stipulation would mean the areas defined as periphery ridgetops were included). This zone is divided into:

(a) Valley bottoms — main creeks (VB-MC)

Mangrove Creek up to Ramas Arm, part of Bucketty Gully and Deep Creek, and Boomerang Creek up to its junction with Sharp Gully, are classified as 'main creek', based principally on the width of the valley bottom.

(b) Valley bottoms — subsidiary creeks (VB-SC)

Sections of the creeks and gullies between the upper limit of 2(a) and the boundary of 1(a).

The main creek zones are generally in the wide valleys with alluvial flats, while the subsidiary creeks are in narrow steep-sided valleys and, if alluvial flats are present, they are very small and usually at creek or gully junctions. For sampling purposes, several small areas at the headwaters of creeks were treated as separate zones and were called subsidiary creek ends (VB-SCE).

3. RIDGESIDES

The land remaining between the ridgetops and the valley bottoms (i.e., the area of sloping ground 10m below the ridgetop and 40m above the valley bottom). It is divided into:

(a) Ridgesides — main creeks (RS-MC)

(b) Ridgesides — subsidiary creeks (RS-SC)

depending on whether the land is above a section of a main creek or a subsidiary creek as defined above. In the upper reaches of some creeks, where the elevation between valley floor and ridgetop is 40m or less (e.g., the headwaters of Bucketty Gully), there are no units classified as ridgesides and the boundary of 'valley bottoms' adjoins 'ridgetops'.

The sampling units selected under this stratified random sampling scheme are irregular in shape since they follow the morphology of the creeks and ridges. The shape and area of the units selected proved ideal in practical terms during the field survey. Sampling units consisting of square grids and straight line transects placed over dissected sandstone countryside would have been more awkward and would have taken longer to survey in the field than the irregularly shaped units of the adopted scheme.

Survey fieldwork undertaken

Two large-scale site survey programs have been undertaken in the Upper Mangrove Creek catchment: the intensive survey of the storage area which was carried out by the NSW NPWS (Furey 1978), and the stratified random sample of the total catchment undertaken by myself, which is described here. In future discussions, these surveys are referred to respectively as the 'storage area survey' and the 'random sample survey'. Because the random sampling units were selected disregarding the fact that the storage area had previously been surveyed for sites, some or part of some of the random sampling units fall within the storage area. There is thus some overlap of the areas covered by the two surveys and some sites fall into both

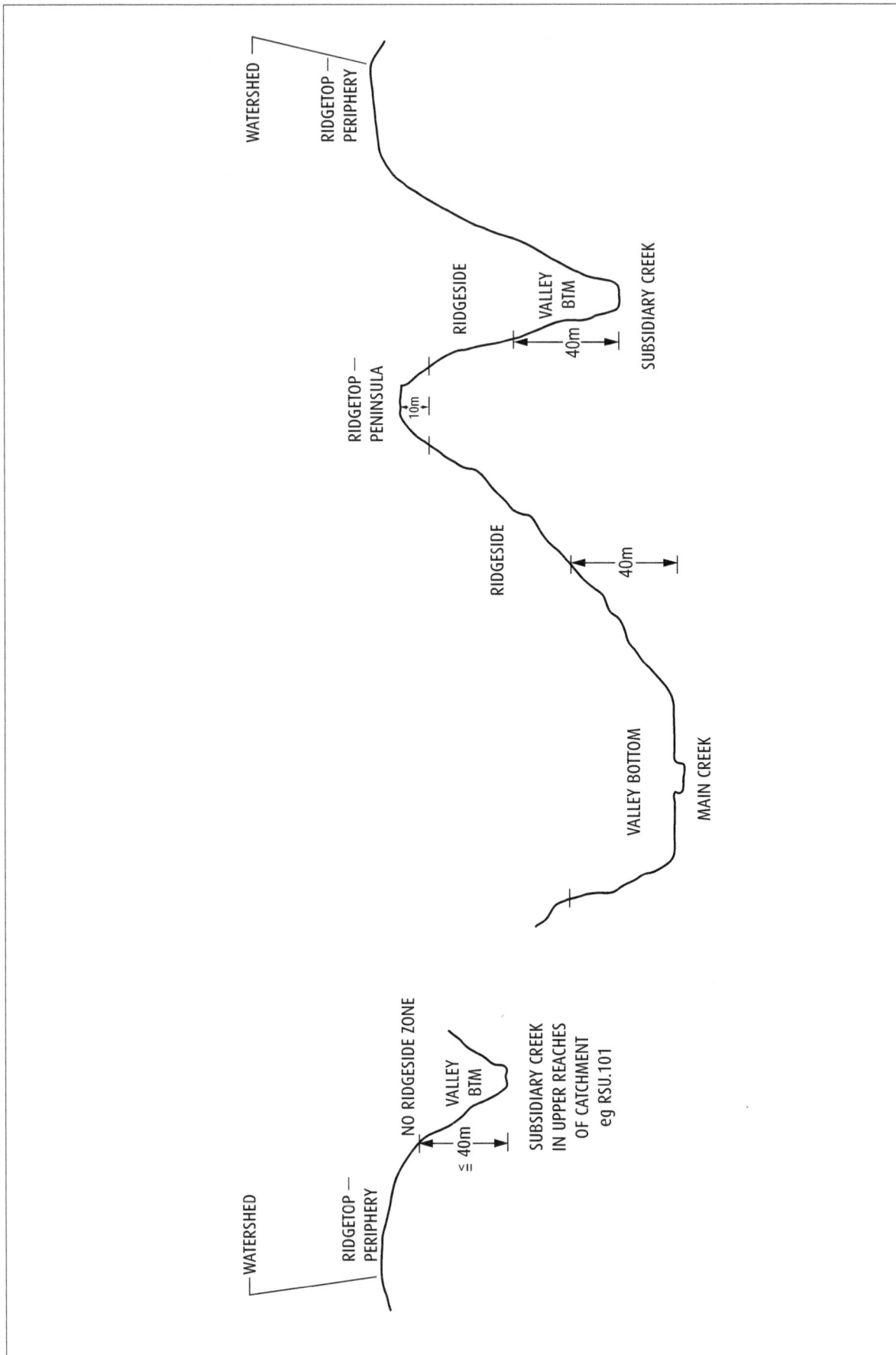

Figure 3.13 Upper Mangrove Creek catchment: schematic cross-section of catchment showing topographic zones.

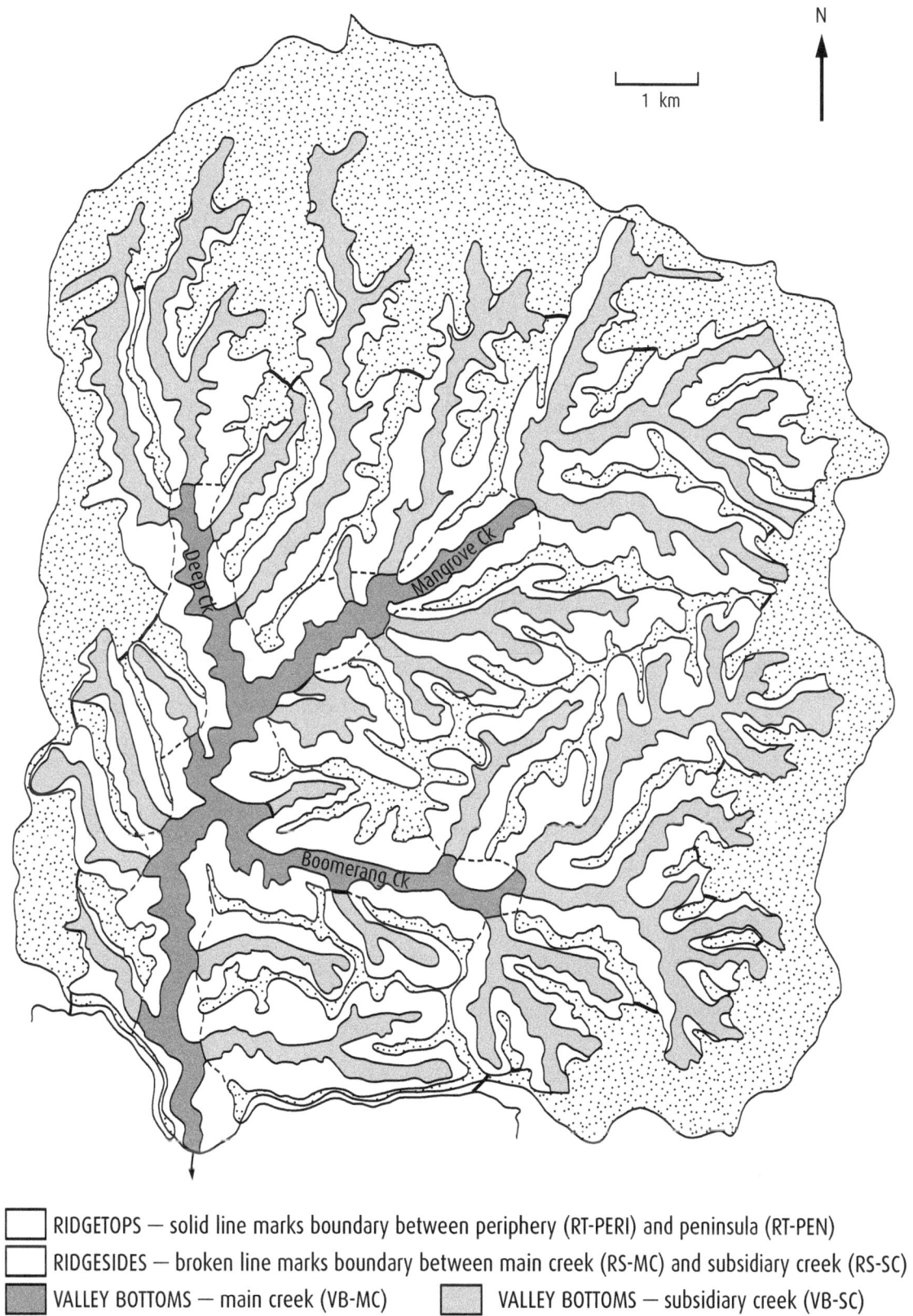

N

1 km

RIDGETOPS — solid line marks boundary between periphery (RT-PERI) and peninsula (RT-PEN)

RIDGESIDES — broken line marks boundary between main creek (RS-MC) and subsidiary creek (RS-SC)

VALLEY BOTTOMS — main creek (VB-MC)   VALLEY BOTTOMS — subsidiary creek (VB-SC)

Figure 3.14 Upper Mangrove Creek catchment: topographic zones. Table 3.2 has descriptions.

sampling schemes. Vegetation conditions had changed by the time the random sampling units were being surveyed for my research project and so units which fell within the storage area were surveyed again. The period between the two surveys was extremely dry, the understorey and ground cover was less dense and visibility was greater in many parts of the catchment for the later survey.

During the random sample survey, 28 of the 31 selected sampling units were surveyed (Table 3.3). The three sampling units not surveyed were RSU.92 (VB-SC), RSU.110a (VB-SCE) and RSU.210 (RS-SC). Of the 28 sampling units surveyed, a small area of four was not finished (RSU.57, RSU.156, RSU.177 and RSU.263). On several occasions, extra ground was covered in the field and so the areas surveyed were slightly larger than the original sampling unit. However, the additional areas and the locations recorded outside the sampling units are not included in the research project analyses. With regard to the strata into which the study area was divided, the sample size and sampling fraction achieved are slightly lower than proposed in three zones: subsidiary valley bottoms (VB-SC), subsidiary creek ends (VB-SCE) and subsidiary ridgesides (RS-SC) (Table 3.3).

Table 3.3 Upper Mangrove Creek catchment: details of stratified random sample. [1] prop/ach indicates proposed/achieved

Area of catchment	101 sq km	
Area of land sampled	10.1 sq km (10%)	
Sample type	stratified random sample (without replacement) (of land)	
	stratified random cluster sample (of sites)	
Stratification	8 zones based on 6 main topographic zones (Table 2)	
Sampling unit	quadrat (irregular in shape)	
Sampling unit sizes	Size A: approx. 0.25 sq km	RT-PEN, VB-MC, VB-SC, RS-MC, RS-SC
	Size B: approx. 1 sq km	RT-PERI
	Size C: <0.25 sq km	RT-SP and VB-SCE
Sampling frame	291 units	
Sample size	proposed: 31	achieved: 28
Sampling fraction	proposed: 10%	achieved: 9.6%
	selected: 10.7%	
Survey intensity	distance between team members	10m to 30m
	area/person-day	ca 6ha

STRATIFICATION (figures taken to nearest 0.1)

Topozone	Total area	Total no. of units	Sample size prop/ach [1]		Sample fraction prop/ach		Area surveyed	
	sq km		%	%	%	%	sq km	%
Catchment	101.0	291	31	28	10.0	9.6	10.1	10.0
RT-PERI	29.3	27	3	3	11.1	11.1	3.2	10.9
RT-PEN	8.5	30	3	3	10.0	10.0	1.0	11.8
RT-SPEN	0.7	9	1	1	11.1	11.1	0.1	14.3
RT-PEN +SPEN	9.2	39	4	4	10.3	10.3	1.1	12.0
VB-MC	4.8	17	2	2	11.8	11.8	0.6	12.5
VB-SC	16.9	59	6	5	10.2	8.5	1.5	8.9
VB-SCE	2.5	15	2	1	13.3	6.7	0.2	8.0
VB-SC +SCE	19.4	74	8	6	10.8	8.1	1.7	8.8
RS-MC	7.2	24	3	3	12.5	12.5	0.8	11.1
RS-SC	31.1	110	11	10	10.0	9.1	2.7	8.7

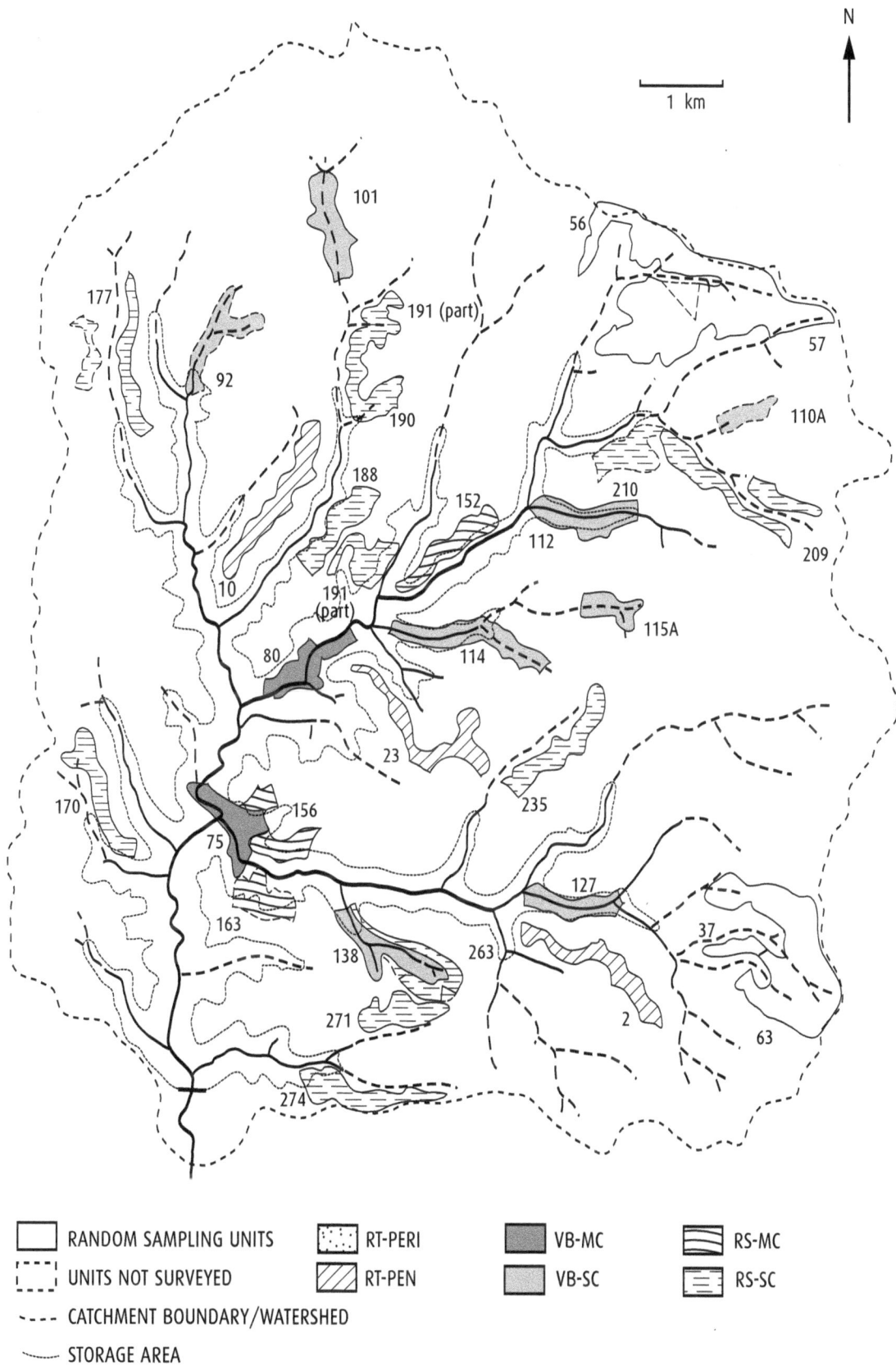

N

1 km

RANDOM SAMPLING UNITS   RT-PERI   VB-MC   RS-MC

UNITS NOT SURVEYED   RT-PEN   VB-SC   RS-SC

CATCHMENT BOUNDARY/WATERSHED

STORAGE AREA

Figure 3.15 Upper Mangrove Creek catchment: location of random sampling units.

In terms of the total catchment, the unfinished and unsurveyed units resulted in a sampling fraction and sample size that are slightly lower than that proposed — 9.6% and not 10%, and 28 instead of 31, respectively (Table 3.3). However, because a mathematical error caused a slightly larger sampling fraction (10.7%) to be selected than that originally proposed (10%), the total area actually surveyed in the sampling units represents 9.96% of the total catchment. When the figures are rounded off, this represents 10.1 sq km, which is 10% of the catchment area.

Because the number of unsurveyed units represents a low percentage of the total units and land area, I was advised that their exclusion does not invalidate the results under probability sampling theory (Brian O'Toole, Sample Survey Centre, University of Sydney, pers. comm, 8 July, 1985).

Field survey methods

Field methods used during the survey of the storage area (Furey 1978) were adopted, but were modified slightly to suit my specific aims. Fieldwork for the random sample survey was undertaken in three main periods: May 1979 (seven days), August 1979 (12 days) and May 1981 (six days) — a total of 25 days. This is actual survey time excluding establishment time, rest days and a day spent at the beginning of each survey period familiarising new survey teams with sites likely to be found. The survey team consisted of archaeology/prehistory students from Sydney and New England Universities, as well as NSW NPWS personnel, graduate archaeologists, consultants and interested people — a total of 19 different people participated in the surveys at various times. A total of 172 person-days was spent surveying the random sampling units; that is, one person-day for about six hectares. It was usually possible to cover one 0.25 sq km random sampling unit per day, except where many locations had to be recorded and/or it took a long time to travel to the sampling unit. Heavy undergrowth in some areas and the rugged nature of the terrain also made progress slow. In some cases, it took one or two hours to travel by vehicle and/or on foot to a random sampling unit.

At the time the survey was carried out, it was considered to be 'high intensity' (Attenbrow 1987: 72). Teams of between two and six, but normally four to five, people surveyed each sampling unit. Each person walked along a 'contour' of the ridgeside in a zigzag manner inspecting the zone on either side of the midpoint of the contour. The distance between team members varied from about 10m to 30m depending on the terrain. Each sampling unit was usually a long narrow area which was covered in one sweep, but in some cases two sweeps were necessary to cover the sampling unit. Team members kept together in a line down the slope so that each adjacent member knew where the other was and what ground had been covered. Team members inspected:

- all rockshelters for archaeological deposit, images and grinding grooves, and if no such evidence was found, their potential for habitation was assessed (see below);
- all flat to flattish open ground for open archaeological deposits — particularly those areas where ground sediments (soil) were exposed due to disturbance or lack of vegetation by natural or human processes;
- all exposed sandstone areas for engravings, and sandstone areas near water sources (i.e., creeks and gullies, or rock pools and seepage zones on ridgetops and ridgesides) for grinding grooves;
- trees, of suitable size and type, for scars.

Potential habitation shelters (PH shelters), in addition to archaeological sites, were recorded during the survey; this added to the time required for the survey. On average, 10 to 15 minutes were spent recording a PH shelter by one or two members, while the rest of the team stood by or inspected nearby likely locations. When a site was found, all team members helped in the recording and, on average, this took about an hour for each site.

In addition to the above, five days were spent relocating several sites which were not fully recorded during the survey. Approximately two days were spent looking specifically for open archaeological deposits along the alluvial flats and banks of Upper Mangrove Creek from the dam wall to the junction of Wattle Creek. The initial storage area survey was undertaken while vegetation was quite lush and the valley bottoms relatively undisturbed. As the drought progressed and as works associated with the dam took place (tree-felling and bulldozing of the 70m contour road), the ground visibility and sub-surface exposure became greater. The section of Mangrove Creek between Wattle Creek junction and Bucketty Creek junction (in which RSU.80 occurs) was re-surveyed intensively, and the banks of the remainder of the creek were re-inspected intermittently and opportunistically whenever possible. These 're-surveys' under the changed conditions located several additional open archaeological deposits (Attenbrow 1997 [1998]). Unfortunately, detailed investigation of most of the open archaeological deposits was not possible before the storage area was inundated.

Many sites were recorded outside the two survey 'areas'. Sites were found during walks in the catchment, from information given by local residents, and while trying to find already recorded sites. Local residents also took me to sites they knew in the catchment. Information about sites outside the random sampling units and those recorded within the storage area has been used as a check on the results of the analysis of the evidence recorded in the random sampling units (Chapter 5, Discussion).

Excavation

Excavation strategy and methods

I originally intended that all *sites* in the random sampling units recorded as having archaeological deposit or potential archaeological deposit would be included in the excavation program. In addition, the deposits in a random sample of PH shelters were to be test excavated to assess the incidence of PADs in PH shelters being archaeological deposits. However, not all of the sites recorded as having archaeological deposit (17 in rockshelters, five in open locations) or potential archaeological deposit (nine rockshelters with images) in the random sampling units were included in the excavation program. The sites excluded were:

- three rockshelters which technically have archaeological deposit (i.e., stone artefacts and/or a hearth and/or some sand present on their sandstone floors), but which in reality have no deposit or no depth to the deposit (Axehead, Button and Firestick);
- one open archaeological deposit at which there is no depth of deposit, that is, a ridgetop situation with skeletal soils (Kyola Road);
- two open archaeological deposits in totally disturbed locations (Palmers Crossing, Willow Tree Gully);
- a rockshelter initially recorded as a PH shelter but identified late in the research project as having archaeological deposit (Token Male).

Four PH shelters with deposit were purposefully selected for excavation. It was not possible to include a larger randomly selected sample within the available fieldwork time. I thus considered it was better to choose PH shelters to answer specific questions, rather than to randomly select a small number out of the 164 with potential archaeological deposit. PH.166, PH.204, PH.233 and PH.425 were selected:

- *PH.166* was chosen as no archaeological deposits had been recorded in RSU.191 and, of the PH shelters that had been recorded in this sampling unit, PH.166 appeared the most likely to contain archaeological materials;
- *PH.204* was chosen as a possible artefact had been noted on the surface during the survey, and no archaeological deposits had been recorded in RSU.112;
- *PH.233* in RSU.63 was chosen to test the proposal that all available rockshelters in the periphery ridgetops were inhabited;

- *PH.425* was chosen as many PH shelters had been recorded in RSU.209, but archaeological evidence had been recorded in very few of the rockshelters in this sampling unit.

The deposit in 29 locations was excavated. Excavation methods used during the research project were essentially the same as those used in the salvage program (Attenbrow 1981: 37–8).

In *the salvage program*, excavation was undertaken at two levels:

1. test pits between $0.25m^2$ and $0.5m^2$ were excavated, the latter as contiguous $0.25m^2$ pits;

2. larger scale excavations, where between $2m^2$ and $13m^2$ was excavated.

The larger scale excavations were carried out in the archaeological deposits which contained a relatively greater amount of cultural material than other sites: Black Hands, Deep Creek, Loggers, Mussel and Wattle Creek. Four of the excavated archaeological deposits in the storage area are within the random sampling units: Loggers, Black Hands Shelter, Black Hands Open Deposit and Geebung.

Initial excavations at Loggers and Black Hands were based on 1m squares (Attenbrow 1981: 38, 98, Fig. 6.4). However, during later work at Loggers (September 1981) and at Mussel and Deep Creek, the 1m squares were divided and dug as contiguous $0.25m^2$ pits (Attenbrow 1981: 89, 1982b: 8–9, 1982a: 2). The smaller squares provide greater horizontal resolution in provenancing excavated archaeological materials than the 1m squares.

For *the research project*, the only larger scale excavations were those in archaeological deposits which lay within both the storage area and a random sampling unit, that is, Loggers and Black Hands. In the remaining archaeological deposits in the random sampling units, usually one or two separate $0.25m^2$ pits or an area 100cm × 50cm were excavated (Table 3.4). In three archaeological deposits, a $1m^2$ pit was started initially, but excavation was restricted to $0.25m^2$ in the lower half of the deposit.

During the research project, sequential sampling was adopted during the excavation of some archaeological deposits (cf. Read 1975: 60). Based on the salvage excavations, I considered it was necessary to retrieve at least 200 artefacts if I wanted to make statements about the presence or absence of artefact types (particularly backed artefacts, which comprised 0.5 to 2% of assemblages at already excavated catchment sites) or about the predominance of certain raw material types in a particular spit, level or site (Attenbrow 1981: 124, Table 8.3; see also discussions in Hiscock 2001: 59). Therefore, if the first $0.25m^2$ pit produced less than 200 artefacts and it was calculated that a $1m^2$ pit would not produce at least that number, no further squares were excavated (principally due to fieldwork time limitations). However, if it was considered that excavation of a pit up to $1m^2$ would provide = />200 artefacts, then further squares were excavated. At two of the shelters (Emu Tracks 2 and Uprooted Tree), even though an initial $0.25m^2$ pit produced in excess of 200 artefacts, it was necessary to excavate an additional adjacent pit in order to reach the bottom of the deposit.

Where a single $0.25m^2$ pit was dug in an archaeological deposit it was designated T (for test pit, e.g., BC/T). If two separate $0.25m^2$ pits were dug, they were called T1 and T2 (e.g., CW/T1 and CW/T2), but if the two $0.25m^2$ pits formed a 100cm × 50cm trench, the squares were called Ta and Tb. Where the test pit was $1m^2$, the four 50cm squares were called Ta, Tb, Tc and Td. At Loggers and Black Hands, where the larger excavations took place before this system was instigated, the 1m×1m pits were called A, B, C, etc.

In Loggers and Black Hands, the deposit in each square was excavated in spits taken to a depth of ca 10cm unless a stratigraphic change (i.e., a change in colour, texture or content of the deposit) was observed before that depth. In all other sites, spits were dug to a depth of ca 5cm except where a stratigraphic change was observed before that depth, though in some cases, where deposits appeared to be sterile, spits up to 10cm deep were dug.

The excavations and subsequent analyses of material recovered from the archaeological deposits were directed towards obtaining stone artefact sequences, the date of earliest habitation at each site, inter-site variability in stone artefacts and faunal collections, and temporal changes in the rate of artefact accumulation. No attempt was made during the analyses to identify variations in the horizontal distribution of artefacts within individual archaeological deposits.

Excavation was also technically a sampling exercise — at no site was the total deposit excavated (Table 3.4). The square/s excavated in each archaeological deposit were selected purposively. Since probability sampling was not employed in selecting the square/s to be excavated, the assumptions of probability sampling cannot be upheld for the excavated data in the same manner as for the site survey results. Nonetheless, the results can still be used to evaluate hypotheses on a valid statistical basis as long as appropriate statistical methods are applied; that is, those which allow the assumption of random sampling to be retained (M. Hall 1981: 651–4). Despite this predicament, given the ways in which the data from each archaeological deposit were to be used, I considered it preferable to adopt the idea of 'constancy' in selecting the area of deposit to be excavated.

In Loggers and Black Hands, the excavated squares were laid out so that the back and the front of the rockshelter floors were included, as well as areas outside the dripline. At Black Hands, the upper deposit inside the rockshelter (in squares A and B) had previously been removed (by unknown people) and only the lowermost 45cm was in situ. Square F, the contents of which were analysed for this research, is immediately outside the dripline and its deposit was in situ throughout its depth.

At other rockshelters, the area to be excavated was selected because:

1.   primarily, it was the area where I assumed human activity would most likely have been focused in the rockshelter (a subjective assumption); that is, an attempt was made to select similar 'activity zones' in each shelter (cf. Morwood 1981: 41);
2.   the deposit in that area appeared to be undisturbed;
3.   it appeared to be the area which would have the greatest depth of deposit;
4.   it was inside the dripline — unless the floor inside the rockshelter was rock (e.g., in the case of McPherson and Delight).

Locating the excavation pit inside the rockshelter also meant that the chance of slopewashed charcoal dominating the dated samples was less than if the area straddled or was outside the dripline. The dripline was avoided, since in terms of point two above, the dripline zone is usually a 'disturbed' zone, often subjected to some degree of scouring. Driplines have been described as areas where the highest densities of artefacts occur (Morwood 1981: 34, 41; Kohen et al. 1984: 68) and thus in some ways it is the best area to obtain a sample of a deposit that would contain the highest numbers of artefacts per volume excavated. However, since the areas being excavated in some archaeological deposits were small — 100cm × 50cm and 50cm × 50cm — I considered it best to avoid areas in which problems with stratigraphic integrity were likely to occur.

The principal motive in selecting the area to be excavated, however, was that it should be the same in each rockshelter. This was considered necessary to keep at least one variable (i.e., the 'activity zone' sampled in each rockshelter) constant when investigating inter-site variability in cultural remains (cf. Johnson 1979: 106; Morwood 1981: 41) and site use within the catchment, and variations in the timing of changes in the artefact accumulation rates in individual archaeological deposits.

The deposit from all excavations was sifted through nested 9mm or 8mm and 3mm sieves, or a single 3mm sieve. Nested sieves were used in the larger scale excavations to facilitate sorting of the materials retained in the sieves. The weight of sandstone rubble retained in each of the sieves was recorded for use in characterising the deposits.

Table 3.4 Upper Mangrove Creek catchment: details of excavations in sites with archaeological deposit and potential archaeological deposit, and potential habitation shelters with potential archaeological deposit. Figures rounded to nearest 0.5cm. [1] First figure listed against Black Hands and Loggers represents percentage for the excavated square for which artefacts have been analysed; the second figure is total proportion of deposit excavated. [2] Depth is the measurement between the ground surface and the often-sloping base of the excavated pit.

SITE NAME/ LOCATION	Area excavated		Proportion of arch. deposit excavated[1]	Depth excavated[2]		Base of excavation
	Square	Size (cm)	%	Max. (cm)	Min. (cm)	
Andara	T1	50 x 50]	1.0	12.5	8.5	Bedrock (weathered)
	T2	50 x 50]		24.0	7.0	Discontinued — sand
Axehead		------				
Bird Tracks	T	50 x 50	1.0	43.0	39.5	Sterile sand
Black Hands SH	F	100 x 100	4.0 [12]	101.0	56.0	Sterile colluvial
Black Hands OD	T1	100 x 50	?	104.0	65.0	Discontinued — water
	T2	100 x 50	?	33.0	30.0	Sterile colluvial
Boat Cave	T	50 x 50	1.0	39.0	30.5	Bedrock
Boronia	Ta-c]	100 x100	4.0	[14.0	6.0	Sterile sand
	Td]			[37.5	37.5	Sterile sand
Button		-------				
Caramel Wave	T1	50 x 50]	3.0	25.5	9.0	Bedrock
	T2	50 x 50]		17.5	6.5	Bedrock
Delight SH	Ta	30 x 20]	7.0	31.5	20.0	Bedrock/sterile sand/rubble
	Tb	50 x 40]		20.5	11.0	Bedrock/sterile sand/rubble
Delight OD	A	60 x 35]		25.0	23.0	Sterile colluvial
	B	75 x 50	?	18.0	18.0	Sterile colluvial
	C	100 x 50]		9.0	9.0	Sterile colluvial
Dingo	Ta	50 x 50]	3.0	22.5	20.0	Discontinued — burial
	Tb	50 x 50]		39.0	15.0	Bedrock/sterile sand
Elngarrah	Ta-d	100 x100	3.0	33.0	0.0	Bedrock, stepped
Elongated Figure	T	50 x 50	1.5	40.0	19.0	Bedrock, sloping
Emu Tracks 2	T1	50 x 50]	3.5	44.5	19.0	Bedrock/sterile sand
	T2a	50 x 50]		79.5	28.0	Rock/bedrock/rubble
	T2b	50 x 50]		35.0	25.5	Rock
Firestick		------				
Geebung	T1	50 x 50]	2.0	5.0	5.0	Sterile colluvial
	T2	50 x 50]		5.0	5.0	Sterile colluvial
Harris Gully/PH.204	T	50 x 50	2.0	49.0	23.0	Bedrock, sloping/sterile sand
Kangaroo and Echidna	T1	50 x 50]	0.5	43.0	36.0	Sterile sand
	T2a	50 x 50]		29.2	26.2	Rock/sterile sand
	T2b	50 x 50]		71.0	66.0	Sterile sand
	T2c	50 x 50]		14.5	9.3	Rock
	T2d	50 x 50]		29.0	28.0	Sterile sand
Kyola Road OD		------				
Loggers	E-F	200 x100	4.0 [24.5]	206.0	160.0	Sterile colluvial
Low Frontage	Ta	50 x 50]	2.0	23.5	16.5	Sterile sand
	Tb	50 x 50]		47.8	30.0	Bedrock
McPherson	T	50 x 50	1.0	19.5	10.0	Rubble
Mangrove Mansions	T1	50 x 50]	0.5	27.0	13.0	Rubble
	T2	50 x 50]		28.0	22.0	Discontinued — sterile sand
One Tooth	T	50 x 50	1.0	37.5	25.0	Bedrock (weathered)
Palmers Crossing N OD		------				
Sunny/PH.233	Ta-b	100 x 50	1.5	71.0	32.5	Rubble

Table 3.4 (continued)

SITE NAME/ LOCATION	Area excavated		Proportion of arch. deposit excavated[1]	Depth excavated[2]		Base of excavation
	Square	Size (cm)	%	Max. (cm)	Min. (cm)	
Ti-tree	T1	50 x 50]	2.0	11.5	5.5	Rock
	T2	50 x 50]		38.0	0.5	Rubble
Token Male/PH.235		------				
Two Moths/PH.425	T	50 x 50	1.0	52.5	34.0	Rubble
Uprooted Tree	Ta	50 x 50]	3.0	72.0	67.0	Discontinued — Tb continued
	Tb	50 x 50]		114.0	77.5	Bedrock, sloping/sterile sand
	Tc	50 x 50]		12.0	8.0	Discontinued — Ta-b continued
Venus	Ta	50 x 50]	3.0	25.0	22.0	Rock/sterile sand
	Tc	50 x 50]		32.0	22.0	Rock
White Figure	Ta-b	100 x 50	3.0	55.0	15.0	Bedrock
Willow Tree Gully OD		-------				
Wolloby Gully	T	50 x 50	<0.5	33.0	17.0	Bedrock/rubble
PH.166	T	50 x 50	1.0	62.0	49.5	Bedrock (weathered)

Excavations undertaken

Excavating the archaeological deposits in the random sampling units (i.e., excluding those which lay inside the storage area) took place in three periods totalling 40 days between June and August 1982. Recording of the rockshelters (i.e., the locations) and images was carried out during the same field seasons. Fifteen different people (all volunteers) were involved — students from Sydney, New England and the Australian National Universities and archaeological consultants — providing a total of 170 person-days. Excavation of archaeological deposits in the three rockshelters which lay in both the storage area and the random sampling units (Loggers, Black Hands and Geebung) was undertaken within the salvage program.

Details of the fieldwork undertaken at each of the 29 excavated locations are set out in Table 3.4. The locations were 27 rockshelters and two open deposits; 23 of the rockshelters were sites and four were potential habitation shelters with deposit (PAD) (Table 3.5). Archaeological materials were retrieved from all but one of the excavated locations.

The area of deposit excavated at each of the rockshelter sites (excluding Black Hands and Loggers) was between 0.2% and 7% (Table 3.4). Three archaeological deposits had <1% of the deposit excavated, 20 had between 1% and 4% (inclusive), and one had 7%. The area excavated at Black Hands and Loggers was 12% and 24.5% respectively, though the artefacts from all excavated squares were not analysed for this study. The first percentage given in column three of Table 3.4 represents the area of the pit from which the analysed artefacts were retrieved. The figures represent the percentage of the total area of the archaeological deposit; the latter not always being the same as the area within the shelter (see next chapter). It was not feasible to calculate the percentage of deposit dug at the two open archaeological deposits.

Of the 23 excavated deposits in rockshelter sites, 14 had surface evidence to indicate that they were archaeological deposits (stone artefacts and/or shell) and nine were rockshelters with images which had potential archaeological deposit. A total of 13 rockshelters with potential archaeological deposit were therefore excavated — four PH shelters and nine rockshelters with images; the latter being classified as sites on the basis of the images.

Artefacts were found on the surface of the deposit outside the excavated areas in many shelters (see next chapter and Appendix 1). In some cases, these artefacts had not been noticed during the site survey, but were found during the excavation phase. They became exposed through treadage and scuffage during excavation activities, which moved leaf-litter about and led to loss of some vegetation ground cover. The number of archaeological deposits noted as having surface artefacts in the final lists therefore does not coincide with the number presented above, which is the number of archaeological deposits where surface artefacts were found during the site survey.

The area and depth excavated at each of the locations is also given in Table 3.4. The base of most excavated pits was not a horizontal area — it was often sloping bedrock or partially sloping rock or rubble — and thus maximum and minimum depths (or thickness) of the excavated deposits are provided. At some sites, although the excavation started as a 1m square, the final deposit excavated was restricted to 50cm × 50cm. When sterile deposits were encountered, if no cultural materials were found after at least 20cm of sterile deposit had been excavated, digging ceased and bedrock was not always reached. The nature of the base of each excavated pit — for example, whether bedrock, rock (possible bedrock or very large boulder/slab), rubble, sterile sand or colluvial — is given in Table 3.4 as well. Where more than one category is given, a greater part of the base consists of the first-mentioned category.

Excavation at Black Hands Open Deposit stopped when the then-rising water from the adjacent storage area was encountered in the excavation pit. Excavation was discontinued before bedrock or sterile deposit was reached in two other archaeological deposits (Anadara and Mangrove Mansions) as, once excavation progressed, it was apparent that the deposit was very disturbed. Probing with a skewer suggested that there was only another 20cm or so depth of deposit at Mangrove Mansions and about 12cm at Anadara before bedrock, and at both shelters this lower deposit appeared disturbed. At both rockshelters, there were very few artefacts in the deposit excavated, and it seemed that additional information would not be gained if the disturbed basal deposits were excavated or another square was excavated in a different part of the shelter. This decision was reinforced by the fieldwork time available and the additional time which would have been required to return to the sites to dig additional pits.

Classification of contents of archaeological deposits

Except for a few pieces of historical (European) material found in surface spits, the cultural elements recovered from the archaeological deposits were of Aboriginal origin. They consist of:

- *stone and bone artefacts*
- *faunal remains*: (bone, shell and exoskeleton) considered to be the remains of animals eaten by the Aboriginal inhabitants of the sites, as well as some faunal remains from non-human predators (see Appendix 3);

Table 3.5 Upper Mangrove Creek catchment: locations and types of deposit excavated.

	LOCATION		TOTAL
Type of deposit	*Rockshelter*	*Open deposit*	
Archaeological deposit	9	2	11
Archaeological deposit associated with images	5	–	5
Potential archaeological deposit associated with images	9	–	9
Potential archaeological deposit	4	–	4
Total sites excavated	23	2	25
Total archaeological deposits excavated	14	2	16
Total PADs excavated	13	–	13
Total locations excavated	27	2	29

- *plant remains*: parts of plants known to be eaten by Aboriginal people and which thus may be humanly derived, and modified wood;

- *ochreous materials*: haematite-rich fine-grained stone, or a series of rock types ranging from shale to muddy sandstone, ranging in colour from red-brown (containing unhydrated iron oxides such as haematite) to yellow (containing hydrated iron oxides such as limonite) (Attenbrow 1982a: 19–20). Only a small amount of this material shows any evidence of use;

- *charcoal*: assumed to be primarily from fires used for cooking, warmth or artefact manufacture.

The manner in which these materials were classified for the salvage program has been outlined previously (Attenbrow 1981: 39–44, 1982b; Stern 1981, 1982; Aplin 1981; Aplin and Gollan 1982); however, some changes were made for the research project and so details are provided below. Details of the recording procedures for images and grinding areas have been excluded from this monograph (see Attenbrow 1987: 116–18 for details).

Stone artefacts

For **the salvage program,** the stone artefacts were classified into the following types: backed artefacts (Bondi points, geometrics, miscellaneous backed pieces, elouera), other flaked implements, bipolar pieces, ground-edged implements and ground pieces (i.e., fragments), cores (with and without pebble cortex), waste and hammerstones (Attenbrow 1981: 39–43, 1982a: Appendix 2). The category 'other flaked implements', which included amorphous pieces with retouch and/or use wear (i.e., non-backed artefacts), was divided into edge-trimmed flakes, thick flake tools, steep-edged scrapers (definitions in Attenbrow 1981: 41–2). Subdivision of the 'other flaked implements' in this manner was made to investigate whether changes identified by Stockton (1977a: 215–217, 1977c) also occurred in the Upper Mangrove Creek catchment. By dividing the non-backed implements at various late-Pleistocene to mid-Holocene aged sites in eastern Australia into pebble and core tools, thick flake tools and edge-trimmed flake tools, Stockton (1977a: 216) documented a gradual shift through time from a predominance of core, pebble and thick flake tools to a predominance of edge-trimmed flake tools.

For **the research project**, stone artefacts from the archaeological deposits in the random sampling units have been classified into the following artefact types: backed artefacts (Bondi points, geometrics, elouera, backed miscellaneous), other flaked artefacts with retouch/use wear (R/UW), bipolar cores, bipolar flakes, cores (hand-held percussion), waste artefacts (which includes redirecting flakes as well as flakes [hand-held percussion] and flaked pieces), ground-edged artefacts and ground fragments, an ochre palette, hammerstones and manuports (see key and notes to Appendix 1). Bipolar artefacts from Loggers and Black Hands were not reclassified into flakes and cores, and the artefact distribution tables for these two sites retain the salvage program classification system. Since inter-site comparisons of artefact assemblages were not carried out for the research project, this has not affected results presented in this volume. A *Bulga* knife (McCarthy 1976: 53, Fig. 39 [4, 5]) was among the ground-edged artefacts retrieved from Kangaroo and Echidna (Fig. 3.16).

Heat-shattered and other fractured pieces, as well as broken flakes, were included with flaked pieces during the analyses (see definitions in Appendix 1). Current technological approaches to stone artefact analyses (e.g., Hiscock 1985) advocate the categorisation of heat-shattered and 'fractured pieces' separate from flaked pieces. Fractured pieces and heat-shattered pieces were not numerous, and it is unlikely that combining these categories together will have affected the artefact accumulation rates to the extent that the documented trends would radically alter. However, this remains to be tested.

The stone artefacts have been classified according to raw material and size categories as well. The raw material categories are: quartz, quartzite, igneous, silcrete, chert/indurated mudstone/tuff, and 'unidentified fine-grained siliceous' (FGS) (see definitions in Appendix 1). Quartz, in pebble form, is present and erodes out of the Hawkesbury sandstone. Quartz, quartzite, some cherts and the FGS stone materials are all available in pebble/cobble form after they have eroded out of the Narrabeen Group (sandstone) conglomerate layers within the catchment and can be collected from lower ridgesides and particularly creek beds within that geological stratum (pers. obs.). Tuffaceous materials, which have been included under chert/indurated mudstone/ tuff, and silcrete do not come from the catchment and possibly come from the Hunter Valley or the Hawkesbury–Nepean River–Cumberland Plain. Constant accessibility to and availability of tuff-type chert and silcrete cannot be assumed to have existed throughout time. The majority of the bipolar artefacts are quartz, but many silcrete and chert specimens were also recovered.

The size categories into which the artefacts are grouped are 0–1cm, 1–2cm, 2–4cm, +4cm; very few artefacts are more than 4cm long. Size is recorded as the length along the percussion axis of a flake, or the longest measurement on other artefacts. For the salvage program, size was recorded as the longest dimension, irrespective of the direction of the percussion axis (Attenbrow 1981: 43). A check was made during the recent analysis and the number of occurrences where the length classes of wider-than-long flakes differed from the width class was monitored. The small number of times the percussion length fell into a different size class to the maximum dimension did not alter the overall percentage figures for the size distribution of artefacts. I therefore consider that data on the size distribution of artefacts from both projects are comparable.

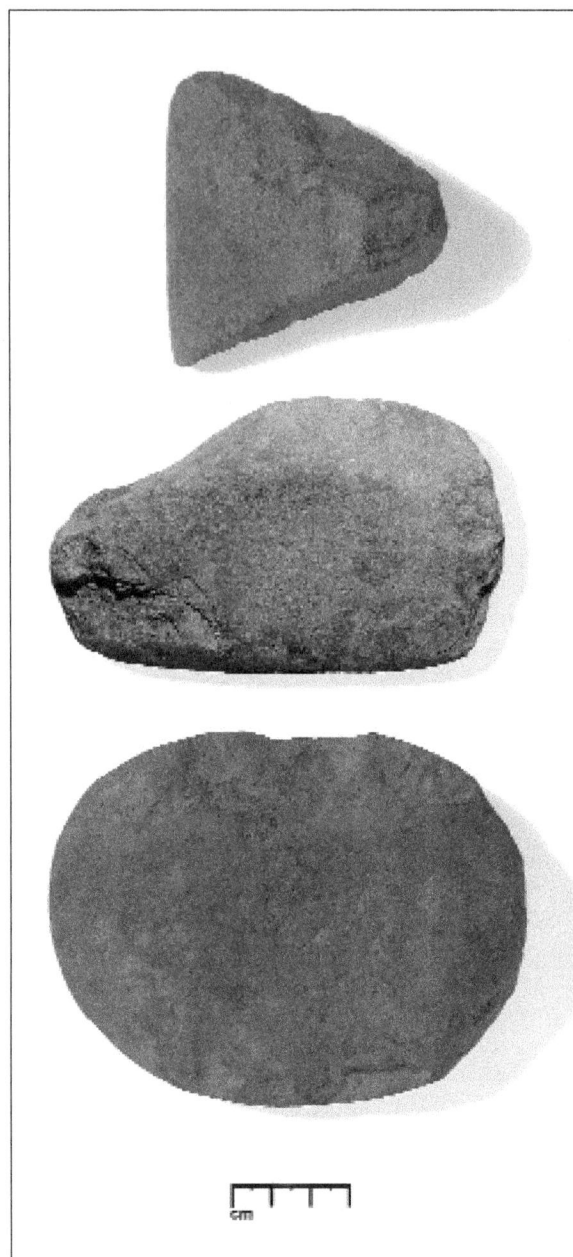

Figure 3.16 Ground-edged artefacts from Kangaroo and Echidna (test pit 2, spit 3): two hatchet heads (top and bottom) and Bulga knife (centre). Photographer Carl Bento, Australian Museum.

Unusual stone implements include a resin-hafted flake from Loggers (Fig. 3.17), which was found in deposit between rocks against the back wall of the lower ceilinged alcove in the shelter (LS/Lb/1), and a broken sandstone ochre palette from Sunny (Sus/T/6) (Fig. 3.18). Based on a depth/age curve (Table A2/14), the ochre palette could be between 1400 and 1600 years old.

Bone artefacts

Very few bone artefacts have been identified (Fig. 3.19). Four bone artefacts were found in the upper levels of Loggers: two with pointed ends (one in LS/Lb/1 and another in LS/Bk/1) and two with a spatulate-like end (one found on the surface in the small alcove and the other in LS/A/3). Three worked small slivers/fragments of bone, each less than 2.5cm long, were found in Bird Tracks Shelter (BT/T/3).

Wooden objects

Wooden objects which may derive from Aboriginal activities were found in three rockshelters, though each of the three items requires further investigation to verify its origin. In Firestick, part of a thick branch with several cut marks was found in association with the remains of a small fireplace. The branch was partially burnt and was possibly taken into this small, relatively inaccessible shelter as firewood. The cut marks are on a section of its unburnt surface. The rockshelter is in a part of the catchment and in a location that suggest it was unlikely that the wood was taken in there recently by non-Aboriginal people, and thus it has been identified tentatively as an Aboriginal artefact. A hand stencil is on the shelter wall.

In Wolloby Gully, a small section of wood with a cut end was excavated in spit 2 of the test pit, and in Button Shelter what may be part of a 'firestick' base was found on bedrock forming the shelter floor (Fig. 3.20).

Figure 3.17 Hafted retouched flake from Loggers Shelter found in lower ceilinged area at rear of shelter (square Lb, spit 1). Photographer Carl Bento, Australian Museum.

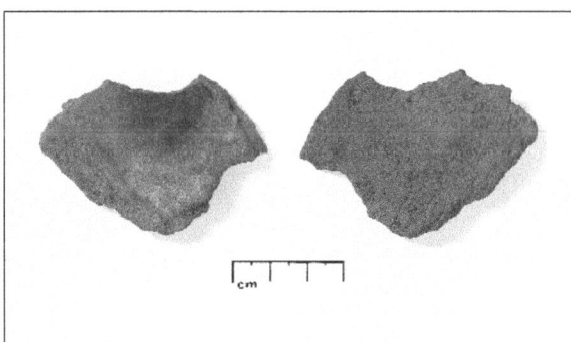

Figure 3.18 Fragment of red ochred sandstone palette from Sunny Shelter (test pit, spit 6). Photographer Carl Bento, Australian Museum.

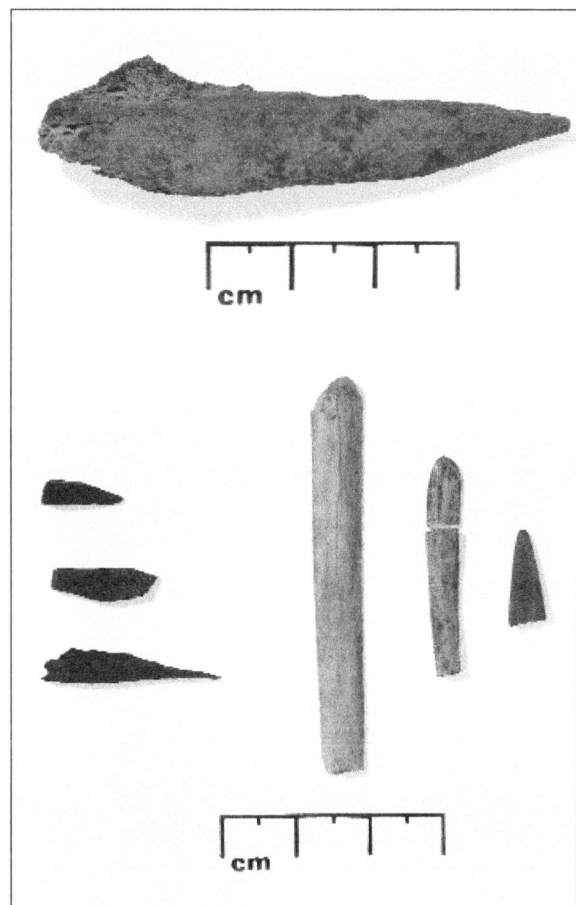

Figure 3.19 Bone artefacts from Loggers Shelter (top: Square Lb, spit 1; and three at right: surface at rear of shelter, square A, spit 3-brown, and square Bk, spit 1) and Bird Tracks (three at left: from test pit, spit 3). Photographer Carl Bento, Australian Museum.

Faunal remains

Faunal remains from the archaeological deposits in the random sampling units were analysed by Aplin (1985, reproduced in Appendix 3) in a similar manner to that used for the salvage excavations. Although the majority of fragments are unidentifiable, a large number of animals was identified (see next chapter). Fragments of shellfish were also present — estuarine cockle (*Anadara trapezia*), freshwater mussel (probably *Hyridella* sp. and/or *Velesunio ambiguus*; Ian Lock, Malacology Department, Australian Museum, pers. comm.), as well as unidentified landsnail and yabbies/crayfish (*Euastacus australiensis*, *E. nobilis* and/or *E. spinifer*; Merrick 1993: 61, 72, 76; Jones and Morgan 1994: 93).

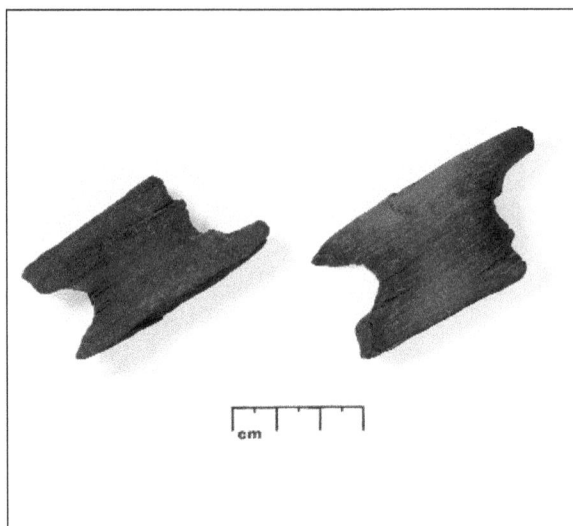

Figure 3.20 Fragment of a possible firestick (base) found on raised section of sandstone floor in Button Shelter. Photographer Carl Bento, Australian Museum.

The landsnails probably have a non-human origin, and the cockles can only have reached the catchment by human means, given the distance between the estuarine environment and the catchment. However, the medium by which freshwater mussels entered the archaeological deposits needs some clarification since they inhabit Upper Mangrove Creek and its tributaries. Several species of birds and the water rat eat freshwater mussel, and they are likely to take shells into rockshelters (Haglund 1981a: 6; Ken Aplin, pers. comm.). Dingoes may also be responsible for the addition of some shell, since they are known to eat shellfish and eat the species of birds which eat shellfish. Shell from primary and secondary ingestion may be defecated by dingoes in rockshelters, though the chance of this is minimal (Su Solomon, pers. comm., 25 November, 1986).

It is most likely that shell fragments in the archaeological deposits in the catchment are all humanly derived, since:

1.   birds are unlikely to deposit shell in the catchment rockshelters, as the species of birds eating freshwater mussel in the catchment are not the species that take their food into rockshelters (P. Smith, NPWS, pers. comm., 1986) and the chance of them dropping inside from above (i.e., while the bird is flying or sitting on the shelter overhang) would be so negligible as to be archaeologically invisible. The chance of non-humanly derived shell being mixed with humanly derived archaeological material is more likely to occur along the coast (Horton 1978: 31; Jones and Allen 1978) and along major inland rivers and lagoons where some species of birds create 'shell middens' (shell dumps) by returning successively to the same location to eat shellfish (Vestjens 1973; Van Tetz, pers. comm., 1985). These latter situations, however, are usually in the open.

2.   the distance between the rockshelters containing shell fragments and the creeks is sufficient that water rats would not have carried shellfish into them. For the same reason, it is unlikely that water birds would have carried shellfish into some of the rockshelters.

3.   dingoes have not been noted to defecate in their dens and tend to use their faeces as territorial markers on paths and bushes in the open (Su Solomon, pers. comm., 25 November, 1986).

Plant remains

Unmodified plant remains include leaves, twigs, bark, grass, seeds, seed pods, eucalypt fruits, casuarina cones, flowers, bracken fronds and small fragments of paperbark. Most plant remains have been classified as 'leaf-litter' which has blown into the rockshelters as the remains usually come from plant species which grow in or in close proximity to the particular location in which they were found: for example, *Eucalyptus* sp., *Angophora* sp., *Acacia* sp., *Persoonia* sp., *Macrozamia* sp., *Melaleuca* sp., *Syncarpia* sp. Paperbark fragments are the only as yet recognised exception to this statement, but many of the seeds are still unidentified. Leaf-litter was present in the upper few centimetres of most archaeological deposits, although it varied in quantity depending on the morphology of the rockshelter mouth (i.e., whether it allowed access to windblown materials) and the dryness of the deposit. Very few organic remains were found below a depth of 30cm.

None of the excavated plant remains can be definitely attributed to human activities, though in some excavated archaeological deposits there is material which could be humanly derived. The identified seeds are from *Acacia filicifolia* (fernleaf wattle) and *Persoonia* sp. (geebung). Seeds of other species of acacia (but not *A. filicifolia*) have been recorded as being eaten by Aboriginal people. It has not been possible to determine whether the seeds and seed pods in the catchment archaeological deposits were taken into the shelters by humans rather than being blown in by the wind. The fruit of *Persoonia* sp. is known to have been eaten by Aboriginal people and these seeds may be food remains. It is also possible that *Persoonia* seeds were deposited in the shelter in the faeces of birds (magpies, currawongs, crows, parrots, bower birds) or, more likely, small rodents (bush rats, possums), which are known to eat such fruits (D. Lunney, NSW NPWS, pers. comm., 1986).

Paperbark is known to have been used by Aboriginal people in the Sydney region and elsewhere for a variety of purposes, for example, as 'blankets' for newborn babies, bedding and wrapping (Collins 1798 [1975]: 465, 612, n14; Phillip in Hunter 1793 [1968]: 544; Macarthur 1791 [1893]: 504; Zola and Gott 1992: 63). The paperbark fragments may thus have been brought into the shelter by humans. The fragments retrieved may be from *Melaleuca* sp. or, less likely, from *Leptospermum attenuatum* (J. Thompsom, NSW Herbarium, pers. comm., 1986).

Analysis of the unmodified plant remains has not been undertaken, and they are not discussed further in this monograph.

Charcoal

The status of charcoal when it is the only material recovered is not always clear. It can occur in a rockshelter as the residue from Aboriginal campfires, but it can also occur in some rockshelters where slopewashed sediments can gain entry. Charcoal could also enter during fierce bushfires, depending on the dimensions and configuration of the mouth of the shelter and the location of the rockshelter on the land — small particles may be windblown or burning branches may fall into the shelter. Where artefacts are present in a shelter, the status of the charcoal is not important in determining whether the shelter is a site or whether the deposit is called 'archaeological deposit' or sterile sediment (although its origin has to be considered when selecting samples for radiocarbon dating and when interpreting radiocarbon dates). However, in shelters where no stone artefacts or humanly derived faunal remains are retrieved, the origin of the charcoal has to be more definitely determined before the site can be said to contain an 'archaeological deposit'.

In determining whether rockshelter deposits which contain large amounts of charcoal, but which do not contain stone artefacts or humanly derived faunal remains, should be classified as 'archaeological deposits', the following were considered:

1.   did the rockshelter have an entry point for slopewashed sediments, and/or was the section of the deposit excavated likely to have been contaminated by slopewashed sediments? And,

2.   did the morphology of the rockshelter mouth suggest that burning branches would be able to fall into the rockshelter?

These criteria had to be considered at only one rockshelter — PH.166. At this rockshelter, I consider that point 2. could have applied and possibly point 1. Since no stone artefacts or other humanly derived materials were found in the deposit, and there are no other traits in PH.166, the rockshelter is not classified as having archaeological deposit or as being a site.

Temporal Sequence

Four cultural phases were identified in the catchment (Table 3.6). These phases were identified and dated on the basis of typological and raw-material changes in the stone artefact assemblages in four radiocarbon-dated sites which were excavated during the salvage program (Attenbrow 1981, 1982a). These four sites have large stratified assemblages and habitation extending back at least 3000 radiocarbon years: Loggers (ca 11,300 BP), Mussel (ca 8700 BP), Deep Creek (ca 6200 BP) and Black Hands (ca 3000 BP). These four phases can be correlated with sequences found in other south-eastern Australian sites and with McCarthy's (1962, 1964a, 1964b, 1976: 96–8) Eastern Regional Sequence (Table 3.7), though minor variations occur in the implements found in different regions as well as in the timing of the transition from one phase to another. The results of other studies in south-eastern NSW (e.g., Megaw 1965, 1968a, 1974; Bowdler 1970, 1976; Lampert 1971a; Stockton and Holland 1974; Kohen et al. 1984) were also considered when defining the phases and in assigning dates for the beginning and/or end of each phase.

In future discussions, I refer to the four phases as the typological phases or the phased sequence. The following attributes and diagnostic artefacts characterise the assemblages belonging to each of the phases as set out in Table 3.8:

— presence, absence or relative abundance of Bondi points;
— presence or absence of ground implements/fragments;
— relative percentage frequency of bipolar artefacts;
— predominance of either quartz or FGS material; and/or,
— presence or absence of igneous material.

Table 3.6 Upper Mangrove Creek catchment: cultural phases and duration based on typological and raw-material changes in stone artefact assemblages.

PHASE	DATES	DURATION
1	from ca 11,300 BP to ca 5000 BP	ca 6300 years
2	between ca 5000 BP and ca 2800 BP	ca 2200 years
3	between ca 2800 BP and ca 1600 BP	ca 1200 years
4	between ca 1600 BP and 110 BP [1840 AD]	ca 1500 years

Table 3.7 Upper Mangrove Creek catchment: sequence of typological phases and dating, and correlation with terminology of other researchers.

UMCC PHASE	STOCKTON AND HOLLAND 1974: 53; ATTENBROW 1981	LAMPERT 1971a: 68	LAMPERT 1971b: 120	McCARTHY 1964b: 202, 234–9 1976: 96–7	JONES, ALLEN AND GOULD IN MULVANEY 1975: 174, 212
1	Capertian	Phase I	Pre-Bondaian	Capertian	Core Tool and Scraper Tradition
2	Early Bondaian	Phase II	Bondaian	Bondaian	]
3	Middle Bondaian	Phase II	Bondaian	Bondaian	] Small Tool Tradition
4	Late Bondaian	Phase III	Post-Bondaian	Eloueran	]

Table 3.8 Upper Mangrove Creek catchment: diagnostic criteria used as basis for dating typological phases. Number of •• indicates relative frequency within assemblages; Y, N indicates yes, no.

PHASE	DIAGNOSTIC CRITERIA						DURATION (YEARS BP)
	Bondi points	Other backed	Ground/ igneous	Bipolar artefacts	Quartz predom.	FGS predom.	
1	•		–	•	N	Y	ca 11,200–ca 5000
2	••	•	•	•	N	Y	ca 5000–ca 2800
3	•••	••	••	••	Y	N	ca 2800–ca 1600
4	–	•	•••	•••	Y	N	ca 1600–ca 110

Phase 1

Catchment assemblages of this phase consist principally of flakes, cores and flaked pieces. Implements include amorphous flakes with retouch/use wear ('scrapers') and dentated saws. A small number of backed artefacts was retrieved from pre-5000 BP contexts in two sites — Loggers Shelter and Mussel Shelter (Fig. 3.21). These artefacts are unlikely to be intrusive from higher levels and are taken as an indication that the manufacture of backed artefacts in Australia began much earlier than 4000 BP, albeit not very frequently (Attenbrow 1982a: 30; Hiscock and Attenbrow 1998, 2004; McNiven 2000; Hiscock 2001). No ground-edged implements occur. Bipolar artefacts are relatively uncommon. The average size of flaked artefacts in this phase is larger than those of later phases (Attenbrow 1981: Fig. 6.13), though the majority are still less than 3cm maximum dimension.

Figure 3.21 Early Holocene backed artefacts from Mussel (a: square B, spit 20; b: square A, spit 23) and Loggers Shelters (c: square F, spit 7; d: square F, spit 9). Scale has 1mm divisions. Photographer Carl Bento, Australian Museum.

The presence of 'saws' suggests affinities with other pre-Bondaian assemblages at Burrill Lake, Blue Mountains sites and Capertee (cf. Lampert 1971a: 65). The catchment assemblages differ from those described as the 'Core Tool and Scraper Tradition' (Bowler et al. 1970) in that no horsehoof cores have been identified and uniface pebble tools are rare or absent in most sites. In this respect, they are similar to the Blue Mountain's Capertian assemblages (McCarthy 1964: 222–5, 1976: 96; Stockton and Holland 1974: 54–5).

Quartz and FGS dominate the assemblages though quartz is less abundant than FGS. Chert, quartzite and silcrete are present in low proportions, and igneous artefacts are a very infrequent occurrence.

Phase 2

For Phase 2 (Early Bondaian), a date of ca 5000 BP has been adopted rather than the date of the earliest backed artefact in Loggers (ca 8500 BP). Backed artefacts occur more frequently after 5000 BP, and it is assumed that by this time they were being manufactured in sufficient numbers to be more frequently visible in archaeological contexts, though they become even more common after 3000 BP. Phase 2 is thus not defined as the period when backed artefacts first appear, but when they are more likely to be archaeologically visible. On this basis, I have assumed that the presence of backed artefacts in the small catchment assemblages is statistically more likely to indicate an age of post-5000 BP, and thus a Phase 2 or 3 (Early or Middle Bondaian) assemblage. Ground-edged implements first appear in this phase, ca 4000 years ago.

FGS stone dominates the assemblages. Quartz is the second-most abundant material. Silcrete, chert (including tuff-type materials) and quartzite are present in increasing numbers, though percentages are still small. Igneous materials increase in abundance compared with Phase 1.

Phase 3

In Phase 3, backed artefacts proliferate and ground-edged implements continue to be present, but quartz is the dominant stone material (by number). At Loggers, Mussel and Deep Creek, there was a gradual change in the relative abundance of FGS and quartz over time (for Loggers, see Appendix 1, Table A1/34). At all three sites, the level in which quartz predominates over FGS (while still continuing to increase in abundance, i.e., in number) is dated to 2700–2800 BP. In sites where initial habitation began earlier than 3000 BP, a change from the predominance of FGS artefacts to the predominance of quartz artefacts is used to indicate the beginning of Phase 3, and the temporal boundary between Phases 2 and 3 is placed at ca 2800 BP.

Phase 4

Backed artefacts are rare. Bondi points are absent from all assemblages dating to this phase, though some geometric microliths and elouera occur in Loggers and Black Hands, which have large assemblages. Bipolar artefacts increase further as do ground-edged implements and fragments from them. Quartz is the dominant raw material (by number) in large assemblages. Compared with Phase 3, igneous waste increases in abundance, and silcrete, chert and FGS decrease in abundance.

The date of ca 1600 BP for the transition from Phase 3 to Phase 4 given above differs from that used in the salvage report (i.e., 1000–1200 BP, Attenbrow 1981: 127). For the salvage program, the phases were identified and dated initially on the basis of the typological sequence and radiocarbon dates at only one site, Loggers. Further excavations and artefact analyses (particularly from Mussel and Deep Creek) since the salvage report was written, as well as further consideration of the data from sites along the coast and hinterland of south-eastern NSW (e.g., Lampert 1971a; Hughes and Djohadze 1980), led to revision of the original decision. The absence of Bondi points and / or rarity of other backed artefacts, or a radiocarbon age of ca 1600 BP, are taken as the beginning of Phase 4 in the catchment.

The date of 110 BP (1840 AD) adopted for the end of Phase 4 is the date that Threlkeld's mission at Lake Macquarie was abandoned as he believed there were no Aboriginal people left in the district to evangelise (Gunson 1974, Vol. 1: 168–9; Ferry 1979: 27, 34). However, Aboriginal people continued living in the Hawkesbury region beyond this date (V. Ross 1981: 204). The pigment sailing ships in two rockshelters and a glass bipolar core in another shelter attest to continuing use of the catchment after British colonisation. In the late 1880s, R. H. Mathews (1897: 1) identified some of his informants, who lived on a reserve near Windsor, as being Darginung. Even so, they were unlikely to have been following the pre-colonial subsistence, habitation or land-use patterns to the extent that they were still inhabiting the rockshelters and manufacturing stone implements in the Upper Mangrove Creek catchment after the mid-1800s.

Dating the archaeological deposits and periods of habitation

Radiocarbon determinations were received for 15 of the archaeological deposits (see Chapter 6). Where radiocarbon dates were not available, I identified the typological phase or phases represented in a site by using the assemblage attributes listed above as diagnostic 'time-markers' (cf. fossile directeur of Johnson 1979: 114; temporal types of Thomas 1979: 222–5). The radiocarbon determinations and diagnostic time-markers provide the basis for estimating the period in which the deposit began to accumulate and the length of time over which the deposit accumulated (in later chapters these periods are referred to as the 'date or period at which habitation was established', and the 'length of time over which a habitation was used'). McDonald (1994: 75) stated that using the absence of backed artefacts to assign a recent phase/millennium to particular habitations is a problem, given the small sample size in some sites and the low probability of their retrieval. This is a valid comment, but, as outlined below, other evidence and criteria were taken into account in assigning an age to habitations and deposits which were not dated by radiocarbon means.

The depth to which archaeological deposit had accumulated was also considered when assessing 'the length of time over which a habitation was used' (see Chapter 6). This was calculated for sites individually by extrapolating from the deposition rates in radiocarbon-dated deposits in rockshelters with similar morphology and location and similar access to sources of sediment; for example, whether cavernously weathered with no opportunity for slopewashed sediments to enter, or open at one side allowing entry of sediments from the adjacent slope.

Support for this method of assigning a 'recent' (late-Holocene) age to these deposits is given by the additional radiocarbon determinations obtained for four habitations since 1987 — Boat Cave, One Tooth, Ti-tree and Venus Shelters. For three of these four sites, the radiocarbon ages were all less than 1000 years BP and for Boat Cave it was earlier, that is, ca 2370 BP (third millennium BP). Ages of these habitations were originally estimated as <1000 BP (Boat Cave, Ti-tree and Venus) and ca 2000–1000 BP (One Tooth) (Attenbrow 1987: Table 7.2). Possible reasons for the greater difference between the estimated and radiocarbon ages for Boat Cave are discussed in Chapter 5.

Radiocarbon dates: conventional versus calibrated
Conventional radiocarbon dates have been used in this study for two principal reasons. Firstly, after calibrating the radiocarbon ages and recalculating each of the indices (the number of habitations used, rate of site establishment, artefact accumulation rate for individual sites, and local artefact accumulate rate) for the Upper Mangrove Creek catchment sites and several

of the regions investigated in Chapter 7, it was seen that calibrating the dates would not alter the conclusions. Secondly, calibrating all radiocarbon ages for all sites included in the examination of other regions was too time-costly for what appeared would be very little if any gain. (This can be seen partially by comparing the conventional and calibrated radiocarbon dates in Table 6.1.)

Calibrations were calculated using Calib Rev 4.3(2000) (Stuiver and Reimer 1993b; Stuiver et al. 1998). Stuiver and Reimer (1993a: 1.3.8) recommended that conventional radiocarbon ages for Southern Hemisphere samples be reduced by 40 years. However, dendrochronological studies by Barbetti et al. (1992) on Tasmanian samples indicate this reduction may not be necessary. Conventional dates for the catchment sites were therefore calibrated twice, the first after reduction by 40 years and the second without reduction. This exercise showed no major differences in the temporal trends produced by each method for the three indices, and calibrations presented in Table 6.1 do not have the 40-year reduction.

The effect of calibration is to stretch out the time scale for periods before 2000 BP, and to shorten the periods after 2000 BP. The main differences to the results of the Upper Mangrove Creek data after calibration are:

1. *Rates of artefact accumulation.* For periods before 2000 BP, the artefact accumulation rates are lower, and after 2000 BP they are higher. However, these variations do not substantially alter the trends. For sites with small numbers of artefacts there is a negligible effect, even when extrapolated to the estimated total numbers of artefacts in them. For sites with larger numbers of artefacts, the changes are more substantial, but the effect on the overall trends is not significant for my arguments. The decrease in the local artefact accumulation rate in the past 1000 years is just as substantial (i.e., the decrease is in the same order of magnitude) as it was before calibration. In addition, the significant or dramatic increases occur in the same millennium as they did before calibration.

2. *Habitation indices.* The calibrated intercepts for the catchment radiocarbon dates less than 5000 BP fall within the same millennium BP as did the intercepts for the conventional dates. For dates above 5000 BP, the intercept falls within the previous millennium except for Loggers. The intercept for the oldest date for Loggers (12,963 CAL BP), while within the previous millennium to that of the conventional date (i.e., 13th rather than 12th millennium BP), is in fact almost 2000 years older than the radiocarbon date (11,050±135 BP [SUA-931]) (Table 6.1). Within the Upper Mangrove Creek catchment, calibration of the radiocarbon dates had no significant impact on the trends in the habitation establishment rates or the number of habitations used for the purposes for which they are used in this study. Although the chronology is extended, the dramatic changes still occur at the same time.

The results of this exercise suggest that calibration of other radiocarbon dates used in this study and reanalysis of the data were unlikely to affect the conclusions reached at the scale of the analyses employed.

4

Upper Mangrove Creek catchment: random sampling units. Fieldwork results and evidence from the archaeological deposits

During the fieldwork, several different types of archaeological evidence relating to Aboriginal occupation of the catchment were located and recorded in the random sampling units: archaeological deposits, images, grinding areas, a burial and isolated finds. Only those archaeological traits that are used to estimate the temporal trends in the quantitative changes in the catchment's archaeological record are described below; that is, the archaeological deposits and isolated finds. Data presented in this chapter provide the bases for calculations in future chapters, for example, for producing depth/age curves and estimated total numbers of artefacts in archaeological deposits. In addition, data are presented about the recorded potential habitation shelters and potential archaeological deposits. To provide a context for these locations, a summary of the fieldwork results is first outlined below (Attenbrow 1987, Chapters 5 and 6, has a full account of fieldwork results relevant to other traits).

Summary of fieldwork results

The fieldwork results as at the end of the excavations — that is, once all fieldwork was complete — are presented below. It is more practical to present the final results in this way rather than discussing the survey, recording and excavation results separately since the status of several locations and sites changed during the course of the excavation and recording work:
- eight potential archaeological deposits in rockshelters with images became archaeological deposits once excavation showed they contained archaeological materials;
- three potential archaeological deposits in PH shelters became archaeological deposits once excavation showed they contained archaeological materials;
- one PH shelter was reclassified as a rockshelter with archaeological deposit when stone artefacts were found on the surface of the deposit (the archaeological deposit was not excavated due to lack of time);
- one PH shelter was reclassified as a rockshelter with images when drawings were found during an impromptu visit subsequent to the site survey.

In future discussions, the term fieldwork thus refers collectively to survey, recording and excavation unless otherwise stated.

By the end of the fieldwork, 80 archaeological traits at 59 archaeological sites, 10 isolated finds and 167 potential habitation shelters had been recorded in the random sampling units (Fig. 4.1, Tables 4.1 and 4.2; see also Attenbrow 1987: Tables 5.2: 4RSU and 5.3, and Appendix 3, Table A3/3). The archaeological traits were 35 archaeological deposits, 22 images, 22 grinding areas, and one burial. Thirty-two traits were in rockshelters, five in open deposits and 22 on open rock (sandstone exposures or rock platforms) (Table 4.2A). The ten isolated finds were all stone artefacts on open deposits (Attenbrow 1987: Appendix 3, Table A3/2). The average density of sites and traits in the random sampling units, and therefore the inferred density of sites and traits in the total catchment, is ca 6/sq km and ca 8/sq km respectively (Tables 4.2A and 4.2B). In following discussions the numbers and densities quoted as being 'in each topographic zone' relate to the sites, traits and artefacts recorded in the random sampling units; extrapolations have not been made to the total catchment.

Sites/archaeological traits were recorded in all topographic zones. However, the number and density of sites in each topographic zone varies, as does the number and density of each type of trait and the contents of each of the traits (Fig. 4.2; Attenbrow 1987: Chapter 6). Two of the three main traits — archaeological deposits and images — are found in all topographic zones. Grinding areas have a more restricted distribution in the random sampling units being recorded in only the periphery ridgetops, subsidiary valley bottoms and subsidiary ridgesides. However, they have been found in other zones in the catchment outside the random sampling units — albeit in small numbers (two on peninsula ridgetops and two in the main valley bottom).

The number of sites in each zone varies between two and 24, and the site density between 2/sq km and 12/sq km (Table 4.2A). The total number of traits in each zone varies from three to 26, while their density varies from 3/sq km to 15/sq km (Table 4.2B and Fig. 4.2). The highest frequencies of sites and traits are found on periphery ridgetops, though subsidiary ridgesides also have a high frequency of traits. The high frequencies of sites and traits in these two zones are a function of the larger area of land within these categories. The highest density of sites and traits is in the main valley bottoms. The lowest frequency and density of sites and traits were recorded on the peninsula ridgetops and the main ridgesides.

Archaeological deposits

The 35 archaeological deposits occur in all topographic zones in the catchment (Fig. 4.2). They were recorded more frequently on subsidiary ridgesides; 31% (11 of the 35) archaeological deposits occur in this zone. The peninsula ridgetops and the main ridgesides, with two archaeological deposits each (6%), have the lowest number of archaeological deposits. The remaining three topographic zones had similar numbers — six, seven and seven archaeological deposits (17%, 20% and 20%).

The density values show a different perspective. The highest density of archaeological deposits occurs in the main valley bottoms — at 10/sq km, it is more than twice that of any other zone (Fig. 4.2 and Table 4.2B). Peninsula ridgetops, the periphery ridgetops and main ridgesides can be grouped together as having the lowest density values (2–3/sq km). The other two topographic zones (subsidiary valley bottoms and subsidiary ridgesides) both have 4/sq km. The average density for archaeological deposits is 3.5/sq km.

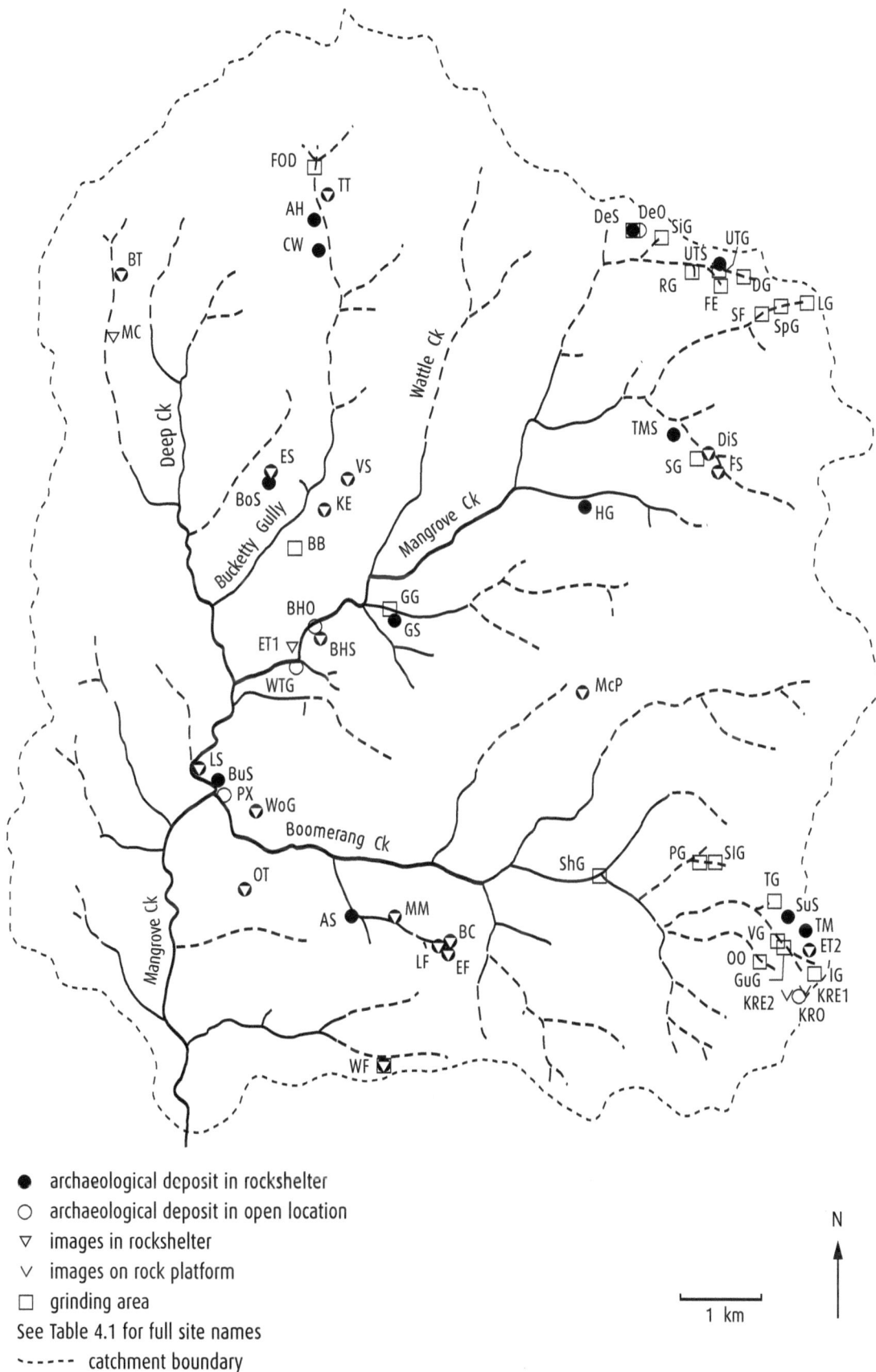

Figure 4.1 Upper Mangrove Creek catchment: archaeological sites recorded in the random sampling units.

Table 4.1 Upper Mangrove Creek catchment: archaeological sites in random sampling units. Tables 3.1 and 3.2 have full names of abbreviated locations, archaeological traits and topographic zones; ENG indicates engraving; SA indicates storage area.

SITE NAME	ABBREVIATED SITE NAME	LOCATION	ARCHAEOLOGICAL TRAIT	RANDOM SAMPLING UNIT	TOPO-ZONE
Anadara	AS	SH	AD	RSU.138	VB-SC
Axehead	AH	SH	AD	RSU.101	VB-SC
Bird Tracks	BT	SH	AD/IM	RSU.177	RS-SC
Black Hands Open Deposit	BHO	OD	AD	RSU.80/SA	VB-MC
Black Hands Shelter	BHS	SH	AD/IM	RSU.80/SA	VB-MC
Boat Cave	BC	SH	AD/IM	RSU.263	RS-SC
Boring Boring	BB	OR	GA	RSU.188	RS-SC
Boronia	BoS	SH	AD	RSU.10	RT-PEN
Button	BuS	SH	AD	RSU.75/SA	VB-MC
Caramel Wave	CW	SH	AD	RSU.101	VB-SC
Delight Open Deposit	DeO	OD	AD	RSU.56	RT-PERI
Delight Shelter	DeS	SH	AD/GA	RSU.56	RT-PERI
Dingo	DiS	SH	AD/IM/BR	RSU.209	RS-SC
Double Grooves	DG	OR	GA	RSU.56	RT-PERI
Elngarrah	ES	SH	AD/IM?	RSU.10	RT-PEN
Elongated Figure	EF	SH	AD/IM	RSU.263	RS-SC
Emu Tracks 1	ET1	SH	ND/IM+ENG	RSU.80/SA	VB-MC
Emu Tracks 2	ET2	SH	AD/IM = ENG	RSU.63	RT-PERI
Firestick	FS	SH	AD/IM	RSU.209	RS-SC
First of Day	FOD	OR	GA	RSU.101	VB-SC
Frogs Eggs	FE	OR	GA	RSU.56	RT-PERI
Geebung Grooves	GG	OR	GA	RSU.114/SA	VB-SC
Geebung Shelter	GS	SH	AD	RSU.114/SA	VB-SC
Gurgling Gully	GuG	OR	GA	RSU.63	RT-PERI
Harris Gully	HG	PH/SH	AD	RSU.112	VB-SC
Isolated Groove	IG	OR	GA	RSU.63	RT-PERI
Kangaroo and Echidna	KE	SH	AD/IM	RSU.188	RS-SC
Kyola Road Open Deposit	KRO	OD	AD	RSU.63	RT-PERI
Kyola Road Engravings 1	KRE1	OR	IM = ENG	RSU.63	RT-PERI
Kyola Road Engravings 2	KRE2	OR	IM = ENG	RSU.63	RT-PERI
Loggers	LS	SH	AD/IM	RSU.75/SA	VB-MC
Lonesome	LG	OR	GA	RSU.57	RT-PERI
Low Frontage	LF	SH	AD/IM	RSU.263	RS-SC
Mangrove Mansions	MM	SH	AD/IM	RSU.138	VB-SC
Manning Creek	MC	PH/SH	PAD/IM	RSU.177	RS-SC
McPherson	McP	SH	AD/IM	RSU.235	RS-SC
One Tooth	OT	SH	AD/IM	RSU.163	RS-MC
Optimus Octavus	OO	OR	GA	RSU.63	RT-PERI
Palmers Crossing North	PX	OD	AD	RSU.75/SA	VB-MC
Petra	PG	OR	GA	RSU.63	RT-PERI
Rusty	RG	OR	GA	RSU.56	RT-PERI
Sharp Gully	ShG	OR	GA	RSU.127	VB-SC
Single Groove	SiG	OR	GA	RSU.56	RT-PERI
Slime Gully	SlG	OR	GA	RSU.63	RT-PERI
Slip Gully	SpG	OR	GA	RSU.57	RT-PERI
Solitary	SG	OR	GA	RSU.209	RS-SC
Star Fern	SF	OR	GA	RSU.56	RT-PERI
Sunny	SuS	PH/SH	AD	RSU.63	RT-PERI
Ti-tree	TT	SH	AD/IM	RSU.101	VB-SC
Token Male	TM	PH/SH	AD	RSU.63	RT-PERI
Two Grooves	TG	OR	GA	RSU.63	RT-PERI

Table 4.1   (Continued)

SITE NAME	ABBREVIATED SITE NAME	LOCATION	ARCHAEOLOGICAL TRAIT	RANDOM SAMPLING UNIT	TOPO- ZONE
Two Moths	TMS	PH	SH/AD	RSU.209	RS-SC
Uprooted Tree Grooves	UTG	OR	GA	RSU.56	RT-PERI
Uprooted Tree Shelter	UTS	SH	AD	RSU.56	RT-PERI
Variety	VG	OR	GA	RSU.63	RT-PERI
Venus	VS	SH	AD/IM	RSU.188	RS-SC
White Figure	WF	SH	AD/IM/GA	RSU.274	RS-SC
Willow Tree Gully	WTG	OD	AD	RSU.80/SA	VB-MC
Wolloby Gully	WoG	SH	AD/IM	RSU.156	RS-MC

Table 4.2 Upper Mangrove Creek catchment: (A) site locations, (B) archaeological deposits and (C) potential habitation shelters in random sampling units. Number, percentage frequency and density in each topographic zone (density is number/sq km). See also Figure 4.1. Tables 3.1 and 3.2 have full names of abbreviated topographic zones; Sh indicates number with shallow deposit <10cm; F indicates number with flood-affected deposit.

A. SITE LOCATIONS

Topozone	Area (sq km)	Shelters No.	%	Dens.	Open deposit No.	%	Dens.	Open rock No.	%	Dens.	Trees No.	%	Dens.	All locations No.	%	Dens.
RT-PERI	3.2	5	15.6	1.6	2	40	0.6	17	77.3	5.3				24	40.7	7.5
RT-PEN	1.1	2	6.3	1.8										2	3.4	1.8
VB-MC	0.6	4	12.5	6.7	3	60	5							7	11.9	11.7
VB-SC	1.7	7	21.9	4.1				3	13.6	1.8				10	16.9	5.9
RS-MC	0.8	2	6.3	2.5										2	3.4	2.5
RS-SC	2.7	12	37.5	4.4				2	9.1	0.7				14	23.7	5.2
Total	10.1	32	100	3.2	5	100	0.5	22	100	2.2	0	0	0	59	100	5.8

B. ARCHAEOLOGICAL TRAITS

Topozone	Arch. deposits No.	%	Dens.	Images No.	%	Dens.	Grinding areas No.	%	Dens.	Burials No.	%	Dens.	Scarred trees No.	%	Dens.	All traits No.	%	Dens.
RT-PERI	7	20.0	2.2	3	13.6	0.9	16	72.7	5.0							26	32.5	8.1
RT-PEN	2	5.7	1.8	1?	4.5	0.9										3	3.7	2.7
VB-MC	6	17.1	10.0	3	13.6	5.0										9	11.3	15.0
VB-SC	7	20.0	4.1	2	9.1	1.2	3	13.6	1.8							12	15.0	7.1
RS-MC	2	5.7	2.5	2	9.1	2.5										4	5.0	5.0
RS-SC	11	31.4	4.1	11	50.0	4.1	3	13.6	1.1	1	100	0.4				26	32.5	9.6
Total	35	100	3.5	22	100	2.2	22	100	2.2	1	100	0.1	0	0	0	80	100	7.9

C. POTENTIAL HABITATION SHELTERS

Topozone	Sh/PAD No.		Dens.	Sh/ND or SD No.		Dens.	All PH shelters No.		Dens.
RT-PERI	8	(1Sh)	2.5				8	(1Sh)	2.5
RT-PEN	7	(4Sh)	6.4	2		1.8	9	(4Sh)	8.2
VB-MC	1	(1F)	1.7				1	(1F)	1.7
VB-SC	21	(4Sh)	12.4	1		0.6	22	(4Sh)	13.0
RS-MC	35	(6Sh)	43.8	2		2.5	37	(6Sh)	46.3
RS-SC	87	(17Sh)	32.2	3		1.1	90	(17Sh)	33.3
Total	159	(32Sh) (1F)	15.8	8		0.8	167	(32Sh) (1F)	16.5

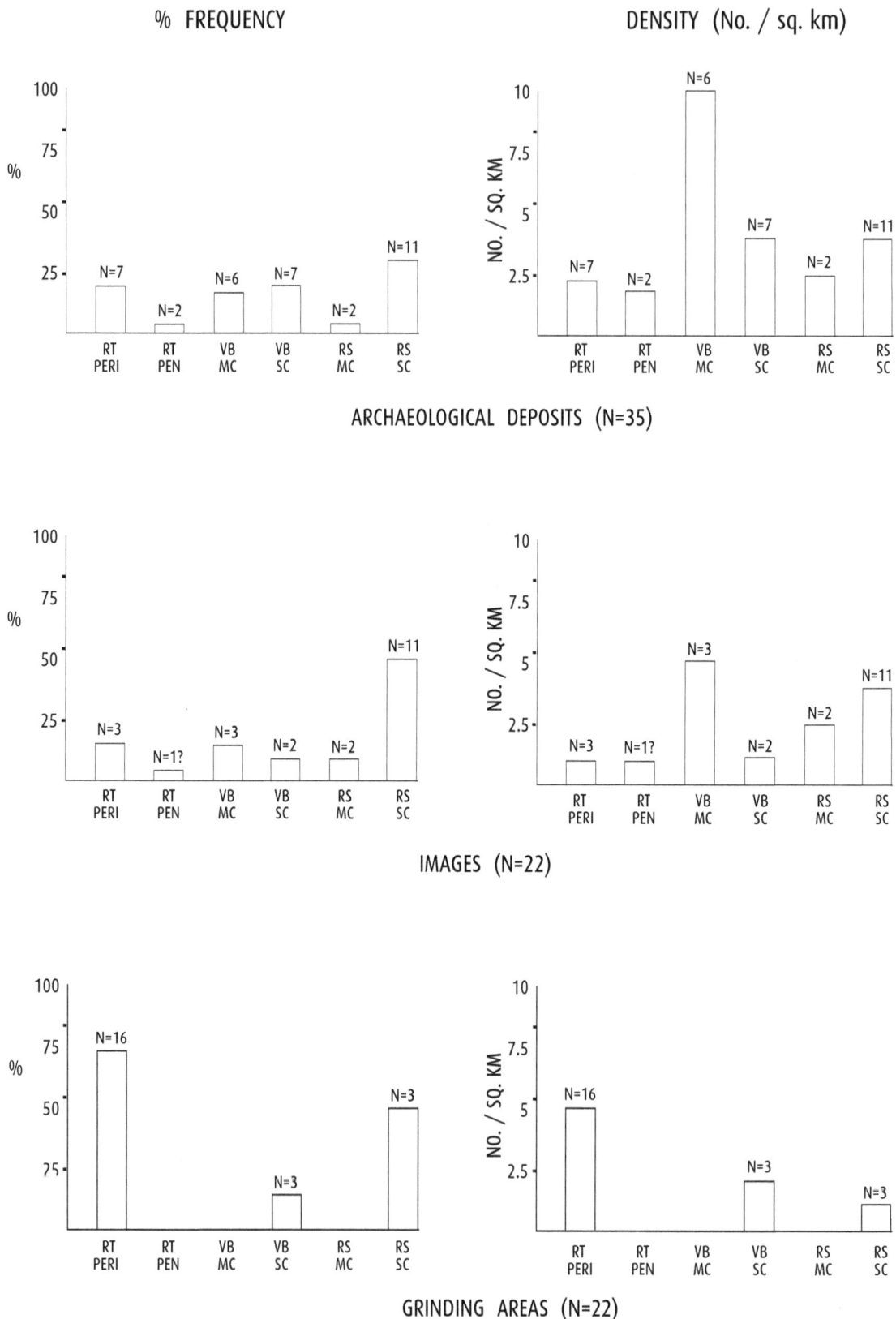

Figure 4.2 Upper Mangrove Creek catchment: random sampling units. Percentage frequency and density of archaeological traits in each topographic zone.

Variations in the frequency of archaeological deposits in different topographic zones are not significant, but variations in the numbers of stone artefacts within the archaeological deposits in each topographic zone are much greater (see below under *Stone artefacts*).

Other information about the archaeological deposits, which was gained from the fieldwork data and is presented below, includes:

1. the number and type of locations in which archaeological deposits occur in the catchment;
2. the area and depth of the archaeological deposit at each location;
3. the contents of each archaeological deposit — that is, the number and type of stone artefacts, as well as the number of bone fragments and animal species identified in the faunal remains.

Thirty of the archaeological deposits were in rockshelters and five in the open. The size and aspect of the rockshelters varied as did the area and depth of the archaeological deposit at each of the excavated locations and the contents (that is, the size of the stone artefact and faunal assemblages). The archaeological deposits were classified into size categories according to the estimated total number of stone artefacts in each in order to assess the distribution of this class of evidence across the catchment (see *Stone artefacts* below).

The rockshelters

The rockshelters in which archaeological deposit was recorded range in size from 3m long by 2.8m deep to 46m long by 9.8m deep (Table 4.3). These measurements represent the maximum lengths and widths of the rockshelters taken from scaled floor plans. Maximum dimensions also include concavities or ledges in the walls which are above floor height.

The habitable area is the area in which it is assumed that use of the shelter would have occurred. It is the area in which a person can sit up (i.e., a ceiling height greater than 80cm) and which has a relatively flat, dry floor. The habitable floor area is usually much less than the area included within the maximum rockshelter length and width, as it excludes areas of low ceiling, shallow overhang, permanently damp deposit or steeply sloping deposit. The habitable area within the rockshelter was noted on floor plans in the field, and then calculated on a digitiser from scaled plans.

Sixty-one per cent of the rockshelters with archaeological deposit face west (11) and north-west (8). Others face north (5, 16%), north-east (2, 6.5%), south (3, 10%) and south-west (2, 6.5%) (Table 4.3).

Nineteen rockshelters contain other archaeological traits: 18 images, one burial and two grinding areas. At the remaining 11 rockshelters and five open deposits, no other archaeological trait was recorded (Table 4.1).

The open deposits

Open archaeological deposits occur on alluvial flats and valley-fill forming creek banks in the main valley bottoms (3) and on ridgetops (2) (Table 4.2A). Outside the random sampling units, they were also found on structural benches on ridgesides, but still within the main valley bottom zones. The locations on which the open archaeological deposits were recorded each had different aspects: north, north-west, north-north-east, west, and south-west.

Area of archaeological deposits

The largest area of deposit in a rockshelter is 273m², though not all of the deposit in this particular rockshelter (Kangaroo and Echidna) is expected to contain abundant archaeological material. The smallest area is 1m² (Firestick) (Table 4.4). The area of deposit at the majority of rockshelters is

Table 4.3 Upper Mangrove Creek catchment: dimensions and aspects of rockshelters with archaeological deposit.
[1] Dimensions are from scaled plans, except for rockshelters noted [2]. [2] 'e' indicates maximum height is at the extent of overhang; 'i' indicates maximum height is inside rockshelter. [3] Dimensions are field estimates; n/c indicates not calculated. [4] Wolloby Gully has two areas under one overhang, each area facing a slightly different direction.

| SITE NAME | AREA OF ROCKSHELTER [1] | | | | HEIGHT [2] | | ASPECT | |
	Length (m)	Width (m)	Total area (m²)	Habitable (m²)	Maximum (m)		(degrees)	
Anadara	33.0	7.0	231.0	58.3	10.6	e	307	NW
Axe Head	10.3	3.3	34.0	11.8	3.3	e	240	SW
Bird Tracks	13.0	4.5	58.5	20.8	2.7	i	270	W
Black Hands	6.3	3.5	22.0	8.5	2.3	i	270	W
Boat Cave	9.0	4.7	42.3	19.7	3.0	e	258	W
Boronia [3]	15.0	2.7	40.5	n/c	1.6	e	n/r	W
Button	7.8	4.4	34.3	26.0	2.6	e	295	NW
Caramel Wave	7.0	3.3	23.1	14.3	3.2	e	40	NE
Delight	8.5	2.8	23.4	7.8	2.8	e	266	W
Dingo	6.8	4.8	32.6	7.4	1.6	e	330	NW
Elngarrah [3]	8.5	2.5	21.3	n/c	1.2	e	300	NW
Elongated Figure	9.3	33.8	34.9	9.9	2.4	e	346	N
Emu Tracks 2	8.3	2.2	18.3	12.0	2.0	e	170	S
Firestick	3.0	2.8	8.3	n/c	2.5	i	30	NE
Geebung	12.0	4.0	48.0	28.5	2.6	e	360	N
Harris Gully	7.8	5.0	39.0	11.5	2.2	i	331	NW
Kangaroo and Echidna	46.0	9.8	450.8	49.9	13.5	e	265	W
Loggers	10.0	3.5	35.0	13.5	5.8	e	315	NW
Low Frontage	10.3	3.8	38.6	15.6	1.5	i	5	N
McPherson	10.0	3.8	38.0	23.6	1.3	e	282	W
Mangrove Mansions	23.0	6.5	149.5	91.9	2.4	e	200	S
One Tooth	6.5	6.2	40.3	24.8	2.5	e	5	N
Sunny	12.8	3.0	38.3	21.7	2.2	e	275	W
Ti-tree	11.5	1.7	20.0	10.3	1.7	e	240	SW
Token Male [3]	9.0	3.0	27.0	n/c	1.8	e	n/r	W
Two Moths	10.0	7.9	79.0	24.1	1.7	i	343	N
Uprooted Tree	14.0	2.2	30.8	9.9	2.2	e	172	S
Venus	12.0	4.6	55.2	10.4	2.6	i	280	W.
White Figure	25.0	7.0	175.0	85.3	9.3	e	330	NW
Wolloby Gully [4]	16.3	10.8	[176.0	119.0	10.8	e	290	W
Wolloby Gully [4]	29.0	4.7	[136.3		9.2	e	320	NW

between 13.5m² and 65.7m². The area of deposit in each rockshelter (which often differed from the habitable area) was digitised from scaled floor plans.

The deposit at some rockshelters extends beyond the overhang. In these instances, the area of archaeological deposit (or potential archaeological deposit) may be greater than the area of the rockshelter itself. In others, part of the rockshelter floor is rock or very shallow deposit, and thus the area of deposit is smaller than the rockshelter floor.

It was not feasible to estimate the potential areas for the open archaeological deposits because of the 'unbounded' nature of the alluvial flats and ridgetops. Time was also not available to undertake a testing program to determine the limits of the archaeological deposit in open sites. The area over which exposed artefacts were recorded is thus provided; the greatest extent of exposed artefacts was at Black Hands Open Deposit — 1200m² (Table 4.5). However, in all open locations, it is probable that buried artefacts extend over a much greater area than the dimensions provided in Table 4.5.

Open archaeological deposits with larger dimensions have been recorded outside the random sampling units (but still within the catchment). At Stockyards Open Deposit,

Table 4.4 Upper Mangrove Creek catchment: random sampling units. Archaeological deposits in rockshelters: area (m²), status and depth of archaeological deposits.

Upper Mangrove Creek catchment: random sampling units. Fieldwork results and evidence from the archaeological deposits

SITE NAME	STATUS OF DEPOSIT					DEPTH OF ARCH. DEPOSIT (MAX.)		COMMENTS
	Area of deposit (m²)	Inside as excav. (m²)	Shallow (m²)	Eroded (m²)	Outside shelter (m²)	Square	cm	
Anadara	46.3	46.3				T1 / T2	7 / 24	
Axehead	5.5	-					<10	Unexcavated
Birdtracks	24.1	24.1		[6.9]			15	Gullied (eroded) area not included as part of deposit for calculations
Black Hands	24.3	11.5	4.3			AB / F	110 / 101	
Boat Cave	22.7	3.3	19.4		8.5		38/<5	Depth as excavated/depth of shallow deposit
Boronia	24.5	24.5					19	
Button	3.0	-					<10	Unexcavated
Caramel Wave	17.0	17.0				T1 / T2	22 / 11	
Delight	3.7	Nil			3.7		32	
Dingo	15.9	13.7			2.2		39	
Elngarrah	34.0	34.0					33	
Elongated Figure	19.8	12.3			7.5		38	
Emu Tracks 2	21.1	12.8			8.3		80	
Firestick	1.0	-					<3	Unexcavated
Geebung	25.0	25.0					5	
Harris Gully	>13.5	13.5			?		42	Deposit outside shelter is an extensive area of flat land, the area of which is indefinable
Kangaroo and Echidna	273.1	49.9/223.2					43/43	Deposit as excavated [dry deposit/damp deposit]
Loggers	53.3	13.5			39.8	A / EF	70 / 206	
Low Frontage	23.3	23.3					18	
Mangrove Mansions	65.7	51.0	14.7				13/<10	Excavated deposit/shallow deposit
McPherson	32.2	-	15.0		17.2		<5/15	Excavated pit was on flat area immediately outside dripline
One Tooth	28.4	8.2	9.1		11.1		24	
Sunny	34.9	19.7		[2.5]	15.2		71	Gullied (eroded) area not included as part of deposit for calculations
Ti-tree	22.4	11.0			11.4	T1 / T2	Nil / 38	
Token Male	20.0	-					?	Depth unknown — unexcavated and no surface indications
Two Moths	34.9	32.4			2.5	T/5	5	T/5 is the spit in which the freshwater mussel was found
Uprooted Tree	17.9	10.8			7.1		81	
Venus	16.6	6.6					18	Deposit consists of three separate areas of sediment in shelter
White Figure	16.0	16.0					55	
Wolloby Gully	150.3	52.7	97.6				5	Artefact density for shallow area assumed to be 10% of excavated area

artefacts were recorded over an area of about 7200m². Their discontinuous exposure in disturbed patches of ground within this area suggests artefacts are present over the whole area, but are simply buried.

Depth of archaeological deposits

The depth, or thickness, of sediment throughout which archaeological materials were found (Tables 4.4 and 4.5) is not always the same as the total depth of the deposit excavated (Table 3.4). Sterile deposits were encountered at the bottom of some excavation pits. In addition, the top spit of pits dug in eight of the rockshelters, which were initially recorded as having potential archaeological deposit, contained no archaeological materials (i.e., no stone artefacts or faunal remains): Elongated Figure, Harris Gully, Low Frontage, McPherson, Mangrove Mansions, Two Moths, Venus Shelter, Wolloby Gully. Other excavated potential archaeological deposits did have archaeological materials in their top spit.

The 'depth of archaeological deposit' is thus the deposit or sediment from which archaeological materials were retrieved. The measurement is based on the combined depth of those spits which contained archaeological materials. Where sterile spits occur either at the top or bottom of the excavated area, their depth is excluded, but in situations where a sterile spit is sandwiched between spits with archaeological materials, it has been included in the depth measurement.

The greatest depth of archaeological deposit was recorded at Loggers (ca 206cm); the shallowest deposit is ca 3cm at Firestick (Table 4.4). The majority of archaeological deposits are between 10cm and 60cm deep.

Contents of archaeological deposits

The relative size and richness of the assemblages in each of the archaeological deposits varies greatly in:

1. the type and range of contents present; for example, stone artefacts, faunal remains, plant remains, ochreous material and charcoal (Table 4.6). Open archaeological deposits have only stone artefacts, with some having charcoal, whereas the range of contents in archaeological deposits in rockshelters is often greater, particularly those with areas of dry deposit where better conditions prevail for the preservation of organic materials such as faunal and plant remains;

2. the range of stone artefact types and animal species represented in the faunal remains (Tables 4.7 to 4.11). The fact that there is an increase in the range of identified stone artefact types and animal species as the size of the assemblages increases, indicates that inter-site and intra-site variations may be related as much to sample size (i.e., to the number of stone artefacts or bone fragments retrieved) as to past human behaviour and specific site functions (Attenbrow 1981: 170, Table 6.2; Grayson 1984: 116–30; Hiscock 2001).

The location and nature of the archaeological deposit, as well as the number of artefacts and bone fragments from each archaeological deposit and each level within a deposit, thus has to be taken into account when analysing and interpreting these data sets (see also Smith 1982: 110; Owen 1984: 69; Owen and Merrick 1994: 3).

There is no correlation between the size of the stone artefact assemblage retrieved from an archaeological deposit and the size of its faunal assemblage.

(a) Only two of the six archaeological deposits with the greatest estimated number of artefacts (Loggers and White Figure) have large faunal assemblages; one has none (Sunny) and two have almost no faunal remains (Uprooted Tree and Emu Tracks 2). The limited amount or lack of bone in most archaeological deposits can be attributed to poor conditions for the preservation of organic materials.

Table 4.5 Upper Mangrove Creek catchment: random sampling units. Open archaeological deposits: area (m²) over which artefacts were exposed and depth of archaeological deposits.

SITE NAME	AREA OVER WHICH EXPOSED ARTEFACTS RECORDED (approx. dimensions – m)	ESTIMATED DEPTH OF ARCHAEOLOGICAL DEPOSIT	COMMENTS
Black Hands	40 x 30	T1 5cm	Alluvial flats
		T2 24cm	Colluvial foot-slopes
Delight	15 x 1	Surface only — <20cm ?	Ridgetop/structural bench — skeletal soil
Kyola Road	5 x 5	Surface only — <20cm ?	Ridgetop — skeletal soil
Palmers Crossing	10 x 1	Unknown — unexcavated	Valley fill (highly disturbed)
Willow Tree Gully	10 x 5	Unknown — unexcavated	Valley fill (highly disturbed)

Table 4.6 Upper Mangrove Creek catchment: random sampling units. Contents recorded in/retrieved from the archaeological deposits. Weights rounded to nearest 0.1g. [1] Exc. indicates artefacts from excavated deposit (– indicates deposit not excavated); Surfgen — artefacts on surface of deposit outside excavated squares. [2] HD — humanly derived faunal remains; NHD — non-humanly derived remains. [3] P — present; N/c — not collected or not counted.

SITE NAME	STONE ARTEFACTS [1] EXC. No.	SURFGEN No.	FAUNAL REMAINS [2] TOTAL BONE AND SHELL No.	Wght (g)	HD No.	NHD No.	PLANT REMAINS [3]	CHARCOAL [3]	OTHER MATERIALS
Anadara	20	3	8	20.5	3	5		P	
Axe Head	–	1							
Bird Tracks	0	0	15	2.0	2	13	P	P	3 bone artefacts
Black Hands OD	12	14						P	1 button
Black Hands SH (Sq F)	3302	n/c	377	44.4	377			P	
Boat Cave	21	3						P	
Boronia	4	1	1	4.3	1			P	
Button	–	4					P		1 button; firestick?
Caramel Wave	14	0	45	9.6	44	1?	P	P	
Delight OD	0	9	n/c	52.8	Hist			n/c	Tinfoil
Delight SH	353	14	1	0.1	1		P	P	
Dingo (Sq Ta+Tb)	12+40	2	647	48.8	638	9	P	P	
Elngarrah	3	4	3	0.3	1	2		P	
Elongated Figure	12	0	5	0.3		5	P	P	
ET-2 (Sq T1+T2)	7397	39	7	0.9	7		P	P	
Firestick	–	0					P	n/c	
Geebung	8	0	2	0.2	2			P	
Harris Gully	34	2	5	0.5	3	2	P	P	
Kangaroo and Echidna	63	1	3	1.3	3		P	P	Resin/gum?
Kyola Road OD	–	4							
Loggers (Sq E+F)	4803	n/c	9704	1309.3	9704		P	P	3 bone artefacts
Low Frontage	6	0					P	P	
McPherson	23	1	1	1.1		1	P	P	
Mangrove Mansions	13	0	53	6.0	53		P	P	Resin/gum
One Tooth	8	4	42	>16.5	39	3	P	P	
Palmers Crossing Nth OD	–	2							
Sunny	1260	7					P	P	Ochre palette
Ti-tree	11	0					P	P	
Token Male	–	3							
Two Moths	0	0	86	11.6	1	85	P	P	
Uprooted Tree	875	3	1	0.3	1		P	P	
Venus	21	1					P	P	
White Figure	1087	0	1205	69.1	1202	3	P	P	
Willow Tree Gully	–	7							
Wolloby Gully	9	0	27	4.8	27		P	P	1 piece cut wood?
Totals	19,411	129							

(b)   Two sites which contain no stone artefacts have faunal remains (Bird Tracks and Two Moths). Bird Tracks has several pieces of burnt bone, as well as three small bone artefacts, and substantial amounts of charcoal. Two Moths has one large and several smaller fragments of freshwater mussel shell. In each case, the species of fauna and/or the size of the fragments were such that Aplin considered them to be humanly derived (Appendix 3), and thus the shelters are classified as having archaeological deposit. Solomon (pers. comm., 22 November, 1986) advised that the largest shell fragment she observed in dingo scats measured 4cm; the large fragment in Two Moths measured ca 6cm.

Table 4.7 Upper Mangrove Creek catchment: random sampling units. Artefact types retrieved from archaeological deposits, including artefacts excavated and collected from surface of deposit outside test pits. [1] Letters after site name refer to excavated square/s from which the artefacts listed were retrieved; other squares and artefacts exist. [2] Key and Notes to Appendix 1 have full names of abbreviated artefact types; x under heading FBI indicates counts for bipolar cores and flakes are combined under CBI.

SITE NAME [1]	BP	GEO	BMS	EL	R/UW	GRF	GRI	CHH	CBI	FBI	H/M	WSTE	SP	TOTAL
Anadara	0	0	0	0	3	1	0	1	1	1	0	16	0	23
Axe Head	0	0	0	0	0	0	1	0	0	0	0	0	0	1
Bird Tracks	0	0	0	0	0	0	0	0	0	0	0	0	0	0
Black Hands OD	0	0	0	0	2	1	0	2	4	7	0	7	3	26
Black Hands SH (F)	8	2	6	0	71	7	0	18	172	x	0	3005	13	3302
Boat Cave	0	0	0	1	2	1	0	0	1	0	0	19	0	24
Boronia	0	0	0	0	0	1	1	1	0	0	0	2	0	5
Button	0	0	0	0	0	0	0	0	1	0	0	3	0	4
Caramel Wave	0	0	0	0	0	0	0	0	0	5	0	9	0	14
Delight OD	0	0	0	0	0	0	0	4	2	0	0	1	2	9
Delight SH	2	2	3	0	8	1	0	12	0	3	0	336	0	367
Dingo (Ta+Tb)	0	0	0	0	0	0	0	4	0	2	0	48	0	54
Elngarrah	0	0	0	0	0	0	0	0	0	0	0	7	0	7
Elongated Figure	0	0	0	0	0	0	0	1	0	0	0	11	0	12
Emu Tracks 2 (T1+T2)	33	11	21	0	111	14	0	61	113	166	0	6874	32	7436
Firestick	0	0	0	0	0	0	0	0	0	0	0	0	0	0
Geebung	0	0	0	0	0	0	0	1	0	1	0	6	0	8
Harris Gully	0	0	0	0	0	2	0	2	0	0	0	31	1	36
Kangaroo and Echidna	1	0	0	0	2	0	3	1	2	3	3	49	0	64
Kyola Road	0	0	0	0	0	0	0	1	0	0	0	3	0	4
Loggers (EF)	8	2	2	2	84	6	1	148	134	x	2	4256	158	4803
Low Frontage	0	0	0	0	0	1	0	0	0	1	0	3	1	6
McPherson	0	0	0	0	0	0	0	1	0	0	0	23	0	24
Mangrove Mansions	0	0	0	0	1	0	0	0	1	0	0	11	0	13
One Tooth	0	0	0	0	0	0	1	0	1	2	0	8	0	12
Palmers Crossing Nth	0	0	0	0	1	0	0	0	0	0	0	1	0	2
Sunny	2	0	1	0	9	9	2	9	20	21	0	1191	3	1267
Ti-tree	0	0	0	0	0	0	0	0	1	1	0	9	0	11
Token Male	0	0	0	0	0	1	0	1	0	0	0	1	0	3
Two Moths	0	0	0	0	0	0	0	0	0	0	0	0	0	0
Uprooted Tree Ta+Tb	0	1	1	0	4	4	1	1	13	9	0	844	0	878
Venus	0	0	0	0	0	0	0	0	1	3	0	18	0	22
White Figure	3	0	1	0	3	4	0	7	13	3	0	1043	10	1087
Willow Tree Gully	0	0	0	0	0	0	0	2	0	0	0	4	1	7
Wolloby Gully	0	0	0	0	0	0	0	0	0	0	0	9	0	9

Table 4.8 Upper Mangrove Creek catchment: random sampling units. Mammal remains retrieved from archaeological deposits: number of fragments. Appendix 3 has full scientific name and common names of animal species; Table 4.1 has full site names. Q indicates echidna quill/s; FT — furred tail; H — hairs.

SITE NAMES	ANIMAL SPECIES	AS	BHS	BT	BoS	CW	DeO	DeS	DiS	ES	EF	ET2	GS	HG	KE	LS	McP	MM	OT	TMS	UTS	WF	WoG
Acrobatidae	*Acrobates pygmaeus*																			1			
Buramyidae	*Cercartetus nanus*			1																			
Dasyuridae	Small dasyurid							1														1	
Macropodidae	*Macropus robustus*															3							
	Large Macropodid		1						1							36				10			
	Macropus rufogriseus															3							
	Wallabia bicolor			1												8							
	Medium Macropodid	5	1			1			6							108			1			2	
	Petrogale penicillata		3													4							
	Thylogale sp.															3							
	Small Macropodid	1	4	1		1			4						1	146		3	4			14	
	Macropodid (unsized)								2														
Muridae	*Pseudomys oralis*																			3			
	Rattus sp. cf. *fuscipes*			2							2												
	Murid unidentified			4					5		3							1	1	12			
Peramelidae	*Isoodon* sp.															2			1				
	Perameles nasuta			2																			
	Peramelid unidentified								2							10		2		1		3	1
Petauridae	*Petaurus* cf. *breviceps*																		FT				
	Petaurus sp.															1							
Phalangeridae	*Trichosurus vulpecula*															12							
Potoroidae	*Potorous* sp.															3						5	
	Potoroid unidentified															17							
Pseudocheiridae	*Pseudocheirus pereginus*															1							
	Pseudocheirine/petaurid		1						2							10						1	
	Large and unsized possum																	4					
Pteropodidae	*Pteropus scapulatus*															1							
Tachyglossidae	*Tachyglossus aculeatus*																	Q					
Vombatidae	*Vombatus ursinus*															1				H+2		1?	1
	Microchiroptera																			4			

Table 4.9 Upper Mangrove Creek catchment: random sampling units. Non-mammal vertebrate remains retrieved from archaeological deposits: number of fragments. Appendix 3 has scientific name and common names of animal species; Table 4.1 has full site names; F indicates bird feather/s.

ANIMAL SPECIES	SITE NAMES																										
	AS	BHS	BT	BoS	CW	DeO	DeS	DiS	ES	EF	ET2	GS	HG	KE	LS	McP	MM	OT	TMS	UTS	WF	WoG
REPTILES																						
Lacertilia																						
Agamidae															2							
Scincidae, e.g., *Egernia* sp.															1							
Small agamid																					1	
Medium lizard																					1	
Unsized lizard			1																1			
Ophidia															7							
Boidae															5							
Elapidae															2							
Medium snake								1													4	
Small snake																			1			
Unsized snake																						1
BIRDS																						
cf. *Dromaius novaehollandiae*															1							
Medium bird																	4					1
Unidentified bird										F							F		F			
FROGS																						
Anura								2											1			
Unidentified frog			1																			
FISH																						
Teleost fish															8							
UNIDENTIFIED FRAGMENTS	2	366	2	0	18	0	0	380	2	0	0	1	4	0	9098	1	35	25	46	1?	1013	14

Table 4.10 Upper Mangrove Creek catchment: random sampling units. Invertebrate faunal remains retrieved from archaeological deposits: number of fragments. Appendix 3 has further details; Table 4.1 has full site names; n/c indicates not counted.

ANIMAL SPECIES	AS	BHS	BT	BoS	CW	DeO	DeS	DiS	ES	EF	ET2	GS	HG	KE	LS	McP	MM	OT	TMS	UTS	WF	WoG
SHELLFISH AND LANDSNAILS																						
Hyriidae	1		1		3			84	1		6	1		2	194			10	1		92	7
Anadara trapezia						n/c		5			1				9			2		1	8	
Saccostrea glomerata						n/c																
Terrestrial landsnail (unidentified)								7				1			8				1		3	
CRUSTACEA																						
Parastacidae (yabby)					22			152													61	2

Table 4.11 Upper Mangrove Creek catchment: random sampling units. Summary of total numbers and weights (g) of all faunal remains retrieved from archaeological deposits. Table 4.1 has full site names.

CATEGORIES OF FAUNAL REMAINS	AS	BHS	BT	BoS	CW	DeO	DeS	DiS	ES	EF	ET2	GS	HG	KE	LS	McP	MM	OT	TMS	UTS	WF	WoG
Total number of bones (whole and fragments)	8	376	15	0	20	0	1	405	2	5	0	1	4	1	9493	1	49	32	82	0	1046	18
Total weight of bone (g)	19.5	55	2	0	4.8	0	0.1	39.6	0.2	0.3	0	0.1	0.4	0.3	1289.2	1.1	5.9	14.1	4.4	0	62.8	4
Total number of quills, feathers and hair/fur samples										1							3	1	2			
Total number of shell fragments	0	1	0	1	3	n/c	0	96	1	0	7	2	1	2	211	0	1	12	2	1	103	7
Total weight of shell fragments (g)	0	0.1	0	4.3	4.3	52.8	0	5.5	0.1	0	0.9	0.1	0.1	1	20.1	0	0.1	2.4	7.2	0.2	5.1	0.6
Total number of yabby fragments	0	0	0	0	22	0	0	152	0	0	0	0	0	0	0	0	0	0	0	0	61	2
Total weight of yabby fragments (g)	0	0	0	0	0.5	0	0	3.7	0	0	0	0	0	0	0	0	0	0	0	0	1.2	0.2

Stone artefacts

Stone artefacts were recorded at 32 of the 35 sites with archaeological deposit. The number of artefacts retrieved ranged from one (in Axe Head) to 7436 (in Emu Tracks 2) (Tables 4.6 and 4.7). The three sites without stone artefacts are Bird Tracks and Two Moths (see b. above) and Firestick in which a piece of modified wood was found (see Chapter 3, Wooden objects).

The stone artefact types are typical of those which occur in stone artefact assemblages in archaeological sites in the Sydney Basin, and include backed artefacts (Bondi points, geometric microliths, eloueras and backed miscellaneous), bipolar artefacts and ground-edged axes/hatchets (see Chapter 3, Temporal sequences). Not all artefact types are found in each archaeological deposit, and sample size probably plays a large part in this variation (see comments under 2. above). The type and number of stone artefacts retrieved from each archaeological deposit is presented in Table 4.7. The distribution of artefact types and raw materials according to spits within each archaeological deposit is presented in Appendix 1.

The estimated total numbers of artefacts in each archaeological deposit in each topographic zone were combined to provide an estimated total number for each zone (Fig. 4.3). The estimated number of artefacts in each zone ranges from 250 to 374,050. The density of artefacts in each zone ranges from 250 to 341,850/sq km. Periphery ridgetops and the main valley bottoms stand out as having the highest estimated number and density of accumulated artefacts. Periphery ridgetops have the highest estimated number of accumulated artefacts, but the main valley bottoms have the highest density. This pattern parallels the distribution of AD-3 category archaeological deposits (see below), which were slightly more frequent in the periphery ridgetops than in the main valley bottoms.

The topographic zones with the highest number and density of artefacts (the periphery ridgetops and main valley bottoms), however, are not the same zones that have the highest number of archaeological deposits (subsidiary ridgesides). That is, the higher number of archaeological deposits in some zones (e.g., the subsidiary ridgesides) does not necessarily compensate for the large size of the assemblages in archaeological deposits in others.

Faunal remains

Faunal remains were retrieved from 22 archaeological deposits and consist of fragments of animal bone, shell and crustacean exoskeleton (Tables 4.6, 4.8 to 4.11; Appendix 3); all categories were not present at each site. As mentioned previously, preservation conditions at individual sites varied considerably and this is likely to account for the variations in number and weight of fragments as much as reasons attributable to human behaviour. The majority of sites had poor conditions for the preservation of organic materials such as bone (Hughes and Sullivan 1979: 22; Aplin 1981: 1). The greatest depth below ground surface at which faunal remains were found in any of the archaeological deposits was 80cm to 90cm at Loggers, where the deposit had a total depth of ca 2m.

The remains from a wide range of animals were found: mammals, birds, fish, reptiles, freshwater and marine shellfish and yabbies. The number of bone fragments retrieved from each site varies from one to 9493; the weight varies from <1g to 1289g. Most fragments are <1cm long. A summary list of the species and/or genus identified at each site is provided in Tables 4.8 to 4.11. Data in Tables 4.6 and 4.8 to 4.11 for Black Hands relate only to Square F, and for Loggers only to Squares E–F. Further details are provided in Aplin's 1981 and 1985 faunal reports reproduced in Appendix 3.

Fragmented shell was retrieved from 15 archaeological deposits and small fragments of freshwater crayfish/yabby carapace from only four. Shell weights range from 0.1g to 20.1g, whereas the maximum weight of yabby carapace is only 3.7g. The shell

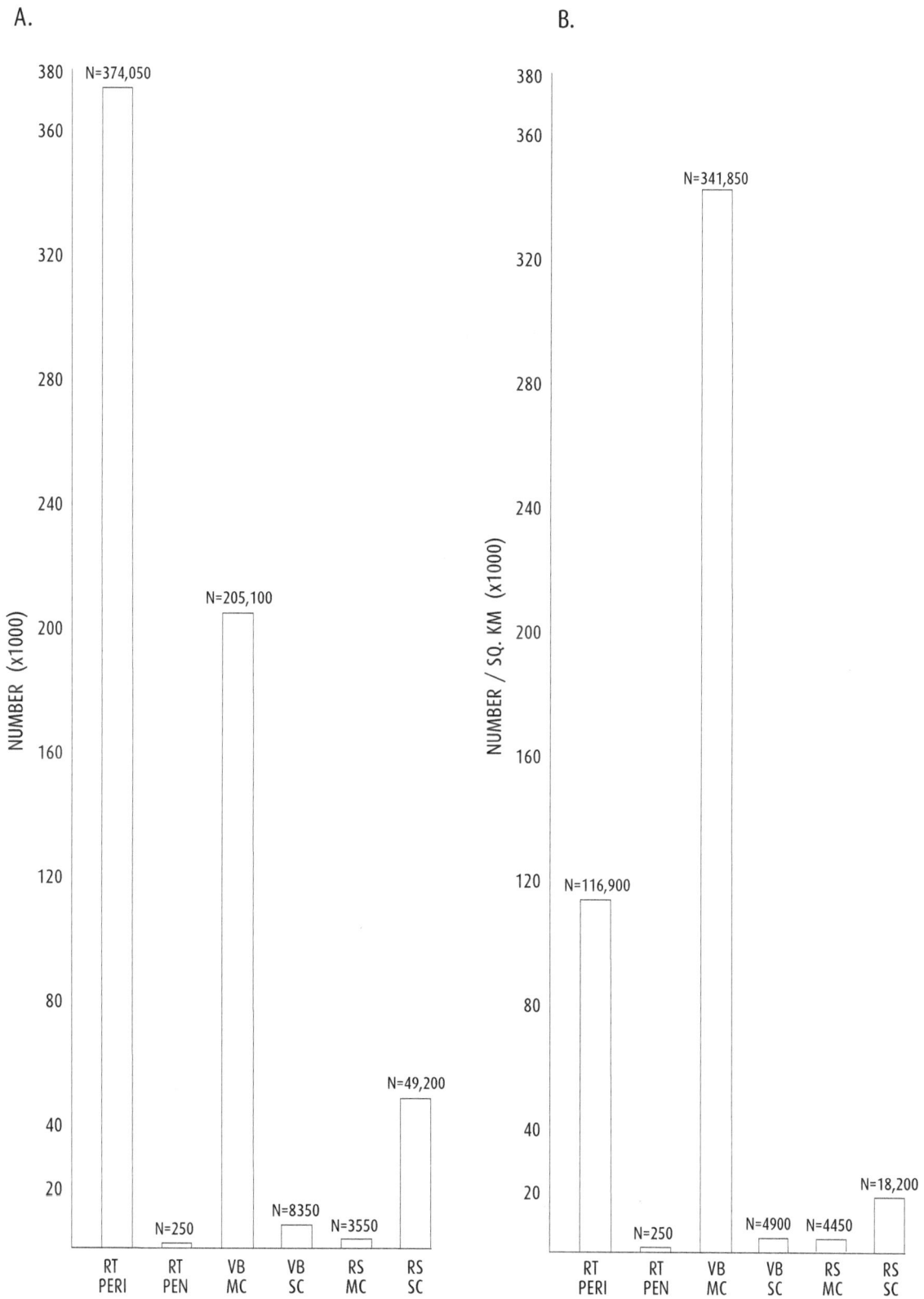

Figure 4.3 Upper Mangrove Creek catchment: random sampling units. (A) Estimated total number and (B) density of artefacts accumulated in each topographic zone.

included estuarine as well as freshwater species. The shell found at Delight Open Deposit is of recent and non-Aboriginal origin. A furred possum tail found on the surface in One Tooth was not weighed.

Categorisation of archaeological deposits

Since stone artefacts were the only category of evidence retrieved in the majority of the archaeological deposits, the number of stone artefacts is used to categorise the archaeological deposits into 'size' classes. The classification is based on the estimated total number of artefacts present in each archaeological deposit (Table 4.12). This was calculated by multiplying the number of artefacts per square metre of excavated deposit by the number of square metres of deposit at the site. The number of artefacts per square metre was calculated by dividing the number of artefacts retrieved by the number of square metres excavated.

In calculating the estimated number of artefacts in each deposit, recorded variations in artefact density throughout the depth of the excavated deposit were taken into account. In addition, where it could be seen that the unexcavated deposits would not contain a similar density of artefacts as the excavated deposit, or that they would not be of similar depth/thickness to the excavated deposits, these observations were taken into account. As well, factors which indicated that there were likely to be spatial variations in the number and/or density of artefacts across the area of the deposit were considered; for example,
1.	whether there were very shallow areas, or eroded/gullied areas with gravel lag; or,
2.	whether there was an area of deposit outside the shelter that was also likely to contain archaeological materials (Table 4.4).

The estimated total number of artefacts in each archaeological deposit is used in the analyses to overcome problems which may result from the wide variation in the area excavated in each archaeological deposit and in the area of archaeological deposit at each site.

Based on the estimated number of artefacts present, a K-means cluster analysis (undertaken by Richard Wright; Orton 1980: 52–4) suggested the archaeological deposits could be divided into three clusters, which I called AD-1, AD-2 and AD-3 (Table 4.13).

In general, the archaeological deposits fall into similar categories if classified on the basis of the actual number of artefacts retrieved or the number of artefacts per square metre, although the ordering within the categories changes slightly in some cases (Table 4.12).

The six sites in category AD-3 have a restricted distribution occurring in only three of the topographic zones: periphery ridgetops (3), the main valley bottoms (2), and the subsidiary ridgesides (1) (Attenbrow 1987: Table 6.3). Most of the archaeological deposits in the periphery ridgetops and main valley bottoms are category AD-3 (i.e., three of five, and two of three respectively). On the subsidiary ridgesides, only one of the 11 sites is category AD-3 and this archaeological deposit lies just within the lower boundary of the sampling unit; that is, just above the boundary of the valley bottom zone. The two archaeological deposits with the highest estimated number of artefacts in category AD-2 (Delight and White Figure, both with ca 5000 artefacts) are also in two of these three topographic zones (periphery ridgetops and subsidiary ridgesides).

The numbers of stone artefacts recorded at open archaeological deposits are quite small (<26), but, in most cases, the area over which buried artefacts could be present is relatively large with ill-defined and/or undefinable boundaries. It was thus not feasible to estimate either the extent of the area over which the open archaeological deposits may exist or the total number of artefacts in them. The five open archaeological deposits are therefore not included in this categorisation, nor in analyses where this breakdown is used. The

Table 4.12 Upper Mangrove Creek catchment: random sampling units. Archaeological deposits: number of artefacts retrieved, number of artefacts/square metre, and estimated total number of artefacts present. [1] Excludes surface artefacts outside excavated squares.

SITE NAME	No. OF ARTEFACTS RETRIEVED [1]	No. OF ARTEFACTS PER SQUARE METRE	ESTIMATED TOTAL No. OF ARTEFACTS IN ARCHAEOLOGICAL DEPOSIT (TAKEN TO NEAREST 50)	
OPEN AND/OR UNEXCAVATED DEPOSITS				
Firestick	0		0	(or very low)
Axe Head	1		–	(very low)
Palmers Crossing Nth OD	2		n/c	
Token Male	3		n/c	
Kyola Road OD	4		n/c	
Button	4		n/c	(very low)
Willow Tree Gully OD	7		n/c	
Delight OD	7		n/c	
Black Hands OD	12 Exc + 14 Surf	12	–	
Total	42			
EXCAVATED DEPOSITS				
Bird Tracks	0	0	0	(or very low)
Two Moths	0	0	0	(or very low)
Elngarrah	3	3	100	
Boronia	4	4	150	
Low Frontage	6	12	300	
Geebung	8	16	400	
Wolloby Gully	9	36	2250	
One Tooth	8	32	750	
Ti-tree	11	22	500	
Elongated Figure	12	48	950	
Mangrove Mansions (East, T1)	13	52	3250	
Caramel Wave	14	28	500	
Anadara	20	40	1850	
Boat Cave	21	84	500	
Venus	21	42	700	
McPherson	23	92	1600	
Harris Gully	34	136	1850	
Dingo (Sq Tb only)	40	160	2600	
Kangaroo and Echidna (T1+T2)	2+61	8+66	5500	
Delight SH	353	1358	5000	
Uprooted Tree (Ta+Tb)	875	1754	31,250	
White Figure	1087	2174	37,050	
Sunny	1260	2520	88,150	
Black Hands SH (Sq F)	3302	3843	77,050	
Loggers (Sq E+F)	4803	2402	128,050	
Emu Tracks 2 (I1+I2)	119+7278	11,830	249,650	
Total	19,399		639,950	

Table 4.13 Upper Mangrove Creek catchment: assemblages grouped according to K-means analysis.

CATEGORY	ESTIMATED TOTAL NUMBER OF ARTEFACTS	No. OF ARCHAEOLOGICAL DEPOSITS
AD-1	0 to 100	7
AD-2	101 to 5500	18
AD-3	>31,000	6

information recorded to date, however, suggests that the largest open archaeological deposits (in terms of both area and potential depth of deposit) occur along the main valley bottoms.

Isolated finds

Ten isolated finds (IFs) were recorded in the random sampling units (Attenbrow 1987: Tables 5.2 and A3/2; 1997 [1998]: Appendix 2). They were all stone artefacts — one ground-edged implement (IF.20), one chert flake (IF.3), three flaked pieces (IF.6; IF.17 with possible R/UW; IF.13 a possible 'axe preform'), two hand-held cores (IFs. 12, 26), a bipolar core (IF.70), one probable manuport (IF.8, a broken basalt pebble), a rejuvenation flake with possible R/UW or edge damage (IF.35).

The isolated finds were all recorded in random sampling units which occur within the storage area. The lack of isolated finds in other random sampling units and the lower frequency recorded in areas outside the storage area is probably due to three main factors:
1. the greater amounts of ground disturbance in the storage area;
2. the greater length of time spent undertaking archaeological work in the storage area;
3. the greater amount of ground/vegetation cover in areas above the storage area.

Although I suggested earlier (Chapter 3, Isolated finds) that isolated finds could provide clues to locations of open archaeological deposits, sub-surface investigations were not undertaken at these locations. It is too late to undertake such a program in the catchment since the isolated finds recorded are in the now-flooded valley bottoms. Sub-surface testing in such locations (as well as locations identified as open archaeological deposits) could, however, and perhaps should, be incorporated into future projects in this region (e.g., in the lower Mangrove Creek or Macdonald River Valley), particularly since open archaeological deposits in Sydney/Hawkesbury sandstone environments are so elusive (Attenbrow 1997 [1998]).

Potential habitation shelters and potential archaeological deposits (PH shelters and PADs)

One hundred and seventy-two potential habitation (PH) shelters were recorded within the random sampling units during the survey period (Attenbrow 1987: Appendix 3, Table A3/3). They are typical sandstone rockshelters, which meet the criteria described in Chapter 3.

The deposit in four of the PH shelters was test excavated — archaeological materials were found in three deposits and one test pit was sterile. On reinspection of other PH shelters, one was found to contain an archaeological deposit and another to have images. Thus, 167 rockshelters in the random sampling units remain classified as 'potential habitation shelters' — a density of 16.5/sq km (Table 4.2C).

Of the 167 PH shelters, 159 have potential archaeological deposit (PAD). Thirty-two rockshelters with PAD have only a shallow depth of sediment (<10cm) and one has a flood-affected deposit (Table 4.2C). Although rockshelters with PAD were recorded in all topographic zones, they are not evenly distributed across the catchment. Their density ranges from 2/sq km in the main valley bottoms to 46/sq km on the main ridgesides.

From the excavations carried out, it is anticipated that rockshelters with shallow deposit are unlikely to have abundant archaeological materials. Of the 30 rockshelters in the random sampling units which are classified as having archaeological deposit, three have only very shallow unconsolidated sediment — Axehead, Button, Firestick). At another three, the deposit with some depth is either outside the rockshelter (McPherson) or restricted to within the dripline zone (Boat Cave, Delight). It was possible to excavate within the dripline zone at Boat Cave, Delight and outside the rockshelter at McPherson, but, apart from Delight, very few stone artefacts or faunal remains were retrieved from the test pits in these archaeological deposits.

Twenty-five locations with PAD were test excavated during the salvage program and the research project (14 PH shelters and 11 rockshelters with images). Eighteen of these (72%) contain definite archaeological material (stone artefacts and/or faunal remains; the deposit in one rockshelter with images [Casper] was classified as doubtful as the test excavation retrieved only one doubtful stone artefact). Extrapolation from these figures suggests there may be a further 91 to 115 rockshelters with archaeological deposit in the random sampling units (i.e., between 9/sq km and 11.5/sq km). However, the PH shelters included in the excavation program were a purposeful sample, and test excavation of a random sample of all PH shelters is necessary before more accurate inferences can be made. Szpak's comparative analysis of the attributes of recorded PH shelters against those of shelters known to have been used concluded that:

> ...it must be assumed that all these rockshelters **have** been used until it is known otherwise, always bearing in mind that in some rockshelters, ie those with bare rock floors and no archaeological evidence, it will be impossible to prove or disprove this contention. (Szpak 1997: 112)

Some rockshelters with PAD may fall outside the PH criteria outlined in the last chapter. For example, rockshelters or overhanging cliffs where the 'sheltered' floor area is smaller than stipulated but a large flattish area of deposit suitable for habitation exists, and the cliff/overhang would provide shelter from, say, strong winds and intense heat, if not from rain. Such locations were not recorded during the survey. There is no way of assessing how many exist, without repeating the survey, and recording and/or test excavating rockshelters with these and/or other characteristics.

5

Upper Mangrove Creek catchment: random sampling units.

Possible biases in the archaeological record and data sets

Biases that may have been introduced into the archaeological record and data sets by both natural events and human behaviour were examined to help establish the degree of reliability that can be placed on the results of the analyses. Incidents — taphonomic processes — affecting the deposits may have occurred during the course of each habitation's use and its abandonment. In addition, methodological procedures adopted for the research project may have affected the results, e.g., during the fieldwork (outside procedures relating to sample selection) and analysis of data.

Methodological factors — fieldwork

Methodological factors which may have affected the fieldwork results concern the way in which sites and archaeological traits were defined, the survey design, sample size, observer bias and whether excavation stopped before the base of an archaeological deposit was reached.

Definitions
It was thought that density figures (i.e., the number of sites per square kilometre) may have become biased due to the way sites and archaeological traits were defined (Chapter 3, Defining sites), in particular, criteria relating to the distance between sites. The following assessment, however, indicates that the site definitions have not significantly affected the results of the analyses relating to site densities.

There are three situations where two archaeological traits less than 50m apart were defined as separate sites:
- Delight Shelter and Delight Open Site;
- Kyola Road Images 1 and Kyola Road Open Site; and,
- Uprooted Tree Shelter and Uprooted Tree Grinding Area.

Each situation involves different types of archaeological traits and/or different types of locations (SH/AD and OD/AD; OR/IM and OD/AD; SH/AD and OR/GA respectively). If these traits are classified as three sites instead of six, the total number of sites in the random sampling units becomes 56 instead of 59, and the average site density becomes 5.5/sq km rather than 5.8/sq km. If, in addition, the original classification of Kyola Road Images as one site (as on the NPWS site card) is retained rather than classifying them as two, the number of sites is reduced to 55, but the site density remains 5.5/sq km; the density of images on open rock drops from 0.2 to 0.1/sq km (Attenbrow 1987: Table 5.11). All of the abovementioned sites are on periphery ridgetops. If the total number of sites on the periphery ridgetops is reduced by four (from 24 to 20), this zone still has the highest number of sites and the second-highest density of sites (Table 4.2A).

Survey design

Problems arose with two of the sampling units: RSU.101 in the northern part of the catchment and RSU.75 at the junction of Mangrove and Boomerang Creeks (Fig. 3.15).

RSU.101

A section of periphery ridgetop was inadvertently included in the subsidiary valley bottom zone when marking the map into topographic zones in the sampling design stage; the subsidiary valley bottom zone was extended too far upstream in this particular creek. This was realised only once in the field. This section of the periphery ridgetop is in the northern half of the RSU.101, a subsidiary valley bottom sampling unit. A grinding area, First of Day, recorded in RSU.101 is therefore just within the periphery ridgetop zone rather than subsidiary valley bottom. In this instance, that part of the sampling unit and the site were not deleted from the analyses. This boundary error does not affect the data and trends presented in this monograph.

RSU.75

This unit is in the main valley bottom at the junction of Mangrove and Boomerang Creeks — it extends along Mangrove Creek both above and below the junction. When surveying commenced in RSU.75, it was found that logging had begun in this section of the storage area, and fallen logs rendered the southern half of the unit below the junction with Boomerang Creek inaccessible. An on-the-spot decision was made to survey an equivalent section along Boomerang Creek which was part of RSU.74. The area actually surveyed has been called RSU.75/74.

The 'abandoned' southern section of RSU.75, which was surveyed during the salvage program, had four recorded sites. A comparison between the evidence recorded in RSU.75 and in RSU.75/74 was made to check whether the results would have been very different (Attenbrow 1987: Table 5.13). Some differences occur: a scarred tree and two open archaeological deposits were found in RSU.75-south, whereas no scarred trees and only one open archaeological deposit occur in the part of RSU.74 surveyed. One of the open archaeological deposits in RSU.75-south, Stockyards Open Deposit, has a much larger number of recorded artefacts (152) and a much larger area (7200m²) than Palmers Crossing in RSU.74 and all other open archaeological deposits in the random sampling units (Tables 4.5 and 4.6). As well as a surface collection, test excavations were undertaken at Stockyards, but there were no materials appropriate to date. The presence of a single Bondi point indicates occupation occurred most likely in Phase 2 or possibly Phase 3 — that is, sometime between ca 5000 and ca 1600 years BP, but it could have occurred up to ca 8000 years ago (Table 3.8; Hiscock and Attenbrow 1998). The limited and disturbed evidence at Palmers Crossing did not allow it to be included in the analyses. If Stockyards had been included, the numbers of sites established and/or used, and the artefact accumulation rates would have increased in the late-Holocene periods. However, the magnitude of the increase would not have been sufficient to substantially alter the trends presented in future chapters.

Sample size

The affect of sample size (Grayson 1984: 116–30; Hiscock and Allen 2000: 100; Hiscock 2001) in relation to the site survey was discussed in Attenbrow 1987 (Chapter 4). With regard to excavation, trends in the habitation and artefact indices may have become biased because of the small area excavated in some of the archaeological deposits (i.e., 0.25m²). For example, small sample sizes may mean that the evidence retrieved from the pit as a whole, or from particular levels, is not representative of the whole deposit. If so, then the number and type of artefacts and raw material retrieved, as well as the estimated total numbers of artefacts which were extrapolated from that sample may be inaccurate, or assignment to a particular phase or millennium may be incorrect. In addition, in shelters with sloping sandstone floors (see next section), it is possible that the earliest time periods are not represented by the excavated basal deposits. These questions can be tested only by further excavation in those archaeological deposits.

Explanations for inter-site variability as well as intra-site temporal variability in the range of stone artefact types and animal species present in each archaeological deposit may also be prejudiced if sample size is not taken into account. In this regard, intra-site comparison of the stone artefact assemblage composition and density figures from individual 0.25m² pits in Mussel, Deep Creek and Confluence, three sites in the storage area, are relevant. In the deposit in each of these rockshelters, more than two adjoining pits were excavated. Temporal trends in the direction and magnitude of changes in density figures were similar in each pit, suggesting trends in artefact accumulation rates in deposits in small to medium shelters are unlikely to be biased. It is assumed, on the basis of this exercise, that numbers and densities of artefacts in a test pit reflect numbers and densities in the deposit as a whole and that the calculations of the estimated total numbers of artefacts (Tables 4.12, 6.11–6.16) based on extrapolations from the test pits are not widely divergent from reality.

In contrast with the density figures, the presence/absence of specific artefact types in particular levels does sometimes vary, and this was kept in mind where the ages of deposits are based on diagnostic artefact types in single 0.25m² pits.

Excavation stopped prematurely

In six sites, excavation stopped before reaching bedrock, or rock/rubble or colluvial sediment which could be assumed to be the original ground surface (Chapter 3, Table 3.4). At Black Hands Open Deposit, digging ceased when water from rising stored water in adjacent Mangrove Creek filled the pit. At two sites, Anadara (T2) and Mangrove Mansions (T2), excavation was not continued due to the clearly shallow and disturbed nature of their deposits. At three of the sites (Bird Tracks, Boronia, and Kangaroo and Echidna), excavation was stopped after about 20cm of sterile deposit was dug.

At a further three sites (Elongated Figure, Harris Gully, Uprooted Tree), the base of the excavation was sloping bedrock which suggests the adjacent deposit may be deeper. At each of these sites it is possible that earlier levels with stone artefacts are present.

The implications of these situations are discussed in the following chapter when changes in the habitation establishment rates are analysed.

Observer bias

This term covers non-detection of archaeological traits due to the inexperience of fieldworkers and/or 'end-of-day' tiredness. Both can affect survey and excavation results.

Survey results

Both inexperience and tiredness can cause evidence to go unnoticed during site survey. For example, one or two stone artefacts in a rockshelter dripline, or particularly faint remnant drawings or scratched outlines on a rockshelter wall/ceiling, could be missed.

During the excavation stage and/or during visits to rockshelters for other reasons, some pigment images were noticed in shelters that had been missed during the site survey (Chapter 4, Summary of fieldwork results). This suggests that some PH shelters which were not revisited may have images. An estimation of how many may have been missed can be gained from the following observations. At the end of the random sample survey, of the 27 rockshelter sites recorded, 11 were without images. After revisiting these 11 sites for test excavations, two were found to have pigment images (Dingo and One Tooth) and a third to have a possible image (Elngarrah); these represent 18% or possibly 27% of the rockshelter sites. By extrapolation, between one-fifth and one-quarter of the recorded PH shelters may contain images, which suggests there are another 30 to 45 rockshelters with images in the random sampling units. However, the 11 sites which were reinspected are a probably biased sample as they all had some other evidence of Aboriginal use (i.e., archaeological deposit). Thus, the number of images in rockshelters that are likely to have been missed is probably <27%.

Excavation results

Three factors may have affected the excavation results of some archaeological deposits.

1. The varying levels of experience and diligence of individual field assistants. Volunteers who assisted in the field varied in their experience, expertise and dedication. Care was taken to ensure people achieved the same level of retrieval, however, the same people were not present throughout each excavation period and some variation in the amounts recovered from the sieves at different sites may have resulted.

2. Field sorting versus laboratory sorting. The sieved residues from some archaeological deposits were sorted in the field and others were taken back to the laboratory for sorting. The level of recovery for sites where excavated materials were sorted in the laboratory may be higher than for those where sorting took place on site.

3. The presence of abundant organic matter and small rubble. The upper spits of some deposits contain a lot of leaf-litter and/or charcoal. Because of their bulk, these materials can hinder the visibility of other archaeological materials. In addition, charcoal tends to colour everything grey, making all the materials appear similar (e.g., this was the case in the upper levels of Loggers and White Figure). Archaeological materials are also less visible in deposits with large amounts of small rubble.

The above statements are based on the observations at two sites where it was possible to check results: White Figure and Deep Creek (the latter is in the storage area [Attenbrow 1982b]). Both have rich archaeological deposits with relatively large assemblages. A sample of the sieved residues from these two sites were returned to the laboratory — a check revealed that the 0–1cm stone artefact category and small bone fragments in some spits may be under-represented because of the factors listed above.

In the case of Deep Creek, the analysis indicated the 'shortfall' would have made no difference to the overall percentage of the artefact types and raw materials within individual excavation units or within analytical levels (combined spits) (horizontally and vertically). This suggests that where large numbers of stone artefacts are recovered, observer bias may not have substantially affected the results.

At White Figure, all three of the above factors were involved. Large amounts of organic matter (leaf-litter and charcoal) in the upper spits made thorough checking of the sieved materials a difficult and lengthy process. When work started on site, the person initially sieving the excavated deposit did not realise that residues should be bagged for later sorting if it was not possible to check the sieved residues thoroughly without holding up the excavation process. The field-sorted residues from the surface and upper two spits were thrown out before I realised they had not been thoroughly checked. From spit 3 onwards, sieve residues were kept and a final sort undertaken in the laboratory. Results gained from excavation units sorted in both the field and laboratory suggest that about 50% of the stone artefacts in the upper two spits may have been missed. The figures used in the analyses were adjusted where necessary to compensate for this (e.g., when estimating the total numbers of artefacts in the archaeological deposits in White Figure — Tables 4.12, 6.11 to 6.13, and A2/16).

Methodological factors — analyses

Calculating artefact accumulation rates

Artefact accumulation rates were calculated for each of the excavated deposits in the catchment (Chapter 6) as well as for sites in the comparative regions in eastern Australia (Chapter 7). The method adopted, using depth/age curves, is described in Chapter 6. Rates derived by this method are very much dependent on (a) the position of dated levels, and (b) the assumptions that deposition rates for sediments remained relatively constant between the dated levels or dated materials, and that gross sediment deposition and erosion patterns are well approximated by the net rate (Morwood 1981: 32; Davidson 1997: 217). Since we often do not know whether these assumptions are true, there are, as Morwood states, limits to the precision of the method. In addition, the small number or lack of radiocarbon ages for some of the catchment deposits may have led to inaccuracies in the trends in the artefact accumulation rates. Various alternatives, involving the way spits were combined into phases of millennial units, were examined for some sites before accepting those presented (Chapter 6). The existence of uneven stratigraphy, sterile layers, disconformities and the integrity of the deposits were taken into account (cf. Rosenfeld et al. 1981: 11–13).

Any biases in the artefact accumulation rates of individual deposits would have been extrapolated across to the local artefact accumulation rates. Again, however, various alternatives were examined before adopting those presented. In calculating the artefact accumulation rates for the eastern Australian sites (Chapter 7), if any of my assumptions about the published information are in error, there may be inaccuracies in the trends presented for these regions.

Natural processes

Natural processes which can affect archaeological evidence include chemical, geomorphological and biological (animal and vegetation) processes. The effect of weather conditions at the time of site survey and recording has also been included under this section, although it could be seen as 'methodological'. These processes can cause the archaeological record to become biased in several ways.

1.   Materials in an archaeological deposit can be disturbed or redistributed by faunal activity and vegetation growth. Fauna which can affect archaeological traits include beetles, ants, termites, wasps, cicadas, as well as larger animals such as wallabies, small rodents, rabbits, wombats, bower birds, lyrebirds and emus. People also dug holes in archaeological deposits for various purposes (including burials), cleared areas and caused general treadage and scuffage during habitation of a site.

2.   Organic materials decay; groundwater causes decomposition of materials.

3.   Deposits and sandstone in or on which archaeological materials were present can become totally or partially removed or destroyed by erosion and/or weathering.

4.   Subsequent sediment deposition or vegetation growth can restrict visibility and thus hinder visual observation of materials and sites in open as well as shelter contexts.

5.   Poor lighting conditions during overcast weather or at the end of the day can affect visibility of archaeological traits during fieldwork.

6.   Charcoal from past bushfires (either natural or humanly-initiated) which has existed in/on the ground for long periods of time (environmental charcoal) can become incorporated into more recent archaeological deposits through fluvial and slope processes (cf. Blong and Gillespie 1978).

Ironically, the erosion and/or disturbance of sediments (1 and 3 above) probably does as much 'good' as 'harm', in that it is these processes which are instrumental in exposing materials which are obscured by deposition of sediment and vegetation (4).

Points 3 and 4 have been put forward as explanations for the lower numbers of archaeological sites dating to the late-Pleistocene and early-Holocene periods (refer to Chapter 2; Worrall 1980: 81–3; Bonhomme 1985: 33; cf. Mellars 1973: 269–70 for similar discussion for Palaeolithic Europe). These points bear on the questions:

1.   were all sites that existed at the time of fieldwork found in the random sampling units during the site surveys and excavations?

2.   of the sites that were formed in the past, what type and number are no longer likely to exist?

Question 1 relates to questions of visibility and question 2 to processes of destruction. Each of these circumstances is discussed below, as well as the problem of older 'environmental' charcoal being incorporated into more recent archaeological deposits.

Visibility

The visibility of archaeological traits that occur in the catchment can be impaired partially or restricted totally by vegetation growth and sediment cover (Sullivan 1983: 6). In addition, bad light at the end of the day or in overcast weather can also affect visibility. These in turn can be accentuated by the factors discussed above under observer bias (inexperience and end-of-day tiredness).

Archaeological deposits in rockshelters

In rockshelters, archaeological materials can be totally covered by sediment and the mouths of small rockshelters can be obscured by dense vegetation. Recording and test excavating potential archaeological deposits in PH shelters has overcome (to a certain extent) some of the difficulties which result from archaeological materials in rockshelters being totally buried. As discussed in the previous chapter, the results of test excavations of potential archaeological deposits provide an estimate of the number of archaeological deposits in rockshelters which may have been missed.

Open archaeological deposits

Five open archaeological deposits were found during the random sample survey. Two are on periphery ridgetops (Delight and Kyola Road) and three in the main valley bottom (Black Hands OD, Palmers Crossing and Willow Tree Gully). The two on the ridgetops were found in areas with sparse leaf-litter and skeletal soils. Those on the valley bottom were all found in disturbed locations on deep deposits forming the creek banks (Attenbrow 1997 [1998]). Other open archaeological deposits probably exist within the random sampling units but are buried under fill in the valley bottoms, and under slopewashed sediments and leaf-litter on the ridgetops and structural benches on ridgesides (see also Vinnicombe 1984: 110). A recording and testing program similar to that for the PH shelters would be required to investigate locations with potential open archaeological deposit in order to assess how many open archaeological deposits are unrecorded. Unfortunately, as previously stated, this is not possible now in the main valley bottom zones of the catchment, but such a program could be carried out above the storage area.

Isolated finds may provide clues to the occurrence of open archaeological deposits in places other than those at which they have been recorded. In addition, site records in many other regions (e.g., the Hunter Valley and Cumberland Plain to the north and south of the catchment) indicate that open archaeological deposits are commonly found on river banks and terraces. However, for both ridgetops and structural benches on ridgesides there are no definite clues as yet to the specific places where open archaeological deposits may occur in the catchment. Although studies such as those by Byrne (1983, 1984), Egloff (1984), Packard (1992) and Hall and Lomax (1996) describe site distribution patterns with open artefact scatters predominantly along ridgetops for many of the NSW east coast forests, a similar pattern has not been documented in the Upper Mangrove Creek catchment or other parts of the sandstone country of the greater Sydney region (e.g., Vinnicombe 1980; Sefton 1988; Illawarra Prehistory Group 1990, 1995, 1996; McDonald 1994; Kinhill Engineers 1995). The reasons for this variance can be seen in the differences in the geology and terrain whereby different types of potential site locations are available in the catchment than in the other NSW east coast forests. The most significant difference is the lack of rockshelters (or the much smaller number of rockshelters) in forests in non-sandstone environments.

Grinding areas and engraved images
Dense understorey shrubs along the creek banks and around rock platforms may obscure the existence of exposed sandstone surfaces where grinding grooves and engraved images typically occur. Grooves and engraved images can also be covered by silt and soil mobilised by slopewash processes.

Destruction
Destruction refers to the removal of archaeological materials, engraved or pigment images, or grinding areas from their original place of deposition or creation. It can be total or partial.

Worrall, in discussing geoarchaeological issues relevant to the catchment, stated:

> … that the likelihood of survival of an occupational deposit of a given age decreases with time. The relatively small number of early sites located in the catchment may thus be explained solely in terms of contemporary geomorphic process without recourse to speculation concerning prehistoric population size. (Worrall 1980: 82–3)

> It is suggested that the operation of a process of discontinuous aggradation and denudation of deposits in the majority of archaeological sites in the catchment may be sufficient in itself to explain the trend towards fewer sites from progressively earlier periods (Worrall 1980: 89).

In contrast, other researchers state that it is unlikely that archaeological deposits within rockshelters, once formed, would have suffered severely from erosion (Hughes and Lampert 1982: 19). In the random sampling units, the majority of the archaeological deposits (30 out of 35) were located in rockshelters. Processes affecting archaeological deposits in the open differ to some extent from those affecting rockshelter deposits.

Archaeological deposits in rockshelters

Worrall (1980: 81–2) made three points about archaeological deposits in rockshelters:

1.   Rockshelters in valley floor situations that were filled during deposition of Unit A (late-Pleistocene in age) may have been repeatedly filled or flushed or the deposit cliffed during events of Unit B deposition (Holocene events). Worrall refers to Bracken and Deep Creek as examples where this could have occurred; both sites are in the storage area and outside the random sampling units.

2.   Archaeological deposits in rockshelters which are on slopes may be subject to intermittent episodes of scour and fill of varying intensity. Worrall places Black Hands Shelter in this category. Worrall adds that the probability of a major scour event severely truncating or flushing the deposit from a rockshelter is obviously a function of time.

3.   The activation or cessation of deposition in rockshelters which are located in talus zones or cliff faces (on slopes) may be closely related to the operation of structural controls and thus may be relatively stable.

The situation, however, is more complex than Worrall's tripartite breakdown suggests. The stratigraphy at Deep Creek does not indicate that its deposits have been affected by filling, flushing or cliffing. The base of the deposits is 3m above present creek level and above flood level. In addition, it is a relatively large shelter (12.4m × 5m) and inside the dripline the shelter is dry and not open to slopewash processes. The deposits at Bracken comprise alluvium derived principally from slopewash (Hughes and Sullivan 1979: 10). Though subject to inundation and deposition of sediments by low-energy floodwaters, there was no evidence of cliffing in the stratigraphy (contrary to Worrall's statement, 1980: 64), scours or erosional lags of gravel and artefacts.

The degree to which the catchment rockshelters are exposed to slope processes also depends on the direction in which their mouth faces (i.e., downslope or across slope) and whether the rockshelter has closed or open sides. Rockshelters facing downslope and those which have closed sides are less prone to slopewash processes than those facing other directions and with open sides.

To assess the processes operating in the rockshelters in the random sampling units, it was recorded whether or not each rockshelter was:

1.   on the valley floor and liable to inundation during floods; or,

2.   on a ridgeside and its morphology was such that it was vulnerable to slope processes which could scour its deposits.

In many rockshelters, the deposit is partially affected by erosional/slope processes, for example, along the dripline from water coming over the overhang, or by water coming downslope and entering the rockshelter from an 'open' side (Table 5.1). In these instances, only a small part of the deposit is affected, not the entire shelter floor.

Worrall (1980: 40, 73) said, on the basis of a stratigraphic section in a road cutting downslope of Black Hands, that the 'shelter deposits ... comprise the infill sediments of a prior scour channel directed along the back wall of the shelter'. Worrall's interpretation suggests the archaeological deposits built up (i.e., habitation took place) in a scour channel within the rockshelter. The stratigraphic sections of the deposit excavated within Black Hands Shelter (squares A and B) and just outside the dripline (square F) do not support an interpretation that earlier materials were scoured out and the later archaeological deposit built up within a scour channel. Unless the hypothesised torrent swept through the rockshelter with such force that it removed all artefacts and small rubble which was deposited within the shelter before the scouring event, a layer of lagged rubble with an artefact density higher than other levels would be expected. No lag of artefacts or rubble was found within or at the base of the excavations to suggest large amounts of sediment had been removed. Worrall may have

Table 5.1 Upper Mangrove Creek catchment: random sampling units. Archaeological deposits in rockshelters and geomorphological processes. [1] Other details about radiocarbon ages are provided in Table 6.1.

SITE NAME	RADIOCARBON AGE (BP) [1]	DEPOSIT LIABLE TO INUNDATION	SHELTER OPEN TO SLOPE PROCESSES — DEPOSITS EXPOSED TO SCOURING		SHELTER MOUTH FACES DOWNSLOPE — FLOOR DEPOSITS NOT SUSCEPTIBLE TO SCOURING
			SUBSTANTIAL	LIMITED	
VALLEY BOTTOM					
Anadara				X	
Axehead					X
Black Hands	3040±85		X		
Button				X	
Geebung				X	
Harris Gully			X		
Loggers	11,050±135		X ⟵⟶ X		
Mangrove Mansions		X			
Ti-tree	490±50				X
RIDGESIDE					
Bird Tracks				X	
Boat Cave	2370±60				X
Caramel Wave	1430±60				X
Dingo	1840±60				X
Elongated Figure	1810±80				X
Firestick					X
Kangaroo and Echidna	6700±150				X
Low Frontage				X	
McPherson					X
One Tooth	350±40				X
Two Moths					X
Venus	560±50				X
White Figure	5230±70				X
Wolloby Gully	400±60			X	
RIDGETOP					
Boronia	1880±60				X
Delight					X
Elngarrah					X
Emu Tracks 2				X	
Sunny	3500±80			X	
Token Male				X	
Uprooted Tree	8430±130			X	
Totals — No.		1	2	11	16
%		3	7	37	53

misinterpreted the sides of the unknown excavator's trench in Black Hands Shelter (see Chapter 3, Excavation strategy and methods) as a scour channel.

Stone artefacts occur outside the rockshelter for a distance of at least 2m across the slope and 2m downslope (i.e., in square F outside the shelter and in the 70m contour road cutting below the shelter). These artefacts are just as or more likely to be from activities carried out within and in close proximity to the rockshelter as from geomorphological movement of artefacts downslope. Several artefacts were recovered from the slightly steeper slopes further below the rockshelter (through either slopewash movement or perhaps being thrown out from the shelter), but their morphology, size and raw material suggests they are of similar age to those in the rockshelter deposits.

Only one other rockshelter in the random sampling units (Harris Gully) is open substantially to slope processes in the same way as Black Hands Shelter (Table 5.1), though there the slope gradient is much lower. Only one rockshelter occurs within the valley floor zone in a position liable to creek overbanking (Mangrove Mansions). Most rockshelters in the catchment are formed in cliffs or low bands of sandstone on the ridgesides. These rockshelters, unless at the end of the cliff or band of sandstone, invariably face downslope and slope materials cannot enter (16, 53%).

At rockshelters such as Bird Tracks, Low Frontage, Sunny and Uprooted Tree, water passes over the overhang and affects a limited part of the deposit along the dripline. Other rockshelters, such as Anadara, have an open side, which allows slope processes to affect a small part of the deposit at one end. In all of these rockshelters, the affected areas were a small portion of the total deposit. If, in the past, the water 'course' was different and affected different and/or greater areas before the deposit built up to its present depth, then it was not apparent in the stratigraphy of the test excavated area.

Of the 30 rockshelters classified as having archaeological deposit, three do not have deposit within the rockshelter but archaeological materials were recovered in the deposit immediately outside the dripline area (Button, Delight, McPherson). At another two, the archaeological materials were present on very shallow sandy sediment overlying bedrock (Axehead and Firestick). A further rockshelter has only images (both pigment and engraved) and no archaeological deposit (Emu Tracks 1). In those sites where there is no deposit within the rockshelter, the floor is steeply sloping bedrock on which sediment could not be retained and/or no rocks are present to help retain the deposit within the rockshelter (Button, Emu Tracks 1, Delight and McPherson). Except for Axehead and Button, they are semicircular, cavernously weathered rockshelters in clifflines facing downslope.

Layers of lagged rubble and/or lagged artefacts were not found in any of the archaeological deposits excavated in the random sampling units. This suggests that there were no putative earlier sediments which might have been washed out. Of the sites excavated in the catchment, only one, Wattle Creek, has evidence of water scouring or channelling and subsequent refilling — this site was dug during the salvage program. No radiocarbon dates were obtained from Wattle Creek, but on the basis of the artefact types retrieved, the earliest assemblages were estimated at less than ca 3000 BP.

The fact that the two rockshelters with the earliest dates are in positions that are vulnerable (Loggers) and partially open (Uprooted Tree) to slopewash processes, and that the majority of the recent archaeological deposits are in rockshelters not subject to slopewash processes, suggests that the larger number of recent archaeological deposits is not the result of the early deposits being scoured out. At Loggers, only a small proportion of the archaeological deposit is sheltered beneath the overhang. This supports the conclusion reached by Hughes and Lampert for the NSW south coast:

> ... that it is unlikely that the archaeological deposits within them [i.e., rockshelters], once formed, would have suffered severely from erosion. (Hughes and Lampert 1982: 19)

Open archaeological deposits

In the catchment, situations where open archaeological deposits are susceptible to destruction are creek banks (valley fill) where flooding can remove and redeposit sediments in which archaeological materials may have accumulated, and ridgesides where slope processes operate. Relatively flat ridgetops are less prone to these processes.

Valley fill. Worrall (1980: 56) divided the valley fill in the catchment into two major units, A and B. The oldest, Unit A, she said (1980: 58) is of late-Pleistocene age, and Unit B is Holocene in age (1980: 74). Worrall (1980: 81) suggested that prehistoric vegetation cover on the Holocene Unit B deposits was probably shrub thickets and thus the likelihood of sites being formed on these deposits was small.

After completion of the salvage program, bulldozing operations took place on the valley floor. Inspections at disturbed locations resulted in the detection of several open archaeological deposits (see previous chapter and Attenbrow 1997 [1998]). They did not appear to be as rich in artefacts as sites such as Loggers and Black Hands, but insufficient work was undertaken on these sites prior to inundation to place any credence on such observations. The majority, if not all, of the more recently recorded open archaeological deposits on the valley bottom are on what I believe Worrall calls Unit B deposits. (No map of the areal extent of Unit A and Unit B deposits was presented by Worrall.)

The geomorphological processes involved in the accumulation and scouring of valley fills was probably of sufficient magnitude to have caused the loss of many sites of all ages. Radiocarbon dates for valley fill in the catchment indicate that fill dating back to at least 7000 BP is present (Sullivan and Hughes 1983: 123, Table 2). It is possible that in situ areas of fill of an older age have survived and that such deposits contain archaeological materials.

Ridgesides. Open archaeological deposits on the slopes of ridgesides would be subject to natural geomorphological processes and occasionally to periods of accelerated erosion (Bonhomme 1985). Bonhomme (1985: 14) reasoned that 'as a result, the material evidence of open sites is continually being reworked and probably lost from the slopes altogether'. Although Bonhomme's first observation may be true, the present archaeological record indicates that all materials have not been lost.

It is clear that the surviving open archaeological deposits in the catchment are unlikely to comprise a comprehensive record of such sites that have existed over time — much less so than the rockshelter deposits, which have greater protection from destruction. The question as to whether the rockshelter deposits by themselves can be accepted as representing the changing trends in catchment habitation patterns over time is raised again when interpretations and explanations for the documented archaeological trends in the catchment are discussed.

Further comments on visibility

The foregoing discussion highlights the fact that, irrespective of whether some sites have been destroyed in the past, all of the archaeological sites that presently exist in the random sampling units are unlikely to have been recorded during the fieldwork undertaken. This is a situation which no doubt exists for all archaeological programs. For some sets of data — in particular, the archaeological deposits and images in rockshelters — estimates of the numbers unrecorded can be made. It can be assumed that the images which were overlooked do not contain numerous figures, but it cannot be assumed that unexcavated potential archaeological deposits do not have abundant archaeological materials (e.g., as found in Bracken and Sunny). For traits on open deposit and open rock, there is, as yet, no data on which to estimate the number of unrecorded sites.

With respect to rockshelters, it would be fruitful to undertake an intensive testing program of the PH shelters to assess more accurately the numbers of unrecorded archaeological deposits and images in rockshelters, and to test Szpak's conclusion 'that it must be assumed that all these rockshelters have been used' (1997: 112). A random sample of PH shelters could be selected, their deposits test excavated and the walls re-inspected for images.

To investigate more rigorously the lack of recorded open archaeological deposits due to visibility problems, a program of site survey followed by shovel and/or backhoe testing in open locations with potential archaeological deposits could be undertaken. Fieldwork could perhaps specifically target flat areas along creek banks, structural benches on ridgesides, and ridgetops. Since most of the alluvial flats in the catchment valley bottom zones have been inundated, a testing program in such locations would have to be undertaken above the storage area in the catchment, downstream of the dam wall, or perhaps in an adjacent river valley.

Incorporation of older charcoal

The mouth of Black Hands Shelter faces across-slope, which means the shelter deposit may have been prone to slopewash processes at some stages of their accumulation, and to incorporation of 'environmental charcoal' from the surrounding slopes. If charcoal in the shelter deposit includes material that had been accumulating on the surrounding slopes for centuries, radiocarbon determinations received for the submitted charcoal samples may indicate an age that is older than the real age of the excavated level from which they were collected (cf. Blong and Gillespie 1978). Consequently, any cultural materials associated with that dated sample may be placed incorrectly into a period earlier than that to which they belong. However, it is possible that the submitted sample from near the base of Black Hands was not contaminated by environmental charcoal because, for example, the surface of the shelter deposit at that time was higher than the surrounding land surface. Alternatively, if it was, any charcoal washed in from the surrounding slopes may have been very much less than that from Aboriginal fires built within the rockshelter, and its influence on the age of the 'combined' sample was not critical. What can be said is that the age obtained for the charcoal sample submitted from near the base of Black Hands (3040±85 BP [SUA–932] from a depth of 90–100cm) is consistent with the type of artefacts present at that depth and the sequence of assemblages above it.

It is unlikely that slopewashed charcoal has contaminated many of the other rockshelter deposits except areas around and outside the dripline areas. Excavated pits were placed well inside the rockshelters except at Loggers and in the three cases where no deposit, or no substantial depth of deposit, existed inside the rockshelter. At Delight and Boat Cave, the only feasible place to excavate was in the dripline zone, and at McPherson the test pit had to be placed in front of the shelter. Of these sites, charcoal from only Boat Cave was used for dating purposes. The charcoal submitted for dating other archaeological deposits came from pits well inside the rockshelters and most probably derives from fires built within the rockshelters. In addition, in all samples, the largest pieces of charcoal available were submitted for dating.

A radiocarbon age of 2370±60 BP (Beta-81625) was obtained for a charcoal sample from near the base of the excavated pit at Boat Cave. This is earlier than my estimate of <1000 BP, based on the artefact types present and the nature and depth of deposit (Attenbrow 1987: Table 7.2). It may be that the earlier than estimated age is due to the inclusion of older charcoal from the ridgeside above (cf. Blong and Gillespie 1978) or simply that the deposits accumulated more slowly than my extrapolations and calculations predicted.

Ages were not obtained from either of the excavated open archaeological deposits on the valley bottom (Black Hands and Stockyards Open Archaeological Deposits). At Stockyards OAD, which was outside the random sampling units, a Bondi point was found which suggests the valley fill and habitation in that location pre-dates ca 1600 BP (see above). Charcoal in these two locations was scattered throughout the deposit — no hearths or hearth-like features were recorded. Using charcoal from these open archaeological deposits to estimate their age was not considered warranted.

Focus on rockshelters

Because of the few open archaeological deposits initially found, and the little if any datable material in those recorded, the analyses of changes over time in habitations has focused on the archaeological deposits in rockshelters. However, many aspects about the use of the catchment rockshelters are not known: for example, the extent to which rockshelters rather than open locations were used for habitation purposes; what other functions besides being habitations/campsites did the rockshelters serve; what size groups visited the catchment and used the rockshelters; and was the use of rockshelters related to seasonal or climatic conditions, or other events. Even for the early colonial period, there are no direct observations about life and activities undertaken in the catchment that can be used as a 'benchmark' from which to work backwards to assess changes over time.

Historical observations indicate that Aboriginal people in many parts of Australia preferred living in the open rather than in enclosed structures (Koettig 1976: 142–60). Even so, where they were available, rockshelters were commonly used, in particular, as refuges from rain, sun or wind, though not specifically from cold (e.g., Mulvaney 1960: 53; White and Peterson 1969: 59; Koettig 1976: 142–60; Jones and Johnson 1985a: 167; Flood 1997: 194–5). In northern Australia, rockshelters were used particularly in the wet season when travel was difficult and relatively permanent camps were established (Tresize 1971: 7, and Haviland and Haviland 1979 in Morwood and Hobbs 1995a: 179; Veth 1993: 77; Flood 1997: 194).

In the Sydney region, McDonald (1994: 348–9) suggested that open locations would have been preferred campsites at the time of British colonisation as the historical records for this region indicate there were large territorial groupings. However, the early historical sources for the coastal zone between Broken Bay and Botany Bay indicate that in terrain where rockshelters are prolific, they were frequently used as campsites (e.g., Bradley 1786–92 [1969: 74,140]; Extract … 1788 in HR.NSW 1892 [1978: 222]; Worgan 1788 [1978: 15–17]; Tench 1789: 80 [1961: 47–8]; White 1790 [1962: 157]; Hunter 1793 [1968: 59–60, 80]; Collins 1798 [1975: 460]). In addition, although large groups were occasionally observed in this area — up to 300 people were seen on some occasions (Collins 1798 [1975: 25]; Tench 1789: 90–1 [1979: 52]) — they were 'seldom seen more than 20 or 30 & frequently two & three together' (Bradley 1786–92 [1969]: 141–2). Resource abundance in the catchment would have been much less than in the coastal zone, where marine/estuarine resources are available in addition to terrestrial plants and animals. The size of groups visiting the catchment would have been at the smaller end of the scale.

In the catchment, it is likely that opportunities would have been taken to use a nearby rockshelter rather than constructing a hut of bark or other materials, especially in periods of bad weather (e.g., extremely wet, rainy, cold, windy or very hot weather). Along the NSW central coast and its hinterland, such conditions are not restricted to any particular season. Frosts and fog can be relatively thick on the catchment's river flats in winter (pers. obs.) and so those areas would most probably have been avoided at that time of the year. Catchment rockshelters were probably used in all seasons, by groups of varying but relatively small size.

Climatic changes that occurred throughout the Holocene (Chapter 9) may have affected the degree to which each type of location was inhabited in different periods of time (cf. Stockton and Holland 1974: 56, 60; cf. Hiscock 1988b: 228). McDonald (1994: 75) said that the decreased artefact accumulation rates in the catchment in the first millennium BP is 'suggestive of a change in preference to outdoor camping, or more specifically outdoor knapping' and 'could be interpreted as indicating that there was a shift in settlement patterns, from shelter locations to open locations during the last millennium'.

However, it is not possible to say from the historical and (as will be seen later) the archaeological evidence whether rockshelters were used more frequently than open locations, and/or whether the use of rockshelters versus open locations remained constant throughout the Holocene. It is thus not possible to say whether rockshelters by themselves provide an accurate or biased record of the changing use of the catchment over time. In general, however, rockshelter deposits are less prone to destruction than open deposits. The catchment rockshelter deposits therefore provide reliable evidence on which to make statements about changes in the rate at which habitations were established in rockshelters, the number of habitations in rockshelters in each time period, and the rate at which artefacts accumulated in rockshelters. Moreover, as will be seen in the final chapters, other behaviours, besides preference for either open or rockshelter camping locations depending on climatic conditions, can be shown to account for increases and decreases in the habitation and artefact indices.

Discussion

This study of factors that are likely to have influenced the results of analyses suggests that it is highly likely there are unrecorded sites in the random sampling units due to observer bias and visibility problems and that some sites (particularly open archaeological deposits) will have been destroyed in the past or remain buried. The exact way in which this knowledge effects the results presented in later chapters is not entirely clear. However, the number and density of locations and/or archaeological traits from all time periods is likely to have been higher in the past than presently exists, and to be higher than currently documented.

The incorporation of older 'environmental' charcoal into archaeological deposits may have occurred at some rockshelters, but excavated pits were usually placed away from the dripline zone and outside scoured and other zones where such contamination could occur. Radiocarbon determinations from such charcoal samples would give an age older than the 'real' age of the associated stone artefact assemblage. Thus, if such situations do occur, the bias introduced by the incorporation of older 'environmental' charcoal will not produce a trend towards a greater number of more recent habitations.

Comparison between results from random sampling units, storage area and the total catchment

Comparing the results from the random sampling units, the storage area and the total catchment enables a number of comments to be made about the results of the random sample survey (Fig. 5.1). The 'total catchment' consists of all sites in the catchment; that is, those in the random sampling units, in the storage area, as well as all other recorded sites outside those intensively surveyed areas.

Archaeological traits

In all three data sets (random sampling units, storage area and the total catchment), archaeological deposits are the most common trait. However, they represent a greater percentage of the traits in the storage area (73%) than in the other two data sets (44% and 48% respectively — Fig. 5.1A).

In the total catchment and random sampling units, images and grinding areas occur in similar proportions, whereas in the storage area they occur in much lower percentages. In addition, grinding areas are less common than images in the storage area, and form a much smaller component in the total catchment sample.

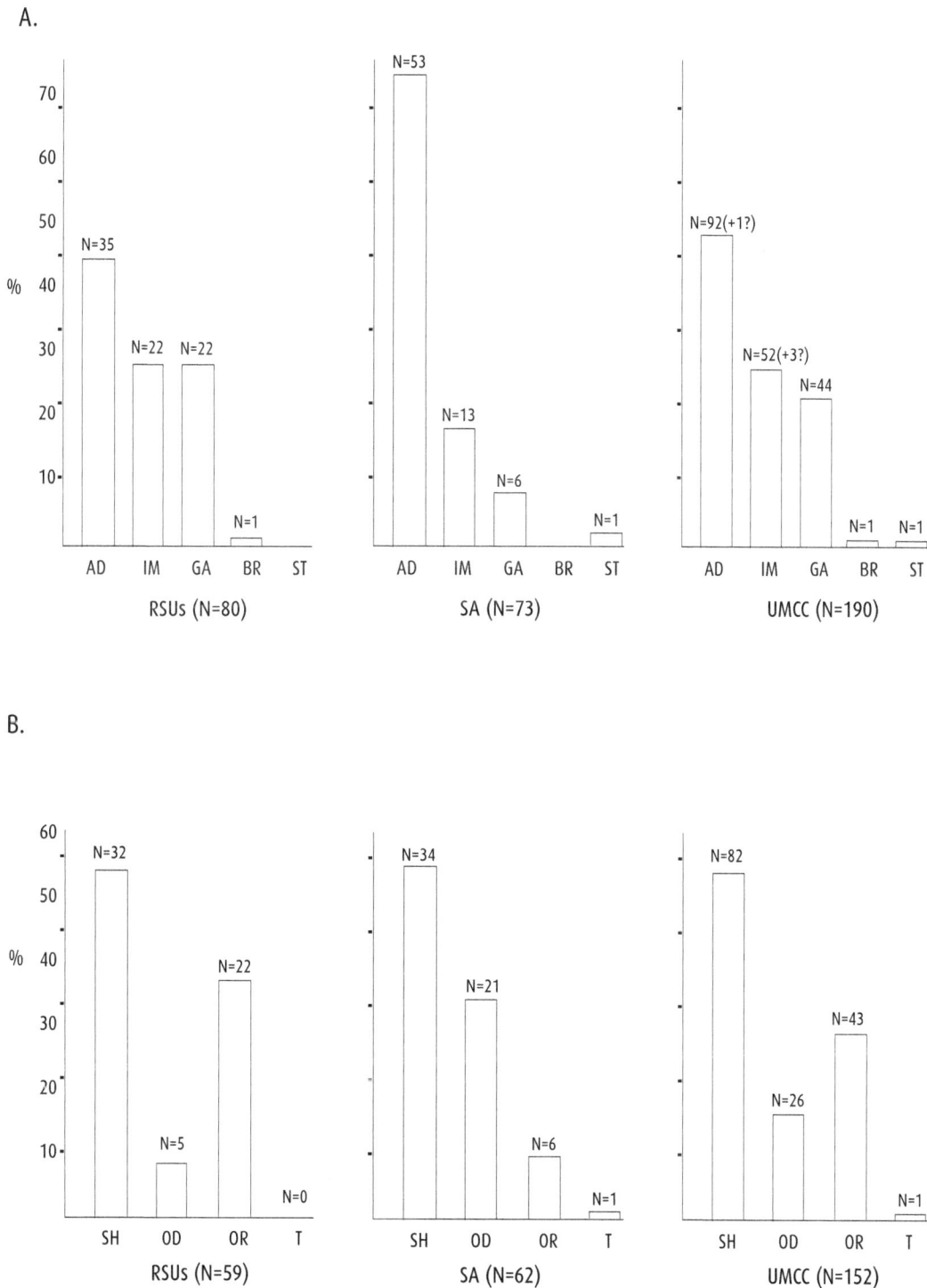

A.

B.

Figure 5.1 Upper Mangrove Creek catchment: percentage frequency of each type of (A) archaeological trait and (B) location in the random sampling units (RSUs) compared with the storage area (SA) and the total catchment (UMCC).

Locations

In all three data sets, rockshelters are the most commonly recorded location (random sampling units 54%, storage area 55%, total catchment 54%). The percentage of open deposit and open rock in each sample varies; for example, the storage area has a higher percentage of open deposit sites and a lower percentage of open rock sites than the random sampling units (Fig. 5.1B). This is probably due to the fact that the storage area:

1. has many large alluvial flats (where open archaeological deposits are more likely to occur);

2. has a greater degree of ground disturbance (and hence greater visibility of open archaeological deposits) than ridgesides and the periphery ridgetops; and,

3. is principally within the Narrabeen Group of sandstones and has less area of Hawkesbury sandstone than the random sampling units. Hawkesbury sandstone overlies the Narrabeen Group and occurs only on the ridgetops and upper ridgesides in the catchment. In the Sydney/Hawkesbury region, most grinding areas and open images (engravings) are recorded on Hawkesbury sandstone (Vinnicombe 1980 XI: 5–6; pers. obs.).

The selected sampling strategy was adopted so that an unbiased, and hopefully representative, sample of not only the valley bottoms (the alluvial flats and lower ridgesides) but also the middle and upper ridgesides and ridgetops was included in the survey program. The above comparison between the data sets from the storage area, the random sampling units and the total catchment indicates that the valley bottoms by themselves are unlikely to contain an unbiased or representative sample of the archaeological evidence within the total catchment.

Problems brought about by restricted visibility and destruction of archaeological traits are common to all three data sets. Thus, the comparison does not help in determining the effect of these factors on the ability to detect sites in the random sampling units. However, the comparison does validate the need for the fieldwork to have been undertaken outside the storage area and for the catchment to be the area of study for this project.

6

Temporal distribution: quantitative changes in the Upper Mangrove Creek catchment

Radiocarbon ages were obtained for 15 of the 35 archaeological deposits in the random sampling units (Table 6.1). Eleven of these ages were reported in Attenbrow 1987 (Table 7.1) and an additional four were obtained in 1995. All dated samples were charcoal. The depth from which each sample came is shown in the tables in Appendix 2. Radiocarbon ages for SUA-1124, SUA-1125 and SUA-1206 from Loggers Shelter were revised after completion of the salvage excavation report and the ages given for these samples in Table 6.1 differ from those in Attenbrow 1981 (p. 70).

The earliest date, 11,050±135 BP (SUA-931), which comes from the base of Loggers Shelter, provides a terminal Pleistocene date for Aboriginal use of the Upper Mangrove Creek catchment. Though SUA-931 provides the earliest evidence for occupation of the catchment, earlier dates from other sites in Australia, and particularly from the NSW central and south coasts, indicate that people were inhabiting coastal south-eastern Australia well before this time (Appendix 4, Table A4/2).

For this study, the 11,000-year period of occupation in the catchment has been divided into four phases based on typological and raw material changes in the artefact assemblages (Table 3.8). In addition, to document changes at different times of the archaeological record at a finer scale, a millennial sequence was calculated for each of the archaeological deposits using depth/age curves (Appendix 2 has calculations).

The stone artefact assemblages in 27 of the archaeological deposits (all in rockshelters) were assigned to a particular phase or phases on the basis of radiocarbon ages and/or diagnostic artefacts and assemblage attributes (Table 6.2, Chapter 3). Three other archaeological deposits in rockshelters without stone artefacts were assigned to a particular phase or phases using other criteria: for Bird Tracks and Two Moths, the phase in which habitation occurred was estimated on the depth of deposit (see Chapter 3); for Firestick, the state of preservation of the modified wood suggests a recent date and it was assigned to Phase 4.

None of the open archaeological deposits were radiocarbon-dated; nor was it possible to assign any of them to specific phases or millennia. Delight OD, Kyola Road, Palmers Crossing North and Willow Tree Gully each had small numbers of undiagnostic artefacts in unstratified or disturbed deposits (Tables 4.5 and 4.7). At Black Hands OD, the ground fragment suggests only that this location was used at least within the last 4000 years. These five archaeological deposits are excluded from the temporal analyses, and the data set analysed in this chapter consists of 30 archaeological deposits in rockshelters.

Table 6.1 Upper Mangrove Creek catchment: random sampling units. Radiocarbon dates, all from full-sized charcoal samples, calibrated using Radiocarbon Calibration Program Rev 4.3 (Stuiver and Reimer 1993b; Stuiver et al. 1998) and rounded to nearest five years.

SITE NAME	PROVENANCE	LAB. NO.	CONVENTIONAL AGE (BP)	CALIBRATED AGE (BP) INTERCEPT/S	TWO SIGMA
Black Hands SH	BH/B/10	SUA-932	3040± 85	3315, 3310, 3255	3445–2960
Boat Cave	BC/Ta/6	Beta-81625	2370± 60	2350	2710–2210
Boronia	BoS/Td/4	SUA-2169	1880± 60	1820	1965–1630
Caramel Wave	CW/T1/6	SUA-2173	1430± 60	1310	1415–1260
Dingo	DiS/Tb/8	SUA-2166	1840± 60	1815, 1790, 1780, 1755, 1740	1920–1610
Elongated Figure	EF/Ta/7	SUA-2170	1810± 80	1715	1920–1535
Kangaroo and Echidna	KE/T2a/4	SUA-2172	6700±150	7570	7820–7315
Loggers	LS/F/2	SUA-1124	530± 90	540	665–335
	LS/F/4	SUA-2165	2480± 60	2705, 2635, 2610, 2595, 2535, 2492	2750–2350
	LS/F/7	SUA-2412	7950± 80	8930, 8920, 8895, 8885, 8850, 8830, 8775	9025–8545
	LS/F/9	SUA-1125	8380±120	9465, 9450, 9430, 9335	9550–9030
	LS/F/13	SUA-1206	9450±120	10,690, 10,645	11,165–10,290
	LS/F/20-21	SUA-931	11,050±135	13,015	13,385–12,660
One Tooth	OT/T/3	Beta-81626	350± 40	435, 350, 335	505–305
Sunny	SuS/Ta-b/13 +Tb/12	SUA-2171	3560± 80	3835	4085–3640
Ti-tree	TTS/T2/3	Beta-81627	490± 50	520	620–470
Uprooted Tree	UTS/T1b/15	SUA-2174	8430±130	9470	9675–9035
Venus	VS/Tc/3	Beta-81628	560± 50	545	650–510
White Figure	WF/Tb/8	SUA-2167	5230± 70	5985, 5970, 5945	6185–5775
Wolloby Gully	WGS/Ta/4	SUA-2168	400± 60	480	535–310

For the salvage program, I presented two sets of data which illustrated changes in the number of archaeological deposits over time (Attenbrow 1981: Tables 7.1 to 7.4; see also Attenbrow 1982b: 76, Tables 2 to 4, but note in Table 2, the boundary between Early and Middle Bondaian is missing and the heading for the first half of MB/IIB is incorrectly placed). The first data set included 15 archaeological deposits, eight of which had radiocarbon ages and seven of which had their time of establishment estimated on the basis of artefact types and/or stone materials. The second data set had 26 archaeological deposits, which included the first data set, plus another 11 which had much smaller artefact assemblages. Assigning the time of establishment of the additional 11 sites to specific periods was thus more speculative than those in the first data set.

Changes over time for these two storage area data sets were presented using a four-phased sequence based on typological changes in the stone artefact assemblages. On the basis of the first data set, I stated that 'there was an increase in the number of shelters which were used over time', but that 'more new shelters were occupied during the latter half of the Middle Bondaian phase than in other phases' (Attenbrow 1981: 127; see also Attenbrow 1982b: 76). Inclusion of 'the more speculative data' to form data set 2 suggested 'there was a gradual increase in the number of new shelters being occupied throughout the Bondaian period although during the Late Bondaian period there was a marked increase'; that is:

> ... very few shelters were occupied before 5000 years ago. About 5000 years ago the number of new shelters being occupied began to increase. Between 2750 and 1200 BP there may have been a greater number of [new] shelters occupied than during the other phases of the Bondaian period, or if the more speculative data is accepted, during the Late Bondaian phase there was a dramatic increase in the number of new shelters being occupied. (Attenbrow 1981: 127–8)

For the salvage program, artefact accumulation rates were calculated only for Loggers Shelter (Attenbrow 1981: 73–4, Tables 6.4 and 6.5). In this rockshelter, there was either 'a gradual increase in the number of artefacts discarded, then a decrease prior to a final increase' or 'a continuing increase in the amount of stone artefacts discarded over time, particularly in the latter phase of occupation' (Attenbrow 1981: 129; 1982b: 77). I noted that the trend towards increasing artefact discard probably would not be seen in the most recent phase at Mussel or Deep Creek, where artefact densities in the upper units were significantly lower than in the middle units. In the salvage report, I concluded:

> ... before any suggestions can be made as to how the evidence from UMC should be interpreted, the combined evidence from individual sites, as well as the seeming increase in the number of sites occupied over time, will have to be considered ... to see if the evidence suggests an increase in the intensity of occupation of the area as a whole. (Attenbrow 1981: 131)

I later suggested that if the low artefact densities in the upper levels of sites such as Deep Creek and Mussel did reflect a low rate of artefact discard, then they may 'cancel out' the higher numbers in the upper levels in Loggers when calculating the trends in the catchment as a whole (Attenbrow 1982b: 77).

These statements are reviewed below in the light of archaeological evidence from the random sampling units. The terminology used differs from that in the salvage report. The terms 'archaeological deposit' and 'habitation' are used rather than 'site' or 'shelter'. 'Archaeological deposits' were initially assumed to be the debris from activities or processes associated with habitation and thus, in this and the following chapters, sites with archaeological deposit are referred to as 'habitations'. Sites with archaeological deposit are also referred to as 'inhabited sites'. Whether some of these 'habitations' were base camps and others transit camps or locations where other daytime activities were undertaken is explored in the final chapter, when explanations and interpretations for dramatic changes in the catchment's habitation and artefact indices are proposed.

In the salvage report, I specifically used the term 'shelter/s' to indicate that the documented trends related only to habitation in rockshelters, and that the trends in the use of open locations for habitation purposes may have been quite different. I still assume this may be the case, though the term 'habitation' has been used in the title to data sets and indices to indicate that the quantitative changes relate only to archaeological deposit (cf. Ross 1985: 84) and not to the other types of archaeological trait recorded in the catchment. On occasions where the term 'site' is used, it refers only to those sites with archaeological deposit (i.e., habitations or inhabited sites). Unless otherwise stated, the term 'artefact' refers to stone artefacts (flaked and ground) and does not include implements of organic materials.

Data from the random sampling units are presented in two different ways:
1. according to typological phases (as used in the salvage report); and,
2. according to successive millennia.

These are referred to as the phased sequence and the millennial sequence respectively. Using these two different methods of presentation illustrates how the trends documented in each of the habitation and artefact indices can vary in a manner which may lead to different interpretations, particularly in respect to the timing and coincidence of various changes in the archaeological record (cf. Frankel 1988; Ulm and Hall 1996).

The data sets

The data sets include all deposits for which it was possible to assign an age of establishment and abandonment, whether through radiocarbon determinations or other methods (Chapter 3, Table 6.2). To use only the archaeological deposits with radiocarbon ages was considered inappropriate as they are a biased selection of the habitations. For my PhD thesis, the percentage of habitations with small assemblages in shallow deposits that was selected for radiocarbon dating was lower (i.e., 37%) than the percentage of multi-phase (multi-millennium) habitations with abundant artefacts.

McDonald (1994: 76–8) was critical of the inclusion of the undated habitations with small numbers of artefacts in the habitation indices and, for her study, she recalculated the indices using only seven sites with >100 excavated artefacts. On this basis, she concluded that no new shelters were established and there was no increase in the number of habitations used in the second and first millennia BP — thus showing 'a consistent or stable use of the same shelters over the last three thousand years' (McDonald 1994: 77). However, in her recalculations, McDonald ignored the existence of four habitations which have radiocarbon ages, two of which are in the second millennium BP and one in the first millennium BP. There is no reason why habitations with radiocarbon ages should not be included in any reanalysis of the data. Inclusion of these sites into her data set would show an increase in habitation establishment and number of habitations used in the last 2000 years, albeit still not as substantial as the increase seen in Figure 6.2B — but still an increase. Inclusion of the undated habitations with shallow deposits and small numbers of artefacts in my 1987 data sets, and interpretation of the land and resource-use patterns in the catchment based on 'all datable deposits', is supported by the four additional radiocarbon ages obtained in 1995 (see Chapter 3).

The following analyses are based therefore on data sets which include all 'possible' archaeological deposits; that is, all deposits for which it was possible to assign an age of establishment and abandonment. Trends in both of the habitation indices have also been presented for data sets including only the habitations with radiocarbon ages. Use of these data sets is not considered appropriate for interpreting the catchment's archaeological record, but they have been included to show the trends if such data sets are used.

The indices

To measure change over time in the numbers of habitations (archaeological deposits) and stone artefacts, the following data sets and indices were calculated for both the phased sequence and the millennial sequence:
Archaeological deposits (habitations):
1. the number of habitations established in successive time periods;
2. the rate of habitation establishment in successive time periods;
3. the number of habitations used in successive time periods;

4.   the rate of habitation establishment in each topographic zone in successive time periods;

5.   the number of habitations used in each topographic zone in successive time periods;

6.   millennial growth rates for habitation establishment and number of habitations used in each period;

7.   average annual growth rates for habitation establishment and number of habitations used in each period.

Stone artefacts:

8.   the estimated number of artefacts accumulated in individual habitations in successive time periods;

9.   the rate of artefact accumulation in individual habitations in successive time periods;

10.   the estimated number of artefacts accumulated in the catchment in successive time periods;

11.   the rate of artefact accumulation in the catchment as a whole (referred to as the local artefact accumulation rate) in successive time periods;

12.   the number of artefacts accumulated in each topographic zone of the catchment in successive time periods;

13.   the rate of artefact accumulation in the catchment in each topographic zone in successive time periods;

14.   millennial growth rates; and,

15.   average annual growth rates.

The number of habitations established and the number of artefacts accumulated in each time period (i.e., each phase or millennium) were converted into rates (the rate of habitation establishment and the rate of artefact accumulation) which take account of variation in the lengths of time in each typological phase. Rate is calculated as the number of habitations established or the number of artefacts accumulated per millennium. I am principally concerned with four indices:

- *the rate of habitation establishment;*
- *the number of habitations used;*
- *the rate of artefact accumulation; and,*
- *the local rate of artefact accumulation.*

They are referred to collectively as the habitation and artefact indices. The term 'habitation indices' has been used when referring collectively to more than one of the indices relating to habitations. Where I refer simply to 'the indices', I mean the indices relating to artefacts as well as habitations. The magnitude of increases or decreases in the indices has been referred to as: marked, substantial or dramatic, with dramatic being the greatest in magnitude. In general discussions, to avoid unwieldy sentences, the term 'dramatic' is used sometimes in a 'generic' sense to refer collectively to changes in several sites or regions, some of which may be marked or substantial.

The habitation indices

The time or period in which an archaeological deposit began to accumulate is taken as the date at which habitation began; it is referred to as the date of habitation establishment. Some images or grooves in some rockshelters may have been created before habitation was 'established' in them, but this cannot be identified.

The term 'number of habitations used in successive time periods' refers to the number of habitations in use by the end of each period (phase or millennium). It does not imply that the number of habitations stated as being used in each particular period were all inhabited at the same time — simply that they were all inhabited at some time during or by the end of that particular period. Although habitations are described as being used in successive time periods, it is assumed they were inhabited discontinuously or intermittently.

In the salvage report, the concepts 'number of habitations used' and 'rate of habitation establishment' are not clearly differentiated. The rate at which habitations were established and the number of habitations used per unit time are treated separately in this monograph and provide different sets of information about habitation and land-use patterns. If all habitations continued to be used once they were established (albeit discontinuously, intermittently or cyclically), the establishment of further habitations would mean an increasing number of habitations were used in successive periods of time. The number of habitations used can increase no matter whether the habitation establishment rates remain stable, increase or decrease. However, if all habitations were used for a short time in only one period, the habitation establishment rate has to have increased in order for the number of habitations used to increase. To calculate the number of habitations used within a particular period of time, it was therefore necessary to know the date at which the habitations were established, the total length of time over which they were inhabited, and whether there were any sustained periods of abandonment.

The artefact indices

The rates of artefact accumulation are based on the estimated total number of artefacts accumulated in each period in each archaeological deposit. The artefact accumulation rates were calculated at three levels: for individual habitations, for the catchment as a whole and for each topographic zone. For the catchment as a whole, this is referred to as the *local rate of artefact accumulation*.

Calculating artefact accumulation rates

Artefact accumulation rates were calculated by a commonly adopted method in which the 'rate' for each spit or level is expressed as the number of artefacts accumulated (or discarded) per millennium or century (e.g., Hughes and Djohadze 1980: Figs 11–13; Morwood 1981: 32; Kelly 1982: 31–49; David and Chant 1995; papers in Morwood and Hobbs 1995b). The following information was used:

1. the number of artefacts (or implements) in each spit or level;
2. the estimated length of time over which each spit or level accumulated; and,
3. the area of each spit or level excavated.
   To gain 2., a depth/age curve was drawn based on:
4. the depth of each spit or level;
5. the age of one (preferably basal or near basal) but ideally more levels throughout the depth of deposit, and an estimate of the time when the site was last used; and,
6. the depth to which the age estimations relate.
   Where the area excavated was not constant in each spit or level, rates were standardised as the number of artefacts/square metre/unit time (e.g., Hughes 1977: Table 5.6, Fig. 5.12; Johnson 1979: Fig. 5, Table 3).

The artefact accumulation rate for the total catchment in each phase and each millennium was estimated by combining the estimated total number of artefacts accumulated in all archaeological deposits for each phase and each millennium. Catchment trends are referred to as the *local rate of artefact accumulation* to differentiate them from the artefact accumulation rates in individual deposits. Combining the total number of artefacts in levels of comparable age in all archaeological deposits is considered valid for several reasons:

- in the same way that it is valid to combine the total number of artefacts in levels of the same age from all excavated squares in a single archaeological deposit to produce a unitary trend for that site. The catchment is viewed as a single unit in the same way that an archaeological deposit or site is;

- at a regional level in 1788, the catchment was within the territory of a single language group (Darginung) and probably only part of the territory of a single clan (though their social, subsistence, economic and trading networks would have extended over a much wider area than the lands associated with both of these groups);

- subsistence activities are assumed to have been dispersed across the land and not restricted to a single specific location during periods of occupation. During each visit to the catchment, except when transiting through the country via the major ridge lines forming the catchment watershed, people are likely to have visited more than one topographic zone and may have 'used' more than one site/archaeological trait of the same or different nature.

Where relevant data are available, calculating artefact accumulation rates is a fairly straightforward exercise. It is often more difficult to decide what constitutes a dramatic increase, when the 'most dramatic increase' occurred, and/or when it began and ended. In some cases, this uncertainty means varying interpretations can be made as to when significant quantitative change occurred and with what other events or processes it was correlated. The shortcomings and limits in using artefact accumulation rates are discussed in Chapter 5.

Growth rates

Growth rates have also been calculated for the rates of habitation establishment, the numbers of habitations used and the local rates of artefact accumulation. Growth rates for these indices assist in illustrating the nature and magnitude of changes and are pertinent to later discussions about the use of archaeological evidence as measures of population change (Chapter 8). They were calculated to determine whether there were variations in the 'rate' at which changes took place in the indices over time; that is, variations in the growth rates indicate whether the rate of change slowed down or accelerated. The rate of change can slow down even though 'increases' still occur; for example, increases from 2 to 3 to 4 to 5 to 7/millennium represent growth rates of +50%, +33%, +25% and +40%.

The growth rates thus help to describe the nature of the quantitative changes which occurred and can assist in determining whether the dramatic increases in the more recent periods were produced simply by exponential population increase; that is, if there was a constant growth rate. Changes in the growth rates for the indices may be as important as the actual size of the increases and decreases and need explaining in investigating dramatic quantitative changes in the archaeological record.

Calculating growth rates

Millennial growth rates are calculated for the habitation and artefact indices, but average annual growth rates were the most expedient growth rates to calculate for local artefact accumulation rates. Growth rates can be expressed in two ways: as a percentage figure (+50%) or a multiplier (×1.5). Both have been presented as each are used in the literature cited; archaeologists often use multipliers (e.g., Hughes and Lampert 1982; Ross 1984), while demographers usually quote average annual growth rates for population increase as percentages (e.g., Ammerman et al. 1976; Hassan 1981; Gray 1985). Percentage figures were calculated using the following equation: the habitation establishment rate for the later period minus the rate for the earlier period divided by the rate for the earlier period multiplied by 100. The multiplier can be derived by dividing the rate for the later period by the rate for the earlier period; for example, a change from 3 habitations/millennium to 6 habitations/millennium, a twofold (×2) increase, represents a growth rate of 100%.

Average annual growth rates were calculated using a small computer program written for this purpose. For the habitation indices, they are based on the number in each phase/millennium and the length of the period (i.e., phase or millennium). Growth rates for the local artefact accumulation rates are based on the duration of the period (i.e., phase or millennium) and estimated total number of artefacts accumulated during that period. Average annual growth rates were not calculated for individual archaeological deposits.

Changes in the rates of habitation establishment

Changes in the rates of habitation establishment are based on the period in which habitations were established according to both the phased and millennial sequence (i.e., the period in which they were first inhabited) (Table 6.2). The estimated period of establishment of habitation is based on:

1. radiocarbon dates:
(a) if the charcoal sample dated was obtained from the basal spit, this was taken as the approximate date at which the archaeological deposit began to accumulate (but note discussion in Hughes and Lampert 1982: 19–20);
(b) if the charcoal sample was not from the basal spit, extrapolation back to the basal spit was made on the basis of a depth/age curve;
2. the phase or millennium into which the stone artefact assemblage in the basal spits was assigned; and,
3. where necessary, the depth of accumulated deposit.

Phased sequence
Eleven of the 30 habitations have more than one phase represented (multi-phase habitations). The remaining 19 have only one phase and are referred to as single-phase habitations. In each of the multi-phase habitations, the phases are successive and the most recent phase is always represented. The dates, artefacts and nature of the deposits indicate that the single-phase habitations all belong to the most recent phase.

The *number* of habitations established varied in each successive typological phase — it was relatively low in the first three phases (four, three and four respectively), but jumped dramatically in the final phase to 19 (Tables 6.2 and 6.3).

The *rate of habitation establishment* increased in each successive phase, with the most recent phase (4) having the highest. The rate increased from 0.6/millennium during Phase 1, to 1.4 in Phase 2, 3.3 in Phase 3 and 12.7 in Phase 4 (Table 6.3 and Fig. 6.1A).

These rates according to the typological phases suggest that substantial change took place in each of the phases, that is, after three points in time — ca 5000 BP, ca 2800 BP and ca 1600 BP — and that the most dramatic increase occurred after 1600 BP.

If only the 15 *radiocarbon-dated archaeological deposits* are used, the habitation establishment rates are, of course, much lower (0.6, 0.9, 2.5 and 4.0/millennium for Phases 1 to 4 respectively) (Table 6.4, marked as * in Fig. 6.1A). Increases still occur, but the increase for Phase 4 is not as dramatic as that based on all habitations.

Growth rates. The *growth rate* for the habitation establishment rate in Phase 4 is substantially greater than in Phases 3 and 2. In Phase 4, it is almost four times that of the previous phase, whereas in Phases 2 and 3 the establishment rate is more than double that of the previous phase (Table 6.5).

Table 6.2 Upper Mangrove Creek catchment: random sampling units. Archaeological deposits: estimated period of habitation establishment.

SITE NAME	PHASE	MILLENNIUM (BP)		BASIS FOR ESTIMATION
Loggers	1	12,000	– 11,000	Radiocarbon date.
Uprooted Tree	1	9000	– 8000	Radiocarbon date.
Kangaroo and Echidna	1	7000	– 6000	Radiocarbon date + extrapolation to base, poss. 10,000–9000 BP.
White Figure	1	6000	– 5000	Radiocarbon date + extrapolation to base.
Sunny	2	5000	– 4000	Radiocarbon date + extrapolation to base.
Emu Tracks 2	2	4000	– 3000	Diagnostic artefact types/raw materials.
Black Hands SH	2	4000	– 3000	Radiocarbon date + extrapolation to base.
Boat Cave	3	3000	– 2000	Radiocarbon date + extrapolation to base.
Delight SH	3	3000	– 2000	Diagnostic artefact types/raw materials.
Dingo	3	2000	– 1000	Radiocarbon date.
Elongated Figure	3	2000	– 1000	Radiocarbon date.
Caramel Wave	4	2000	– 1000	Radiocarbon date.
Boronia	4	2000	– 1000	Radiocarbon date.
Harris Gully	4	2000	– 1000	Diagnostic artefact types/raw materials/Depth of arch. deposit and estimated accumulation rate.
Elngarrah	4	2000	– 1000	Depth of arch. deposit and estimated accumulation rate.
Two Moths	4	2000	– 1000	Depth of arch. deposit and estimated accumulation rate.
McPherson	4	<1000		Diagnostic artefact types/raw materials/Depth of arch. deposit and estimated accumulation rate.
Bird Tracks	4	<1000		Depth of arch. deposit and estimated accumulation rate.
Low Frontage	4	<1000		Diagnostic artefact types/raw materials/Depth of arch. deposit and estimated accumulation rate.
One Tooth	4	<1000		Radiocarbon date + extrapolation to base.
Venus	4	<1000		Radiocarbon date + extrapolation to base.
Ti-tree	4	<1000		Radiocarbon date + extrapolation to base.
Anadara	4	<1000		Diagnostic artefact types/raw materials/Depth of arch. deposit and estimated accumulation rate.
Wolloby Gully	4	<1000		Radiocarbon date.
Geebung	4	<1000		Diagnostic artefact types/raw materials/Depth of arch. deposit and estimated accumulation rate.
Mangrove Mansions	4	<1000		Diagnostic artefact types/raw materials/Depth of arch. deposit and estimated accumulation rate.
Token Male	4	<1000		Diagnostic artefact types/raw materials/Surface evidence only.
Axehead	4	<1000		Diagnostic artefact types/raw materials/Surface evidence only.
Button	4	<1000		Diagnostic artefact types/raw materials/Surface evidence only.
Firestick	4	<1000		Surface evidence only/state of preservation of modified wood.

Millennial sequence

The millennial sequence indicates that there was a marked increase in *the habitation establishment rate* in the fourth millennium BP, a particularly dramatic rise in the second millennium BP and a further substantial increase in the first millennium BP (Fig. 6.1B). The period of habitation can be divided into three: 12,000 BP to 7000 BP, 7000 BP to 2000 BP and 2000 BP to contact. The seventh millennium BP is taken as the period in which change begins as it is from that time onwards that habitations were established in each successive millennium.

Table 6.3 Upper Mangrove Creek catchment: random sampling units. Number of habitations established, rate of habitation establishment and number of habitations used (A) in each phase and (B) millennium (N = 30). See also Figures 6.1 and 6.2. Numbers in square brackets represent totals if habitation in Kangaroo and Echidna extended back to 10th millennium BP. [1] This total for first millennium BP excludes Two Moths, inhabited only in the second millennium BP.

A. PHASED SEQUENCE

Phase	Length of phase (years)	No. of habitations established	Rate of habitation establishment	No. of habitations used
1	ca 6300	4	0.6	4
2	ca 2200	3	1.4	7
3	ca 1200	4	3.3	11
4	ca 1500	19	12.7	30
Total	11,200	30		

B. MILLENNIAL SEQUENCE

Millennium BP	No. of habitations established	Rate of habitation establishment	No. of habitations used
12,000–11,000	1	1	1
11,000–10,000	0	0	1
10,000–9000	0 (1)	0 (1)	1 (2)
9000–8000	1	1	2 (3)
8000–7000	0	0	2 (3)
7000–6000	1 (0)	1 (0)	3
6000–5000	1	1	4
5000–4000	1	1	5
4000–3000	2	2	7
3000–2000	2	2	9
2000–1000	7	7	16
<1000	14	14	[1] 29
Total	30		

Except for the last 1000 years, trends based on only the 15 *archaeological deposits with radiocarbon dates* are similar to those based on all habitations (marked as * in Fig. 6.1B). The most recent millennium shows stability in the habitation establishment rate rather than the increase which is indicated when all habitations are included.

Growth rates. Because habitation establishment was infrequent and the number involved was very low in the period 12,000 BP to 7000 BP, it was not considered meaningful to calculate the millennial growth rates for this period (Table 6.6). In the fourth and first millennia BP the growth rate doubles, whereas in the second millennium BP the increase is three- to fourfold. The second millennium BP thus had the highest growth rate throughout the catchment's period of recorded use.

Comments on rates of habitation establishment

At one habitation (Kangaroo and Echidna), the period of establishment could fall within one of two different millennia. The extrapolated date does not alter the phase in which habitation began, but places the date of establishment some three millennia earlier (i.e., from the seventh to the 10th millennium BP). I use the more recent date in discussions and the conclusions since

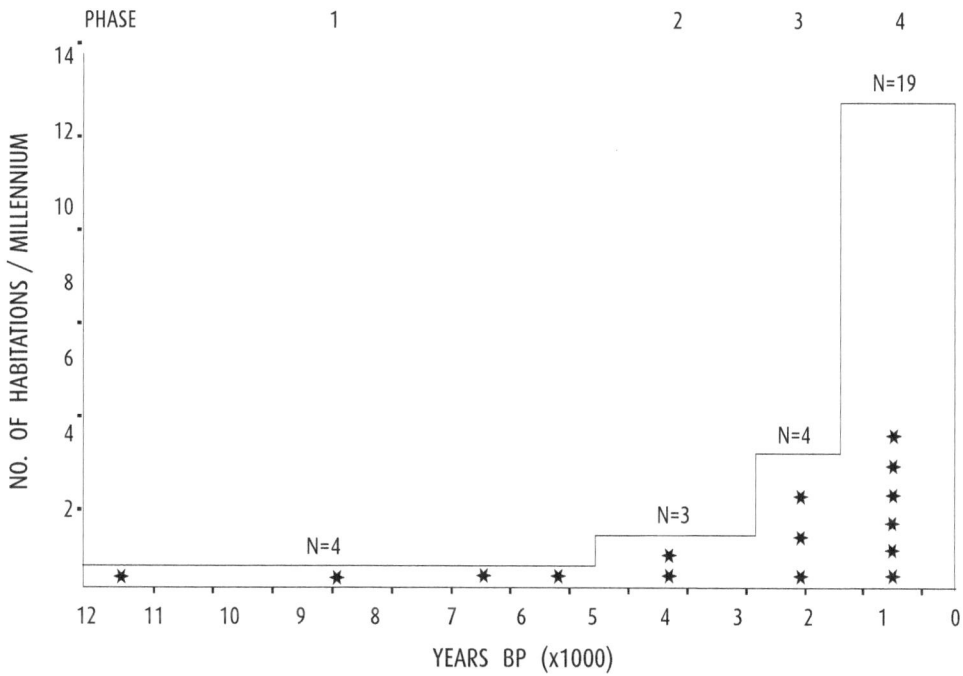

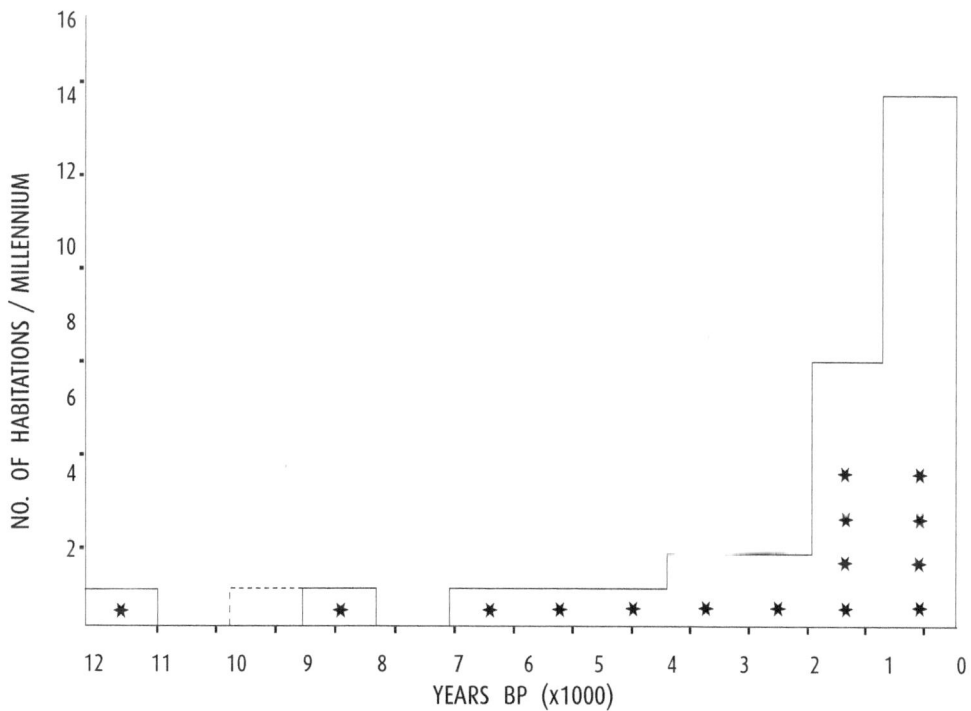

Figure 6.1 Upper Mangrove Creek catchment: random sampling units. Rate of habitation establishment in each (A) phase and (B) millennium. N = 30, stars indicate numbers of radiocarbon-dated archaeological deposits in each period. Dashed outline in millennial sequence indicates extrapolated dating for Kangaroo and Echidna. Tables 6.1 to 6.4 have details.

Table 6.4 Upper Mangrove Creek catchment: random sampling units. Radiocarbon-dated archaeological deposits only: number of habitations established, rate of habitation establishment, and number of habitations used (A) in each phase and (B) each millennium (N = 15). See also Figures 6.1 and 6.2.

A. PHASED SEQUENCE

Phase	Length of phase (years)	No. of habitations established	Rate of habitation establishment	No. of habitations used
1	ca 6300	4	0.6	4
2	ca 2200	2	0.9	6
3	ca 1200	3	2.5	9
4	ca 1500	6	4.0	15
Total	ca 11,200	15		

B. MILLENNIAL SEQUENCE

Millennium BP	No. of habitations established	Rate of habitation establishment	No. of habitations used
12,000–11,000	1	1	1
11,000–10,000	0	0	1
10,000–9000	0	0	1
9000–8000	1	1	2
8000–7000	0	0	2
7000–6000	1	1	3
6000–5000	1	1	4
5000–4000	1	1	5
4000–3000	1	2	6
3000–2000	1	2	7
2000–1000	4	4	11
<1000	4	4	15
Total	15		

Table 6.5 Upper Mangrove Creek catchment: random sampling units. Phased sequence: growth rates for rates of habitation establishment, numbers of habitations used and local rates of artefact accumulation, based on Table 6.3A. # indicates habitations were first established and artefacts first accumulated in this phase.

| Phase | Growth rates for: | | | | | |
| | Rate of habitation establishment | | Number of habitations used | | Local rate of artefact accumulation | |
	X	%	X	%	X	%
1	#		#		#	
2	2.33	+133	1.75	+75	1.35	+35
3	2.36	+136	1.57	+57	19.17	+1817
4	3.85	+285	2.72	+172	0.50	-49

Table 6.6 Upper Mangrove Creek catchment: random sampling units. Millennial sequence: growth rates for rates of habitation establishment, numbers of habitations used and local rates of artefact accumulation, plus average annual growth rates for local rates of artefact accumulation, based on Table 6.3B. # indicates habitations were first established and artefacts first accumulated in this millennium.

Millennium BP			Growth rates for:				
	Rate of habitation establishment		Number of habitations used		Local rate of artefact accumulation		
					Millennial		Av. annual
	X	%	X	%	X	%	%
12th	#		#		#		
11th			1.00	0	25.70	+2470	+0.33
10th			1.00	0	6.40	+540	+0.19
9th			2.00	+100	0.97	-3	0.00
8th			1.00	0	0.23	-77	-0.15
7th			1.50	+50	0.73	-27	-0.03
6th	1.0	0	1.33	+33	1.18	+18	+0.02
5th	1.0	0	1.25	+25	1.43	+43	+0.04
4th	2.0	+100	1.40	+40	2.28	+128	+0.08
3rd	1.0	0	1.29	+29	14.39	+1339	+0.27
2nd	3.5	+250	1.78	+78	0.93	-7	-0.01
1st	2.0	+100	1.81	+81	0.57	-43	-0.06

the date based on the depth/age curve is very much earlier than the radiocarbon date, but the depth between the dated level and the base of the archaeological deposit is not very great.

Excavation ceased at Kangaroo and Echidna and four other archaeological deposits before bedrock was reached (Anadara, Bird Tracks, Boronia and Mangrove Mansions) (see Chapter 5, Table 3.4). In addition, in three other rockshelters (Elongated Figure, Harris Gully and Uprooted Tree), the base of the excavations is sloping bedrock. It is possible therefore that there may be earlier evidence of habitations in other parts of the deposits at these eight sites. However, the area of deposit in the rockshelters is small and the slope gradients are low, so the extra depth of deposit and/or time may not be great. The period of establishment for these eight archaeological deposits was assigned on the basis of the archaeological materials recovered and the radiocarbon dates at three of the sites: five to Phase 4, one to Phase 3 (Elongated Figure) and two (Kangaroo and Echidna and Uprooted Tree) to Phase 1. If the period of habitation establishment for the archaeological deposits assigned to Phases 3 and 4 was earlier than assumed, this would only add support to the argument that early deposits were not necessarily scoured out of rockshelters. Habitation in ALL these shelters would have had to have begun earlier and to have begun in the SAME phase, for trends in the habitation establishment rates to be affected. Because of the nature and estimated remaining depth of the deposit, and the stone artefact assemblages in the basal spits at these archaeological deposits, this situation is considered unlikely (see Chapter 3, Excavations undertaken). Similar arguments can be made about trends according to the millennial sequence.

Changes in the numbers of habitations used

The stratigraphy of each of the archaeological deposits suggests that, except in one case, once a habitation was established, it continued to be used into the most recent phase — not necessarily continuously, but without any major long-term breaks in habitation. That is, there were no breaks which were of sufficient length to allow sterile layers to form or one of the assemblages in the stone artefact sequence to be missing. The exception is Two Moths, where the only evidence for habitation is freshwater mussel shell (Appendix 3). The shell occurs in a single level mid-depth within the excavated deposit. The age of this level has been estimated as some time within the second millennium BP. Two Moths is thus excluded as a habitation in use in the first millennium BP (e.g., in Table 6.10).

Phased sequence

The *number of habitations used* by the end of each successive phase increased markedly so that the number of habitations used during the most recent phase was greater than in any previous phase. Four habitations were used in Phase 1, seven in Phase 2, 11 in Phase 3, and 30 in the final phase (4) (Fig. 6.2A). The *growth rate* between the two final phases (×2.72) was greater than at other times (×1.75 and ×1.57) (Table 6.5).

Millennial sequence

According to the millennial sequence, the increase in the number of habitations used was very slow until the ninth millennium BP, after which there was a gradual increase until the third millennium BP. There were then substantial increases in both the second and first millennia BP (Fig. 6.2B). The increase in the first millennium BP was slightly greater than that in the second millennium BP.

When only the 15 *radiocarbon-dated archaeological deposits* are used (marked as * in Fig. 6.2B), the trend in the number of habitations used is similar to that shown when all habitations are included, though the increases in the second and first millennia BP are not as substantial.

Growth rates. The highest growth rates occurred in the second and first millennia BP (×1.78 and ×1.81 respectively), as well as the ninth millennium BP (×2) — though the latter situation represents an increase from one to two sites (Table 6.6).

Changes in the habitation indices in each topographic zone by the end of each successive time period

Phased sequence

The distribution of habitations in each of the topographic zones in each phase varied over time (Fig. 6.3 and Tables 6.7 and 6.9):

Phase 1 — four habitations were established in three of the topographic zones (the main valley bottoms [VB-MC], subsidiary ridgesides [RS-SC], and periphery ridgetops [RT-PERI]). The four habitations were spread widely over the catchment;

Phase 2 — seven habitations used; the additional three habitations were established in only two of the three topographic zones in which the Phase 1 habitations were recorded (the main valley bottoms [VB-MC] and periphery ridgetops [RT-PERI]);

Phase 3 — 11 habitations used; the additional four habitations were established in only two of the three topographic zones in which the Phase 1 habitations were established (subsidiary ridgesides [RS-SC] and periphery ridgetops [RT-PERI]).

A.

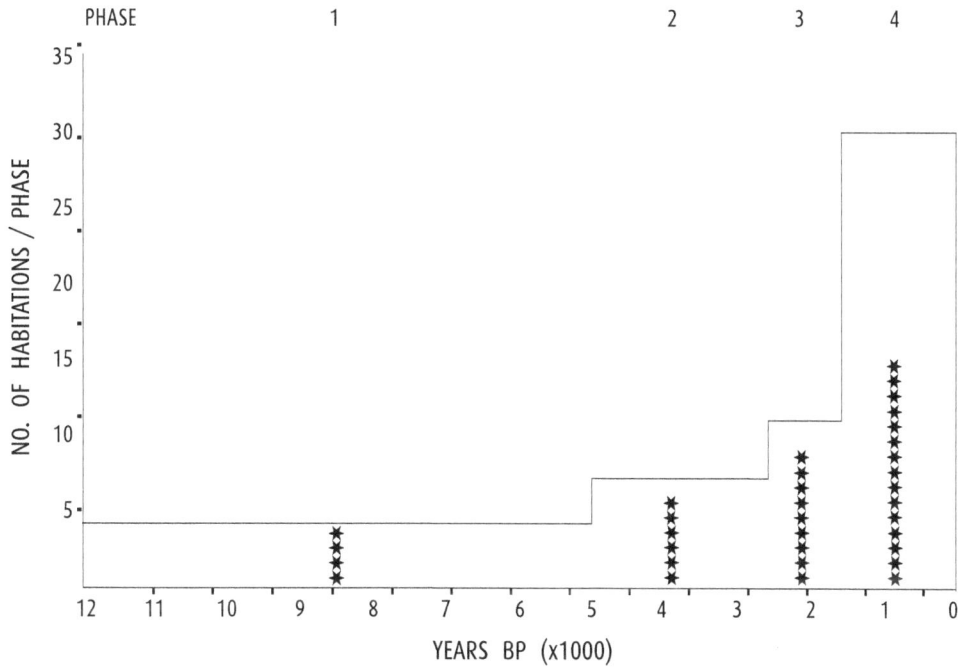

B.

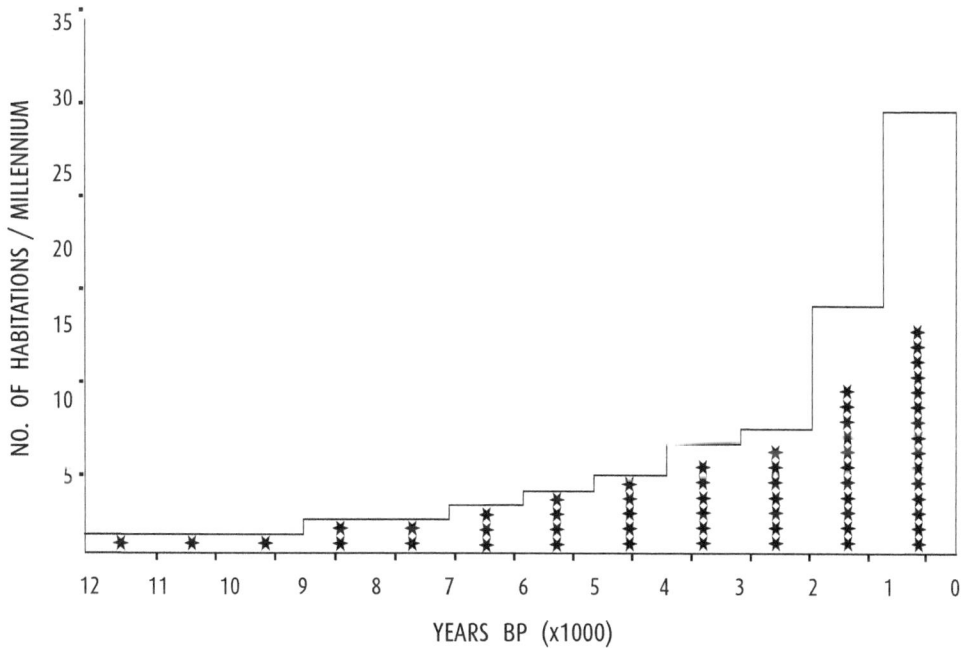

Figure 6.2 Upper Mangrove Creek catchment: random sampling units. Number of habitations used in each (A) phase and (B) millennium. N = 30, stars indicate numbers of radiocarbon-dated habitations. In millennial sequence, first millennium BP excludes Two Moths, which was not inhabited in that period. Tables 6.1 to 6.4 have details.

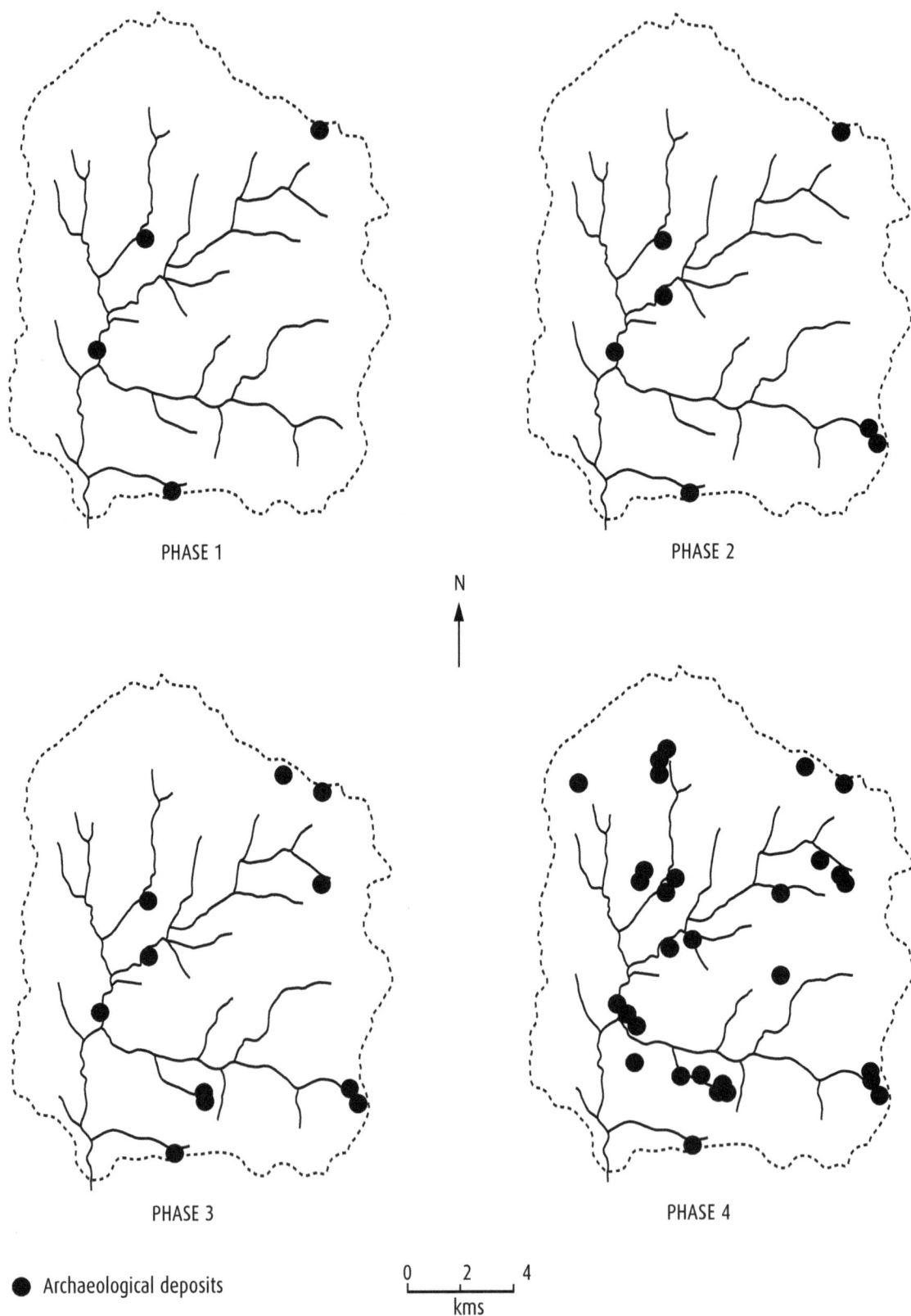

Figure 6.3 Upper Mangrove Creek catchment: random sampling units. Distribution of habitations used in each phase.

Phase 4 — 30 habitations used. Habitations now established in all six of the topographic zones — that is, habitations were established in three zones which were previously uninhabited: peninsula ridgetops (RT-PEN), the main ridgesides (RS-MC) and the subsidiary valley bottoms (VB-SC). These three zones are those in which the least archaeological evidence was recorded.

Thus, the first habitations established were widely and sparsely distributed but in a restricted number of topographic zones (three). It was only in the most recent phase (4) that all six topographic zones were inhabited. That is, in the most recent phase, habitation occurred in topographic zones which were previously uninhabited (or had not been inhabited to a degree or in a manner which was archaeologically visible at the level of fieldwork undertaken).

Millennial sequence

Trends shown in the millennial sequence reveal that the main valley bottom was the first zone in which habitations were established; then the periphery ridgetops and later the subsidiary ridgesides (or vice versa, if the extrapolated date for Kangaroo and Echidna is proved correct) (Fig. 6.4 and Tables 6.8 and 6.10). Establishment of habitations in the subsidiary valley bottoms and the peninsula ridgetops takes place in the second millennium BP and it is not until the first millennium BP that the main ridgesides are finally inhabited.

Table 6.7 Upper Mangrove Creek catchment: random sampling units. Number of habitations established in each topographic zone in each phase (N = 30).

Phase	Total	Topographic zones					
		RT-PERI	RT-PEN	VB-MC	VB-SC	RS-MC	RS-SC
1	4	1		1			2
2	3	2		1			0
3	4	1		0			3
4	19	1	2	1	7	2	6
Total	30	5	2	3	7	2	11

Table 6.8 Upper Mangrove Creek catchment: random sampling units. Number of habitations established, also equals rate of habitation establishment, in each topographic zone in each millennium (N = 30).

Millennium BP	Total	Topographic zones					
		RT-PERI	RT-PEN	VB-MC	VB-SC	RS-MC	RS-SC
12,000–11,000	1			1			
11,000–10,000	0			0			
10,000–9000	0(1)			0			0(1)
9000–8000	1	1		0			0
8000–7000	0	0		0			0
7000–6000	1(0)	0		0			1(0)
6000–5000	1	0		0			1
5000–4000	1	1		0			0
4000–3000	2	1		1			0
3000–2000	2	1		0			1
2000–1000	7	0	2	0	2		3
<1000	14	1	0	1	5	2	5
Totals	30	5	2	3	7	2	11

Table 6.9 Upper Mangrove Creek catchment: random sampling units. Number of habitations used in each topographic zone in each phase (N = 30).

Phase	Total habitations	Topographic zones					
		RT-PERI	RT-PEN	VB-MC	VB-SC	RS-MC	RS-SC
1	4	1		1			2
2	7	3		2			2
3	11	4		2			5
4	30	5	2	3	7	2	11

Table 6.10 Upper Mangrove Creek catchment: random sampling units. Number of habitations used in each topographic zone in each millennium (N = 30). [1] These figures exclude Two Moths, which was inhabited in only the second millennium BP.

Millennium BP	Total habitations	Topographic zones					
		RT-PERI	RT-PEN	VB-MC	VB-SC	RS-MC	RS-SC
12,000–11,000	1			1			
11,000–10,000	1			1			
10,000–9000	1(2)			1			0(1)
9000–8000	2(3)	1		1			0(1)
8000–7000	2(3)	1		1			0(1)
7000–6000	3	1		1			1
6000–5000	4	1		1			2
5000–4000	5	2		1			2
4000–3000	7	3		2			2
3000–2000	9	4		2			3
2000–1000	16	4	2	2	2		6
<1000	29[1]	5	2	3	7	2	10[1]

Changes in the rates of artefact accumulation — individual habitations

At some habitations, very few artefacts were retrieved in the excavations while in others several thousand were recovered (between one and 7436) (Table 4.6). Estimated total numbers of artefacts accumulated in individual habitations varied equally widely (from <100 to almost 250,000) (Table 4.12).

Artefact accumulation rates for individual habitations have been calculated for each of the phases and millennia in which the habitations were used (Figs 6.5 and 6.6; Tables 6.12 and 6.13 respectively). Artefact accumulation rates are based on the estimated total number of artefacts in an archaeological deposit and on the estimated total number within each spit/phase/millennium (Tables 6.11 and 6.13). The estimated total number of artefacts was used to avoid problems associated with inter-site variability in both the amount excavated in each site and the area of each archaeological deposit (i.e., in the number of square metres likely to contain cultural materials) at each site.

The artefact accumulation rates did not always continue to increase in each of the habitations (i.e., a similar trend to that seen in the salvage program [Attenbrow 1981, 1982b]). Each habitation had its own 'history of accumulation' or 'habitation history'. Variations occurred not only in the date at which each habitation was established and the estimated total number of artefacts accumulated, but also in:

1. the rates at which artefacts accumulated in particular periods; and,
2. the direction and timing of the dramatic or substantial changes in the artefact accumulation rates.

At habitations used for more than one phase or more than two millennia, long-term changes in the artefact accumulation rates are evident.

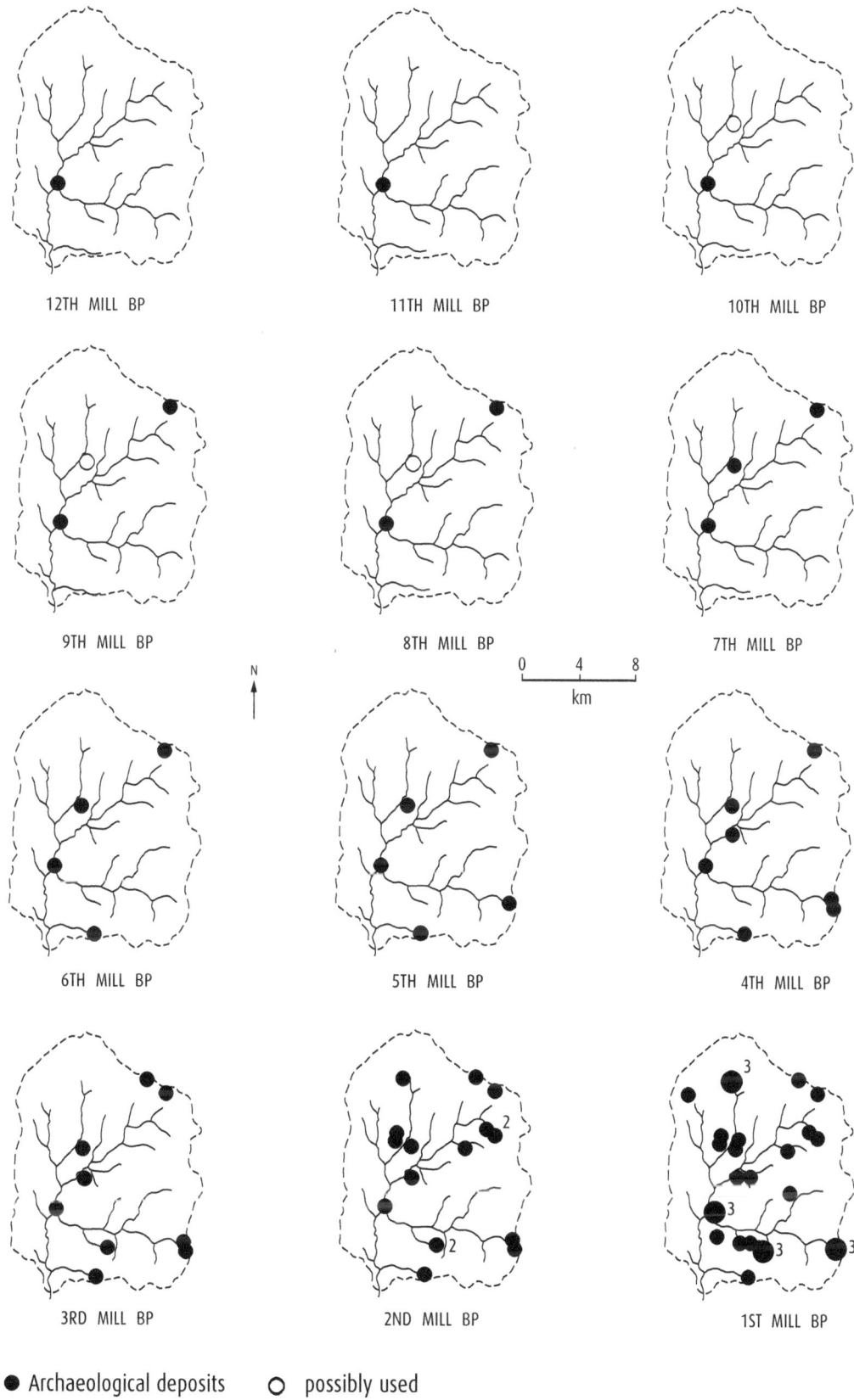

Figure 6.4 Upper Mangrove Creek catchment: random sampling units. Distribution of habitations used in each millennium.

Table 6.11 Upper Mangrove Creek catchment: random sampling units. Archaeological deposits: estimated total number of artefacts accumulated in each phase, rounded to nearest 50.

SITE NAME	TOTAL	PHASE 1	PHASE 2	PHASE 3	PHASE 4
Loggers	128,050	63,000	5600	22,950	36,500
Kangaroo and Echidna	5500	1850	1600	1450	600
Uprooted Tree	31,250	850	3250	4650	22,500
White Figure	37,050	500	2100	19,250	15,200
Sunny	88,150		3500	38,550	46,100
Emu Tracks 2	249,650		14,500	199,050	36,100
Black Hands SH	77,050		1000	41,700	34,350
Boat Cave	500			100	400
Delight SH	5000			3200	1800
Dingo	2600			200	2400
Elongated Figure	950			250	700
Totals: multi-phase habitations	625,700	66,200	31,550	331,350	196,650
Caramel Wave	500				500
Boronia	150				150
Harris Gully	1850				1850
Elngarrah	100				100
Two Moths	0				0
McPherson	1600				1600
Bird Tracks	0				0
Low Frontage	300				300
One Tooth	750				750
Venus	700				700
Ti-tree	500				500
Anadara	1850				1850
Wolloby Gully	2250				2250
Geebung	400				400
Mangrove Mansions	3250				3250
Token Male	>3				>3
Axehead	1				1
Button	4				4
Firestick	0				0
Totals: single-phase habitations	14,200				14,200
Totals: all habitations	639,950	66,200	31,550	331,350	210,850

Table 6.12 Upper Mangrove Creek catchment: random sampling units. Archaeological deposits: rate of artefact accumulation in each phase (number per millennium), rounded to nearest 50. See also Figure 6.5.

SITE NAME	PHASE 1	PHASE 2	PHASE 3	PHASE 4
Loggers	10,150	2550	19,150	24,350
Kangaroo and Echidna	300	750	1200	400
Uprooted Tree	150	1500	3900	15,000
White Figure	100	950	16,050	10,150
Sunny		1600	32,150	30,750
Emu Tracks 2		6600	165,850	24,050
Black Hands SH		450	34,750	22,900
Boat Cave			100	250
Delight SH			2650	1200
Dingo			150	1600
Elongated Figure			200	450
Caramel Wave				350
Boronia				100
Harris Gully				1250
Elngarrah				50
Two Moths				0
McPherson				1050
Bird Tracks				0
Low Frontage				150
One Tooth				500
Venus				450
Ti-tree				350
Anadara				1250
Wolloby Gully				1500
Geebung				250
Mangrove Mansions				2150
Token Male				>2
Axehead				1
Button				3
Firestick				0
Totals: all habitations	10,700	14,350	276,150	140,550

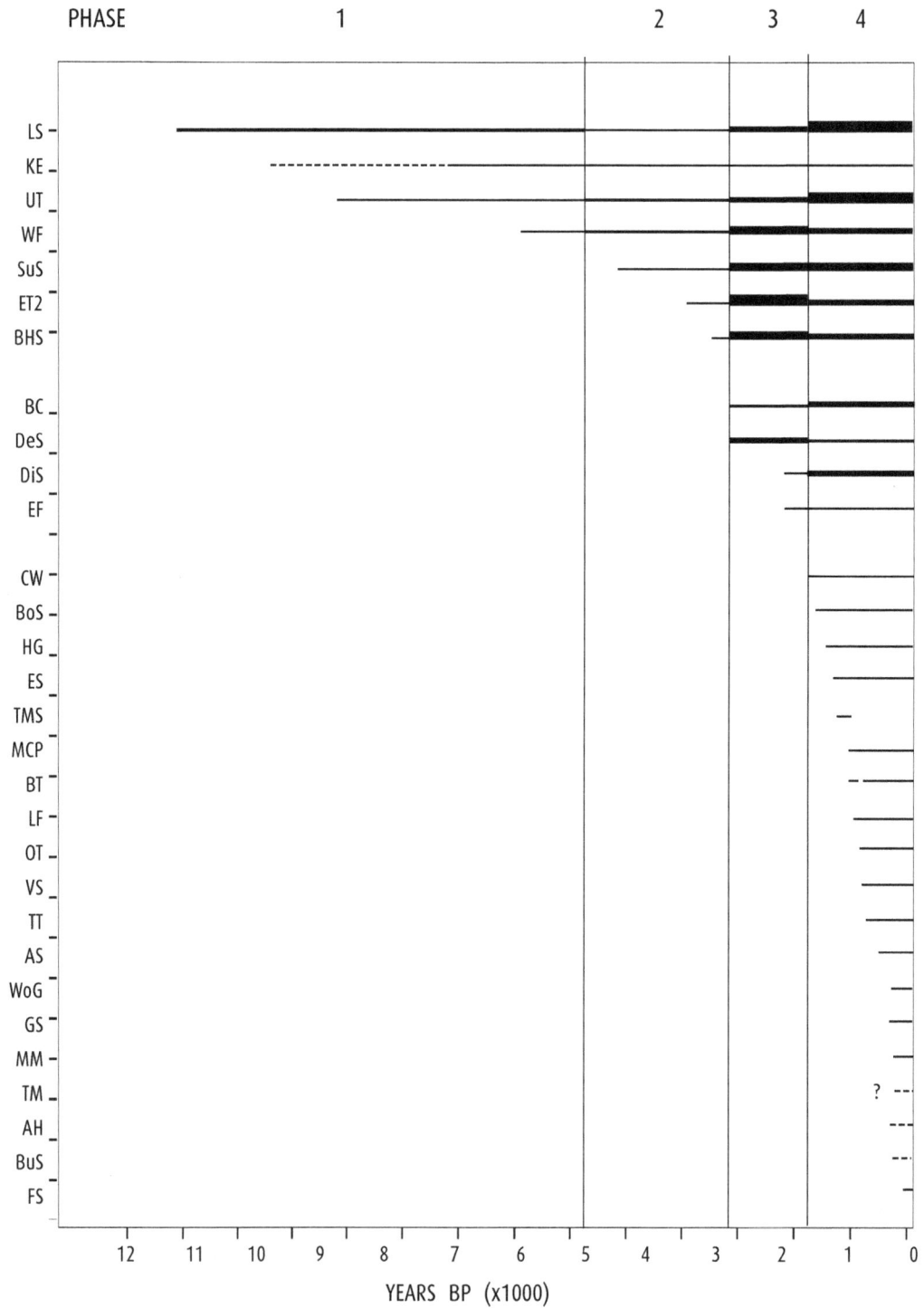

Figure 6.5 Upper Mangrove Creek catchment: random sampling units. Rate of artefact accumulation in each phase in individual archaeological deposits. Time is represented to scale, but frequency is schematic only. Table 6.12 has details.

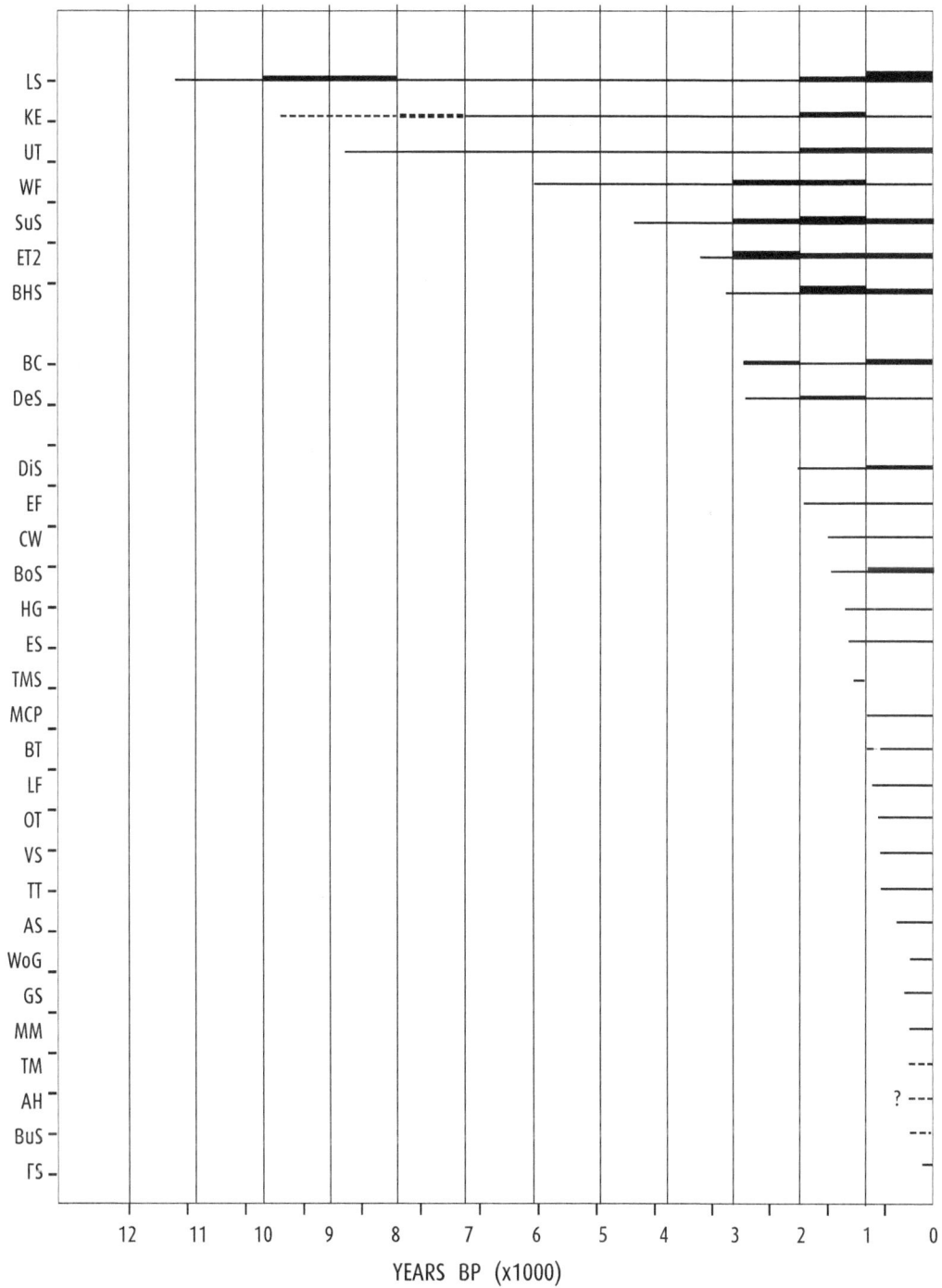

Figure 6.6 Upper Mangrove Creek catchment: random sampling units. Rate of artefact accumulation in each millennium in individual archaeological deposits. Time is represented to scale, but frequency is schematic only. Table 6.13 has details.

Table 6.13 Upper Mangrove Creek catchment: random sampling units. Archaeological deposits: estimated total number of artefacts accumulated in each millennium and rate of artefact accumulation for millennial sequence, rounded to nearest 50; based on calculations in Appendix 2. See also Figure 6.6.

SITE NAME	ESTIMATED TOTAL NO. OF ARTEFACTS	ESTIMATED TOTAL NUMBER OF ARTEFACTS IN EACH MILLENNIUM (BP)											
		12TH	11TH	10TH	9TH	8TH	7TH	6TH	5TH	4TH	3RD	2ND	1ST
Loggers (EF)	128,050	150	3850	24,100	23,200	4300	3650	3550	4150	5850	7000	11,800	36,450
Kangaroo and Echidna (T1+T2)	5,500			[400]	[400]	[950]	50	50	750	700	450	1400	350
Uprooted Tree (Ta+Tb)	31,250				50	200	300	800	1150	1300	2350	13,050	12,050
White Figure	37,050							300	450	1550	11,550	17,200	6000
Sunny	88,150								150	2150	25,250	44,450	16,150
Emu Tracks 2 (T1+T2)	249,650									3650	165,200	66,350	14,450
Black Hands SH (F)	77,050									100	16,050	46,300	14,600
Boat Cave	500										100	50	350
Delight SH	5000										1250	2650	1100
Dingo	2600											600	2000
Elongated Figure	950											550	400
Caramel Wave	500											50	450
Boronia	150											50	100
Harris Gully	1850											700	1150
Elngarrah	100											50	50
Two Moths	0											0	n/u
McPherson	1600												1600
Bird Tracks	0												0
Low Frontage	300												300
One Tooth	750												750
Venus	700												700
Ti-tree	500												500
Anadara	1850												1850
Wolloby Gully	2250												2250
Geebung	400												400
Mangrove Mansions	3250												3250
Token Male	>3												>3
Axehead	1												1
Button	>4												>4
Firestick	0												0
Totals: all habitations	639,950	150	3850	24,500	23,650	5450	4000	4700	6650	15,300	229,200	205,250	117,250

Phased sequence

Eleven habitations were used in more than one phase. The estimated total number of artefacts accumulated at each habitation in each phase is set out in Table 6.11 and the rates of artefact accumulation in Figure 6.5 and Table 6.12. At all but two of the seven habitations used for more than two phases, there were substantial or dramatic increases in the rate at which artefacts accumulated in Phase 3. The exceptions were Kangaroo and Echidna and Uprooted Tree, where the rates increased, but on a smaller scale than elsewhere.

At five of the 11 multi-phase habitations, the artefact accumulation rates continued to increase in successive periods. At the other six habitations, there was a decrease, sometimes relatively dramatic, in the accumulation rates in the upper levels.

Millennial sequence

Fifteen habitations were used for more than two millennia, and seven for more than 3000 years (Fig. 6.6 and Table 6.13). At the seven habitations used for more than 3000 years:

1.   a dramatic or substantial increase in the artefact accumulation rates can be seen; this occurred within the last 3000 years and usually in the third or second millennium BP. At only one habitation (Loggers, where the rate of artefact accumulation continued to increase until contact) did a substantial increase occur in the first millennium BP;

2.   there was also a dramatic or substantial decrease in the artefact accumulation rate in all habitations except Loggers and Uprooted Tree; at the other five habitations, this decrease occurred after the dramatic increase mentioned in 1. above. At one habitation (Emu Tracks 2) it began in the second millennium BP and at the other four it was in the first millennium BP. At Uprooted Tree a decrease occurred in the first millennium BP, but it was not marked.

In the two sites where habitation is estimated to have begun in the third millennium BP, Delight and Boat Cave, the former had a decrease while the latter had an increase in the first millennium BP.

The millennial sequence also indicates that:

1.   decreased artefact accumulation rates occurred at a greater number of habitations in the most recent period (i.e., all but Loggers and Boat Cave), although the decrease at Uprooted Tree was not very great;

2.   the substantial increases and decreases in the accumulation rates did not necessarily occur at the same time in all habitations — at some the increase began in the third millennium BP and in others the second millennium BP. The substantial decrease occurred in most habitations in the last 1000 years, but at Emu Tracks 2 it began in the second millennium BP — at the same time as increases were beginning at others;

3.   at Loggers, there was a period with relatively high artefact accumulation rates in the 10th and ninth millennia BP, that is, within Phase 1. At Kangaroo and Echidna, there may have been a period of relatively high artefact accumulation in the eighth millennium BP, but the presence of artefacts dating back to 10,000 BP at this habitation is equivocal at present; and,

4.   the growth rates at individual habitations varied widely.

The millennial sequence reveals that the relationships between the use of the various habitations within the catchment were more complex than those indicated by the phased sequence. Variability in the timing, direction and magnitude of the changes in the artefact accumulation rates in individual habitations, as documented for the catchment, have not been documented in the same detail anywhere else in Australia. The variability documented for the catchment suggests that local habitation and land-use patterns in other regions are likely to be more complex than models based on less detailed site and artefact distribution studies.

Changes in the local rate of artefact accumulation — the catchment

While trends at individual habitations reflect the manner in which people inhabited specific locations within the catchment and how they occupied the catchment once they were there, the catchment trends are pertinent to discussions about long-term use of the catchment in a regional context (cf. Foley 1981b: 175–6). So, in assessing changes in the catchment as a whole, and at a topographic level, I used a non-site approach (Foley 1981a, 1981b, 1981c; Thomas 1975) — an approach now more commonly used in eastern Australia, especially with open archaeological deposits (Robins 1997; MacDonald et al. 1998: 37; MacDonald and Davidson n.d: 153–5; Holdaway et al. 1998; Doelman et al. 2001).

A.

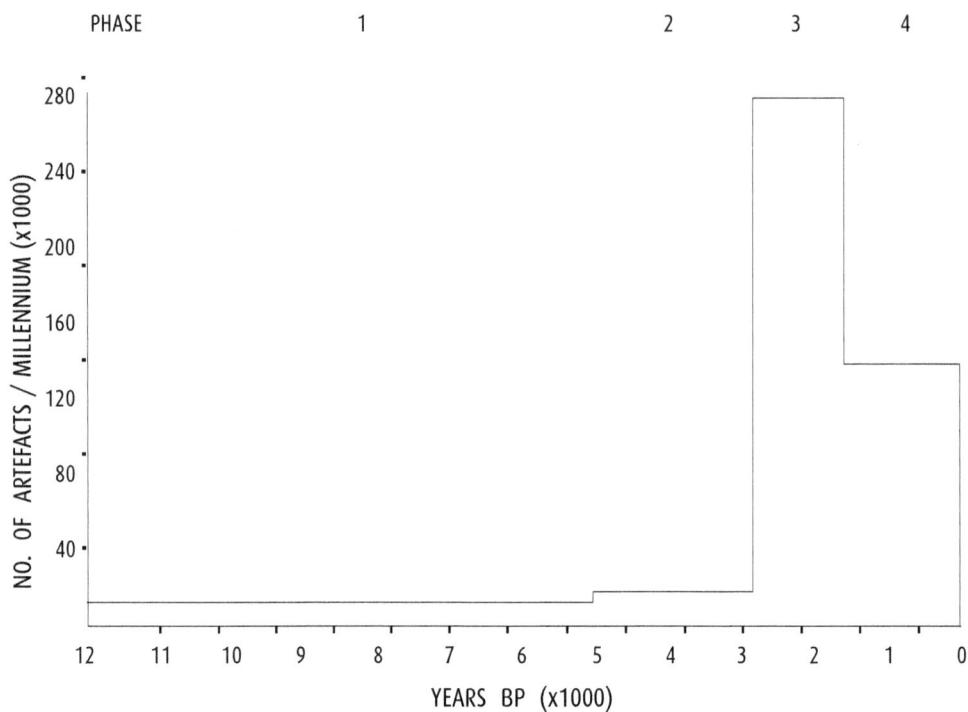

B.

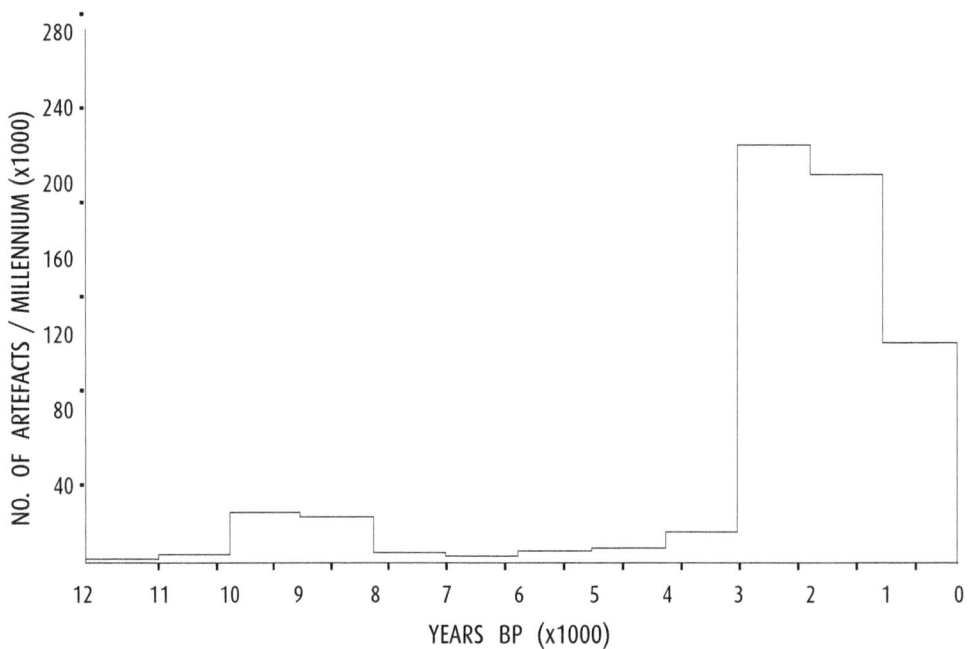

Figure 6.7 Upper Mangrove Creek catchment: random sampling units. Local rate of artefact accumulation in each (A) phase and (B) each millennium. Tables 6.12 and 6.13 have details.

Phased sequence

According to the phased sequence, the *local artefact accumulation rate* was higher in Phase 3 than in any other phase; that is, there was a peak accumulation period between ca 2800 BP and ca 1600 BP, and in the most recent phase the artefact accumulation rates decreased (Fig. 6.7A).

Growth rates. The growth rates for the local artefact accumulation rates varied dramatically over time (Table 6.5). Between Phases 1 and 2 the growth rate was low (x1.35), but in Phase 3 it was almost 20 times higher than in Phase 2. In Phase 4, the local artefact accumulation rate was half that of Phase 3 (x0.5).

Millennial sequence

The millennial sequence shows that there was an initial slow but steady increase in the local artefact accumulation rate, but then it increased dramatically in the third millennium BP (Fig. 6.7B). A similarly high rate was maintained in the second millennium BP, after which it decreased substantially in the first millennium BP. In the 10th and ninth millennia BP, there was also a minor peak in the local artefact accumulation rates, which is masked in the phased sequence.

Growth rates. The local artefact accumulation rate in the third millennium BP was more than 14 times higher than that of the fourth millennium BP (Table 6.6). The growth rate in the 10th millennium was also very high (x6.4), though the actual numbers of artefacts involved were lower than in the more recent periods. The exceptionally high growth rate in the 11th millennium BP (x25.7) does not warrant undue emphasis since it is presently based on small numbers of artefacts from a single habitation, i.e., Loggers.

The decline in the growth rate in the eighth millennium BP (x0.23) was also greater than the decline that occurred in the first millennium BP (x0.57). These figures suggest that dramatic changes also occurred in the early-Holocene and were not restricted to the late-Holocene.

Comments on local artefact accumulation rates

Variations in the direction of trends in individual archaeological deposits in the most recent period were noted in the storage area data set (Attenbrow 1981: 131; 1982b: 77). Although I speculated that the decreases in the upper levels of some archaeological deposits may 'cancel out' the increases in others, at that time I did not envisage that the overall trend would be towards such a substantial decrease in the local artefact accumulation rate in the last 1000 years. The substantial decrease in the local artefact accumulation rate during the most recent phase and millennium is in strong contrast with the continuing increases which are documented for the habitation establishment rates and numbers of habitations used in the successive periods of time. It is possible that the documented trends are biased because of the small area excavated in some archaeological deposits (discussed in Chapter 3, Excavation strategy and methods, and Chapter 5, Sample size), but it appears unlikely and can be tested only by further excavation in each archaeological deposit.

Much of the variation between Phase 3 and 4 is due to the large difference between these phases at Emu Tracks 2. If this habitation was excluded from the data set, Phase 4 would have had a higher rate of artefact accumulation than Phase 3. In the millennial sequence, if Emu Tracks 2 was excluded from the figures, the rate for the third millennium BP would drop dramatically, but the second millennium BP still has a higher rate than the first. However, there is no reason why Emu Tracks 2 — as opposed to any other archaeological deposit — should be excluded from the sample, given the nature of the selection procedures.

To check whether the observed pattern in the local artefact accumulation rates (in particular, the lower number of artefacts in the most recent period) was due to mis-allocation of spits to a wrong phase, various ways of combining the totals were calculated. Mis-allocation could occur where diagnostic artefacts were not present; it could also occur if the vertical distribution of such artefacts had been altered by subsequent disturbance, such as treadage and scuffage. The most drastic situation that could have occurred is that all top spits in Phase 3 belong to Phase 4 and all bottom spits in Phase 3 belong to Phase 2. In this situation, Phase 4 does have a greater artefact accumulation rate than Phase 3. However, there is no reason to believe this happened in ALL archaeological deposits. In addition, many archaeological deposits have only two spits in Phase 3, and, if diagnostic artefacts representing Phase 3 are present, then at least one of the spits must fall into Phase 3. If the Phase 4 habitations without diagnostic features belonged elsewhere, this would only accentuate the decrease in Phase 4.

Although mis-allocating spits and/or assemblages to specific millennia may have occurred for the reasons outlined above, the fact that both sequences produced similar trends indicates that the status of the postulated trends are secure enough to use as a basis for interpretative and explanatory models for the temporal changes in the habitation and land-use patterns in the catchment.

Changes in the rate of artefact accumulation in each topographic zone in successive time periods

The number of artefacts accumulated in each topographic zone varied widely, with the highest number being on the periphery ridgetops (Tables 6.14 to 6.16). The number of artefacts and the rate at which they accumulated in each zone also varied considerably over time.

Phased sequence

The periphery ridgetops had the highest number of artefacts accumulated and the highest artefact accumulation rates in all phases except Phase 1 (Tables 6.14 and 6.15). In Phase 1, the highest number and highest rate were in the main valley bottoms.

In Phase 2, although there was a slight increase in the local accumulation rate, the rate decreased in the main valley bottoms while increasing in the other two inhabited zones (subsidiary ridgesides and periphery ridgetops). In Phase 3, the increase in artefact accumulation rates is dramatic in all zones, but the growth rate is much greater in the main valley bottoms and periphery ridgetops than on the subsidiary ridgesides (×18, ×21 and ×10 respectively).

Phase 4 had several changes — at the same time as there were decreased rates in all zones previously inhabited (with the periphery ridgetops having a much greater decrease than the main valley bottoms and subsidiary ridgesides), the remaining three zones were inhabited for the first time (peninsula ridgetops, main ridgesides and subsidiary valley bottoms). However, the accumulation rates in these three zones are very much lower than in the three zones inhabited throughout the sequence.

Changes in the artefact accumulation rates which occurred in each phase therefore did not happen uniformly in each of the topographic zones.

Millennial sequence

The millennial sequence shows a similar long-term pattern to the phased sequence. However, it reinforces the habitation indices, indicating that artefact accumulation first began in the main valley bottom, did not begin on the peninsula ridgetops and in the subsidiary valley bottoms until the second millennium BP, and it was only in the first millennium BP that it began on the main ridgesides (Table 6.16). It also shows that the peak in the artefact accumulation rates in the 10th and ninth millennia BP took place in the main valley bottoms.

Table 6.14 Upper Mangrove Creek catchment: random sampling units. Estimated total number of artefacts accumulated in each phase in each topographic zone, rounded to nearest 50.

Phase	Topographic zones						Total:
	RT-PERI	RT-PEN	VB-MC	VB-SC	RS-MC	RS-SC	all zones
1	850		63,000			2350	66,200
2	21,250		6600			3700	31,550
3	245,450		64,650			21,250	331,350
4	106,500	250	70,850	8350	3000	21,900	210,850
Total: all phases	374,050	250	205,100	8350	3000	49,200	639,950

Table 6.15 Upper Mangrove Creek catchment: random sampling units. Rate of artefact accumulation (number per millennium) in each phase in each topographic zone, rounded to nearest 50; based on Table 6.14.

Phase	Topographic zones						Total:
	RT-PERI	RT-PEN	VB-MC	VB-SC	RS-MC	RS-SC	all zones
1	150		10,150			400	10,700
2	9650		3000			1700	14,350
3	204,550		53,900			17,700	276,150
4	71,000	150	47,250	5550	2000	14,600	140,550
Total catchment	33,700	50	18,500	750	250	4450	57,650

Table 6.16 Upper Mangrove Creek catchment: random sampling units. Estimated total number of artefacts accumulated in each millennium in each topographic zone and rate of artefact accumulation (number per millennium) for millennial sequence, rounded to nearest 50.

Millennium BP	Topographic zones						Total: all zones
	RT-PERI	RT-PEN	VB-MC	VB-SC	RS-MC	RS-SC	
12th			150				150
11th			3850				3850
10th			24,100			(400)	24,500
9th	50		23,200			(400)	23,650
8th	200		4300			(950)	5450
7th	300		3650			50	4000
6th	800		3550			350	4700
5th	1300		4150			1200	6650
4th	7100		5950			2250	15,300
3rd	194,050		23,050			12,100	229,200
2nd	126,500	100	58,100	750		19,800	205,250
1st	43,750	150	51,050	7600	3000	11,700	117,250
Total No.	374,050	250	205,100	8350	3000	49,200	639,950
Catchment rate	33,700	50	18,500	750	250	4450	57,650

Discussion

In the above analyses of the habitation and artefact indices, several observations are made:

1. the trends observed when millennial divisions are used as the basis for presenting the quantitative changes differ in their timing and nature from those based on typological phases;

2. data sets including only habitations with radiocarbon ages indicate different late-Holocene trends compared with data sets including 'all datable habitations';

3. the timing and direction of the catchment trends in the habitation establishment rates, the number of habitations used, and the local artefact accumulation rates, were not uniform;

4. the growth rates in each of the three indices were not constant over time;

5. timing and direction of the changes in the artefact accumulation rates at individual habitations varied widely;

6. the trends in the habitation establishment rates, the number of habitations used and artefact accumulation rates in each topographic zone varied widely; and,

7. the timing of the quantitative changes and the appearance of changes in typology, technology and raw material did not necessarily coincide.

Typological phases versus millennial divisions

Use of the *typological phases* suggests that either marked, substantial or dramatic changes occurred in both habitation indices and the local artefact accumulation rates at or after three points in time: **ca 5000 BP** (the beginning of Phase 2), **ca 2800 BP** (the beginning of Phase 3) and **ca 1600 BP** (the beginning of Phase 4) (Figs 6.1A, 6.2A and 6.7A).

The *millennial sequence* indicates slightly different timing for the changes (Fig. 6.1B, 6.2B and 6.7B):

1. in the *habitation establishment rates*, there was:

*   an increase in the **seventh** millennium BP (represented by the beginning of habitation establishment in each millennium), which is not identifiable in the phased sequence;

*   a marked increase in the **fourth**, rather than the fifth millennium BP; and,

*   dramatic increases in both the **second** and **first** millennia BP, so that the increases appear as a continual process, rather than a single dramatic increase occurring only halfway through the second millennium BP with the same level being maintained into the first millennium BP;

2. in *the numbers of habitations used*, there was:

*   a gradual increase over time until the **second** millennium BP, rather than a marked and sudden increase in the fifth millennium BP after a period of no or very little change; and,

*   dramatic increases in both the **second** and **first** millennia BP, which are part of a continuing process rather than only one dramatic increase occurring halfway through the second millennium BP with the same level being maintained in the first millennium BP;

3. in *the local artefact accumulation rates* there was:

*   a small peak in the local artefact accumulation rates in the **ninth** and **10th** millennia BP (i.e., in the early Holocene), which is not apparent in the phased sequence;

*   a sudden and dramatic increase in the **third** millennium BP;

*   the rate remained high in the **second** millennium BP, i.e., the high rates extended over a longer period than in the phased sequence;

*   a substantial decrease in the most recent period, but it was in the **first** millennium BP, rather than in second millennium BP (i.e., after 1600 BP).

The above comparison of the millennial and phased sequences enables variations in the trends produced by each method to be observed. While the overall trends remain the same in terms of direction, use of millennial sequences brings out differences (sometimes subtle) in the timing of the changes, as well as the nature of the changes (i.e., whether a change was gradual or sudden). Temporal boundaries for the phased sequence can in some sense accommodate the interpretations based on the millennial sequence; that is, the changes occurred **within** the dates of the phased sequence. However, when changes are stated as occurring in a phase or in any dated period, there is usually an assumption (explicit or implicit) that the change took place at the beginning of the specified period — which need not be the case.

In general, analyses based on data from the random sampling units support the 1981 postulated trends for the storage area habitations which included 'the more speculative data' and indicate that there was a dramatic increase in the number of habitations being established in the Late Bondaian (Phase 4). In addition, the *phased sequences* suggest that in Phase 4 there was an inverse relationship between changes in the two habitations indices and the local artefact accumulation rate (the former continuing to increase and the latter decreasing dramatically), and that these changes coincided in time. In contrast, trends based on the *millennial sequences* indicate that (a) the rates of increase during the early-Holocene were more even than the phased sequences indicate; and (b) ca 5000 BP was not a time of significant change in any of the indices, with the dramatic changes occurring after 3000 BP. The *millennial sequences* also enable the complex relationships between habitation establishment, habitations used and local artefact accumulation rates in the late-Holocene to be more clearly identified. For example, initially, in the third millennium BP, a dramatic increase occurred in the local artefact accumulation rate while the habitation establishment rate and the number of habitations used were relatively low. It was only in the second millennium BP that the habitation establishment rate and the number of habitations used increased dramatically (i.e., while the local artefact accumulation rate was almost stable). Then, in the first millennium BP, the habitation establishment rate and number of habitations used continued to increase whereas the local artefact accumulation rate dropped substantially. Use of millennial divisions demonstrates that major quantitative changes in habitation and artefact indices did not necessarily coincide in time, direction or magnitude.

The above comparative analysis of the trends in the phased and millennial sequences illustrates how grouping materials from several excavation units into phases based on typological (or other) changes, which may have extended over several millennia, can mask the time at which changes in other events and processes took place. In addition, it can suggest they were sudden, or even gradual or long-term processes rather than short-term events; the reverse may equally apply (but cf. Morwood 1981: 30). It could be argued that using millennial divisions still forces changes to appear as if they occurred either earlier or later than they actually did — that is, at the millennial boundary rather than at some time within a millennium — but this will also depend on how an author describes and/or interprets the graphs. An alternative may be to combine dated boundaries (where available) and millennial divisions within units that extend over several millennia. However, the main implication of this comparison is that each aspect of the archaeological record is likely to have its own trajectory and temporal sequence, and therefore should not be presented in terms of previously constructed sequences designed for other purposes. Each strand of evidence from the archaeological record (e.g., artefact types, technological traits, raw materials, artefact accumulation rates, habitation establishment rates, numbers of habitations used and faunal assemblages) should be analysed separately and have its own sequence established before comparisons are made and correlations, if any, identified. Different methods of presentation and different analytical methods may also contribute to apparent regional variations in the timing of different events, particularly if researchers in different regions are not using the same methods.

Future discussions, unless indicated, are based on millennial sequences.

Artefact accumulation rates in individual habitations

Comparison of the trends in *individual habitations* shows that the *artefact accumulation rates* in each varied widely in timing, direction and magnitude (Fig. 6.6 and Table 6.13); they also often differed from those of the *local artefact accumulation rates* (Fig. 6.7). At the seven habitations used for more than 3000 years, the following patterns can be seen:

1.   a dramatic or substantial increase in the artefact accumulation rates within the last 3000 years, but usually within the third or second millennium BP. The magnitude of the increase varied from habitation to habitation;

2.   at only one of these seven habitations (Loggers) (14% of the habitations) did the artefact accumulation rates continue to increase gradually throughout the depth of the deposit, and the highest artefact accumulation rate occurred in the first millennium BP;

3.   at the other six habitations (86% of habitations), a decrease in the artefact accumulation rates is apparent in the first or second millennium BP, and the peak in the artefact accumulation rates occurred sometime within the third and second millennium BP. The magnitude of the decrease varied from habitation to habitation; in most it was substantial but in others (e.g., Uprooted Tree) it was minor in nature.

These differences indicate that the history of use and/or at least the amount of stone knapping at each habitation varied over time. The inter-site variability in this index further confirms the often-made statement that regional or local prehistories should not be based on the sequence of evidence from 'single sites' (e.g., Struever 1971; Thomas 1979: 283; Attenbrow 1981: 119; Davidson 1983: 94–5; Cosgrove 1995: 108–9).

Inter-zonal variability within the catchment

Inter-zonal variability is seen in the habitation establishment rates, the numbers of habitations used and the artefact accumulation rates. In the 12th millennium BP, habitations were established initially in only one zone, the main valley bottoms. In the ninth millennium BP, a second zone (the periphery ridgetops) was used, and then in the seventh millennium BP a third zone (the subsidiary ridgesides; that is, if it was not inhabited in the 10th millennium BP). It was not until the second millennium BP that habitations were established in another two zones and only in the first millennium BP that all zones were used.

In each zone, the habitation establishment rate and the number of habitations used in each millennium increased over time. However, the timing, direction and magnitude of the changes in the artefact accumulation rates were not the same in each zone. In the first three zones inhabited (main valley bottoms, periphery ridgetops and subsidiary ridgesides), the accumulation rates increased until the second millennium BP — then in the first millennium BP the rates decreased, but at varying magnitudes. In contrast, the two zones which were not inhabited until the second millennium BP had increased accumulation rates in the first millennium BP.

Thus, habitations were not established in all topographic zones at the same time, and three of the zones were used only within the last 2000 years. This pattern suggests there was a greater dispersal of activities within the catchment over time. It also appears visually, when mapped (Figs 6.3 and 6.4), to be simply a denser or more concentrated habitation pattern, particularly in the last 2000 years, which is due partially to the distribution of the last-used zones (main ridgesides, peninsula ridgetops, and subsidiary valley bottoms). Establishment of habitations in these three zones could be viewed as 'movement into marginal areas' or 'an intensification of land-use' as proposed by Lourandos (see Chapter 2). If so, it is on a much smaller scale than the examples given by Lourandos, but this presumably would not preclude it from being part of the same process. As with the individual habitations, each zone appears to have had its own history of use (Tables 6.15 and 6.16).

Variations over time in the millennial growth rates

Growth rates for the habitation and artefact indices reinforce the trends and complexity outlined above (Table 6.6). In the three indices there are some consecutive millennia in which growth rates were constant, but as a general rule they fluctuated quite markedly over the 11,000-year period and varied dramatically between some periods of time. The growth rates for the habitation establishment rates varied from zero (×1) to ×3.5 and for the number of habitations used from zero (×1) to ×1.81. The highest growth rates were in the artefact accumulation rates — they varied from ×0.23 to ×14.39 — where there were decreases as well as increases.

Because of the larger numbers of sites and artefacts in the more recent millennia, the quantitative changes that occurred in the habitation and artefact indices are usually numerically much larger than those that occurred earlier (i.e., pre-4000 BP). However, the growth rates associated with these larger increases and decreases in recent millennia are not always greater than the growth rates of early-Holocene levels. The highest growth rates in the local artefact accumulation rates are recorded in the 10th and third millennia BP. Substantial declines in the growth rates occurred in the eighth and first millennia BP.

These variations in growth rates are pertinent to later discussions concerning interpretations which are based on the assumption that increases in numbers of habitations and/or artefacts are the product or material manifestation of increases in numbers of people — either general or local population increase, or increased use of a particular habitation.

Relationship between the timing of the quantitative changes and the appearance of qualitative changes in the stone artefact assemblages

The quantitative changes over time (i.e., in numbers of sites and artefacts) have been explained in terms of the qualitative changes in the stone artefact assemblages, that is, by changes in typology, technology and raw material (Chapter 2). In the catchment, however, the timing of the quantitative changes did not coincide with the appearance of new artefact types and technological features or with changes in raw materials, for example:

1.   *backed artefacts* appeared long before the dramatic increases in both the artefact accumulation rates at individual habitations in the third or second millennium BP and the local artefact accumulation rate in the third millennium BP;

2.   *the disappearance of Bondi points* and decrease in other backed artefacts occurred about 1600 BP (i.e., in the second millennium BP), whereas at most habitations the decrease in the artefact accumulation rates occurred in the first millennium BP. This 'typological' change thus occurred earlier than the dramatic decrease in the artefact accumulation rates; and,

3.   *bipolar artefacts increase markedly in frequency percentage* about 2800 BP; this 'typological' change is related to *an increase in bipolar working* (a 'technological' change), which is also correlated with *an increase in the percentage frequency of quartz* (a 'raw material' change). Bipolar working is seen on quartz material more often than on other types of raw material, such as silcrete and chert/tuff, and increases relative to hand-held percussion. The predominance of quartz over FGS which occurred ca 2800 BP was used as the criterion for the beginning of Phase 3 (see Chapter 3, Temporal sequences). The dramatic increase in the local artefact accumulation rate in

the third millennium BP appears to coincide with the beginning of Phase 3 (ca 2800 BP). The dramatic changes in the artefact accumulation rates, however, are unlikely to be caused directly by the increased use of quartz and / or bipolar working, for the following reasons:

(a)   a dramatic increase in the artefact accumulation rates does not necessarily occur in the same level in which quartz dominates over FGS in individual archaeological deposits — that is, the two events did not occur at the same time (see also Attenbrow 1981, 1982a; Stern 1982);

(b)   the increase in percentage frequency of quartz artefacts at individual habitations indicates that the change in dominance from FGS to quartz was a gradual one, beginning about 5000 or 4000 BP and continuing until contact with some minor oscillations (e.g., Loggers, Attenbrow 1981: Fig. 6.13; Deep Creek, Stern 1982: Graph 3);

(c)   artefact accumulation rates did not always increase over time in all archaeological deposits. An increase in the percentage frequency of quartz did not always occur in all archaeological deposits, but there is no correlation between those archaeological deposits in which increased artefact accumulation rates occurred and those in which the percentage frequency of quartz increased, and vice versa.

Concluding comments

The evidence presented above indicates that habitation patterns in the Upper Mangrove Creek catchment varied over time, as did the accumulation of artefacts in individual habitations. The relationships between the late-Holocene dramatic changes in the habitation and artefact indices are not obvious and are likely to have been complex. Subsistence and land-use patterns associated with the changing habitation distribution patterns and changing artefact accumulation rates were probably equally complex.

Grinding areas and images are also indicators of land-use and their creation would have varied over time as well, though identifying quantitative changes over time in their creation and the use of locations with these traits is much more difficult than is the case with archaeological deposits. The only evidence that suggests a date for pigment images in the catchment comes from outside the random sampling units. At Dingo and Horned Anthropomorph, polished dark-red ochre of similar colour to images on the walls was found in the deposits of the southern shelter below an excavated context dated to ca 580 BP (581±120 BP, GX-0070; Macintosh 1965: 85, 96–7). In the immediately adjacent northern shelter of this site, charcoal directly above a layer with ochre of a light-red colour similar to line drawings on the walls of that shelter was dated to between 144±125 BP and 120±155 BP (GX-0069). Macintosh considered that these dates indicated the northern images were created between AD 1750 and AD 1830, and the southern images ca AD 1400.

In the random sampling units, a broken ochred palette was found in Sunny Shelter in levels with an estimated date of 1400–1600 BP (Fig. 3.18, see Chapter 3). In addition, outside the random sampling units, a piece of utilised ochre, dark-red haematite-rich material, was found in Deep Creek Shelter in a level dated to ca 2000 years ago (Attenbrow 1982a: 19–20, 27). However, pigment images were not seen on the walls or ceilings of either of these shelters. After his study of the rates of weathering and roof-fall in NSW south coast rockshelters, Hughes (1978: 41) stated, 'decorated surfaces in shelters not used as habitations, especially engravings, might well have survived for hundreds or thousands of years.' However, he concluded that 'it is unlikely that painting and drawings in such occupied shelters would have survived more than a few decades and even rock engravings would probably have been completely removed within a few hundred years'. It is possible that pigment images once existed in Deep Creek and Sunny Shelters, but the surfaces are presently irregular and not favourable for creating pigment images. It is also possible the ochre used in these shelters was used for decorating tools, weapons or people's bodies.

Some information about the grinding grooves, which are assumed to be associated with making and maintaining ground-edged implements, can be obtained from the catchment's archaeological deposits. Ground-edged implements (e.g., axes/hatchets) and fragments from them occur in the deposits only in levels dating to the last 4000 years, and, increasingly, the last 2000 years (Appendix 1). Stone types used to manufacture ground-edged implements occur increasingly in levels dating to the last 4000 years; grinding grooves are thus assumed to have been made in the catchment some time within the last 4000 years, and principally in the last 2000 years.

The introduction of ground-edged implements into south-eastern Australia some 4000 years ago, and the subsequent increase in their manufacture, would have brought about changes in land-use patterns in the catchment since:

1. the raw materials from which they were made (usually an igneous or an indurated metamorphic rock) differed from that used to make flaked stone implements; and,

2. areas of suitable sandstone (i.e., uniform and coarse-grained) were required to shape and/or sharpen the axe/hatchet heads.

Basalt sources, the rock from which many of the ground implements in the catchment were made (pers. obs.), are not present within the catchment, but exist within a short distance (<10km) to the west (Mogo Creek) and to the south (e.g., Basalt Hill, Kulnura Hymix quarries and Popran Creek), as well as elsewhere in the region. The nearby outcrops may not be the specific sources of basalt used for the catchment implements since the surface exposures were probably deeply weathered (as at the unquarried Basalt Hill). However, basalt pebbles of useable size and quality occur in creeks below these sources (Mogo, Warre Warren and Popran Creeks respectively) (local residents Lionel Young and Robert Thompson [pers. comm.] and pers. obs.). The need for this type of raw material and the restricted locations in which it occurs are likely to have influenced or altered the movements of people as well as trading patterns and networks.

Grinding grooves in the catchment have a more restricted distribution pattern than other archaeological traits. They occur on sandstone, in particular, the Hawkesbury sandstone, which is more uniform and coarser-grained than the Narrabeen Group of sandstones, though exposed surfaces of the latter are sometimes suitable. In the catchment, the Hawkesbury sandstone is restricted to the ridgetops and upper ridgesides. Whether the introduction of ground-edged implements and their manufacture initiated use of different (previously unused) topographic zones is not clear. However, it would have meant increased use of certain areas and an increase in the range of activities undertaken in areas which previously may only have been used for, say, hunting and gathering food resources.

Many eastern Australian studies in the 1970s and 1980s documented dramatic or substantial increases in the late-Holocene in the number of habitations used and the number of artefacts accumulated over time (see Chapter 2). The catchment data similarly indicate a continuing increase in the number of habitations established and used, but the artefact accumulation rates in many individual habitations and in the catchment as a whole did not continue to increase, and there was a dramatic decrease in the first millennium BP. Such decreases were rarely acknowledged in the 1970s and 1980s, but they are, however, common in many other regions and localities in eastern Australia, as will be seen in the following chapter and as has been shown in more recent studies.

7

Quantitative changes in other regions of eastern Australia: a review

Chronological changes in the numbers of habitations and/or artefacts were assumed by many researchers in the 1970s and 1980s to have been produced by changes in the size of populations. Explanations entailing continuing population increase were based, in some cases, on the belief that the rate of artefact production and/or the number of habitations used continued to increase throughout the period of Aboriginal occupation until European colonisation. Archaeological evidence for quantitative changes in several eastern Australian regions is reviewed below with two aims in mind:

- firstly, to show that trends identified in the Upper Mangrove Creek catchment are not anomalous. That is, (a) substantial decreases in artefact accumulation rates also occurred in other regions in the last 1000 years, and (b) dramatic or substantial increases in the artefact accumulation rates, the rate of habitation establishment and the number of habitations occurred in other regions later than 4000 BP; and,
- secondly, to examine data used by researchers of the 1970s and 1980s as support for their propositions that quantitative changes in the archaeological record indicated (a) that the population continued to increase in size until contact; and/or (b) that dramatic increases in the numbers of habitations and/or artefacts coincided in time with the introduction of the 'Small Tool Tradition' and/or Bondaian phases of the Eastern Regional Sequence.

The review, initially undertaken in 1987, includes sites and regions studied or used as supporting evidence for the interpretations and explanations presented in Chapter 2, but also includes other regions and several other sites for which habitation and/or artefact indices could be calculated. The regions, and the regions in which the sites were located, are: the NSW south coast-Sydney, south-western Victoria, central Queensland highlands, south-eastern Queensland, NSW–ACT–Victorian southern uplands-tablelands, the Mallee in north-western Victoria, the NSW Hunter Valley, NSW Blue Mountains, and the lower Murray Valley in South Australia (Tables 7.1 and 7.2, Figs 7.1 and 7.2; Appendix 4). The review was considered comprehensive at the time. There were (and still are) few regions for which data are available to estimate regional habitation establishment rates and/or to calculate artefact accumulation rates for a number of sites within the same region.

Table 7.1 Eastern Australian regions used as comparative case studies for habitation indices.

REGION	NO. OF SITES
NSW south coast and Sydney (NSW SC-S)	58
South-western Victoria (SW VIC)	23
Central Queensland highlands (CQH)	11
South-eastern Queensland (SEQ)	23
NSW–ACT–Victorian southern uplands-tablelands (NSW SU-T)	14
The Mallee, north-western Victoria (VIC MALLEE)	9
NSW Hunter Valley — Mt Arthur north and south (HV-MANS)	15
— Singleton area (HV-SING)	12

Table 7.2 Eastern Australian regions and sites used in comparative case studies for rates of artefact accumulation.

REGION AND SITE NAMES	NO. OF SITES
NSW south coast and Sydney: Burrill Lake, Bass Point, Currarong 1, Currarong 2, Sassafras 1	5
NSW Hunter Valley and adjacent areas: Sandy Hollow, Milbrodale, Bobadeen, Big L, Yango Creek, Macdonald River	6
NSW Blue Mountains and adjacent areas: Springwood, Kings Table, Walls Cave, Capertee 1 and 3, Shaws Creek K1 and K2	7
South-western Victoria: Bridgewater, Seal Point	2
Lower Murray Valley, South Australia: Devon Downs, Fromms Landing 1 and 6	3
Central Queensland highlands: Kenniff Cave, The Tombs, Natives Well 1 and 2	4
South-eastern Queensland: Maidenwell, Gatton, Platypus, Bushrangers	4

Although numerous large-scale surveys have been carried out in eastern Australia in the last 25–30 years (particularly for consulting projects), changes in habitation establishment rates and the numbers of habitations used cannot be ascertained for many projects because:

(a)   the surveys have not been followed by an excavation program (e.g., Vinnicombe 1980, 1984 — excluding the Upper Mangrove Creek catchment; Sydney Prehistory Group 1983; Sefton 1988; Illawarra Prehistory Group 1990, 1995, 1996; English and Gay 1993; see also other examples in Attenbrow 1987: Chapters 2 and 4);

(b)   only a few selected archaeological deposits were excavated and/or dated (e.g., Haglund 1981a, 1981b, 1984, 1996; Attenbrow and Hughes 1983; Byrne 1983, 1984; Attenbrow 1984; Egloff 1984; McNiven 1992; Corkill and Edgar 1996; Lilley and Ulm 1999; Ulm and Lilley 1999: 69 [though others are proposed or in progress]; White 2001); and/or

(c)   the documented length of habitation is not long enough for quantitative changes to be discernible (e.g., Coutts 1982).

In addition, in many areas where only open archaeological deposits/stone artefact scatters occur, artefact assemblages are frequently in deflated or unstratified shallow sediments, and/or materials suitable for radiometric determinations are not present (e.g., Hiscock 1982a in Lilley and Ulm 1999: 6; Lilley 1985: 95; Hiscock 1986, 1988a, 1993; Jo McDonald CHM 1997: 91–2, 96; Baker 2000: 74; Haglund 2001a: 18; Kuskie 1999: 47; Haglund 2002: 19–20).

Open archaeological deposits have been excavated in eastern Australia where datable materials were recovered, for example: on the NSW Cumberland Plain-Sydney region (Kohen et al. 1984: 57; Kohen 1986: 204; Smith 1986: 21; McDonald 1986b; Koettig 1990: 16; McDonald and Rich 1993: Vol. 2: Beta Analytic Lab. Report; McDonald et al. 1994: Table 5, 1996: 33–5, Table 20; White 1997 [1998]: Lab. Report; Jo McDonald CHM 1999: 21); in the NSW Hunter Valley (Koettig 1987, 1989, 1992, 1994; Haglund 1992; Rich 1992: 110; Kuskie and Kamminga 2000: 523–4; Haglund 2002: 19–20); the NSW south coast-Sydney (Boot 1993b, 1994, 1996a; Godden Mackay and Austral Archaeology 1997: 25); the NSW southern tablelands (Packard 1984; Koettig 1985a; Kamminga et al. 1989); western NSW (Holdaway et al. 1998: 16); and in

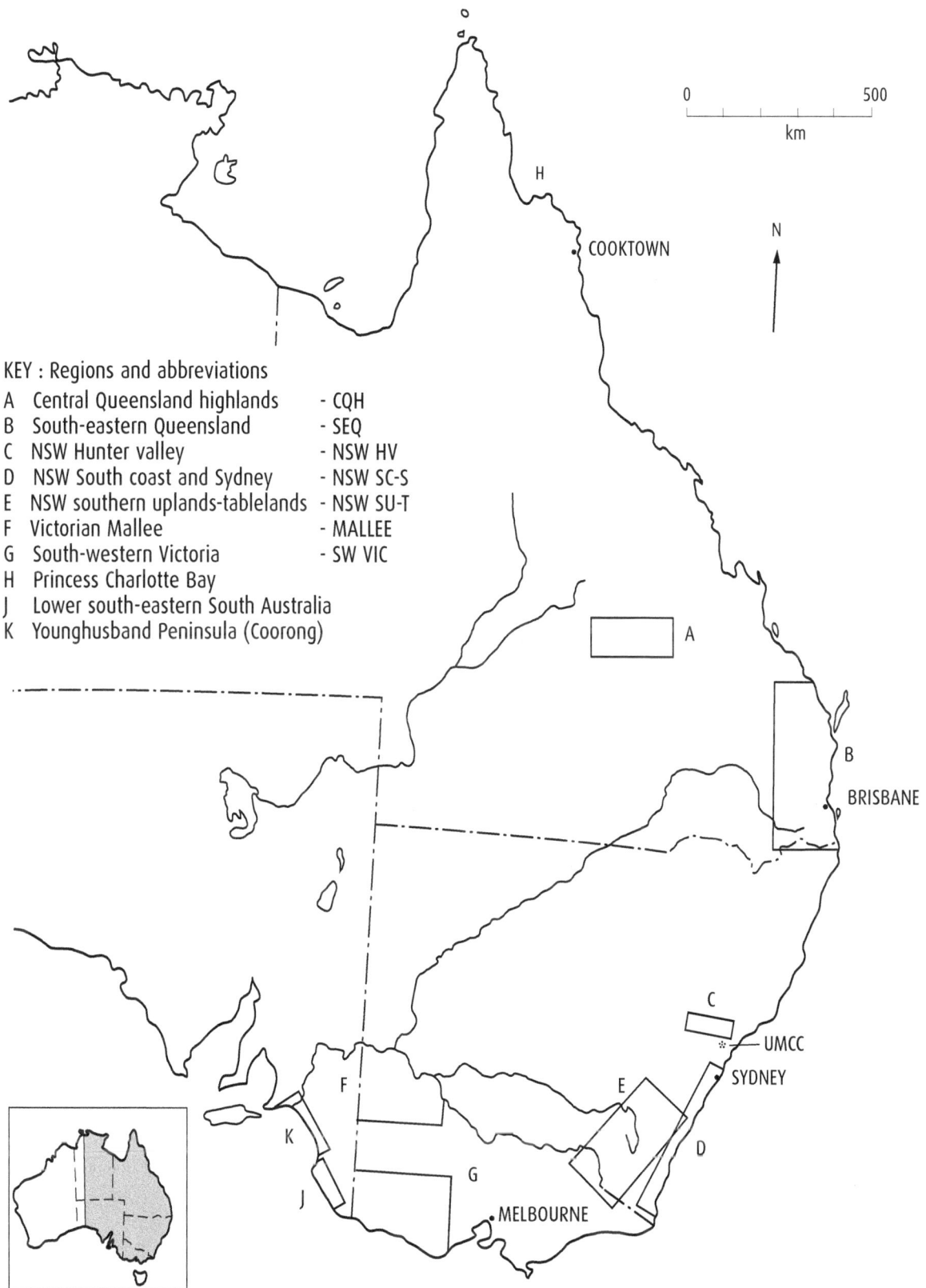

KEY : Regions and abbreviations
A   Central Queensland highlands   - CQH
B   South-eastern Queensland   - SEQ
C   NSW Hunter valley   - NSW HV
D   NSW South coast and Sydney   - NSW SC-S
E   NSW southern uplands-tablelands - NSW SU-T
F   Victorian Mallee   - MALLEE
G   South-western Victoria   - SW VIC
H   Princess Charlotte Bay
J   Lower south-eastern South Australia
K   Younghusband Peninsula (Coorong)

Figure 7.1 Regions reviewed in eastern Australia.

KEY: Site names and abbreviations

1   Kenniff Cave (KC)
2   The Tombs (TT)
3   Native Well 1 (NW1)
4   Native Well 2 (NW2)
5   Maidenwell (Mai)
6   Gatton (Gat)
7   Bobbadeen (Bob)
8   Sandy Hollow (SH)
9   Milbrodale (Mil)
10 Big L (Big)
11 Yango Creek (YC)
12 Macdonald River (MR)
13 Capertee 1
14 Capertee 3 (Cap3)
15 Kings Table (KT)

16 Walls Cave (WC)
17 Springwood (SC)
18 Shaws Creek
19 Shaws Creek (K2)
20 Burrill Lake (BL)
21 Currarong 1 (Cur1)
22 Currarong 2 (Cur2)
23 Bass Point (BP)
24 Sassafras (Sas)
25 Bridgewater
26 Seal Point
27 Devon Downs (DD)
28 Fromms Landing 1
29 Fromms Landing 6 (FL6)

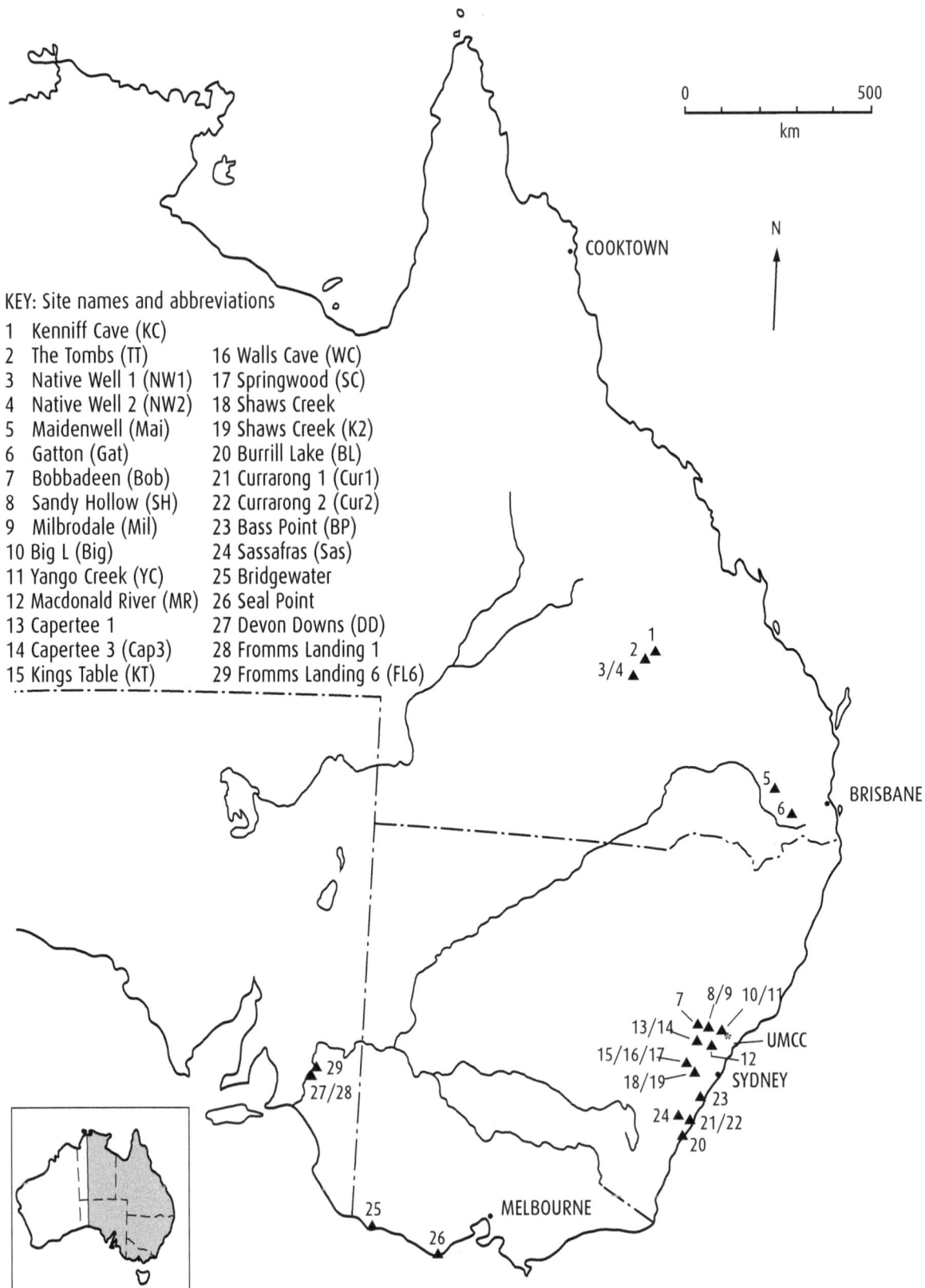

Figure 7.2 Sites reviewed in eastern Australia.

other eastern states (Ross 1981, 1984; Robins 1996). However, incorporating open archaeological deposits into an analysis of habitation establishment rates or numbers of habitations used based on radiocarbon ages can sometimes be problematic (see below). Other ways of estimating the age of open archaeological deposits through identification of diagnostic features in stone artefact assemblages have been attempted (Hiscock 1986, 1988a, 1993: 74; Holdaway et al. 1998: 16; Ulm and Hall 1996: 54), though not yet successfully (Baker 1992: 10, 64).

To compare the habitation establishment rates, the numbers of habitations used and artefact accumulation rates for the Upper Mangrove Creek catchment with trends in the other regions meant recalculating available data where these indices had not been calculated for the original studies. However, indices for both habitations and artefacts could not be calculated for all regions reviewed. For the Victorian Mallee and the NSW–ACT–Victorian southern uplands-tablelands, data were available for calculating trends in only habitation establishment and/or use and not the artefact accumulation rates. For the lower Murray Valley and NSW Blue Mountains, the few excavated archaeological deposits allowed calculation of only artefact accumulation rates. Data on which to produce inter-site and inter-zonal trends, as well as local artefact accumulation rates (as calculated for the catchment), are not available for any of the regions. In some case studies, I comment on the original data and methods used, and present alternative ways of analysing or interpreting the data (Appendix 4). Time and space constraints restrict comments about the limitations of the data, but those made illustrate some of the problems and difficulties faced in using quantitative data on sites and artefacts to indicate changes in population size and aspects of human behaviour. For some case studies, more recently radiometrically dated archaeological deposits are added to data sets of earlier researchers and the data reanalysed (e.g., NSW south coast-Sydney and NSW–ACT–Victorian southern uplands-tablelands). For others, e.g., south-eastern Queensland and south-western Victoria, the results of recent studies are also reported.

Millennial and average annual growth rates for habitation and artefact indices are also presented for each region (see Chapter 6 for methods of calculation). These rates were calculated to assess claims for dramatic increases in the rate at which change took place; for example, a six- to tenfold increase in artefact accumulation rates stated by Hughes and Lampert (1982) for the NSW south coast, and a tenfold increase in sites by Ross (1984) for the Victorian Mallee. Average annual growth rates were the most expedient growth rates to calculate for artefact accumulation rates, and are relevant to discussions about the evidence for population change. Population growth rates are usually discussed in terms of average annual growth rates (Ammerman et al. 1976: 29–30; Hassan 1981: 200–2; Gray 1985). Gray (1985: 23) says that a tenfold population increase over 2000 years implies an average annual growth rate of only 0.1% p.a., which is 'hardly a population explosion', and evidence for figures in excess of 0.5% p.a. are required 'to signify a considerable departure from near-stationarity'.

In this and future chapters, the word 'site/s' refers only to sites with archaeological deposit (i.e., habitation/s) unless specifically mentioned. Other archaeological traits (e.g., grinding areas, images, burials and quarries) are not included in the analyses. The term archaeological deposit includes shell middens, and those referred to as 'dated' may have had their age estimated by radiometric methods or on the basis of diagnostic artefacts or other traits. Archaeological deposits or artefact assemblages which do not have specific ages but which were estimated to be, say, ca 7000 BP or ca 3000 BP, are assigned to the seventh millennium BP or third millennium BP respectively, and not to the eighth millennium BP or fourth millennium BP.

Changes in the habitation indices

In analysing the Upper Mangrove Creek data, the term 'habitation indices' was used to refer collectively to two or more of the indices relating to habitations; that is, the habitation establishment rate and the number of habitations used. For this review, a third index — the rate of known-habitation use — has been used for some areas. Trends in these three indices in several regions of eastern Australia were investigated to determine:

1. whether there were dramatic changes in the indices in the latter half of the Holocene (as in the Upper Mangrove Creek catchment) and, if so, the timing of such changes;
2. the nature of these changes; that is, whether there were dramatic increases or dramatic decreases in these rates in the latter half of the Holocene; and,
3. whether growth rates in the habitation indices changed dramatically over time, and what the magnitude of such changes was.

For the Upper Mangrove Creek catchment, the habitation establishment rate and the number of habitations used in each millennium were described separately. In this review, these two indices are discussed together since many authors did not distinguish between the two concepts; 'an increase in site numbers' was the term most commonly used. In addition, the habitation establishment rate and/or the number of habitations used in each millennium could not be calculated for all regions. In deep and/or stratified archaeological deposits (usually in rockshelters or as shell middens), it can usually be ascertained whether the habitation continued to be used regularly and/or whether there were long periods of abandonment, for example, by the presence or absence of sterile layers. (By this, I don't mean to imply that habitations were used continuously throughout each millennium or that all the habitations noted as being used during a particular millennium were all used contemporaneously; habitation is assumed to be discontinuous or intermittent.) However, it is usually not possible to make such assumptions in the case of shallow open archaeological deposits.

Using age determinations from open habitations which consist of unstratified shallow stone artefact or shell scatters for the type of analysis undertaken here is more problematic than using those from deep stratified archaeological deposits in bounded locations such as rockshelters. Firstly, at extensive open habitation sites, materials from successive visits may not have been superimposed in the same area and so it is often not possible to ascertain the total length of time over which individual open habitations were used. Even if several dates are obtained, it is usually not possible to state whether the earliest radiocarbon age relates to the habitation's establishment or to some other time during its use. Dates gained by radiometric means or based on diagnostic features for a shallow open habitation can usually indicate only that it was used at that particular time or during that particular period/phase. In fact, the habitation may have been established much earlier, and/or it may have been used over a longer period of time than the date/s indicate/s. The most that can be calculated for regional studies where only open habitations have been recorded is the 'the number of habitations known to be used' at particular times or in particular periods. Secondly, the relationship between artefact assemblages in open habitations and datable materials (say, charcoal) is often less secure than in rockshelter deposits. For example, unless the charcoal comes from a humanly derived feature (e.g., a heat-treatment or cooking pit, or hearth), there is always the possibility that it has survived in/on the ground for a very long period of time and that bioturbation or geomorphological slope processes have moved it into association with cultural material of a later age. Thirdly, many shallow unstratified archaeological deposits do not have diagnostic artefact types or material suitable for radiometric dating. Fourthly, the way artefact scatters have been defined and/or interpreted in a particular project may influence the calculation of indices. For example, two artefact scatters visible on eroded land surfaces along a creek bank may have been described as two archaeological sites, but there may be unexposed buried artefacts between the two 'archaeological sites' and they are actually one site in physical and behavioural terms. If dates in the same millennium were obtained for both artefact scatters and they were actually part of the same site, including both dates when calculating the number of habitations used may skew the trends.

Within eastern Australia, evidence for changes in the number of habitations established or used is available for only a few widely dispersed regions. Seven regions within the area stretching from the central Queensland highlands to south-western Victoria (Table 7.1, Fig. 7.1, Appendix 4) are included in this review of habitation indices. Trends for these seven regions, along with those for the Upper Mangrove Creek catchment, are summarised in Table 7.3. Archaeological evidence from Princess Charlotte Bay, lower south-eastern South Australia and the Younghusband Peninsula (southern and northern Coorong) was also used as the basis for proposing demographic change over time, usually in association with local shifts in

Table 7.3 Regions in eastern Australia: summary of habitation indices. *Italics* indicates millennia with highest rate or largest number of habitations/millennium in region; underline – millennium in which greatest/most dramatic increase occurred in region; # – millennium in which highest growth rate occurred in region. Table 7.1 has full names of regions.

Mill. BP	Rate of habitation establishment in each millennium						Number of habitations used in each millennium					Rate of known-habitation use in each millennium		
	Regions						Regions					Regions		
	UMCC	NSW SC-S	SW VIC	CQH	SEQ	NSW SU-T	UMCC	NSW SC-S	CQH	SEQ	NSW SU-T	VIC MALLEE STH	NTH	NSW HV(SING)
25th		1						1						
24th								1						
23rd								1						
22nd				1				1	1					
21st					1	1		1	1	1	1			
20th								1	1	1	1			
19th								2	1	1	1			
18th		1				1		3	1	1	2			
17th								3	1	1	2			
16th								3	1	1	2			
15th		1						4	1	1	2			
14th								4	1	1	2			
13th		1	1	1				4	2	1	2	—	—	
12th	1		1				1	4	2	1	2	↑	↑	
11th		2		1			1	6	3	1	2	?	?	
10th	(1)0			1			(2)1	6	4	1	2			
9th	1							2	6	3	1	2-3	_2-3_	
8th		2	1				2	8	3	l	2	low	low	
7th	(0)1	2					3	10	3	1	2	↓	↓	
6th	1	3	1		1		4	13	3	2	2			
5th	1	2	1	2	#4		5	15	#5	#6	2	—	—	
4th	2	#9	1	#2	1	2	7	#24	*7*	7	# 4	↑?	↑?	2
3rd	2	9	2	#2	3	1	9	33	*9*	10	5	_24_	2	4
2nd	#7	*17*	*#11*	#2	5	2	16	*49*	*11*	14	7	high	low	5
1st	_14_	8	5	0	*9*	*#7*	*#29*	55	11	_23_	*#14*	↓	↓	7
Total habitations	30	58	24	11	23	14						121	20	12

population from one environmental zone to another (Chapter 2, Fig. 7.1). However, these studies have not been included in this review, as data were not presented that enabled calculation of artefact indices for individual habitations and habitation indices for the study area as a whole and for different environmental zones.

Because of constraints discussed above, I have calculated both the habitation establishment rate and the number of habitations used in each millennium for only four regions in which the sample consists of archaeological deposits in rockshelters and/or relatively deep/stratified open archaeological deposits (NSW south coast and Sydney, central Queensland highlands, south-eastern Queensland, and NSW–ACT–Victorian southern uplands-tablelands) (Table 7.3). For south-western Victoria, where basal dates are quoted for open archaeological deposits but not always for the length of habitation, only habitation establishment rates were calculated. For the NSW Hunter Valley and Victorian Mallee, I calculated only the rate of known-habitation use.

Changes in the rate of habitation establishment

In the five regions for which the habitation establishment rates were calculated, the rates in the late-Pleistocene and first half of the Holocene were low, as in the Upper Mangrove Creek catchment (Table 7.3, Figs 7.3 to 7.7).

In only two regions (south-eastern Queensland and NSW–ACT–Victorian southern uplands-tablelands) did the rates continue to increase until contact, as in the catchment (Figs 7.6A and 7.7A). In the other three (NSW south coast-Sydney, south-western Victoria and central Queensland highlands), they decreased in the first millennium BP (Figs 7.3A to 7.5A). Decreases in the habitation establishment rates also occurred at other times in the late Holocene; for example, in the fifth millennium BP in the NSW south coast-Sydney region, fourth millennium BP in south-eastern Queensland and third millennium BP in NSW–ACT–Victorian southern uplands-tablelands (Figs 7.3A, 7.6A and 7.7A). It is interesting to note that the low habitation establishment rate in the fifth millennium BP in the NSW south coast-Sydney, which was present in Hughes and Lampert's (1982: Fig. 6) and Attenbrow's (1987: Fig. 9.4) data sets, still remains despite the increased size of the data set used here. Since the sample includes rockshelters as well as sites in the coastal hinterland, it seems unlikely that this decrease/low rate is due entirely to coastal erosion (cf. Head 1987: 455–8).

In each region, the most dramatic or greatest increase in the habitation establishment rate occurred in the same millennium as the highest habitation establishment rate. However, this did not happen in the same millennium in each region. It was in the first millennium BP (as in the Upper Mangrove Creek catchment, Fig. 6.1B) in two regions (south-eastern Queensland and NSW–ACT–Victorian southern uplands-tablelands, Figs 7.6A and 7.7A), and in the second millennium BP in two regions (NSW south coast-Sydney and south-western Victoria, Figs 7.3A and 7.4B). In the central Queensland highlands, there is no 'highest' rate or 'dramatic' increase (Fig. 7.5A) — two sites were established in four successive millennia from the fifth millennium BP onwards.

Although the highest establishment rates and the greatest increases occurred after 5000 BP, there were also substantial increases in the habitation establishment rates in some regions (e.g., NSW south coast-Sydney) as early as the eighth millennium BP (Tables 7.3 and A4/1).

Changes in the number of habitations used

In the four regions for which the number of habitations used was calculated, the numbers increased during successive millennia (Table 7.3). All major increases occurred in the late-Holocene. There were no decreases, but numbers remained stable in the central Queensland highlands in the second and first millennia BP (Fig. 7.5B).

A.

B.

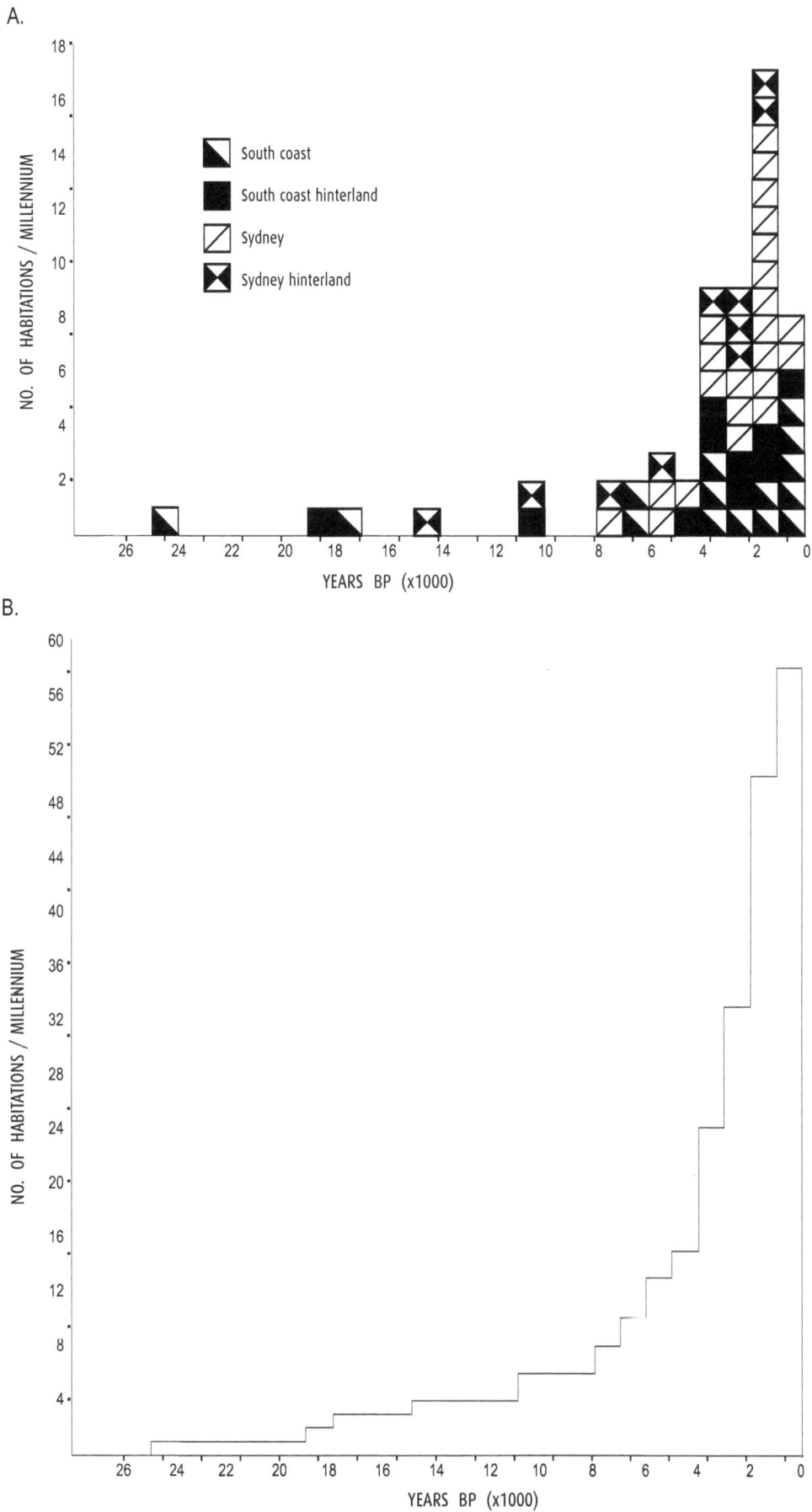

Figure 7.3 NSW south coast and Sydney: (A) Rate of habitation establishment in each millennium. (B) Number of habitations used in each millennium. N = 58, Tables A4/1 and A4/2 have sites included.

A.

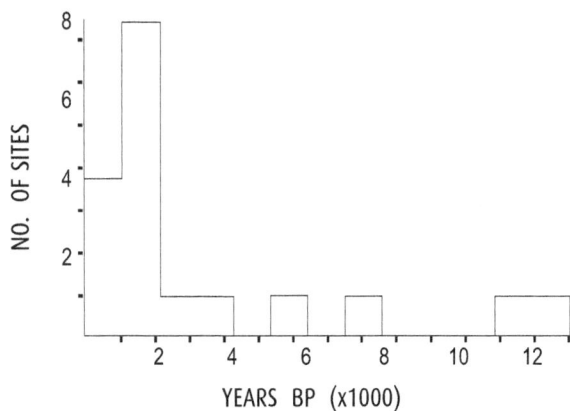

B.

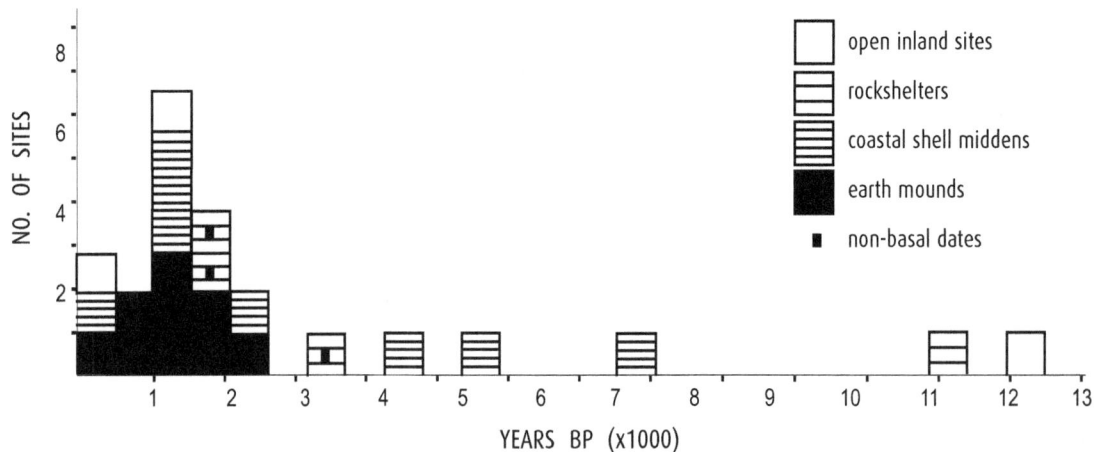

Figure 7.4 South-western Victoria: number of habitations established in each millennium. (A) Redrawn from Lourandos 1983: 86, Fig. 3: basal radiocarbon dates from a sample of 19 archaeological sites. (B) Redrawn from Williams 1988: Fig. 10.1: basal radiocarbon dates from a sample of 25 archaeological sites. Tables A4/3 and A4/4 have sites included; Toolondo drainage system and Werribee burials have been excluded from graphs.

A.

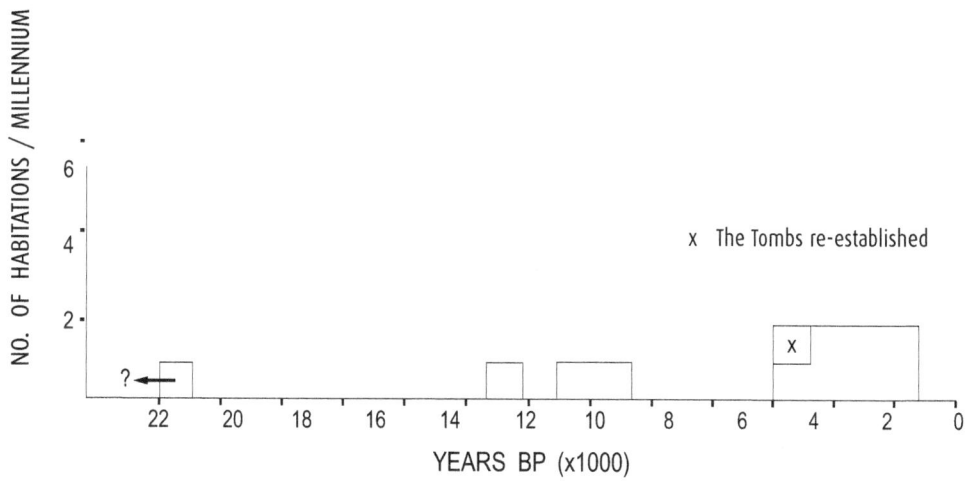

B.

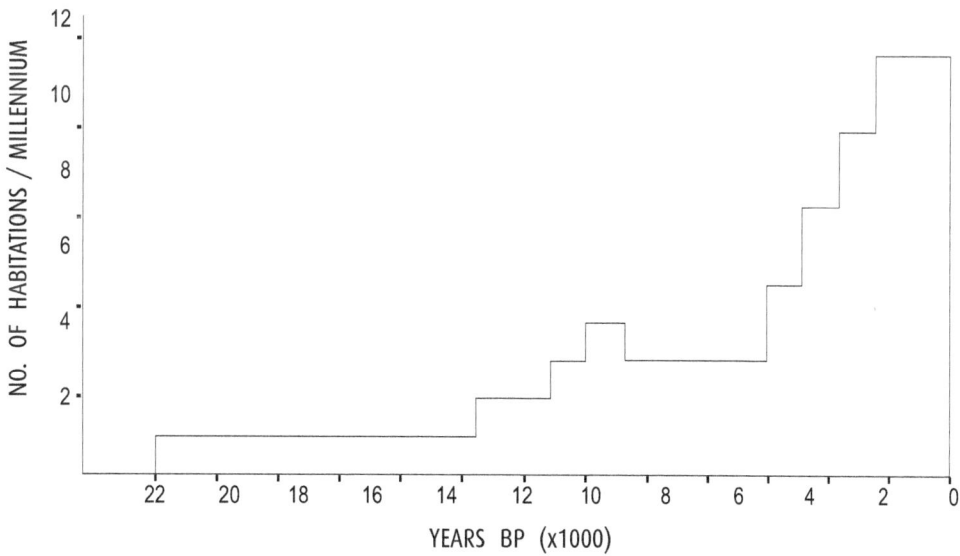

Figure 7.5 Central Queensland highlands: (A) Rate of habitation establishment in each millennium. (B) Number of habitations used in each millennium. N = 11, Table A4/5 and A4/6 have sites included.

A.

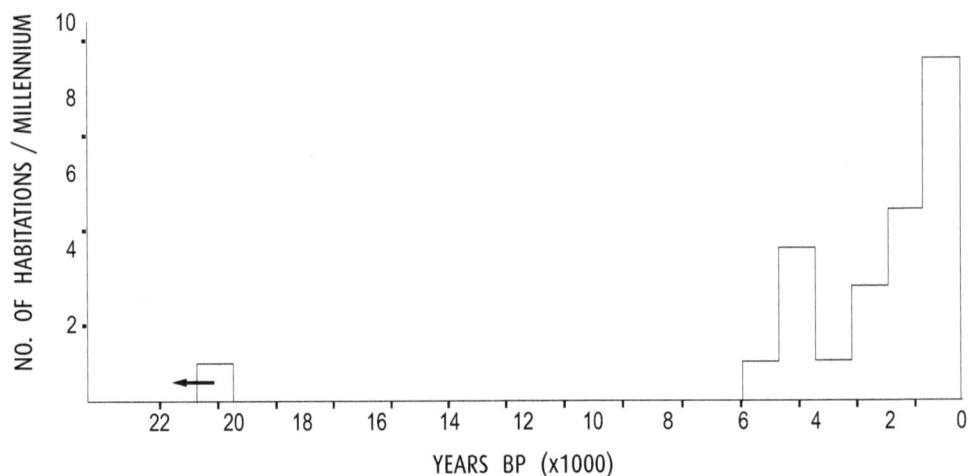

B.

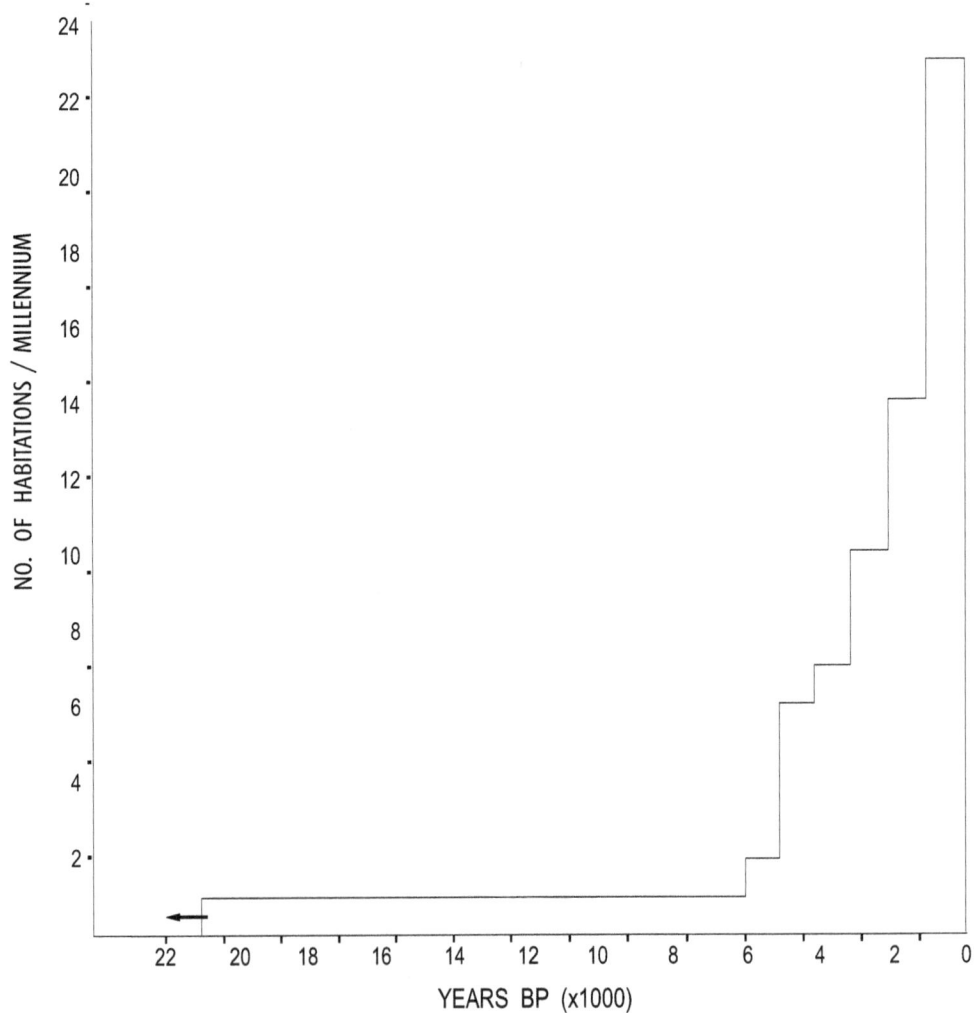

Figure 7.6 South-eastern Queensland: (A) Rate of habitation establishment in each millennium. (B) Number of habitations used in each millennium. N = 23, Tables A4/7 and A4/8 have sites included.

A.

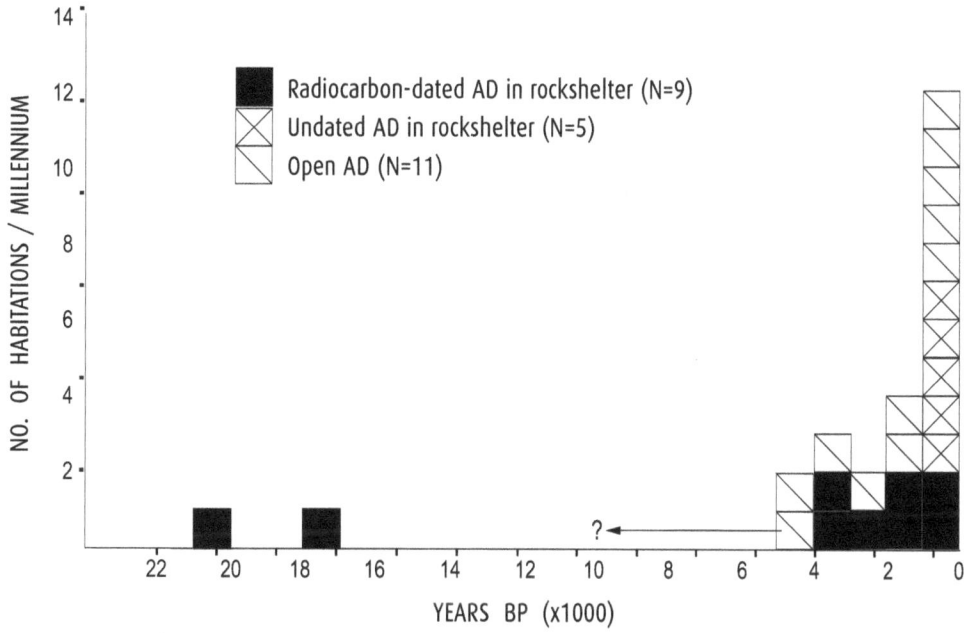

B.

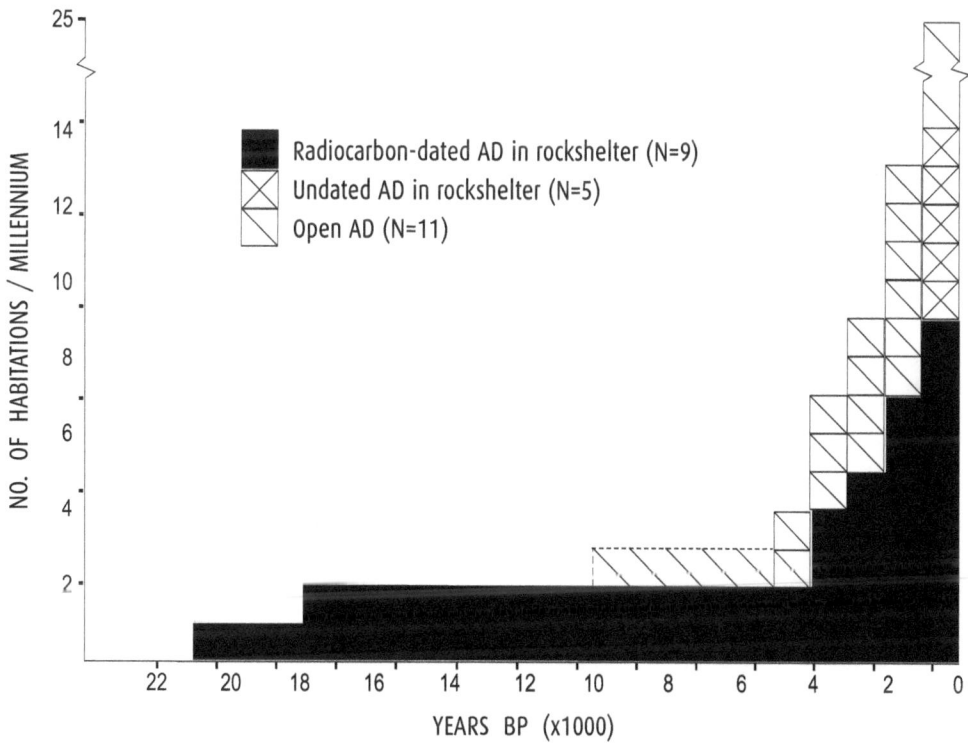

Figure 7.7 NSW–ACT–Victorian southern uplands-tablelands: (A) Rate of habitation establishment in each millennium. (B) Number of habitations used in each millennium. N = 25, Tables A4/9 and A4/10 have sites included.

In the NSW south coast-Sydney, south-eastern Queensland and NSW–ACT–Victorian southern uplands-tablelands, the highest number of habitations used was in the first millennium BP (Figs 7.3B, 7.6B, 7.7B).

In south-eastern Queensland and the NSW–ACT–Victorian southern uplands-tablelands, the greatest increase in the number of habitations used was in the first millennium BP, and in NSW south coast-Sydney it was in the second millennium BP. In the central Queensland highlands, there was a uniform increase (+2) in the fifth, fourth, third and second millennia BP.

Changes in the rate of known-habitation use

For the Victorian Mallee, Ross' data suggest a dramatic increase in the rate of known-habitation use in the southern area during the Late Phase (4500 BP to contact). In the northern area, the Early Phase (ca 12,000 to 6000 BP) rates were similar to (or possibly slightly higher or slightly lower, depending on the method of calculation) than those of the Late Phase (Table 7.3, Fig. 7.8). The timing and nature of the increase in the rate of known-habitation use in the southern Mallee is, however, equivocal (see case study in Appendix 4). Although Ross placed it at ca 4500 BP, it could have been later or spread out over a number of millennia.

The trend in the NSW Hunter Valley, according to Hiscock's (1986) analysis of the Mount Arthur North and South (MANS) sites near Muswellbrook (Fig. 7.9A, Table A4/14), appears to differ from that in other regions. In Hiscock's analysis, the most significant increase in the rate of known-habitation use occurred at a relatively late date (ca 1300 BP) and was followed by a subsequent decrease ca 800 BP; that is, both the initial increase and the subsequent decrease occurred within the last 1500 years. However, depending on when the habitations were used and how the dates are used, the trend in Hiscock's figures could be seen as a substantial increase in the second millennium BP and a decrease in the first millennium BP.

In contrast with Hiscock's figures, trends based on recent radiocarbon dates from sites in the Singleton area suggest a continuing, relatively steady increase in the rate of known-habitation use over the last 4000 years (Fig. 7.9B, Tables 7.3, A4/15 and A4/16).

Changes in the growth rates for habitation indices

Growth rates for habitation establishment rates of the late-Pleistocene and the first half of the Holocene were not calculated because of the low frequency at which habitations were established in all regions (Tables 7.4 and 7.6). However, data on the number of habitations used (Table 7.5) suggest that in most regions the trend in the growth rates altered substantially during the early Holocene, and that changes in the last 2000 years were part of this longer term trend. The following analyses exclude situations in which a twofold increase represents an increase from one to two sites.

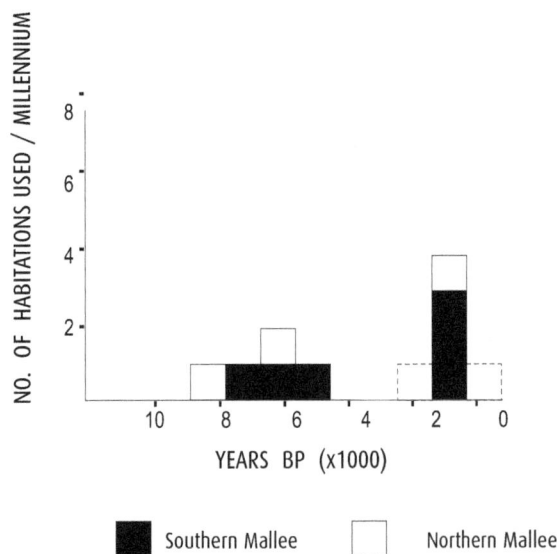

Figure 7.8 The Mallee, north-western Victoria: rate of known-habitation use in each millennium based on radiometrically dated sites, which were assigned to a millennium on the basis of calibrated radiocarbon dates and TL dates. N = 9, Table A4/11 has sites included.

A.

B.

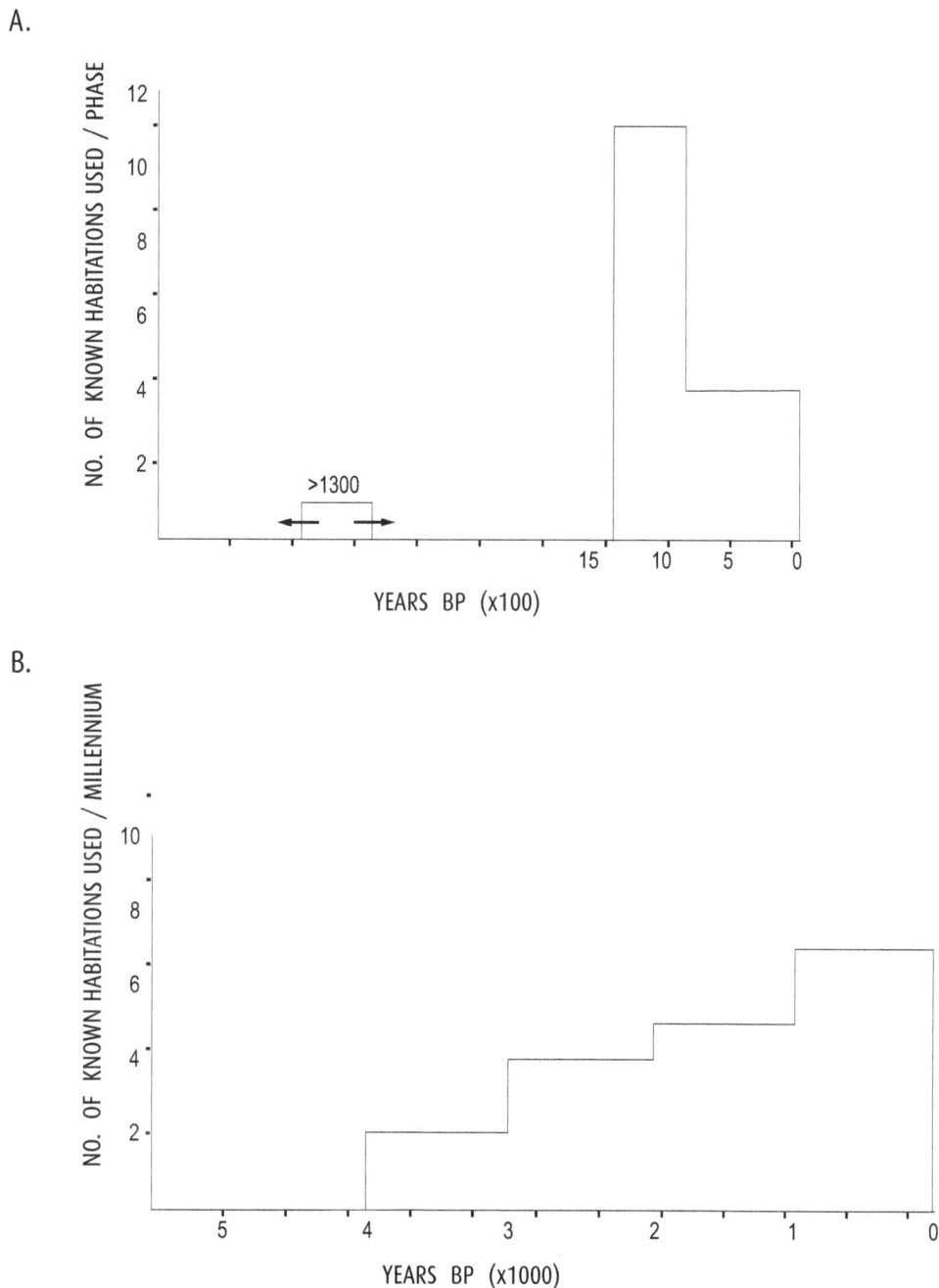

Figure 7.9 NSW Hunter Valley: number of habitations known to be used. (A) Mount Arthur North and South, Muswellbrook. N = 15. (B) Central lowlands (Singleton area). N = 12. Tables A4/14 and A4/15 have sites included.

Habitation establishment rates: Changes in the millennial growth rates varied regionally (Table 7.4). The increases ranged between +50% (×1.5) and +450% (×5.5) and the decreases between -33% p.a. (×0.7) and -100% p.a. (×0), although periods of zero growth (stability, 0%, ×1) were also recorded. The highest millennial growth rate did not occur in the same millennium in every region: fifth millennium BP in south-eastern Queensland, fourth millennium BP in NSW south coast-Sydney, second millennium BP in south-western Victoria, and first millennium BP in NSW–ACT–Victorian southern uplands-tablelands. In three of the five regions, the growth rates decreased with negative rates in the first millennium BP.

Table 7.4 Regions in eastern Australia. Millennial growth rates for rates of habitation establishment. *Italics* indicates highest millennial growth rates in sequence, except where a twofold increase represents an increase from one site to two sites; # – millennium in which first habitation established (the earliest millennium for which evidence is presently documented); ^^ – millennium after which habitations are established in every millennium thereafter.

MILLENNIUM BP	REGIONS											
	UMCC		NSW SC-S		SW VIC		CQH		SEQ		NSW SU-T	
	X	%	X	%	X	%	X	%	X	%	X	%
25th			#									
24th												
23rd												
22nd							#					
21st									#			
20th												
19th												
18th											#	
17th												
16th												
15th												
14th												
13th					#							
12th	#											
11th												
10th												
9th												
8th			^^									
7th	^^		1.0	0								
6th	1	0	1.5	-50	^^				^^			
5th	1	0	0.7	-33	1.0	0	^^		*4.0*	*+300*		
4th	2	+100	*4.5*	*+350*	1.0	0	*1*	*0*	0.3	-75	^^	
3rd	1	0	1.0	+0	2.0	+100	*1*	*0*	3.0	+200	0.5	-50
2nd	*3.5*	*+250*	1.9	+89	*5.5*	*+450*	*1*	*0*	1.7	+67	2.0	+100
1st	2	+100	0.5	-53	0.5	-55	0	-100	1.8	+80	*3.5*	*+250*

Average annual growth rates ranged between +0.04% and +0.17% p.a. for the increases and from -0.04% to -0.14% p.a. for the decreases (Table 7.6). All regions, except the central Queensland highlands, had millennia in which the average annual growth rate was >0.1%, but no region had rates greater than 0.5%. In some regions, there were periods of zero growth (stability) over two millennia.

Number of habitations used: The highest millennial growth rate was +200% (×3) (Table 7.5). The highest growth rates in each region were not restricted to a particular millennium, though they were all within the last 5000 years: the fifth millennium BP for central Queensland highlands and south-eastern Queensland, fourth millennium BP for NSW south coast-Sydney, and the fourth and first for NSW–ACT–Victorian southern uplands-tablelands. Millennial growth rates for increases in the number of habitations used range from +12% (×1.1) to +200% (×3). In many periods, there was zero growth, particularly in the earlier millennia of a sequence. A negative growth rate is recorded only once — in the central Queensland highlands in the ninth millennium BP (-25%, ×0.8). In south-eastern Queensland, the growth rates for the number of habitations used fluctuated slightly in each of the last four millennia, and, although there was an increase in the last 1000 years, the growth rate did not reach that of the fifth millennium BP (Table 7.5).

Table 7.5 Regions in eastern Australia. Millennial growth rates for number of habitations used, and for NSW Hunter Valley known-habitation use. *Italics* indicates highest millennial growth rates in sequence, except where a twofold increase represents an increase from one to two habitations.

MILLENNIUM BP	UMCC		NSW SC-S		CQH		SEQ		NSW SU-T		HV[SING]		HV[MANS]	
	X	%	X	%	X	%	X	%	X	%	X	%	X	%
25th			1.0											
24th			1.0	0										
23rd			1.0	0										
22nd			1.0	0	1.0									
21st			1.0	0	1.0	0	1.0		1.0					
20th			1.0	0	1.0	0	1.0	0	1.0	0				
19th			2.0	+100	1.0	0	1.0	0	1.0	0				
18th			1.5	+50	1.0	0	1.0	0	2.0	+100				
17th			1.0	0	1.0	0	1.0	0	1.0	0				
16th			1.0	0	1.0	0	1.0	0	1.0	0				
15th			1.3	+33	1.0	0	1.0	0	1.0	0				
14th			1.0	0	1.0	0	1.0	0	1.0	0				
13th			1.0	0	2.0	+100	1.0	0	1.0	0				
12th		1	1.0	0	1.0	0	1.0	0	1.0	0				
11th	1.0	0	1.5	+50	1.5	+50	1.0	0	1.0	0				
10th	1.0	0	1.0	0	1.3	+33	1.0	0	1.0	0				
9th	2.0	+100	1.0	0	0.8	-25	1.0	0	1.0	0				
8th	1.0	0	1.3	+33	1.0	0	1.0	0	1.0	0				
7th	1.5	+50	1.3	+25	1.0	0	1.0	0	1.0	0				
6th	1.3	+33	1.3	+30	1.0	0	2.0	+100	1.0	0				
5th	1.3	+25	1.2	+15	*1.7*	*+70*	*3.0*	*+200*	1.0	0				
4th	1.4	+40	*1.6*	*+60*	1.4	+40	1.2	+17	*2.0*	*+100*				
3rd	1.3	+29	1.4	+38	1.3	+30	1.4	+43	1.3	+25	*2.0*	*+100*		
2nd	1.8	+78	1.5	+48	1.2	+22	1.4	+40	1.4	+40	1.3	+30	?	?
1st	*1.8*	*+81*	1.1	+12	1	0	1.6	+64	*2.0*	*+100*	1.4	+40	*0.3*	*-74*

Table 7.6 Regions in eastern Australia. Average annual growth rates (excluding 0% p.a. growth rates) for habitation establishment rates. ^^ – indicates millennium after which habitations were established in each successive millennium; *italics* – highest growth rates in sequence, except where a twofold increase represents an increase from one to two habitations.

MILLENNIUM BP	UMCC %	NSW SC-S %	SW VIC %	CQH %	SEQ %	NSW SU-T %
8th		^^				
7th	^^					
6th		+0.04	^^		^^	
5th		-0.04		^^	*+0.14*	
4th	+0.07	*+0.15*			-0.14	^^
3rd	0.00	0	+0.07		+0.11	-0.07
2nd	*+0.13*	+0.06	*+0.17*		+0.05	+0.07
1st	+0.07	-0.08	-0.08	-100	+0.05	*+0.13*

The millennial growth rate for the first millennium BP was lower than that of the second millennium BP in the NSW south coast-Sydney and central Queensland highlands. Decreases of similar magnitude occurred in the growth rates in earlier periods in some regions. It is thus not possible to say whether the decreases in the last 1000 years represent the beginning of what may have been a long-term cumulative decrease or are simply part of an 'unfinished' fluctuation.

Average annual growth rates for the number of habitations used ranged from +0.01% to +0.11% p.a. for the increases, with -0.03% p.a. for the only negative growth rate, which was in the ninth millennium BP in the central Queensland highlands (Table 7.7). Only one region had an average annual growth rate of >0.1%.

Rate of known-habitation use: Millennial and average annual growth rates for the rates of known-habitation use were calculated only for the NSW Hunter Valley. For Hiscock's (1986) MANS model, where the length of the pre-Bondaian phase is not known, the millennial growth rate (×0.26) and the average annual growth rate (-0.19% p.a.) for the most recent phase are well below those calculated for the number of habitations used/millennium in other regions (Tables 7.5 and 7.7). For the radiometrically dated sample of Singleton habitations, the millennial growth rates (×1.3 to ×2) and average annual growth rates (+0.02% to +0.07%) are similar to those of other regions.

Table 7.7   Regions in eastern Australia. Average annual growth rates (excluding 0% p.a. growth rates) for number of habitations used, and for NSW Hunter Valley known-habitation use. *Italics* indicates highest growth rates in sequence, except where a twofold increase represents an increase from one site to two sites; # – millennium in which habitations were first established.

MILLENNIUM BP	REGIONS						
	UMCC %	NSW SC-S %	CQH %	SEQ %	NSW SU-T %	HV[SING] %	HV[MANS] %
25th		#					
22nd			#				
21st				#	#		
20th							
19th		+0.07					
18th		+0.04			+0.07		
17th							
16th							
15th		+0.03					
14th							
13th			+0.07				
12th	#						
11th		+0.04	+0.04				
10th			+0.03				
9th	+0.07		−0.03				
8th		+0.03					
7th	+0.04	+0.02					
6th	+0.03	+0.03		+0.07			
5th	+0.02	+0.01	*+0.05*	*+0.11*			
4th	+0.03	*+0.05*	+0.03	+0.02	*+0.07*	#	#?
3rd	+0.03	+0.03	+0.03	+0.04	+0.02	*+0.07*	
2nd	*+0.06*	+0.04	+0.02	+0.03	+0.03	+0.02	?
1st	*+0.06*	+0.01		+0.05	*+0.07*	+0.03	−0.19

Changes in the artefact accumulation rates

Variations in the rate at which artefacts accumulated over time were the subject of attention in the early 1980s, particularly in discussions on variations in the 'intensity of site use' (Hughes and Djohadze 1980; Hiscock 1981, 1986; Smith 1982; Morwood 1981, 1984). For this review, I examine changes in the artefact accumulation rates at several sites in eastern Australia to ascertain whether:

1.   decreased artefact accumulation rates occurred in the uppermost levels of archaeological deposits, and the timing of such decreases;

2.   dramatic increases occurred in the artefact accumulation rates, and the timing of such increases; and,

3.   the growth rates in this index changed dramatically over time, as did the magnitude of such changes.

For many excavated sites, insufficient information is available with which to calculate the artefact accumulation rates for each level/spit, which requires the use of depth/age curves (see Chapters 5 and 6 for method of calculation and limits). Data for 31 sites from seven

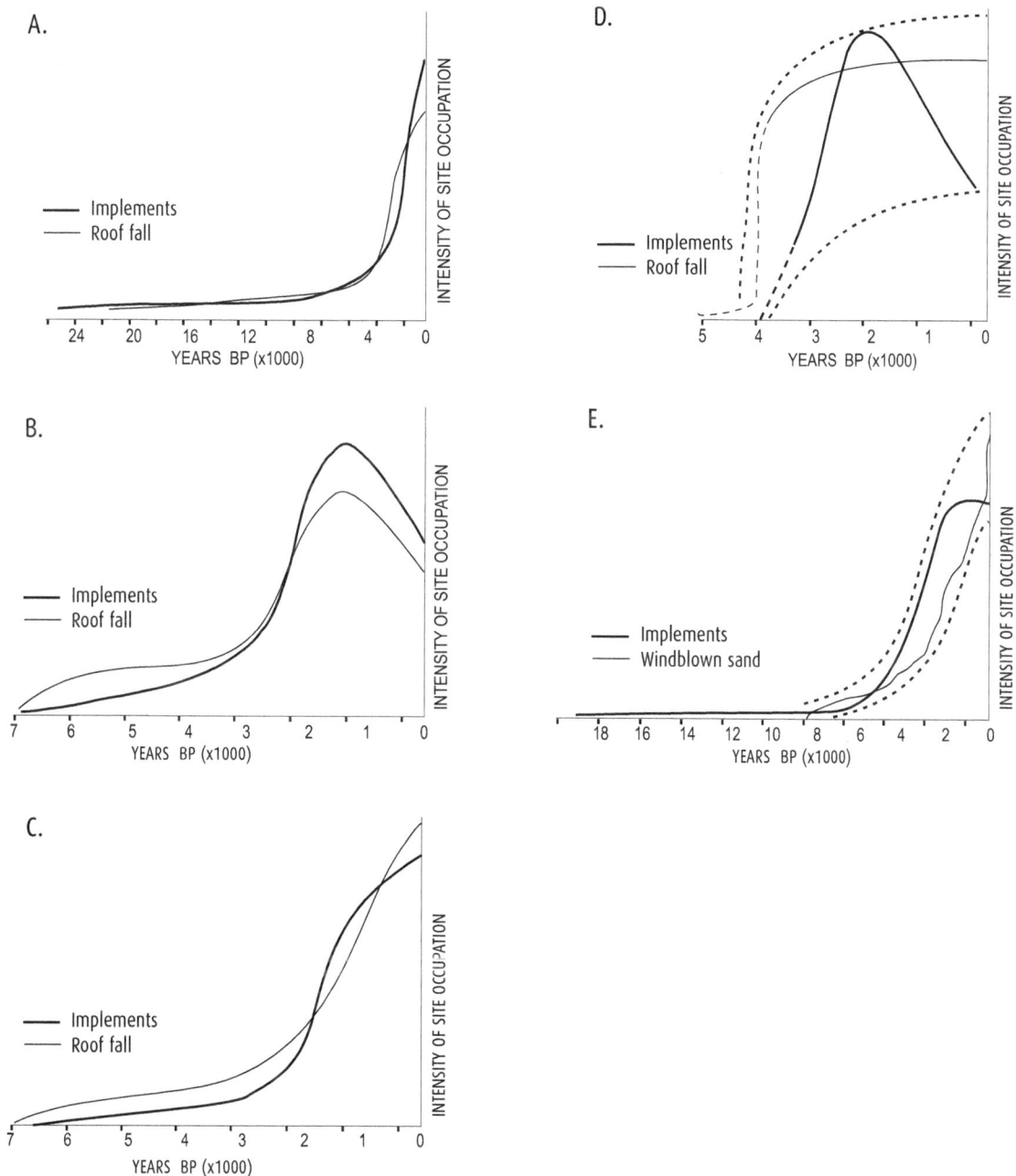

Figure 7.10 NSW south coast: (A) Burrill Lake, (B) Currarong 1, (C) Currarong 2, (D) Sassafras and (E) Bass Point. Redrawn from Hughes and Lampert 1982: Figs 1 to 5.

NO. OF ARTEFACTS / MILLENNIUM (x100)

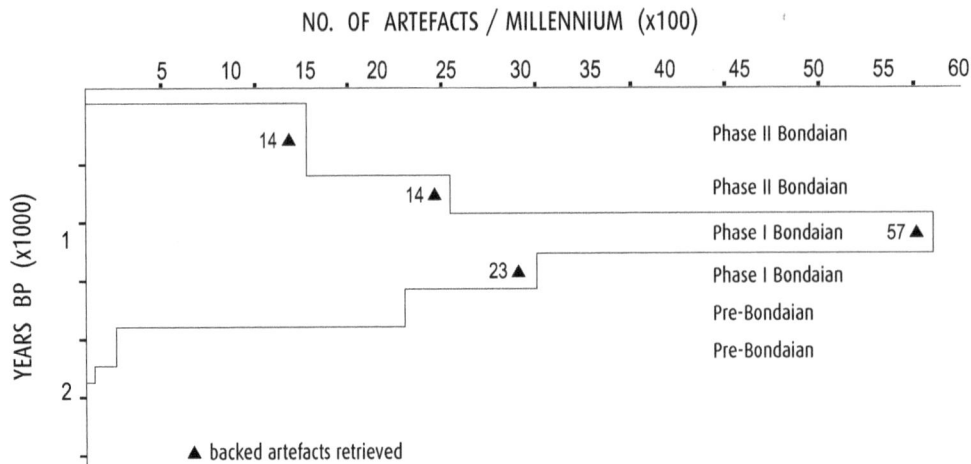

Figure 7.11 Sandy Hollow, NSW Hunter Valley: rates of artefact accumulation (number per millennium). Table A4/22 has details. Phases after Hiscock 1986.

regions in eastern Australia were examined (Table 7.2, Figs 7.2, 7.10 to 7.29). For 24 of these sites, data are summarised in Figure 7.30. Fuller details about the archaeological evidence at each of these sites and the artefact accumulation rates are provided in Appendix 4.

Artefact accumulation rates for the Upper Mangrove Creek catchment (for the catchment as a whole and individual archaeological deposits) are based on the estimated total number of artefacts accumulated in each phase and millennium in each archaeological deposit. However, for the sites included in this review, artefact accumulation rates based on excavated assemblages were not extrapolated to the whole deposit since only the trends for regions and individual sites were being compared, not the 'actual' rates. Variations in the area of each spit or level were taken into account, or, where nothing to the contrary was stated in the published reports, the area was assumed to be constant or that any variations were of such small magnitude that the results were not overly distorted. The accumulation rates are based on artefact numbers, except for the NSW south coast-Sydney sites, where implement numbers were used in the 1982 Hughes and Lampert study; for these sites, accumulation rates for total numbers of artefacts may differ.

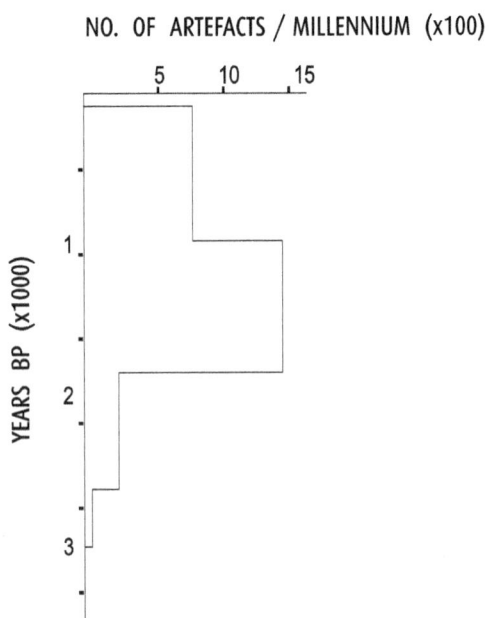

NO. OF ARTEFACTS / MILLENNIUM (x100)

Figure 7.12 Milbrodale, NSW Hunter Valley: rates of artefact accumulation (number per millennium). Table A4/23 has details.

NO. OF ARTEFACTS / MILLENNIUM (x100)

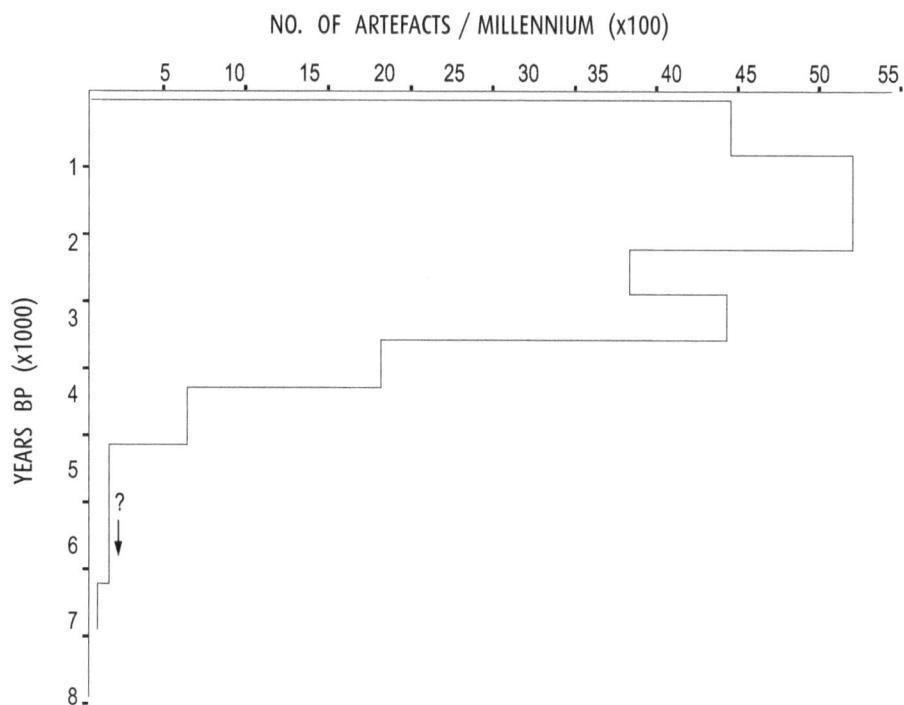

Figure 7.13 Bobadeen, Ulan, upper Goulburn River, NSW: rates of artefact accumulation (number per millennium). Table A4/24 has details.

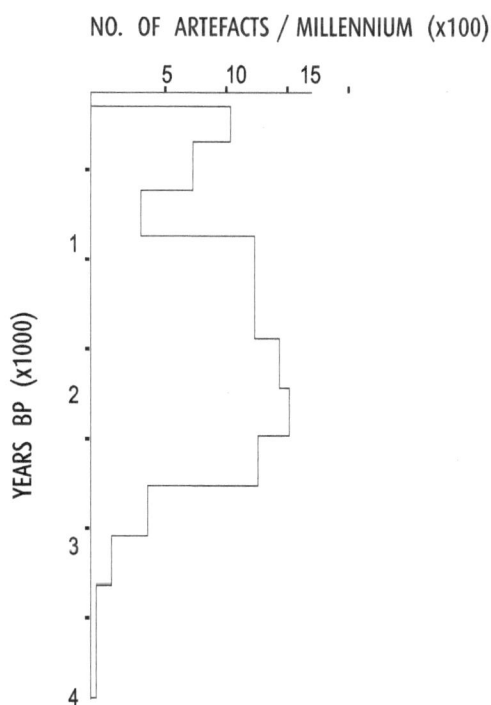

NO. OF ARTEFACTS / MILLENNIUM (x100)

NO. OF ARTEFACTS / MILLENNIUM (x100)

Figure 7.14 Big L, NSW Hunter Valley (southern rim): rates of artefact accumulation (number per millennium). Table A4/25 has details.

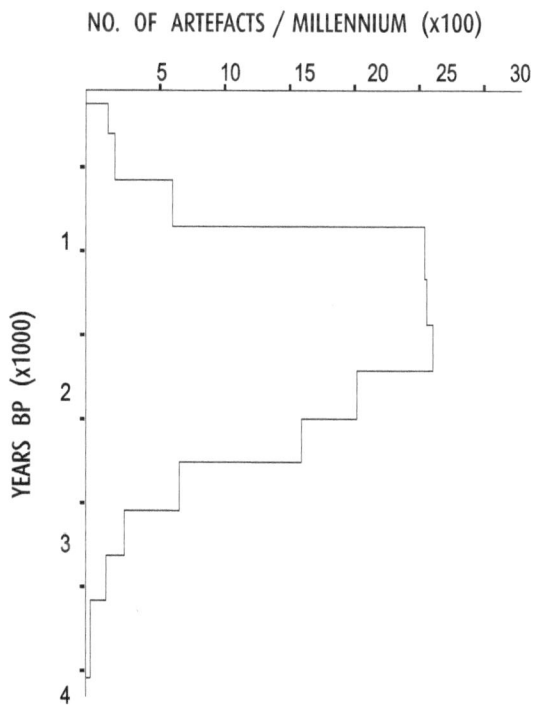

Figure 7.15 Yango Creek, NSW Hunter Valley (southern rim): rates of artefact accumulation (number per millennium). Table A4/26 has details.

NO. OF ARTEFACTS / MILLENNIUM (x1000)

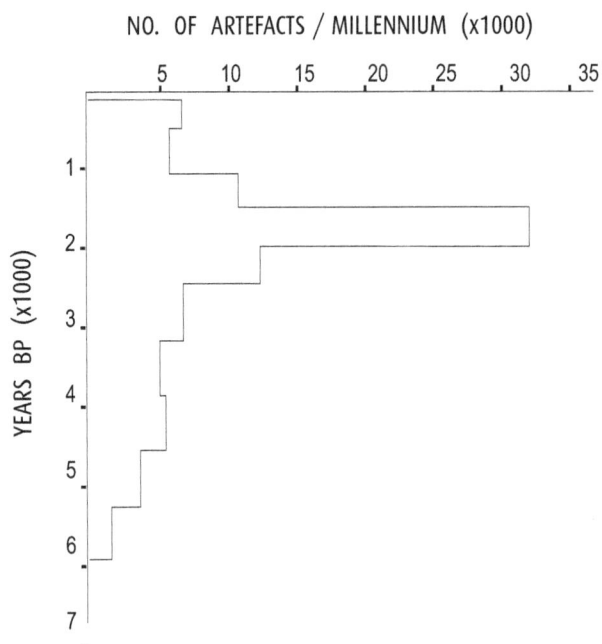

Figure 7.16 Macdonald River, NSW: rates of artefact accumulation (number per millennium). Table A4/27 has details.

Only the density or concentration of artefacts in each spit or level (usually expressed as the number of artefacts per cubic metre or kilogram of deposit) was provided for some sites. In most sites reviewed below, where I have calculated artefact accumulation rates, the rates tend to follow the same trend as the density figures; that is, increases and decreases in density figures occur in the same spits or levels in which increases and decreases occur in the rate of accumulation. However, there are cases where they do not coincide, for example, Springwood Creek. For a few sites, where artefact accumulation rates or data on which to calculate artefact accumulation rates were not available, I used density figures; for example, Shaws Creek K1 and K2, Capertee 1 and 3. Sediment accumulation rates in these sites may not have been constant over time, and thus these figures may not equate to artefact accumulation rates. However, they were included in order to increase the size of the data sets for some regions.

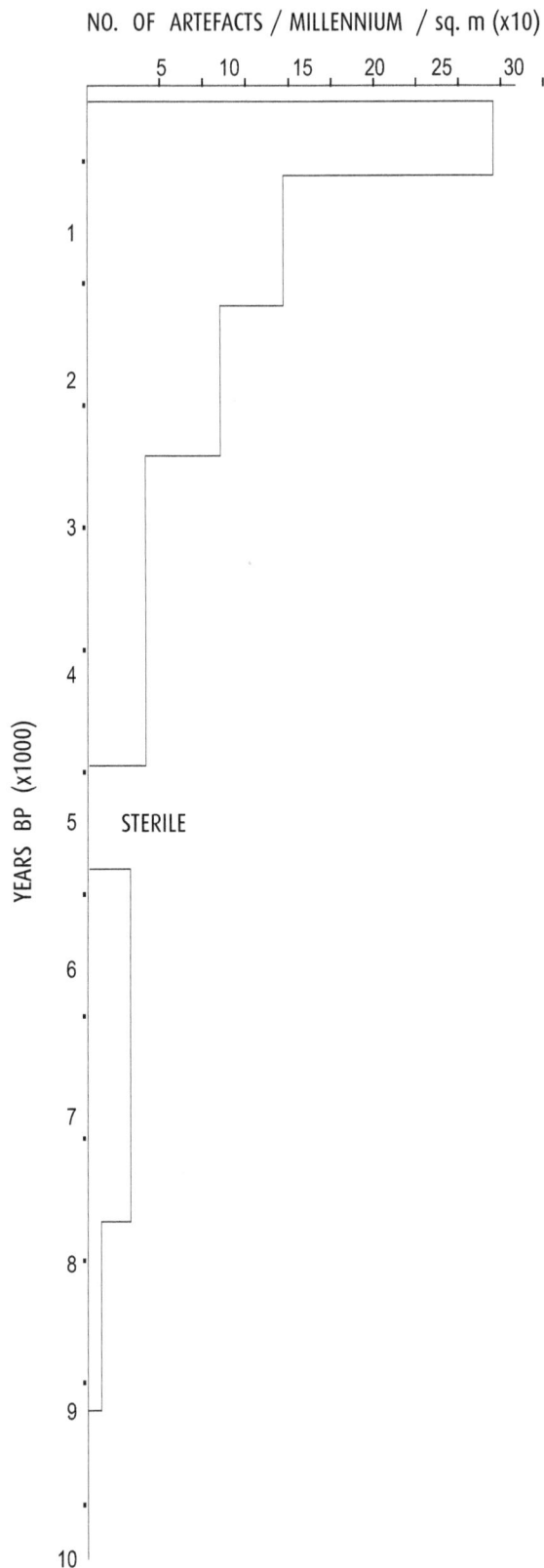

NO. OF ARTEFACTS / MILLENNIUM / sq. m (x10)

Figure 7.17 Springwood Creek, NSW Blue Mountains: rates of artefact accumulation (number per millennium). Table A4/28 has details.

NO. OF ARTEFACTS / MILLENNIUM (x100)

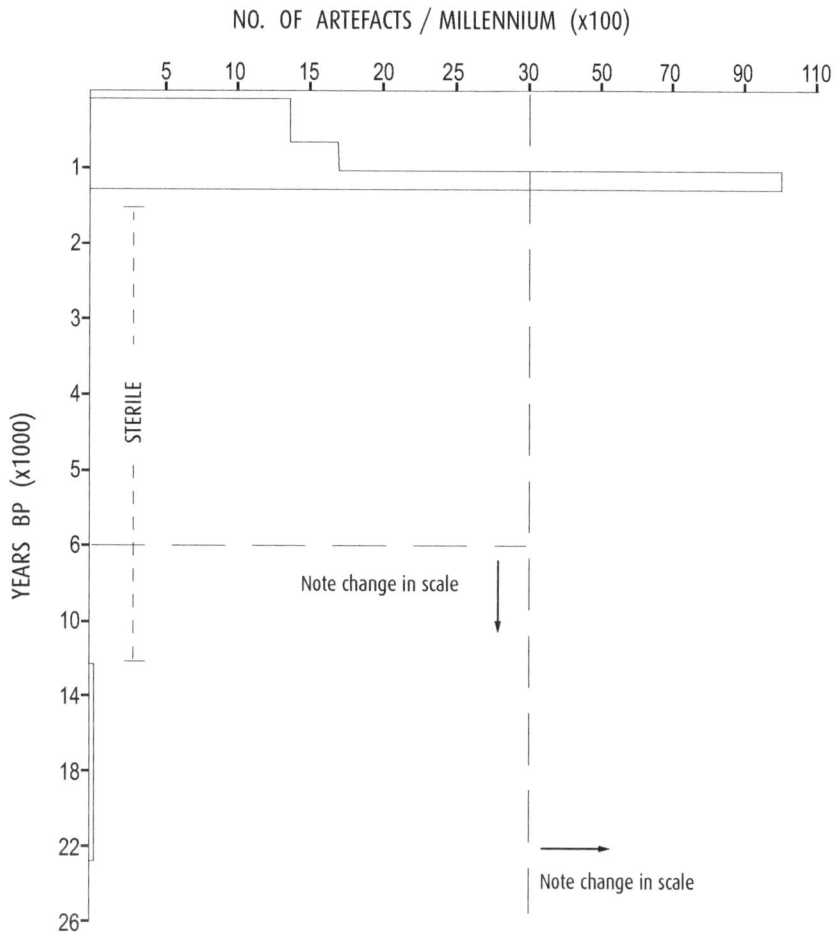

Figure 7.18 Kings Tableland, NSW Blue Mountains: rates of artefact accumulation (number per millennium). Table A4/29 has details.

Growth rates, standardised as average annual growth rates, are calculated for those sites where artefact accumulation rates are presented. The growth rates are calculated for each spit/level, except for the earlier levels at some sites where dating is equivocal and/or sterile layers exist.

Dramatic decreases in artefact accumulation rates

All regions have habitation sites with decreased artefact accumulation rates or densities in their most recent levels (Fig. 7.30, Table 7.8). In a majority of the sites (65%), the artefact accumulation rates in the most recent level/s are lower than those in earlier late-Holocene levels. Decreasing accumulation rates in the uppermost levels of habitation sites are a widespread and common trend, though their existence was overlooked in many 1970s and 1980s interpretations and explanations of the Holocene archaeological record.

The greatest or most dramatic decrease in artefact accumulation rates (or densities) occurred more frequently in the first millennium BP (excluding those associated with sterile layers), but at some sites it occurred in the second, third or fourth millennium BP.

Dramatic increases in artefact accumulation rates

In all 31 sites, the highest artefact accumulation rates occurred in the latter half of the Holocene (Figs 7.10 to 7.29; Tables A4/17 to A4/42; summarised in Fig. 7.30). However, very

Table 7.8 Regions in eastern Australia. Number of habitations and direction of change in artefact accumulation rates in the most recent/upper levels of habitations in each region (+1 indicates habitations with an increasing trend but not highest rate in sequence), based on Tables A4/17 to A4/42.

REGION	DIRECTION OF CHANGE IN ARTEFACT ACCUMULATION RATES IN UPPER LEVELS				TOTAL NUMBER OF SITES
	DECREASE	INCREASE	STABLE	UNCERTAIN	
NSW south coast-Sydney	2	2	1		5
NSW Hunter Valley	5 +1				6
Blue Mountains and adjacent areas	4 +1	1	1		7
South-western Victoria	1	1			2
Lower Murray Valley	2			1	3
Central Queensland highlands	3 +1				4
South-eastern Queensland	2 +1	1			4
Total number of sites	19 +4	5	2	1	31

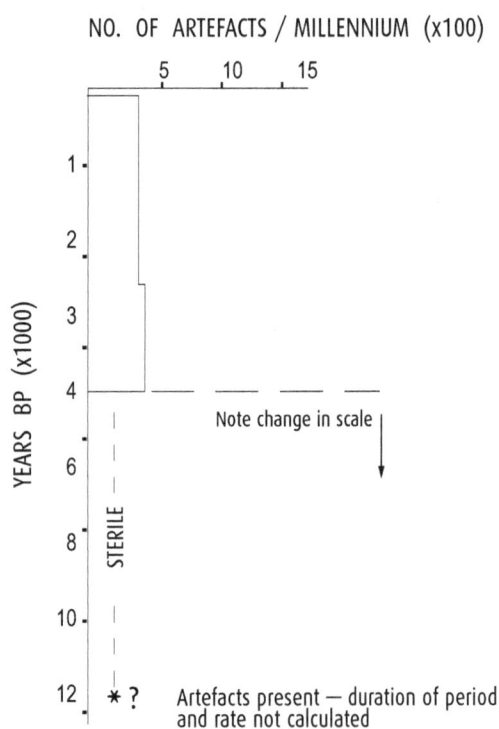

Figure 7.19 Walls Cave, NSW Blue Mountains: rates of artefact accumulation (number per millennium). Table A4/30 has details.

few sites had their highest artefact accumulation rates in the most recent uppermost levels (e.g., Burrill Lake, Currarong 2, Springwood: Figs 7.10A, 7.10C and 7.17 respectively). Two sites had stable or slightly decreasing rates/densities (Bass Point, Walls Cave: Figs 7.10E and 7.19), and another four had fluctuating rates in their upper levels. So, although there was an increase in the uppermost level/s, the highest rates occurred in an earlier period (marked as +1 on Table 7.8). High artefact accumulation rates were usually associated with dramatic or substantial increases and decreases in artefact numbers.

At all sites, the most dramatic increase in the artefact accumulation rates occurred in the latter half of the Holocene, usually after 4000 BP, though the timing of these dramatic changes varied at individual sites. For example, at Kenniff Cave, it began in the latter part of the sixth millennium BP, and at Macdonald River at the end of the fifth millennium BP; at nine sites it was in the fourth millennium BP, and at five in the third and at five (possibly six) in the second millennium BP. At only one site, the most dramatic increase occurred in the first millennium BP (Springwood Creek).

At sites where initial habitation began in the early-Holocene or late-Pleistocene, artefact accumulation rates were initially low but gradually increased over time. Minor fluctuations occurred during this period in some sites and in a few there were substantial peaks in the artefact accumulation rates or artefact concentrations as at Loggers in the catchment — for example, at Capertee 3, Shaws Creek K2, Native Well 1 and Kenniff Cave (Figs 7.20, 7.22, 7.24 and 7.26 respectively).

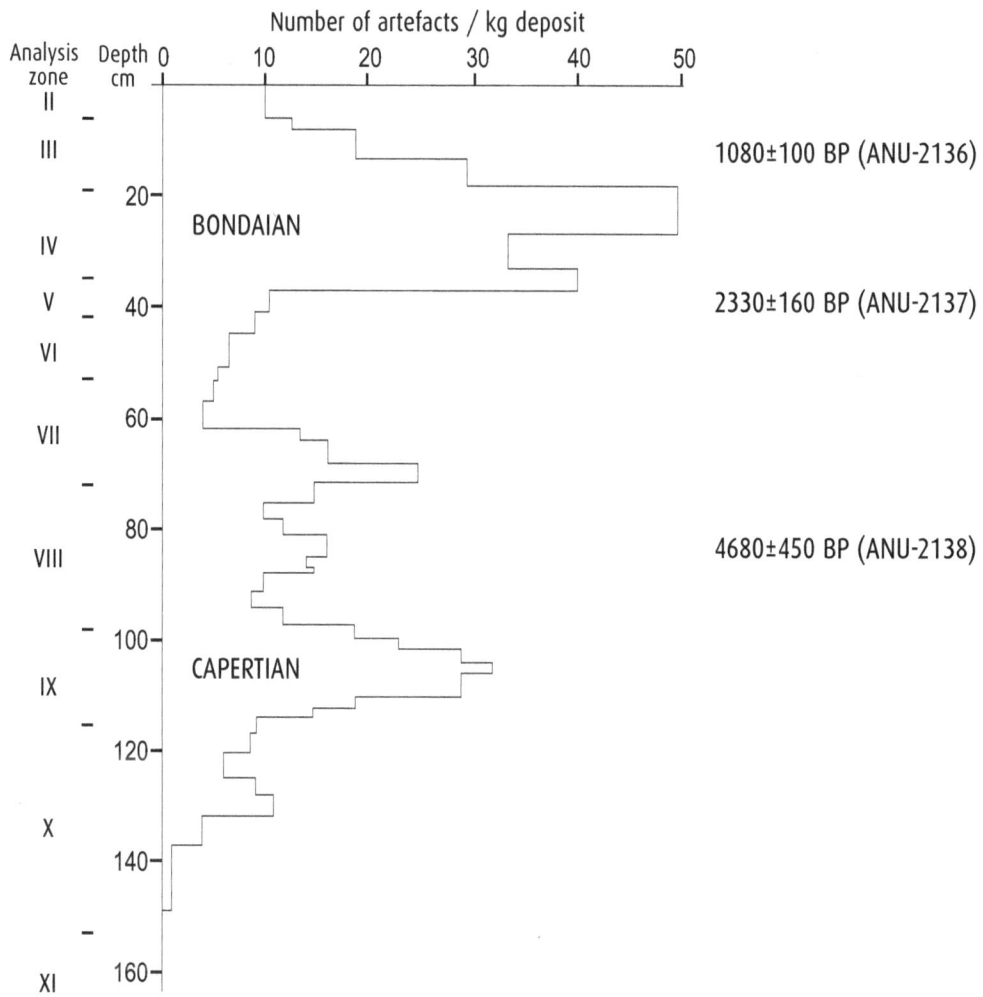

Figure 7.20 Capertee 3 (Square Q13), Capertee Valley, NSW: density of artefacts in each level (number per kilo of deposit). Redrawn from Johnson 1979: Fig. 35.

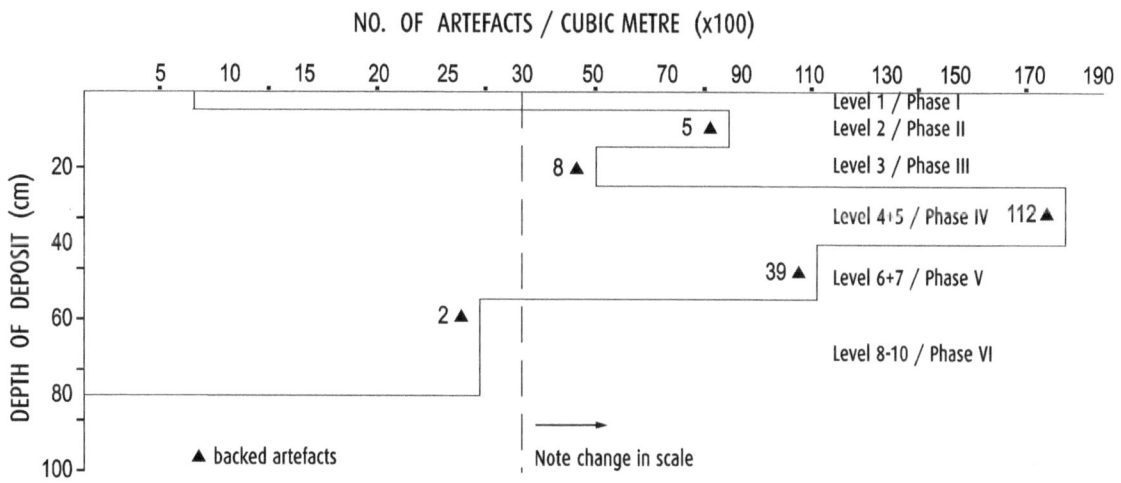

Figure 7.21 Shaws Creek K1, NSW: density of artefacts in each level (number per cubic metre). Table A4/31 has details.

NO. OF ARTEFACTS / CUBIC METRE (x100)

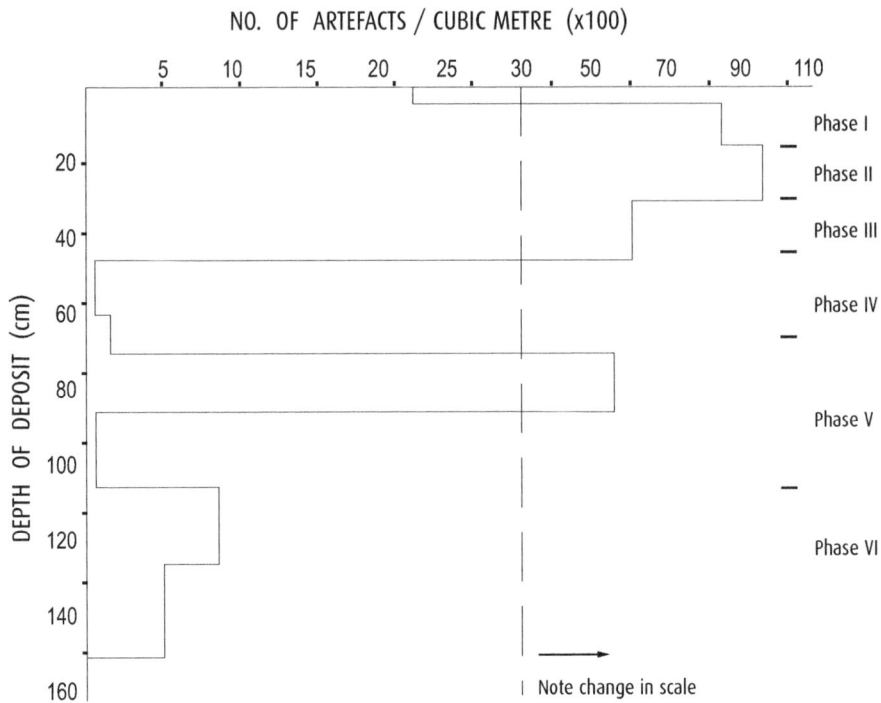

Figure 7.22 Shaws Creek K2 (Square A), NSW: density of artefacts in each level (number per cubic metre). Table A4/32 has details.

Average annual growth rates for the artefact accumulation rates

Average annual growth rates for the artefact accumulation rates, which were calculated for 22 habitation sites, varied widely (Appendix 4, Tables A4/17 to A4/42). The positive values ranged from +0.01% to +3.45%, with most (84%) less than +0.5%. However, most habitations had one or more levels in which the growth rate was +0.1% p.a. or greater. Negative growth rates occurred at many habitations, particularly in the most recent upper level/s. They ranged from -0.003% to -1.98%, with most (88%) less than -0.5%.

The highest growth rates usually occurred during the latter half of the Holocene. However, they were not restricted to any particular millennium — at four sites, they began in the fifth millennium BP, at seven in the fourth millennium BP, at four in the third, four in the second and one in the first millennium BP. At some sites the highest rates continued into the next millennium. Still, figures for Kenniff Cave, where the period with the highest growth rate began at the end of the sixth millennium BP (Table A4/39), and Native Well 1, which also had high growth rates in the early Holocene (Table A4/37), suggest substantial change was not restricted to the latter half of the Holocene. High artefact concentrations at Shaws Creek K2 and Capertee 3 in the 13th and seventh millennia BP respectively may also reflect high rates of accumulation and may be associated with high growth rates.

In general, high average annual growth rates are associated with the highest artefact accumulation rates and dramatic increases in the accumulation rates. However, the trend towards higher artefact accumulation rates did not always begin with a dramatic increase in the rates or with the highest growth rate, and the most dramatic increase in the artefact accumulation rates was not always associated with the highest growth rate.

For the artefact accumulation rates, the duration of a particular growth rate is influenced by factors such as the rate of sediment accumulation, the depth of individual excavation units, and, in particular, the estimated length of time over which a spit/level accumulated and the analytical methods used in specific studies to portray change over time.

NO. OF ARTEFACTS / MILLENNIUM (x100)

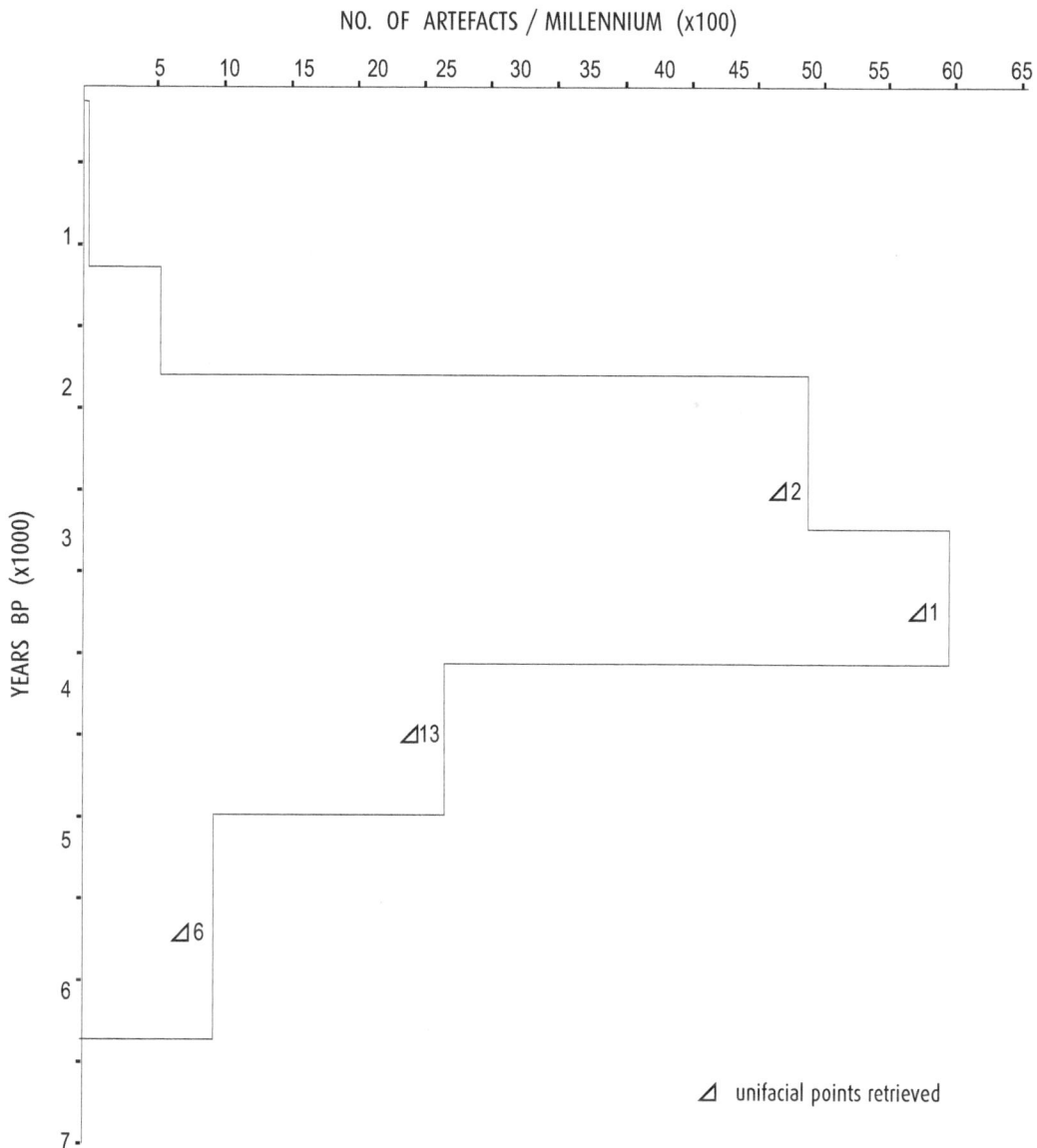

Figure 7.23 Devon Downs, lower Murray Valley, South Australia: rates of artefact accumulation (number per millennium). Table A4/34 has details.

For example, the two extremes are Hughes and Lampert's study, in which rates were presented for stratigraphic units which accumulated over periods in excess of 1000 years (Tables A4/17 to A4/21), and Gatton, for which the period of accumulation for many spits is calculated as 55 years (Table A4/42). Such factors have not been taken into account or explored in this review.

Relationships between the habitation indices and the artefact accumulation rates: directions and timing

For only five of the regions reviewed are both habitation indices and artefact accumulation rates for individual sites available: NSW south coast-Sydney, NSW Hunter Valley, central Queensland highlands, south-eastern Queensland, and south-western Victoria. In these regions, trends in the habitation indices and artefact accumulation rates at individual

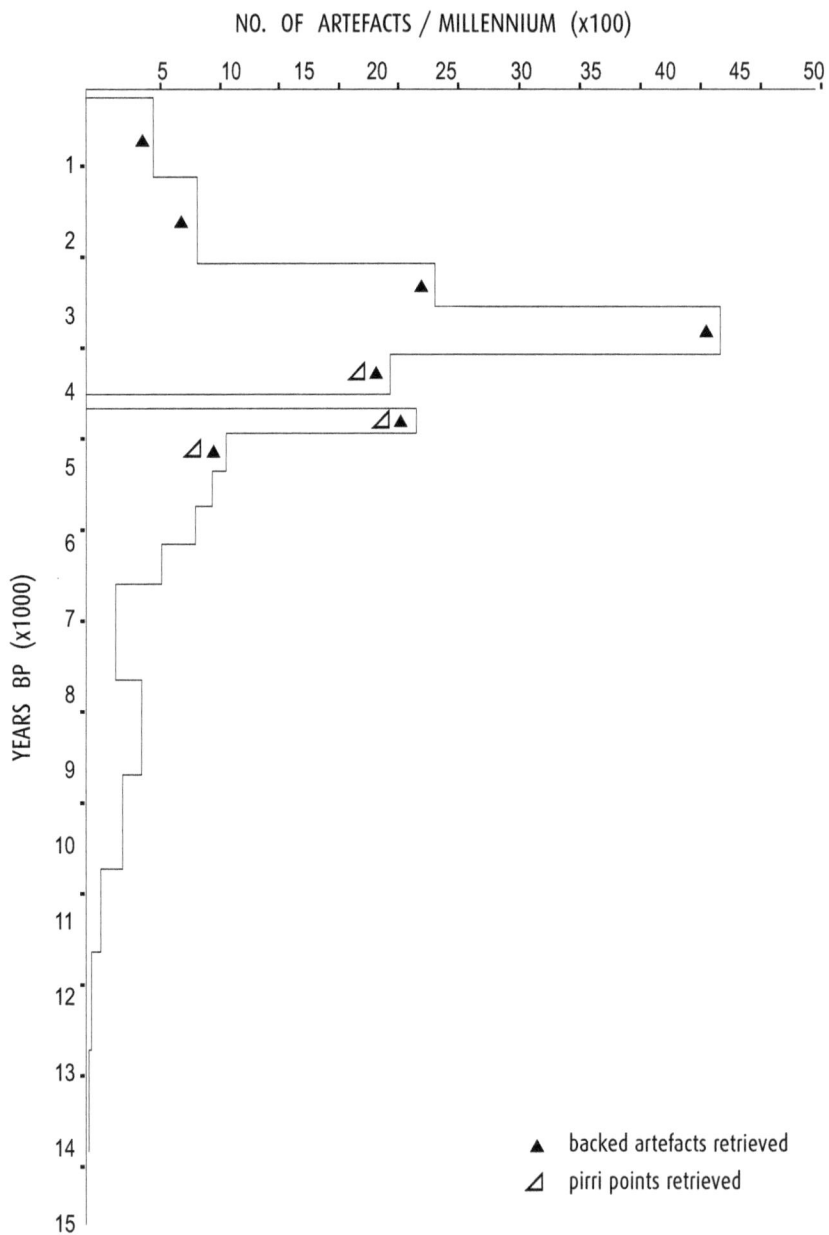

Figure 7.24 Native Well 1, central Queensland highlands: rates of artefact accumulation (number per millennium). Table A4/37 has details.

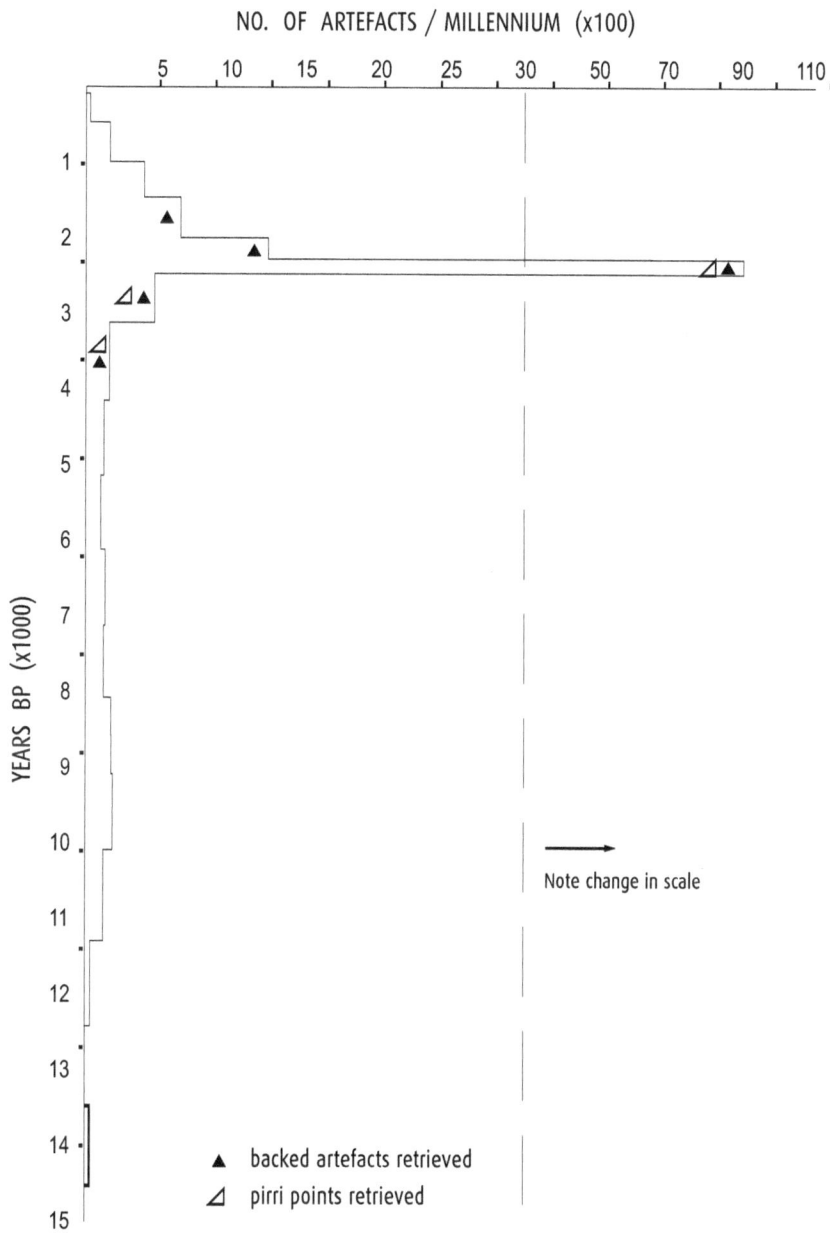

Figure 7.25 Native Well 2, central Queensland highlands: rates of artefact accumulation (number per millennium). Table A4/38 has details.

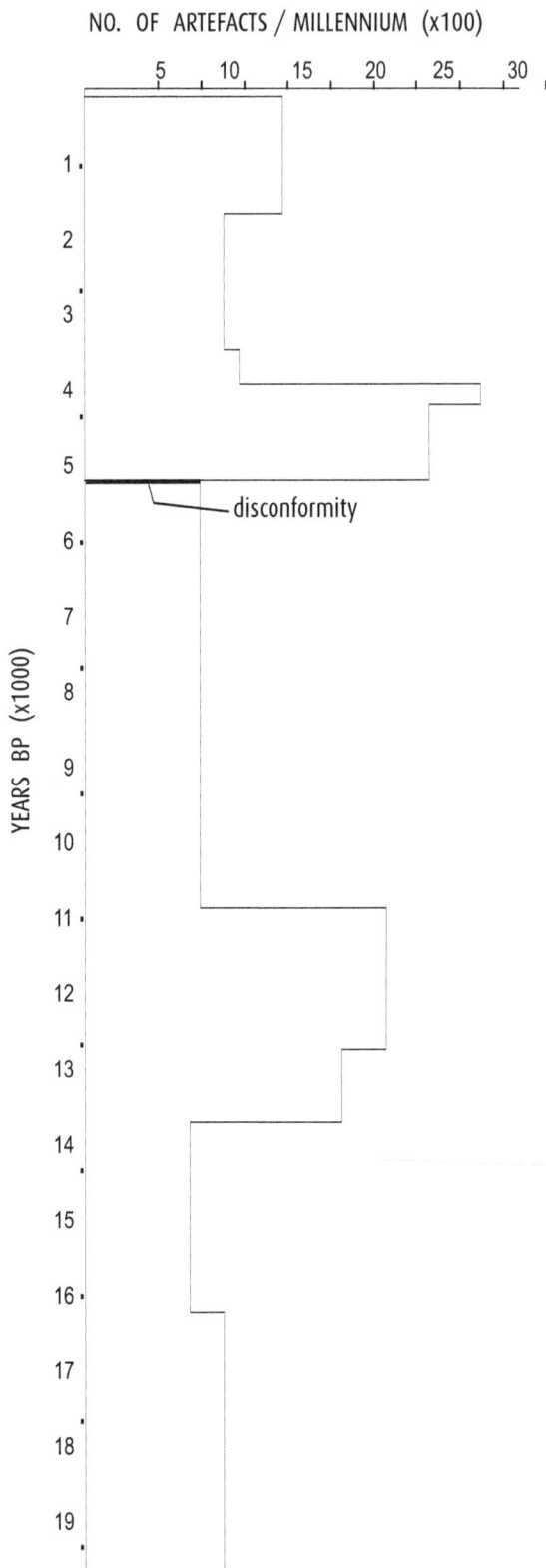

habitations in the last 1000 or so years did not always follow the same direction. The timing at which dramatic changes occurred in the habitation and artefact indices also varied.

Direction of trends

- In no region did both the habitation indices and the artefact accumulation rates for all sites continue to increase until contact;

- in the NSW Hunter Valley, the artefact accumulation rates decreased in all sites in the last 1000 years or so, in contrast with the rate of known-habitation use, which varied — increasing in the Singleton area but decreasing in the Muswellbrook area;

- in south-eastern Queensland, the habitation indices continued to increase while the artefact accumulation rates in the most recent period decreased at two sites, increased at one site, and at another fluctuated while generally increasing;

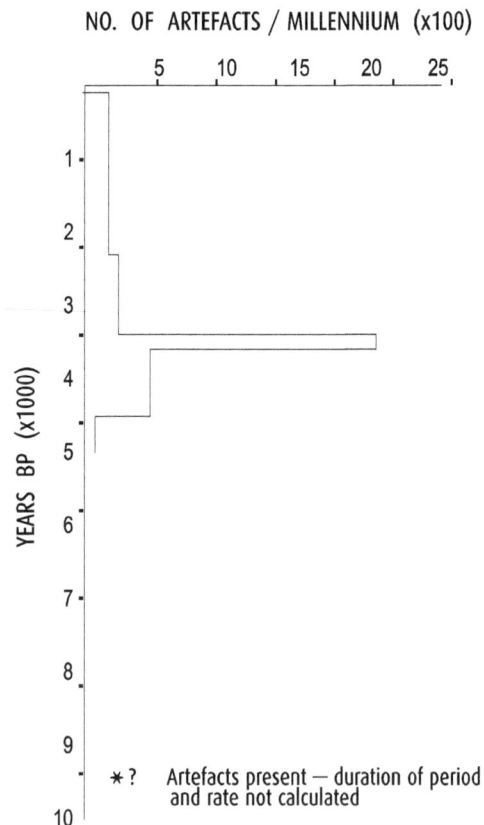

Figure 7.26 Kenniff Cave, central Queensland highlands: rates of artefact accumulation (number per millennium). Table A4/39 has details.

Figure 7.27 The Tombs, central Queensland highlands: rates of artefact accumulation (number per millennium). Table A4/40 has details.

- in three regions — NSW south coast-Sydney, south-western Victoria and central Queensland highlands — the habitation establishment rates decreased in the last 1000 years while the direction of artefact accumulation rates at individual sites varied (rates increased at some sites, whereas at others they decreased and at one they remained stable);
- the numbers of habitations used continued to increase until contact in NSW south coast-Sydney, while in the central Queensland highlands they remained stable.

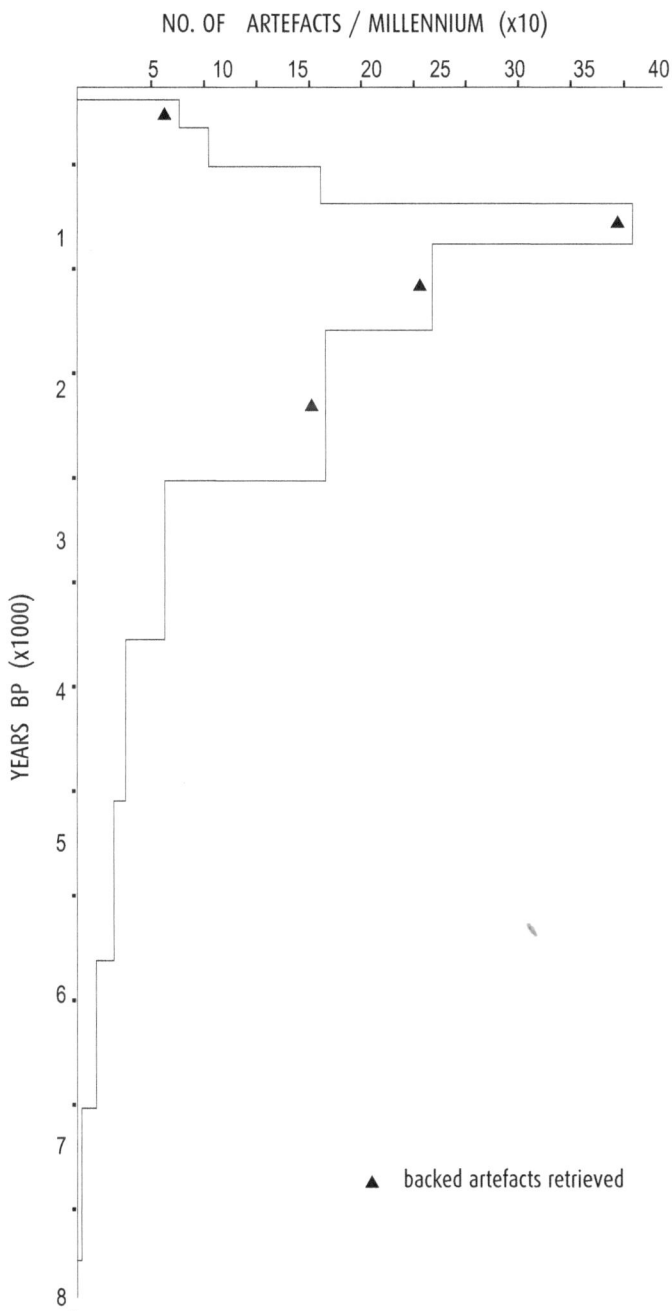

NO. OF ARTEFACTS / MILLENNIUM (x10)

Timing

- In none of the regions did the dramatic increase in the habitation indices coincide in time with the majority of dates at which the dramatic increases in the artefact accumulation rates occurred in individual habitations. In general, the dramatic increase in the artefact accumulation rate was earlier than the dramatic change in the habitation establishment rate — a pattern seen also in the Upper Mangrove Creek catchment;
- the most dramatic increases in the artefact accumulation rates in individual habitations did not always coincide in time with the appearance of artefacts accepted as diagnostic of the 'Small Tool Tradition' and/or Bondaian assemblages. This is discussed further in the following chapter.

Trends in the direction and timing of the habitation and/or artefact indices that I identified for some regions differed from those apparently perceived by other researchers according to their interpretations and explanations: for example, the artefact accumulation rates in individual habitations on the NSW south coast by Hughes and Lampert (1982), and in south-western Victoria by Lourandos (1983a: 85).

It is clear that the trends observed in the Upper Mangrove Creek catchment are not atypical. The lack of correlation in the timing of the dramatic quantitative changes in the habitation and artefact indices is seen also in other regions in eastern Australia. Many have habitation establishment rates which increased dramatically in the latter half

Figure 7.28 Maidenwell, south-eastern Queensland: rates of artefact accumulation (number per millennium). Table A4/41 has details.

of the Holocene and then continued to increase until contact, as well as having archaeological deposits in which artefact accumulation rates decreased in the uppermost levels. It is also apparent that there was much regional variation, and that the timing of 'events' and the direction of changes in the archaeological record were not uniform across eastern Australia (see also Lampert 1971a: 68–9; Williams 1985: 328–9).

Discussion and conclusions

An examination of the evidence relating to changing site and artefact numbers in several eastern Australian regions shows that some of the interpretations and explanations proposed by researchers in the 1970s and 1980s are no longer sustainable. In particular, although dramatic or substantial increases did occur in the habitation establishment rates, the numbers of habitations used and/or the artefact accumulation rates, the timing varied regionally and the indices did not always continue to increase from the period of initial occupation until the time of European contact.

Dramatic or substantial increases in the habitation establishment rates and the numbers of habitations in other regions did not occur at ca 5000 BP or ca 4000 BP. The dramatic or most substantial increases did not occur in the same period in each region, but were usually in the second or first millennium BP. Data for some of the regions suggest there were intra-regional variations in the trends in the establishment and use of habitations, for example, in the Victorian Mallee, NSW Hunter Valley and NSW south coast-Sydney.

Dramatic increases in the artefact accumulation rates all occurred in the late-Holocene; though it was usually after ca 4000 BP, the timing varied at individual sites. Substantial decreases in artefact accumulation rates in individual habitations were also documented in the last 1000 years in other regions, as in the catchment. Substantial decreases are also documented in the artefact indices in some regions in earlier periods when fluctuations in the rates occurred, but the most dramatic decreases usually occurred in the first millennium BP.

High growth rates and the highest growth rates for the habitation and artefact indices in each region were not restricted to any particular millennium BP (Tables 7.4 to 7.7, A4/17 to A4/42, Fig. 7.30). The highest growth rates all occurred in the latter half of the Holocene, but high growth rates also occurred in earlier periods. However, even where the habitation establishment rate and/or the number of habitations used continued to increase into the first millennium BP, the millennial and annual growth rates did not necessarily do so. Some regions had declining and

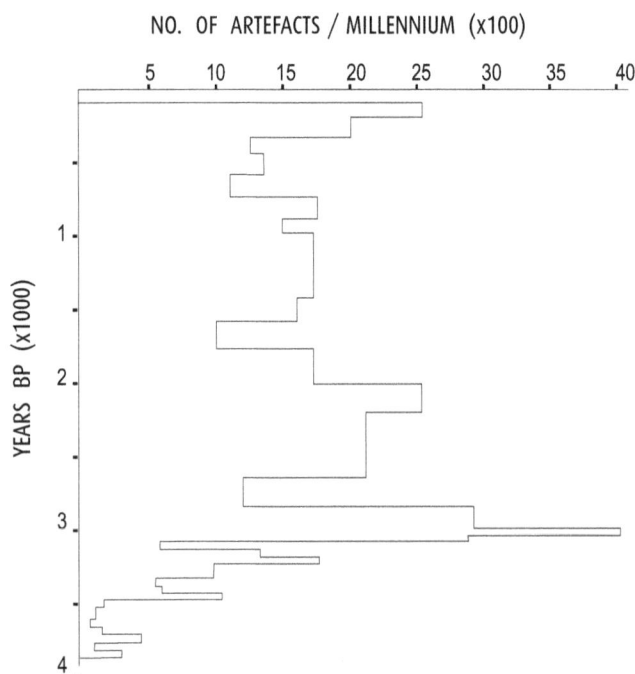

Figure 7.29 Gatton, south-eastern Queensland: rates of artefact accumulation (number per millennium). Table A4/42 has details.

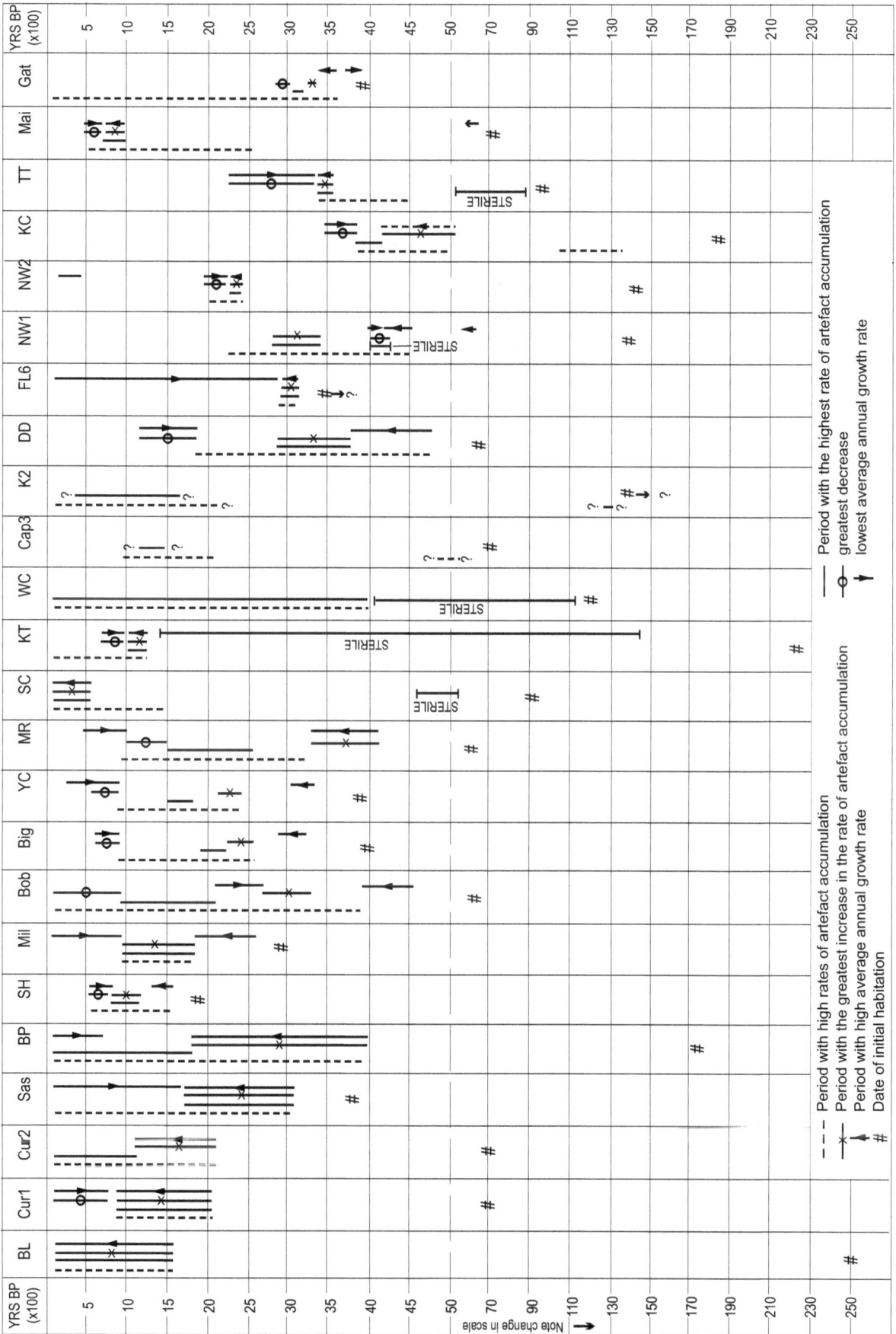

Figure 7.30 Habitations in eastern Australia: summary of changes in the rates of artefact accumulation and changes in growth rates in the artefact accumulation rates.

negative growth rates for the habitation indices in the first millennium BP. Decreasing and negative average annual growth rates for artefact accumulation also occurred in the upper level/s of most habitations in all regions.

For the habitation indices, the millennial growth rates are usually much less than the two- to threefold increases quoted by Hughes and Lampert (1981: 20) and the tenfold increase proposed by Ross (1984: 198–9). Nevertheless, millennial growth rates of between ×2 and ×5.5 do occur, particularly in the habitation establishment rates, in all regions except the central Queensland highlands, but the highest rates are usually restricted to one millennium and no more than two millennia. Average annual growth rates greater than 0.1% occurred in the habitation indices in all regions, though they were restricted to one millennium; no regions had growth rates of 0.5% or greater — all were less than 0.2%.

In the case of the artefact accumulation rates, most habitations had some levels for which the average annual growth rate was 0.1% or greater; such growth rates extended for periods between 110 and 2150 years. Only seven habitations had levels with positive rates of more than 0.5%, and two had negative rates of more than 0.5%, but in all cases (mostly in Gatton) these rates existed for short periods of between 55 and 500 years. Thus, for both habitation and artefact indices, the average annual growth rates are usually much less than the 0.5% Gray (1985: 23) considered necessary 'to signify a considerable departure from near-stationarity' in human populations. The significance of the millennial and average annual growth rates is discussed more fully in the next chapter.

Although some case studies involve large numbers of habitations (e.g., 141 in the Victorian Mallee), the number of dated excavated archaeological deposits in each region is small — particularly when the size of the regions in which the sites occur is considered. Of the regions studied, the NSW south coast-Sydney had the largest number of radiometrically dated sites (58), though Ulm and Hall's (1996: Fig. 4, Appendix 1) recent data set for south-eastern Queensland has 57. The number of habitations used in the analyses for the Upper Mangrove Creek catchment (30) is not as large as that recorded in some other studies, but it is as yet the only study where:

1.   the sample of sites occurs within a relatively small bounded area (ca 100 sq km);
2.   an attempt has been made to ascertain the establishment date for all habitations in the sample and to estimate the length of habitation at each site; and,
3.   the majority of 'dated' archaeological deposits (26 of 30) can be assumed on probability sampling grounds to be an unbiased sample from the locality. Four sites were originally recorded as potential habitation shelters with potential archaeological deposit and were purposefully selected for excavation.

In the case of the habitation indices, data for many regions are likely to be biased because of

(a)   the small numbers of sites and the large size of most regions (e.g., central Queensland highlands with 11 sites in 21,000 sq km); and,

(b)   the procedures adopted in selecting the sites excavated or analysed — the excavated or radiocarbon-dated sites were purposefully selected for particular projects and within these areas many other undated habitations occur.

Comparison of (a) the Upper Mangrove Creek catchment trends when based on a data set in which only radiocarbon-dated archaeological deposits are used with (b) the trends when all sites are included (Figs 6.1 and 6.2) suggests that the decrease in the habitation establishment rates in regions such as the NSW south coast-Sydney, south-western Victoria and the central Queensland highlands, may be due to bias in the selection of sites excavated. That is, sites with assumed short habitation periods and/or shallow deposits are less likely to be selected for excavation and/or dating than sites with multi-phase, deep stratified deposits.

If this is so, then most regions may have had an increase in the habitation establishment rate in the final 1000 years before contact (though the growth rates could still have declined). At present, however, when dates become available from newly excavated sites in any of the regions discussed above, their inclusion could easily change the trends — as in the case of the NSW south coast-Sydney region, and south-western Victoria (see Appendix 4). Empirical data from projects based on site surveys in defined areas using intensive probability sampling methods and the excavation and dating of unbiased samples of archaeological deposits are required to test whether regional trends documented to date are valid or need to be revised.

Similarly, data on artefact accumulation rates come from only a relatively few widespread sites in each of the seven regions — the maximum number of sites reviewed in any one region is seven. In addition, data available for each region and site are not uniform. Thus, whether the trends from these few individual sites are representative of the locality or region as a whole and/or whether they provide a valid basis on which to propose regional chronological changes in, for example, habitation and land-use patterns, is arguable.

Other Australian regions and sites, and later studies

Despite doubts being raised about the validity of currently documented trends in other regions of eastern Australia because of sampling issues, studies in other parts of the continent and recent studies of the 1990s support the conclusions outlined above. Dramatic increases have been documented in the habitation establishment rate and in the number of habitations used at varying times in the late-Holocene, for example, in south-western Western Australia (Hallam 1977), western NSW (Allen 1972: 321 in Hughes and Lampert 1982: Fig. 10), and in south-eastern Cape York and south-eastern Queensland by David and Chant (1995: Fig. 38), Morwood and Hobbs (1995a: Fig. 15.1), Ulm and Hall (1996: Fig. 4), and David and Lourandos (1997).

Decreased artefact accumulation rates and/or artefact densities have been documented in recent levels in many sites in many parts of Australia, for example, on the central Queensland coast (Cania Gorge — Eales et al. 1999: 39, Figs 8 and 9; Westcott et al. 1999: 51, Fig. 9), and the Victoria River district, Northern Territory (Attenbrow et al. 1995: Fig. 7). In some cases, Pleistocene levels have very much higher artefact accumulation rates than Holocene levels (e.g., Fern Cave, south-east Cape York, David 1991: 45, Table 2, Fig. 5).

Intra-regional variations in the late-Holocene trends, with artefact accumulation rates increasing throughout the sequence in some sites and decreasing in the most recent levels in others, have been documented in regions such as Arnhem Land, northern Australia (Jones 1985: 291, 293, 296; Jones and Johnson 1985a: 183, 1985b: 71; Allen 1996: 199); in south-western Western Australia (Ferguson 1985); in Central Australia (Thorley 1999: 66–67); south-east Cape York (David and Chant 1995; Morwood and Hobbs 1995b); and the NSW south coast (Boot 1996b).

The trends identified in the Upper Mangrove Creek catchment are clearly not anomalous — intra-regional variations in the trends in late-Holocene artefact accumulation rates are a common occurrence in Australia, and substantial decreases in artefact accumulation rates occurred in many individual sites in other regions in the last 2000–1000 years. Dramatic or relatively substantial increases in the habitation indices also occurred later than 4000 BP in other regions, but usually in the second or first millennium BP.

If the artefact accumulation rates by themselves are accepted as indicators of demographic change, then the trends in some regions indicate that populations may not have continued to increase in size until contact in all regions of Australia. In a similar vein, if habitation indices are accepted as indicators of demographic change, then the trends in some regions indicate that populations may have increased dramatically in the late-Holocene.

However, such increases occurred much later than ca 4000 BP, the time when some researchers advocate that the 'Small Tool Tradition' appeared. The differences in direction and timing of the dramatic changes in the habitation and artefact indices also indicate that such changes may not have always coincided in time with the appearance of artefacts accepted as diagnostic of the 'Small Tool Tradition' or the Bondaian phases of the Eastern Regional Sequence. Late-Holocene trends in habitation and artefact indices, however, may be indicators of other behavioural changes — for example, modifications to habitation, subsistence and land-use patterns influenced by climatic and environmental changes that were occurring in this period. Each of these issues is discussed more fully in the following chapters.

8

A re-examination of interpretations and explanations for changes in habitation and artefact indices in eastern Australia

A review of 1970s and 1980s archaeological studies showed there were numerous interpretations and explanations for dramatic changes in habitation and artefact indices in several regions of eastern Australia (Chapter 2). In this chapter, these explanations and interpretations are compared with the archaeological evidence on which they were based (presented in Chapter 7 and Appendix 4). This comparison shows that in many instances the explanations and interpretations cannot be sustained. Equally, it shows that a wide range of interpretations and explanations are possible, but that simplistic relationships between numbers of sites/artefacts and numbers of people, or between numbers of artefacts and the introduction of the 'Small Tool Tradition' or Bondaian assemblages, are unlikely to describe the full complexity of a region's prehistory.

Population-change explanations

Assumptions underlying the population-change explanations

Most behavioural-change explanations are based on the assumption that quantitative changes in the habitation and artefact indices were produced by a change in the number of artefacts manufactured and habitations used by each person. That is, there were changes in the ratio of habitations to people and in the ratio of artefacts to people. Population-change explanations tend to assume (or imply) that those ratios were relatively constant throughout time and thus a change in the number of habitations and/or artefacts is evidence of a change in population size.

Many researchers of the 1970s and 1980s perceived or assumed that the long-term direction of the quantitative changes in the archaeological records of eastern Australia was only towards 'increase', or assumed that decreases in the most recent millennium BP were not significant. On this basis, they proposed that the quantitative changes indicated a trend towards increasing population size, which continued until European contact. The population increases were usually seen as part of a general continent-wide phenomenon, though local shifts in population from one environmental zone or geographic area to another, or shifts from one type of habitation to another without the inference of a general population increase, were also proposed.

Very few advocates of the population-change explanations were explicit about the assumptions on which they based their conclusions; authors who were explicit include Beaton (1985), Ferguson (1985), Ross (1985) and Morwood (1986: 117, 1987: 343; see also O'Connell and Allen 1995: 857).

Beaton (1985: 16) stated that 'Archaeological sites ultimately mean people, and questions about the presence or absence of sites may just as well be phrased in terms of the presence or absence of people'. Beaton's (1985: 17–18) discussions about the relationship between trends indicated by 'a histogram of sites occupied per thousand year period' and population-growth models show that he accepted changes in population size were reflected in that index.

Ross (1984: 234; 1985: 87) believed an increase in the number of sites to be 'the most suitable indicator' of population increase, 'where it can be demonstrated that behavioural change and archaeological visibility have not biased the archaeological record'. She qualified this by citing one of three conditions which Bailey (1983b: 163) stipulated should be established if one is to accept an increase in site density as evidence of population increase: that is, that the average number of inhabitants per site remained unchanged. Ross concluded:

> In other words, it must be possible to demonstrate that a greater number of sites in the landscape was not a function of purely behavioural change. (Ross 1985: 87)

Ross argued further:

> The only behavioural change which could produce more occupation sites in an area, and a concomitant expansion of people into previously unoccupied or rarely occupied regions, without involving an increased number of people, would be a change involving the same number of people spending shorter periods of time at more sites. The obvious expression of this would be **more sites, but with each site containing sparser occupation debris.** (1985: 87) (my emphasis)

Ross then stated, 'This is clearly not the case in the middle to late Holocene in south-eastern Australia.' However, this is exactly the evidence that is documented in the Upper Mangrove Creek catchment for the first millennium BP — more sites, but with many containing 'sparser occupation debris'. The evidence presented in the previous chapter suggests this may also be the case in other regions in eastern Australia. Ross' statements assume that the ultimate measure of the number of people inhabiting either individual sites or specific areas of land is the total amount of habitation debris accumulated. In addition, Ross' statement does not allow for the possibility that two behavioural changes may have occurred at the same time; for example, people may have begun to move more frequently at the same time as they began to make more artefacts per head of population.

Ferguson (1985: 11–12) analysed artefact distributions in the late-Pleistocene through mid-Holocene levels at several sites in south-western Western Australia to test the assumption that 'since artefacts are products of human activity, the frequency of artefact finds can be seen to indicate the intensity of that activity'. He (1985: 492) stated that it is unlikely that the evidence from individual sites in his study area suggests only a change in local settlement pattern or that some other raw material could have been substituted for stone. He (1985: 491–2) argued that the artefacts were 'essential components of the prehistoric society's cultural core' and that there was sufficient continuity in the stone-working process to legitimise comparison of the relevant late-Pleistocene through to mid-Holocene levels. Ferguson (1985: 492–3) concluded, as a result of his analyses, that 'the drop in artefacts suggests a corresponding drop in the amount of human activity', and that 'the region-wide drop in artefact finds during the mid-Holocene suggests a comparable region-wide drop in human population'. However, he (1985: 12) expressed reservations about whether comparable statements could be made about the increase in the artefact accumulation rate in the late-Holocene levels of sites since new stone-reduction techniques and artefact types occurred in this period.

Morwood (1987) argued that archaeological criteria for population increases could include increases in the rate of site formation processes and in occupational intensity at sites, as well as more intensive economic exploitation as indicated by the use of new habitats, resource types, extractive technologies and management strategies. Following Ross (1985) and Hughes and Lampert (1982), Morwood said that in south-eastern Queensland 'The growth of site numbers over time ... provides a general measure of population increase' (1987: 343).

Each of these researchers was assuming that changes in the numbers of habitations and/or artefacts are evidence of changes in the number of people across the land or in sites. There are many problems in accepting this assumption — apart from the fact that valid alternative explanations to population change can be proposed for these quantitative changes (as acknowledged by Ferguson for the late-Holocene). For example, it has not been established that changes in the number of people inhabiting a site or region or the amount of time spent (e.g., person-days) in a site or region are the only mechanisms that produced changes in the habitation establishment rate, the number of habitations used or the rate of artefact accumulation. It has not been demonstrated yet, nor can it yet be assumed, that (a) knapping was such a constant part of the activities in a habitation that the debris from this activity can act as a measure of the whole range of activities undertaken at a site, and/or time spent at a site, and/or number of people who used a habitation (Bettinger 1981; M. C. Hall 1981; Hiscock 1981: 31–2, 1984: 133–5; Smith 1982: 114–15; see also Chapter 2, Increases in the archaeological record, Population change); (b) there was a direct relationship between artefact use and discard behaviour (Binford 1973; Foley 1981a: 16, 1981b: 165, 1981c: 197); or (c) the rates of use and discard of stone artefacts are known (Foley 1981b: 175).

Implications of population-change premises

If it is ESTABLISHED or researchers CONTINUE TO ASSUME that changes in the habitation indices and the artefact accumulation rates were produced by changes in population size, the decreases in the indices that are presently documented for the latter half of the Holocene throw doubt on explanations which propose that the population continued to increase throughout Australian prehistory.

Many researchers tended to accept that changes in the habitation indices and artefact accumulation rates acted in concert; that is, they followed the same trends in timing and direction. This was not necessarily the case in all areas. In the Upper Mangrove Creek catchment, changes in the habitation indices and the local artefact accumulation rate did not coincide in time or direction, and this was also the case with the habitation indices and artefact accumulation rates for individual habitations in other eastern Australian regions.

If the documented changes in both the habitation and artefact indices for the eastern Australian regions were EACH produced by a change in population size, then various scenarios can be constructed. For example, assuming a three-phase sequence with group size and the magnitude of changes in each index remaining the same, only if there was an increase in both the habitation indices and the artefact accumulation rates in the most recent period could the trends be taken as an indication that population continued to increase until contact. If there was a decrease in one index and an increase in the other, it would suggest population size remained the same in the final phase as in the second phase; a decrease in both habitation and artefact indices would suggest a decrease in the population size in the final phase.

Following from this, if the regional trends based on the habitations and artefact indices for other regions in eastern Australia have any validity, then one can speculate as to likely changes that occurred in the population size in each region in the first millennium BP. If only the habitation indices are measures of population change, then there was an increase in population size in the majority of regions in the last 1000 years: in the NSW south coast-Sydney region, in south-eastern Queensland, NSW southern uplands-tablelands, southern Victorian Mallee, as well as the Upper Mangrove Creek catchment. In two regions there was no change in the size of the population (central Queensland highlands and the northern Victorian Mallee), and in the NSW Hunter Valley there was a decrease in population in one area and an increase in another.

In the case of the artefact accumulation rates, rates for individual habitation sites in these regions did not always follow the same direction in the last 1000 years or so, and for none of the regions (except the Upper Mangrove Creek catchment) has a local artefact accumulation rate been calculated. So, if it is assumed that where more than 50% of the sites have decreased rates in the final phase the local artefact accumulation rate decreased, and if only the local artefact accumulation rates are indicators of population change, then there was a decline in population in most regions in the last 1000 years: in the central Queensland highlands, south-eastern Queensland, NSW Hunter Valley, NSW Blue Mountains, South Australian lower Murray Valley, as well as the Upper Mangrove Creek catchment. Only two regions had stable populations: the NSW south coast-Sydney and south-western Victoria.

If the habitation indices and local artefact accumulation rates are both measures of population change, then in most regions the population was either stable (south-eastern Queensland, Upper Mangrove Creek catchment) or had declined (central Queensland highlands and NSW Hunter Valley); in only one region did the population increase in the last 1000 years (NSW south coast-Sydney).

Based on the above, the minimum implication is that in the first millennium BP the population did not increase, or did not continue to increase in all regions. Such simplistic interpretations of the data are, of course, not tenable. However, they were presented to show the type of conclusions that can be reached with the type of data currently available, IF the population-change premise is adopted.

Although the above scenarios are presented in terms of general population change, under the population-change premise, the presently documented trends could also be explained as:

1. local shifts in population from one geographic or topographic zone to another for a variety of reasons (e.g., as in Moore 1970; Luebbers 1978, 1981; Beaton 1985; Lourandos 1985a; Ferguson 1985); or,

2. in some regions, particularly country where rockshelters exist, a shift in preference from inhabiting one type of location for another, that is, rockshelters versus open deposits (e.g., as in Stockton 1970a; Stockton and Holland 1974), in regions such as the Upper Mangrove Creek catchment, central Queensland highlands, NSW south coast-Sydney; or preference for one habitation over another, but of the same type, because of changed local environmental conditions (Smith 1982) or a change in the cultural 'status' of the location (Morwood 1986).

Under the population-change premise, only if one assumes that the gaps in the archaeological record contain a different trend from that already documented (i.e., that the present studies are biased or unrepresentative of the locality or region itself or of the continental trends) can one avoid the conclusion that the presently documented trends indicate that in some regions of eastern Australia there were periods of decreasing population, and that in the last 1000 or 2000 years, the population was less than that of the preceding millennia.

Growth rates

Some researchers associated dramatic increases in habitation indices and/or artefact accumulation rates with dramatic increases in their growth rates (e.g., Hughes and Lampert 1982; Ross 1984).

IF ever it is demonstrated that the relationship between numbers of habitations and people, as well as between stone artefacts and people, was such that the ratio between these variables remained constant over time, then it could be assumed that the growth rates in the indices represent the growth rates in the human population. This would allow changes in relative population size to be proposed, but would not relate to actual population size (for which the actual ratio between people and habitations and/or artefacts is required). Average annual growth rates were calculated for the habitation and artefact indices (Chapters 6 and 7, Appendix 4) so that comparisons could be made with the rates which are normally cited by demographers in discussions on population growth.

Examination of the average annual growth rates for the habitation indices (Tables 7.6 and 7.7) suggests that in some regions lower growth rates prevailed in the first millennium BP than in earlier millennia. In two regions — NSW southern uplands-tablelands and south-eastern Queensland — late-Holocene growth rates continued increasing into the first millennium BP, though in the latter region the rates did not return to the high values of the fifth and sixth millennia BP.

Average annual growth rates for artefact accumulation rates in the first millennium BP in individual habitations varied within each region (Tables A4/17 to A4/42). Growth rates for local artefact accumulation rates could not be calculated for each region, as they were for the catchment (Table 6.6). The large number of regions with numerous habitations with decreasing growth rates in the first millennium BP, however, may indicate decreasing or stable populations existed in many regions in this period, or, if there was an increase in population size, the actual rate of population growth may have declined or remained relatively stable (stationary).

Hughes and Lampert (1982: 20) stated that there was a two- to threefold increase in site numbers and a six- to tenfold increase in 'the intensity of occupation' (i.e., rate of implement accumulation) after 5000 BP. Ross (1984: 198–9) stated that there was a tenfold increase in site numbers after 4000 BP. Although these authors concluded that the most likely explanation for the increases was population increase, none claimed that the population growth rate was the same as that for the habitations and/or artefacts. Hughes and Lampert made no comment about the difference in the growth rates that they calculated for habitation and implement numbers. If the increase in the growth rate for human populations was not the same as that for habitations and/or artefacts, this implies that the ratio between numbers of people and numbers of habitations and/or artefacts changed at the same time as the growth rates for the habitations and artefacts changed. If so, the relationship between changes in population size and changes in material behaviour and habitation patterns is obviously more complex than implied by many of the explanations reviewed here.

The increases in the growth rates referred to by Hughes and Lampert and Ross took place over several millennia — that is, over 2000 years for the artefacts and 5000 years for habitations on the NSW south coast, and over 4000 years for habitations in the Victorian Mallee. The growth rates are very much lower when standardised as millennial or average annual growth rates. For Hughes and Lampert's 1982 data, the average annual growth rates for south coast habitations are between ×1.0001 and ×1.0002 (+0.01% and +0.02%), and for the implements ×1.0009 and ×1.0012 (between +0.09% and +0.12%); for the southern Mallee the average annual growth rate based on Ross' figures is ×1.0006 (0.06%).

The average annual growth rates for the eastern Australian regions (including the NSW south coast-Sydney using my recalculated figures, and the Victorian Mallee) can be summarised as follows:

Habitation indices (i.e., numbers of habitations used and rates of known-habitation use) (Table 7.7):

The average annual growth rates were all less than +0.11% p.a., with positive values ranging from +0.01% to +0.11%; only one region had a value >0.1%. Only two regions had negative growth rates (a decrease) in one period — central Queensland highlands with a growth rate of –0.03% in the ninth millennium BP, and NSW Hunter Valley (MANS), with –0.19% in the most recent phase.

Artefact accumulation rates (Tables A4/17 to A4/42):

Most average annual growth rates with positive values ranged between +0.01% and +0.94%, with the highest being +3.45%. Most negative values ranged from 0.003% to -0.66%, with the lowest being -1.98%. Four habitations with sterile layers had values of -100%. Most habitations had one or more levels in which the growth rate was +0.1% or greater; seven had levels with positive values greater than +0.5%. Two habitations had negative values greater than –0.5%.

The average annual growth rates for the habitation indices are the average for a period of one millennium. The growth rates for the artefact accumulation rates are the average for the estimated length of time over which a single spit or level accumulated, which is usually less than 1000 years.

There is much temporal and regional variation in the growth rates. As a rule, the highest growth rates in the indices occur within the last 5000 years, but high growth rates are not restricted to this period. If these indices indicate population growth rates, then there was also much temporal and regional variation in population growth, and all major population increases were not restricted to the last 5000 years.

The percentage figures that constitute significant growth rates in demographic and social terms for hunter-gatherer populations have been discussed by Ammerman et al. (1976), Weiss (1978: 774), Hassan (1981, 1982) and Gray (1985). Hassan (1981: 143) calculated the average annual rate of world population growth during the Pleistocene at well below 0.01% (a figure he says is 'exceedingly low'). He (1981: 208; 1982: 244–5, Table 3.2) said that during the Lower Palaeolithic it was 0.00007%, during the Middle Palaeolithic 0.005% and during the Upper Palaeolithic 0.01%. The acceleration in rates from Lower to Upper Palaeolithic, he said, perhaps reflects greater evolutionary adaptability and biological development from *Homo erectus* to *H. sapiens*. Hassan (1981: 140, 201, 221) argued that the maximum rate of growth for hunter-gatherers should be placed at about 0.5% p.a. with an average of 0.1% p.a. He considered that a growth rate of 0.1% is well below the explosive rates of today, which often exceed 1% and 2% p.a. in many nations. A rate of 0.5%, however, is sufficiently rapid to alter demographic conditions in a short time (Hassan 1981: 221). He (1981: 140, 221, 259) pointed out that prehistoric populations were not incapable of rapid rates of population increase — at a rate of 0.5% p.a., the doubling time would be ca 130 years or about seven generations; at a rate of 0.1%, doubling would take about 35 generations (ca 650 years). Birdsell (1957 in Hassan 1981: 203) proposed an annual growth rate for waves of immigrants sweeping over newly discovered territory in Australia of 3.6% (the equivalent to doubling every generation), but Hassan (1982: 257) said this figure is unrealistically high and that the rate could not have been higher than between 0.5% and 1%. Hassan (1981: 142, 260; 1982: 245) emphasised that the above figures are average rates and small populations would have been subject to stochastic fluctuations in size, and changes in mortality and fertility rates could have led to population increase or decline if no other mechanisms dampened the effect of such fluctuations.

Gray (a demographer) said the apparent population changes referred to by Lourandos (1983a, 1984) and Hughes and Lampert (1982) imply a near-stationary state, and that a tenfold population increase over 2000 years, as suggested by the recent archaeological evidence in south-eastern Australia, implies an average annual growth rate of only 0.1% p.a. This, Gray (1985: 23) pointed out, was hardly a population explosion, and local occurrences of growth or decline at this rate actually support the 'near-stationarity' hypothesis. He commented further that a tenfold population increase over a much shorter period (say 500 years) would be needed to signify a considerable departure from 'near-stationarity'; such an increase represents a growth rate of 0.5% p.a. Gray (1985: 26) concluded that over time we should expect to find very considerable changes (increases) in the sizes of Aboriginal populations (local and continental), but that such changes over very long periods of time are relatively insignificant and do not contradict the hypothesis of long-term 'stationarity'.

Ammerman et al. (1976: 29) stated that it was unreasonable to expect a regional population to continue growing at a rate of 1% to 3% a year over a period as long as 1000 years. However, he believed that even an apparently low rate of growth such as 0.1% a year would lead to major changes in population size and probably to socioeconomic changes as well, if it was maintained over periods in the order of 2000 years.

Thus, the significance that can be assigned to a particular growth rate depends as much on the length of time over which it was maintained, as on the actual growth rate itself.

Population-change conclusions

If the regional changes in the number of habitations and/or artefacts over time are assumed to indicate changes in population size, and if it is accepted that either a 0.1% p.a. growth rate over 2000 years or a 0.5% p.a. growth rate over 500 years may have brought about significant demographic, social or economic changes, what conclusions can be drawn from the archaeological evidence? Did growth rates of either 0.1% p.a. over 2000 years or 0.5% p.a. over 500 years occur in many or any regions in eastern Australia? Conclusions that can be drawn depend on which set of evidence is taken as the indicator of population change — the habitation indices or the artefact accumulation rates.

- If the habitation indices (number of habitations used and rate of known-habitation use) are taken as the indicators, then the calculated growth rates suggest significant change did not occur in any region. All average annual growth rates were less than +0.11% p.a. (Table 7.7). The growth rates for 500-year periods have not been calculated, but the raw data do not appear to indicate growth rates of greater than 0.5% p.a. were maintained for periods of more than 500 years.

- If the artefact accumulation rates are taken as the indicators, then although average annual growth rates greater than +0.1% occurred at many times, it is not often that they were maintained for periods of 2000 years or more (i.e., Bass Point for ca 2150 years and Devon Downs for ca 1900 years). Growth rates of +0.5% p.a. or greater occurred less frequently and at only one site were they maintained for a period greater than 500 years (Sandy Hollow for ca 510 years) (Appendix 4, Tables A4/17 to A4/42). At other sites, growth rates of +0.5% or greater were all associated with periods of less than 220 years (Native Wells 2 and Gatton). Three sites had negative values of –0.1% or less which were maintained over 2000 years: at Kenniff Cave between ca 16,200 BP and ca 13,700 BP (ca 2500 years), at Native Well 2 between ca 2300 BP and ca 100 BP (ca 2200 years), and Fromms Landing 6 between ca 2950 BP and ca 100 BP (ca 2850 years). No sites indicate growth rates of -0.5% or less for periods of 500 years or more.

The evidence from individual sites is, however, likely to represent only the changes in each particular site and may not be representative of the changes within a locality or region as a whole. In addition, the length of time over which a growth rate appears to have been sustained (e.g., as at Bass Point and Devon Downs) is a function of the temporal units into which the site's deposits were divided for other analytical purposes. Reanalysis of the data grouped according to other units may show other trends.

The above conclusions suggest that the 'dramatic' increases in the archaeological record which are documented in the previous chapters may not necessarily indicate that demographically or socially significant changes occurred in the population growth rates at certain points in time. Claims for dramatic increases in population growth rates during specific periods of time in the late-Holocene may be unfounded. However, even though a growth rate may not change over time, the size of the increase in a population after a long period of time could become relatively substantial (Gray 1985: 26). Thus if a prevailing system or systems (e.g., social, economic or technological) could not operate effectively beyond a certain population size, then a steady increase in the size of a population over the long-term eventually may have brought about social, economic and/or material changes. Although I argue elsewhere in this monograph that quantitative changes in the archaeological record may not be produced by population change, there is no doubt that the population increased in size from the time of initial colonisation to the time of British colonisation in 1788. In addition, over this time, the increasing size of the population would have resulted in larger amounts of cultural debris being created and larger numbers of sites being inhabited. However, populations no doubt also declined in many regions and perhaps continent-wide at various times, and some arid and semi-arid regions may have been abandoned in some periods, for example, during the Last Glacial Maximum (Davidson 1990: 53–5; and recent studies, see below). In addition, growth rates associated with these increases and decreases in population need not have been uniform in direction, magnitude or timing in different areas across the continent.

If changes in the habitation and artefact indices are evidence of population change, then the 'population changes' were principally small in scale, that is, <0.1% p.a., and where they reached >0.5% p.a. they were not sustained over long periods of time, that is, for periods exceeding 500 years. The growth rates do not indicate any periods which were above 'near stationarity' — that is, the archaeological evidence does not support dramatic increases or decreases in population sizes during particular periods in time. Investigating theoretical issues associated with the identification of archaeological indices that measure population growth and decline (see discussion in Beaton 1990: 32) was beyond the scope of this study. However, these issues need to be addressed, as well as the nature and size of samples of sites on which the trends are based, in order to identify archaeological measures of population change in hunter-gatherer communities. Associated with these concerns is the identification of factors or processes that would have brought about changes in the growth rate and perhaps resulted in 'rapid' population changes (Hassan 1982: 263).

Behavioural change: qualitative changes in stone artefact assemblages

Explanations and interpretations relating to behavioural change are based on the assumption that during the Holocene the population size remained stable or fluctuated within only a narrow range. Most of these explanations assume that there were changes in the ratio of habitations to people and in the ratio of artefacts to people; that is, the average number of habitations used or artefacts manufactured by individual people altered.

Typological, technological and raw material changes are the focus of interpretations and explanations involving qualitative changes in the stone artefact assemblages. Many researchers associated dramatic increases in the habitation indices with the introduction of artefacts diagnostic of the Bondaian assemblages or 'Small Tool Tradition' (Lampert and Hughes 1974: 233; Bowdler 1981: 108, 1983: 12–13; Morwood 1981, 1984; Hughes and Lampert 1982: 26; Rowland 1983: 73; Ross 1984: 200). However, the causal relationships proposed between these events were often indirect; for example, the qualitative changes in the stone artefact assemblages resulted in larger numbers of artefacts which in turn made the archaeological deposits more visible. Other explanations, which suggest direct relationships between qualitative changes in the stone artefact assemblages and quantitative changes in the archaeological record, concern only the dramatic changes in artefact accumulation rates.

Qualitative changes in the stone artefact assemblages have been proposed as explanations for both the dramatic increases in the artefact accumulation rates in the last 5000 or 4000 years BP and for the decreases in the artefact accumulation rates in the last 1000 years or so. Some of the explanations were discussed during presentation of the evidence from the Upper Mangrove Creek catchment (Chapter 6), and are apparent in the review of quantitative changes in eastern Australia (Chapter 7, Appendix 4). Examples quoted below demonstrate that qualitative changes in the stone artefact assemblages cannot be used as a universal explanation for the quantitative changes in the archaeological record.

Increases in the artefact accumulation rates in the last 5000 or 4000 years BP

Qualitative changes in the stone artefact assemblages in south-eastern Australia that researchers have related to increases in artefact accumulation rates were said to occur at the beginning of the 'Small Tool Tradition' or Bondaian Phase of the Eastern Regional Sequence (i.e., Phase 2 in the Upper Mangrove Creek catchment), as well as at the transition from the Middle to Late Bondaian Phase (referred to as Bondaian and post-Bondaian Phases by some researchers [Table 3.7], and as Phases 3 and 4 in the Upper Mangrove Creek catchment).

Introduction of Bondaian assemblages/'Small Tool Tradition'

Increased artefact accumulation rates were said to coincide with or be associated with the introduction of the 'Small Tool Tradition' (e.g., Lampert and Hughes 1974: 233; Bowdler 1981: 108, 1983: 12–13; Morwood 1981, 1984; Hughes and Lampert 1982: 26). Introduction of the 'Small Tool Tradition'/Bondaian assemblages has been identified by the appearance (addition) of new implements into the assemblages — a typological change; a change in technology; and a change in raw materials.

While some of the new implements can be interpreted as innovations, the changes in technology and raw materials do not represent the introduction of new technology or new raw materials. They are simply a change in the frequency (number of times) that a technique or raw material was used.

1. Typological change — the addition of new implements into the assemblages. New implements which are said to appear in eastern Australia with the 'Small Tool Tradition' include backed artefacts such as Bondi points and geometric microliths (but see Hiscock and Attenbrow 1998). Ground-edged artefacts appear for the first time in south-eastern Australia; in Queensland, South Australia and western NSW, unifacial (pirri) points also appear.

Increases in the artefact accumulation rates are usually related to changes in the flaked artefacts and not the ground-edged artefacts. However, the appearance and then subsequent increase in the use of ground-edged artefacts probably also impacted on many aspects of Aboriginal life, which may be reflected in the amount of stone artefact manufacturing debris accumulated at sites. McBryde (1977: 234–6) associated an increase in ground-edged implements with a decline in the representation of macropodids and a rise in that of phalangeridae in the food refuse at sites in the New England region. An association between the increase in ground-edged implements and the increase in total numbers of artefacts has not been raised by other researchers and is not discussed here.

Hughes and Lampert (1982: 25) and Ross (1984: 200) stated that the new stone implements introduced with the 'Small Tool Tradition' expanded the existing range of stone implements and did not just replace existing types. Ross as well as Hughes and Lampert argued against the suggestion that these additions resulted in an increase in the number of artefacts discarded per head of population at a site, not only because of the increased range of implements per person but also as a result of the greater quantity of manufacturing debris created. Hughes and Lampert (1982: 25) argued that the curves 'for only maintenance tools (flake scrapers, core tools and elouera)' at Burrill Lake and Currarong 1 (both on the NSW south coast) showed no appreciable divergence from those for 'all implements' and thus the addition of the 'new tool types' did not affect the trends.

In addition, the evidence from other regions indicates that the appearance of new implement types (e.g., backed artefacts, unifacial points) did not always coincide in time with a 'dramatic' increase in the artefact accumulation rates in all sites and/or regions; for example, not at Sandy Hollow in the NSW Hunter Valley (Fig. 7.11; Table A4/22), Native Well 1 and 2 in the central Queensland highlands (Figs 7.24 and 7.25; Tables A4/37 and A4/38) or Maidenwell in south-eastern Queensland (Fig. 7.28; Table A4/41).

In contrast, at Devon Downs, while the disappearance of points in the upper two spits coincides with a dramatic decrease in the artefact accumulation rate (and may be due to the smaller sample size in these units, Smith 1982: 110–11), there was a more substantial earlier decrease in the number of unifacial points which appears to coincide in time with a substantial increase in the artefact accumulation rate (in spit 4). At Native Well 1, pirri points disappeared from the assemblage in the same level (4) as the most dramatic increase in the artefact accumulation rate (though it was not the period with the highest growth rate). Thus dramatic increases in artefact accumulation rates were associated in one site with the disappearance of an implement type, and at the other with a reduced frequency of an implement type.

The lack of simultaneity in the appearance of new artefact types and substantial changes in the artefact accumulation rates is also seen in sites outside eastern Australia. For example, at Nauwalabila I (the Lindner Site), Arnhem Land, the main concentration of bifacial points occurred in units with the highest number of artefacts per kilo of sediment (units 17 to 9), but they first appeared (a single occurrence) in a much earlier level (unit 27) (Jones and Johnson 1985a: Tables 9.4 and 9.6; Jones 1985: 296). The first appearance of adze/chisel slugs occurred at the beginning of an upward trend in the concentration figures (unit 19) though a substantial increase in the concentrations and the highest concentration figures occurred later (units 17 to 9). The adze/chisel slugs remained in the assemblage throughout the sequence and did not decline in number or disappear with the decrease in artefact concentrations in the upper eight units.

2. Technological changes. The appearance of Bondaian assemblages are described as being characterised by the increased control in flaking, and changes in the preparation of cores and retouched flakes (Stockton 1977a: 216; Johnson 1979: 95, 110–11; Kohen et al. 1984: 66–7; Hiscock 1986: 42–4).

At Sandy Hollow in the Hunter Valley, Hiscock (1986: 44) said technological changes accompanied each of three phases which he called Pre-Bondaian, Phase I Bondaian and Phase II Bondaian. The technological features include faceted platforms (which were introduced and were present only in the Phase I Bondaian spits) and overhang removal. The latter was present throughout the sequence, but the percentage of flakes with overhang removal increased in Phase II Bondaian spits. Pre-Bondaian spits have a virtual absence of platform preparation (Hiscock 1986: 42–4, Table 6). However, although these technological and typological features are present in the spits with the highest artefact accumulation rates, their appearance did not coincide with the most dramatic increase in the artefact accumulation rate (Fig. 7.11, Table A4/22). There was a marked increase in the artefact accumulation rates at the beginning of Phase I Bondaian, but it was not as dramatic as that which occurred within the pre-Bondaian phase or midway through Phase I Bondaian.

At Devon Downs, the technological change was described as a change in the 'reduction processes from flake technology to an opportunistic mode of stone working' (Smith 1982: 114). Smith concluded, however, that this change was not correlated with changes in the 'amount of stone in the deposit' (Fig. 7.23, Table A4/34).

The evidence from Sandy Hollow and Devon Downs suggests that the appearance of a technological change and a dramatic change in the artefact accumulation rates did not always coincide in time. Artefact accumulation rates also increased at times when technological change was not identified.

3. Raw material change. The increased relative frequency of fine-grained materials such as silcrete, chert and indurated mudstone/tuff, which are usually associated with the introduction of the Bondaian assemblages and 'Small Tool Tradition', was not suggested as a reason for the increased accumulation rates. Smith (1982: 110–11) suggested that 'the availability of suitable stone' may be a reason for quantitative changes, but at Devon Downs he argued that there were no obvious changes in the types of raw materials utilised and thus this type of change did not explain the observed variation.

Transition from Middle to Late Bondaian (Bondaian to post-Bondaian)

The disappearance of or a decline in backed artefacts, as well as an increase in the percentage frequency of ground-edged artefacts, bipolar artefacts and quartz as a raw material have been documented at the transition from Middle to Late Bondaian (from Bondaian to post-Bondaian; from Phase 3 to 4 in the Upper Mangrove Creek catchment). The increase in bipolar artefacts represents an increase in bipolar working.

The increase in bipolar artefacts (a 'typological' change), due to an increase in bipolar working (a technological change) is usually associated with an increase in the percentage frequency of quartz (a change in raw material usage). Bipolar working is seen more often on quartz material than on other types of raw material (e.g., silcrete, chert, indurated mudstone/tuff), and increased at the expense of hand-held percussion.

Assemblages in the uppermost levels at many sites in south-eastern Australia (referred to as Late Bondaian, post-Bondaian, Late Small Tool Phase or 'Recent') are quartz-dominant (McCarthy 1948: 22; Lampert 1971a: 16, 44–7, Table 5; Flood 1980: 250, 329; Attenbrow 1981: 45–52). The increased percentage frequency of quartz artefacts in 'recent assemblages' was used by some to explain the continuing increase in rates of artefact accumulation at some sites. For example, Williams (1985) suggested that significant increases in the rates of sedimentation and artefact discard did not occur until after 2000 BP on the NSW south coast and that:

> Perhaps these changes were associated with shifts in technology ... where backed blades tended to drop out of assemblages and were replaced by quartz artefacts, which are mostly unretouched. (Williams 1985: 327–8)

Hiscock (1982b: 43) considered that quartz domination may have been due to the fact that quartz was more highly reduced than other stone types and therefore may reflect only changes in knapping behaviour. An increase in the use of quartz and bipolar technology may result in a greater quantity of debitage being produced per unit time. Individual sites in the Upper Mangrove Creek catchment (Chapter 6) and several other sites in eastern Australia (e.g., Currarong 1 [Lampert 1971a: 67]; Sassafras [Flood 1980: 328]; Shaws Creek K2 [Kohen et al. 1984: Fig. 6]) have quartz-dominant assemblages with decreased rates of artefact accumulation in the upper levels. This shows that increases in the percentage frequency of quartz artefacts at individual sites were not always associated with increases in the artefact accumulation rates.

Conclusion relating to increases in the artefact accumulation rate

It is clear that typological, technological and/or raw material changes, which have been used to identify the introduction of the Bondaian assemblages or the 'Small Tool Tradition' and the transition from middle to late Bondaian (Bondaian to post-Bondaian), did not always coincide in time with the onset of dramatic changes and/or continuing increases in the artefact accumulation rates. Quantitative changes occurred at some sites at the same time as typological, technological or raw material changes, but as a general rule it cannot be said that quantitative changes occurred in all sites or all regions at the same time as the appearance of the Bondaian assemblages/'Small Tool Tradition'.

Decreases in the artefact accumulation rates in the last 1000 years

Decreases in the artefact accumulation rates were explained in terms of typological, technological and raw material changes. Some explanations incorporate a change from stone to another type of raw material, rather than the exchange of one stone type for another (i.e., simple raw material change, as discussed in the previous section).

Typological change

The decrease or disappearance of backed or other artefacts has not been advocated as a reason for decreased artefact accumulation rates — possibly because the latter went unrecognised or was considered unimportant. However, the following examples indicate that it was unlikely there is any association between the two events.

At Maidenwell, the loss of/decrease in backed artefacts coincided in time with a substantial decrease in the artefact accumulation rate at the beginning of the Recent Period, when there was also the greatest decline in the growth rate (Fig. 7.28; Table A4/41). (Morwood 1986: 98, believes the backed artefact in the uppermost excavation unit was 'scuffed up' from earlier levels.) At Native Well 1 and Native Well 2, backed artefacts and pirri points respectively disappear from the assemblages subsequent to dramatic decreases (Figs 7.24 and 7.25, Tables A4/37 and A4/38). In contrast, in the Upper Mangrove Creek catchment, the decline in backed artefacts began before the dramatic decrease in the artefact accumulation rate (Chapter 6).

Technological change

Again, as with the other qualitative changes, whether or not there was a correlation between changes in technology and decreases in artefact accumulation rates varied from site to site. Technological change was investigated by Smith (1982: 111, 114–15) as a cause for the quantitative changes at Devon Downs: a 'change from a well-developed flake technology, including unifacial points, to a more casual approach to stone working in units 1 to 3'. He concluded that the decrease in the artefact accumulation rate was not correlated with the technological change (Fig. 7.23, Table A4/34).

At Sandy Hollow, reanalysis of the artefact distribution patterns by Hiscock (1986: 44, Fig. 3) and myself (Chapter 7, Appendix 4) show that the beginning of the Phase II Bondaian coincided with a substantial decrease in the artefact accumulation rate and the greatest decline in the growth rate (Fig. 7.11, Table A4/22).

Raw material change

Smith (1982: 110–11) proposed that changes in the 'availability of stone' were likely to affect the amount of stone in a site. However, for the sequence at Devon Downs, he (1982: 111–12) concluded that the lack of variation in the index used to measure this aspect indicated that changes in the availability of stone did not explain the observed variations in either the decrease or the increase in the artefact accumulation rate.

A change in the nature of the raw materials used was also proposed as an explanation for decreased amounts of stone in the recent levels of archaeological deposits, i.e., the replacement of stone by another raw material but one which has not survived (Mulvaney 1975: 243), or one which was not left behind (Schrire 1972: 664–6). Both of these explanations are essentially the same (changes in preferred raw materials) except that the new raw materials differ and the reason for the change from the original raw material differs. Although Mulvaney's explanation may partially explain a change in technology (i.e., the 'degeneration' in stone-working), the fact that all archaeological deposits in the area do not have a decline in the artefact accumulation rates in the upper levels make it appear less plausible. It remains a difficult hypothesis to test, unless sites are found which have long histories of habitation and excellent preservation of organic materials throughout.

Conclusions concerning qualitative changes in the stone artefact assemblages

There are some instances where temporal correlations between quantitative and qualitative changes in the artefact assemblages are documented. However, as a general rule, the dramatic quantitative changes in the artefact accumulation rates in the latter half of the Holocene did not occur at the same time (i.e., in the same spit or level in a site) as the appearance or disappearance of backed artefacts, the increased use of bipolar working, an increased use of quartz or changes in other raw materials, or changes in technology. The quantitative changes did not always coincide in time with the appearance of the Bondaian assemblages/'Small Tool Tradition' or the transition from the Middle to Late Bondaian (Bondaian to post-Bondaian).

Such a conclusion implies that

1. if dramatic changes in the artefact accumulation rates are indicative of changes in the population size, then the increase in population was not necessarily associated with the introduction of the 'Small Tool Tradition' or Bondaian assemblages, or any of the other qualitative changes examined above (see also Williams 1985: 5, 327–9).

2. Bowdler's (1981) hypothesis that the association of increases in archaeological phenomena with the appearance of the 'Small Tool Tradition' in the eastern Australian highlands is an indicator that ceremonial activities were associated with the first successful occupation of the highlands is not supported. In addition, the evidence presented in previous chapters indicates that dramatic increases in the habitation establishment rates, the numbers of habitations used and the artefact accumulation rates were not geographically restricted and occurred over a much wider area and diversity of environments than the eastern Australian highlands.

Dramatic increases in the habitation establishment rates, the numbers of habitations used and the artefact accumulation rates may be said to be associated with Bondaian assemblages and the 'Small Tool Tradition' in so far as they often occur within the period in which these assemblages have been identified. However, the dramatic changes in the artefact accumulation rates cannot necessarily be explained by typological, technological or raw material changes in the stone artefact assemblages (or at least those aspects examined above). The appearance of Bondaian assemblages/the 'Small Tool Tradition' and the qualitative changes in the stone artefact assemblages examined above cannot be used as universal explanations for the quantitative changes in the archaeological record.

Conclusions and post-1980s studies

During the past 22 years, many other studies have been carried out which incorporate some of the explanations and interpretations addressed in this and earlier chapters. These more recent regional studies reinforce the results of 1970s and 1980s studies in documenting increasing numbers of habitations established and used during the Holocene, and also the fact that artefact accumulation rates increased in the upper levels of some sites and decreased in others within the same region. Many explanatory models for these quantitative changes still include intensification and increasing social complexity (Lourandos 1997: 240–3), though such processes are often said to begin much later than originally proposed by Lourandos. For example, Ulm and Hall (1996: 54–5) put forward intensification of resource use associated with changes in land-use as late as 1200 BP to explain the increase in shell middens and bevelled pounders that occurred in south-eastern Queensland at that time. Sociodemographic models have also been proposed (Lourandos 1997: 243, 318–21, 327–30; David and Lourandos 1997).

Continent-wide demographic changes are still proposed (e.g., Beaton 1990; Dodson et al. 1992: 119–23; O'Connor et al. 1993: 96, 102; Flood 1995: 248–9), though regional changes, sometimes involving local shifts of population, have been proposed more frequently (e.g., McNiven 1992a; David and Chant 1995: 514; Morwood 1995: 39; Morwood and Hobbs 1995a: 180–2; Morwood and L'Oste-Brown 1995: 175; Ulm and Hall 1996: 55). Researchers still base conclusions on the assumption that changing numbers of sites or artefacts provide a general measure of population increase, for example: O'Connor et al. (1993: 101) state that:

> when the magnitude and direction of change in discard rates are **internally consistent** at the regional level, this must signal fundamental changes in the regional system ... we explicitly assume that regional changes in discard rates of a large order of magnitude do reflect population change (cf. Ferguson 1985).

Changes in site use, that is, in the 'intensity of site use', also remains a common theme (Barker 1991; Lourandos 1993: 74; Boot 1996b: 77–8; David 1991; Morwood and Jung 1995: 97–9; Morwood and Hobbs 1995a: 180–1), as well as periods of abandonment (Morwood, Hobbs and Price 1995: 81, 85). A change from the preferential use of rockshelters to open locations within the same locality was still proposed (McDonald 1994: 74–8, 80, 348–9); and human taphonomic processes (treadage) were investigated to account for changes in artefact accumulation rates (Jung 1992; Morwood and Jung 1995: 99; Morwood and Hobbs 1995a: 181; Lamb 1996b). Natural processes, including the rising sea-level and coastal erosion were still advocated to explain the documented increases in site numbers (e.g., Bird and Frankel 1991a: 3, 5–6, 1991b: 187–8; Dodson et al. 1992: 119–23; Ulm and Hall 1996: 52–3).

Researchers have begun increasingly to undertake detailed investigations which assess changes in site numbers and artefact numbers in individual sites, as well as the abundance and paucity of particular artefact types and stages of reduction at a regional level, in terms of responses to changing risk factors (e.g., Hiscock 1994, 2002; Lamb 1996a; Thorley 1999: 67; Clarkson 2001: 67–8), mobility patterns (e.g., McNiven 1992b, 1994; Hiscock 1996; Barton 2000: 38–9; Thorley 2001), and tool manufacturing and maintenance behaviour (Barton 2000: 38–40). Hiscock (1993: 65, 75) described the transition from pre-Bondaian to Bondaian as representing 'an increase in the regularity and precision of knapping related to raw material conservation'. Many recent consulting reports involving Aboriginal sites on the Cumberland Plain (Sydney region) and in the NSW Hunter Valley incorporate discussions about site function, land-use and mobility patterns. They were among the themes White (2001) explored in addressing reasons why changes in a rockshelter assemblage occurred over time. However, most consulting reports deal with stone artefact assemblages in open contexts and their explanations for assemblage variation in different parts of their study area (e.g., according to stream order) do not address temporal change (e.g., Craib et al. 1999: 138–42; Kuskie and Kamminga 2000; AMBS 2002a, 2002b, 2002c, 2000d, 2003).

Studies have increasingly used more than one 'measure of intensity of site use' (e.g., stone artefacts, faunal remains, ochre, sediment) (e.g., Barker 1991: 105–7; David and Chant 1995: 514; Morwood and Hobbs 1995b; Morwood and Jung 1995; Mulvaney and Kamminga 1999: 272). Some studies have included regional and temporal variations in engraved and pigment images to identify long-term social and demographic changes including changes to territorial boundaries (e.g., David and Chant 1995: 514; Morwood and Hobbs 1995a, 1995b; Morwood and Jung 1995).

At a more continental scale, decreased artefact accumulation rates and sterile layers/disconformities at and about the time of the Last Glacial Maximum have been interpreted as periods of site or regional abandonment or lower population densities (i.e., local shifts in population) and contraction in the size of territories due to increased aridity, particularly in arid and semi-arid regions in northern Australia (e.g., Hiscock 1988b; Ross et al. 1992: 109; Smith 1989; Veth 1989, 1993: 103–14; Allen 1990: 300; O'Connor et al. 1993; Thorley 1999: 66–7; O'Connor 1999: 48–9, 121–2) and Cape York (e.g., Morwood and Hobbs 1995a: 180), as well as after the Last Glacial Maximum in south-west Tasmania (Cosgrove et al. 1990; Cosgrove 1995).

On the other hand, evidence from many regions indicates a richness, complexity and variability in the archaeological record of the late-Pleistocene prior to the Late Glacial Maximum comparable with that documented in many late-Holocene sites in, for example, south-west Tasmania (e.g., Cosgrove et al. 1990; McNiven et al. 1993; McNiven 1994; Cosgrove 1995; Holdaway and Porch 1995); the Kimberley and north-west Western Australia (O'Connor 1999: 199, 122; Balme 2000; Veth et al. 2000: 56); northern Queensland (David 1991; Hiscock 1984; Lamb 1996b); and the NSW south coast (Boot 1996b: 77–8); though David and Chant (1995: 423–4) present an opposing view. The archaeological evidence for the late-Pleistocene and early-Holocene periods of 'intensification' in eastern mainland Australia as speculated by O'Connor (1999: 119, 122) for the Kimberley needs more detailed examination. However, discussions in the final chapters concentrate on explanations for the quantitative changes in the Holocene archaeological record of the Upper Mangrove Creek catchment.

9

Climatic and environmental change in eastern Australia during the late Pleistocene and Holocene

Environmental changes associated with global climatic changes of the late-Pleistocene and Holocene in south-eastern Australia included changes to vegetation patterns and lake levels, as well as rising sea-level. Along the NSW central coast, these changes were of sufficient magnitude to affect both the land and subsistence resources available to inhabitants of the Upper Mangrove Creek catchment and the surrounding regions. People would have responded to these changes, but in doing so, climatic and environmental conditions were determining variables only in so far as they provided a series of options/opportunities and constraints within which the societies operated. Decisions about which options to take, when to adopt them and how resources were utilised were probably based on factors such as social, economical, political and ideological preferences, as well as technological capacities (Fletcher 1977b: 138–40; McBryde 1977: 249; Thomas 1981: 171–2; Gamble 1982: 99–103, 1983: 202, 1984: 250, 256, 1986: 29–31; Bailey 1983b: 150, 164–5; Lourandos 1983b: 43; Rowland 1983: 63; Head 1986: 122).

These environmental changes would have altered the relative abundance and/or spatial distribution of resources across the land, and thus influenced land and resource-use patterns. For example, they would have influenced which parts of the land people used and the methods they adopted to obtain their subsistence needs (including land management practices such as the use of fire and burning patterns), and may have influenced the size of the population which inhabited and exploited particular resource zones (Birdsell 1953, 1971; Hayden 1972; Lampert and Hughes 1974: 231; Bailey 1983b: 149–50; Gamble 1983: 208–9; Ross 1981: 145, 1984: 94; Jones 1985: 293–4; Mooney 1997: 148). In this way, environmental factors may have influenced people's decisions about their subsistence practices which then led to changes in habitation patterns, the size of local populations, land-management practices, and/or the tool kits made, used and maintained within the catchment. Firing vegetation to aid hunting and/or promote plant growth may have exacerbated or altered changes initiated by climatic effects. Environmental change thus indirectly affected the archaeological record by bringing about changes in human behaviour and material culture and the nature and/or amount of physical evidence that was left behind.

Climatic and environmental factors are examined therefore in exploring possible reasons for the observed temporal changes in the catchment's archaeological record. The discussions concentrate on the nature and timing of climatic and environmental changes in the Holocene in south-eastern Australia, and on changes to the morphology of the coastline which were associated with the rise in sea-level after the Last Glacial Maximum. Discussions concentrate on the last 11,000 years, the period for which there is archaeological evidence of human occupation in the catchment.

However, there is very little data on climatic and environmental change available for the catchment, with the only specific information coming from excavated faunal remains (Aplin 1981; Aplin and Gollan 1982; Butler 2000). Information about the effect of sea-level rise on the NSW coastline (e.g., Roy 1984, 1994; Ferland and Roy 1994; Roy et al. 1997) and some vegetational histories for the lower Hawkesbury River and its tributaries (e.g., Dodson and Thom 1992; Johnson 2000) are available. Nevertheless, since the latter studies are limited in number and duration, and refer only to pollen evidence, the following discussions also draw on evidence from several widespread regions in south-eastern Australia as well as global trends.

Climate change

The present climate of the Gosford–Wyong region has been described as temperate maritime, with warm to hot summers and cool to mild winters (NSW Department of Public Works 1977, Vol. 2: 55–6). The Commonwealth Bureau of Meteorology (2003) records for Kulnura, on the eastern watershed of the catchment, indicate mean daily temperatures range from a maximum of 26.4°C in summer to a minimum of 5.6°C in winter. More rainfall is experienced during the summer months than the rest of the year and this rainfall is generally of high intensity as it occurs during summer storms. Monthly rainfall ranges from a mean of 169mm in summer to 51.7mm in winter. February is the time of highest mean and median rainfall. In the Mangrove Creek valley, frosts occur regularly in mid-winter as well as fog and mist, which can remain for much of the morning. Maritime effects of the adjacent coast are modified by the intervening terrain. Compared with the coast, the valley is somewhat drier, has a slightly greater seasonal and diurnal temperature range and less strong winds.

The 10,000 years of the Holocene have been regarded by many as stable with very little or no climatic or environmental change (Costin 1971: 33; McBryde 1977: 225; Wasson 1982: 1). However, climatic and environmental changes have been documented for this period, though the observed variations are both smaller in magnitude and shorter in duration than those recorded for the late-Pleistocene (Bowler et al. 1976: 388; Kershaw 1982: 79; de Menocal 2001: 668; Dodson and Mooney 2002). Some researchers consider the Holocene changes were of insufficient magnitude to affect human behavioural patterns (e.g., Pearson 1981: 58–61; Smith 1982: 115), except perhaps at higher elevations (Costin 1971: 37), whereas others argue the changes were significant in terms of their impact on human resources and subsistence and habitation patterns (Stockton and Holland 1974: 48, 56, 58, 60; Pearson 1981: 61; Lourandos 1983b: 43; Rowland 1983: 62, 70–4, 1999: 146; Ross 1984: 81; Williams 1985: 315–16, 1988: 218, 220; Head 1986: 124).

Broad climatic trends in south-eastern Australia during the late-Pleistocene were much drier and colder between ca 25,000 and 15,000 BP than present, with periods of extreme cold and aridity about the time of the Last Glacial Maximum (Fig. 9.1). At the transition from late-Pleistocene to Holocene, ca 10,000 BP, conditions were similar to or still a little drier and perhaps cooler than present, but they became warmer and wetter during the early-Holocene

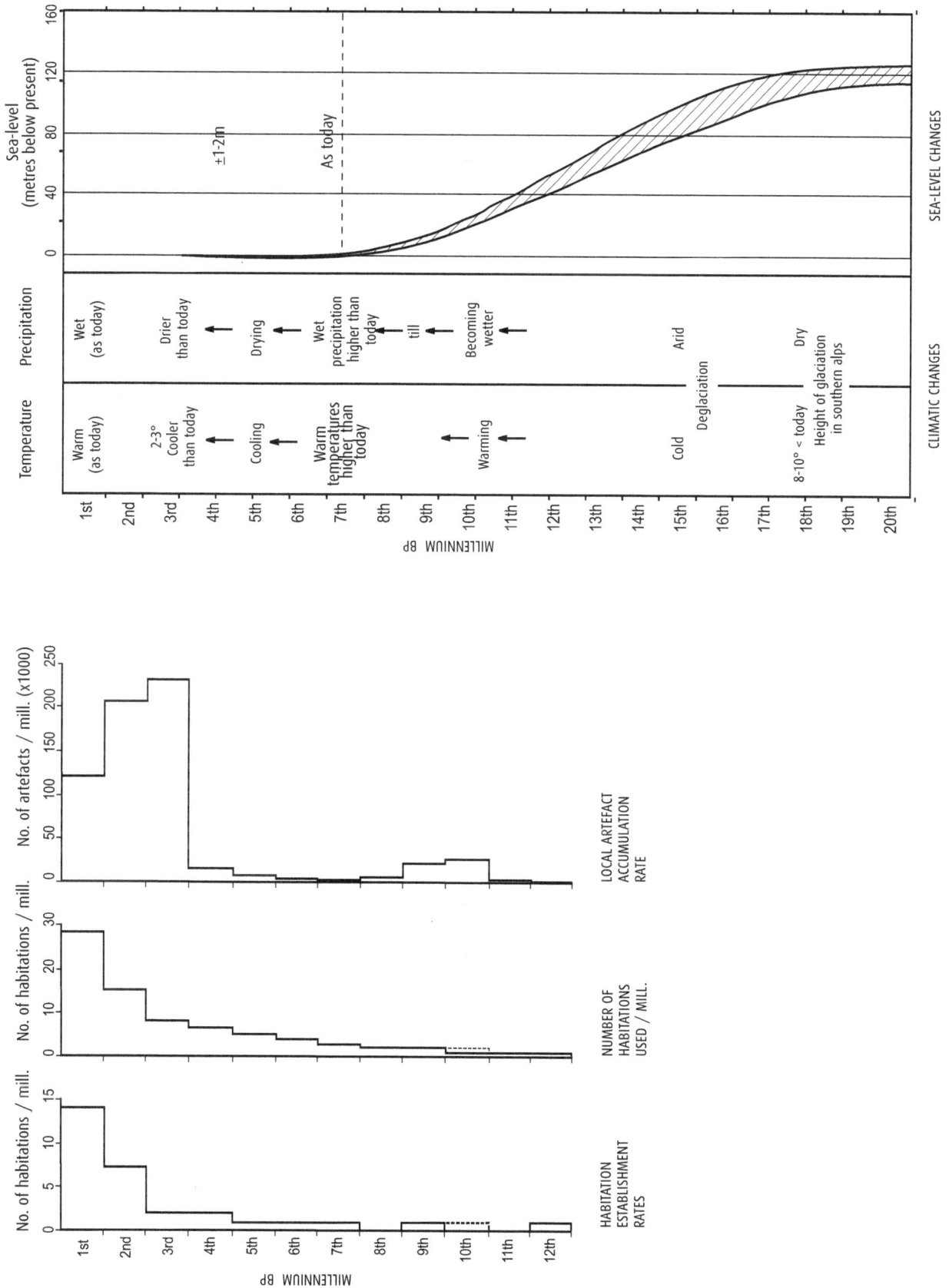

Figure 9.1 Upper Mangrove Creek catchment: comparison between timing of changes in habitation and artefact indices and general climatic shifts and sea-level rise in south-eastern Australia. Sea-level curve based on Roy 1998: Fig. 25.5C.

so that from ca 7000 BP to 5000 BP the climate was warmer and wetter than today. In the late-Holocene, temperatures and effective precipitation fluctuated, but for a time became on average colder and drier than today. The reported timing of colder–drier conditions varies regionally, but occurred between 3800 BP and 1500 BP. During the last 1500–1000 years, average temperature and precipitation again increased to values similar to those of today. Wind direction and intensity are not immediately relevant to my current investigations and therefore discussions on climate focus on temperature and precipitation.

The above trends show broad temporal correlation with data from other southern Pacific-Rim countries which are linked to El Niño–Southern Oscillation (ENSO) events indicating that the general long-term climatic changes in Holocene south-eastern Australia were part of global climate changes. ENSO's mode of operation has not been constant over time, and probably did not operate in its present-day fashion during the period of lower sea-level associated with the Last Glacial Maximum (Markgraf et al. 1992: 194). Timing of the cycles and their strength may also have varied globally. Typical ENSO cycles started to be an influencing factor only about 7000 years ago (albeit weakly at first). They began to exercise a strong presence only about 5000 years ago and were not fully developed until about 3000 years ago (McGlone et al. 1992: 436, 457–8; Rodbell et al. 1999: 519). Onset of its current state in the last 5000 years (Kershaw et al. 2000: 502; or 6000 years according to Markgraf and Diaz 2000: 465; Moy et al. 2002: 164) produced an increase in climate and environmental variability. The South American evidence indicates peak event frequency occurred ~1200 cal BP and then decreased towards the present (Moy et al. 2002: 164). The dominant effect of ENSO in south-eastern Australia was to increase the variability of precipitation (McGlone et al. 1992: 435).

Within the broad climatic trends in eastern Australia, some regional variations, particularly after 5000 BP, were linked to ENSO phenomena, and it has been suggested that changes occurred later in time in north-eastern Australia than in south-eastern Australia (McGlone et al. 1992: 446; Markgraf and Diaz 2000: 474). In addition, there were regional differences, particularly in effective precipitation, which were due to variations in altitude (e.g., southern highlands versus coastal lowlands), geography (e.g., inland versus coastal; semi-arid versus temperate), and hydrologic conditions (Bowler et al. 1976: 388; Chappell and Grindrod 1983b: 2, 1983c: 27–8; Kodela 1992; Markgraf et al. 1992: 195; Harrison and Dodson 1993; Kershaw et al. 2000: 492; Markgraf and Diaz 2000: 474). Variations in the timing and duration of peak conditions have also been reported, sometimes depending on the palaeoenvironmental records used; for example, lake levels or pollen data (Bowler et al. 1976: 388; Harrison and Dodson 1993: 280; Dodson and Mooney 2002: 456, 460).

Late Pleistocene

During the late Pleistocene (ca 35,000 BP to ca 10,000 BP), glacial and periglacial conditions developed in south-eastern Australia and then retreated. This phase of glaciation began about 34,000–31,000 years ago. Mean annual temperatures were probably only 3°C below present at that time, but during the period from ca 25,000 to ca 15,000 BP, they would have been between 6°C to 10°C lower than present (Galloway 1965: 603–6; Costin 1971: 33, 1972: 581, 588–9; Bowler et al. 1976: 359, 370; Singh 1983a: 66, 1983b: 24; Markgraf et al. 1992: 194–5; Kershaw 1995: 660; Kershaw et al. 2000: 490). Throughout the late-Pleistocene, conditions were generally drier than today in the south-east of the continent (Bowler et al. 1976; Rognon and Williams 1977: 301–2; Dodson and Thom 1992: 121, 132). Absolute and effective precipitation during the Last Glacial Maximum has been estimated as being about 50% of today's values (Kershaw et al. 2000: 491).

Glacial conditions and periglacial conditions existed above 1000m, and periglacial conditions existed along the Great Dividing Range as far north as the NSW New England

Tablelands. Along the eastern coast and foothills of the Great Dividing Range, conditions may not have been as extreme during the Last Glacial Maximum due to the ameliorating effect of oceanic influences and, in post-glacial times, may have been ameliorated by the rising sea-level (Costin 1971: 35; Kershaw et al. 2000: 490–1).

By about 15,000 BP, temperatures were rising and deglaciation was in progress, though the colder-than-present conditions lasted until about 10,000-9000 BP (Costin 1971: 33, 36, 1972: 589; Bowler et al. 1976: 387, 389). In southern Australian coastal areas, the evidence indicates a gradual increase in rainfall and vegetation growth conditions between ca 15,000 BP and ca 10,000 BP rather than an abrupt change (Dodson and Hope 1983: 75).

The Holocene

At the beginning of the Holocene, ca 10,000 BP, conditions in many coastal areas in southern Australian were similar to those at present, though some areas remained drier, possibly until ca 9000 BP (Dodson and Hope 1983: 75; Harrison and Dodson 1993: 282; Markgraf and Diaz 2000: 471). Most changes at this time in southern coastal areas can be attributed to decreased continentality associated with the rising sea-level, which in general resulted in an improvement in the rainfall/evaporation ratio, which continued into the Holocene.

The increasing temperatures and precipitation culminated in an early- to mid-Holocene 'optimum', which was warmer and wetter than the preceding 10,000 or so years, and had the highest temperatures and precipitation in the Holocene period (Bowler et al. 1976: 378, 388; Rognon and Williams 1977: 305; Kershaw 1995: 667–9). It was up to 25% or 30% wetter and 1°C warmer than present (Kershaw et al. 2000: 490; Dodson and Mooney 2002: 456). These conditions lasted from about 8000 BP to 4000 BP, although timing of peak conditions varied regionally, being reached earlier in the south of the continent than in the north (McGlone et al. 1992: 435, 446; Markgraf and Diaz 2000: 474; see also Costin 1971: 33; Bowler 1976: 73; Chappell and Grindrod 1983d: 87; Kershaw 1982: 79, 1989: 89; Harrison and Dodson 1993: 282, 287–8). In the south-eastern lowlands, maximum moisture conditions existed between ca 7000 BP to 5000 BP (Bowler et al. 1976: 378; Markgraf et al. 1992: 195–6; Markgraf and Diaz 2000: 474).

The evidence generally points to a return to a cooler drier climate from about 5000 or 4500 BP. It is in this period, especially after 3000 BP, that ENSO began to operate as now and there is evidence for increasing seasonality and variability in precipitation, leading to more marked winter–summer precipitation patterns in some areas (Markgraf et al. 1992: 196, 208; McGlone et al. 1992: 435–6, 457; Markgraf and Diaz 2000: 475). Temperatures and precipitation continued to drop until conditions became cooler and drier than at present. Dates attributed to the duration of this 'colder-drier' period fall between 3800 BP to 1500 BP, with most between 3500 BP and 2000 BP (e.g., Costin 1971: 36–7, 1972: 589; Bowler et al. 1976: 371, 373; Dodson 1987: 79; McGlone et al. 1992: 446; Harrison and Dodson 1993: 276, 279–80). Costin (1971: 36; 1972: 589) estimated temperatures in the Snowy Mountains from ca 4000–3000 to 1500 BP to be about 2°C or 3°C lower than today.

With moister conditions, some vegetation zones may have expanded at the expense of others: more closed vegetation communities increased in area and more open conditions decreased; for example, rainforests and wet sclerophyll forests increased and dry sclerophyll forest decreased, forest expanded into woodland areas, woodland expanded into grasslands, and swamps increased in size and some perhaps became lakes (Bowler et al. 1976: 371–3; Williams 1985: 316; Kodela and Dodson 1988 [1989]: 324–5; Dodson and Thom 1992: 133; McGlone et al. 1992: 446; Jones and Dodson 1997: 20). Alternatively, changes may have occurred as variations in species abundance within vegetation communities (Scott Mooney, pers. comm., 2003). With drier, more arid conditions, the reverse of these conditions would have applied and more open conditions prevailed. Changes in water availability and vegetation patterns brought on by climatic change would in turn have influenced the animal distribution patterns. Fire regimes (natural and/or human) may have altered as well.

Locally, pollen and charcoal records come from cores from swamps on Mill Creek, a tributary of the Hawkesbury River near its junction with Mangrove Creek, and in Ku-ring-gai Chase National Park on the southern side of Broken Bay. These suggest drier conditions occurred between 2900 BP and 1800–1900 BP. At Mill Creek, one core dating from ca 9100 BP to ca 2500 BP indicates that about 2800 BP to 2500 BP the forest was more open than in the preceding period, 9000 BP to 2800 BP, and that the rainforest elements, locally at least, declined at this time (Dodson and Thom 1992: 127–31, 133). Dodson and Thom (1992: 133) suggest that abundant charcoal in the core sections containing rainforest elements indicates that the decline in rainforest and development of more open vegetation was in part due to increased occurrences of either anthropogenic or natural wildfires, and make no reference to climatic change. Another Mill Creek core extending over 863 years to 1993 indicates the presence prior to 1790 AD of dry sclerophyll forest on the valley sides with wetland communities on the valley floor (Johnson 2000). There was little charcoal input during the prehistoric period compared with that of the subsequent European agricultural period beginning in the 1790s (Johnson 2000: 217, 223). In Ku-ring-gai Chase National Park, pollen evidence from a core extending back ca 6000 years suggests there was a possible dry period about 2900 BP, that climatic conditions ca 2000 BP may have been drier than present, and that conditions possibly became slightly drier and the eucalypt canopy opened towards a more woodland type about 1800–1900 BP (Kodela and Dodson 1988 [1989]: 324–5). In contrast with Mill Creek, charcoal declined in Ku-ring-gai Chase National Park within the last 200 years (p. 323), perhaps reflecting the absence of Aboriginal burning and/or the lack of agricultural opportunities in this catchment.

Aboriginal burning patterns have been proposed by several environmental scientists as being responsible for some vegetation and geomorphological changes (or at least for accelerating changes) during the late-Holocene, though their impact is much debated (Bowler et al. 1976: 388; Hughes and Sullivan 1979: 24–5, 1981, 1986; Hughes 1981; Colhoun 1983: 93; Hope 1983: 98; Sullivan and Hughes 1983: 124; Head 1989; Dodson and Thom 1992: 133; McGlone et al. 1992: 449, 455–6, 458; Kershaw et al. 2000: 490, 503). However, others state that in many Australian, New Zealand and South American pollen records, evidence for increasing fire frequency cannot be ascribed to anthropogenic factors alone, and were likely to be the result of increasing climatic variability (Markgraf and Diaz 2000: 475; Dodson and Mooney 2002: 456).

During the last 1000 years, climatic conditions in eastern Australia appear to have been relatively stable with slight increases in precipitation compared with the preceding period (Harrison and Dodson 1993: 276, 279), and slight increases in temperature until those of today were reached (Dodson 1987: 79–80). Marked climatic fluctuations have been documented in the Northern Hemisphere; for example, Europe's Medieval Warm Period in the 11th and 12th centuries AD (950–750 BP), and the subsequent Little Ice Age of the 16th to 19th centuries AD (450–100 BP) (Markgraf and Diaz 2000: 478–9; de Menocal 2001: 668; Jones et al. 2001: 663–5). However, such periods have not been identified in south-eastern Australian records to date (Jones et al. 2001: 664; Mooney 1997: 140), though they have in other Southern Hemisphere regions (e.g., the Little Ice Age in South America [Peru] and New Zealand, Mooney 1997: 147).

Palaeoenvironmental evidence from the Upper Mangrove Creek catchment

Temporal changes in excavated faunal assemblages from the catchment may provide some evidence for environmental change during the last 3000 years, the period during which faunal remains have been preserved. Three excavated archaeological deposits — Loggers, Mussel and Deep Creek — have sufficient faunal remains for changes over time to be investigated. In two of these rockshelter sites — Mussel and Deep Creek — there was a change in the faunal assemblages, particularly in the macropodid component, about 1200–1000 BP (Aplin 1981: 33–4, 51–3; Aplin and Gollan 1982: 20–6; Butler 2000: 85–8). However, it was not identified in the sequence at Loggers, which is in a more open section of the valley system. In some south-eastern Australian regions — e.g., the Snowy Mountains — colder–drier conditions have been recorded as persisting as late as 1500 BP, but as described above, such conditions have not been documented this late in local pollen cores.

In both Mussel and Deep Creek, the lower assemblages are characterised by the presence of *Macropus giganteus* (eastern grey kangaroo) and the relative importance of *M. rufogriseus* (red-necked wallaby). In the upper assemblages, *M. giganteus* and *M. rufogriseus* are absent (the latter is presently uncommon in the catchment) and there is a corresponding rise in *Wallabia bicolor* (swamp wallaby) and *Thylogale* sp. (pademelon) (Aplin 1982: 20–1). In present-day faunal studies, the two species characterising the earlier levels are observed most often in areas of relatively dry, open forest and woodland; both are grazers feeding on grasses, herbs and forbs (Strahan 2000: 335–8, 350–2). The two species characterising the later levels are commonly associated with dense, wet understorey communities; the swamp wallaby is primarily a browser of shrubs and bushes rather than grass, and pademelons have a varied diet of leaves and fruit, or feed on the grassy edges of dense forest (Strahan 2000: 397–400, 404–5).

Aplin suggested that this change in the faunal assemblages could be interpreted as either (1) a shift in the catchment vegetation patterns involving the areal expansion of wet, closed communities at the expense of drier, more open vegetation (Aplin 1981: 52–3; Aplin and Gollan 1982: 21), or (2) a shift in subsistence activities, within a stable environment, towards the resources of wetter, more closed forests (Aplin and Gollan 1982: 21). He (1981: 53) suggested that two factors may account for the postulated variation in vegetation: either variations in magnitude and frequency of firing events, or water-table fluctuations in the valley fill and associated changes to the hydrologic regime of the drainage system. Subsequently, Aplin and Gollan (1982: 24) said, 'a reduction in the frequency of firing events would probably be sufficient to bring about the envisaged vegetational change in the Deep Creek valley.' However, they (1982: 21) argued that since the faunal changes involved 'the local extinction of at least one species of mammal, the grey kangaroo', it was strong support for an environmental interpretation of the sequence. A change in the Aboriginal burning regime seems an unsatisfactory explanation because of the small distances between Deep Creek, Mussel and Loggers shelters (<5km) and because of the implications that the burning was restricted to the vicinity of shelters which show a decrease in the accumulation rates for both artefact and faunal assemblages at this time (Attenbrow 1982a: 42–4).

An environmental interpretation for the change in the faunal assemblages accords with the evidence for a generalised widespread climatic change in the later Holocene from very dry conditions to the moister present-day regime. However, the date for the faunal change in Mussel and Deep Creek (ca 1200–1000 BP) is much later than that indicated by the local palaeoenvironmental records (ca 2000 BP). The reason for this difference is not known. It is possible that the pollen records, which are from swamp contexts, may not reflect exactly the changes that were occurring in the surrounding forests or higher up in the river catchment (e.g., Kodela and Dodson 1988: 324). Further excavated faunal sequences as well as more detailed palaeoenvironmental records from within or near the catchment are needed to establish the nature of the vegetation changes that occurred during this period. Until such data are available, it is not possible to say unequivocally that the excavated faunal sequence is a consequence of environmental changes or changing fire regimes, or whether it represents a change in the animal species people preferred to hunt and eat, which occurred for purely social reasons.

Changes in sea-level

The eastern boundary of the Upper Mangrove Creek catchment is presently ~33km from the ocean coastline (in the closest direct line), and, to the western shores of Tuggerah Lake and Lake Macquarie, it is ~25km and ~28km respectively. The catchment's southern boundary is presently ~18km from estuarine conditions in the lower reaches of Mangrove Creek, and ~28km from the Hawkesbury River.

Although the entire catchment is within the freshwater reaches of Mangrove Creek, its use and occupation would have been affected by physical changes to the adjacent country brought about by the rising sea-level associated with late-Pleistocene and Holocene climatic events. Rising sea-level affected NSW coastal regions in two main ways: by reducing the area of dry land, and altering the configuration of the coastline. The reduction in landmass and westward movement of the coastline in turn affected the degree of continentality experienced by the coastal hinterland. Even after the sea-level stabilised ca 6500 BP, the coastline did not remain a stable environment.

Changes to country

During the Last Glacial Maximum, between 25,000 BP and 15,000 BP, when the sea was between 110m and 130m below its present level (Ferland and Roy 1994: 184–5; Roy 1998: 368), the coastline at Broken Bay would have been between 20km and 25km further east and the Hawkesbury River and its present estuary would have been freshwater (Roy and Thom 1981: Figs 5 and 6; Roy 1983: Fig. 4A). As the sea-level rose during the period ca 18,000–17,000 BP to ca 6500 BP, the catchment itself was not directly impacted by the changes in sea-level, but land between the former (LGM) and current coastline was gradually inundated. At the same time, estuarine conditions gradually extended into the Hawkesbury River valley, with its mouth becoming and remaining marine-dominated. The Hawkesbury River is the largest drowned river estuary on the NSW coast.

The rise in sea-level was not constant: the sea rose rapidly until about 8000 BP (ca 1m/century), but then slowed down to about half that rate between 8000 BP and 6500 BP (Roy 1998: 368). By ca 10,000 BP, it had fallen to –35m; by ca 9000 BP to between –15m and –20m; and, by ca 7000 BP, to between –4m and –6m (Chappell 1983: 121; Chappell and Grindrod 1983d: 87; Roy 1994: 255, 1998: 368). Although it reached its present level and stabilised ca 6500 BP, the sea had reached the base of the cliffs which form the present coastline about 10,000–9000 BP (Roy 1994: 241). When Loggers Shelter was first inhabited, about 11,000 BP, the sea-level was still rising and the shoreline was about 4km to 8km east of the present coastline. To the south, the ocean waters were already extending into the lower sections of the Hawkesbury River palaeo-valley.

On its south-eastern margin, the continental shelf is steeper and narrower than in other parts of Australia and the loss of land along the NSW coastline was not as extensive as it was along the continent's northern or southern coastlines. The rising sea drowned the river valleys along the NSW coast forming 'rias' such as the Broken Bay–Hawkesbury River and Sydney Harbour (Port Jackson) systems. The present NSW coast is essentially a drowned embayed coast where prior bedrock valleys are partially infilled by sandy barriers, tidal flats, lagoons (often called lakes) and deltaic plains (Roy 1984: 99–100, 1994; Roy and Thom 1981: 471). The drowning of these river valleys substantially increased the length of shore with estuarine conditions, and extended the availability of estuarine resources further into the coastal hinterland. By 6500 BP, estuarine conditions extended ~29km up the Hawkesbury River and into the lower reaches of Mangrove Creek; and brackish conditions reached upstream some 50km inland (as far as Windsor).

Although sea-level is usually described as having stabilised ca 6500 years ago, there is evidence that between 4100 BP and 3200 BP the sea-level along the NSW coast was at least 1m, and possibly 2m above the present level due to hydrostatic readjustments (e.g., Chappell 1983: 122; Flood and Frankel 1989; Baker and Haworth 1997, 1999, 2000a, 2000b; Roy 1998: 368, 371). Evidence for higher sea-levels in this period comes from Valla Beach on the NSW north coast (Flood and Frankel 1989) as well as Port Jackson (Sydney Harbour) and Port Hacking (Baker and Haworth 1997, 1999, 2000a, 2000b).

Changes to the southern Australian shoreline after ca 8500 BP have been described as minor compared with those in the period between 15,000 BP and 10,000 BP, and, after ca 6500 BP, to be negligible except for local progradation in some areas (Chappell and Grindrod 1983d: 87) or to be related to gains or losses to the coastal sediment budget (Chapman et al. 1982: 42). However, locally, along the NSW central coast, mid- and late-Holocene changes were somewhat greater and more diverse than these statements imply. They included the formation and/or modification of rock platforms, the building of coastal barriers, the infilling of estuaries, as well as the formation of lagoons when barriers developed across the mouths of drowned valleys (Langford-Smith and Thom 1969; Roy 1984, 1994). The coastline east of the Upper Mangrove Creek catchment includes large barrier estuaries such as Lake Macquarie, Tuggerah and Munmorah Lakes, and Brisbane Waters (Roy 1994: 247). Lake Macquarie, one of the deepest barrier estuaries in NSW, began to form as the sea-level was rising and was ca 5m deep about 8000 BP (Roy 1994: 250–1, 255, Fig. 8).

Coastal productivity and resource availability

In presenting their case for population increase (see Chapter 2), Lampert and Hughes (1974: 228) stated that when the sea-level was rising before ca 7000 BP, any barrier systems that existed on the inner continental shelf would have been less well developed and would have held back smaller bodies of water than those of more recent times; there were probably fewer lagoons and they may even have been ephemeral. There were also fewer rock platforms at that time than in the later period of stable sea-level, and the inter-tidal/near-tidal zone was therefore narrower. Thus, they said, within the period of human occupation, inter-tidal rock platforms and coastal lagoons of reasonable size seem to have been restricted to periods of stable sea-level and perhaps the period just before the sea began its most recent transgression, that is, during the last 7000 or 5000 years. Lampert and Hughes concluded that coastal resources would have been less accessible during the initial period of rising sea-level, but marine resources, particularly molluscs, would have become more abundant in the late-Holocene as a result of coastal developments.

Callaghan (1980: 47) posited that it took 2000 years, between ca 6000 BP and ca 4000 BP, for the marine coastal ecology to stabilise and become favourable for fishing and shellfishing. He based his proposition on basal radiocarbon dates for mid-north coast middens containing some molluscan remains, which cluster ca 4000 BP, and a similar date for a drastic increase in deposition rates in shell middens at Bass Point and Burrill Lake. White and O'Connell (1982: 99) argued that when south-eastern Australian littoral environments were less extensive, shellfish would have been significantly less numerous than they are today, and were thus unlikely to have been as important to coastal populations of 6000 years ago as they were later. Extensive progradation is also said to have changed the nature of subsistence resources over time in Princess Charlotte Bay in north-eastern Australia (Chappell 1982: 75), where Beaton (1985: 13) argued that the 'food base offered during the transgressive intertidal period' was much less productive in terms of numbers of individuals of all shellfish species than in the late-Holocene.

The probability that the late-Holocene shoreline was more productive than shorelines of earlier periods has been substantiated by geological investigations on the continental shelf (e.g., Roy 1984, 1994, 1998, pers.comm. 1986; Pye and Bowman 1984). Present-day rock platforms are the product of long periods of erosion during highstands of the sea and are composite features formed over hundreds and thousands of years, but there were no equivalents to them at the time of the lowest Last Glacial sea-level. The inner continental shelf has bedrock reefs and rocky headlands that extend to depths of 50m to 70m below present sea-level, but below this the inner and outer shelf consists of sediment with few outcrops. At the height of the Last Glacial Period, the coastline was a relatively unbroken sandy beach without the current configuration of headlands, cliffs, beaches, lagoons and deep invasive estuaries and rock platforms. Estuaries in the palaeo-valleys extending across the continental shelf would have been much smaller than today and, combined with the less extensive rock platforms, there would have been correspondingly less abundant fish and shellfish resources. Transgressive barrier estuaries and lagoons did exist throughout the marine transgression, but initially the coastal lagoons would have been small with low productivity. They would have attained their maximum size only towards the end of the transgression and at the beginning of the stillstand period (ca 7000–5000 BP). During stillstand, they have been progressively decreasing in size as they infill with sediment (Roy 1984: 115, Fig. 5; 1994).

With regard to the effects of progradation on the NSW central and south coast, the Shoalhaven and the Hunter Rivers are the only large rivers in areas of subdued coastal topography where relatively extensive estuarine sedimentation has occurred (Roy 1994, 1998; Roy and Thom 1981). Many other smaller areas of infill have occurred in both embayments and estuaries, such as Brisbane Waters and in Lake Macquarie. The degree and effects of progradation vary from estuary to estuary depending on their stage of infilling (Roy 1984); and, in large, deep and steep-sided estuaries such as the Broken Bay–Hawkesbury River system, it would not have been as great as in the smaller barrier estuaries. Roy (1984: 117–18) states that population densities of marine fauna would be highest in estuaries in youthful stages, and that in mature estuaries, estuarine plant and animals experience a general decline in distribution, population numbers and species diversity. In contrast with other parts of the coastline, maximum estuarine productivity was probably reached about 7000 to 5000 years ago.

Coastline modifications associated with the rising sea-level over the last 11,000 years affected the availability of land and subsistence resources on the NSW central coast, though the exact nature and magnitude of the variations in resource abundance are still largely unknown.

The effect of sea-level change on occupation of the Upper Mangrove Creek catchment

The land

The area of land lost from the coastal plain (i.e., land which now forms part of the continental shelf) as the sea-level rose between ca 11,000 BP and ca 6500 BP was not as great as that lost in the previous 7000 or so years (i.e., between 4km or 8km compared with 16km or 17km). People would have moved from the lands being inundated, but the area lost after 11,000 BP was probably insufficient to influence in any major way the distribution of people within a region which would have included the catchment. The loss of land between 18,000 BP and 11,000 BP is more likely to have affected population distributions.

The Hawkesbury River valley experienced changes of a different and more dramatic nature than those of the continental shelf. Drowning of the Hawkesbury palaeo-valley started when the sea-level was at –50m between 12,000 and 11,000 BP. The long, narrow valley bottoms were flooded rapidly up to about Wisemans Ferry. The flooded valley reached its maximum size about 9000 BP or 8000 BP, after which shoaling and infilling began as river sediments were deposited in standing water bodies and point bars began forming.

The formation of Broken Bay and the presence of a broader and deeper Hawkesbury River had several implications. The land lost through inundation may have included alluvial terraces forming river banks (Langford-Smith and Thom 1969: 578), which may have been used as access routes for movement along the river as well as habitation locations. It is more likely, however, that the Hawkesbury River excavated its valley fill during the sea-level lowstand, and few terraces were left when the sea-level started to rise (P. Roy, pers. comm., 1986). The river may also have formed a greater barrier to movement between areas north and south of the river than previously existed, or alternatively, provided an easier mode of crossing the valley — that is, crossing by boat as opposed to having to walk up and down the sides of a deep valley.

Loss of the broad river terraces, if present, may have affected subsistence strategies and the movement of people for other activities, and the presence of the broad river may have affected relationships between local groups of people north and south of the river. No archaeological evidence for either of these possibilities is apparent in the data retrieved to date from the Upper Mangrove Creek catchment.

Availability of resources

Environmental changes associated with the rising sea-level would have affected the distribution and abundance of resources available for people who utilised the catchment in several ways. The land lost due to the sea-level rise meant loss of terrestrial resources, that is, animals and plant foods in the coastal zone. However, in hinterland areas such as the catchment, rainfall/evaporation improved due to decreased continentality and this is likely to have increased water availability and possibly productivity of the timbered lands. In addition, the increased length of estuarine shoreline produced a greater abundance of marine resources. The rise in sea-level also brought abundant marine resources (both ocean and estuarine) much closer to the Upper Mangrove Creek catchment.

These changes in the location, morphology and productivity of the ocean shoreline and estuarine reaches of the Hawkesbury River, lower Mangrove Creek and Brisbane Waters must have influenced the subsistence movements of those people using the catchment. The nature of the effects would have depended on the distribution of local groups (clans and language groups), their subsistence ranges and the 'territorial' boundaries within which they operated. If, in any period, the range of the group/s that inhabited the catchment extended to the coast and/or Hawkesbury River, then changes in the productivity of the ocean and estuary shorelines may have contributed (wholly or partially) to the changing site and artefact distribution patterns in the catchment.

If decreasing continentality in areas such as the Upper Mangrove Creek catchment increased productivity of the forests as well as water availability, it may have encouraged people to extend into or increase their use of these hinterlands by the end of the Pleistocene period. Redistribution of marine resources, both before and after stabilisation of the sea-level, may have influenced local and regional subsistence patterns in the hinterland, including the catchment, as well as along the coastline itself. There is no direct archaeological evidence to indicate that life in the catchment after 11,000 BP was affected by environmental changes associated with the rise in sea-level in a way that would have altered the distribution of habitations, the habitation establishment rate, the number of habitations used or the artefact accumulation rates. However, general correspondence between the earliest date for a catchment habitation and the time when the Hawkesbury River palaeo-valley began to be flooded (ca 12,000 BP to 11,000 BP) suggests there may be an association between initial occupation of the catchment (or at least a level of occupation that is now archaeologically visible) and sea-level rise at this time. People would have been moving westward from inundated coastal lands and also northwards from the inundated Hawkesbury Valley.

Conclusions: correlations between climate and environmental changes and catchment trends in habitation and artefact indices

The earliest evidence for occupation in the Upper Mangrove Creek catchment dates to the terminal Pleistocene, ca 11,200 BP, when conditions were warming up after the glacial conditions of the Last Glacial Maximum and rainfall-evaporation ratios were improving as continentality decreased due to the rising sea-level (Fig. 9.1). The initial or increased level of occupation in the Upper Mangrove Creek catchment just over 11,000 years ago could reflect the last stages of the westward movement of people as the sea-level rose and coastal lands were inundated, combined with their movement into hinterland areas where resource productivity and water availability increased due to decreasing continentality.

As the climate became even warmer and wetter in the early Holocene (reaching a peak sometime between ca 8000 BP and ca 5000 BP, when conditions were warmer and wetter than today), the habitation establishment rate and the number of habitations used increased slowly. An increase in habitation establishment rates is evident in the seventh millennium BP. Early-Holocene trends in the artefact accumulation rates differed slightly to those for both the establishment and use of habitations. They remained low until the fourth millennium BP, apart from a small peak in the 10th and ninth millennia BP, that is, just before the climate became warmer and wetter than today.

Although the climate began to get cooler and drier ca 5000-4500 years ago, it was not until the fourth millennium BP that there was a small increase in the habitation establishment rate; however, the trend in the number of habitations used and the artefact accumulation rate did not change, but continued to increase gradually.

In the last 3000 years, there is not a clear correlation between the timing of the climatic changes and the times at which dramatic changes occurred in the habitation and artefact indices. In the third millennium BP, when the climate became much cooler and drier and more variable than it had been over the previous 7000 years, the local artefact accumulation rate increased dramatically, but the habitation indices continued increasing gradually as before. It was not until later, in the second millenium BP, that there was a dramatic increase in the habitation establishment rate and the number of habitations used. By that time, the climate was still colder and drier than today but average temperatures and rainfall had begun to increase. In contrast with the habitation indices, the local artefact accumulation rate did not increase — it decreased slightly, and remained almost as high as in the second millennium BP. During the first millennium BP, when the climate became yet warmer and wetter until the present climatic regime prevailed, the rate at which habitations were established increased markedly and the number of habitations used rose substantially again, with an increase as great as that in the second millennium BP. In strong contrast with the habitation indices, the artefact accumulation rate dropped substantially, though the rate was still much higher than those before the third millennium BP.

Lack of correlation in the timing and direction of the trends in the catchment's habitation and artefact indices over the last 3000 years could be interpreted as there being no causal relationship between climatic events and the human behaviour which produced the quantitative changes in the archaeological record, but this need not necessarily be the case. The documented trends in habitation and artefact indices in other areas of eastern Australia also indicate much variability. They suggest that dramatic changes in the habitation and artefact indices occurred principally within the latter half of the Holocene, but were not necessarily restricted to that period. A similar pattern is seen in the growth rates for each of the indices indicating that the presently documented dramatic increases are not solely the result of exponential increase. Again, such regional variation could suggest that changes in the archaeological record and the climatic changes were unrelated. However, the extent to which the subsistence resource base was affected would have varied from region to region depending on local factors — in some areas, climatic changes may have been beneficial, but in others detrimental. In addition, the timing of the onset and duration of changed environmental conditions in response to a particular climatic variation was not uniform across the continent. Thus, because of variations in the range of options available to each group, the cultural changes that occurred were unlikely to be uniform in all regions (cf. Allen 1996: 201).

Environments with limited water supplies, or an excess of water, were probably affected more markedly and earlier than richer environments and thus the subsistence strategies of people occupying these areas are likely to have been affected at an earlier date than those of people in other types of environments. In some areas, the change may have promoted movement into previously unoccupied environments or the use of specific resources within the same environment, or prompted changes in exploitation strategies which involved changes in the degree of mobility or the types of material technology used. Regional variation will have occurred because of specific local conditions: geographical, social, technological and the history of events that occurred in the past. For these reasons, the timing and direction of changes in habitation and artefact indices are unlikely to be uniform in all regions.

Even though the exact nature of the impact of climatic changes on resources is often uncertain (cf. Veth et al. 2000: 60, 62), it is generally agreed that variations in the abundance and distribution of subsistence resources occurred at times of climate and environmental change. Warmer–wetter conditions are often referred to as 'optimal', and a change to warmer–wetter conditions as 'ameliorating', whereas a change to colder–drier conditions is seen as 'deteriorating' (e.g., several contributors to Chappell and Grindrod 1983a; Kershaw 1984: 69). Many archaeologists appear to accept or assume that periods of colder–drier conditions had less abundant resources and were more stressful, and that the number of people inhabiting a particular area or region was related to the level of resources available (e.g., Lampert and Hughes 1974: 231; Pearson 1981: 57–8; Ross 1981, 1984). Lourandos, for example, says: 'If there is a close relationship between population and environment, then declining populations could be expected as conditions became drier and more stressful' (1985b: 38), and, 'the early-Holocene was generally more humid than the late-Holocene which, being drier, was a more stressful period' (1997: 311). However, in some regions, the colder–drier period may not have had fewer subsistence resources than the warmer–wetter periods, and may not have had a lower human population. The consequences of climatic changes may have been beneficial in some areas but detrimental in others (White and O'Connell 1982: 99; Rowland 1983: 63; Head 1986: 124, 1987: 457; Bird and Frankel 1991a: 10). Similarly, the effect of sea-level changes will not have been the same in all parts of the continent (Chappell 1982: 70, 78). Although some information is available for the Upper Mangrove Creek catchment, there are still many unknowns, for example:

1. what was the nature of changes in vegetation and faunal distribution patterns at a regional level — did the faunal changes documented in the catchment occur elsewhere and at the same time?

2. how did overall resource availability and/or productivity change with the climatic changes?

3. was resource productivity greater in the recent warmer–wetter period than in the preceding cooler–drier period; that is, was the change advantageous or detrimental to the region's inhabitants?

More detailed studies are needed, but in the meantime, ways of interpreting and explaining the catchment's archaeological record, and of exploring possible influences of the regional climatic and environmental changes on habitation, subsistence and land-use patterns, are addressed in the following chapter.

10

From numbers of sites and artefacts to habitation, subsistence and land-use patterns

Many cultural and natural processes have been proposed as explanations for the type of quantitative changes that have been documented in the habitation and artefact indices of the Upper Mangrove Creek catchment. In interpreting the catchment's long-term trends, general broad-scale demographic changes that affected the whole continent since initial colonisation cannot be discounted as having played a role. However, the catchment's population trends may not have followed continent-wide trends, which have long been debated (Birdsell 1953, 1957, 1977; Beaton 1983, 1985, 1990; Lourandos 1985b; Rowland 1989; Davidson 1990). An interesting aspect of the catchment data set is that trends in the habitation and artefact indices varied, with the dramatic changes in each index occurring in different millennia and the direction of the changes differing from each other in the last 1000 years (Fig. 9.1). In the first millennium BP, habitation indices continued to increase while the local artefact accumulation rate decreased substantially. Therefore, if it is accepted that increasing numbers of artefacts indicate increasing population size, then the decreased numbers of artefacts in the first millennium BP could mean there were fewer people inhabiting the catchment at that time.

Inter- or intra-regional shifts in population in different periods of time also cannot be discounted as having brought about changes in the catchment's habitation and artefact indices. These movements entail people shifting the focus of their lives and daily activities from one environmental or geographic zone to another on a long-term basis. For example, they can take place through changes in seasonal subsistence patterns, changes in territorial/range/domain boundaries, or redistribution of populations in response to long-term global environmental changes. These regional-scale options cannot be investigated for the catchment yet, as appropriate levels of archaeological information are not available in adjacent areas and regions. The presence of estuarine shell (*Anadara trapezia*, Sydney cockle) in the upper levels of some of the catchment shelters indicates contact between the coast and/or estuary and the catchment, at least in the recent past, but not necessarily seasonal movements. Regional ethnohistorical descriptions refer to people travelling into the 'mountains' from Lake Macquarie ca 30km away on the adjacent coast for trading purposes (Threlkeld 1826 in Gunson 1974, Vol. 2: 206), but make no mention of seasonal movements. The 'mountains' referred to were probably the sandstone plateaux of the coastal hinterland and not the Great Dividing Range, but whether this would have included the catchment is not known. Similarly, in the Sydney region to the south, early colonial descriptions of Aboriginal life provide no evidence for seasonal movements (Attenbrow 2002: 53). However, that is not to say that seasonal movements between coast and hinterland could not have occurred in the past. In the terminal Pleistocene and early Holocene for instance, when the coastline was further to the east and more land was available, territories may have been larger and movements perhaps less restricted than in, say, the last 6000 years. However, no archaeological evidence for seasonal movements has been identified in the catchment or elsewhere on the NSW central coast.

Late-Holocene changes in habitation distribution patterns and the way subsistence activities were organised within the catchment, which may have included variations in mobility patterns, are also likely reasons for changes in both the numbers of habitations and the numbers of artefacts within individual habitations and the catchment as a whole. This proposition is examined below with some of the data available for the catchment.

Variations in the 'intensity of site use', which refers to changes in the number of person-days spent at a habitation, through either variation in the number of people, the number of visits or the length of each visit, may also have occurred. Nevertheless, there are other reasons which could account for increasing or decreasing artefact accumulation rates in individual habitations and these need to be addressed before change in 'intensity of site/catchment use' is accepted as an explanation. They cannot be fully addressed, however, until other analyses of the excavated assemblages (some of which are discussed below) are completed.

Dramatic changes in the artefact accumulation rates in the catchment, as in other regions in eastern Australia, were not correlated in time with either the introduction of new implement types or changes in technology or raw materials, all of which were part of geographically widespread, long-term changes in the stone artefact assemblages (Chapters 2, 6, 7 and 8). The reasons for such changes in the stone artefact assemblages are still subject to research and debate. Suggested explanations include changes in the availability of and access to stone materials because of variations in group boundaries and relationships due to social and territorial reorganisation, and/or changes in the nature and level of subsistence risk as a consequence of variations in plant and animal resource availability associated with climatic and environmental changes. Possible causes of subsistence risk, and risk minimisation strategies which may have produced increases and decreases in the artefact accumulation rates, are explored below.

Changing trends in both the habitation and artefact indices reflect the way people lived within only one part of their country: the Upper Mangrove Creek catchment. The catchment (which is only 12km by 10km) would have been only part of a clan territory and part of the range of a band or bands who, at contact, belonged to a language group now known as the Darginung. In 1788 (at the time of British colonisation), and for an unknown time beforehand, the Darginung (and their predecessors) would have belonged to a yet larger 'culture-area' (cf. Lampert 1971a: 70) which was east of the Great Dividing Range and extended from Port Macquarie in the north to the NSW/Victorian border in the south (Fraser 1892: ix, map, 1892 [1893]: 32, map, Appendix X: 92; Eades 1976; Attenbrow 2002: 33) (a smaller area than the south-eastern culture area of Peterson [1976: Fig. 8]). Trends in the catchment's habitation and artefact indices thus cannot be interpreted without reference to what people may have been doing in other parts of their country or their neighbours' country, which lay on each side of the catchment.

In south-eastern Australia, the appearance of new implement types and changes in technology and raw materials (Chapters 2, 7 and 8) were part of a sequence of stone artefact assemblages which McCarthy (1964a, 1964b: 201–2, 1976: 96–8) called the Eastern Regional Sequence, and which is presently under review (Hiscock and Attenbrow in press). There are regional and sometimes local variations in the assemblages of each phase and the phases appear to have begun at slightly different times in different regions. Such regional differences were possibly due to variations in local environmental conditions and the way each region responded to climatic change as well as to regional variations in social organisation, territoriality and subsistence patterns due to historical precedents (Attenbrow 1987: 365–8). In addition, and for the same reasons, there would also have been variations in the habitation–subsistence organisation of each region or locality. These broad-scale behavioural changes, which are reflected in the stone artefact assemblages across the culture-area, would have been a 'background' to habitation and subsistence strategies used in the catchment. The catchment's habitation and subsistence strategies would have been related to its specific environmental characteristics and the role they played in its inhabitants' lives.

In earlier chapters, it has been shown that several explanations for dramatic changes in habitation and artefact indices do not apply to the catchment. For example, the impact of geomorphological processes (e.g., burial, erosion and deflation) on habitation distribution patterns in the catchment were found to be an unlikely source of bias in the observed trends in rockshelter sites, though they may have skewed the recording of open archaeological deposits (Chapter 5). Greater visibility of habitation sites due to an increase in the number of stone artefacts manufactured per person is also unlikely given the fact that the local artefact accumulation rate, as well as the rate in many individual habitations, decreased during the period when substantial increases occur in the habitation indices. Some explanations cannot be investigated without further fieldwork, for example, intra-site changes in the location of discard. Comparison of sequences in individual 50 × 50cm pits within the same rockshelter suggests this is an unlikely reason, particularly given the relatively small size of many catchment rockshelters.

The following discussions therefore focus on behavioural explanations and processes that are likely to have affected the catchment's archaeological record. Interpretations of the dramatic increase in the habitation indices revolve around habitation patterns and subsistence organisation, while those for the artefact accumulation rates centre on subsistence methods and equipment. They include the concepts of mobility and risk, which were highlighted earlier as potentially fruitful avenues to explore the dramatic changes in the catchment's habitation and artefact indices (Attenbrow 1982b: 76–7; 1987: 368–77, 384).

Habitation patterns and subsistence organisation

In earlier chapters, the habitations have all been treated as functionally equal, although it was foreshadowed in Chapter 3 (defining Archaeological Deposits) that they may not all have been used for the same activities. Their likely function is thus explored as a start to investigating the habitation and mobility patterns and subsistence organisation that operated within the catchment.

Base camps, transit camps and activity locations

Binford's (1978, 1980, 1982, 1983) ethnographically based forager–collector model has been important in identifying past habitation, subsistence and land-use patterns from archaeological site distribution patterns. In Binford's model, the principal contexts for discard or abandonment of artefactual remains, and thus places which can be identified archaeologically, were 'residential (home) bases' and 'locations'. Binford (1980: 9) defined residential bases as 'the hub of subsistence activities, the locus out of which foraging parties originate and where most processing, manufacturing, and maintenance activities take place'. Locations, also referred to as 'functionally specific sites', were defined as

> ... a place where extractive tasks are exclusively carried out ... only limited quantities [of food and raw materials] are procured there during any one episode, and therefore the site is occupied for only a very short period of time ... abandonment of tools is at a very low rate. In fact, few if any tools may be expected to remain at such a site. A good example of a *location* generated by foragers, a wood-procurement site ... (Binford 1980: 9–10)

Binford (1980: 10) defined three other places associated with the 'collector end' of the forager–collector continuum: 'field camp' (overnight camps while away from the residential base), 'station' (e.g., ambush locations or hunting stands) and 'cache'. In his model, these latter places were associated with collectors who were characterised by storing food for at least part of the year and who logistically organised procurement parties. Such locations were used rarely by foragers, who typically did not store food but obtained it daily, ranging out on an 'encounter' basis before returning to their home base each afternoon or evening (p. 5); they stayed only occasionally in overnight camps when hunting (p. 7–8).

Binford's model was based on ethnographic studies of the Nunamiut Eskimo of Alaska, the Gwi San and Dobe !Kung of the Kalahari Desert, as well as equatorial groups (Binford 1978). Other researchers, however, based on their own ethnographic observations in other countries, included a much wider range of places as 'activity locations' within forager subsistence strategies; for example: hunting hides, viewing/lookout points, artefact preparation locations, manufacturing localities, tree-felling areas, waterholes, ceremonial locales, burial areas, shade areas, as well as areas associated with food procurement (e.g., kill and butchery sites, and plant gathering areas), firewood and raw material sources (Foley 1981b: 164, 1981c: 11, 107, Table 2.1; Bettinger 1991: 66; Veth 1993: 83, 90). In northern Australia, in addition to base camps used by the present-day Anbarra, Meehan (1988: 179–80) described overnight (transit) camps, and places which she referred to as 'dinner-time camps'. At some 'dinner-time camps', shellfish were processed and the meat was taken back to the base to eat.

Characteristics that have been said to identify base camps or distinguish them from activity locations in archaeological contexts include size (area in square metres) as well as the diversity, richness and nature of artefact types and faunal remains. Binford (1982: 15) proposed that base camps would have the most complex mix of archeological remains since they were commonly used logistically when residential camps were elsewhere. Meehan (1988: 179–80) observed that base camps have a much larger area and much wider range of food species, and, since parts of some animals would be eaten at dinner-time camps, home bases may not have the remains of whole animals. Nelson (1991: 79–81, 85) said locations identified archaeologically as base camps have a greater diversity and richness of artefacts representing a greater range of activities undertaken on site and in the immediate area, in contrast with activity locations that have low diversity of artefact types used for a few specific and focused activities. She cautioned, however, that the nature of the stone artefact assemblages and classes of artefacts representing reduction strategies at base camps would depend on the technological system operating at the time. Evidence of storage was another characteristic she said distinguished base camps from activity locations (Nelson 1991: 82).

For the Upper Mangrove Creek catchment, there are no historical or ethnographic descriptions of subsistence strategies or land-use practices for the early colonial period. Historical sources for adjacent areas suggest that groups moved frequently and those inhabiting the hinterland of the NSW central coast would have employed strategies closer to those of foragers rather than collectors (e.g., Threlkeld 1825–26, 1826; see also Brayshaw 1986; Vinnicombe 1980; Attenbrow 2002). On this basis, it is proposed that the catchment's inhabitants were relatively mobile hunter-gatherers who moved between many short-term base camps within their country, with group size varying according to weather, season and locality. While in the catchment, family groups stayed at base camps for several nights undertaking a range of domestic tasks, members going out daily to obtain food and raw materials. Tasks undertaken at activity locations away from base camps may have included: (a) hunting, butchering, fishing (including eels) and shellfishing (freshwater mussel), plant and honey collecting; (b) procuring raw materials, such as stone, wood, plant fibre and resin; and, (c) religious or ritual responsibilities. During these daily forays, to places inside or outside the catchment, damaged tools and implements would have been mended, and food prepared and/or eaten at locations away from the base camp. People also may have sought protection in rockshelters during the day from the extreme heat of summer, the frosts and cold winds of winter, and the rain at any time of the year. Individuals or small groups would have made occasional longer trips for subsistence, trade or social purposes to places which necessitated the use of overnight/transit camps away from their base camps. Large gatherings for ceremonial purposes probably occurred at locations outside the catchment.

Within the catchment, in addition to the numerous archaeological deposits (habitations), there are also many sites with images (mostly pigment drawings in shelters) and grinding grooves (and a scarred tree outside the random sampling units). Together, this suite of archaeological sites demonstrates that many of the activities described above were carried out. Overnight camping and a range of domestic tasks were undertaken at habitations. The grinding grooves indicate that the shaping and sharpening of ground-edged implements occurred, and the pigment and engraved images were likely created in association with both religious and secular activities. Although there is no outcropping bedrock in the catchment from which stone artefacts can be made, pebbles and cobbles eroded from the Hawkesbury sandstone and conglomerate beds in the Narrabeen sandstones are available on the ridgesides and in creek beds (Chapter 3). Some catchment habitations may have been used as transit camps by people travelling from one locality to another on ceremonial business or to procure raw materials by direct access or trade — for example, along the historically documented route between the Hunter Valley and Brisbane Waters via the Wollombi Valley and the ridge forming the catchment's eastern boundary, which also linked with other routes extending west as far as Mudgee–Rylstone (McCarthy 1936: 2–3, 1939a: 1, 1939b: 407, 1939c: 100).

Identifying base camps, activity locations/transit camps

Although I address only the habitation indices in this section, it is not realistically possible to address the habitation indices by themselves. As mentioned above, the number of artefacts in each habitation varied widely, and the small size of the assemblages in some (even when extrapolated to estimated total numbers) suggests all were not base camps. Even the six long-term habitations (i.e., those used for more than 3000 years) with the most abundant and richest assemblages were unlikely to have been only base camps throughout their history of use. Their earliest use may have been as activity locations or transit camps (cf. Morwood and L'Oste-Brown 1995: 161).

Stone artefact analyses appropriate to investigating whether 'habitations' are base camps, transit camps or activity locations, and whether their function varied over time, have not been undertaken (see below). Therefore, to explore this idea further, I used the breakdown into 'millennial assemblages' for individual habitations, which was used in calculating the local artefact accumulation rates (Table 6.13, Appendix 2). These figures represent the estimated total number of artefacts that accumulated in a habitation site in each millennium. To devise a model based on assemblage size which can be tested later through the archaeological assemblages, a K-means cluster analysis was employed as it provides a good approximation of the number of divisions into which a population can be split (Orton 1980: 52–3; Wright 1992). This analysis indicated that the millennial assemblages could be grouped into either four or seven clusters (Table 10.1). In both series, there are large gaps between the clusters at the higher end of the figures, but at the lower end, there is no obvious break between 'small' and 'large' assemblages. There is thus no clear indication of what can be assigned as activity locations/transit camps or base camps, assuming the former would have a small number of artefacts discarded at them whereas the latter would have had much larger assemblages incorporating debitage from stone implement manufacture. So, for the purpose of model-building, the lowest group in the cluster of seven (0–2350) was taken as activity locations/transit camps, and the other groups as base camps. This assignment on the basis of estimated artefact numbers is still somewhat arbitrary and speculative. However, when the grouping into four clusters was chosen and assemblages in the 0–7000 cluster were assigned as activity locations/transit camps, there were no base camps in the catchment until the third millennium BP, except in Loggers in the 10th and ninth millennia BP. While that is a possibility, it seems a less reasonable basis on which to develop a hypothesis than the one adopted.

Clearly, in testing the proposed habitation and land-use model, one avenue to investigate will be whether the 'habitations' and/or the millennial assemblages in long-term 'habitations' in 'Group 0–2350' are activity locations or transit camps and whether the others are base camps. Assemblages resulting from very short-term or infrequently used base camps could overlap in size with frequently used activity locations. Assemblage/artefact attributes chosen for analysis need to be those that will identify whether assemblages were derived from domestic activities at base camps (e.g., cooking and eating of meals by family groups, and implement manufacture), hunting and gathering tasks that would happen in activity locations (e.g., minor maintenance of hunting equipment and butchery of large animals), or preparation and consumption of food by small groups as would occur in transit camps. Questions to address include: what level of diversity exists in tool types and faunal species (bearing in mind the effect of sample size; Attenbrow 1981: 170, 1987: 134–5, 147; Grayson 1984: 116–30; Thomas 1989: 86; Hiscock 2001)? What activities are represented by the assemblages? What do use-wear and residue analyses tell us about tool functions? What reduction stages are

Table 10.1 Upper Mangrove Creek catchment: millennial assemblages grouped according to K-means analysis.

NO. AND SIZE OF CLUSTER	MILLENNIAL ASSEMBLAGES	SITES
Grouped into 4 clusters		
0–7000	63 [3]	30
11,550–25,250	12	6
36,450–66,350	4	4
165,200	1	1
Grouped into 7 clusters		
0–2350	52 [3]	28
2650–7000	11	5
11,550–17,200	9	6
23,200–25,250	3	2
36,450–46,300	3	3
66,350	1	1
165,200	1	1

represented in the stone artefacts — stone implement manufacture or only tool maintenance? What particular skeletal parts of animals are present? What other cultural features are present, e.g., hearths or heat-treatment pits? Issues relating to measuring 'intensity of site use' could be addressed by analysing deposition rates for more than one set of evidence; for example, faunal as well as stone artefact assemblages, charcoal and sediments (cf. Smith 1982; Hiscock 1984: 134; Morwood 1986). Site location analysis may also identify whether any category is associated with specific environmental or topographic contexts and habitat/resource zones (Foley 1981a: 4–7).

Using the above basis for assigning assemblages as base camps or activity locations/transit camps, only one of the seven long-term 'habitations' appears to have been a base camp throughout it history of use — Emu Tracks 2, first established in the fourth millennium BP. The function (or principal function) of the other long-term 'habitations' changed over time from activity location to base camp. Loggers was used initially as an activity location in the 12th millennium BP (i.e., <2350 artefacts accumulated in that millennium, see Table 6.13), and it was not until the next millennium that a base camp was established there, which was then used for such purposes throughout its history. Three long-term 'habitations' were not used as base camps until the third and another until the second millennium BP. In the first millennium BP, only one 'habitation' was first used and established as a base camp (Mangrove Mansions, though it is its large area that results in a high estimate for the total number of artefacts and places it in this category, rather than the excavated assemblage size), and another used as a base camp in the second millennium BP reverted back to use as an activity location. Of the 22 'habitations' used solely as activity locations, only one was initially used before 3000 BP — Kangaroo and Echidna. This was established by at least 6700 BP, based on a radiocarbon age for a level 28cm deep. Extrapolation of this date to the base of the cultural deposit at 43cm using a depth/age curve would place initial establishment about 9800 BP (Table A2/12), but this seems improbable and here a maximum age of 7000 BP is assumed.

Most activity locations were first used in the last 2000 years — seven in the second millennium BP and 13 in the first millennium BP. Some may have been used only once, whereas others were used on numerous occasions over centuries or millennia. Even once established as a base camp, 'habitations' would have been used occasionally or frequently as an activity location on daily forays, or as a transit camp on long-distance trips for trade, ceremonial or other social purposes (cf. Binford 1982: 15; Ebert 1992: 30–1).

Variations in the number of base camps and activity locations in different millennia (Table 10.2, Fig. 10.1) support the proposition that habitation patterns and subsistence organisation in the catchment changed over the last 11,000 years, and that change of an unprecedented scale and nature began in the third millennium BP. In this period, a substantial increase in base camps occurred which contrasts with the lower number of locations used solely as activity locations/transit camps. The timing of this change, based on the size of assemblages within 'habitations' was earlier than the dramatic increase in the habitation indices, which was in the second millennium BP (Fig. 9.1). As well as an increase in the number of activity locations in the second and first millennia BP, there was also the use of topographic zones which had not been used (or not often used) before (Table 10.2), though given the small size of the catchment this should not be interpreted as movement into marginal environments (Lourandos 1983a: 82; 1985a: 391, 400) or into unfamiliar territory (Hiscock 1994: 277–8, 282).

During the last 4000 years, and perhaps more commonly in the last 2000 years, in addition to activities that occurred within 'habitations', the manufacture and maintenance of ground-edged implements occurred on sandstone where water was available, e.g., in creek-

Table 10.2 Upper Mangrove Creek catchment: distribution of base camps (BC) and activity locations/transit camps (AL/TC) in each topographic zone in each millennium. Numbers in square brackets indicate a location possibly used in that millennium.

MILL. BP	MAIN VALLEY BOTTOMS		PERIPHERY RIDGETOPS		SUBSIDIARY RIDGESIDES		MAIN RIDGESIDES		SUBSIDIARY VALLEY BOTTOMS		PENINSULA RIDGETOPS		RATIO	TOTAL 'HABITATIONS'
	BC	AL/TC	BC	AL/TC	BC	AL/TC	BC	AL/TC	BC	AL/TC	BC	AL/TC	BC:AL/TC	
12th		1											0:1	1
11th	1												1:0	1
10th	1					[1]							1:[1]	1 +[1]
9th	1			1		[1]							1:1+[1]	2 +[1]
8th	1			1		[1]							1:1+[1]	2 +[1]
7th	1			1		1							1:2	3
6th	1			1		2							1:3	4
5th	1			2		2							1:4	5
4th	1	1	1	2		2							2:5	7
3rd	2		2	2	1	2							5:4	9
2nd	2		4		1	5				2		2	7:9	16
1st	2	1	3	2	1	9		2	1	6		2	7:22	29

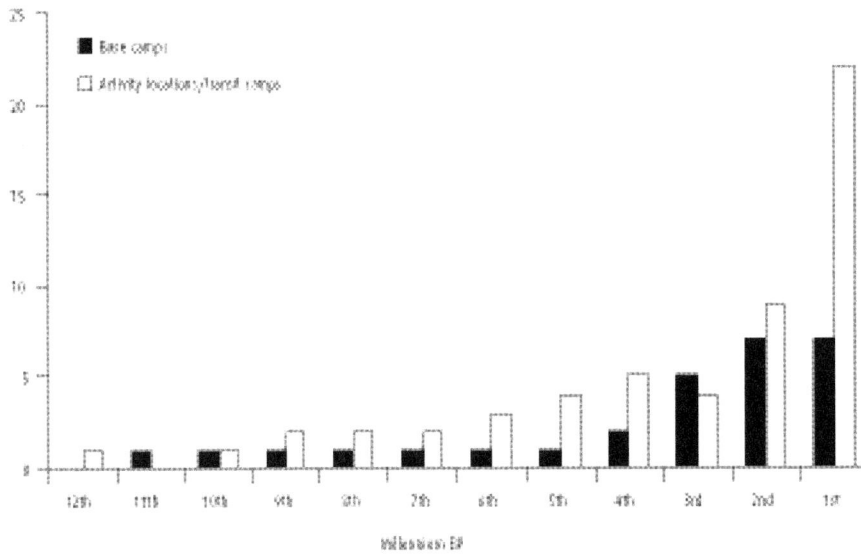

Figure 10.1 Upper Mangrove Creek catchment: number of base camps and activity locations/transit camps used in each millennium.

lines, adjacent to rock pools and seepage areas on rock platforms, and beneath rockshelter driplines. Chronological assignment of these activities is based on the presence of ground implements and ground fragments in stone artefact assemblages dated to the last 4000 years, and increasingly in the last 2000 years, when there is also a greater amount of igneous material in the assemblages (Table 10.3, Figs 10.2 and 10.3). Most sites with grinding grooves (74%) occur in the upper elevations of the catchment — on Hawkesbury sandstone exposed in creek-lines and on rock platforms principally in the periphery ridgetop zones (Table 4.2, Figs 4.1 and 4.2). This grinding groove distribution pattern reinforces the view that activities were increasingly dispersed across the catchment in the last few thousand years.

Half the locations with images (principally pigment in rockshelters) are on ridgesides above subsidiary creeks; the rest are relatively evenly distributed in each of the other zones,

Table 10.3 Upper Mangrove Creek catchment: number and percentage frequency of backed, ground, igneous, bipolar and quartz artefacts in each millennium.

MILLENNIUM BP	TOTAL NO. OF ARTEFACTS	BACKED ARTEFACTS		GROUND ARTEFACTS		IGNEOUS ARTEFACTS		BIPOLAR ARTEFACTS		QUARTZ ARTEFACTS	
		NO.	%	NO.	%	NO.	%	NO.	%	NO.	%
12th	5									2	40.00
11th	145					1	0.69			51	35.17
10th	906					2	0.22	1	0.11	309	34.11
9th	873	1	0.11			3	0.34	1	0.11	332	38.03
8th	167	1	0.60			1	0.60	1	0.60	53	31.74
7th	146					1	0.68			58	39.73
6th	167					2	1.20	3	1.80	53	31.74
5th	219	1	0.46			5	2.28	4	1.83	81	36.99
4th	444	5	1.13	1	0.23	3	0.68	11	2.48	144	32.43
3rd	5936	67	1.13	9	0.15	58	0.98	196	3.30	3079	51.87
2nd	6694	30	0.45	16	0.24	222	3.32	288	4.30	3754	56.08
1st	3455	8	0.23	24	0.69	144	4.17	189	5.47	1942	56.21

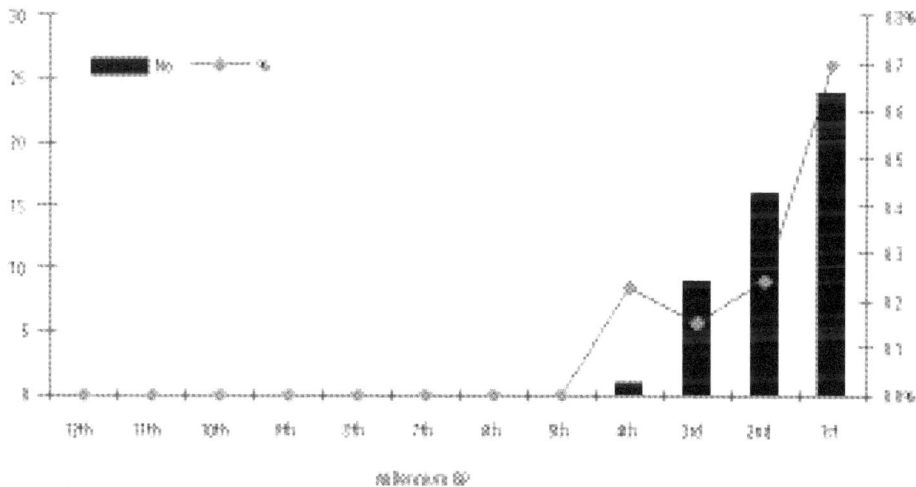

Figure 10.2 Upper Mangrove Creek catchment: number and percentage frequency of ground implements and ground fragments in each millennium.

except peninsula ridgetops. Unfortunately, the creation of pigment and engraved images cannot be incorporated into the chronology. McDonald (1994: 152) assumes pigment images are more likely to 'correspond in age with more intensive occupation' (i.e., the period during which high artefact accumulation rates are documented) in the shelter in which the images occur. However, I have not assumed such a correlation since (as suggested above) the function of many shelters may have changed over time (see also Rosenfeld 2002: 76). The only evidence that indicates an age for pigment images in the catchment is outside the random sampling units, in a shelter called Dingo and Horned Anthropomorph. In this shelter, red ochre of similar colour to images on the shelter walls was found in excavated contexts dated to ca 580 BP and younger (Macintosh 1965: 85, 96–7).

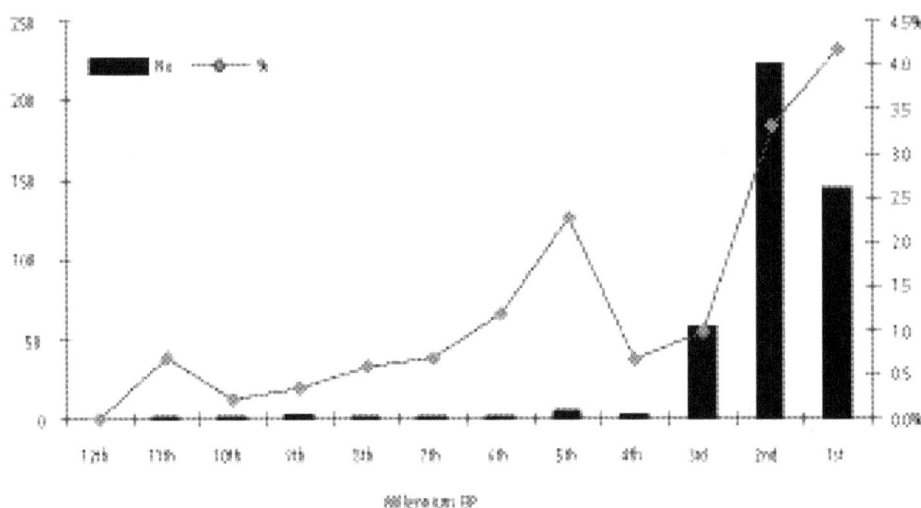

Figure 10.3 Upper Mangrove Creek catchment: number and percentage frequency of igneous artefacts in each millennium.

It is therefore proposed that the number of activity locations/transit camps used in the catchment gradually increased until 3000 BP. Then, particularly after 2000 BP, there was a dramatic increase in their number associated with the use of topographic zones not previously used or only infrequently used (Table 10.2). Base camps were first established in the 11th millennium BP, but the number did not increase until the fourth millennium BP, with the greatest increase in establishment occurring in the third millennium BP.

Mobility — residential or logistical?

In his collector–forager model, Binford (1980, 1982) described residential mobility and logistical mobility as organisational alternatives that could be employed in varying mixes in different settings. Logistical mobility was a strategy adopted by collectors in which base camps were inhabited for relatively long periods, and task groups went out overnight or longer using field camps, stations and caches, and then brought resources back to base camps. Residential mobility related to the movement of people between base camps. It was a strategy used by foragers, who had high residential mobility, in which people moved so that they camped near the resources they were exploiting.

Residentially mobile groups operated within a foraging range around each base camp within which they used a number of activity locations, which included hunting blinds and other special-use locations (Binford 1982: 7, 11, Fig. 2). The field camps, stations and caches used by the logistically mobile groups were beyond their foraging range, but within a logistical range. Highly mobile foragers did not develop a logistical range, although occasional logistical trips were undertaken. Binford states that 'with any condition that restricts residential mobility of either foragers or collectors, we can expect (among other things) a responsive increase in the degree of logistically organised production' (1980: 17; see also Nelson 1991: 85). The several residential bases with their associated foraging ranges and logistical ranges, which were used over the course of a year, were within an 'annual range' (Binford 1982: 7). 'Long-term mobility' involved circulation through a series of annual ranges, perhaps every decade, and the country which encompassed several annual ranges of a community formed an 'extended range' (Binford 1983: 382–3).

The concept of a series of 'ranges' to describe Aboriginal subsistence patterns is well accepted in Australian ethnographic studies (e.g., Stanner 1965; Maddock 1982: 42–7), but Binford's forager–collector model is not without problems and it has often been applied too simplistically (Bamforth 1991; Bettinger 1991: 71–3; Odell 1996: 52–3; Lourandos 1997: 19–20). Kelly (1992: 44–5, 50, 60) pointed out that there are many different dimensions to mobility — individual mobility, group residential, territorial shifts and migrations, each of which can vary independently of the others. He considered it is not useful to speak of a continuum between mobile and sedentary systems, since mobility is not merely variable but multidimensional. The concept of residential mobility involves not just the movement between base camps but also the frequency of movements and distance (km) between them, as well as the duration of visits at base camps (or duration of time between each move). It also involves the total distance covered in residential moves each year (Kelly 1983: 278–9; Shott 1986: 26; Andrefsky 1998: 212), as well as distance covered from the base camps in daily forays, which can vary in length according to circumstances. For example, the longer people stayed at a base camp, the further they had to go each day to gain resources; that is, the distances covered on trips out from the base camp became greater (Kelly 1992: 46–7). Bettinger (1991: 72) questioned Binford's claim that increasing population pressure should lead to an increase in logistical mobility (and a decrease in residential mobility), as surrounding populations would have restricted group movements. However, Australian ethnographic studies (e.g., Gould 1975: 149–50; Maddock 1982: 42–7) show that controlled territorial boundaries are often counterbalanced by social mechanisms based on kinship and exogamous marriage rules, which facilitate subsistence movements across boundaries in times of need — though when such systems came into being is not yet known. Binford's model also does not include a term for groups part-way along the continuum, e.g., those who are residentially mobile but who undertake occasional logistical forays. The terminology in effect imposes a binary view of hunter-gatherer strategies: they are either foragers or collectors. As well, mobility models by Binford and others are based on ethnographic studies of communities who inhabited different environments to that of the catchment (which is forested plateau country with a temperate climate) and who were removed in time for most of the period over which the catchment was used. The mobility patterns and subsistence organisation of groups using the catchment (particularly those of the distant past) were probably quite different to those of the communities on which the models were based.

Although the catchment habitations have been assigned provisionally as either base camps or activity locations/transit camps on the basis of assemblage size, it is more difficult to identify the degree of mobility or the mobility strategy/strategies under which they were formed. Part of the difficulty arises because the catchment is of a size (12km by 10km) that it would have been only part of the daily, annual or extended range over which groups operated (Higgs and Vita Finzi 1982: 30–3; Foley 1981a: 4–9; Binford 1982: 7). However, intensive archaeological fieldwork programs equivalent to that of the catchment have not been carried out in adjacent catchments or regions. The location of base camps in adjacent regions throughout the Holocene is not known. The closest excavated shelters to the catchment are Mogo Creek, ca 7km to the west in the adjacent Macdonald River catchment (Kohen 1995), and Upside-Down Man, ca 18km to the south on Ironbark Creek, a tributary of lower Mangrove Creek (McDonald 1994: Appendix 3). Both may have been within the daily or at least annual range of groups using the catchment. Mogo Creek Shelter, first used at least 2340 years ago (Kohen 1995: 15), has an upper layer which has a very rich and diverse faunal assemblage but very few stone artefacts; unfortunately, this layer is highly disturbed. Upside-

Down Man was first used about 4000 years ago, but it is only in levels post-dating 1500 BP that total estimated numbers of artefacts (based on McDonald 1994: Appendix 3: 264–6, Tables A3.13 and A3.24, Fig. A3.14) are high enough to suggest it was a base camp (according to my methods of categorising catchment habitations).

As stated above, people using the catchment would have been relatively mobile hunter-gatherers — certainly in the recent past, based on early colonial descriptions for the NSW central coast, but probably also throughout the Holocene. Any variation in mobility patterns would have been within the 'forager' end of the spectrum rather than 'collector'. However, many details are not known for any period of time, even the historical period; for example: (a) how long groups stayed at particular base camps or activity locations; (b) how many base camps people used each year; (c) how often groups returned to particular camps or activity locations; (d) how often people moved throughout a year from base camp to base camp; (e) what distance they moved between base camps or, (f) the size of the group/s (band/s) that visited the catchment. Groups may have varied in size and composition when they were in different parts of their annual range according to resource abundance and social/ceremonial occasions. It is also not known how far they ventured out from base camps on daily foraging trips (their daily range); how often they undertook subsistence trips requiring overnight camps away from their base camps (logistical trips); the size of their annual subsistence range; or where clan and language group boundaries were. Oral histories indicate movements from Singleton in the Hunter Valley (ca 60km distant to the north) via the catchment's eastern periphery ridgetop to Brisbane Waters (28km away to the south-east). These trips entailed movement into territories of other clans and language groups, but we do not know the frequency of such special-purpose trips (e.g., to obtain raw materials or attend rituals/ceremonial functions), or whether people travelled yet greater distances. Each variable listed above would not have been constant, but may have varied over the course of a year, seasonally, in different environmental zones, and over the 11,000 years of the catchment's use.

Rowland (1983: 73) proposed that more short-term, briefly occupied sites may result after a change from reasonably stable and semi-sedentary activities to those based on greater mobility and more geographically or seasonally separated resources. Whether changes in the distribution patterns of base camps and activity locations/transit camps in the catchment involved variations in residential mobility patterns and the length of subsistence trips, is not clear from the archaeological evidence. However, since the location and nature of base camps outside the catchment for most of the Holocene is unknown, the nature of any logistical trips undertaken is uncertain. Nevertheless, the archaeological evidence does indicate that land-use patterns changed many times throughout the Holocene, as people reorganised their habitation, subsistence and manufacturing activities within the catchment — a suggested model is presented in Table 10.4.

Other measures of mobility patterns

Habitation patterns by themselves cannot be taken as the only indication of mobility, irrespective of the area over which habitation patterns have been recorded. Modifications to subsistence tools and equipment may also have been associated with or made in response to changes in mobility strategies (Odell 1996: 53). Other proposed measures of residential mobility involve certain characteristics of stone artefact assemblages from habitation sites, as well as the nature of site structure and the presence of specific features or facilities such as heat-treatment pits (Kelly 1992: 56–7) or storage places (Nelson 1991: 82). None are absolute measures that distinguish different levels of mobility in hunter-gatherer communities — most are relative measures between what went before and what came after, and many are interrelated. Advocated measures of mobility involving stone artefact assemblages include variations in tool-kit/assemblage diversity and richness, and multifunctionalism (versatility and flexibility) of tools; curated versus expedient artefacts/technology and longevity; the production/use of blades; the use of bipolar technology; the portability (transportability) of implements; tool/artefact size and weight; and selectivity in raw material use. These issues have been discussed by many authors (e.g., Binford 1977: 34; Ebert 1979; Torrence 1983, 2001: 86; Binford and O'Connell 1984; Bamforth 1986; Shott 1986; Parry and Kelly 1987; Kelly and Todd 1988: 237; Baker 1992: 16; Nelson 1991: 70–1, 74, 76; Kelly 1992: 55; Hiscock 1993, 1994, 1996; McNiven 1994; Morwood and L'Oste Brown 1995: 161; Hayden et al. 1996; O'Dell 1996; Andrefsky 1998: Chapter 9; Jochim 1998: 201–4; Clarkson 2002).

A number of these measures involve the concept of raw material conservatism or stone rationing (Bamforth 1986: 39–40; Nelson 1991: 74–7; Morwood and L'Oste Brown 1995: 161; Hiscock 1996; Bamforth and Bleed 1997, Table 7.3; White 2001: 10–15, Table 3), which is also said to incorporate increasing core reduction, including the use of bipolar technology; selection and procurement of better quality stone material; rotating cores, and re-using/recycling previously discarded cores and flakes; more careful knapping strategies such as platform preparation and overhang removal; reducing tool size, producing blades, and development of hafted tools; and extending the use-life of tools by additional retouch. The adoption of stone rationing strategies such as the use of bipolar technology has been said to be important under conditions of low residential mobility (i.e., increased sedentism), though it depends on the availability and abundance of stone (Parry and Kelly 1987: 300–1; Hiscock 1996).

Many of the above strategies are reflected not only in the catchment's assemblages but also in the stone artefact assemblages in other parts of the south-eastern coastal NSW culture-area, though expressed to varying degrees according to the specific environment and/or availability of resources. As such, these strategies may be indicators of what were general, prevailing regional or culture-area customs and practices and they are not necessarily predictors of the mobility patterns in one small area of a group's range. In addition, the usefulness of some proposed measures has been questioned. Some systems or terms used in the above propositions (e.g., curated/expedient/opportunistic, reliable/maintainable, and flexibility/versatility) are not mutually exclusive and are often interdependent, and some indicators are over-simplifications and sometimes contradictory (e.g., Bamforth 1986, 1991; Jochim 1989; Myers 1989: 86–8; Torrence 1989a: 62–4; Nelson 1991; Kelly 1992: 55–6; Hayden et al. 1996; Nash 1996; Odell 1996; Odell et al. 1996: 378–9, 381–2; Bamforth and Bleed 1997: 134; Andrefsky 1998: 214, 221–9; Mulvaney and Kamminga 1999: 266; Daniel 2001: 239, 250–2). In addition, some terms are not self-explanatory and unless defined in each study are open to ambiguous use and interpretation.

In the case of the catchment, it will ultimately be best to look at the assemblages as a whole to identify relationships between different technological strategies (e.g., within manufacturing as well as subsistence practices) and their place in the total technological system, and then to study how the system changed over time. However, as an initial stage in this process, the use of bipolar technology as an indicator of mobility levels is examined below with presently available catchment data.

Bipolar technology

Expedient technologies, such as the bipolar reduction of cores, are argued to be associated with low residential mobility — in particular, with a shift from high mobility to increased sedentism (Parry and Kelly 1987: 300; Hiscock 1996; Morwood and L'Oste-Brown 1995: 161). However, based on ethnographic analogies from New Guinea, Brazil, Western Australia and

Table 10.4 A habitation, subsistence and land-use model for the Upper Mangrove Creek catchment.

MILLENNIUM BP	HABITATION DISTRIBUTION PATTERN IN CATCHMENT	MOVEMENTS AND MOBILITY
12th millennium BP (11,500–11,000 BP)	An activity location/transit camp was used in the main valley bottom. (1 AL/TC)	The earliest group/s to visit the catchment had their base camp outside the catchment. Members of the group/s visited the catchment occasionally to get food and raw materials or were simply transiting through the catchment staying overnight on their way elsewhere for trade or ceremonial purposes.
11th millennium BP (11,000–10,000 BP)	A base camp was established in the main valley bottom in the shelter previously used as an activity location/transit camp. (1 BC)	Regional subsistence patterns were reorganised in this period. Groups now spent more time in the catchment, camping for several days in at least one base camp around which they hunted, gathered food plants and obtained raw materials.
10th millennium BP (10,000–9000 BP)	The base camp in the main valley bottom continued to be used, and an activity location/transit camp on a subsidiary ridgeside may have been used. (1 BC and 1? AL/TC)	Subsistence patterns were similar to those of the preceding period. The activity location was used from base camps within or outside the catchment.
9th and 8th millennia BP (9000–7000 BP)	The base camp in the main valley bottom continued to be used. An activity location/transit camp was used on the north-eastern sector of the periphery ridgetop (the catchment watershed) and an activity location/transit camp may have been used on a subsidiary ridgeside. (1 BC and 1+1? AL/TC)	Subsistence patterns remained the same. The shelter on the north-eastern periphery ridgetop was used as an activity location, or as a transit camp during use of the ridge as an access route for trade or ceremonial activities between the Hunter Valley and Brisbane Waters, as historically documented.
7th and 6th millennia BP (7000–5000 BP)	The base camp in the main valley bottom and the activity locations on the periphery ridgetop continued to be used and activity locations/transit camps were used increasingly on subsidiary ridgesides. (1 BC and 2–3 AL/TC)	Regional subsistence patterns continued as before. The northern and eastern periphery ridgetops continued to be used as access routes.
5th millennium BP (5000–4000 BP)	The base camp continued to be used in main valley bottom. The number of activity locations/transit camps increased gradually with another being used by the end of this period, again in a previously inhabited zone — the periphery ridgetop. (1 BC and 4 AL/TC)	Regional subsistence patterns began changing. The larger number of activity locations/transit camps suggests an increasing use of the catchment, and increasing use of the access route along the northern and eastern catchment boundary.
4th millennium BP (4000–3000 BP)	The base camp continued in use in main valley bottom with a second base camp established — this time on the periphery ridgetop in a different location to the activity location/transit camp already used in this zone. Use of activity locations/transit camps increased bringing the total to five by the end of the period. All base camps and activity locations/transit camps were in the same topographic zones as before — the main valley bottoms, the periphery ridgetops and subsidiary ridgesides. (2 BC and 5 AL/TC)	Regional subsistence patterns were reorganised with greater catchment use and/or the long-distance access route along the north-eastern boundary was more frequently used. Ground-edged hatchets/implements began to be used, made and/or modified within the catchment.
3rd millennium BP (3000–2000 BP)	The base camps in the main valley bottoms and periphery ridgetops continued to be used, and another three were established — the latter were all in shelters previously used as activity locations/transit camps in the main valley bottoms, the periphery ridgetops and subsidiary ridgesides. Two shelters continued to be used as activity locations/transit camps, and an additional two were used — still on the periphery ridgetops and subsidiary creek ridgesides. (5 BC and 4 AL/TC)	Major re-organisation of regional subsistence patterns and habitation patterns within the catchment. The smaller number of activity locations compared with the number of base camps suggests people did not hunt, fish or gather plant foods far from their base camps, or that the base camps were also used as activity locations from other base camps (within or outside the catchment). As the catchment is only 12km by 10km in area, all parts could have been reached from a single catchment base camp. Alternatively, groups could have moved sequentially from one base camp to another, gaining their resources in the immediate vicinity of each or in a different sector of the catchment (cf. Binford 1982: Fig. 2; McNiven 1992b: 505–6, Fig. 7), with perhaps more intensive coverage of the areas used (Binford 1980: 5). Establishment of extra base camps on the north-eastern catchment boundary may reflect more numerous long-distance movements associated with ceremonial purposes or growth in trade, and firmer establishment of the route between the Hunter Valley and Brisbane Waters.

Table 10.4 (continued)

MILLENNIUM BP	HABITATION DISTRIBUTION PATTERN IN CATCHMENT	MOVEMENTS AND MOBILITY
2nd millennium BP (2000–1000 BP)	Five base camps continued to be used and two additional base camps were established in previous activity locations/transit camps on the periphery ridgetops. There was a very large increase in the number of activity locations/transit camps used – some were in already inhabited zones but others were now along the peninsula ridgetops, the valley bottoms in subsidiary creeks and ridgesides above the main creek. (7 BC and 9 AL/TC)	Further substantial reorganisation of subsistence patterns. The unprecedented number of activity locations used in a greater number of topographic zones, in addition to the increase in base camps, suggests zones from which food and raw materials were obtained around each base camp became larger. Alternatively, an increasing number of trips were made out from catchment base camps, and/or there was a greatly increasing number of trips into the catchment for hunting, gathering or raw materials from base camps in adjacent valleys or further downstream along Mangrove Creek. Manufacture/maintenance of ground-edged axe/hatchet heads increased in the periphery ridgetops.
1st millennium BP (1000 BP–1840 AD)	Six base camps continued to be used, one was used only as an activity location/transit camp, and one new base camp was established. One existing activity location/transit camp ceased to be used, but all others continued to be used with an even greater number of different locations now used for these purposes in all topographic zones within the catchment. (7 BC and 22 AL/TC)	Habitation patterns changed slightly, but activities associated with hunting and gathering, as well as gaining raw materials and tool manufacture, were carried out at an increasingly greater number of areas within the catchment.

South Africa, as well as North American archaeological examples, Parry and Kelly (1987) outline how expedient core technologies can be associated with both high and low residential mobility depending on factors such as the abundance and distribution of raw materials. In regions where stone material is abundant and widely distributed, highly mobiles groups can practice an expedient technology. In contrast, in areas where raw stone sources are scarce, distant and localised, highly mobile groups will design tools to overcome a potential lack of raw material availability and use a formal core technology. Parry and Kelly maintain that, although it is a technology wasteful of stone, more frequent bipolar core reduction was associated with low residential mobility/sedentary groups for whom the main consideration in stone-working was to have an adequate supply of useable stone at locations where it was needed. Such a supply could be maintained at residential locations by stockpiling material obtained through trips to quarries.

Hiscock (1982b: 39–41; 1996: 152) explained that bipolar knapping is not necessarily wasteful, in the sense that it can be used to extend the life span of rocks by enabling flakes to be removed from a core that is too small to be worked by other percussion techniques (see also Parry and Kelly 1987: 301–2; Odell 1996: 70–1, 76; Andrefsky 1998: 227). However, the nature, distribution and availability of stone material can also influence the degree to which bipolar reduction is adopted (Nelson 1991: 75; Andrefsky 1998: 227). Hiscock (1996: 152) considered that bipolar techniques conferred advantages on groups with low residential mobility if they were not camped adjacent to a large quarry, as it reduced the frequency with which stone needed to be transported to a base camp, in that more flakes could be gained from a single core. In a study of sites on the Kakadu flood plain in Arnhem Land, he demonstrated that in assemblages of the same age at different locations in relatively close proximity to each other, evidence for the use of bipolar and hand-held technologies varied in frequency as each site increased in distance from the raw material sources (Hiscock 1996: 152). Hiscock considered that the increased use of bipolar technology during the late-Holocene demonstrates an increased use of expedient technology associated with increased sedentism, or at least decreased mobility during this period. Variations may also occur in assemblages of the same age however, because of the different function of sites in the subsistence system. For example, base camps may contain greater evidence of bipolar core reduction than activity locations at which only a short time (i.e., no more than one night) is spent.

In the catchment, the number of bipolar pieces (cores and flakes) in Loggers and Black Hands increased during the late-Holocene (Tables A1/33 and A1/7 respectively). In Emu Tracks 2, Uprooted Tree and White Figure, in addition to an increase in bipolar cores and flakes, the ratio of hand-held cores to bipolar cores decreased (Tables A1/25, A1/47 and A1/51). Quartz as well as FGS, silcrete and chert were all reduced by bipolar techniques though quartz bipolar cores and flakes are much more abundant in the assemblages. In the catchment as a whole, there was a greater and increasing use of bipolar technology at the expense of hand-held core reduction starting ca 6000 years ago, but more dominantly in the last 3000 years (Table 10.3, Fig. 10.4). The amount of quartz in the assemblages was similar over the last 3000 years (Fig. 10.5), suggesting other stone materials were increasingly reduced by bipolar techniques. If the use of bipolar technology in core reduction was associated with low residential mobility, then this component of the stone artefact assemblages suggests people using the catchment gradually became less residentially mobile from ca 6000 years ago, but especially after 4000 BP.

In many parts of the central and south coast of NSW, the increasing use of bipolar core reduction in the late-Holocene has been documented in numerous stratified rockshelter deposits and is thus associated with broad-scale culture-area changes (e.g., Burrill Lake and Currarong, Lampert 1971a: 38, 46–7, 65–8, Tables 3 and 15; Curracurrang 1, Megaw 1974: 35–7; Curracurrang 2, Glover 1974: 15, Table 2; Lapstone Creek, McCarthy 1948: 22; Macdonald River, Moore 1981, Table 6; Mill Creek 11, Koettig 1985b: 45–9, Table 12, 1990: 1; Mt Yengo, McDonald 1994, Appendix 1: 61, 73–4; Sassafras 1 and 2, Flood 1980: 229, 233, Figs 40, 43; Shaws Creek K2, Kohen et al. 1984: 66, Table 5; Upside-Down Man, McDonald 1994, Appendix 3: 245–6). While bipolar core reduction is well documented in excavated rockshelter deposits in sandstone regions of south-eastern NSW, it is much less common in non-sandstone areas

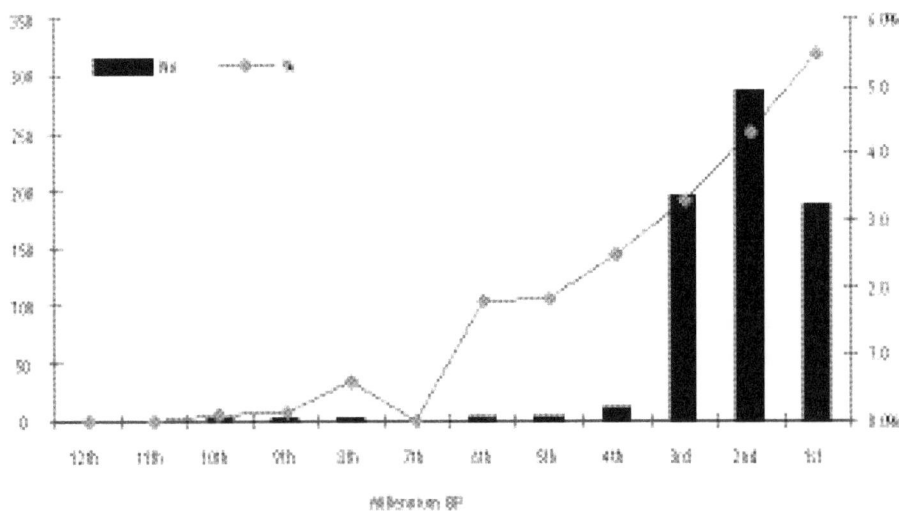

Figure 10.4 Upper Mangrove Creek catchment: number and percentage frequency of bipolar artefacts in each millennium.

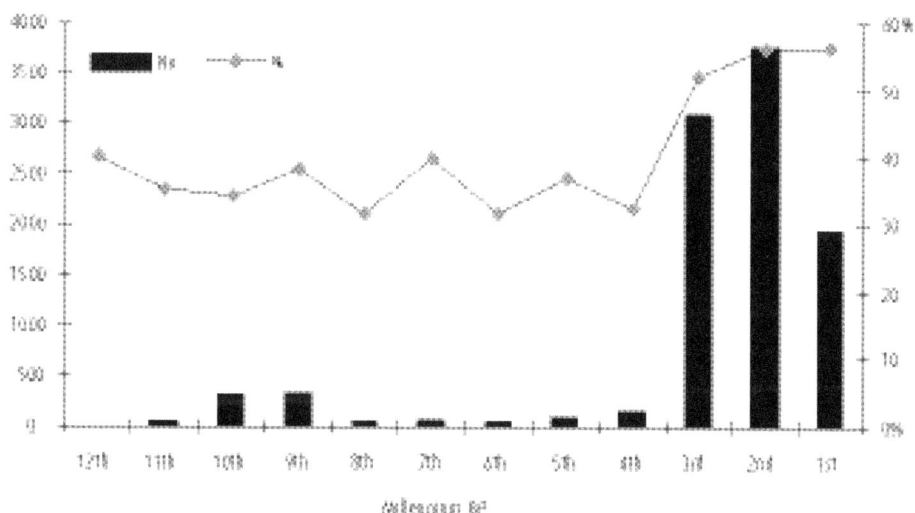

Figure 10.5 Upper Mangrove Creek catchment: number and percentage frequency of quartz artefacts in each millennium.

where silcrete, chert/tuff and other fine-grained siliceous materials are locally available and predominantly used, but quartz is much less readily available and much less commonly used; for example, the Cumberland Plain (AMBS 2002b: 9–11, 32–5, Table 14), Hunter Valley central lowlands (Baker 1992: 7, 20) and upper Shoalhaven River Valley (Attenbrow and Hughes 1983; Attenbrow 1984). Thus, inter-regional variations, which appear to correlate with the availability of certain raw materials, are evident in the use of bipolar technology.

Use of bipolar technology may have been the most efficient way to exploit the stone materials available in the sandstone country. For example, in the catchment, raw material sources suitable for making flaked tools are pebbles and cobbles from the conglomerate beds in the Narrabeen Group sandstones and quartz pebbles from the Hawkesbury sandstone. The largest cobble I observed in the catchment was of FGS and was $160 \times 110 \times 70$mm in size, but the majority were much smaller, particularly the quartz pebbles (generally $< = 25$mm). Silcrete and chert/tuff materials are not available within the catchment, with the nearest sources of the former being in the Hunter Valley lowlands (ca 60km to the north) and the south of the Hawkesbury River (e.g., Cumberland Plain, ca 55km to the south). Sources of chert/tuff are also available in the Hunter Valley lowlands as well as the Colo and Grose River valleys of the Blue Mountains and the Hawkesbury River gravels (35–60km to the south — all distances as the crow flies, but ground travel distances would be longer). Thus, changes in access to and availability of stone material sources which were not available within the catchment may have influenced the degree to which bipolar working was used in core reduction. It may have been used to exploit the imported silcrete and chert/tuff materials to the maximum and, at the same time, would have been the most suitable method to gain useful flakes from the local, small-sized quartz pebbles (Lampert 1971a: 47; Hiscock 1982b). The need to reduce cores of imported materials by the bipolar technique in order to maximise their use may have led to its greater use with other local materials when there was a demand for greater numbers of stone implements (see below). Groups in regions such as the Hunter Valley and Cumberland Plain had no need to adopt bipolar core reduction techniques on a large scale since they had continuing access to quality materials such as silcrete and chert/tuff.

Taçon (1991: 198–9, 203–4) suggested quartz and quartzite were especially valued as raw materials in western Arnhem Land because they were shiny and iridescent, properties associated with Ancestral Beings. In south-eastern Australia, this could be the case with quartz crystals, which are reported as being associated with rituals and ceremonies (Mathews 1897: 2–3; Howitt 1904 [1996]: 357–8). However, quartz in reef and pebble/cobble forms is so ubiquitous in so many areas it is hard to accept that such forms of quartz had symbolic significance or special powers in this part of Australia. Its easy accessibility combined with the absence of preferred raw materials may be the reason for its increased use in sandstone country of the culture-area. Why it increased in the catchment at the expense of FGS where both materials are readily available is presently inexplicable.

It is possible that the increasing use of bipolar core reduction in the catchment in the late-Holocene was initially a response to restrictions in access to preferred raw materials unavailable in the catchment (i.e., silcrete and chert/tuff). Such restrictions may have been a result of reorganisation of social relationships in the culture-area, which led to greater territoriality and/or more tightly controlled territorial boundaries. Newly established boundaries, or more tightly controlled boundaries, may have meant groups inhabiting the sandstone country could no longer make long-distance trips to stone sources in the non-sandstone country without prior permission or outside the context of trading partnerships and marital relationships. Such a scenario suggests long-distance mobility patterns may have changed, but whether reduced residential mobility was also involved is not yet clear.

Subsistence methods and equipment

The proposed habitation, subsistence and land-use model (Table 10.4) based on the tentative assignment of habitations as either base camps or activity locations provides an explanation for late-Holocene trends in the habitation indices. While artefact numbers were used to produce the model, the model does not explain either the dramatic increase in the local artefact accumulation rate in the third millennium BP or the subsequent substantial decrease in the last 1000 years. Changes in the local artefact accumulation rate do not coincide in time, direction or magnitude with changes in the habitation indices. However, the major increase in base camps in the third millennium BP does coincide in time with the dramatic increase in the local artefact accumulation rate (compare Figs 9.1 and 10.1). The question now has to be asked: are the major increases in both numbers of base camps and the local artefact accumulation rates linked and simply due to a greater number of people inhabiting each base camp and the catchment as a whole, or are they due to some other events or circumstances? The following discussion addresses only changes in the local artefact accumulation rates. Variations in the artefact accumulation rates of individual habitations will be addressed elsewhere.

One explanation for changing local artefact accumulation rates that is explored below is that they reflect a change in the number of implements that were made/used by each person in response to changing levels of subsistence risk rather than local, regional or continental population increase. That is, were risk minimisation strategies adopted in the third and first millennia BP that could have led to changes in the tool-kit, which in turn resulted in the dramatic increase in the local artefact accumulation rate in the third millennium BP as well as the substantial decrease in the last 1000 years BP? In fact, advocating population increase at a time when the climate was colder and drier would be incongruous — such conditions are usually described as 'deteriorating' and as being associated with low levels of subsistence resources (e.g., David and Lourandos 1998: 212), although whether resource levels were lower at this time in temperate coastal south-eastern Australia is not certain.

No new flaked implement types appeared in the late-Holocene assemblages; that is, tool-kit diversity remained the same. It appears that an increase occurred in the average number of implements used by each person in the third millennium BP that did not involve an increase in the number of implement types. Flaked implements that did increase in abundance in the catchment in the third millennium BP (both in number and as a percentage of the catchment assemblage) are the backed artefacts (Bondi points, geometric microliths and elouera). Most backed artefacts (85%) were in levels dated to between ca 3000 BP and ca 1000 BP (Table 10.3, Fig. 10.6). The possible use of backed artefacts in risk minimisation strategies is explored below.

The similarity in percentage frequencies for backed artefacts as a proportion of the total catchment assemblage in both the fourth and third millennia BP (despite the large difference in size between the assemblage for each millennium) suggests that there may have been a relationship between the proliferation of backed artefacts and the dramatic increase in the local artefact accumulation rate in the third millennium BP. However, it seems unlikely that backed artefact production was the sole reason for the similarly high local artefact accumulation rate in the second millennium BP as backed artefacts decreased in the number and percentage in this period despite a slight increase in the total number of artefacts. In assemblages of the first millennium BP, backed artefacts are represented only by eloueras and geometric microliths — no Bondi points have been identified in catchment assemblages dating to this period.

Tasks for which Bondi points and geometric microliths were used are still debated. The original view was that Bondi points were 'surgical knives' (Etheridge and Whitelegge 1907: 238), but the most common view now is that they were barbs for hunting spears (McCarthy 1958: 186; Lampert 1971a: 69; McBryde 1974: 264–5, 326, 1977: 234, 1985; Mulvaney 1975: 229; Kamminga 1980: 5, 9, 11; Kohen 1986: 313, 323, 1995: 77, 82; Flood 1999: 224–5; Mulvaney and Kamminga 1999: 236; Moore 2000: 35–6). It has also been suggested that Bondi points were points or barbs for multi-pronged fishing spears (McCarthy 1958: 186, 1965: 79; Branagan and Megaw 1969: 8). Others say they could also be small cutting tools/knives — hafted or even hand-held (Stockton 1970b: 227–9, 1979: 54; Moore 2000: 36–7); awls (needles or

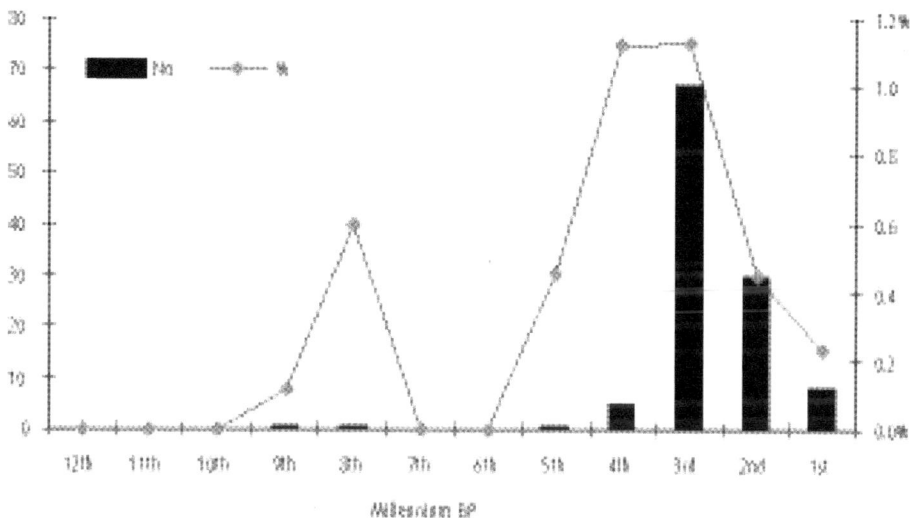

Figure 10.6 Upper Mangrove Creek catchment: number and percentage frequency of backed artefacts in each millennium.

points) for skin-working (Tindale 1957: 27; Stockton 1970b: 227–9, 1979: 54; Kamminga 1980: 5), or ceremonial objects (White and O'Connell 1982: 123). As with other parts of Australian Aboriginal tool-kits, they may have been multifunctional components used in a range of different tools for a range of different tasks (Dickson 1973: 7); though Mulvaney and Kamminga (1999: 266) question this. Examination of use-wear patterns and residues adhering to backed artefacts from eastern NSW assemblages suggests various uses: spear barbs and plant processing (Boot 1993a: Tables 8–11), and hafting as a knife rather than a spear (Therin 2000; Haglund 2001b: 35–6). Robertson's (2002) examination of backed artefacts from the catchment sites Deep Creek and Emu Tracks 2 has revealed traces of bird feathers. For the following discussion, I assume backed artefacts were multi-functional components and their functions included being points and barbs in hunting spears.

Risk minimisation strategies

Risk can be defined as the probability of loss, or, more specifically when related to food resources, it can be seen as the probability of failing to meet dietary requirements and the costs of such failure, for example hunger and malnutrition (Wiessner 1982a: 172–3; Torrence 1989a: 59; Bamforth and Bleed 1997: 117, 133–4). There are thus two components to the concept of risk: the first, the likelihood of an event's occurrence, and the second, the magnitude of that event (Kelly 1992: 47) or the cost or consequence of losing the sought-after resource (Cashdan 1985; Bamforth and Bleed 1997: 112, 117).

In ethnographic studies, mobility is seen as the simplest response to subsistence risk, which works by taking advantage of the spatial and temporal variations in resource abundance and moving away from areas with scarce food resources (Gould 1980: 84–7; Halstead and O'Shea 1989: 3–4; O'Shea and Halstead 1989: 124; Veth et al. 2000). Risk and mobility are thus interconnected (Parry and Kelly 1987; Torrence 1989a, 1989c, 2001: 88; Odell 1996: 53). However, many other strategies aimed at reducing or avoiding subsistence risks have been documented ethnographically (e.g., Colson 1979; Wiessner 1982a: 172–3, 1982b: 65; Cashdan 1983, 1985; Whitelaw 1983: 58–62; Boydston 1989: 75–6; Myers 1989: 84–5; Thorley 2001: 10; Torrence 2001: 80). These include food storage; transmission of information about famine foods; conversion of surplus food into durable valuables which could be stored and traded for food in an emergency; transfer of risk or loss from one party to another; diversification of activities and/or resources rather than specialisation; and, switching to different resources or switching territories (Colson 1979: 21; Wiessner 1982b: 172–3; Kelly and Todd 1988: 233). Other ethnographic examples include pooling or sharing of risk, which combines principles of risk transfer with principles of storage, and storage of obligations (i.e., generalised reciprocity) (Wiessner 1982b: 172–3). This strategy operates at varying levels and involves the establishment of social relationships as well as kinship and exchange networks and political alliances (at inter- and intra-group levels), which enables the use of food resources in the territories of other clans or language groups in times of hardship (i.e., group mobility) (Colson 1979: 21; Gould 1980: 84–7; Maddock 1982: 42–7; Halstead and O'Shea 1989: 3–4; Myers 1989: 85; O'Shea and Halstead 1989: 124). Prevention of loss through measures such as rituals, control of resources through burning, land rights (territoriality) and defence of territory, so that a group can plan a yearly round without the risk that others will come into the area unexpectedly and exhaust critical resources, have also been reported as methods of reducing risk (Wiessner 1982b: 172–3).

Most hunter-gatherer communities have a variety of strategies and have different strategies for use in different contexts, though some categories are mutually incompatible (e.g., food storage and mobility) and others mutually reinforcing (mobility and diversification) (Halstead and O'Shea 1989: 4; O'Shea and Halstead 1989: 124). The two most common strategies mentioned in ethnographic literature are risk pooling (reciprocity) and risk avoidance in the form of local mobility, but Torrence (1989a: 58–9) pointed out that the role of tools and technology was often left out of anthropological and archaeological discussions about risk minimisation. The term technology in this context is used more broadly than I have done in previous chapters and includes the use, transport and discard, as well as all stages in making and maintaining the components of a tool-kit (Nelson 1991: 57).

Technological options

Technological options that have been proposed as subsistence risk minimisation strategies include a reduction in expedient tools and/or opportunistic technological behaviour (Nelson 1991: 64–5; Torrence 2001: 84–5), as well as the introduction or increased use of highly structured tools and techniques (Wiessner 1982a and 1982b). Other suggested options comprise tended and untended facilities (Torrence 2001: 80); tools designed for curation/longevity and portability (transportability) (Nelson 1991: 62–4, 73–6; Torrence 2001: 84, 86–8); diversified assemblages (tool-kit diversity), including special-purpose tools, as well as increased complexity of tools (number of component parts) (Bleed 1986: 743; Myers 1989: 86; Torrence 1989a: 60–2); efficient and specialised tools that require high investment in production time — specialising in a small set of reliable resources (Bamforth and Bleed 1997: 115); reliable, versatile and portable tools that require low investment in production time, used in association with resource diversification (Bamforth and Bleed 1997: 115); multifunctional, readily modifiable, easily portable tools — that is, formal tools (Andrefsky 1998: 214); reliable and maintainable technological systems which, separately or together, ensure tools are available and work when they are needed (Bleed 1986; Torrence 1989a: 60, 62–3, 2001: 82–9; Myers 1989: 87; Nelson 1991: 66–73; Odell 1996: 53; Jochim 1998: 205–6).

As with proposed measures of mobility based on stone artefact assemblage variables, not all of the above propositions have proved useful when applied in archaeological studies (e.g., Hayden et al. 1996). The central problem that technological strategies have to solve is to ensure that the tools are available and are in a useful condition when needed; that is, technology reduces risk by preventing or at least reducing the probability that loss will occur (Torrence 1989a: 59; Bamforth and Bleed 1997: 116). Efforts to devise loss-reducing technology will be greatest where the consequences of resource loss or the frequency with which risk will occur is greatest (Torrence 1989a: 59–60). However, the context in which the risk occurs also needs to be considered; similar events with similar probabilities of occurrence may result in very different costs in different environments/regions and different communities and thus responses will vary (e.g., Jochim 1989: 110–11); choosing one technological option over another, or a technological rather than a social solution, may also impose costs. Alternative technological solutions have to be acceptable within constraints imposed by other demands on time and the resources of the community, and options must be effective as well as feasible; thus some options may not be acceptable in certain circumstances or contexts (Bamforth and Bleed 1997: 125, 133–4). Torrence (1989a: 61–2) considered technological strategies would be used for coping with short-term risk associated with potentially serious consequences but, as the severity and/or frequency of the risk encountered diminished, different forms of social behaviour would be introduced; for example, mobility and information sharing would be adopted for spatial variations in resource availability. Another technological cost, in addition to application failure (i.e., breakage during use or because of poor tool design), is the cost of production. Such costs include the failure to produce sufficient numbers of tools due to, say, breakages during manufacture, the inability to obtain sufficient raw materials because of time, or social constraints (Bamforth and Bleed 1997: 112, 127–8). The necessity to prepare some stone materials by heat treatment also may have incurred considerable wastage (Mulvaney and Kamminga 1999: 266). Thus, high technological costs may constrain some choices, and opportunities and constraints would have been balanced against or perhaps integrated with each other in some circumstances.

Backed artefacts

Several European studies have linked changes in the availability of game with an emphasis on backed artefacts (microlithic tools) in stone artefact assemblages (e.g., Myers 1989: 90–1; Jochim 1989, 1998: 201–14; Torrence 2001: 88–9). These studies interpret the trend as an increase in the number of stone points/barbs on spears, whereby they could easily be replaced and/or the spear could continue in use even if one was broken. Myers (1989: 82, 87–8, 90–1) proposed that the alteration in microliths from large forms in early Mesolithic British assemblages to smaller more abundant late Mesolithic forms represented a change in tool-kit, in which the microliths were standardised components in multi-pronged tools, which were part of a more diverse, reliable and maintainable tool-kit. This change was a response to a climatically associated faunal change — from migratory species that inhabited open vegetation and could be intercepted along known routes, to non-migratory species that inhabited a denser understorey, were dispersed and unpredictable in location. The late Mesolithic microliths were part of a strategy to enable animal resources to be procured quickly and effectively once they were encountered.

The introduction of new tool-kits (including backed artefacts, unifacial/bifacial points and tulas) and stone-working strategies in Australia in the mid-Holocene (between 6000 BP and 3000 BP) has been explained by Hiscock (1994: 268; 2002) as the introduction of technological solutions to risks created by scheduling uncertainties. At that time, he said, organisational difficulties were imposed by particular systems of settlement and mobility (p. 273) during the use and/or colonisation of previously unoccupied or unfamiliar country, the latter including rapidly changing environments, such as areas in Arnhem Land impacted by the final stages of the rising sea-levels (Hiscock 1994: 277–8, 282). Hiscock described these tools as standardised, multifunctional, reliable, maintainable and portable, with their production geared to raw material conservatism (Hiscock 1994: 278, 287). The subsequent decline in backed artefacts and points, he maintained, was 'primarily a response to the economics of raw material usage associated with low residential mobility together with a reduction of uncertainty in landscape use' (Hiscock 1994: 286). In a recent article building on earlier ideas but focusing on backed artefacts, Hiscock (2002: 171, 174) considered that broad chronological trends in the proliferation of their production in many different contexts in southern Australia may well reflect one cultural response to risk incurred by increased environmental variability — a drier and more variable ENSO-controlled late-Holocene climate beginning 5000–4000 BP. This response, he pointed out, was increased production of a pre-existing implement form. He (2002: 172–3) said that other shifts in food resource use in the mid-Holocene in several parts of the continent would have been risk-reduction mechanisms in the face of environmental variation, increased pressure through population increase, and/or reduction of territory size. The subsequent late-Holocene decline in backed artefacts, he said, was, however, not a response to reduction of foraging risk, but to 'the onset of new environmental and social contexts involving factors such as sedentism, territoriality and population increase, that has a more potent effect on the selection of appropriate technology' (Hiscock 2002: 172).

Sources of risk and risk minimisation in the Upper Mangrove Creek catchment

Environmental changes associated with late-Holocene climatic shifts may have altered the levels of subsistence risk experienced by the catchment's inhabitants. The general correlation in timing of late-Holocene climatic changes with the dramatic changes in the local artefact accumulation rates, and the proliferation and decline of backed artefacts, all of which occur within the last 4000 years, suggest an association. Late-Holocene climatic changes (as discussed in the previous chapter) are likely to have affected the catchment's vegetation communities and animal populations, though it would have been the areal extent and/or abundance of certain plants that altered rather than a loss of communities.

Archaeological faunal evidence

Archaeological evidence from Deep Creek and Mussel Shelters indicates that there may have been a change in the macropod populations in the catchment in the late-Holocene. Several macropod species were identified (Aplin 1981: Tables 4 and 7; Aplin and Gollan 1982: Tables 7 and 8). Faunal assemblages dating from ca 3000 BP to ca 1200–1000 BP were characterised by the presence of the eastern grey kangaroo (*Macropus giganteus*) and the relative importance of the red-necked wallaby (*M. rufogriseus*) and later assemblages (less than ca 1200–1000 BP old) by pademelons (either *Thylogale stigmatica*, red-legged pademelon, or *Thylogale thetis*, red-necked pademelon). The later assemblages also have a greater abundance of swamp wallabies (*Wallabia bicolor*) than the early assemblages. The two macropod species distinguishing the earlier assemblages are much larger in size than the macropod species characterising the later faunal assemblages (Table 10.5).

The habitats of these macropod species suggest that the forest understorey in the catchment was generally more open in the early period from ca 3000 BP to 1200–1000 BP than during the last 1000 years or so. Such vegetation changes are in general agreement with regional pollen records, which indicate forests were more open between ca 2800 BP and ca 1800 BP and the climate was colder and drier than in the preceding five or six millennia. In the warmer–wetter millennia of the early to mid-Holocene, the forest understorey may have been as dense as or denser than it was in the last 1000 years. Consequently, both the eastern grey kangaroo and the red-necked wallaby may have been less numerous in the catchment in the early to mid-Holocene than between 3000 to 1200-1000 BP. If so, the transition to a more open forest environment in the late-Holocene may have provided a situation in which the use of stone-barbed spears and/or multi-barbed spears (incorporating Bondi points) became a preferred method of hunting macropods, including the then more common large eastern grey kangaroo and red-necked wallaby.

Backed artefacts

The onset of increasingly colder and drier conditions following the early Holocene 'optimum' began ca 5000 or 4000 BP, and at this time backed artefacts began to increase as a proportion of the catchment's artefact assemblages (Fig. 10.6). However, after ca 3000 BP, when conditions became very much colder and drier than at any other time during the Holocene, the numbers

Table 10.5 Upper Mangrove Creek catchment: size of common macropod species in each period (weights from Strahan 2000).

PERIOD	MACROPOD SPECIES	WEIGHT
Early	*Macropus giganteus*, eastern grey kangaroo	up to 66kg for males/32kg for females
Early	*Macropus rufogriseus*, red-necked wallaby	up to 26.8kg males/15.5kg females
Early-Late	*Macropus robustus*, wallaroo, euro	up to 46.5kg males/25kg females
Early-Late	*Wallabia bicolor*, swamp wallaby	up to 20.5kg males/15.4kg females
Early-Late	*Petrogale penicillata*, brush-tailed rock wallaby	up to 10.9kg males/8.2kg females
Late	*Thylogale thetis*, red-necked pademelon	up to 9.1kg males/4.3kg females
Late	*Thylogale stigmatica*, red-legged pademelon	up to 6.8kg males/4.2kg females

of backed artefacts produced in the catchment increased dramatically — that is, the technological response to climatic change was far greater than earlier on. Weather conditions became more variable with the onset of current ENSO phenomena ca 3000 BP. Increasing seasonality and variability in precipitation, combined with the colder–drier conditions, may have increased the magnitude of resource fluctuations and thus increased the levels of subsistence risk (cf. Bamforth and Bleed 1997: 113). By ca 3000 BP, the probability of failure in the hunt may have become too great to ignore. Macropod populations inhabiting the catchment had changed to the extent that there was a greater level of risk associated with hunting them — the probability of failing to spear (kill) a kangaroo or wallaby had increased. Part of the response was increased production of backed artefacts to act as points and barbs in hunting spears so that each hunter had more stone-barbed spears and/or each spear had more barbs than previously to increase their chance of hunting success. Hunters may have made more stone-barbed spears to ensure against loss or breakage of a spear shaft during the chase. Alternatively, more barbs were inserted in their spears because of the larger size of the animals and/or such a method of manufacture would have enabled the hunter to continue the chase even if one barb had broken or been lost.

The evidence for the end of the colder–drier period is not as easily interpreted. The pollen evidence indicates drier conditions lasted only to ca 1800 BP. The number and percentage of backed artefacts decreased during the second millennium BP, with Bondi points absent after ca 1600 BP. However, the change in the macropod populations, according to the archaeological evidence, did not occur until ca 1200–1000 BP. Macropod species were possibly able to maintain their population levels well after the late-Holocene driest–coldest conditions prevailed. Alternatively, perhaps the hunters continued for as long as they could to catch the species to which they had become accustomed, despite variations in their abundance, but used different equipment and/or moved to strategies that involved the production of fewer backed artefacts.

By ca 1000 BP, climatic conditions had returned to a warmer-wetter regime and vegetation patterns that were similar to those at the time of British colonisation. The macropod species commonly represented in the faunal assemblages of this period — swamp wallaby, pademelon and brush-tailed rock wallaby — are smaller than the eastern grey kangaroo and red-neck wallaby, which are present only in the early assemblage (Table 10.5). The continued decline in backed artefact production (including the abandonment or much reduced use of Bondi points) may have occurred because stone-barbed spears were not as useful or efficient as other methods to catch the smaller macropods, and even the larger species such as the euro, which is present throughout the deposits, in the denser understorey of this period. Other ways of minimising risk, such as the use of traps or communal hunting, may have been more common. The latter were observed in early colonial times in adjacent areas: Macdonald River (Mathew 1833 in Havard 1943: 237); Lake Macquarie (Threlkeld 1825 in Gunson 1974, Vol. 2: 191), and near Maitland in the Hunter Valley central lowlands (Dawson 1830: 8 in Brayshaw 1986: 79, Table B). In some instances, nets were fixed among the trees (Fawcett 1898: 153 in Brayshaw 1986: 79). The use of wooden barbed and/or wooden pointed spears may have increased, or the quartz pieces produced by bipolar core reduction may have begun to replace backed artefacts in stone-barbed hunting spears. Both wooden pointed and quartz barbed hunting spears were used locally on the coast at Lake Macquarie in the early colonial period (Threlkeld 1825–26 in Gunson 1974, Vol. 1: 67).

If the catchment's archaeological record is representative of changes that happened in the forested sandstone plateau of the NSW central hinterland, then similar faunal sequences should be identified in future excavations where conditions are suitable for the preservation of organic remains. Outside the sandstone plateau country, in areas where vegetation and faunal communities were different and responses to climatic changes may have differed, human responses may have varied as well, especially in the adjacent coastal zones where ocean and estuarine resources were available. However, the widespread distribution of backed artefacts and their ubiquitous proliferation ca 3000 BP across the wider culture-area and south-eastern Australia generally, indicates that, if their increased production was due to their adoption in risk minimisation strategies at this time of marked climatic and environmental changes, their pre-existence and multifunctional nature meant they were accepted as 'a universal panacea' ready for a variety of contexts (Hiscock 2002).

So, in seeking explanations for the dramatic increase in the local artefact accumulation rate in the third millennium BP, I propose that it may partially reflect the greatly increased production of backed artefacts as a technological response to variations in subsistence risk. In the catchment, the increased risk may have arisen because of a change in the abundance of specific macropod species, which was brought about by changing climate and vegetation patterns.

It seems likely, however, that variations in the rate of backed artefact production were not the only technological or behavioural change involved in the dramatic changes in the local artefact accumulation rates, particularly in the second and first millennia BP. For example, backed artefacts began to decline in the second millennium BP, whereas the faunal assemblage and local rate of artefact accumulation remained unchanged until the first millennium BP.

Ground-edged implements

Although no new flaked implements appeared in the catchment's late-Holocene assemblages, new stone implements did occur earlier than the third millenium BP proliferation of backed artefacts. In the fourth millennium BP, ground-edged implements appear. They are evidenced as whole implements as well as fragments which increase over time, both in abundance and as a proportion of the catchment assemblages (Table 10.3, Fig. 10.2). Ground-edged implements may have been used in manufacturing wooden food-procurement equipment, such as spears, spear-throwers, clubs, traps or containers, or in gaining possums from tree trunks. Climatic conditions were beginning to get colder and drier in the fourth millennium BP. In these conditions, ground-edged implements may have been adopted as part of risk minimisation strategies to cope with associated environmental changes to vegetation or faunal communities, before strategies and equipment using greater numbers of backed artefacts were devised.

Later again, in the second and first millennia BP, with lesser use of strategies incorporating backed artefacts, there was an increase in subsistence methods using ground-edged implements, or wooden implements or equipment. By the historical period, ground-edged implements were commonly used by both men and women for a wide range of subsistence and manufacturing purposes (Collins 1798 [1975]: 456; Hunter 1793 [1968]: 61; Tench 1793: 191 [1979]: 284).

Unanswered questions and further research

The above model provides plausible reasons why each hunter required more backed artefacts with the onset of the coldest–driest conditions, and why they subsequently declined in use. There are, however, still some areas of uncertainty. For example, the function of the backed artefacts as spear points and barbs still needs to be demonstrated. Although bird feathers have been identified on some backed artefacts from the catchment (Robertson 2002), no evidence for their being hafted as spear points or barbs has been observed. If backed artefacts were not spear points/barbs or were not associated with hunting land animals solely for food as discussed above, what was their function and what promoted their proliferation ca 3000 years ago? Was that function associated with risk of another nature, such as personal health and comfort and the manufacture of skin cloaks for warmth?

In addition, the cost of failure — not killing an animal — is not known because there is insufficient knowledge about alternative reliable food sources (plant and animal) in the catchment. If such technological steps were taken to minimise the risk of failure/loss, it suggests there were possibly fewer alternative reliable food sources than in the preceding period. The effect of the proposed vegetation changes on plant food sources needs to be explored. Did some resources become more restricted or limited in availability and abundance, while others became more widespread and plentiful? Failure in the hunt may also have had a social cost to the hunters — their status as a hunter and food provider was at risk (e.g., Gould 1969: 17).

The series of archaeological changes that occurred at the beginning of the coldest-driest period (ca 3000 BP) differed from those at the end of the period. The decrease in the local artefact accumulation rate in the last 1000 years was not as great as the initial increase in the third millennium BP. Although the decrease in the local artefact accumulation rate correlates relatively well in time with the change in the archaeological faunal assemblages, the decline in backed artefacts began earlier — in the previous millennium, when ground-edged implements increased (Table 10.3, Figs 9.1, 10.2 and 10.6). The nature of these changes suggests that subsistence activities and their associated technologies did not return to those of previous times — a conclusion supported by other long-term changes in the stone artefact assemblages (e.g., the increasing use of bipolar technology) and the habitation distribution patterns. By ca 1000 BP, social behaviour, including the nature of social interactions within and beyond the culture-area, was substantially different from that of the period preceding ca 3000 BP.

Social and territorial organisation

During the first millennium BP, at the same time as technological solutions were being adopted to minimise newly encountered subsistence risk, social and territorial organisation within the region and wider culture-area may have changed too. For example, the effects of modifications to the nature and position of territorial boundaries of clans and language groups, as suggested above in relation to the increased use of bipolar core reduction, might have been offset by developing and extending trading and political alliance networks (cf. Wiessner 1982a: 172–3; David and Lourandos 1998: 198, 212). The alliances, which may have begun initially many millennia before as trading partnerships and networks based initially on relationships between individuals (cf. Gamble 1998), eventually evolved together with the systems of kinship, exogamous marriage and ceremonial life into the social and territorial organisations that existed at the time of European contact. These networks and alliances, therefore, facilitated not only the procurement of raw materials and the performance of ceremonies associated with religious beliefs, but also the sharing of subsistence risk by enabling people to move into the country of other clans and language groups in times of hardship.

The late-Holocene archaeological record of the catchment could be interpreted as a series of diverse measures implemented to minimise subsistence risk in a period of increasing climatic variability — such measures incorporating both technological and social solutions. The dramatic increase in the local artefact accumulation rate ca 3000 BP and the substantial decrease ca 1000 BP may be the consequence not only of an increase and subsequent decrease in the production of backed artefacts, but also of the increasing production and use of ground-edged implements and the increasing number of quartz pieces produced by bipolar core-reduction techniques. Such measures were only some of the actions taken to ameliorate subsistence risk at various points in time. Further research as outlined above is needed to support these claims, particularly those relating to the nature and timing of social and territorial reorganisation, for which there is presently little unambiguous physical evidence.

Conclusions and future research

In the course of investigating interpretations and explanations for the quantitative changes in the catchment's archaeological record — that is, the habitation and artefact indices — several themes have been explored. This has led to the production of explanatory models which will require evaluation and testing by future research.

The provisional assignment of individual 'habitations' as either home bases or activity locations/transit camps, and their spatial distribution within the catchment in different periods of time, suggests that changing habitation and land-use patterns, involving shifts in subsistence and mobility patterns, may explain the dramatic late-Holocene increases in the habitation indices. Very few base camps were established during the early Holocene and it appears that it was not until the fourth millennium BP that increasing numbers of base camps began to be established in the catchment — at a time when ground-edged implements first appeared. Nevertheless, the third millennium BP stands out as a period when something different occurred, with a substantial increase in base camps and a reversal in the ratio of base camps to locations used only as activity locations or transit camps. The dramatic increases in the habitation indices in the last 2000 years appear to be almost totally due to increases in activity locations/transit camps and not in the numbers of base camps. However, activity locations/transit camps are not assumed to be associated only with logistical movements, and consequently are not taken as indicators of frequent logistical mobility and the transformation of foragers into collectors. The inhabitants of the Upper Mangrove Creek catchment continued to be relatively mobile hunter-gatherers throughout the Holocene. Even so, the continually changing 'habitation' distribution pattern indicates that a reorganisation of mobility patterns (in the broadest meanings of the term) relating to camp life and subsistence activities took place in the catchment at frequent intervals and even more frequently and dynamically within the last 4000 years.

If the increasing use of bipolar core reduction in the catchment from ca 4000 BP was related to a reduction in residential mobility, then to some extent this is paralleled in the hypothesised initial increase in the establishment of catchment base camps. The continuing increase in the proportion of bipolar artefacts in the assemblages of the last 1000 years, however, is not paralleled by an increase in the number of catchment base camps. In addition, with present data, it cannot yet be established whether the dramatic increase in activity locations/transit camps in the first millennium BP was associated with greater logistical mobility from within or outside the catchment, or due to some other subsistence strategy. Changes in the abundance of quartz, FGS, silcrete and tuff-type chert in the catchment assemblages suggest that access to and/or availability of non-local stone resources altered over time. Such restrictions may also account for the increased use of bipolar reduction techniques. The stone material changes may have been associated with variations in long-distance movements and/or trade, which were influenced by changing territorial boundaries/trading networks and alliances, as well as culturally determined preferences in raw material use.

In summary, the long-term trends in the habitation indices and in the changing numbers of base camps and activity locations, as well as the increasing use of bipolar core reduction, suggest there was a reorganisation of subsistence strategies and land-use patterns involving changes in habitation and possibly long-distance and local mobility patterns. The changes in habitation patterns and mobility may have been associated with climatically associated environmental changes. Even the initial establishment of a base camp in Loggers in the 12th millennium BP may have been part of a redistribution of populations as they responded to the rising sea-level, which by this time had reached the base of the present coastal clifflines and was extending further up the palaeo-Hawkesbury River Valley.

Comparison of the timing of late-Holocene climatic changes with trends in the habitation indices (Fig. 9.1) shows that dramatic changes in the latter did not correlate with the onset of the increasingly colder and drier conditions (which began ca 4000–3500 years ago), the period that was much colder and drier than the present (ca 3000 BP to ca 1800 BP), or the onset of the current El Niño mode of operation (ca 3000 BP). However, the initial increase in the establishment of base camps in the fourth millennium BP does coincide with the onset of colder–drier conditions. In addition, the major increase in base camp numbers and the local artefact accumulation rate correlate with the beginning of the coldest-driest Holocene period in the third millennium BP. The warmer-wetter conditions of the last 1000 years were not matched by a return to a smaller number of base camps, though artefact numbers decreased in some. More detailed studies of the stone artefact assemblages and 'intensity of site use' are required before concluding that these correlations reflect greater rockshelter use — whether in response to demographic pressures or the need for greater protection from the weather which they would have provided.

The changing Holocene climatic conditions, particularly the period of coldest-driest conditions in the late-Holocene, which brought about changes in the catchment's vegetation patterns and in the catchment's macropod population, is also seen as the impetus for the adoption of a series of risk minimisation strategies (cf. Torrence 2001: 94). These strategies, which were designed to minimise or avoid subsistence risk, initially involved the introduction of ground-edged implements and greatly increased production of backed artefacts possibly used as spear points and barbs, as well as changes in local and long-distance mobility patterns which are reflected in the increasing use of bipolar core reduction. These changes to the tool-kit and stone reduction techniques probably only partially explain the dramatic increase in the local artefact accumulation rate in the third millennium BP and the continuing high rate in the second millennium BP.

The substantial decrease in the local artefact accumulation rate in the first millennium BP can, again, be explained only partially by changes in the tool-kit and technology, such as the reduced production of backed artefacts, the effects of which may have been offset partially by the increasing manufacture and use of ground-edged tools and bipolar pieces. It is likely that subsistence risk was also minimised by the adoption of social solutions which enabled greater mobility (residential, logistical and long-distance) and reciprocity of subsistence resources at the inter- and intra-group level. During this period, network systems based on kinship, trade, ceremonial responsibilities and obligations, and political alliances may have attained the level of organisation and complexity similar to that observed at the time of British colonisation, even though these systems and alliances had their origins many millennia in the past.

The decreased local artefact accumulation rate may also represent decreased catchment use. Decreasing population seems an unlikely correlate of increasingly warmer-wetter conditions if these 'ameliorating' conditions were associated with an increasing abundance of food sources. However, if this was the case, a decline in the catchment population could represent a redistribution of the regional population which led to higher densities in the coastal zone where fish-hooks were introduced some 900 years ago (Attenbrow et al. 1998). Adoption of this small implement may have enabled the resources of the ocean shoreline, estuaries and lagoons to be more efficiently harvested. Such a scenario could accommodate a reduction in catchment use in the last 1000 years, however, demographic change does not have to be invoked to explain or interpret the quantitative changes in the catchment's archaeological record.

The foregoing models go part way to understanding and interpreting the catchment's archaeological record, in terms of the use of habitations, the land and its resources. Only selected data sets were incorporated: the habitations as places where a variety of activities or functions were undertaken and between which people moved in their daily lives; bipolar core reduction as a measure of mobility; and backed artefacts and ground-edged implements as a response to subsistence risk. Each of the studies presented here has looked at different aspects of life and material culture.

Further research using other data sets and with other theoretical contexts is required to establish the strength of the models. Such studies could begin by testing the proposed habitation and land-use model by reanalysing the excavated assemblages to identify the functions of each habitation in each millennium and the activities which took place inside them. Secondly, they would investigate the artefact accumulation rates in individual habitations to explore 'intensity of site use', and, thirdly, they would involve spatial analyses incorporating all archaeological traits in the catchment. Additional studies are also needed to investigate the use, availability and accessibility of the various stone materials to test whether reasons for the increasing use of bipolar core reduction techniques are solely reduced residential mobility, or involve restricted access to distant raw materials. In the context of risk minimisation, it is essential to have more detailed palaeo-ecological data about past vegetation and faunal changes and the availability and abundance of food resources, which will allow identification of options and constraints in different periods of time (cf. Jochim 1989: 108; Veth et al. 2000: 60, 62). Such data would assist in assessing the level of subsistence risk that may have existed. Similarly, the nature of Aboriginal burning regimes in the past and the effect that the people themselves may have had on the vegetation and faunal populations of the catchment also requires further research.

Ideally, and eventually, it will be fruitful to look at the various strands of the catchment's archaeological record as an integrated body of data (cf. Nelson 1991: 57–8, 89–90): all archaeological traits and their assemblages, all materials and manufacturing processes and the tool-kit. Ultimately, they are all related — just as the behaviours and processes that created them were interrelated. For example, with mobility and risk, the degree of risk involved in acquiring a certain resource may influence adoption of particular mobility patterns (Myers 1989: 84, 90–1; Odell 1996: 53; Torrence 1989a: 61–2, 2001: 88). However, before that can be done, studies of individual aspects of the various archaeological traits and excavated materials (faunal remains as well as stone assemblages, sediments and charcoal) are needed. In addition, the catchment has to be set in a wider regional context taking into account changes along the coast and other parts of the region.

While many questions remain to be addressed, this study reaffirms that a region's prehistory cannot be portrayed on the evidence from a single site or a few selected sites. It is not sufficient to look at only habitation indices or only artefact accumulation rates in isolation, particularly when investigating long-term regional habitation, land- and resource-use patterns. I agree with Lourandos (1996: 17–18) that general trends in the use and establishment of habitations must be differentiated from those of stone artefacts, but stone artefacts are not a 'subsidiary indicator' to sites in regional studies seeking to identify long-term trends in habitation and land-use patterns. Both habitation and artefact indices, as well as the nature and diversity of artefact assemblages, and habitation function and distribution patterns, need to be taken into account whether demographic-change or behavioural-change explanations are proposed as part of a region's prehistory.

References

Allen, H. 1972. Where the Crow Flies Backward. Man and Land in the Darling Basin. Unpublished PhD thesis, Australian National University, Canberra.

Allen, H. 1990. Environmental history in south-western New South Wales during the Late Pleistocene. In C. Gamble and O. Soffer (eds), *The World at 18,000 BP*, Vol. 2: *Low Latitudes*, pp. 296–321. Unwin Hyman.

Allen, H. 1996. The time of the mangroves: changes in mid-Holocene estuarine environments and subsistence in Australia and Southeast Asia. In I. C. Glover and P. Bellwood (eds), *Indo-Pacific Prehistory: The Chiang Mai Papers*, Vol. 2, *Indo-Pacific Prehistory Association Bulletin* 15: 193–205.

AMBS (Australian Museum Business Services). 2002a. Archaeological Salvage Excavation of Site HVS38 (37-5-167), Riverview Mine, Hunter Valley. Report to Coal and Allied Pty Ltd, Singleton.

AMBS (Australian Museum Business Services). 2002b. Liverpool–Parramatta Transitway (LPT). Orphan School Creek Archaeological Test Excavations. Unpublished report to the Roads and Traffic Authority Transitway.

AMBS (Australian Museum Business Services). 2002c. Parklea Leisure Centre Stage I. Archaeological Investigation of Site PK/PC6. Vol. 1: Main Report. Unpublished report prepared for Blacktown City Council.

AMBS (Australian Museum Business Services). 2002d. Warkworth Mine Western Extension Archaeological Assessment of Aboriginal Heritage. Unpublished report to Coal and Allied Pty Ltd, Singleton.

AMBS (Australian Museum Business Services). 2003. Extension of West Pit, Hunter Valley Operations. Archaeological Assessment. Unpublished report to Coal and Allied Operations Pty Ltd, Singleton.

Ammerman, A. J., L. L. Cavalli-Sforza and D. K. Wagener. 1976. Toward the estimation of population growth in Old World prehistory. In E. B. W. Zubrow (ed.), *Demographic Anthropology. Quantitative Approaches*, pp. 27–61. Albuquerque: University of New Mexico Press.

Andrefsky, W., Jr. 1998. *Lithics. Macroscopic Approaches to Analysis*. Cambridge University Press.

Aplin, K. 1981. Faunal Remains from Archaeological Sites in Mangrove Creek Catchment. Appendix 4 in V. Attenbrow, Mangrove Creek Dam Salvage Excavation Project, Vol. 2. Unpublished report to NSW National Parks and Wildlife Service on behalf of NSW Department of Public Works.

Aplin, K. 1985. Faunal Remains from Archaeological Sites in the Mangrove Creek Catchment. Report No 3. The Random Sampling Units. Appendix 6B in V. Attenbrow, 1987, The Upper Mangrove Creek Catchment. A Study of Quantitative Changes in the Archaeological Record. Unpublished PhD thesis, University of Sydney.

Aplin, K. and K. Gollan. 1982. Faunal Remains from Archaeological Sites in the Mangrove Creek Catchment II: The Deep Creek Fauna. Appendix 3 in V. Attenbrow, Archaeological Investigation of Deep Creek Shelter, Mangrove Creek Dam. Unpublished report to NSW National Parks and Wildlife Service on behalf of NSW Department of Public Works.

Attenbrow, V. 1976. Aboriginal Subsistence Economy on the Far South Coast of New South Wales, Australia. Unpublished BA(Hons) thesis, University of Sydney.

Attenbrow, V. 1980. Loggers Shelter, Upper Mangrove Creek, near Sydney. *Australian Archaeology* 11: 25–7.

Attenbrow, V. 1981. Mangrove Creek Dam Salvage Excavation Project. 2 vols. Unpublished report to NSW National Parks and Wildlife Service on behalf of NSW Department of Public Works.

Attenbrow, V. 1982a. Archaeological Investigation of Deep Creek Shelter, Mangrove Creek Dam. Unpublished report to NSW National Parks and Wildlife Service on behalf of NSW Department of Public Works.

Attenbrow, V. 1982b. The archaeology of Upper Mangrove Creek catchment: research in progress. In S. Bowdler (ed.), *Coastal Archaeology in Eastern Australia. Proceedings of the 1980 Valla Conference on Australian Prehistory*, pp. 67–78. Canberra: Department of Prehistory, Research School of Pacific Studies, Australian National University.

Attenbrow, V. 1982c. Loggers Shelter, Mangrove Creek Dam. Documentation of Fourth Season of Fieldwork — September 1981. Unpublished report to NSW National Parks and Wildlife Service.

Attenbrow, V. 1984. Welcome Reef Dam Project. Investigations into Aboriginal Archaeological Sites — Stage II. Unpublished report to the Metropolitan Water Sewerage and Drainage Board, Sydney.

Attenbrow, V. 1987. The Upper Mangrove Creek Catchment. A Study of Quantitative Changes in the Archaeological Record. Unpublished PhD thesis, University of Sydney.

Attenbrow, V. 1992a. Port Jackson Archaeological Project — Stage II. Work carried out between January 1990 and 30 June 1992. Unpublished report to Australian Institute of Aboriginal and Torres Strait Islander Studies, Canberra.

Attenbrow, V. 1992b. Shell bed or shell midden. *Australian Archaeology* 34: 3–21.

Attenbrow, V. 1993. Preliminary Report on 1993 Excavations at Balmoral Beach 2. Port Jackson Archaeological Project — Stage II. Unpublished report for NSW National Parks and Wildlife Service, Sydney, and Australian Institute of Aboriginal and Torres Strait Islander Studies, Canberra.

Attenbrow, V. 1994. Port Jackson Archaeological Project — Stage II (1993). Work undertaken between January 1993 and March 1994. Unpublished final report to Australian Institute of Aboriginal and Torres Strait Islander Studies, Canberra.

Attenbrow, V. 1995. Port Jackson Archaeological Project — Stage II (1994). Work undertaken between April 1994 and August 1995. Unpublished final report (with additions and amendments 1996) to Australian Institute of Aboriginal and Torres Strait Islander Studies, Canberra.

Attenbrow, V. 1997 [1998]. The Upper Mangrove Creek Catchment, near Gosford/Wyong, NSW — Open Archaeological Deposits. Unpublished report to the Australian Museum and NSW National Parks and Wildlife Service, Sydney.

Attenbrow, V. 2002. *Sydney's Aboriginal Past. Investigating the Archaeological and Historical Records.* Sydney: UNSW Press.

Attenbrow, V.J. 2003–2004. Potential archaeological deposits in the storage area of the Mangrove Creek Dam in the NSW Central Coast. *Newsletter of the Australian Association of Consulting Archaeologists* 94: 17–18

Attenbrow, V. and B. Conyers. 1983. Off Bindea Street, Bonnet Bay. Proposed Residential Subdivision. Report on Archaeological Investigations. Unpublished report to Stocks and Holdings Pty Ltd, Sydney.

Attenbrow, V., B. David and J. Flood. 1995. Mennge-ya and the origins of points: new insights into the appearance of points in the semi-arid zone of the Northern Territory. *Archaeology in Oceania* 30(3): 105–20.

Attenbrow, V., R. Fullagar and C. Szpak. 1998. Stone files and shell fish-hooks in south-eastern Australia. In R. Fullagar (ed.), *A Closer Look: Recent Australian Studies of Stone Tools*, pp. 127–48. *Sydney University Archaeological Methods Series 6*. Sydney: Archaeological Computing Laboratory, School of Archaeology, University of Sydney.

Attenbrow, V. and P. Hughes. 1983. Welcome Reef Dam Project: Preliminary Investigations into Aboriginal Archaeological Sites. Unpublished report to the Metropolitan Water Sewerage and Drainage Board, Sydney.

Attenbrow, V. and T. Negerevich. 1981. Lucas Heights Waste Disposal Depot: Proposed Extensions. Aboriginal Sites in Bardens Creek Valley. Unpublished report to the Metropolitan Waste Disposal Authority, Sydney.

Attenbrow, V. and T. Negerevich. 1984. The assessment of sites. Lucas Heights Waste Disposal Depot: a case study. In S. Sullivan and S. Bowdler (eds), *Site Surveys and Significance Assessment in Australian Archaeology*, pp. 136–51. Canberra: Department of Prehistory, Research School of Pacific Studies, Australian National University.

Attenbrow, V. and D. Steele. 1995. Fishing in Port Jackson, New South Wales — more than met the eye. *Antiquity* 69 (262): 47–60.

Bahn, P. G. 1983. Late Pleistocene economies of the French Pyrenees. In G. Bailey (ed.), H*unter-Gatherer Economy in Prehistory: A European Perspective*, pp. 168–86. Cambridge University Press.

Bailey, G. N. 1983a. Concepts of time in Quaternary prehistory. *Annual Review of Anthropology* 12: 165–92.

Bailey, G. 1983b. Economic change in late Pleistocene Cantabria. In G. Bailey (ed.), *Hunter-Gatherer Economy in Prehistory: A European Perspective* pp. 149–65. Cambridge University Press.

Bailey, G. 1983c. Hunter-gatherer behaviour in prehistory: problems and perspectives. In G. Bailey (ed.), *Hunter-Gatherer Economy in Prehistory: A European Perspective*, pp. 1–6. Cambridge University Press.

Bailey, G. (ed.), 1983d. *Hunter-Gatherer Economy in Prehistory: A European Perspective*. Cambridge University Press.

Bailey, G., P. Carter, C. Gamble and H. Higgs. 1983. Epirus revisited: seasonality and inter-site variation in the Upper Palaeolithic of north-west Greece. In G. Bailey (ed.), *Hunter-Gatherer Economy in Prehistory: A European Perspective*, pp. 64–78. Cambridge University Press.

Baker, N. 1992. NSW National Parks and Wildlife Service Hunter Valley Aboriginal Sites Assessment Project: Stone Artefact Assessment and Analysis — Recording Techniques and Methodology. Unpublished report to the NSW National Parks and Wildlife Service.

Baker, N. 1994. Analysis of Stone Artefacts from Site W6, Sandy Hollow Creek, Warkworth, Hunter Valley, NSW. Report to Haglund and Associates for Warkworth Mining Ltd.

Baker, N. 2000. Mungerie Park Town Centre. Archaeological Salvage Excavations near Kellyville, Cumberland Plain, NSW. 2 vols. Unpublished report by Australian Museum Business Services to the Department of Urban Affairs and Planning, Sydney.

Baker, N. and G. Martin. 2001. Salt Ash Air Weapons Range Aboriginal Heritage Assessment for Environmental Assessment Report. Unpublished report by Australian Museum Business Services to URS Australia Pty Ltd for the Department of Defence.

Baker, R., S. Feary and P. J. Hughes. 1984. An Archaeological Assessment of Two Proposed Sand Mining Areas at Lake Bathurst, NSW. Unpublished report to Mr L. Maas, 'Gilmour', via Lake Bathurst, NSW.

Baker, R. G. V. and R. J. Haworth. 1997. Further evidence from relic shellcrust sequences for a late-Holocene higher sea level for eastern Australia. *Marine Geology* 141: 1–9.

Baker, R. G. V. and R. J. Haworth. 1999. Evidence for the nature of late-Holocene sea level fall on the New South Wales coast from fixed biological indicators: was the fall smooth or fluctuating? In J. A. Kesby, J. M. Stanley, R. F. McLean and L. J. Olive (eds), *Geodiversity: Readings in Australian Geography at the Close of the 20th Century,* pp. 351–9. School of Geography and Oceanography, University College, University of New South Wales, Australian Defence Force Academy, Canberra, on behalf of the Institute of Australian Geographers Inc., Canberra.

Baker, R. G. V. and R. J. Haworth. 2000a. Smooth or oscillating late-Holocene sea level curve? Evidence from cross-regional statistical regressions of fixed biological indicators. *Marine Geology* 163: 353–65.

Baker, R. G. V. and R. J. Haworth. 2000b. Smooth or oscillating late-Holocene sea level curve? Evidence from the palaeo-zoology of fixed biological indicators in east Australia and beyond. *Marine Geology* 163: 367–86.

Balme, J. 2000. Excavations revealing 40,000 years of occupation at Mimbi Caves, south central Kimberley, Western Australia. *Australian Archaeology* 51: 1–5.

Bamforth, D. B. 1986. Technological efficiency and tool curation. *American Antiquity* 51 (1): 38–50.

Bamforth, D. B. 1991. Technological organisation and hunter-gatherer land use: a California example. *American Antiquity* 56 (2): 216–34.

Bamforth, D. B. and P. Bleed. 1997. Technology, flaked stone technology, and risk. In C. M. Barton and G. A. Clark (eds), *Rediscovering Darwin: Evolutionary Theory and Archaeological Explanation,* pp. 109–39. Arlington: American Anthropological Association.

Barbetti, M., T. Bird, G. Dolezal, G. Taylor, R. Francey, E. Cook and M. Peterson. 1992. Radiocarbon variations from Tasmanian conifers: first results from late Pleistocene and Holocene logs. *Radiocarbon* 34 (3): 806–17.

Barker, B. C. 1991. Nara Inlet 1: coastal resource use and the Holocene marine transgression in the Whitsunday Islands, central Queensland. *Archaeology in Oceania* 26 (3): 102–9.

Barker, G. W. W. 1975. Prehistoric territories and economies in central Italy. In E.S. Higgs (ed.), *Palaeoeconomy,* pp. 111–75. Cambridge University Press.

Barrallier, F. 1801. Letter to Greville, precise date unknown, as translated in part by Greville. Banks Papers–Brabourne Papers, Vol. 4, pp. 78e–83. ML: FM4 1747. Reproduced in A. McQueen, 1993, *Blue Mountains to Bridgetown. The Life and Journeys of Barrallier 1773–1853.* Appendix 2: Report on Bass Strait and the Hunter River, pp. 131–3. Springwood: Andy McQueen.

Barton, H. 2000. The behaviour of raw materials or the behaviour of hunter-gatherers? In T. Denham and S. Blau (eds), *National Archaeology Students' Conference. Proceedings of the Second National Archaeology Students' Conference,* pp. 37–41. Canberra: School of Archaeology and Anthropology, Australian National University.

Beaton, J. M. 1977. Dangerous Harvest. Investigations in Late Prehistoric Occupation of Upland South-east Central Queensland. Unpublished PhD thesis, Australian National University, Canberra.

Beaton, J. M. 1982. Fire and water: aspects of Australian Aboriginal management of Cycads. *Archaeology in Oceania* 17 (1): 51–8.

Beaton, J. M. 1983. Does Intensification account for changes in the Australian Holocene archaeological record? *Archaeology in Oceania* 18 (2): 94–7.

Beaton J. M. 1985. Evidence for a coastal occupation time-lag at Princess Charlotte Bay (North Queensland) and implications for coastal colonisation and population growth theories for Aboriginal Australia. *Archaeology in Oceania* 20 (1): 1–20.

Beaton, J. M. 1990. The importance of past population for prehistory. In B. Meehan and N. White (eds), *Hunter-Gatherer Demography. Past and Present,* pp. 23–40. *Oceania Monograph* 39. Sydney: University of Sydney.

Bender, B. 1978. Gatherer-hunter to farmer: a social perspective. *World Archaeology* 10 (2): 204–22.

Benson, D. H. 1978. Vegetation Survey of Upper Mangrove Creek, Wyong, NSW. Unpublished typescript, National Herbarium of New South Wales, Royal Botanic Gardens, Sydney.

Bettinger, R. L. 1977. Aboriginal human ecology in Owens Valley: prehistoric change in the Great Basin. *American Antiquity* 42 (1): 3–17.

Bettinger, R. L. 1981. Sampling and statistical inference in Owens Valley. *American Antiquity* 46 (3):656–60.

Bettinger, R. L. 1991. *Hunter–Gatherers. Archaeological and Evolutional Theory.* New York: Plenum Press.

Binford, L. R. 1968. Post-Pleistocene adaptations. In S. R. Binford and L. R. Binford (eds), *New Perspectives in Archaeology,* pp. 313–41. Atherton: Aldine.

Binford, L. R. 1973. Interassemblage variability — the Mousterian and the 'functional' argument. In C. Renfrew (ed.), *The Explanation of Culture Change: Models in Prehistory,* pp. 227–54. London: Duckworth.

Binford, L. R. 1975. Sampling, judgment, and the archaeological record. In J.W. Mueller (ed.), *Sampling in Archaeology,* pp. 251–7. Tucson: University of Arizona Press.

Binford, L. R. 1977. Forty-seven trips. A case study in the character of archaeological formation processes. In R. V. S. Wright (ed.), *Stone Tools as Cultural Markers: Change, Evolution and Complexity,* pp. 24–36. Canberra: Australian Institute of Aboriginal Studies and New Jersey: Humanities Press Inc.

Binford, L. R. 1978. Dimensional analysis of behaviour and site structure: learning from an Eskimo hunting stand. *American Antiquity* 43 (3): 330–61.

Binford, L. R. 1980. Willow smoke and dogs' tails: hunter-gatherer settlement systems and archaeological site formation. *American Antiquity* 45 (1): 4–20.

Binford, L. R. 1982. The archaeology of place. *Journal of Anthropological Archaeology* 1 (1): 5–31.

Binford, L. R. 1983. Long-term land-use patterning: some implications for archaeology. In L.R. Binford (ed.), *Working at Archaeology,* pp. 379–86. Academic Press.

Binford, L. R. and J. O'Connell. 1984. An Alyawara day: the stone quarry. *Journal of Archaeological Research* 40: 406–32.

Bird, C. F. M. and D. Frankel. 1991a. Chronology and explanation in western Victoria and south-east South Australia. *Archaeology in Oceania* 26 (1): 1–16.

Bird, C. F. M. and D. Frankel. 1991b. Problems in constructing a prehistoric regional sequence: Holocene south-east Australia. *World Archaeology* 23 (2): 179–92.

Bird, C. F. M. and D. Frankel. 2001. Excavations at Koongine Cave: Lithics and land-use in the terminal Pleistocene and Holocene of South Australia. *Proceedings of the Prehistoric Society* 67: 49–83.

Bird, C. F. M., D. Frankel and N. van Waarden. 1998. New radiocarbon determinations from the Grampians-Gariwerd region, western Victoria. *Archaeology in Oceania* 33 (1): 31–6.

Birdsell, J. B. 1953. Some environmental and cultural factors influencing the structuring of Australian Aboriginal populations. *American Naturalist* 87 (834): 171–207.

Birdsell, J. B. 1957. Some population problems involving Pleistocene man. *Cold Spring Harbor Symposia on Quantitative Biology* 22: 47–69.

Birdsell, J. B. 1971. Australia. Ecology, spacing mechanisms and adaptive behaviour in Aboriginal land tenure. In R. Crocombe (ed.), *Land Tenure in the Pacific,* pp. 334–61. London: Oxford University Press.

Birdsell, J. B. 1977. The recalibration of a paradigm for the first peopling of greater Australia. In J. Allen, J. Golson and R. Jones (eds), *Sunda and Sahul. Prehistoric Studies in Southeast Asia, Melanesia and Australia,* pp. 113–67. Academic Press.

Blackwell, A. 1982. Bowen Island: further evidence for economic change and intensification on the south coast of New South Wales. In S. Bowdler (ed.), *Coastal Archaeology in Eastern Australia. Proceedings of the 1980 Valla Conference on Australian Prehistory,* pp. 46–51. Canberra: Department of Prehistory, Research School of Pacific Studies, Australian National University.

Bleed, P. 1986. The optimal design of hunting weapons: maintainability or reliability? *American Antiquity* 51 (4): 737–47.

Blong, R. J. and R. Gillespie. 1978. Fluvially transported charcoal gives erroneous ^{14}C ages for recent deposits. *Nature* 271 (5647): 739–41.

Bonhomme, T. 1984. An archaeological survey of Boomerang Creek, Mangrove Creek Dam Catchment, NSW. Unpublished report to Gutteridge Haskins and Davey Pty Ltd for the NSW Department of Public Works.

Bonhomme, T. 1985. Excavation of An Aboriginal Open Site at Boomerang Creek, Mangrove Creek Dam, NSW. Unpublished report for the NSW Department of Public Works (Gosford/Wyong).

Boot, P. G. 1993a. Analysis of resins and other plant residues on stone artefacts from Graman, New South Wales. In B. L. Fankhauser and J. R. Bird (eds), *Archaeometry: Current Australasian Research*, pp. 3–12. Canberra: Department of Prehistory, Research School of Pacific Studies, Australian National University.

Boot, P. 1993b. Pleistocene date from archaeological excavations in the hinterlands of the New South Wales south coast. *Australian Archaeology* 37: 59.

Boot, P. 1994. Recent research into the prehistory of the hinterland of the south coast of New South Wales. In M. Sullivan, S. Brockwell and A. Webb (eds), *Archaeology in the North. Proceedings of the 1993 Australian Archaeological Association Conference*, pp. 319–40. Darwin: North Australia Research Unit, Australian National University.

Boot, P. 1996a. Aspects of prehistoric change in the south coast hinterland of New South Wales. In S. Ulm, I. Lilley and A. Ross (eds), *Australian Archaeology '95. Proceedings of the 1995 Australian Archaeological Association Annual Conference*, pp. 63–79. *Tempus* 6. St Lucia, Brisbane: Anthropology Museum, University of Queensland.

Boot, P. 1996b. Pleistocene sites in the south coast hinterland of New South Wales. In S. Ulm, I. Lilley and A. Ross (eds), *Australian Archaeology '95. Proceedings of the 1995 Australian Archaeological Association Annual Conference*, pp. 275–88. St Lucia, Brisbane: *Tempus* 6. Anthropology Museum, University of Queensland.

Bowdler, S. 1970. Bass Point: The Excavation of a South-east Australian Shell Midden showing Cultural and Economic Change. BA(Hons) thesis, University of Sydney.

Bowdler, S. 1971. Balls Head: The excavation of a Port Jackson rock shelter. *Records of the Australian Museum* 28 (7): 117–28.

Bowdler, S. 1976. Hook, line, and dilly bag: an interpretation of an Australian coastal shell midden. *Mankind* 10 (4): 248–58.

Bowdler, S. 1981. Hunters in the highlands: Aboriginal adaptations in the eastern Australian uplands. *Archaeology in Oceania* 16 (2): 99–111.

Bowdler, S. 1983. Aboriginal Sites in the Megalong, Kanimbla and Hartley Valleys, New South Wales. Unpublished report for Roland Breckwoldt.

Bowdler, S. 1993. Views of the past in Australian prehistory. In M. Spriggs, D. E. Yen, W. Ambrose, R. Jones, A. Thorne and A. Andrews (eds), *A Community of Culture. The People and Prehistory of the Pacific*, pp. 123–38. Canberra: Department of Prehistory, Research School of Pacific Studies, Australian National University.

Bowler, J. M. 1976. Recent developments in reconstructing late Quaternary environments in Australia. In R. L. Kirk and A. G. Thorne (eds), *The Origin of the Australians*, pp. 55–77. Canberra: Australian Institute of Aboriginal Studies, and New Jersey: Humanities Press Inc.

Bowler, J. M., G. S. Hope, J. N. Jennings, G. Singh and D. Walker. 1976. Late Quaternary climates of Australia and New Guinea. *Quaternary Research* 6: 359–94.

Bowler, J. M., R. Jones, H. Allen and A. G. Thorne. 1970. Pleistocene human remains from Australia: a living site and human cremation from Lake Mungo, western New South Wales. *World Archaeology* 2 (1): 39–60.

Boydston, R. A. 1989. A cost–benefit study of functionally similar tools. In R. Torrence (ed.), *Time, Energy and Stone Tools*, pp. 67–77. Cambridge University Press.

Bradley, W. 1786–1792 [1969]. *A Voyage to New South Wales, The Journal of Lieutenant William Bradley RN of HMS Sirius 1786–1792*. Facsimile reproduction of original manuscript and charts, the Trustees of the Public Library of New South Wales in association with Ure Smith Pty Ltd, Sydney.

Branagan, D. F. and J. V. S. Megaw. 1969. The lithology of a coastal Aboriginal settlement at Curracurrang, NSW. *Archaeology and Physical Anthropology in Oceania* 4 (1):1–17.

Brayshaw, H. 1986. *Aborigines of the Hunter Valley. A Study of Colonial Records*. Scone, NSW: Scone and Upper Hunter Historical Society.

Butler, R. H. 2000. Bone Mineral Density of Macropodidae: Implications for the Interpretation of Archaeological Assemblages. An Example from the Deep Creek Faunal Assemblage. Unpublished BA(Hons) thesis, La Trobe University, Melbourne.

Byrne, D. 1983. *The Five Forests: An Archaeological and Anthropological Investigation*. 2 vols. NSW National Parks and Wildlife Service.

Byrne, D. 1984. A survey strategy for a coastal forest. In S. Sullivan and S. Bowdler (eds), *Site Surveys and Significance Assessment in Australian Archaeology*, pp. 61–70. Canberra: Department of Prehistory, Research School of Pacific Studies, Australian National University.

Callaghan, M. 1980. Some previously unconsidered environmental factors of relevance to south coast prehistory. *Australian Archaeology* 11: 43–9.

Capell, A. 1970. Aboriginal languages in the south central coast, New South Wales: fresh discoveries. *Oceania* 41:20–7.

Cashdan, E. 1983. Territoriality among human foragers: ecological models and an application to four Bushman groups. *Current Anthropology* 24 (1): 47–66.

Cashdan, E. 1985. Coping with risk: reciprocity among the Basarwa of Northern Botswana. *Man* 20 (n.s.) (3): 454–74.

Chang, K. C. 1972. *Settlement Patterns in Archaeology*. An Addison-Wesley Module in Anthropology 24: 1–26.

Chapman, D. M., M. Geary, P. S. Roy and B. G. Thom. 1982. *Coastal Evolution and Coastal Erosion in New South Wales*. A report prepared for the Coastal Council of New South Wales, Sydney.

Chappell, J. 1982. Sea levels and sediments: some features of the context of coastal archaeological sites in the tropics. *Archaeology in Oceania* 17 (2): 69–78.

Chappell, J. 1983. Sea level changes, 0 to 40KA. In J. M. A. Chappell and A. Grindrod (eds), *Climanz. Proceedings of the First Climanz Conference*, pp. 121–2. Canberra: Department of Biogeography and Geomorphology, Research School of Pacific Studies, Australian National University.

Chappell, J. M. A. and A. Grindrod (eds). 1983a. *Climanz. Proceedings of the First Climanz Conference*. Canberra: Department of Biogeography and Geomorphology, Research School of Pacific Studies, Australian National University.

Chappell, J. M. A. and A. Grindrod. 1983b. 32 +/- 5KA: review. In J. M. A. Chappell and A. Grindod (eds), *Climanz. Proceedings of the First Climanz Conference*, pp. 1–3. Canberra: Department of Biogeography and Geomorphology, Research School of Pacific Studies, Australian National University.

Chappell, J. M. A. and A. Grindrod. 1983c. 25–20KA review. In J. M. A. Chappell and A. Grindod (eds), *Climanz. Proceedings of the First Climanz Conference*, pp. 27–28. Canberra: Department of Biogeography and Geomorphology, Research School of Pacific Studies, Australian National University.

Chappell, J. M. A. and A. Grindrod. 1983d. 7 +/- 2KA review. In J. M. A. Chappell and A. Grindod (eds), *Climanz. Proceedings of the First Climanz Conference*, pp. 87–88. Canberra: Department of Biogeography and Geomorphology, Research School of Pacific Studies, Australian National University.

Chenhall, R. G. 1975. A rationale for archaeological sampling. In J. W. Mueller (ed.), *Sampling in Archaeology*, pp. 3–25. Tucson: The University of Arizona Press.

Chippindale, C. 2001. What are the right words for rock-art in Australia? *Australian Archaeology* 53:12–15.

Clark, G. A. and L. G. Strauss. 1983. Late Pleistocene hunter-gatherer adaptations in Cantabrian Spain. In G. Bailey (ed.), *Hunter-Gatherer Economy in Prehistory: A European Perspective*, pp. 131–48. Cambridge University Press.

Clarkson, C. 2001. Technological change in Wardaman Country: a report on the 1999 field season. *Australian Aboriginal Studies* 2001/1: 63–8.

Clarkson, C. 2002. Holocene scraper reduction, technological organisation and landuse at Ingaladdi Rockshelter, Northern Australia. *Archaeology in Oceania* 37 (2): 79–86.

Clegg, J. K. 1965. A note on the stone industry of Cathedral Cave, Carnarvon Gorge, Queensland. *Mankind* 6 (5): 237.

Clegg, J. K. 1977. The four dimensions of artifactual variation. In R. V. S. Wright (ed.), *Stone Tools as Cultural Markers: Change, Evolution and Complexity*, pp. 60–66. Canberra: Australian Institute of Aboriginal Studies, and New Jersey: Humanities Press Inc.

Clegg, J. 1984. The evaluation of archaeological significance: prehistoric pictures and/or rock art. In S. Sullivan and S. Bowdler (eds), *Site Surveys and Significance Assessment in Australian Archaeology*, pp. 10–18. Canberra: Department of Prehistory, Research School of Pacific Studies, Australian National University.

Clegg, J. 1985. Comments on: The interpretation of prehistoric art, by David Groenfeldt. *Rock Art Research* 2 (1): 35–45.

Cogger, H. 2000. 6th ed. *Reptiles and Amphibians of Australia*. Sydney: Reed New Holland.

Colhoun, E.A. 1983. The climate of Tasmania 7 ± 2KA BP. In J. M. A. Chappell and A. Grindrod (eds), *Climanz. Proceedings of the First Climanz Conference*, pp. 93–4. Canberra: Department of Biogeography and Geomorphology, Research School of Pacific Studies, Australian National University.

Colley, S. 1997. A pre- and post-contact Aboriginal shell midden at Disaster Bay, New South Wales south coast. *Australian Archaeology* 45: 1–19.

Collier, S. 1976. Report on Archaeological Impact Survey of the Proposed Gosford-Wyong Water Supply. Unpublished report to the NSW Department of Public Works.

Collins, D. 1798 [1975]. *An Account of the English Colony in New South Wales* Vol. 1. Edited by B. H. Fletcher. The Strand, London: T. Cadell Jr, and W. Davies. [Republished by A. H. and A. W. Reed in association with the Royal Australian Historical Society, Sydney.]

Colson, E. 1979. In good years and in bad: food strategies of self-reliant societies. *Journal of Anthropological Research* 35 (1): 18–29.

Commonwealth Bureau of Meteorology. 2003. http://www.bom.gov.au/climate/averages/tables/cw_061029.shtm

Conkey, M. W. 1978. Style and information in cultural evolution: towards a predictive model for the Paleolithic. In C. L. Redman, M. J. Berman, E. V. Curtin, W. T. Langhorne Jr, N. M. Versaggi and J. C. Wanser (eds), *Social Archaeology. Beyond Subsistence and Dating*, pp. 61–85. Academic Press.

Conkey, M. W. 1984. To find ourselves: art and social geography of prehistoric hunter gatherers. In C. Schrire (ed.), *Past and Present in Hunter Gatherer Studies*, pp. 253–76. Academic Press.

Corkill, T. 1995. Aboriginal Archaeology of M2 Motorway. Test Excavation and Significance Assessment of Rockshelter PAD X/CF6, Darling Mills State Forest, Carlingford, NSW. Unpublished report to Roads and Transport Authority of NSW, Sydney.

Corkill, T. and J. Edgar. 1996. Aboriginal Archaeology of M2 Motorway Salvage Excavation of Rockshelter Site CF6, Darling Mills State Forest, Carlingford, NSW. Unpublished report to NSW Roads and Traffic Authority, Sydney.

Cosgrove, R. 1995. *The Illusion of Riches. Scale, Resolution and Explanation in Tasmanian Pleistocene Human Behaviour*. British Archaeological Reports, International Series 608. Oxford: Tempus Reparatum, Archaeological and Historical Associates Limited.

Cosgrove, R., J. Allen and B. Marshall. 1990. Palaeo-ecology and Pleistocene human occupation in south central Tasmania. *Antiquity* 64 (242): 59–78.

Costin, A. B. 1971. Vegetation, soils and climate in late Quaternary south-eastern Australia. In D. J. Mulvaney and J. Golson (eds), *Aboriginal Man and Environment in Australia*, pp. 26–37. Canberra: Australian National University Press.

Costin, A. B. 1972. Carbon-14 dates from the Snowy Mountains area, south-eastern Australia, and their interpretation. *Quaternary Research* 2: 579–90.

Coutts, P. J. F. 1982. Victoria Archaeological Survey activities report 1979–80. In P. J. F. Coutts (ed.), *Cultural Resources Management in Victoria 1979–1981. Records of the Victorian Archaeological Survey* 13: 1–27.

Cowgill, G. 1975. A selection of samplers: comments on archaeo-statistics. In J. W. Mueller (ed.), *Sampling in Archaeology*, pp. 258–74. Tucson: The University of Arizona Press.

Craib, J. L., T. Bonhomme, G. R. Mangold and S. S. Williams. 1999. Archaeological Salvage Excavations at Site RS1 (45-5-982), Regentville, western Sydney. Final Report. Unpublished report to TransGrid.

Dallas, M. Consulting Archaeologists. 2002. Sutherland Shire Council. Aboriginal Cultural Heritage Study. Report to Sutherland Shire Council.

Daniel, I. R., Jr. 2001. Stone raw material availability and Early Archaic settlement in the south-eastern United States. *American Antiquity* 66 (2): 237–65.

David, B. 1990. Echidna's Rest, Chillagoe: a site report. *Queensland Archaeological Research* 7: 73–94.

David, B. 1991. Fern Cave, rock art and social formations: rock art regionalisation and demographic models in south-eastern Cape York Peninsula. *Archaeology in Oceania* 26 (2): 41–57.

David, B. and D. Chant. 1995. Rock art and regionalisation in north Queensland prehistory. *Memoirs of the Queensland Museum* 37 (2): 357–528.

David, B. and L. Dagg. 1993. Two caves. *Memoirs of the Queensland Museum* 33 (1): 143–62.

David, B. and H. Lourandos. 1997. 37,000 years and more in tropical Australia: investigating long-term archaeological tends in Cape York Peninsula. *Proceedings of the Prehistoric Society* 63: 1–23.

David, B. and H. Lourandos. 1998. Rock art and socio-demography in northeastern Australian prehistory. *World Archaeology* 30 (2): 193–219.

Davidson, I. 1983. Site variability and prehistoric economy in Levante. In G. Bailey (ed.), *Hunter-Gatherer Economy in Prehistory: A European Perspective*, pp. 79–95. Cambridge University Press.

Davidson, I. 1990. Prehistoric Australian demography. In B. Meehan and N. White (eds), *Hunter-Gatherer Demography. Past and Present*, pp. 41–58. Oceania Monograph 39. University of Sydney.

Davidson, I. 1997. Book review: B. David and D. Chant. 1995. *Rock Art and Regionalisation in North Queensland Prehistory. Memoirs of the Queensland Museum* 37 (2). *Archaeology in Oceania* 32 (3): 217–18.

Dawson, R. 1830. *The Present State of Australia*. London.

de Menocal, P. B. 2001. Cultural response to climate change during the late-Holocene. *Science (Paleoclimate)* 292: 667–73.

Dickson, F. P. n.d. [ca 1973]. Aboriginal prehistory of Botany Bay. In D. J. Anderson (ed.), *The Botany Bay Project. A Handbook of the Botany Bay Region — Some Preliminary Background Papers*, pp. 44–50. Sydney: The Botany Bay Project Committee.

Dickson, F. P. 1973. Backed blades and points. *Mankind* 9 (1): 7–14.

Dodson, J. R. 1987. Mire development and environmental change, Barrington Tops, New South Wales, Australia. *Quaternary Research* 27: 73–81.

Dodson, J., R. Fullagar and L. Head. 1992. Dynamics of environment and people in the forested crescents of temperate Australia. In J. Dodson (ed.), *The Naive Lands*, pp.115–59. Melbourne: Longman Cheshire.

Dodson, J. R. and G. Hope. 1983. Southern Australian coastal areas, 15,000–10,000 BP. In J. M. A. Chappell and A. Grindrod (eds), *Climanz. Proceedings of the First Climanz Conference*, pp. 74–5. Canberra: Department of Biogeography and Geomorphology, Research School of Pacific Studies, Australian National University.

Dodson, J. R. and S. D. Mooney. 2002. An assessment of historic human impact on south-eastern Australian environmental systems, using late-Holocene rates of environmental change. *Australian Journal of Botany* 50: 455–64.

Dodson, J. R. and B. G. Thom. 1992. Holocene vegetation history from the Hawkesbury Valley, New South Wales. *Proceedings of the Linnean Society of New South Wales* 113 (2): 121–34.

Doelman, T., J. Webb and M. Domanski. 2001. Source to discard: patterns of lithic raw material procurement and use in Sturt National Park, north-western New South Wales. *Archaeology in Oceania* 36 (1): 15–33.

Eades, D. K. 1976. *The Dharawal and Dhurga Languages of the New South Wales South Coast*. Canberra: Australian Institute of Aboriginal Studies.

Eales, T., C. Westcott, I. Lilley, S. Ulm, D. Brian, and C. Clarkson. 1999. Roof Fall Cave, Cania Gorge: site report. *Queensland Archaeological Research* 11: 29–42.

Ebert, J. I. 1979. An ethnoarchaeological approach to reassessing the meaning of variability in stone tool assemblages. In C. Kramer (ed.), *Ethnoarchaeology: Implications of Ethnography for Archaeology*, pp. 61–74. New York: Columbia University Press.

Ebert, J. I. 1992. *Distributional Archaeology*. Albuquerque: University of New Mexico Press.

Egloff, B. J. 1984. Sampling the Five Forests. In S. Sullivan and S. Bowdler (eds), *Site Surveys and Significance Assessment in Australian Archaeology*, pp. 71–78. Canberra: Department of Prehistory, Research School of Pacific Studies, Australian National University.

English, T. and L. Gay. 1993. Merriwa Region Archaeological Survey 1992, September 28th to October 9th. Vol. 1. Unpublished report to the Wanaruah Aboriginal Land Council.

Enright, W. J. 1935. Distribution of Merewether chert. *Mankind* 1 (12): 8.

Etheridge, R., Jr, and T. Whitelegge. 1907. Aboriginal workshops on the coast of New South Wales, and their contents. *Records of the Australian Museum* 6 (4): 233–50.

Extract from a letter written by an officer of the marines, dated Port Jackson, 18th November, 1788 (Banks Papers). 1892 [1978]. In *Historical Records of New South Wales* 1 (2) — Phillip 1783–1792, pp. 221–4. Sydney: Government Printer.

Fawcett, J. W. 1898. Notes on the customs and dialect of the Wonnah-Ruah tribe. *Science of Man* 1 (n.s.) 7: 152–4.

Ferguson, W. C. 1985. A Mid-Holocene Depopulation of the Australian South-west. Unpublished PhD thesis, Australian National University, Canberra.

Ferland, M. A. and P. S. Roy. 1994. Lowstand sedimentation on the central NSW outer shelf: description and implications. In C. F. K. Diessel and R. L. Boyd (convenors), *Proceedings of the 28th Newcastle Symposium on Advances in the Study of the Sydney Basin*, pp. 180–87. Newcastle: Department of Geology, University of Newcastle.

Ferry, J. 1979. The failure of the New South Wales Missions to the Aborigines before 1845. *Aboriginal History* 3(1): 25–36.

Fletcher, R. 1977a. Alternatives and differences. In M. Spriggs (ed.), *Archaeology and Anthropology: Areas of Mutual Interest*, pp. 49–67. Oxford: British Archaeological Reports, Supplementary Series 19.

Fletcher, R. 1977b. Settlement studies (micro and semi-micro). In D. L. Clarke (ed.), *Spatial Archaeology*, pp. 47–162. Academic Press.

Fletcher-Jones, N. A. 1985. Across the First Frontier: The Behavioural Ecology of the Sydney Region Aborigines. 2 vols. Unpublished PhD thesis, University of Durham, Britain.

Flood, J. M. 1973. The Moth Hunters — Investigations towards a Prehistory of the Southeastern Highlands of Australia. Unpublished PhD thesis, Australian National University, Canberra.

Flood, J. 1976. Man and ecology in the highlands of south-eastern Australia: a case study. In N. Peterson (ed.), *Tribes and Boundaries in Australia*, pp. 30–49. Canberra: Australian Institute of Aboriginal Studies, and New Jersey: Humanities Press Inc.

Flood, J. 1980. *The Moth Hunters: Aboriginal Prehistory of the Australian Alps*. Canberra: Australian Institute of Aboriginal Studies.

Flood, J. 1999. *Archaeology of the Dreamtime. The Story of Prehistoric Australia and its People*. Sydney: Angus and Robertson.

Flood, J. 1997. Australian Aboriginal use of caves. In C. Bonsall and C. Tolan–Smith (eds), *The Human Use of Caves*, pp. 193–200. British Archaeological Reports, International Series 667. Oxford: Archaeopress.

Flood, J. , B. David, J. Magee and B. English. 1987. Birrigai: a Pleistocene site in the south-eastern highlands. *Archaeology in Oceania* 22 (1): 9–26.

Flood, P. G. and E. Frankel. 1989. Late Holocene higher sea level indicators from eastern Australia. *Marine Geology* 90: 193–5.

Foley, R. 1981a. A model of regional archaeological structure. *Proceedings of the Prehistoric Society* 47:1–17.

Foley, R. 1981b. Off-site archaeology: an alternative approach for the short-sited. In I. Hodder, G. Isaac and N. Hammond (eds), *Pattern of the Past: Studies in Honour of David Clarke*, pp. 157–84. Cambridge University Press.

Foley, R. 1981c. *Off-site Archaeology and Human Adaptation in Eastern Africa: An Analysis of Regional Artefact Density in the Amboseli, Southern Kenya*. A. R. Hands and D. R. Walker (eds), Cambridge Monographs in African Archaeology 3. Oxford: British Archaeological Reports, International Series 97.

Frankel, D. 1988. Characterising change in prehistoric sequences: a view from Australia. *Archaeology in Oceania* 23 (2): 41–8.

Fraser, J. 1892. Map of New South Wales as occupied by Native Tribes (frontispiece), and Introduction. In L. E. Threlkeld, *An Australian Language as spoken by the Awabakal, the People of Awaba or Lake Macquarie (near Newcastle, New South Wales); being an account of their language, traditions, and customs*, pp. ix–lxvi. Edited by J. Fraser [Republication of Threlkeld 1834, unpublished 1857 and 1859 manuscripts, with text rearranged, condensed and edited, plus appendix by J. Fraser]. Sydney: Government Printer.

Fraser, J. 1892 [1893]. *The Aborigines of New South Wales*. Published by authority of New South Wales Commissioners for the World's Columbian Exposition, Chicago, 1893. Sydney: Government Printer.

Furey, L. 1978. Archaeological Survey. Mangrove Creek — Dam Storage Area. Unpublished report to NSW National Parks and Wildlife Service.

Galloway, R. W. 1965. Late Quaternary climates in Australia. *The Journal of Geology* 73 (4): 603–18.

Gamble, C. 1982. Interaction and alliance in Palaeolithic society. *Man* (NS) 17: 92–107.

Gamble, C. 1983. Culture and society in the Upper Palaeolithic of Europe. In G. Bailey (ed.), *Hunter-Gatherer Economy in Prehistory: A European Perspective*, pp. 201–11. Cambridge University Press.

Gamble, C. 1984. Regional variation in hunter-gatherer strategy in the Upper Pleistocene of Europe. In R. Foley (ed.), *Hominid Evolution and Community Ecology. Prehistoric Human Adaptation in Biological Perspective*, pp. 237–60. Academic Press.

Gamble, C. 1986. *The Palaeolithic Settlement of Europe*. Cambridge University Press.

Gamble, C. 1998. Palaeolithic society and the release from proximity: a network approach to intimate relations. *World Archaeology* 29 (3): 426–49.

Gillespie, R. 1982. *Radiocarbon Users Handbook*. Quaternary Research Unit Occasional Publication 1. North Ryde, Sydney: Macquarie University.

Gillespie, R. 1990. The Australian marine shell correction factor. In R. Gillespie (ed.), *Quaternary Dating Workshop 1990*, p. 15. Canberra: Department of Biogeography and Geomorphology, Research School of Pacific Studies, Australian National University.

Gillespie, R. and R. B. Temple. 1976. Sydney University natural radiocarbon measurements III. *Radiocarbon* 18 (1): 96–109.

Glover, E. 1974. Report on the excavation of a second rock shelter at Curracurrang Cove, New South Wales. In J. V. S. Megaw (ed.), *The Recent Archaeology of the Sydney District. Excavations 1964–1967*, pp. 13–18. Canberra: Australian Institute of Aboriginal Studies.

Godden Mackay Pty Ltd and Austral Archaeology Pty Ltd. 1997. POW Project 1995. Randwick Destitute Children's Asylum Cemetery. Archaeological Investigation. Vol. 2: Archaeology, Part 3 — Aboriginal Archaeology. Unpublished report prepared for the South Eastern Sydney Area Health Service, Heritage Council of NSW and NSW Department of Health, Sydney.

Godfrey, M. C. S. 1989. Shell midden chronology in south-western Victoria: reflections of change in prehistoric population and subsistence? *Archaeology in Oceania* 24 (2): 65–9.

Gould, R. A. 1969. *Yiwara: Foragers of the Australian Desert*. London: Collins.

Gould, R. A. 1975. Ecology and adaptive response among the Tolowa Indians of north-western California. *The Journal of California Anthropology* 2 (2): 149–170.

Gould, R. A. 1980. *Living Archaeology*. Cambridge: Cambridge University Press.

Gray, A. 1985. Limits for demographic parameters of Aboriginal populations in the past. *Australian Aboriginal Studies* 1985/1: 22–7.

Grayson, D. K. 1984. *Quantitative Zooarchaeology. Topics in the Analysis of Archaeological Faunas*. Academic Press.

Greer, S. 1985. Salvage Program: Proposed Extensions F3 Freeway (Wahroonga–Berowra). Unpublished report to NSW Department of Main Roads, Sydney.

Gunn, R. 1979. Report on the Aboriginal Rock Art of the Upper Mangrove Creek Catchment Area. (Documentation of 'Art' Sites to be destroyed by the Mangrove Creek Dam storage area.) Unpublished report to NSW National Parks and Wildlife Service.

Gunson, N. (ed.) 1974. *Australian Reminiscences and Papers of L. E. Threlkeld, Missionary to the Aborigines, 1824–1859*. Vol. 1. Canberra: Australian Institute of Aboriginal Studies.

Haglund, L. 1981a. Archaeological Investigations in the Area of the Proposed Kerrabee Dam. Unpublished report to NSW National Parks and Wildlife Service on behalf of the NSW Water Resources Commission.

Haglund, L. 1981b. Archaeological Survey and Sampling at the Site of the Ulan Coal Mine Ulan, NSW. Unpublished report prepared for Longworth and McKenzie Pty Ltd.

Haglund, L. 1984. Archaeological investigations in the area of the proposed Kerrabee Dam, New South Wales: a case study. In S. Sullivan and S. Bowdler (eds), *Site Surveys and Significance Assessment in Australian Archaeology*, pp. 79–87. Canberra: Department of Prehistory, Research School of Pacific Studies, Australian National University.

Haglund, L. 1989. Technological Change. A Comparison of Developments in the Goulburn and Hunter River Valleys. Unpublished report for the Australian Institute of Aboriginal and Torres Strait Islander Studies, Canberra.

Haglund, L. 1992. Archaeological Investigations at Doctors Creek, Warkworth, NSW. Salvage Excavation and Surface Collection in compliance with NPWS Salvage requirements. Sites NPWS 37-6-158, 37-6-162 and 37-6-458. Vol. 6, Appendix G: Reports on radiocarbon and thermoluminescence dating. Unpublished report by Haglund and Associates to Warkworth Mining Limited.

Haglund, L. 1995. The Proposed M2 Motorway: Investigation of Aboriginal Heritage Significance. Test Excavation of Rock Shelter PAD1/DC1 on Devlins Creek, Pennant Hills–Beecroft. Unpublished report prepared by Haglund and Associates Cultural Heritage Consultants for NSW Roads and Traffic Authority, Sydney.

Haglund, L. 1996. Salvage Excavation completed for Ulan Coal Mines Ltd: NPWS site 36-3-177, Ulan Heritage Identifier 116, in compliance with requirements under NPWS Consent No. 786. Unpublished report to Ulan Coal Mines Ltd.

Haglund, L. 2001a. Archaeological Investigations within Warkworth Mining Lease relating to Sullivans and Dights Creek, NSW. Vol. 4: Summary and Discussion of Results. Unpublished report by Haglund and Associates to Warkworth Mining Limited.

Haglund, L. 2001b. Salvage Excavation completed for Ulan Coal Mines Ltd: Site SG5, Aboriginal Rock Shelter Site, in compliance with requirements under NPWS Consent No. 1002. Vol. 1: Overview. With a report on usewear and residue analysis by Michael Therin. Unpublished report by Haglund and Associates to Ulan Coal Mines Ltd.

Haglund, L. 2002. Archaeological Investigations within Warkworth Mining Lease: Aboriginal Sites along Sandy Hollow Creek, NSW. Vol. 1a: Site W6 (NPWS 37-6-151). Unpublished report by Haglund and Associates to Warkworth Mining Limited.

Haglund, L. and J. Stockton. 1983. Archaeological Investigations of Proposed Sandstone Extraction Area at Cattai: Lot 71B and Lot 1, D. P. 40740, Cheesemans Road. Unpublished report to Collin C. Donges and Associates Pty Ltd on behalf of N. L. Perry and Son Pty Ltd.

Hale, H. M. and N. B. Tindale. 1930. Notes on some human remains in the Lower Murray Valley, South Australia. *Records of the South Australian Museum* 4 (2): 145–218.

Hall, J. 1982. Sitting on the crop of the bay: an historical and archaeological sketch of Aboriginal settlement and subsistence in Morton Bay, southeast Queensland. In S. Bowdler (ed.), *Coastal Archaeology in Eastern Australia. Proceedings of the 1980 Valla Conference on Australian Prehistory*, pp. 79–95. Canberra: Department of Prehistory, Research School of Pacific Studies, Australian National University.

Hall, J. and P. Hiscock. 1988. Platypus Rockshelter (KBA: 70), S. E. Queensland: chronological changes in site use. *Queensland Archaeological Research* 5: 42–62.

Hall, J. and P. Hiscock 1988b. The Moreton Regional Archaeological Project (MRAP). Stage II: an outline of objectives and methods. *Queensland Archaeological Research* 5: 4–24.

Hall, M. C. 1981. Land-use changes in Owens Valley prehistory: a matter of statistical inference. *American Antiquity* 46 (3): 648–56.

Hall, R. and K. Lomax. 1996. A regional landscape approach to the management of stone artefact sites in forested uplands in eastern Australia. *Australian Archaeology* 42: 35–8.

Hallam, S. J. 1972. An archaeological survey of the Perth Area, Western Australia: a progress report on art and artefacts, dates and demography. *Australian Institute of Aboriginal Studies Newsletter* 3 (5): 11–19.

Hallam, S. 1977. Topographic archaeology and artifactual evidence. In R. V. S. Wright (ed.), *Stone Tools as Cultural Markers: Change, Evolution and Complexity*, pp. 169–77. Canberra: Australian Institute of Aboriginal Studies, and New Jersey: Humanities Press Inc.

Hallam, S. J. 1979. (reprint) *Fire and Hearth: A Study of Aboriginal Usage and European Usurpation in South-western Australia*. Canberra: Australian Institute of Aboriginal Studies.

Halstead, P. and J. O'Shea. 1989. Introduction: cultural responses to risk and uncertainty. In P. Halstead and J. O'Shea (eds), *Bad Year Economics: Cultural Responses to Risk and Uncertainty*, pp. 1–7. Cambridge: Cambridge University Press.

Harrison, S. P. and J. Dodson. 1993. Climates of Australia and New Guinea since 18,000 yr BP. In H. E. Wright, Jr, J. E. Kutzbach, T. Webb III, W. F. Ruddiman, F. A. Street-Perrott and P. J. Bartlein (eds), *Global Climates since the Last Glacial Maximum*, pp. 265–92. Minneapolis: University of Minnesota Press.

Hassan, F. A. 1981. *Demographic Archaeology*. New York: Academic Press.

Hassan, F. A. 1982. Demographic archaeology. In M. B. Schiffer (ed.), *Advances in Archaeological Method and Theory. Selections for Students from Volumes 1 through 4*, pp. 225–79. Academic Press.

Havard, O. 1943. Mrs Felton Mathew's Journal (continued). *Journal and Proceedings of the Royal Australian Historical Society* 29 (4): 217–52.

Haviland, J. and L. Haviland. 1979. Report on fieldwork at Hopevale, May–August 1979. Reference No. pMs 3185, Australian Institute of Aboriginal Studies Library, Canberra.

Hayden, B. 1972. Population control among hunter/gatherers. *World Archaeology* 4 (2): 205–21.

Hayden, B. 1979. *Palaeolithic Reflections. Lithic Technology and Ethnographic Excavation among Australian Aborigines*. Canberra: Australian Institute of Aboriginal Studies.

Hayden, B., N. Franco and J. Spafford 1996. Evaluating lithic strategies and design criteria. In G. H. Odell (ed.) *Stone Tools. Theoretical Insights into Human Prehistory*, pp. 9–45. New York: Plenum Press.

Head, L. 1983. Environment as artefact: a geographic perspective on the Holocene occupation of south-western Victoria. *Archaeology in Oceania* 18 (2): 73–80.

Head, L. 1985. Pollen analysis of sediments from the Bridgewater Caves archaeological site, south-western Victoria. *Australian Archaeology* 20: 1–15.

Head, L. 1986. Palaeoecological contributions to Australian prehistory. *Archaeology in Oceania* 21 (2): 121–9.

Head, L. 1987. The Holocene prehistory of a coastal wetland system: Discovery Bay, south-eastern Australia. *Human Ecology* 15 (4): 435–62.

Head, L. 1989. Prehistoric Aboriginal impacts on Australian vegetation: an assessment of the evidence. *Australian Geographer* 20 (1): 37–46.

Herbert, C. and R. Helby. 1980. *A Guide to the Sydney Basin. Geological Survey of New South Wales Bulletin* 26. Sydney: Department of Mineral Resources.

Higgs, E. S. and C. Vita-Finzi. 1972. Prehistoric economies: a territorial approach. In E. S. Higgs (ed.), *Papers in Economic Prehistory*, pp. 27–36. Cambridge University Press.

Hiscock, P. 1981. Comments on the use of chipped stone artefacts as a measure of 'intensity of site usage'. *Australian Archaeology* 13: 30–4.

Hiscock, P. 1982a. An Archaeological Assessment of Site 1, Awoonga Dam, Queensland. Unpublished report to the Gladstone Area Water Board.

Hiscock, P. 1982b. A technological analysis of quartz assemblages from the south coast. In S. Bowdler (ed.), *Coastal Archaeology in Eastern Australia. Proceedings of the 1980 Valla Conference on Australian Prehistory*, pp. 32–45. Canberra: Department of Prehistory, Research School of Pacific Studies, Australian National University.

Hiscock, P. 1984. A preliminary report on the stone artefacts from Colless Creek Cave, North-west Queensland. *Queensland Archaeological Research* 1: 120–51.

Hiscock, P. 1985. The need for a taphonomic perspective in stone artefact analysis. *Queensland Archaeological Research* 2: 82–97.

Hiscock, P. 1986. Technological change in the Hunter River valley and the interpretation of late-Holocene change in Australia. *Archaeology in Oceania* 21 (1): 40–50.

Hiscock, P. 1988a. Developing a relative dating system for the Moreton Region: an assessment of prospects for a technological approach. *Queensland Archaeological Research* 5: 113–32.

Hiscock, P. D. 1988b. Prehistoric Settlement Patterns and Artefact Manufacture at Lawn Hill, North-west Queensland. PhD thesis, University of Queensland, Brisbane.

Hiscock, P. 1993 Bondaian technology in the Hunter Valley, New South Wales. *Archaeology in Oceania* 28 (2): 65–76.

Hiscock, P. 1994. Technological responses to risk in Holocene Australia. *Journal of World Prehistory* 8 (3): 267–92.

Hiscock, P. 1996. Mobility and technology in the Kakadu coastal wetlands. In I. C. Glover and P. Bellwood (eds), *Indo-Pacific Prehistory: The Chiang Mai Papers*, Vol. 2. *Indo-Pacific Prehistory Association Bulletin* 15: 151–7.

Hiscock, P. 2001. Sizing up prehistory: sample size and composition of artefact assemblages. *Australian Aboriginal Studies* 2001/1: 48–62.

Hiscock, P. 2002. Pattern and context in the Holocene proliferation of backed artifacts in Australia. In R. G. Elston and S. L. Kuhn (eds), *Thinking Small: Global Perspective on Microlithization. Archaeological Papers of the American Anthropological Association* (AP3A) 12: 163–77.

Hiscock, P. and H. Allen. 2000. Assemblage variability in the Willandra Lakes. *Archaeology in Oceania* 35 (3): 97–103.

Hiscock, P. and V. Attenbrow. 1998. Early Holocene backed artefacts from Australia. *Archaeology in Oceania* 33 (2): 49–62.

Hiscock, P. and V. Attenbrow. 2004. A revised sequence of backed artefact production at Capertee 3, New South Wales. *Archaeology in Oceania,* 39(2): 94–99.

Hiscock, P. and V. Attenbrow. 2004. in press. *Australia's Eastern Regional Sequence Revisited: Technology and Change at Capertree 3.* British Archaeological Reports, International Series. Oxford: Archaeopress.

Hiscock, P. and J. Hall. 1988. Technological change at Bushrangers Cave (LA: A11), southeast Queensland. *Queensland Archaeological Research* 5: 90–112.

Hiscock, P. and M. Koettig. 1985. The Salvage Excavation and Collection of Archaeological Sites. Vol. 3A: in ANUTECH Pty Ltd, Archaeological Investigations at Plashett Dam, Mount Arthur North and Mount Arthur South in the Hunter Valley, New South Wales. Unpublished report prepared for the Electricity Commission of NSW and Mount Arthur South Coal Pty Ltd.

Holdaway, S. and N. Porch. 1995. Cyclical patterns in the Pleistocene human occupation of South-west Tasmania. *Archaeology in Oceania* 30 (2): 74–82.

Holdaway, S., D. Witter, P. Fanning, R. Musgrave, G. Cochrane, T. Doelman, S. Greenwood, D. Pigdon and J. Reeves. 1998. New approaches to open site spatial archaeology in Sturt National Park, New South Wales, Australia. *Archaeology in Oceania* 33 (1): 1–19.

Hope, G. 1983. Southern Australia 7000–5000 BP. In J. M. A. Chappell and A. Grindrod (eds), *Climanz. Proceedings of the First Climanz Conference,* p. 98. Canberra: Department of Biogeography and Geomorphology, Research School of Pacific Studies, Australian National University.

Horton, D. R. 1978. Preliminary notes on the analysis of Australian coastal middens. *Australian Institute of Aboriginal Studies Newsletter* 10. p. 30–3.

Howitt, A. W. 1904 [1996]. *The Native Tribes of South-East Australia.* London: Macmillan and Co. Limited,. [Facsimile edition by Aboriginal Studies Press, Canberra.]

Hughes, P. J. 1977. A Geomorphological Interpretation of Selected Archaeological Sites in Southern Coastal New South Wales. Unpublished PhD thesis, University of New South Wales, Sydney.

Hughes, P. J. 1978. Weathering in sandstone shelters in the Sydney Basin and the survival of rock art. In C. Pearson (ed.), *Conservation of Rock Art,* pp. 36–41. Canberra: Institute for the Conservation of Cultural Material, Canberra College of Advanced Education.

Hughes, P. J. 1981. The impact of bushfires on soils and soil erosion. In P. Stanbury (ed.), *Bushfires. Their Effect on Australian Life and Landscape,* pp. 33–7. The Macleay Museum, the University of Sydney.

Hughes, P. J. 1982. A Geoarchaeological Interpretation of the Deep Creek Shelter Archaeological Site, Mangrove Creek, NSW. Appendix I in V. Attenbrow, Archaeological Investigation of Deep Creek Shelter, Mangrove Creek Dam. Unpublished report to NSW National Parks and Wildlife Service on behalf of NSW Department of Public Works.

Hughes, P. J. 1985. Summary of Investigations, and the Recommendations. In Vol. 1: in ANUTECH Pty Ltd, Archaeological Investigations at Plashett Dam, Mount Arthur North, and Mount Arthur South in the Hunter Valley, New South Wales. Unpublished report prepared for the Electricity Commission of NSW and Mount Arthur South Coal Pty Ltd.

Hughes, P. J. , R. K. Barz and P. Hiscock. 1984. An Archaeological Investigation of the Bungendore Sands Quarry, Lake George, NSW. Unpublished report to Corkhill Bros. Pty Ltd, Fyshwick, ACT.

Hughes, P. J. and V. Djohadze. 1980. *Radiocarbon Dates from Archaeological Sites on the South Coast of New South Wales and the Use of Depth/Age Curves.* Canberra: Department of Prehistory, Research School of Pacific Studies, Australian National University.

Hughes, P. J., M. Hermes, and A. Lance. 1984. North Head Shell Midden, Batemans Bay, NSW. Analyses of Midden Contents. A report to NSW National Parks and Wildlife Service, South East Region, Queanbeyan.

Hughes, P. J. and R. J. Lampert. 1982. Prehistoric population change in southern coastal New South Wales. In S. Bowdler (ed.), *Coastal Archaeology in Eastern Australia. Proceedings of the 1980 Valla Conference on Australian Prehistory*, pp. 16–28. Canberra: Department of Prehistory, Research School of Pacific Studies, Australian National University.

Hughes, P. J. and M. E. Sullivan. 1979. A Geoarchaeological Investigation of Sandstone Shelter Archaeological Sites in the Mangrove Creek Catchment, New South Wales. Appendix 2 in V. Attenbrow (1981), Mangrove Creek Dam Salvage Excavation Project, Vol. 2. Unpublished report to NSW National Parks and Wildlife Service on behalf of NSW Department of Public Works.

Hughes, P. J. and M. E. Sullivan. 1981. Aboriginal burning and late-Holocene geomorphic events in eastern NSW. *Search* 12 (8): 277–8.

Hughes, P. J. and M. E. Sullivan. 1986. Aboriginal landscape. In J. S. Russell and R. F. Isbell (eds), *Australian Soils: The Human Impact*, pp. 117–33. University of Queensland Press in association with the Australian Society of Soil Science Incorporated.

Hunter, J. 1793 [1968]. *An Historical Journal of the Transactions at Port Jackson and Norfolk Island, ... including the journals of Governors Phillip and King, and of Lieut. Ball; and the voyages from the first sailing of the Sirius in 1787 to the return of that Ship's company to England in 1792.* Printed for John Stockdale, Piccadilly, London. [Australiana Facsimile Editions No. 148, reproduced by Libraries Board of South Australia, Adelaide.]

Illawarra Prehistory Group. 1990. 1989–1990 Archaeological Survey of the Cordeaux River and Woronora River. Unpublished report for Australian Institute of Aboriginal and Torres Strait Islander Studies, Canberra.

Illawarra Prehistory Group. 1995. 1994–1995 Archaeological Survey of Kangaroo Creek, Royal National Park. Unpublished report for Australian Institute of Aboriginal and Torres Strait Islander Studies, Canberra.

Illawarra Prehistory Group. 1996. 1995–1996 Archaeological Survey of the North and Western Side of the Hacking River including Royal National Park and Garrawarra State Recreation Area. Unpublished report for Australian Institute of Aboriginal and Torres Strait Islander Studies, Canberra.

Jochim, M. A. 1989. Optimization and stone tool studies: problems and potentials. In R. Torrence (ed.), *Time, Energy and Stone Tools*, pp. 106–11. Cambridge University Press.

Jochim, M. A. 1998. *A Hunter-Gatherer Landscape. South-west Germany in the Late Paleolithic and Mesolithic.* New York: Plenum Press.

Johnson, A. G. 2000. Fine resolution palaeoecology confirms anthropogenic impact during the late-Holocene in the lower Hawkesbury Valley, NSW. *Australian Geographer* 31 (2): 209–35.

Johnson, I. 1979. The Getting of Data. A Case Study from the Recent Industries of Australia. PhD thesis, Australian National University, Canberra.

Jones, D. S. and G. J. Morgan. 1994. *A Field Guide to Crustaceans of Australian Waters.* Sydney: Reed.

Jones, P. D., T. J. Osborn and K. R. Briffa. 2001. The evolution of climate over the last millennium. *Science (Paleoclimate)* 292: 662–7.

Jones, R. 1977. The Tasmanian paradox. In R. V. S. Wright (ed.), *Stone Tools as Cultural Markers: Change, Evolution and Complexity*, pp. 189–204. Canberra: Australian Institute of Aboriginal Studies, and New Jersey: Humanities Press Inc.

Jones, R. 1985, Archaeological conclusions. In R. Jones (ed.), *Archaeological Research in Kakadu National Park*, pp. 291–8. Australian National Parks & Wildlife Service and the Department of Prehistory, Research School of Pacific Studies, Australian National University, Canberra.

Jones, R. and J. Allen. 1978. Caveat excavator: a sea bird midden on Steep Head Island, north west Tasmania. *Australian Archaeology* 8: 142–5.

Jones, R. and I. Johnson. 1985a. Deaf Adder Gorge: Lindner Site, Nauwalabila I. In R. Jones (ed.), *Archaeological Research in Kakadu National Park*, pp. 165–227. Australian National Parks & Wildlife Service and Department of Prehistory, Research School of Pacific Studies, Australian National University, Canberra.

Jones, R. and I. Johnson. 1985b. Rockshelter excavations: Nourlangie and Mt Brockman massifs. In R. Jones (ed.), *Archaeological Research in Kakadu National Park*, pp. 39–76. Canberra: Australian National Parks & Wildlife Service and Department of Prehistory, Research School of Pacific Studies, Australian National University.

Jones, R. L. and J. R. Dodson. 1997. A Holocene vegetation record from Wrights Creek Valley, New South Wales. *Proceedings of the Linnean Society of New South Wales* 118: 1–22.

Judge, W. J., J. I. Ebert, and R. K. Hitchcock. 1975. Sampling in regional archaeological survey. In J. W. Mueller (ed.), *Sampling in Archaeology*, pp. 82–123. Tucson: University of Arizona Press.

Jung, S. 1992. Trample damage of stone flakes as an index of occupation intensity: a case study from Magnificent Gallery. *Queensland Archaeological Research* 9: 26–8.

Kamminga, J. 1980. A functional investigation of Australian microliths. *The Artefact* 5 (1 and 2): 1–18.

Kamminga, J., R. Paton and I. Macfarlane. 1989. Archaeological Investigations in the Thredbo Valley, Snowy Mountains. Unpublished report to Farabo Pty Ltd.

Kefous, K. 1982. Prehistoric site patterning in the Victorian Mallee. *Archaeology in Oceania* 17 (2): 98–9.

Kelly, M. 1982. *A Practical Reference Source to Radiocarbon Dates obtained from Archaeological Sites in Queensland.* Cultural Resource Management Monograph Series Number 4. Brisbane: Archaeology Branch, Department of Aboriginal and Islander Advancement.

Kelly, R. L. 1983. Hunter-gather mobility strategies. *Journal of Anthropological Research* 39 (3): 277–306.

Kelly, R. L. 1992. Mobility/sedentism: concepts, archaeological measures, and effects. *Annual Review of Anthropology* 21: 43–66.

Kelly, R. L. and L. C. Todd 1988. Coming into the country: early Paleoindian hunting and mobility. *American Antiquity* 53 (2): 231–44.

Kershaw, A. P. 1982. Holocene palaeoecology In B. G. Thom and R. J. Wasson (eds), *Holocene Research in Australia 1978–1982*, pp. 78–82. Duntroon, ACT: Department of Geography, Faculty of Military Studies, University of New South Wales, Royal Military College.

Kershaw, A. P. 1984. Review of Quaternary studies in Australia – plant and invertebrate palaeoecology. In G. E. Wilford (compiler), *Quaternary Studies in Australia: Future Directions. Record 1984/14* p. 69. Bureau of Mineral Resources, Geology and Geophysics.

Kershaw, A. P. 1989. Was there a 'Great Australian Arid Period'? *Search* 20 (3): 89–92.

Kershaw, A. P. 1995. Environmental change in greater Australia. In J. Allen and J. F. O'Connell (eds), *Transitions. Pleistocene to Holocene in Australia and Papua New Guinea. Antiquity* 69 (Special No. 265): 656–75.

Kershaw, P., P. G. Quilty, B. David, S. van Huet, and A. McMinn. 2000. Palaeobiogeography of the Quaternary of Australasia. In A. J. Wright, G. C. Young, J. A. Talent and J. R. Laurie (eds), *Palaeobiogeography of Australasian Faunas and Floras*, pp. 471–515. Memoir 23 of the Association of Australasian Palaeontologists, Canberra.

Kinhill Engineers Pty Ltd. 1995. Morisset Forestry District EIS. An Assessment of Aboriginal Archaeological Sites. Unpublished report to State Forests of New South Wales, Taree.

Kodela, P. G. 1992. Rainforest, pollen and palaeoecological studies in the Robertson area. *Eucryphia* 5: 5–8.

Kodela, P. G. and J. R. Dodson. (1988) 1989. A late-Holocene vegetation and fire record from Ku-ring-gai Chase National Park, New South Wales. *Proceedings of the Linnean Society of NSW* 110 (4): 317–26.

Koettig, M. 1976. Rising Damp: Aboriginal Structures in Perspective. Unpublished MA Qual. thesis. Department of Anthropology, University of Sydney.

Koettig M. 1985a. Archaeological Investigations of the Sites HCA. 11, HCA. 13 and HCA. 14, near Berrima, Southern Tablelands, NSW: Investigation of Sites Along State Highway No 2 — Hume Section. Unpublished report to NSW Department of Main Roads.

Koettig, M. 1985b. Archaeological Investigations of Three Sites on Upper Mill Creek: near Lucas Heights, Sydney. Unpublished report for Metropolitan Waste Disposal Authority, Sydney.

Koettig, M. 1986. Test Excavations at Six Locations along the Proposed Pipeline Route between Singleton and Glennies Creek Dam, Hunter Valley Region, NSW. Unpublished report to NSW Department of Public Works.

Koettig, M. 1987. Monitoring Excavations at Three Locations along the Singleton to Glennies Creek Pipeline Route, Hunter Valley, NSW. (Third report on archaeological investigations along this route.) Unpublished report to the NSW Department of Public Works .

Koettig, M. 1989. Test Excavations at Portion 147 Pokolbin, near Cessnock. Unpublished report to the McInnes Group of Companies.

Koettig, M. 1990. Report on Salvage Excavations at M14, Upper Mill Creek, Near Lucas Heights, Sydney. Unpublished report to the Waste Management Authority, NSW, Sydney.

Koettig, M. 1991. Survey and Test Excavations Bulga Lease Authorisation 219. Unpublished report to Saxonvale Coal Pty Ltd.

Koettig, M. 1992. Salvage Excavations of Aboriginal Sites on the Camberwell Lease. Vol. 3: Table, Illustrations, Photos. Unpublished report to Camberwell Coal Pty Ltd.

Koettig, M. 1994. Bulga Lease Authorisation 219. Salvage Excavations. 5 vols. Unpublished report to Saxonvale Coal Pty Ltd.

Koettig, M. and P. J. Hughes. 1983. An Archaeological Survey of the Proposed Hungry Creek Rural/Residential Subdivision, Upper Wollombi Brook, NSW. A report to John Cameron, Dungeness Pastoral Company, Murrays Run via Laguna, NSW.

Kohen, J. L. 1986. Prehistoric Settlement in the Western Cumberland Plain: Resources, Environment and Technology. Unpublished PhD thesis, Macquarie University, Sydney.

Kohen, J. 1995. Excavation of A Rock Shelter Site at Mogo Creek, Yengo National Park. Unpublished report prepared for NSW National Parks and Wildlife Service, Sydney, and Darkinjung Local Aboriginal Land Council, Wyong.

Kohen, J. , E. Stockton and M. Williams 1981. Where plain and plateau meet: recent excavations at Shaws Creek rock-shelter, eastern New South Wales. *Australian Archaeology* 13: 63–8.

Kohen, J. L., E. D. Stockton, and M. A. J. Williams. 1984. Shaws Creek KII rock-shelter: a prehistoric occupation site in the Blue Mountains piedmont, eastern New South Wales. *Archaeology in Oceania* 19 (2): 57–73.

Kuskie, P. J. 1999. An Aboriginal Archaeological Assessment of the Proposed Mount Arthur North Coal Mine, Near Muswellbrook, Hunter Valley, New South Wales. Vol. A. Unpublished report to Dames and Moore, Brisbane.

Kuskie, P. J. and J. Kamminga. 2000. Salvage of Aboriginal Archaeological Sites in relation to the F3 Freeway near Lenaghans Drive, Black Hill, New South Wales. Vol. A: Report. Unpublished report by South East Archaeology to Roads and Traffic Authority, New South Wales (Major Projects, Northern Region, Newcastle).

Lamb, L. 1996a. A methodology for the analysis of backed artefact production on the South Molle Island quarry, Whitsunday Islands. In S. Ulm, I. Lilley and A. Ross (eds), *Australian Archaeology '95. Proceedings of the 1995 Australian Archaeological Association Annual Conference*, pp. 151–59. *Tempus* 6. St Lucia, Brisbane: Anthropology Museum, University of Queensland.

Lamb, L. 1996b. Investigating changing stone technologies, site use and occupational intensities at Fern Cave, north Queensland. *Australian Archaeology* 42: 1–7.

Lampert, R. J. 1966. An excavation at Durras North, New South Wales. *Archaeology and Physical Anthropology in Oceania* 1 (2): 83–118.

Lampert, R. J. 1971a. *Burrill Lake and Currarong. Coastal Sites in Southern New South Wales. Terra Australis* 1. Canberra: Department of Prehistory, Research School of Pacific Studies, Australian National University.

Lampert, R. J. 1971b. Coastal Aborigines of south-eastern Australia. In D. J. Mulvaney and J. Golson (eds), *Aboriginal Man and Environment in Australia*, pp. 114–32. Canberra: Australian National University Press.

Lampert, R. J. and P. J. Hughes. 1974. Sea level change and Aboriginal coastal adaptations in southern New South Wales. *Archaeology and Physical Anthropology in Oceania* 9 (3): 226–35.

Langford-Smith, T. and B. G. Thom. 1969. New South Wales coastal morphology. In G. H. Packard (ed.), *Geology of New South Wales. Journal of Geological Society of Australia* 16, Part I: 572–80.

Lawrence, R. 1968. *Aboriginal Habitat and Economy*. Canberra: Department of Geography, School of General Studies, Australian National University.

Lawrence, R. J. 1971. Habitat and economy: a historical perspective. In D. J. Mulvaney and J. Golson (eds), *Aboriginal Man and Environment in Australia*, pp. 249–61. Canberra: Australian National University Press.

Lilley, I. 1984. Late Holocene subsistence and settlement in subcoastal southeast Queensland. *Queensland Archaeological Research* 1: 8–32.

Lilley, I. A. 1985. An experiment in statistical location analysis in sub-coastal southeast Queensland. *Australian Archaeology* 21: 91–112.

Lilley, I. 2000. So near and yet so far: reflections on archaeology in Australia and Papua New Guinea, intensification and culture contact. *Australian Archaeology* 50: 36–44.

Lilley, I. and S. Ulm. 1999. The Gooreng Gooreng Cultural Heritage Project: preliminary results of archaeological research, 1993–1997. *Queensland Archaeological Research* 11: 1–14.

Lourandos, H. 1976. Aboriginal settlement and land use in south western Victoria: a report on current field work. *The Artefact* 1 (4): 174–93.

Lourandos, H. 1977. Aboriginal spatial organisation and population: south western Victoria reconsidered. *Archaeology and Physical Anthropology in Oceania* 12 (3): 202–25.

Lourandos, H. 1980a. Change or stability?: hydraulics, hunter-gatherers and population in temperate Australia. *World Archaeology* 11 (3): 245–64.

Lourandos, H. 1980b. Forces of Change: Aboriginal Technology and Population in South Western Victoria. Unpublished PhD thesis, University of Sydney.

Lourandos, H. 1983a. Intensification: a late Pleistocene–Holocene archaeological sequence from south-western Victoria. *Archaeology in Oceania* 18 (2): 81–94.

Lourandos, H. 1983b. 10,000 years in the Tasmanian highlands. *Australian Archaeology* 16: 39–47.

Lourandos, H. 1984. Changing perspectives in Australian prehistory: a reply to Beaton. *Archaeology in Oceania* 19 (1): 29–33.

Lourandos, H. 1985a. Intensification and Australian prehistory. In T. D. Price and J. A. Brown (eds), *Prehistoric Hunter-Gatherers. The Emergence of Cultural Complexity*, pp. 385–423. Academic Press.

Lourandos, H. 1985b. Problems with the interpretation of late-Holocene changes in Australian prehistory. *Archaeology in Oceania* 20 (1): 37–9.

Lourandos, H. 1987. Pleistocene Australia. Peopling a continent. In O. Soffer (ed.), *The Pleistocene Old World. Regional Perspectives*, pp. 147–65. New York: Plenum Press.

Lourandos, H. 1988. Palaeopolitics: resource intensification in Aboriginal Australia and Papua New Guinea. In T. Ingold, D. Riches and J. Woodburn (eds), *Hunters and Gatherers 1. History, Evolution and Social Change*, pp. 148–160. Oxford: Berg.

Lourandos, H. 1993. Hunter-gatherer cultural dynamics: long- and short-term trends in Australian prehistory. *Journal of Archaeological Research* 1 (1): 67–88.

Lourandos, H. 1996. Change in Australian prehistory: scale, trends and frameworks of interpretation. In S. Ulm, I. Lilley and A. Ross (eds), *Australian Archaeology '95. Proceedings of the 1995 Australian Archaeological Association Annual Conference*, pp. 15–21. *Tempus* 6. St Lucia, Brisbane: Anthropology Museum, University of Queensland.

Lourandos, H. 1997. *Continent of Hunter-Gatherers. New Perspectives in Australian Prehistory*. Cambridge University Press.

Lourandos, H. and A. Ross. 1994. The great 'intensification debate': its history and place in Australian archaeology, *Australian Archaeology* 39: 54–63.

Luebbers, R. A. 1978. Meals and Menus: A Study of Change in Prehistoric Coastal Settlements in South Australia. Unpublished PhD thesis, Australian National University, Canberra.

Luebbers, R. A. 1981. The Coorong Report: An Archaeological Survey of the Southern Younghusband Peninsula. Unpublished report prepared for the South Australian Department of Environment and Planning.

Luebbers, R. A. 1984. The Coorong Report. An Archaeological Survey of The Northern Coorong, 1982. Unpublished (draft) report prepared for the South Australian Department for Environment and Planning.

Maddock, K. 1982. 2nd ed. *The Australian Aborigines. A Portrait of their Society*. Ringwood: Penguin Books Australia.

Markgraf, V. and H. F. Diaz. 2000. The past ENSO record: a synthesis. In H. F. Diaz and V. Markgraf (eds), *El Niño and The Southern Oscillation. Multiscale Variability and Global and Regional Impacts*, pp. 465–88. Cambridge: Cambridge University Press.

Markgraf, V., J. R. Dodson, A. P. Kershaw, M. S. McGlone, and N. Nicholls. 1992. Evolution of late Pleistocene and Holocene climates in the circum-South Pacific land areas. *Climate Dynamics* 6: 193–211.

Mathews, R. H. 1896a The Būnăn ceremony of New South Wales. *American Anthropologist* 9 (10): 327–44.

Mathews, R. H. 1896b. Stone cooking-holes and grooves for stone-grinding used by the Australian Aborigines. *Journal of the Anthropological Institute of Great Britain* 25 (3): 255–9.

Mathews, R. H. 1897. *The Burbung of the Darkinung Tribes*. Carlton, Melbourne: Ford and Son, [Reprinted from *Proceedings of the Royal Society of Victoria* 10 (n. s.) (1): 1–12, July 1897.]

Mathews, R. H. 1901. Rock-holes used by the Aborigines for warming water. *Journal and Proceedings of the Royal Society of New South Wales* 35: 213–16.

Mazel, A. D. 1989a. Changing social relations in the Thukela Basin, Natal 7000–2000 BP. *South African Archaeological Society Goodwin Series* 6: 33–41.

Mazel, A. D. 1989b. People making history: the last ten thousand years of hunter-gatherer communities in the Thukela Basin. *Natal Museum Journal of Humanities* 1: 1–168.

Macarthur, E. 1791 [1893]. The Letters — Mrs Macarthur's Letters to Relatives and Friends in England. Sydney, Port Jackson N. S. Wales, March the 7th, 1791 (extracts). In Appendix B. The Macarthur Papers. In F. M. Bladen (ed.), *Historical Records of New South Wales*, Vol. 2: Grose and Paterson 1793–1795, pp. 494–512. Sydney: Government Printer.

McBryde, I. 1974. *Aboriginal Prehistory in New England. An Archaeological Survey of Northeastern New South Wales*. Sydney: Sydney University Press.

McBryde, I. 1977. Determinants of assemblage variation in New England prehistory. Environment, subsistence economies, site activities, or cultural tradition? In R. V. S. Wright (ed.), *Stone Tools as Cultural Markers: Change, Evolution and Complexity*, pp. 225–50. Canberra: Australian Institute of Aboriginal Studies, and New Jersey: Humanities Press Inc.

McBryde, I. 1985. Backed blade industries from the Graman rock shelters, New South Wales: some evidence on function. In V. N. Misra and P. Bellwood (eds), *Recent Advances in Indo-Pacific Prehistory. Proceedings of the International Symposium held at Poona, December 19–21, 1978*, pp. 231–49. New Delhi: Oxford and IBH Publishing Co.

McCarthy, F. D. 1936. Archaeological Reconnaissance of Mangrove Mountain. 28/7/1936. Report dated 31 July, 1936. Australian Museum Archives: Series 10, Correspondence 240/1936.

McCarthy, F. D. 1939a. Archaeological Reconnaissance to Wollombi District. Report dated 18 April 1939. Australian Museum Archives: Series 10, Correspondence 166/39.

McCarthy, F. D. 1939b. 'Trade' in Aboriginal Australia, and 'trade' relationships with Torres Strait, New Guinea and Malaya. *Oceania* 9 (4): 405–38.

McCarthy, F. D. 1939c. 'Trade' in Aboriginal Australia, and 'trade' relationships with Torres Strait, New Guinea and Malaya. B. Articles bartered over wide areas. *Oceania* 10 (1): 80–104.

McCarthy, F. D. 1948. The Lapstone Creek excavation: two culture periods revealed in eastern New South Wales. *Records of the Australian Museum* 22 (1): 1–34.

McCarthy, F. D. 1958. Culture succession in south eastern Australia. *Mankind* 5 (5): 177–90.

McCarthy, F. D. 1961. Australia. *Asian Perspectives* 5 (1): 98–104.

McCarthy, F. D. 1964a. Australia. *Asian Perspectives* 8 (1): 102–11.

McCarthy, F. D. 1964b. The archaeology of the Capertee Valley, New South Wales. *Records of the Australian Museum* 26 (6): 197–246.

McCarthy, F. D. 1965. The Aboriginal past: archaeological and material equipment. In R. M. Berndt and C. H. Berndt (eds), *Aboriginal Man in Australia. Essays in honour of Emeritus Professor A. P. Elkin*, pp. 71–100. Sydney: Angus and Robertson.

McCarthy, F. D. 1976. 2nd ed. revised. *Australian Aboriginal Stone Implements*. Sydney: The Australian Museum Trust.

McCarthy, F. D. 1978. New light on the Lapstone Creek excavation. *Australian Archaeology* 8: 49–60.

McDonald, J. 1985. An Excavation at Cherrybrook. Site 45-6-1649; and Addendum. Unpublished report prepared for the Metropolitan Water, Sewerage and Drainage Board, NSW.

McDonald, J. 1986a. Maroota Historic Site Archaeological Survey. Part I. Unpublished report to the NSW National Parks and Wildlife Service.

McDonald, J. 1986b. Preliminary Archaeological Reconnaissance of the Proposed Schofields Regional Depot, Plumpton, NSW. Unpublished report prepared by Brayshaw and Associates for the Metropolitan Waste Disposal Authority, Sydney.

McDonald, J. 1992a. *The Archaeology of the Angophora Reserve Rock Shelter*. Environmental Heritage Monograph Series 1. Sydney: NSW National Parks and Wildlife Service.

McDonald, J. 1992b. The Great Mackerel Rockshelter excavation: women in the archaeological record? *Australian Archaeology* 35: 32–50.

McDonald, J. 1994. Dreamtime Superhighway: An Analysis of Sydney Basin Rock Art and Prehistoric Information Exchange. Unpublished PhD thesis, Australian National University, Canberra.

McDonald, Jo, Cultural Heritage Management Pty Ltd. 1997. Archaeological Salvage of Site RM1 at Richmond, NSW. Test and Salvage Excavation Report. Unpublished report prepared for Restifa and Partners on behalf of Woolworths.

McDonald, Jo, Cultural Heritage Management Pty Ltd 1999. Test Excavation of PAD 5 (RH/SP9) and PAD 31 (RH/CC2) for the Rouse Hill (Stage 2) Infrastructure Project at Rouse Hill and Kellyville, NSW. Unpublished report to Rouse Hill Infrastructure Consortium.

McDonald, J., P. Mitchell and E. Rich. 1996. A Further Investigation of Site RS1 (45-5-892) at Regentville, Mulgoa Creek, Western Sydney. Unpublished report for Environmental Services, Pacific Power, Sydney.

McDonald, J. and E. Rich. 1993. Archaeological Investigations for the Rouse Hill Infrastructure Project (Stage I) Works along Caddies, Smalls and Second Ponds Creeks, Rouse Hill and Parklea, NSW. Final Report on Test Excavation Program. 2 vols. Unpublished report for Rouse Hill (Stage I) Pty Ltd.

McDonald, J., E, Rich and H. Barton. 1994. The Rouse Hill Infrastructure Project (Stage 1) on the Cumberland Plain, western Sydney. In M. Sullivan, S. Brockwell and A. Webb (eds), *Archaeology in the North. Proceedings of the 1993 Australian Archaeological Association Conference*, pp. 259–93. Darwing: North Australia Research Unit, Australian National University.

MacDonald, K. and I. Davidson. n.d. [ca 1998]. The Bayswater Archaeological Research Project. Vol. 1. School of Human and Environmental Studies, University of New England, Armidale.

MacDonald, K., M. Ridges and I. Davidson. 1998. Report on the 1997 field season of the Bayswater Archaeological Research Project, NSW Hunter Valley. *Australian Archaeology* 46: 37–8.

McGlone, M. S., A. P. Kershaw and V. Markgraf. 1992. El Niño/Southern Oscillation climatic variability in Australasian and South American paleoenvironmental records. In H. F. Diaz and V. Markgraf (eds), *El Niño: Historical and Paleoclimatic Aspects of the Southern Oscillation*, pp. 435–62. Cambridge University Press.

Macintosh, N. W. G. 1965. Dingo and horned anthropomorph in an Aboriginal rock shelter. *Oceania* 36 (2): 85–101

McManamon, F. P. 1984. Discovering sites unseen. In M. B. Schiffer (ed.), *Advances in Archaeological Method and Theory* 7: 223–92. Academic Press.

MacNeish, R. S. 1964. Ancient Mesoamerican civilization. *Science* 143 (3606): 531–7.

MacNeish, R. S. 1973. The evolution of community patterns in the Tehuacán Valley of Mexico and speculations about the cultural processes. In R. Tringham (ed.), *Ecology and Agricultural Settlements: An Ethnographic and Archaeological Perspective*, pp. R2: 1–27. Massachusetts: Warner Modular Publications Inc.

McNiven, I. 1992a. Sandblow sites in the Great Sandy Region, coastal southeast Queensland: implications for models of late-Holocene rainforest exploitation and settlement restructuring. *Queensland Archaeological Research* 9: 1–16.

McNiven, I. J. 1992b. Shell middens and mobility: the use of off-site faunal remains, Queensland, Australia. *Journal of Field Archaeology* 19: 495–508.

McNiven, I. J. 1994. Technological organisation and settlement in south-west Tasmania after the glacial maximum. *Antiquity* 68 (258): 75–82.

McNiven, I. J. 2000. Backed to the Pleistocene. *Archaeology in Oceania* 35 (1): 48–52.

McNiven, I., B. Marshall, J. Allen, N. Stern and R. Cosgrove. 1993. The Southern Forests Archaeological Project: An overview. In M. A. Smith, M. Spriggs and B. Fankhauser (eds), *Sahul in Review. Pleistocene Archaeology in Australia, New Guinea and Island Melanesia*, pp. 213–24. Canberra: Department of Prehistory Research School of Pacific Studies, Australian National University.

Meehan, B. 1982. *Shell Bed to Shell Midden*. Canberra: Australian Institute of Aboriginal Studies.

Meehan, B. 1988. The 'dinnertime camp'. In B. Meehan and R. Jones (eds), *Archaeology with Ethnography: An Australian Perspective*, pp. 171–81. Canberra: Department of Prehistory, Research School of Pacific Studies, Australian National University.

Megaw, J. V. S. 1965. Excavations in the Royal National Park, New South Wales: a first series of radiocarbon dates from the Sydney district. *Oceania* 35 (3): 202–7.

Megaw, J. V. S. 1968a. A dated culture sequence for the south Sydney region of New South Wales. *Current Anthropology* 9 (4): 325–9.

Megaw, J. V. S. 1968b. Trial excavations in Captain Cook's Landing Place Reserve, Kurnell, NSW. *Australian Institute of Aboriginal Studies Newsletter* 2 (9): 17–19.

Megaw, J. V. S. 1974. The recent archaeology of the south Sydney district — a summary. In J. V. S. Megaw (ed.), *The Recent Archaeology of the Sydney District. Excavations 1964–1967*, pp. 35–8. Canberra: Australian Institute of Aboriginal Studies.

Megaw, J. V. S. and A. Roberts. 1974. The 1967 excavations at Wattamolla Cove — Royal National Park, New South Wales. In J. V. S. Megaw (ed.), *The Recent Archaeology of the Sydney District. Excavations 1964–1967*, pp. 1–12. Canberra: Australian Institute of Aboriginal Studies.

Megaw, J. V. S. and R. V. S. Wright. 1966. The excavation of an Aboriginal rock-shelter on Gymea Bay, Port Hacking, NSW. *Archaeology and Physical Anthropology in Oceania* 1 (1): 23–50.

Mellars, P. A. 1973. The character of the Middle-Upper Palaeolithic transition in south-west France. In C. Renfrew (ed.), *The Explanation of Culture Change: Models in Prehistory*, pp. 255–76. London: Duckworth.

Merrick, J. R. 1993. *Freshwater Crayfishes of New South Wales*. Sydney: The Linnean Society of New South Wales.

Miller, R. D. 1983. Bull Cave: Its Relevance to the Prehistory of the Sydney Region. Unpublished BA(Hons) thesis, University of Sydney.

Mooney, S. 1997. A fine-resolution palaeoclimatic reconstruction of the last 2000 years, from Lake Keilambete, south-eastern Australia. *The Holocene* 7 (2): 139–149.

Moore, D. R. 1970. Results of an archaeological survey of the Hunter River Valley, New South Wales, Australia. Part I: The Bondaian Industry of the Upper Hunter and Goulburn River Valleys. *Records of the Australia Museum* 28: 25–64.

Moore, D. R. 1981. Results of an archaeological survey of the Hunter River Valley, New South Wales, Australia. Part II: Problems of the lower Hunter and contacts with the Hawkesbury Valley. *Records of the Australian Museum* 33 (9): 388–442.

Moore, M. W. 2000. Technology of Hunter Valley microlith assemblages, New South Wales. *Australian Archaeology* 51: 28–39.

Morphy, H. 1999. Encoding the Dreaming — a theoretical framework for the analysis of representational processes in Australian Aboriginal art. *Australian Archaeology* 49: 13–22.

Morwood, M. J. 1979. Art and Stone. Towards a Prehistory of Central Western Queensland. Unpublished PhD thesis, Australian National University, Canberra.

Morwood, M. J. 1981. Archaeology of the central Queensland highlands: the stone component. *Archaeology in Oceania* 16 (1): 1–52.

Morwood, M. J. 1984. The prehistory of the central Queensland highlands. In F. Wendorf and A. Close (eds), *Advances in World Archaeology* 3: 325–80.

Morwood, M. J. 1986. The archaeology of art: excavations at Maidenwell and Gatton shelters, southeast Queensland. *Queensland Archaeological Research* 3: 88–132.

Morwood, M. J. 1987. The archaeology of social complexity in south-east Queensland. *Proceedings of the Prehistoric Society* 53: 337–50.

Morwood, M. J. 1995. Aboriginal ethnography, S. E. Cape York peninsula. In M. J. Morwood and D. R. Hobbs (eds), In *Quinkan Prehistory. The Archaeology of Aboriginal Art in S. E. Cape York Peninsula, Australia*, pp. 33–9. *Tempus* 3. St Lucia, Brisbane: Anthropology Museum, University of Queensland.

Morwood, M. J. and D. R. Hobbs. 1995a. Conclusions. In *Quinkan Prehistory. The Archaeology of Aboriginal Art in S. E. Cape York Peninsula, Australia*, pp. 178–85. *Tempus* 3. St Lucia, Brisbane: Anthropology Museum, University of Queensland.

Morwood M. J. and D. R. Hobbs (eds) 1995b. In *Quinkan Prehistory. The Archaeology of Aboriginal Art in S. E. Cape York Peninsula, Australia*. *Tempus* 3. St Lucia, Brisbane: Anthropology Museum, University of Queensland.

Morwood, M. J. , D. R. Hobbs and D. M. Price. 1995. Excavations at Sandy Creek 1 and 2. In *Quinkan Prehistory. The Archaeology of Aboriginal Art in S. E. Cape York Peninsula, Australia*, pp. 71–91. *Tempus* 3. St Lucia, Brisbane: Anthropology Museum, University of Queensland.

Morwood, M. J. and S. Jung. 1995. Excavations at Magnificent Gallery. In *Quinkan Prehistory. The Archaeology of Aboriginal Art in S. E. Cape York Peninsula, Australia*, pp. 93–100. *Tempus* 3. St Lucia, Brisbane: Anthropology Museum, University of Queensland.

Morwood, M. J. and S. L'Oste-Brown. 1995. Chronological changes in stone artefact technology. In *Quinkan Prehistory. The Archaeology of Aboriginal Art in S. E. Cape York Peninsula, Australia*, pp. 161–77. *Tempus* 3. St Lucia, Brisbane: Anthropology Museum, University of Queensland.

Moy, C. M., G. O. Seltzer, D. T. Rodbell and D. M. Anderson. 2002. Variability of El Niño/Southern Oscillation activity at millennial timescales during the Holocene epoch. *Nature* 420: 162–5.

Mueller, J. W. 1975. Archaeological research as cluster sampling. In J. W. Mueller (ed.), *Sampling in Archaeology*, pp. 33–41. Tucson: University of Arizona Press.

Mulvaney, D. J. 1960. Archaeological excavations at Fromm's Landing on the lower Murray River, South Australia. *Proceedings of the Royal Society of Victoria* 72 (2): 53–85.

Mulvaney, D. J. 1969. 1st ed. *The Prehistory of Australia*. London: Thames and Hudson.

Mulvaney, D. J. 1975. 2nd ed. *The Prehistory of Australia*. Australia: Penguin Books.

Mulvaney, D. J. and E. B. Joyce. 1965. Archaeological and geomorphological investigations on Mt Moffatt Station, Queensland, Australia. *Proceedings of the Prehistoric Society* 31: 147–212.

Mulvaney, D. and J. Kamminga. 1999. *Prehistory of Australia*. Sydney: Allen and Unwin.

Mulvaney, D. J., G. H. Lawton and C. R. Twidale. 1964. Archaeological excavation of rock shelter No 6 Fromm's Landing, South Australia. *Proceedings of the Royal Society of Victoria* 77 (2): 479–516.

Murray-Wallace, C. V. and S. M. Colley. 1997. Amino acid racemisation and radiocarbon dating of a contact period midden, Greenglade rock-shelter, New South Wales. *Archaeology in Oceania* 32 (2): 163–9.

Myers, A. 1989. Reliable and maintainable technological strategies in the Mesolithic of mainland Britain. In R. Torrence (ed.), *Time, Energy and Stone Tools*, pp. 78–91. Cambridge University Press.

Nanson, G. C., R. W. Young and E. D. Stockton. 1987. Chronology and palaeoenvironment of the Cranebrook Terrace (near Sydney) containing artefacts more than 40,000 years old. *Archaeology in Oceania* 22 (2): 72–8.

Nash, S. E. 1996. Is curation a useful heuristic? In G. H. Odell (ed.), *Stone Tools. Theoretical Insights into Human Prehistory*, pp. 81–99. New York: Plenum Press.

NSW Department of Public Works. 1977. Gosford–Wyong Water Supply. Mangrove Creek Dam Environmental Impact Statement: Vol. 1: Summary of Investigations for Water Supply to the Gosford–Wyong Region. Vol. 2: Environmental Impact of the Proposed Mangrove Creek Dam. NSW Department of Public Works.

NSW National Parks & Wildlife Service. 1979. *For Planners and Developers. Aboriginal Sites in NSW*. NSW National Parks & Wildlife Service.

Neal, R. and E. Stock. 1986. Pleistocene occupation in the south-east Queensland coastal region. *Nature* 323 (6089): 618–21.

Nelson, M. C. 1991. The study of technological organisation. In M. B. Schiffer (ed.), *Archaeological Method and Theory* 3: 57–100. Tucson: University of Arizona Press.

Nolan, A. 1986. Sandstone Point: Temporal and Spatial Patterns of Aboriginal Site Use at a Midden Complex, South-east Queensland. Unpublished BA(Hons) thesis, University of Queensland, Brisbane.

O'Connell, J. F. and J. Allen. 1995. Human reactions to the Pleistocene–Holocene transition in Greater Australia: a summary. In J. Allen and J. F. O'Connell (eds), *Transitions. Pleistocene to Holocene in Australia and Papua New Guinea. Antiquity* 69 (Special No. 265): 855–62.

O'Connor, S. 1999. *30,000 Years of Aboriginal Occupation: Kimberley, North West Australia. Terra Australis* 14. Canberra: Department of Archaeology and Natural History and Centre for Archaeological Research, Australian National University.

O'Connor, S., P. Veth, and N. Hubbard. 1993. Changing interpretations of postglacial human subsistence and demography in Sahul. In M. A. Smith, M. Spriggs, and B. Fankhauser (eds), *Sahul in Review. Pleistocene Archaeology in Australia, New Guinea and Island Melanesia*, pp. 95–105. Canberra: Department of Prehistory, Research School of Pacific Studies, Australian National University.

Odell, G. H. 1996. Economizing behaviour and the concept of 'curation'. In G. H. Odell (ed.), *Stone Tools. Theoretical Insights into Human Prehistory*, pp. 51–80. New York: Plenum Press.

Odell, G. H., B. D. Hayden, J. K. Johnson, M. Kay, T. A. Morrow, S. E. Nash, M. S. Nassaney, J. W. Rick, M. F. Rondeau, S. A. Rosen, M. J. Shott and P. T. Thacker. 1996. Some comments on a continuing debate. In G. H. Odell (ed.), *Stone Tools. Theoretical Insights into Human Prehistory*, pp. 337–92. New York: Plenum Press.

O'Donnell, G. and M. J. Walker. 1982. Archaeological Excavation at Reef Beach, Balgowlah, NSW. Unpublished report for NSW National Parks and Wildlife Service.

Orton, C. 1980. *Mathematics in Archaeology*. Cambridge University Press.

O'Shea, J. and P. Halstead. 1989. Conclusions: bad year economics. In P. Halstead and J. O'Shea (eds), *Bad Year Economics: Cultural Responses to Risk and Uncertainty*, pp. 123–26. Cambridge University Press.

Owen, J. F. 1984. Bones to scale: the interpretation of fish remains from New South Wales coastal middens. Unpublished BA (Hons) thesis, University of Sydney.

Owen, J. F. and J. R. Merrick. 1994. Analysis of coastal middens in south-eastern Australia: sizing of fish remains in Holocene deposits. *Journal of Archaeological Science* 21: 3–10.

Packard, P. W. 1984. With A Pinch of Salt: The Archaeology of Saline–Seepage Erosion Sites in the Yass River Basin. Unpublished B. Litt. thesis, Australian National University, Canberra.

Packard, P. 1992. An Archaeological Assessment of State Forests in the Kempsey and Wauchope Forestry Management Areas. Unpublished report to Forestry Commission of New South Wales, Sydney.

Parry, W. J. and R. L. Kelly. 1987. Expedient core technology and sedentism. In J. K. Johnson and C. A. Morrow (eds), *The Organization of Core Technology*, pp. 285–304. Boulder: Westview Special Studies in Archaeological Research. Westview Press.

Paton, R. and I. Macfarlane. 1989. An Excavation of Abrahams Bosom Rockshelter 1 near Currarong, Jervis Bay, New South Wales. Unpublished report to the NSW National Parks and Wildlife Service and the NSW Department of Lands.

Pearson, M. 1981. Seen Through Different Eyes: Changing Land Use and Settlement Patterns in the Upper Macquarie Region of NSW, from Prehistoric Times to 1860. Unpublished PhD thesis, Australian National University, Canberra.

Peterson, N. 1976. The natural and cultural areas of Aboriginal Australia: a preliminary analysis of population groupings with adaptive significance. In N. Peterson (ed.), *Tribes and Boundaries in Australia*, pp. 50–71. Canberra: Australian Institute of Aboriginal Studies, and New Jersey: Humanities Press Inc.

Poiner, G. 1971. Process of The Year. Unpublished BA(Hons) thesis, University of Sydney.

Poiner, G. 1974. The trial excavation of an estuarine rock shelter at Yowie Bay. In J. V. S. Megaw (ed.), *The Recent Archaeology of the Sydney District. Excavations 1964–1967*, pp. 28–34. Canberra: Australian Institute of Aboriginal Studies.

Poiner, G. 1976. The process of the year among Aborigines of the central and south coast of New South Wales. *Archaeology and Physical Anthropology in Oceania* 11 (3): 186–206.

Pye, K. and G. M. Bowman. 1984. The Holocene marine transgression as a forcing function in episodic dune activity on the eastern Australian coast. In B. G. Thom (ed.), *Coastal Geomorphology in Australia*, pp. 179–96. Academic Press.

Read, D. W. 1975. Regional sampling. In J. W. Mueller (ed.), *Sampling in Archaeology*, pp. 45–60. Tucson: University of Arizona Press.

Rich, E. 1992. Narama Salvage Project, Lower Bayswater Creek, Hunter Valley, NSW. Vol. 1: Overview. Unpublished report by Brayshaw McDonald Pty Ltd for Envirosciences Pty Ltd and Narama Joint Venture, Sydney/Newcastle.

Richardson, N. 1992. Conjoin sets and stratigraphic integrity in a sandstone shelter: Kenniff Cave (Queensland, Australia). *Antiquity* 66 (251): 408–18.

Richardson, N. 1996. Seeing is believing: a graphical illustration of the vertical and horizontal distribution of conjoined artefacts using DesignCAD 3D. In S. Ulm, I. Lilley and A. Ross (eds), *Australian Archaeology '95. Proceedings of the 1995 Australian Archaeological Association Annual Conference*, pp. 81–95. *Tempus* 6. St Lucia, Brisbane: Anthropology Museum, University of Queensland.

Rivett, L. 1980. The Photogrammetric Recording of Aboriginal Art Sites in the North Metropolitan and Hawkesbury Districts. Unpublished report by Department of Surveying, University of Melbourne, to NSW National Parks & Wildlife Service.

Roberts, A. L. and F. D. Pate. 1999. Late Holocene climatic changes recorded in macropod bone collagen stable carbon and nitrogen isotopes at Fromms Landing, South Australia. *Australian Archaeology* 49: 48–9.

Robertson, G. 2002. Birds of a feather stick: microscopic feather residues on stone artefacts from Deep Creek Shelter, New South Wales. In S. Ulm, C. Westcott, J. Reid, A. Ross, I. Lilley, J. Prangnell and L. Kirkwood (eds), *Barrier, Borders, Boundaries. Proceedings of the 2001 Australian Archaeological Association Annual Conference*, pp. 175–182. *Tempus 7*. St Lucia, Brisbane: Anthropology Museum, The University of Queensland.

Robins, R. 1996. A report on archaeological investigations of open hearth sites in south-west Queensland. *Queensland Archaeological Research* 10: 25–35.

Robins, R. P. 1997. Patterns in the landscape: a case study in nonsite archaeology from south-west Queensland. *Memoirs of the Queensland Museum, Cultural Heritage Series* 1 (1): 23–56.

Rodbell, D. T., G. O. Seltzer, D. M. Anderson, M. B. Abbott, D. B. Enfield and J. H. Newman. 1999. An ~15,000-year record of El Niño-driven alluviation in south-western Ecuador. *Science* 283: 516–20.

Rognon, P. and M. A. J. Williams. 1977. Late Quaternary climatic changes in Australia and North Africa: a preliminary interpretation. *Palaeogeography, Palaeoclimatology, Palaeoecology* 21: 285–327.

Rosenfeld, A. 2002. Rock-art as an indicator of changing social geographies in Central Australia. In B. David and M. Wilson (eds), *Inscribed Landscapes. Marking and Making Place*, pp. 61–78. Honolulu: University of Hawai'i Press.

Rosenfeld, A., D. Horton and J. Winter. 1981. *Early Man in North Queensland. Art and Archaeology in the Laura Area. Terra Australis* 6. Canberra: Department of Prehistory, Research School of Pacific Studies, Australian National University.

Rosenfeld, A., J. Winston-Gregson and K. Maskell. 1983. Excavations at Nursery Swamp 2, Gudgenby Nature Reserve, Australian Capital Territory. *Australian Archaeology* 17: 48–58.

Ross, A. 1976. Inter-tribal Contacts — What The First Fleet Saw. Unpublished BA(Hons) thesis, University of Sydney.

Ross, A. 1981. Holocene environments and prehistoric site patterning in the Victorian Mallee. *Archaeology in Oceania* 16 (3): 145–54.

Ross, A. 1982. Absence of evidence: reply to Keryn Kefous. *Archaeology in Oceania* 17 (2): 99–101.

Ross, A. 1984. If There Were Water: Prehistoric Settlement Patterns in the Victorian Mallee. Unpublished PhD thesis, Macquarie University, Sydney.

Ross, A. 1985. Archaeological evidence for population change in the middle to late-Holocene in south-eastern Australia. *Archaeology in Oceania* 20 (3): 81–9.

Ross, A. 1988. Tribal and linguistic boundaries: a reassessment of the evidence. In G. Aplin (ed.), *A Difficult Infant. Sydney before Macquarie*, pp. 42–53. Sydney: New South Wales University Press.

Ross, A., T. Donnelly and R. Wasson. 1992. The peopling of the arid zone: human–environment interactions. In J. Dodson (ed.), *The Naive Lands*, pp. 77–114. Longman Cheshire.

Ross, A. and J. Specht. 1976. An archaeological survey on Port Jackson, Sydney. *Australian Archaeology* 5: 14–17.

Ross, V. 1981. *A Hawkesbury Story*. Sydney: Library of Australian History.

Rowland, M. J. 1983. Aborigines and environment in Holocene Australia: changing paradigms. *Australian Aboriginal Studies* 1983/2: 62–77.

Rowland, M. J. 1989. Population increase, intensification or a result of preservation? Explaining site distribution patterns on the coast of Queensland. *Australian Aboriginal Studies* 1989/2: 32–42.

Rowland, M. J. 1999. The Keppel Islands — 'a 3000 year' event revisited. In J. Hall. and I. J. McNiven (eds), *Australian Coastal Archaeology*, pp. 141–55. Canberra: ANH Publications, Department of Archaeology and Natural History, Research School of Pacific and Asian Studies, Australian National University.

Roy, P. S. 1983. Quaternary geology. In C. Herbert (ed.), *Geology of the Sydney 1: 100,000 Sheet 9130*, pp. 41–91. Sydney: Geological Survey of New South Wales, Department of Mineral Resources.

Roy, P. S. 1984. New South Wales estuaries: their origin and evolution. In B. G. Thom (ed.), *Coastal Geomorphology in Australia*, pp. 99–121. Academic Press.

Roy, P. S. 1994. Holocene estuary evolution — stratigraphic studies from south-eastern Australia. *Incised-valley Systems: Origin and Sedimentary Sequences* SEPM Special Publication 51: 241–63. Society for Sedimentary Geology.

Roy, P. S. 1998. Cainozoic geology of the coast and shelf. In E. Scheibner, H. Basden (eds), *Geology of New South Wales — Synthesis. Vol. 2: Geological Evolution*, pp. 361–85. Geological Survey of New South Wales Memoir Geology 13 (2).

Roy, P. S. and B. G. Thom. 1981. Late Quaternary marine deposition in New South Wales and southern Queensland — an evolutionary model. *Journal of the Geological Society of Australia* 28: 471–89.

Roy, P. S., W. -Y. Zhuang, G. F. Birch, P. J. Cowell and L. Congxian. 1997. *Quaternary Geology of the Forster–Tuncurry Coast and Shelf, Southeast Australia*. Geological Survey Report: GS 1992/201. Final Report on the Marine Minerals Investigation — 1990 to 1991 — A Joint Government/Industry Research Project. Sydney: Geological Survey of New South Wales, Department of Mineral Resources.

Schiffer, M. B. 1976. *Behavioural Archaeology*. Academic Press.

Schrire, C. 1972. Ethno-archaeological models and subsistence behaviour in Arnhem Land. In D. L. Clarke (ed.), *Models in Archaeology*, pp. 653–70. London: Methuen and Co Ltd.

Schrire, C. 1982. *The Alligator Rivers. Prehistory and Ecology in Western Arnhem Land. Terra Australia 7*. Canberra: Department of Prehistory, Research School of Pacific Studies, Australian National University.

Schwartz, D. W. 1956. Demographic changes in the early periods of Cohonina prehistory. In G. R. Willey (ed.), *Prehistoric Settlement Patterns in the New World*, pp. 26–31. Viking Fund Publications in Anthropology 23. Wenner Gren Foundation for Anthropological Research Inc.

Sefton, C. E. 1988. Site and Artefact Patterns on the Woronora Plateau. Unpublished MA thesis, University of Sydney.

Shott, M. J. 1986. Technological organisation and settlement mobility: an ethnographic examination. *Journal of Anthropological Research* 42: 15–51.

Shott, M. J. 1989. Shovel-test sampling in archaeological survey: comments on Nance and Ball, and Lightfoot. *American Antiquity* 54 (2): 396–404.

Singh, G. 1983a. Late Quaternary vegetation and lake level record from Lake George, New South Wales: 18 +/- 2KA. In J. M. A. Chappell and A. Grindrod (eds), *Climanz. Proceedings of the First Climanz Conference*, p. 66. Canberra: Department of Biogeography and Geomorphology, Research School of Pacific Studies, Australian National University.

Singh, G. 1983b. Late Quaternary vegetation and lake level record from Lake George, New South Wales: 32 +/- 5KA. In J. M. A. Chappell and A. Grindrod (eds), *Climanz. Proceedings of the First Climanz Conference*, pp. 23-4. Canberra: Department of Biogeography and Geomorphology, Research School of Pacific Studies, Australian National University.

Smith, L. J. 1986. Artefact analysis of a 3450 year old open site at Quaker's Hill on the Cumberland Plain, New South Wales. *Australian Archaeology* 23: 11–24.

Smith, M. A. 1982. Devon Downs reconsidered: changes in site use at a lower Murray Valley rock-shelter. *Archaeology in Oceania* 17 (3): 109–16.

Smith, M. A. 1989. The case for a resident human population in the Central Australian Ranges during full glacial aridity. *Archaeology in Oceania* 24 (3): 93–105.

Stanner, W. E. H. 1965. Aboriginal territorial organisation: Estate, range, domain and regime. *Oceania* 36 (1): 1–26.

Steele, D. 1987. Intra-site Refuse Disposal and Australian Rock Shelters. Unpublished BA(Hons) thesis, University of Sydney.

Stern, N. 1981. A Preliminary Analysis of the Retouched/Use-wear Component of the Loggers Stone Assemblage. Appendix 3 in V. Attenbrow, Mangrove Creek Dam Salvage Excavation Project, Vol. 2. Unpublished report to NSW National Parks & Wildlife Service on behalf of NSW Department of Public Works.

Stern, N. 1982. Analysis of the Stone Artefact Component from Deep Creek Shelter, Mangrove Creek, NSW. Appendix 2 in V. Attenbrow, Archaeological Investigation of Deep Creek Shelter, Mangrove Creek Dam. Unpublished report to NSW National Parks & Wildlife Service on behalf of NSW Department of Public Works.

Stockton, E. D. 1970a. An archaeological survey of the Blue Mountains. *Mankind* 7 (4): 295–301.

Stockton, E. D. 1970b. Some observations on Bondi points. *Mankind* 7 (3): 227–9.

Stockton, E. D. 1973. Shaws Creek shelter: human displacement of artefacts and its significance. *Mankind* 9 (2): 112–17.

Stockton, E. D. 1977a. Pre-microlithic industries in south-east Australia. *The Artefact* 2 (4): 209–19.

Stockton, E. D. 1977b. Review of early Bondaian dates. *Mankind* 11 (1): 48–51.

Stockton, E. D. 1977c. Taxonomy at the service of prehistory. In R. V. S. Wright (ed.), *Stone Tools as Cultural Markers: Change, Evolution and Complexity*, pp. 340–3. Canberra: Australian Institute of Aboriginal Studies, and New Jersey: Humanities Press Inc.

Stockton, E. D. 1979. The search for the first Sydneysiders. In P. Stanbury (ed.), *10,000 Years of Sydney Life. A Guide to Archaeological Discovery*, pp. 49–54. University of Sydney: The Macleay Museum.

Stockton, E. D. 1981. Reflections around the campfire. *The Artefact* 6: 3–16.

Stockton, E. D. 1993. Archaeology of the Blue Mountains. In E. Stockton (ed.), *Blue Mountains Dreaming. The Aboriginal Heritage*, pp. 23–52. Winmalee, NSW: A Three Sisters Publication.

Stockton, E. D. n.d. [ca 1973]. Kings Table Shelter. Report submitted to NSW National Parks and Wildlife Service.

Stockton, E. D. and W. Holland. 1974. Cultural sites and their environment in the Blue Mountains. *Archaeology and Physical Anthropology in Oceania* 9 (1): 36–65.

Strahan, R. (ed.) 2000. *The Mammals of Australia: The National Photographic Index of Australian Wildlife*. Sydney: The Australian Museum and Reed New Holland.

Straus, L. G. and G. A. Clark. 1983. Further reflections on adaptive change in Cantabrian prehistory. In G. Bailey (ed.), *Hunter-Gatherer Economy in Prehistory: A European Perspective*, pp. 166–67. Cambridge University Press.

Struever, S. 1968. Woodland subsistence-settlement systems in the Lower Illinois Valley. In S. R. Binford and L. R. Binford (eds), *New Perspectives in Archaeology*, pp. 285–312. Atherton: Aldine.

Struever, S. 1971. Comments on archaeological data requirements and research strategy. *American Antiquity* 36 (1): 9–19.

Stuiver, M. and P. J. Reimer. 1993a. *CALIB User's Guide Rev. 3. 0. 1*. Seattle: Quaternary Research Centre AK-60, University of Washington.

Stuiver, M. and P. J. Reimer. 1993b. Extended 14C data base and revised CALIB 3. 0 ^{14}C calibration program. *Radiocarbon* 35 (1): 215–230.

Stuiver, M., P. J. Reimer, E. Bard, J. W. Beck, G. S. Burr, K. A. Hughen, B. Kromer, F. G. McCormac, J. van der Plicht and M. Spurk. 1998 INTCAL98: Radiocarbon age calibration 24,000 — 0 cal BP. *Radiocarbon* 40 (3): 1041–1083.

Sullivan, M. E. 1982a. Aboriginal Shell Middens in the Coastal Landscape of New South Wales. Unpublished PhD thesis, Australian National University, Canberra.

Sullivan, M. E. 1982b. Exploitation of offshore islands along the New South Wales coastline. *Australian Archaeology* 15: 8–19.

Sullivan, M. E. 1984. A shell midden excavation at Pambula Lake on the far south coast of New South Wales. *Archaeology in Oceania* 19 (1): 1–15.

Sullivan, M. E. and P. J. Hughes. 1983. The geoarchaeology of the Sydney Basin sandstones. In R. W. Young and G. C. Nanson (eds), *Aspects of Australian Sandstone Landscapes*, pp. 120–26. Australian and New Zealand Geomorphology Group Special Publication 1. Department of Geography, University of Wollongong.

Sullivan, S. 1983. Making a discovery: the finding and reporting of Aboriginal sites. In G. Connah (ed.), *Australian Field Archaeology. A Guide to Techniques*, pp. 1–9. Canberra: Australian Institute of Aboriginal Studies.

Sutton, S. A. 1990. Pleistocene axes in Sahul: a response to Morwood and Tresize. *Queensland Archaeological Research* 7: 95–109.

Sydney Prehistory Group 1983. *In Search of the Cobrakall. A Survey of Aboriginal Sites in the Campbelltown Area, South of Sydney.* 2 vols. Sydney: NSW National Parks and Wildlife Service.

Szpak, C. 1997. But… has it been used? An Analysis of the Attributes of Shelters with Evidence of Use and Shelters with the Potential for Use. Unpublished Diploma of Arts thesis, University of Sydney.

Taçon, P. 1991. The power of stone: symbolic aspects of stone use and tool development in western Arnhem Land, Australia. *Antiquity* 65 (247): 192–207.

Tench, W. 1789 and 1793 [1979]. *Sydney's First Four Years, being a reprint of a Narrative of the Expedition to Botany Bay, and A Complete Account of the Settlement at Port Jackson.* Republished by Library of Australian History in association with the Royal Australian Historical Society, Sydney.

Therin Archaeological Consulting. 2000. Spring Gully 5 Salvage Excavation. Use-wear and Residue Report, prepared for Haglund and Associates. Appendix in: Laila Haglund (2001), Salvage Excavation completed for Ulan Coal Mines Ltd: Site SG5, Aboriginal Rock Shelter Site, in compliance with requirements under NPWS Consent No. 1002. Vol. 1: Overview.

Thomas, D. H. 1975. Non-site sampling in archaeology: up the creek without a site? In J. W. Mueller (ed.), *Sampling in Archaeology*, pp. 61–81. Tucson: University of Arizona Press.

Thomas, D. H. 1979. *Archaeology.* USA: Holt, Rinehart and Winston.

Thomas, N. 1981. Social theory, ecology and epistomology: theoretical issues in Australian prehistory. *Mankind* 13 (2): 165–77.

Thomas, D. H. 1989. Diversity in hunter-gatherer cultural geography. In R. D. Leonard and G. T. Jones (eds), *Quantifying Diversity in Archaeology*, pp. 85–91. Cambridge: Cambridge University Press.

Thorley, P. 1999. Regional archaeological research in the Palmer River catchment. *Australian Aboriginal Studies* 1999/2: 62–8.

Thorley, P. 2001. Uncertain supplies: water availability and regional archaeological structure in the Palmer River catchment, central Australia. *Archaeology in Oceania* 36 (1): 1–14.

Threlkeld, L. E. 1825. London Missionary Society. Aboriginal Mission, New South Wales, December, 1852[sic]. LMS Report December 1825 [printed, Sydney]. In N. Gunson (ed.), 1974. *Australian Reminiscences and Papers of L. E. Threlkeld, Missionary to the Aborigines, 1824–1859,* Vol. 2: 189–94. Canberra: Australian Institute of Aboriginal Studies.

Threlkeld, L. E. 1825–26. Reminiscences of the Aborigines of New South Wales. Traits of the Aborigines of New South Wales. In N. Gunson (ed.), 1974 *Australian Reminiscences and Papers of L. E. Threlkeld, Missionary to the Aborigines, 1824–1859,* Vol. 1: 41–80. Canberra: Australian Institute of Aboriginal Studies.

Threlkeld, L. E. 1826. Second Half Yearly Report of the Aboriginal Mission supported by the London Missionary Society. L. E. Threlkeld, Missionary to the Aborigines New South Wales, Newcastle, June 21st 1826 [LMS Report 21 June 1826] [LMS Australia Letters]. In N. Gunson (ed.), 1974 *Australian Reminiscences and Papers of L. E. Threlkeld, Missionary to the Aborigines, 1824–1859* Vol. 2: 204–10. Canberra: Australian Institute of Aboriginal Studies.

Tindale, N. B. 1957. Culture succession in south eastern Australia from late Pleistocene to the present. *Records of the South Australian Museum* 13 (1): 1–49.

Tindale, N. B. 1964. Radiocarbon dates of interest to Australian archaeologists. *Australian Journal of Science* 27 (1): 24.

Torrence, R. 1983. Time budgeting and hunter-gatherer technology. In G. Bailey (ed.), *Hunter-Gatherer Economy in Prehistory. A European Perspective*, pp. 11–22. Cambridge University Press.

Torrence, R. 1989a. Retooling: towards a behavioural theory of stone tools. In R. Torrence (ed.), *Time, Energy and Stone Tools*, pp. 57–66. Cambridge University Press.

Torrence, R. (ed.) 1989b. *Time, Energy and Stone Tools.* Cambridge University Press.

Torrence, R. 1989c. Tools as optimal solutions. In R. Torrence (ed.), *Time, Energy and Stone Tools*, pp. 1–6. Cambridge University Press.

Torrence, R. 2001. Hunter-gatherer technology: macro- and microscale approaches. In C. Panter-Brick, R. H. Layton and P. Rowley-Conwy (eds), *Hunter-gatherers: An Interdisciplinary Perspective*, pp. 73–98. Cambridge University Press.

Tracey, R. 1974. Three minor sites near Curracurrang Cove with a preliminary note on a rock shelter at Newport. In J. V. S. Megaw (ed.), *The Recent Archaeology of the Sydney District. Excavations 1964–1967*, pp. 19–27. Canberra: Australian Institute of Aboriginal Studies.

Tresize, P. 1971. *Rock Art of South-east Cape York*. Canberra: Australian Institute of Aboriginal Studies.

Ulm, S. and J. Hall. 1996. Radiocarbon and cultural chronologies in southeast Queensland prehistory. In S. Ulm, I. Lilley and A. Ross (eds), *Australian Archaeology '95. Proceedings of the 1995 Australian Archaeological Association Annual Conference*, pp. 45–62. *Tempus* 6. St Lucia, Brisbane: Anthropology Museum, University of Queensland.

Ulm, S. and I. Lilley 1999. The archaeology of the southern Curtis Coast: an overview. *Queensland Archaeological Research* 11: 59–73.

Vestjens, W. J. M. 1973. Feeding of White Ibis on freshwater mussels. *The Emu* 73 (2): 71–2.

Veth, P. 1989. Islands in the interior: a model for the colonization of Australia's arid zone. *Archaeology in Oceania* 24 (3): 81–92.

Veth, P. M. 1993. *Islands in the Interior. The Dynamics of Prehistoric Adaptations within the Arid Zone of Australia*. Michigan: International Monographs in Prehistory.

Veth, P., S. O'Connor and L. A. Wallis. 2000. Perspectives on ecological approaches in Australian archaeology. *Australian Archaeology* 50: 54–66.

Vinnicombe, P. 1980. Predilection and Prediction: A Study of Aboriginal Sites in the Gosford–Wyong Region. Unpublished report to NSW National Parks & Wildlife Service.

Vinnicombe, P. 1984. Single sites or site complexes? A case study from north of the Hawkesbury, New South Wales. In S. Sullivan and S. Bowdler (eds), *Site Surveys and Significance Assessment in Australian Archaeology*, pp. 107–18. Canberra: Department of Prehistory, Research School of Pacific Studies, Australian National University.

Wade, J. P. 1967. Excavation of a rock-shelter at Connels Point, New South Wales. *Archaeology and Physical Anthropology in Oceania* 2 (1): 35–40.

Wasson, R. J. 1982. Holocene terrestrial stratigraphy. In B. G. Thom and R. J. Wasson (eds), *Holocene Research in Australia, 1978–1982* pp. 1–4. Duntroon ACT: Department of Geography, Faculty of Military Studies, University of New South Wales, Royal Military College.

Watchman, A. 1982. A Brief Inspection of the Preservation of Aboriginal Rock-art at Mangrove Creek, New South Wales. Unpublished report sent to Val Attenbrow.

Webb, S. and S. Cane. 1986. An Excavation and Analysis of 2 Aboriginal Shell Middens near Merimbula, New South Wales. Unpublished report to Sinclair Knight and Partners Pty Ltd.

Weiss, K. M. 1978. Archaeological approaches to population inference. *American Antiquity* 43 (4): 773–6.

Westcott, C., I. Lilley, S. Ulm, C. Clarkson and D. Brian. 1999. Big Foot Art Site, Cania Gorge: site report. *Queensland Archaeological Research* 11: 43–58.

White, C. and N. Peterson. 1969. Ethnographic interpretations of the prehistory of western Arnhem Land. *South-western Journal of Anthropology* 25 (1): 45–67.

White, E. 1997 [1998]. Archaeological Salvage of Site WGO3-2 (NPWS No. 45-5-971) at Wattle Grove, NSW. Unpublished report prepared for Jo McDonald Cultural Heritage Management for Delfin Management Services Pty Ltd.

White, E. 2001. Stone Artefact Analysis. Volume 2 in L. Haglund, Salvage Excavation completed for Ulan Coal Mines Ltd: Site SG5, Aboriginal Rock Shelter Site, in compliance with requirements under NPWS Consent No. 1002. Unpublished report to Ulan Coal Mines Ltd.

White, J. 1790 [1962]. *Journal of a Voyage to New South Wales*. Piccadilly: J. Debrett. [Republished by Angus and Robertson in association with the Royal Australian Historical Society, Sydney.]

White, J. P. and P. J. Habgood. 1985. La préhistoire de l'Australie. *La Recherche* 167: 730–7.

White, J. P. and J. F. O'Connell. 1982. *A Prehistory of Australia, New Guinea and Sahul*. Academic Press.

White, J. P. and C. Wieneke. n.d. [ca 1975.]. Henry Lawson Drive Rockshelter: Excavation Report. Unpublished report to NSW National Parks & Wildlife Service.

Whitelaw, T. 1983. People and space in hunter-gatherer camps: a generalizing approach in ethnoarchaeology. *Archaeological Review from Cambridge* 2 (2): 48–66.

Wiessner, P. 1982a. Beyond willow smoke and dogs' tails: a comment on Binford's analysis of hunter-gatherer settlement systems. *American Antiquity* 47 (1): 171–8.

Wiessner, P. 1982b. Risk, reciprocity and social influence on !Kung San economics. In E. R. Leacock and R. B. Lee (eds), *Politics and History in Band Societies*, pp. 61–84. Cambridge University Press and Editions de la Maison des Sciences de l'Homme, Paris.

Willey, G. R. 1953. *Prehistoric Settlement Patterns in the Virú Valley, Perú.* Smithsonian Institution, Bureau of American Ethnology Bulletin 155. Washington: United States Government Printing Office.

Willey, G. R. 1956. Problems concerning prehistoric settlement patterns in the Maya lowlands. In G. R. Willey (ed.), *Prehistoric Settlement Patterns in the New World,* pp. 107–14. Wenner-Gren Foundation for Anthropological Research Inc.

Willey, G. R. and P. Phillips. 1962. *Method and Theory in American Archaeology.* Phoenix Books, the University of Chicago Press.

Williams, E. 1985. Wet Underfoot? Earth Mound Sites and the Recent Prehistory of South-western Victoria. Unpublished PhD thesis, Australian National University, Canberra.

Williams, E. 1987. Complex hunter-gatherers: a view from Australia. *Antiquity* 61 (232): 310–21.

Williams, E. 1988. *Complex Hunter-Gatherers. A Late Holocene Example from Temperate Australia.* Oxford: British Archaeological Reports, International Series 423.

Williamson, C. 1998. Late Holocene Australia and the writing of Aboriginal history. In T. Murray (ed.), *Archaeology of Aboriginal Australia. A Reader,* pp. 141–8. Sydney: Allen and Unwin.

Wobst, H. M. 1983. We can't see the forest for the trees: sampling and the shapes of archaeological distributions. In J. A. Moore and A. S. Keene (eds), *Archaeological Hammers and Theories,* pp. 37–85. Academic Press.

Worgan, G. B. 1788 [1978]. *Journal of a First Fleet Surgeon.* The William Dixson Foundation: Publication 16. Sydney: the Library Council of New South Wales in association with the Library of Australian History.

Worrall, L. 1980. Geoarchaeological Investigations at Mangrove Creek, NSW. Unpublished BA(Hons) thesis, Australian National University, Canberra.

Wright, R. V. S. 1992. 2nd ed. *Doing Multivariate Archaeology and Prehistory: Handling Large Data Sets with MV-Arch.* Balmain: R. V. S. Wright.

Yoffee, N. 1985. Perspectives on 'trends toward social complexity in prehistoric Australia and Papua New Guinea'. *Archaeology in Oceania* 20 (2): 41–9.

Zola, N. and B. Gott. 1992. *Koorie Plants Koorie People. Traditional Aboriginal Food, Fibre and Healing Plants of Victoria.* Melbourne: Koorie Heritage Trust.

APPENDIX 1

The Upper Mangrove Creek catchment — random sampling units

Distribution of artefact types and raw materials in each archaeological deposit

Key to abbreviations in Appendix 1 tables

Stone artefact types and abbreviations used in tables:

BP   Bondi point

Geo   Geometric microlith

BMs   Miscellaneous backed artefact

El   Elouera

Ruw   Other flaked artefact with retouch and/or use wear (on conchoidal or bipolar flake, or flaked piece)

GrF   Fragment of ground implement, for example, flake or flaked piece with ground surface

CHh   Core — hand-held percussion

CBi   Bipolar core

FBi   Bipolar flake or fragment

FP   Flaked piece — see notes below

GrI   Ground implement — whole or broken/damaged

H/M   Hammerstone or manuport

SP   Split pebble — see notes below

FrP   Fractured piece — see notes below

Wste   Waste — see notes below

Notes on artefact types

Bipolar cores, flakes and flaked pieces

For Loggers and Black Hands, which were analysed during the salvage project, artefacts showing evidence of bipolar reduction were grouped together under the heading 'bipolar pieces' and were not classified separately into bipolar core, flake or fragment.

Waste

This category includes whole and broken flakes as well as flaked pieces. The category *flaked piece* includes:

(a)   pieces which are clearly artefacts, in that they have surfaces with remnants of the flaking process — for example, partial flake scars — but lack clear features (such as striking platforms, impact points, bulbs of percussion, ring cracks or distinct ventral surfaces which show the direction of blow) to enable their definite identification as cores or flakes. These pieces may derive from either hand-held cores or bipolar techniques, and many probably result from uncontrolled fracturing along incipient fracture planes in the raw material during knapping. Most of the catchment artefacts are made from river pebbles, which were probably derived from the sandstone conglomerates in the catchment. Because of their geological history, many of the pebbles have distinct fracture planes running through their bodies as well as visible impact points on the outer cortex.

(b)   heat-fractured fragments. They were not separated out or quantified, but appeared to be relatively few in number.

Split pebbles are pebbles with a single break (i.e., as if the pebble had been split in half). The broken surface has a fresh appearance with unworn/unrounded edges, but there are no discernible impact points or flake scars. There was thus no clear sign that they were humanly produced artefacts. However, since they occur mainly in sites with large assemblages — for example, Loggers, Black Hands, Emu Tracks 2 — it seems likely they are present through human activities rather than being roof-fall. Their presence principally in large assemblages may well be a result of sample size. However, if they were roof-fall or slopewashed materials their abundance would relate more to the area excavated rather than assemblage size, which is not always the case.

Fractured pieces, as with split pebbles, do not show any distinguishing features. However, because of their angular shape, the fresh appearance of their fractures and surfaces, and/or raw material type (usually quartz), they are considered more likely to be humanly produced artefacts derived from uncontrolled shatter during knapping than naturally broken pebbles derived from roof-fall or slopewash. Obvious naturally fractured pebbles which had rounded edges or 'stained' inner surfaces, or where two half pebbles could conjoin, were not included in this category.

Raw material categories and abbreviations used in tables:

Qz   Quartz
FGS   Fine-grained siliceous — see notes below
Cht   Chert — see notes below
Silc   Silcrete
Qzte   Quartzite — also includes meta-quartzite, orthoquartzite/indurated sandstone
        and possibly some coarse-grained silcrete
Ign   Igneous — principally basalt

Notes on raw materials

Most artefacts are made from pebbles and cobbles of quartz, FGS, chert (excluding tuff) and quartzite which have eroded out of the Narrabeen Group (sandstone) conglomerate layers within the catchment and can be collected from lower ridgesides and particularly creek beds within that geological stratum (pers. obs.).

The chert category in the following tables includes jasper, chalcedony, indurated siltstone/mudstone, as well as volcanic tuff. The volcanic tuff is similar to and may be Nobbys tuff (or tuffite), which is exposed in various places in the Hunter Valley, such as the cliffs at the mouth of the Hunter River (Herbert and Helby 1980: 465–72), and the Blue Mountains, such as the Grose Valley, which drains into the Hawkesbury River. Enright (1935: 8) and Moore (1981: 422–3) referred to this material as Merewether chert. Sources of similar tuffaceous material occur in the Upper Grose Valley and in the gravels of the Grose and Hawkesbury Rivers.

Other terms used in tables

Surfgen   The general surface of the shelter deposit, outside the excavated squares or
            test pits
T/Surf   The surface of the excavated square or test pit

Table A1/1 Artefact types in surface collections from rockshelters and open locations. [1] GRI is a preform for an axe/hatchet, flaked and possibly partially ground. [2] GRI is a broken ground-edged implement ca 9 x 6 x 1.5cm.

SITE NAME							ARTEFACT TYPES							
	BP	GEO	BMS	EL	RUW	GRF	CHH	CBI	FBI	WSTE	GRI	H/M	SP/FRP	TOTAL
Axehead Shelter	0	0	0	0	0	0	0	0	0	0	[1]1	0	0	1
Button Shelter	0	0	0	0	0	0	0	1	0	3	0	0	0	4
Kyola Road Open Deposit	0	0	0	0	0	0	1	0	0	3	0	0	0	4
Palmers Crossing Open Deposit	0	0	0	0	1	0	0	0	0	1	0	0	0	2
Token Male Shelter	0	0	0	0	0	0	1	0	0	1	[2]1	0	0	3
Willow Tree Gully Open Deposit	0	0	0	0	0	0	2	0	0	4	0	0	1	7

Table A1/2 Raw materials in surface collections from rockshelters and open locations.

SITE NAME	RAW MATERIALS							
	QZ	FGS	CHT	SILC	QZTE	IGN	OTHER	TOTAL
AXEHEAD SHELTER	0	0	0	0	0	1	0	1
BUTTON SHELTER	4	0	0	0	0	0	0	4
KYOLA ROAD OPEN DEPOSIT	1	0	0	0	3	0	0	4
PALMERS CROSSING OPEN DEPOSIT	0	0	2	0	0	0	0	2
TOKEN MALE SHELTER	1	1	0	0	0	1	0	3
WILLOW TREE GULLY OPEN DEPOSIT	2	3	2	0	0	0	0	7

Table A1/3 Anadara Shelter: distribution of artefact types.

SQ/SPIT	BP	GEO	BMS	EL	RUW	GRF	CHH	CBI	FBI	WSTE	GRI	H/M	SP/FRP	TOTAL
AS/SURFGEN	0	0	0	0	0	0	1	0	0	2	0	0	0	3
AS/T1/SURF-4	0	0	0	0	0	0	0	0	0	0	0	0	0	0
AS/T2/SURF	0	0	0	0	0	0	0	0	0	0	0	0	0	0
AS/T2/1	0	0	0	0	0	0	0	0	0	0	0	0	0	0
AS/T2/2-BRN	0	0	0	0	0	0	0	0	0	0	0	0	0	0
AS/T2/2-RB	0	0	0	0	1	0	0	0	0	1	0	0	0	2
AS/T2/3-BRN	0	0	0	0	0	0	0	0	0	0	0	0	0	0
AS/T2/3-RB (STH)	0	0	0	0	0	0	0	0	0	1	0	0	0	1
AS/T2/4-BRN	0	0	0	0	1	0	0	0	0	1	0	0	0	2
AS/T2/5-BRN	0	0	0	0	1	1	0	1	1	11	0	0	0	15
TOTAL EXC+SURFGEN	0	0	0	0	3	1	1	1	1	16	0	0	0	23

Table A1/4 Anadara Shelter: distribution of raw materials.

SQ/SPIT	QZ	FGS	CHT	SILC	QZTE	IGN	OTHER	TOTAL
AS/SURFGEN	2	1	0	0	0	0	0	3
AS/T1/SURF–4	0	0	0	0	0	0	0	0
AS/T2/SURF	0	0	0	0	0	0	0	0
AS/T2/1	0	0	0	0	0	0	0	0
AS/T2/2-BRN	0	0	0	0	0	0	0	0
AS/T2/2-RB	1	0	1	0	0	0	0	2
AS/T2/3-BRN	0	0	0	0	0	0	0	0
AS/T2/3-RB (STH)	1	0	0	0	0	0	0	1
AS/T2/4-BRN	1	1	0	0	0	0	0	2
AS/T2/5-BRN	6	4	4	0	0	1	0	15
TOTAL EXC+SURFGEN	11	6	5	0	0	1	0	23

Table A1/5 Black Hands Open Deposit: distribution of artefact types.

SQ/SPIT	BP	GEO	BMS	EL	RUW	GRF	CHH	CBI	FBI	WSTE	GRI	H/M	SP/FRP	TOTAL
BHO/SURFGEN	0	0	0	0	2	1	2	2	2	2	0	0	3	14
BHO/T1/SURF	0	0	0	0	0	0	0	0	0	0	0	0	0	0
BHO/T1/1	0	0	0	0	0	0	0	0	0	0	0	0	0	0
BHO/T1/2	0	0	0	0	0	0	0	1	0	1	0	0	0	2
BHO/T1/3-8	0	0	0	0	0	0	0	0	0	0	0	0	0	0
BHO/T2/SURF	0	0	0	0	0	0	0	0	0	0	0	0	0	0
BHO/T2/1	0	0	0	0	0	0	0	0	2	2	0	0	0	4
BHO/T2/2	0	0	0	0	0	0	0	1	3	1	0	0	0	5
BHO/T2/3	0	0	0	0	0	0	0	0	0	1	0	0	0	1
BHO/T2/4	0	0	0	0	0	0	0	0	0	0	0	0	0	0
TOTAL EXC+SURFGEN	0	0	0	0	2	1	2	4	7	7	0	0	3	26

Table A1/6 Black Hands Open Deposit: distribution of raw materials.

SQ/SPIT	QZ	FGS	CHT	SILC	QZTE	IGN	OTHER	TOTAL
BHO/SURFGEN	6	6	1	0	0	1	0	14
BHO/T1/SURF	0	0	0	0	0	0	0	0
BHO/T1/1	0	0	0	0	0	0	0	0
BHO/T1/2	2	0	0	0	0	0	0	2
BHO/T1/3-8	0	0	0	0	0	0	0	0
BHO/T2/SURF	0	0	0	0	0	0	0	0
BHO/T2/1	2	1	0	1	0	0	0	4
BHO/T2/2	3	1	0	1	0	0	0	5
BHO/T2/3	0	1	0	0	0	0	0	1
BHO/T2/4	0	0	0	0	0	0	0	0
TOTAL EXC+SURFGEN	13	9	1	2	0	1	0	26

Table A1/7 Black Hands Shelter (Square F): distribution of artefact types. [1] Surface artefacts present but not collected or recorded. [2] Artefacts in this assemblage were analysed during the salvage program and bipolar flakes were included with bipolar cores in a category bipolar pieces.

SQ/SPIT	BP	GEO	BMS	EL	RUW	GRF	CHH	CBI	FBI[2]	WSTE	GRI	H/M	SP/FRP	TOTAL
BHS/SURFGEN[1]														
BHS/F/SURF+1	0	0	0	0	1	1	1	4	X	29	0	0	0	36
BHS/F/2	0	0	0	0	3	2	0	18	X	153	0	0	5	181
BHS/F/3	0	0	0	0	11	0	0	20	X	311	0	0	1	343
BHS/F/4	0	1	0	0	13	1	2	19	X	449	0	0	0	485
BHS/F/5	0	0	0	0	23	0	2	36	X	599	0	0	4	664
BHS/F/6	3	1	4	0	18	3	8	60	X	977	0	0	2	1076
BHS/F/7-S	4	0	1	0	1	0	5	12	X	353	0	0	1	377
BHS/F/8-S	0	0	0	0	0	0	0	1	X	82	0	0	0	83
BHS/F/9-S	1	0	1	0	0	0	0	2	X	41	0	0	0	45
BHS/F/10-SE	0	0	0	0	1	0	0	0	X	9	0	0	0	10
BHS/F/11-SE	0	0	0	0	0	0	0	0	X	2	0	0	0	2
TOTAL EXC+SURFGEN	8	2	6	0	71	7	18	172	X	3005	0	0	13	3302

Table A1/8 Black Hands Shelter (Square F): distribution of raw materials. [1] Surface artefacts present but not collected or recorded.

SQ/SPIT	QZ	FGS	CHT	SILC	QZTE	IGN	OTHER	TOTAL
BHS/SURFGEN[1]								
BHS/F/SURF+1	24	7	2	1	0	2	0	36
BHS/F/2	116	40	11	2	2	10	0	181
BHS/F/3	258	70	10	2	1	2	0	343
BHS/F/4	311	143	21	1	1	9	0	485
BHS/F/5	410	204	36	2	6	6	0	664
BHS/F/6	741	246	57	6	9	17	0	1076
BHS/F/7-S	205	118	44	4	5	1	0	377
BHS/F/8-S	80	27	6	0	0	0	0	83
BHS/F/9-S	25	14	3	1	2	0	0	45
BHS/F/10-SE	5	4	0	1	0	0	0	10
BHS/F/11-SE	2	0	0	0	0	0	0	2
TOTAL EXC+SURFGEN	2177	873	190	20	26	47	0	3302

Table A1/9 Boat Cave: distribution of artefact types.

SQ/SPIT	BP	GEO	BMS	EL	RUW	GRF	CHH	CBI	FBI2	WSTE	GRI	H/M	SP/FRP	TOTAL
BC/SURFGEN	0	0	0	1	0	0	0	1	0	1	0	0	0	3
BC/T/SURF	0	0	0	0	0	0	0	0	0	0	0	0	0	0
BC/T/1	0	0	0	0	0	0	0	0	0	3	0	0	0	3
BC/T/2	0	0	0	0	0	0	0	0	0	7	0	0	0	7
BC/T/3	0	0	0	0	0	0	0	0	0	0	0	0	0	0
BC/T/4	0	0	0	0	0	0	0	0	0	1	0	0	0	1
BC/T/5	0	0	0	0	0	1	0	0	0	2	0	0	0	3
BC/T/6	0	0	0	0	2	0	0	0	0	4	0	0	0	6
BC/T/7	0	0	0	0	0	0	0	0	0	1	0	0	0	1
BC/T/8	0	0	0	0	0	0	0	0	0	0	0	0	0	0
TOTAL EXC+SURFGEN	0	0	0	1	2	1	0	1	0	19	0	0	0	24

Table A1/10 Boat Cave: distribution of raw materials. [1] Other is glass.

SQ/SPIT	QZ	FGS	CHT	SILC	QZTE	IGN	OTHER	TOTAL
BC/SURFGEN	0	0	2	0	0	0	[1]1	3
BC/T/SURF	0	0	0	0	0	0	0	0
BC/T/1	1	2	0	0	0	0	0	3
BC/T/2	3	3	1	0	0	0	0	7
BC/T/3	0	0	0	0	0	0	0	0
BC/T/4	0	0	0	0	0	1	0	1
BC/T/5	1	1	0	0	0	1	0	3
BC/T/6	1	1	4	0	0	0	0	6
BC/T/7	0	1	0	0	0	0	0	1
BC/T/8	0	0	0	0	0	0	0	0
TOTAL EXC+SURFGEN	6	8	7	0	0	2	1	24

Table A1/11 Boronia Shelter: distribution of artefact types.

SQ/SPIT	BP	GEO	BMS	EL	RUW	GRF	CHH	CBI	FBI2	WSTE	GRI	H/M	SP/FRP	TOTAL
BoS/SURFGEN	0	0	0	0	0	0	1	0	0	0	0	0	0	1
BoS/T/SURF	0	0	0	0	0	0	0	0	0	0	1	0	0	1
BoS/T/1	0	0	0	0	0	0	0	0	0	0	0	0	0	0
BoS/T/2	0	0	0	0	0	0	0	0	0	1	0	0	0	1
BoS/T/3	0	0	0	0	0	1	0	0	0	1	0	0	0	2
BoS/T/4	0	0	0	0	0	0	0	0	0	0	0	0	0	0
BoS/T/5	0	0	0	0	0	0	0	0	0	0	0	0	0	0
TOTAL EXC+SURFGEN	0	0	0	0	0	1	1	0	0	2	1	0	0	5

Table A1/12 Boronia Shelter: distribution of raw materials.

SQ/SPIT	QZ	FGS	CHT	SILC	QZTE	IGN	OTHER	TOTAL
BoS/SURFGEN	0	1	0	0	0	0	0	1
BoS/T/SURF	0	0	0	0	0	1	0	1
BoS/T/1	0	0	0	0	0	0	0	0
BoS/T/2	1	0	0	0	0	0	0	1
BoS/T/3	0	1	0	0	0	1	0	2
BoS/T/4	0	0	0	0	0	0	0	0
BoS/T/5	0	0	0	0	0	0	0	0
TOTAL EXC+SURFGEN	1	2	0	0	0	2	0	5

Table A1/13 Caramel Wave Shelter: distribution of artefact types.

SQ/SPIT	BP	GEO	BMS	EL	RUW	GRF	CHH	CBI	FBI2	WSTE	GRI	H/M	SP/FRP	TOTAL
CW/SURFGEN	0	0	0	0	0	0	0	0	0	0	0	0	0	0
CW/T1/SURF	0	0	0	0	0	0	0	0	0	0	0	0	0	0
CW/T1/1	0	0	0	0	0	0	0	0	0	0	0	0	0	0
CW/T1/2	0	0	0	0	0	0	0	0	0	0	0	0	0	0
CW/T1/3-OB	0	0	0	0	0	0	0	0	1	1	0	0	0	2
CW/T1/3-P	0	0	0	0	0	0	0	0	1	3	0	0	0	4
CW/T1/4	0	0	0	0	0	0	0	0	0	2	0	0	0	2
CW/T1/5	0	0	0	0	0	0	0	0	0	0	0	0	0	0
CW/T1/6	0	0	0	0	0	0	0	0	1	0	0	0	0	1
CW/T2/SURF	0	0	0	0	0	0	0	0	0	0	0	0	0	0
CW/T2/1	0	0	0	0	0	0	0	0	0	0	0	0	0	0
CW/T2/2	0	0	0	0	0	0	0	0	0	1	0	0	0	1
CW/T2/3	0	0	0	0	0	0	0	0	2	2	0	0	0	4
CW/T2/4-OB	0	0	0	0	0	0	0	0	0	0	0	0	0	0
CW/T2/4-P	0	0	0	0	0	0	0	0	0	0	0	0	0	0
TOTAL EXC+SURFGEN	0	0	0	0	0	0	0	0	5	9	0	0	0	14

Table A1/14 Caramel Wave Shelter: distribution of raw materials.

SQ/SPIT	QZ	FGS	CHT	SILC	QZTE	IGN	OTHER	TOTAL
CW/SURFGEN	0	0	0	0	0	0	0	0
CW/T1/SURF	0	0	0	0	0	0	0	0
CW/T1/1	0	0	0	0	0	0	0	0
CW/T1/2	0	0	0	0	0	0	0	0
CW/T1/3-OB	2	0	0	0	0	0	0	2
CW/T1/3-P	4	0	0	0	0	0	0	4
CW/T1/4	2	0	0	0	0	0	0	2
CW/T1/5	0	0	0	0	0	0	0	0
CW/T1/6	1	0	0	0	0	0	0	1
CW/T2/SURF	0	0	0	0	0	0	0	0
CW/T2/1	0	0	0	0	0	0	0	0
CW/T2/2	0	1	0	0	0	0	0	1
CW/T2/3	2	0	2	0	0	0	0	4
CW/T2/4-OB	0	0	0	0	0	0	0	0
CW/T2/4-P	0	0	0	0	0	0	0	0
TOTAL EXC+SURFGEN	11	1	2	0	0	0	0	14

Table A1/15 Delight Open Deposit: distribution of artefact types.

SQ/SPIT	BP	GEO	BMS	EL	RUW	GRF	CHH	CBI	FBI	WSTE	GRI	H/M	SP/FRP	TOTAL
DeO/SURFGEN	0	0	0	0	0	0	4	2	0	1	0	0	2	9
DeO/A/SURF-2	0	0	0	0	0	0	0	0	0	0	0	0	0	0
DeO/B/SURF-3	0	0	0	0	0	0	0	0	0	0	0	0	0	0
DeO/C/SURF-2	0	0	0	0	0	0	0	0	0	0	0	0	0	0
TOTAL EXC+SURFGEN	0	0	0	0	0	0	4	2	0	1	0	0	2	9

Table A1/16 Delight Open Deposit: distribution of raw materials.

SQ/SPIT	QZ	FGS	CHT	SILC	QZTE	IGN	OTHER	TOTAL
DeO/SURFGEN	5	2	0	0	2	0	0	9
DeO/A/SURF-2	0	0	0	0	0	0	0	0
DeO/B/SURF-3	0	0	0	0	0	0	0	0
DeO/C/SURF-2	0	0	0	0	0	0	0	0
TOTAL EXC+SURFGEN	5	2	0	0	2	0	0	9

Table A1/17 Delight Shelter: distribution of artefact types.

SQ/SPIT	BP	GEO	BMS	EL	RUW	GRF	CHH	CBI	FBI	WSTE	GRI	H/M	SP/FRP	TOTAL
DeS/SURFGEN	0	0	0	0	1	0	5	0	0	8	0	0	0	14
DeS/T/SURF	0	0	1	0	3	0	4	0	0	47	0	0	0	55
DeS/T/1	0	0	0	0	2	0	2	0	1	67	0	0	0	72
DeS/T/2	1	0	2	0	1	0	0	0	0	78	0	0	0	82
DeS/T/3	1	2	0	0	1	0	1	0	2	90	0	0	0	97
DeS/T/4	0	0	0	0	0	1	0	0	0	33	0	0	0	34
DeS/T/5	0	0	0	0	0	0	0	0	0	11	0	0	0	11
DeS/T/6	0	0	0	0	0	0	0	0	0	1	0	0	0	1
DeS/T/7	0	0	0	0	0	0	0	0	0	1	0	0	0	1
TOTAL EXC+SURFGEN	2	2	3	0	8	1	12	0	3	336	0	0	0	367

Table A1/18 Delight Shelter: distribution of raw materials.

SQ/SPIT	QZ	FGS	CHT	SILC	QZTE	IGN	OTHER	TOTAL
DeS/SURFGEN	7	6	0	0	1	0	0	14
DeS/T/SURF	24	20	6	1	4	0	0	55
DeS/T/1	43	21	3	1	40	0	0	72
DeS/T/2	41	25	5	7	3	0	1	82
DeS/T/3	48	34	5	6	4	0	0	97
DeS/T/4	18	13	0	1	1	1	0	34
DeS/T/5	8	1	0	1	1	0	0	11
DeS/T/6	1	0	0	0	0	0	0	1
DeS/T/7	0	1	0	0	0	0	0	1
TOTAL EXC+SURFGEN	190	121	19	17	18	1	1	367

Table A1/19 Dingo Shelter (Squares Ta and Tb): distribution of artefact types. [1] I–III refers to levels; the spits cross-cut stratigraphic layers, but excavation units within spits were dug according to the stratigraphic boundaries. For analysis the excavation units have been grouped according to the stratigraphic layers and designated Analytical Levels I to III. [2] Artefacts were not collected but were recorded in the field as 'flakes'.

SQ/LEVEL[1]	BP	GEO	BMS	EL	RUW	GRF	CHH	CBI	FBI	WSTE	GRI	H/M	SP/FRP	TOTAL TA+TB	TOTAL TB
DiS/SURFGEN	0	0	0	0	0	0	0	0	0	[2]2	0	0	0	2	0
DiS/I SURF	0	0	0	0	0	0	2	0	0	2	0	0	0	4	4
DiS/I-GB	0	0	0	0	0	0	1	0	0	7	0	0	0	8	1
DiS/II-GB	0	0	0	0	0	0	0	0	0	3	0	0	0	3	3
DiS/II-PB	0	0	0	0	0	0	0	0	0	21	0	0	0	21	21
DiS/III-GB UPR	0	0	0	0	0	0	0	0	1	12	0	0	0	13	8
DiS/III-GB LWR	0	0	0	0	0	0	1	0	1	1	0	0	0	3	3
TOTAL EXC+SURFGEN	0	0	0	0	0	0	4	0	2	48	0	0	0	54	40

Table A1/20 Dingo Shelter (Squares Ta and Tb): distribution of raw materials. [1] I–III refers to levels; spits cross-cut stratigraphic layers, but excavation units within spits were dug according to the stratigraphic boundaries. For analysis, excavation units have been grouped according to the stratigraphic layers and designated Analytical Levels I to III.

SQ/LEVEL[1]	QZ	FGS	CHT	SILC	QZTE	IGN	OTHER	TOTAL
DiS/SURFGEN	2	0	0	0	0	0	0	2
DiS/I SURF	1	3	0	0	0	0	0	4
DiS/I-GB	2	6	0	0	0	0	0	8
DiS/II-GB	0	1	2	0	0	0	0	3
DiS/II-PB	2	14	4	0	1	0	0	21
DiS/III-GB UPR	8	2	3	0	0	0	0	13
DiS/III-GB LWR	2	0	0	0	1	0	0	3
TOTAL EXC+SURFGEN	17	26	9	0	2	0	0	54

Table A1/21 Elngarrah Shelter: distribution of artefact types.

SQ/SPIT	BP	GEO	BMS	EL	RUW	GRF	CHH	CBI	FBI	WSTE	GRI	H/M	SP/FRP	TOTAL
ES/SURFGEN	0	0	0	0	0	0	0	0	0	4	0	0	0	4
ES/T/SURF	0	0	0	0	0	0	0	0	0	0	0	0	0	0
ES/T/1	0	0	0	0	0	0	0	0	0	2	0	0	0	2
ES/T/2	0	0	0	0	0	0	0	0	0	1	0	0	0	1
TOTAL EXC+SURFGEN	0	0	0	0	0	0	0	0	0	7	0	0	0	7

Table A1/22 Elngarrah Shelter: distribution of raw materials.

SQ/SPIT	QZ	FGS	CHT	SILC	QZTE	IGN	OTHER	TOTAL
ES/SURFGEN	3	1	0	0	0	0	0	4
ES/T/SURF	0	0	0	0	0	0	0	0
ES/T/1	1	0	0	0	0	1	0	2
ES/T/2	0	1	0	0	0	0	0	1
TOTAL EXC+SURFGEN	4	2	0	0	0	1	0	7

Table A1/23 Elongated Figure: distribution of artefact types.

SQ/SPIT	BP	GEO	BMS	EL	RUW	GRF	CHH	CBI	FBI	WSTE	GRI	H/M	SP/FRP	TOTAL
EFS/SURFGEN	0	0	0	0	0	0	0	0	0	0	0	0	0	0
EFS/T/SURF	0	0	0	0	0	0	0	0	0	0	0	0	0	0
EFS/T/1	0	0	0	0	0	0	0	0	0	0	0	0	0	0
EFS/T/2	0	0	0	0	0	0	1	0	0	4	0	0	0	5
EFS/T/3	0	0	0	0	0	0	0	0	0	0	0	0	0	0
EFS/T/4	0	0	0	0	0	0	0	0	0	0	0	0	0	0
EFS/T/5	0	0	0	0	0	0	0	0	0	2	0	0	0	2
EFS/T/6	0	0	0	0	0	0	0	0	0	2	0	0	0	2
EFS/T/7	0	0	0	0	0	0	0	0	0	3	0	0	0	3
TOTAL EXC+SURFGEN	0	0	0	0	0	0	1	0	0	11	0	0	0	12

Table A1/24 Elongated Figure Shelter: distribution of raw materials.

SQ/SPIT	QZ	FGS	CHT	SILC	QZTE	IGN	OTHER	TOTAL
EFS/SURFGEN	0	0	0	0	0	0	0	0
EFS/T/SURF	0	0	0	0	0	0	0	0
EFS/T/1	0	0	0	0	0	0	0	0
EFS/T/2	0	5	0	0	0	0	0	5
EFS/T/3	0	0	0	0	0	0	0	0
EFS/T/4	0	0	0	0	0	0	0	0
EFS/T/5	2	0	0	0	0	0	0	2
EFS/T/6	2	0	0	0	0	0	0	2
EFS/T/7	1	2	0	0	0	0	0	3
TOTAL EXC+SURFGEN	5	7	0	0	0	0	0	12

Table A1/25 Emu Tracks 2 Shelter: distribution of artefact types. [1] WOB refers to 'wombat overburden', which was deposit on surface of square T2 and which came from a wombat hole at the back of the shelter.

SQ/SPIT	BP	GEO	BMS	EL	RUW	GRF	CHH	CBI	FBI	WSTE	GRI	H/M	SP/FRP	TOTAL
ET2/SURFGEN	0	0	0	0	0	0	1	3	0	11	0	0	0	15
ET2/T2/WOB[1]	0	0	0	0	0	2	0	2	1	18	0	0	1	24
ET2/T2/SURF	0	0	0	0	0	0	0	0	0	0	0	0	0	0
ET2/T2/1	0	0	0	0	0	0	1	1	1	93	0	0	1	97
ET2/T2/2	0	0	0	0	0	1	0	0	0	80	0	0	2	83
ET2/T2/3	0	0	0	0	5	3	1	7	6	463	0	0	4	489
ET2/T2/4	0	0	0	0	8	1	1	7	10	551	0	0	0	578
ET2/T2/5	1	0	0	0	6	0	1	6	22	477	0	0	1	514
ET2/T2/6	2	0	1	0	17	3	1	28	19	810	0	0	2	883
ET2/T2/7	0	0	0	0	2	0	5	13	23	723	0	0	1	777
ET2/T2/8	2	0	2	0	14	0	6	16	18	840	0	0	2	900
ET2/T2/9	5	4	7	0	14	1	19	18	43	1038	0	0	4	1153
ET2/T2/10	8	2	6	0	18	0	16	12	15	745	0	0	5	827
ET2/T2/11	11	3	5	0	10	0	7	0	6	583	0	0	8	633
ET2/T2/12	1	2	0	0	6	0	1	0	0	246	0	0	1	257
ET2/T2/13	3	0	0	0	0	0	0	0	0	51	0	0	0	54
ET2/T2/14	0	0	0	0	0	0	0	0	0	20	0	0	0	20
ET2/T2/15	0	0	0	0	0	0	0	0	0	13	0	0	0	13
TOTAL T2	33	11	21	0	110	9	59	108	163	6733	0	0	31	7278
ET2/T1/SURF	0	0	0	0	0	0	0	0	0	0	0	0	0	0
ET2/T1/1	0	0	0	0	0	0	0	0	0	1	0	0	0	1
ET2/T1/2	0	0	0	0	0	0	0	0	0	2	0	0	0	2
ET2/T1/3	0	0	0	0	0	0	1	0	0	7	0	0	0	8
ET2/T1/4	0	0	0	0	1	1	0	0	1	22	0	0	0	25
ET2/T1/5	0	0	0	0	0	1	0	0	0	6	0	0	0	7
ET2/T1/6	0	0	0	0	0	1	0	0	0	24	0	0	0	25
ET2/T1/7	0	0	0	0	0	0	0	0	1	15	0	0	0	16
ET2/T1/8	0	0	0	0	0	0	0	0	0	35	0	0	0	35
TOTAL T1	0	0	0	0	1	3	1	0	2	112	0	0	0	119
TOTAL EXC+ SURFGEN +WOB	33	11	21	0	111	14	61	113	166	6874	0	0	32	7436

Table A1/26 Emu Tracks 2 Shelter: distribution of raw materials. [1] WOB refers to 'wombat overburden', which was deposit on surface of square T2 and which came from a wombat hole at the back of the shelter.

SQ/SPIT	QZ	FGS	CHT	SILC	QZTE	IGN	OTHER	TOTAL
ET2/SURFGEN	9	2	2	1	0	1	0	15
ET2/T2/WOB[1]	13	3	0	0	0	8	0	24
ET2/T2/SURF	0	0	0	0	0	0	0	0
ET2/T2/1	60	19	4	1	2	11	0	97
ET2/T2/2	44	28	5	0	2	4	0	83
ET2/T2/3	219	93	50	4	19	103	1	489
ET2/T2/4	265	180	51	4	21	57	0	578
ET2/T2/5	283	158	32	5	20	16	0	514
ET2/T2/6	443	298	69	5	45	22	1	883
ET2/T2/7	396	275	53	3	42	8	0	777
ET2/T2/8	494	250	97	11	39	9	0	900
ET2/T2/9	648	255	144	32	60	9	5	1153
ET2/T2/10	422	215	117	30	34	6	3	827
ET2/T2/11	306	150	91	31	47	0	8	633
ET2/T2/12	70	96	39	30	22	0	0	257
ET2/T2/13	20	19	7	4	2	2	0	54
ET2/T2/14	11	4	1	2	2	0	0	20
ET2/T2/15	6	4	2	0	1	0	0	13
TOTAL T2	3687	2044	762	162	358	247	18	7278
ET2/T1/SURF	0	0	0	0	0	0	0	0
ET2/T1/1	0	1	0	0	0	0	0	1
ET2/T1/2	1	1	0	0	0	0	0	2
ET2/T1/3	6	1	0	0	0	1	0	8
ET2/T1/4	10	9	2	1	0	3	0	25
ET2/T1/5	3	2	0	1	0	1	0	7
ET2/T1/6	10	10	2	0	0	3	0	25
ET2/T1/7	9	3	3	0	1	0	0	16
ET2/T1/8	18	11	5	1	0	0	0	35
TOTAL T1	57	38	12	3	1	8	0	119
TOTAL EXC T1+T2+ SURFGEN+WOB	3766	2087	776	166	359	264	18	7436

Table A1/27 Geebung Shelter: distribution of artefact types.

SQ/SPIT	BP	GEO	BMS	EL	RUW	GRF	CHH	CBI	FBI	WSTE	GRI	H/M	SP/FRP	TOTAL
GS/SURFGEN	0	0	0	0	0	0	0	0	0	0	0	0	0	0
GS/T1/SURF	0	0	0	0	0	0	1	0	0	0	0	0	0	1
GS/T1/1	0	0	0	0	0	0	0	0	0	5	0	0	0	5
GS/T2/SURF	0	0	0	0	0	0	0	0	0	0	0	0	0	0
GS/T2/1	0	0	0	0	0	0	0	0	1	1	0	0	0	2
TOTAL EXC+SURFGEN	0	0	0	0	0	0	1	0	1	6	0	0	0	8

Table A1/28 Geebung Shelter: distribution of raw materials.

SQ/SPIT	QZ	FGS	CHT	SILC	QZTE	IGN	OTHER	TOTAL
GS/SURFGEN	0	0	0	0	0	0	0	0
GS/T1/SURF	0	1	0	0	0	0	0	1
GS/T1/1	3	0	1	0	1	0	0	5
GS/T2/SURF	0	0	0	0	0	0	0	0
GS/T2/1	2	0	0	0	0	0	0	2
TOTAL EXC+SURFGEN	5	1	1	0	1	0	0	8

Table A1/29 Harris Gully Shelter: distribution of artefact types.

SQ/SPIT	BP	GEO	BMS	EL	RUW	GRF	CHH	CBI	FBI	WSTE	GRI	H/M	SP/FRP	TOTAL
HG/SURFGEN	0	0	0	0	0	1	1	0	0	0	0	0	0	2
HG/T/SURF	0	0	0	0	0	0	0	0	0	0	0	0	0	0
HG/T/1	0	0	0	0	0	0	0	0	0	0	0	0	0	0
HG/T/2	0	0	0	0	0	0	0	0	0	1	0	0	0	1
HG/T/3	0	0	0	0	0	0	0	0	0	8	0	0	0	8
HG/T/4	0	0	0	0	0	1	0	0	0	3	0	0	0	4
HG/T/5	0	0	0	0	0	0	0	0	0	0	0	0	0	0
HG/T/6	0	0	0	0	0	0	0	0	0	4	0	0	0	4
HG/T/7	0	0	0	0	0	0	0	0	0	7	0	0	0	7
HG/T/8	0	0	0	0	0	0	1	0	0	7	0	0	1	9
HG/T/9	0	0	0	0	0	0	0	0	0	1	0	0	0	1
HG/T/10	0	0	0	0	0	0	0	0	0	0	0	0	0	0
HG/T/11	0	0	0	0	0	0	0	0	0	0	0	0	0	0
TOTAL EXC+SURFGEN	0	0	0	0	0	2	2	0	0	31	0	0	1	36

Table A1/30 Harris Gully Shelter: distribution of raw materials.

SQ/SPIT	QZ	FGS	CHT	SILC	QZTE	IGN	OTHER	TOTAL
HG/SURFGEN	0	1	0	0	0	1	0	2
HG/T/SURF	0	0	0	0	0	0	0	0
HG/T/1	0	0	0	0	0	0	0	0
HG/T/2	0	1	0	0	0	0	0	1
HG/T/3	1	0	1	0	6	0	0	8
HG/T/4	2	1	0	0	0	1	0	4
HG/T/5	0	0	0	0	0	0	0	0
HG/T/6	4	0	0	0	0	0	0	4
HG/T/7	4	3	0	0	0	0	0	7
HG/T/8	8	1	0	0	0	0	0	9
HG/T/9	0	1	0	0	0	0	0	1
HG/T/10	0	0	0	0	0	0	0	0
HG/T/11	0	0	0	0	0	0	0	0
TOTAL EXC+SURFGEN	19	8	1	0	6	2	0	36

Table A1/31 Kangaroo and Echidna Shelter: distribution of artefact types.

SQ/SPIT	BP	GEO	BMS	EL	RUW	GRF	CHH	CBI	FBI	WSTE	GRI	H/M	SP/FRP	TOTAL
KE/SURFGEN	0	0	0	0	1	0	0	0	0	0	0	0	0	1
KE/T1/SURF	0	0	0	0	0	0	0	0	0	0	0	0	0	0
KE/T1/1	0	0	0	0	0	0	0	0	0	0	0	0	0	0
KE/T1/2	0	0	0	0	0	0	0	0	0	1	0	0	0	1
KE/T1/3	0	0	0	0	0	0	0	0	0	0	0	0	0	0
KE/T1/4	0	0	0	0	0	0	0	0	0	0	0	0	0	0
KE/T1/5	0	0	0	0	0	0	0	0	0	0	0	0	0	0
KE/T1/6	0	0	0	0	0	0	0	0	0	1	0	0	0	1
TOTAL T1	0	0	0	0	0	0	0	0	0	2	0	0	0	2
KE/T2/SURF	0	0	0	0	0	0	0	0	0	0	0	0	0	0
KE/T2/1	0	0	0	0	0	0	0	1	2	9	0	0	0	12
KE/T2/2	0	0	0	0	0	0	0	0	0	11	0	0	0	11
KE/T2/3	1	0	0	0	1	0	1	1	1	21	3	3	0	32
KE/T2/4	0	0	0	0	0	0	0	0	0	1	0	0	0	1
KE/T2/5	0	0	0	0	0	0	0	0	0	5	0	0	0	5
KE/T2/6	0	0	0	0	0	0	0	0	0	0	0	0	0	0
KE/T2/7	0	0	0	0	0	0	0	0	0	0	0	0	0	0
KE/T2/8	0	0	0	0	0	0	0	0	0	0	0	0	0	0
TOTAL T2	1	0	0	0	1	0	1	2	3	47	3	3	0	61
TOTAL EXC+SURFGEN	1	0	0	0	2	0	1	2	3	49	3	3	0	64

Table A1/32 Kangaroo and Echidna Shelter: distribution of raw materials.

SQ/SPIT	QZ	FGS	CHT	SILC	QZTE	IGN	OTHER	TOTAL
KE/SURFGEN	0	1	0	0	0	0	0	1
KE/T1/SURF	0	0	0	0	0	0	0	0
KE/T1/1	0	0	0	0	0	0	0	0
KE/T1/2	1	0	0	0	0	0	0	1
KE/T1/3	0	0	0	0	0	0	0	0
KE/T1/4	0	0	0	0	0	0	0	0
KE/T1/5	0	0	0	0	0	0	0	0
KE/T1/6	0	1	0	0	0	0	0	1
TOTAL T1	1	1	0	0	0	0	0	2
KE/T2/SURF	0	0	0	0	0	0	0	0
KE/T2/1	11	0	0	0	1	0	0	12
KE/T2/2	2	8	0	0	1	0	0	11
KE/T2/3	9	18	1	0	1	3	0	32
KE/T2/4	0	1	0	0	0	0	0	1
KE/T2/5	0	3	0	1	0	1	0	5
KE/T2/6	0	0	0	0	0	0	0	0
KE/T2/7	0	0	0	0	0	0	0	0
KE/T2/8	0	0	0	0	0	0	0	0
TOTAL T2	22	30	1	1	3	4	0	61
TOTAL EXC+SURFGEN	23	32	1	1	3	4	0	64

Table A1/33 Loggers Shelter (Squares E/F): distribution of artefact types. [1] Surface artefacts present but not collected or recorded. [2] Artefacts in this assemblage were analysed during the salvage program; bipolar flakes were included with bipolar cores in a category bipolar pieces.

SQ/SPIT	BP	GEO	BMS	EL	RUW	GRF	CHH	CBI	FBI[2]	WSTE	GRI	H/M	SP/FRP	TOTAL
LS/SURFGEN[1]														
LS/EF/SURF+1	0	0	0	0	9	1	2	29	X	617	0	0	0	678
LS/EF/2	0	2	0	2	11	3	12	46	X	604	1	0	9	690
LS/EF/3	2	0	1	0	10	2	13	23	X	361	0	0	17	429
LS/EF/4	2	0	0	0	8	0	18	24	X	376	0	0	4	432
LS/EF/5	2	0	1	0	3	0	3	6	X	193	0	1	2	211
LS/EF/6	0	0	0	0	5	0	14	3	X	237	0	0	3	262
LS/EF/7	1	0	0	0	2	0	6	1	X	179	0	0	4	193
LS/EF/8	0	0	0	0	1	0	6	0	X	66	0	0	11	184
LS/EF/9	1	0	0	0	8	0	10	1	X	170	0	1	15	206
LS/EF/10	0	0	0	0	2	0	17	0	X	235	0	0	24	278
LS/EF/11	0	0	0	0	3	0	15	0	X	295	0	0	11	325
LS/EF/12	0	0	0	0	12	0	6	1	X	320	0	0	19	358
LS/EF/13	0	0	0	0	6	0	7	0	X	312	0	0	8	333
LS/EF/14	0	0	0	0	0	0	3	0	X	31	0	0	2	36
LS/EF/15	0	0	0	0	2	0	2	0	X	24	0	0	10	38
LS/EF/16	0	0	0	0	0	0	1	0	X	38	0	0	3	42
LS/EF/17	0	0	0	0	0	0	1	0	X	27	0	0	4	31
LS/EF/18	0	0	0	0	1	0	2	0	X	29	0	0	0	32
LS/EF/19	0	0	0	0	0	0	0	0	X	17	0	0	0	17
LS/EF/20	0	0	0	0	0	0	0	0	X	21	0	0	2	23
LS/EF/21	0	0	0	0	1	0	0	0	X	4	0	0	0	5
TOTAL EXC EF														
+SURFGEN	8	2	2	2	84	6	148	134	X	4256	1	2	158	4803

Table A1/34 Loggers Shelter (Squares E/F): distribution of raw materials. [1] Surface artefacts present but not collected or recorded.

SQ/SPIT	QZ	FGS	CHT	SILC	QZTE	IGN	OTHER	TOTAL
LS/SURFGEN[1]								
LS/EF/SURF+1	380	232	24	12	16	14	0	678
LS/EF/2	330	266	44	11	21	18	0	690
LS/EF/3	211	161	25	7	15	10	0	429
LS/EF/4	197	172	25	7	25	4	2	432
LS/EF/5	87	96	8	3	12	5	0	211
LS/EF/6	104	123	8	6	16	3	2	262
LS/EF/7	53	107	10	8	13	1	1	193
LS/EF/8	42	111	12	0	16	0	3	184
LS/EF/9	63	112	18	1	12	0	0	206
LS/EF/10	106	123	23	8	17	1	0	278
LS/EF/11	121	135	42	5	18	1	3	325
LS/EF/12	154	133	38	3	25	1	4	358
LS/EF/13	129	135	40	8	17	1	3	333
LS/EF/14	16	13	2	0	3	0	2	36
LS/EF/15	10	22	4	0	2	0	0	38
LS/EF/16	17	20	2	0	3	0	0	42
LS/EF/17	12	12	3	0	4	0	0	31
LS/EF/18	8	16	5	0	3	0	0	32
LS/EF/19	5	8	2	0	0	0	2	17
LS/EF/20	9	10	3	0	0	1	0	23
LS/EF/21	2	1	1	0	1	0	0	5
TOTAL EXC EF								
+SURFGEN	2056	2008	339	79	239	60	22	4803

Table A1/35 Low Frontage Shelter: distribution of artefact types.

SQ/SPIT	BP	GEO	BMS	EL	RUW	GRF	CHH	CBI	FBI	WSTE	GRI	H/M	SP/FRP	TOTAL
LF/SURFGEN	0	0	0	0	0	0	0	0	0	0	0	0	0	0
LF/T/SURF	0	0	0	0	0	0	0	0	0	0	0	0	0	0
LF/T/1	0	0	0	0	0	0	0	0	0	0	0	0	0	0
LF/T/2	0	0	0	0	0	1	0	0	1	1	0	0	0	3
LF/T/3	0	0	0	0	0	0	0	0	0	1	0	0	0	1
LF/T/4	0	0	0	0	0	0	0	0	0	1	0	0	0	1
LF/T/5	0	0	0	0	0	0	0	0	0	0	0	0	0	0
LF/T/6	0	0	0	0	0	0	0	0	0	0	0	0	0	0
LF/T/7	0	0	0	0	0	0	0	0	0	0	0	0	1	1
LF/T/8	0	0	0	0	0	0	0	0	0	0	0	0	0	0
TOTAL EXC+SURFGEN	0	0	0	0	0	1	0	0	1	3	0	0	1	6

Table A1/36 Low Frontage Shelter: distribution of raw materials.

SQ/SPIT	QZ	FGS	CHT	SILC	QZTE	IGN	OTHER	TOTAL
LF/SURFGEN	0	0	0	0	0	0	0	0
LF/T/SURF	0	0	0	0	0	0	0	0
LF/T/1	0	0	0	0	0	0	0	0
LF/T/2	1	0	1	0	0	1	0	3
LF/T/3	1	0	0	0	0	0	0	1
LF/T/4	1	0	0	0	0	0	0	1
LF/T/5	0	0	0	0	0	0	0	0
LF/T/6	0	0	0	0	0	0	0	0
LF/T/7	1	0	0	0	0	0	0	1
LF/T/8	0	0	0	0	0	0	0	0
TOTAL EXC+SURFGEN	4	0	1	0	0	1	0	6

Table A1/37 McPherson Shelter: distribution of artefact types.

SQ/SPIT	BP	GEO	BMS	EL	RUW	GRF	CHH	CBI	FBI	WSTE	GRI	H/M	SP/FRP	TOTAL
McP/SURFGEN	0	0	0	0	0	0	1	0	0	0	0	0	0	1
McP/T/SURF	0	0	0	0	0	0	0	0	0	0	0	0	0	0
McP/T/1	0	0	0	0	0	0	0	0	0	0	0	0	0	0
McP/T/2	0	0	0	0	0	0	0	0	0	4	0	0	0	4
McP/T/3	0	0	0	0	0	0	0	0	0	19	0	0	0	19
TOTAL EXC+SURFGEN	0	0	0	0	0	0	1	0	0	23	0	0	0	24

Table A1/38 McPherson Shelter: distribution of raw materials.

SQ/SPIT	QZ	FGS	CHT	SILC	QZTE	IGN	OTHER	TOTAL
McP/SURFGEN	0	1	0	0	0	0	0	1
McP/T/SURF	0	0	0	0	0	0	0	0
McP/T/1	0	0	0	0	0	0	0	0
McP/T/2	3	1	0	0	0	0	0	4
McP/T/3	10	6	2	0	1	0	0	19
TOTAL EXC+SURFGEN	13	8	2	0	1	0	0	24

Table A1/39 Mangrove Mansions Shelter (East and West): distribution of artefact types.

SQ/SPIT	BP	GEO	BMS	EL	RUW	GRF	CHH	CBI	FBI	WSTE	GRI	H/M	SP/FRP	TOTAL
MME/SURFGEN	0	0	0	0	0	0	0	0	0	0	0	0	0	0
MME/T1/SURF	0	0	0	0	0	0	0	0	0	0	0	0	0	0
MME/T1/1	0	0	0	0	0	0	0	0	0	0	0	0	0	0
MME/T1/2	0	0	0	0	11	0	0	0	0	18	0	0	0	9
MME/T1/3	0	0	0	0	0	0	0	0	0	1	0	0	0	1
MME/T1/4	0	0	0	0	0	0	0	1	0	2	0	0	0	3
MME/T1/5-Y	0	0	0	0	0	0	0	0	0	0	0	0	0	0
MME/T1/5-M	0	0	0	0	0	0	0	0	0	0	0	0	0	0
MME/T1/6-MX	0	0	0	0	0	0	0	0	0	0	0	0	0	0
MME/T1/6-Y	0	0	0	0	0	0	0	0	0	0	0	0	0	0
MMW/SURFGEN	0	0	0	0	0	0	0	0	0	0	0	0	0	0
MMW/T2/SURF–4	0	0	0	0	0	0	0	0	0	0	0	0	0	0
TOTAL EXC+SURFGEN	0	0	0	0	1	0	0	1	0	11	0	0	0	13

Table A1/40 Mangrove Mansions Shelter (East and West): distribution of raw materials.

SQ/SPIT	QZ	FGS	CHT	SILC	QZTE	IGN	OTHER	TOTAL
MME/SURFGEN	0	0	0	0	0	0	0	0
MME/T1/SURF	0	0	0	0	0	0	0	0
MME/T1/1	0	0	0	0	0	0	0	0
MME/T1/2	0	0	9	0	0	0	0	9
MME/T1/3	0	0	1	0	0	0	0	1
MME/T1/4	2	1	0	0	0	0	0	3
MME/T1/5-Y	0	0	0	0	0	0	0	0
MME/T1/5-M	0	0	0	0	0	0	0	0
MME/T1/6-MX	0	0	0	0	0	0	0	0
MME/T1/6-Y	0	0	0	0	0	0	0	0
MMW/SURFGEN	0	0	0	0	0	0	0	0
MMW/T2/SURF–4	0	0	0	0	0	0	0	0
TOTAL EXC+SURFGEN	2	1	10	0	0	0	0	13

Table A1/41 One Tooth Shelter: distribution of artefact types.

SQ/SPIT	BP	GEO	BMS	EL	RUW	GRF	CHH	CBI	FBI	WSTE	GRI	H/M	SP/FRP	TOTAL
OT/SURFGEN	0	0	0	0	0	0	0	0	1	2	1	0	0	4
OT/T/SURF	0	0	0	0	0	0	0	0	0	0	0	0	0	0
OT/T/1	0	0	0	0	0	0	0	0	1	1	0	0	0	2
OT/T/2	0	0	0	0	0	0	0	1	0	1	0	0	0	2
OT/T/3	0	0	0	0	0	0	0	0	0	3	0	0	0	3
OT/T/4	0	0	0	0	0	0	0	0	0	0	0	0	0	0
OT/T/5	0	0	0	0	0	0	0	0	0	1	0	0	0	1
OT/T/6	0	0	0	0	0	0	0	0	0	0	0	0	0	0
OT/T/7	0	0	0	0	0	0	0	0	0	0	0	0	0	0
TOTAL EXC+SURFGEN	0	0	0	0	0	0	0	1	2	8	1	0	0	12

Table A1/42 One Tooth Shelter: distribution of raw materials.

SQ/SPIT	QZ	FGS	CHT	SILC	QZTE	IGN	OTHER	TOTAL
OT/SURFGEN	0	3	0	0	0	1	0	4
OT/T/SURF	0	0	0	0	0	0	0	0
OT/T/1	2	0	0	0	0	0	0	2
OT/T/2	1	0	0	0	0	1	0	2
OT/T/3	1	1	0	0	0	1	0	3
OT/T/4	0	0	0	0	0	0	0	0
OT/T/5	0	0	0	1	0	0	0	1
OT/T/6	0	0	0	0	0	0	0	0
OT/T/7	0	0	0	0	0	0	0	0
TOTAL EXC+SURFGEN	4	4	0	1	0	3	0	12

Table A1/43 Sunny Shelter: distribution of artefact types. [1] GRI in SS/T/6 is a broken sandstone slab with ochre on it (an ochre palette).

SQ/SPIT	BP	GEO	BMS	EL	RUW	GRF	CHH	CBI	FBI	WSTE	GRI	H/M	SP/FRP	TOTAL
SuS/SURFGEN	0	0	0	0	1	0	0	2	1	2	1	0	0	7
SuS/T/SURF	0	0	0	0	0	0	0	0	0	0	0	0	0	0
SuS/T/1	0	0	0	0	0	0	0	0	0	25	0	0	1	26
SuS/T/2	0	0	0	0	0	1	0	2	1	73	0	0	0	77
SuS/T/3-5	0	0	0	0	0	5	0	4	10	263	0	0	0	282
SuS/T/6	0	0	0	0	5	1	2	7	3	255	[1]1	0	0	274
SuS/T/7	1	0	0	0	0	2	0	5	1	176	0	0	0	185
SuS/T/8	1	0	0	0	0	0	5	0	5	173	0	0	0	184
SuS/T/9	0	0	0	0	1	0	2	0	0	99	0	0	0	102
SuS/T/10	0	0	1	0	1	0	0	0	0	77	0	0	1	80
SuS/T/11	0	0	0	0	1	0	0	0	0	28	0	0	0	29
SuS/T/12	0	0	0	0	0	0	0	0	0	8	0	0	0	8
SuS/T/13	0	0	0	0	0	0	0	0	0	9	0	0	1	10
SuS/T/14	0	0	0	0	0	0	0	0	0	3	0	0	0	3
TOTAL EXC+SURFGEN	2	0	1	0	9	9	9	20	21	1191	12	0	3	1267

Table A1/44 Sunny Shelter: distribution of raw materials. [1] Other raw material in SS/T/6 is a broken sandstone slab with ochre on it (an ochre palette).

SQ/SPIT	QZ	FGS	CHT	SILC	QZTE	IGN	OTHER	TOTAL
SuS/SURFGEN	4	2	0	0	0	1	0	7
SuS/T/SURF	0	0	0	0	0	0	0	0
SuS/T/1	16	5	3	0	1	1	0	26
SuS/T/2	53	18	2	0	0	4	0	77
SuS/T/3-5	170	66	9	1	1	35	0	282
SuS/T/6	157	78	22	2	6	7	[1] 2	274
SuS/T/7	114	45	14	2	3	7	0	185
SuS/T/8	115	35	17	6	10	1	0	184
SuS/T/9	74	15	5	8	0	0	0	102
SuS/T/10	52	14	5	9	0	0	0	80
SuS/T/11	23	1	4	1	0	0	0	29
SuS/T/12	7	0	0	1	0	0	0	8
SuS/T/13	9	1	0	0	0	0	0	10
SuS/T/14	3	0	0	0	0	0	0	3
TOTAL EXC+SURFGEN	797	280	81	30	21	56	12	1267

Table A1/45 Ti-tree Shelter: distribution of artefact types.

SQ/SPIT	BP	GEO	BMS	EL	RUW	GRF	CHH	CBI	FBI	WSTE	GRI	H/M	SP/FRP	TOTAL
TT/SURFGEN	0	0	0	0	0	0	0	0	0	0	0	0	0	0
TT/T1/SURF–3	0	0	0	0	0	0	0	0	0	0	0	0	0	0
TT/T2/SURF	0	0	0	0	0	0	0	0	0	0	0	0	0	0
TT/T2/1	0	0	0	0	0	0	0	1	1	5	0	0	0	7
TT/T2/2	0	0	0	0	0	0	0	0	0	1	0	0	0	1
TT/T2/3	0	0	0	0	0	0	0	0	0	2	0	0	0	2
TT/T2/4	0	0	0	0	0	0	0	0	0	0	0	0	0	0
TT/T2/5	0	0	0	0	0	0	0	0	0	1	0	0	0	1
TOTAL EXC+SURFGEN	0	0	0	0	0	0	0	1	1	9	0	0	0	11

Table A1/46 Ti-tree Shelter: distribution of raw materials.

SQ/SPIT	QZ	FGS	CHT	SILC	QZTE	IGN	OTHER	TOTAL
TT/SURFGEN	0	0	0	0	0	0	0	0
TT/T1/SURF–3	0	0	0	0	0	0	0	0
TT/T2/SURF	0	0	0	0	0	0	0	0
TT/T2/1	1	16	0	0	0	0	0	7
TT/T2/2	1	0	0	0	0	0	0	1
TT/T2/3	0	2	0	0	0	0	0	2
TT/T2/4	0	0	0	0	0	0	0	0
TT/T2/5	1	0	0	0	0	0	0	1
TOTAL EXC+SURFGEN	3	8	0	0	0	0	0	11

Table A1/47 Uprooted Tree Shelter: distribution of artefact types. [1] Ground implement is a pebble with ground/abraded areas.

SQ/SPIT	BP	GEO	BMS	EL	RUW	GRF	CHH	CBI	FBI	WSTE	GRI	H/M	SP/FRP	TOTAL
UTS/SURFGEN	0	0	0	0	0	0	0	1	0	2	0	0	0	3
UTS/T/SURF	0	0	0	0	0	0	0	0	0	0	0	0	0	0
UTS/T/1	0	0	0	0	1	1	0	2	0	47	[1]1	0	0	52
UTS/T/2	0	0	0	0	0	0	0	2	0	77	0	0	0	79
UTS/T/3	0	1	0	0	0	3	0	2	2	199	0	0	0	207
UTS/T/4	0	0	0	0	1	0	0	4	3	177	0	0	0	185
UTS/T/4+5-TN	0	0	0	0	0	0	0	0	0	2	0	0	0	2
UTS/T/5	0	0	1	0	1	0	0	0	2	103	0	0	0	107
UTS/T/6	0	0	0	0	0	0	0	1	0	71	0	0	0	72
UTS/T/7	0	0	0	0	0	0	1	1	1	37	0	0	0	40
UTS/T/8	0	0	0	0	0	0	0	0	0	18	0	0	0	18
UTS/T/9	0	0	0	0	0	0	0	0	1	3	0	0	0	34
UTS/T/10	0	0	0	0	0	0	0	0	0	30	0	0	0	30
UTS/T/11	0	0	0	0	1	0	0	0	0	26	0	0	0	27
UTS/T/12	0	0	0	0	0	0	0	0	0	11	0	0	0	11
UTS/T/13	0	0	0	0	0	0	0	0	0	7	0	0	0	7
UTS/T/14	0	0	0	0	0	0	0	0	0	3	0	0	0	3
UTS/Tb/15	0	0	0	0	0	0	0	0	0	1	0	0	0	1
UTS/Tb/16	0	0	0	0	0	0	0	0	0	0	0	0	0	0
UTS/Tb/17	0	0	0	0	0	0	0	0	0	0	0	0	0	0
UTS/Tb/18	0	0	0	0	0	0	0	0	0	0	0	0	0	0
TOTAL EXC+SURFGEN	0	1	1	0	4	4	1	13	9	844	11	0	0	878

Table A1/48 Uprooted Tree Shelter: distribution of raw materials.

SQ/SPIT	QZ	FGS	CHT	SILC	QZTE	IGN	OTHER	TOTAL
UTS/SURFGEN	3	0	0	0	0	0	0	3
UTS/T/SURF	0	0	0	0	0	0	0	0
UTS/T/1	18	22	3	2	0	6	1	52
UTS/T/2	32	34	4	2	2	5	0	79
UTS/T/3	94	78	15	7	1	12	0	207
UTS/T/4	78	80	8	6	2	11	0	185
UTS/T/4+5-TN	0	2	0	0	0	0	0	2
UTS/T/5	50	40	8	4	2	3	0	107
UTS/T/6	35	30	1	3	3	0	0	72
UTS/T/7	18	14	4	1	3	0	0	40
UTS/T/8	9	6	2	1	0	0	0	18
UTS/T/9	10	16	0	2	6	0	0	34
UTS/T/10	7	16	2	2	3	0	0	30
UTS/T/11	7	13	2	1	4	0	0	27
UTS/T/12	0	7	1	1	2	0	0	11
UTS/T/13	1	1	0	0	5	0	0	7
UTS/T/14	0	3	0	0	0	0	0	3
UTS/Tb/15	0	1	0	0	0	0	0	1
UTS/Tb/16	0	0	0	0	0	0	0	0
UTS/Tb/17	0	0	0	0	0	0	0	0
UTS/Tb/18	0	0	0	0	0	0	0	0
TOTAL EXC+SURFGEN	362	363	50	32	33	37	1	878

Table A1/49 Venus Shelter: distribution of artefact types.

SQ/SPIT	BP	GEO	BMS	EL	RUW	GRF	CHH	CBI	FBI	WSTE	GRI	H/M	SP/FRP	TOTAL
VS/SURFGEN	0	0	0	0	0	0	0	1	0	0	0	0	0	1
VS/T/SURF	0	0	0	0	0	0	0	0	0	0	0	0	0	0
VS/T/1	0	0	0	0	0	0	0	0	0	0	0	0	0	0
VS/T/2	0	0	0	0	0	0	0	0	0	10	0	0	0	10
VS/T/3	0	0	0	0	0	0	0	0	1	5	0	0	0	6
VS/T/4	0	0	0	0	0	0	0	0	2	3	0	0	0	5
VS/T/5	0	0	0	0	0	0	0	0	0	0	0	0	0	0
TOTAL EXC+SURFGEN	0	0	0	0	0	0	0	1	3	18	0	0	0	22

Table A1/50 Venus Shelter: distribution of raw materials.

SQ/SPIT	QZ	FGS	CHT	SILC	QZTE	IGN	OTHER	TOTAL
VS/SURFGEN	1	0	0	0	0	0	0	1
VS/T/SURF	0	0	0	0	0	0	0	0
VS/T/1	0	0	0	0	0	0	0	0
VS/T/2	1	9	0	0	0	0	0	10
VS/T/3	2	4	0	0	0	0	0	6
VS/T/4	3	1	1	0	0	0	0	5
VS/T/5	0	0	0	0	0	0	0	0
TOTAL EXC+SURFGEN	7	14	1	0	0	0	0	22

Table A1/51 White Figure Shelter: distribution of artefact types.

SQ/SPIT	BP	GEO	BMS	EL	RUW	GRF	CHH	CBI	FBI	WSTE	GRI	H/M	SP/FRP	TOTAL
WF/SURFGEN	0	0	0	0	0	0	0	0	0	0	0	0	0	0
WF/T/SURF	0	0	0	0	0	0	0	0	0	7	0	0	0	7
WF/T/1	0	0	0	0	1	0	2	2	0	22	0	0	1	28
WF/T/2	0	0	0	0	0	0	0	1	0	30	0	0	2	33
WF/T/3	0	0	0	0	0	0	0	0	0	83	0	0	0	83
WF/T/4	0	0	0	0	0	1	1	1	1	248	0	0	2	254
WF/T/5	3	0	1	0	0	1	1	5	2	388	0	0	5	406
WF/T/6	0	0	0	0	1	2	3	4	0	185	0	0	0	195
WF/T/7	0	0	0	0	0	0	0	0	0	65	0	0	0	65
WF/T/8	0	0	0	0	1	0	0	0	0	12	0	0	0	13
WF/T/9	0	0	0	0	0	0	0	0	0	3	0	0	0	3
TOTAL EXC+SURFGEN	3	0	1	0	3	4	7	13	3	1043	0	0	10	1087

Table A1/52 White Figure Shelter: distribution of raw materials.

SQ/SPIT	QZ	FGS	CHT	SILC	QZTE	IGN	OTHER	TOTAL
WF/SURFGEN	0	0	0	0	0	0	0	0
WF/T/SURF	0	7	0	0	0	0	0	7
WF/T/1	3	14	9	0	2	0	0	28
WF/T/2	6	21	3	0	2	1	0	33
WF/T/3	28	46	6	1	1	1	0	83
WF/T/4	115	103	20	4	0	12	0	254
WF/T/5	196	156	21	12	4	16	1	406
WF/T/6	88	78	11	6	2	10	0	195
WF/T/7	20	31	5	6	2	1	0	65
WF/T/8	5	5	0	2	1	0	0	13
WF/T9	0	3	0	0	0	0	0	3
TOTAL EXC+SURFGEN	461	464	75	31	14	41	1	1087

Table A1/53 Wolloby Gully Shelter: distribution of artefact types.

SQ/SPIT	BP	GEO	BMS	EL	RUW	GRF	CHH	CBI	FBI	WSTE	GRI	H/M	SP/FRP	TOTAL
WoG/SURFGEN	0	0	0	0	0	0	0	0	0	0	0	0	0	0
WoG/T/SURF	0	0	0	0	0	0	0	0	0	0	0	0	0	0
WoG/T/1	0	0	0	0	0	0	0	0	0	0	0	0	0	0
WoG/T/2	0	0	0	0	0	0	0	0	0	0	0	0	0	0
WoG/T/3	0	0	0	0	0	0	0	0	0	9	0	0	0	9
WoG/T/4	0	0	0	0	0	0	0	0	0	0	0	0	0	0
WoG/T/5	0	0	0	0	0	0	0	0	0	0	0	0	0	0
WoG/T/6	0	0	0	0	0	0	0	0	0	0	0	0	0	0
TOTAL EXC+SURFGEN	0	0	0	0	0	0	0	0	0	9	0	0	0	9

Table A1/54 Wolloby Gully Shelter: distribution of raw materials.

SQ/SPIT	QZ	FGS	CHT	SILC	QZTE	IGN	OTHER	TOTAL
WoG/SURFGEN	0	0	0	0	0	0	0	0
WoG/T/SURF	0	0	0	0	0	0	0	0
WoG/T/1	0	0	0	0	0	0	0	0
WoG/T/2	0	0	0	0	0	0	0	0
WoG/T/3	0	9	0	0	0	0	0	9
WoG/T/4	0	0	0	0	0	0	0	0
WoG/T/5	0	0	0	0	0	0	0	0
WoG/T/6	0	0	0	0	0	0	0	0
TOTAL EXC+SURFGEN	0	9	0	0	0	0	0	9

APPENDIX 2

The Upper Mangrove Creek catchment — random sampling units

Number of artefacts in each millennium and estimated total number of artefacts accumulated in each archaeological deposit

Notes

The number of artefacts accumulated in each millennium/excavated pit is obtained by adding together the numbers of artefacts in spits which can be assigned to the same millennium. Where the boundary between two millennia falls within a spit, the number of artefacts in that spit is divided proportionately. For example, if the depth/age duration of a spit is 750 BP to 1750 BP and the number of artefacts in the spit is 40, then 25% (10) are assigned to the first millennium BP and 75% (30) to the second millennium BP.

The estimated total number of artefacts accumulated in the archaeological deposit is obtained by firstly converting *the number of artefacts accumulated in each millennium/excavated pit* into the 'number of artefacts accumulated in each millennium per square metre' (cf. Table 4.12). That figure is then multiplied by the estimated area over which the deposit is likely to extend at the same level across the site (Table 4.4). These extrapolations take into account the known and assumed variations in depth of deposit across the shelter, as well as the potential for the deposit to contain archaeological materials (see Chapter 4). Figures are rounded to the nearest 50.

The average depth of deposit is used in the calculations rather than the maximum depth of deposit (Table 3.4) or the depth of archaeological deposit (Table 4.4). This is because the depth across the base of the excavated squares, and also the base of individual spits, was often not uniform, and so the average depth of the spits/base of square has been used. The depth quoted in these tables for the basal spits thus often varies from those in Tables 3.4 and 4.4 (see also Chapters 3 and 4). Figures are rounded to the nearest 0.5cm.

The duration over which a deposit is estimated to have accumulated is based on depth/age curve projections using radiocarbon ages where they are available. For archaeological deposits without radiocarbon ages, the estimated period over which the archaeological deposit accumulated was based on diagnostic traits and/or the depth of the deposit. Where deposit depth was used, the estimated duration was extrapolated from archaeological deposits in rockshelters with similar morphologies (e.g., whether or not open to slope processes) and where the length of time over which the deposit accumulated had been radiocarbon-dated (see Chapter 3).

Several archaeological deposits considered to have accumulated within the first millennium BP (whether estimates are based on radiocarbon ages or other criteria) are listed together in Table A2/17.

Table A2/1 Black Hands Shelter (Square F): number of artefacts accumulated in each millennium and estimated total number of artefacts accumulated in the archaeological deposit.

SPIT	AVERAGE SPIT DEPTH (cm)	C14 AGES (years BP)/ DIAGNOSTIC TRAIT	D/A DATES (years BP)	DURATION (years)	NO. OF ARTEFACTS	NO. OF ARTEFACTS ACCUMULATED IN EACH MILLENNIUM IN EXCAVATED PIT	ESTIMATED TOTAL NUMBER OF ARTEFACTS ACCUMULATED IN THE ARCHAEOLOGICAL DEPOSIT
BHS/F/1	4.5		0–175	175	36		
BHS/F/2	13.5		175–500	325	181		
BHS/F/3	23.5		500–875	375	343	722	14,600
BHS/F/4	34.0		875–1250	375	485 (162/323)		
BHS/F/5	44.0		1250–1600	350	664		
BHS/F/6	54.0		1600–1900	300	1076	2189	46,300
BHS/F/7	64.0		1900–2200	300	377 (126/251)		
BHS/F/8	74.0		2200–2500	300	83		
BHS/F/9	84.0		2500–2800	300	45		
BHS/F/10	94.0		2800–2975	175	10	390	16,050
BHS/F/11	99.0	3040±85	2975–3100	125	2 (1/1)		
						1	100
				3100	3302	3302	77,050

Table A2/2 Boat Cave: number of artefacts accumulated in each millennium and estimated total number of artefacts accumulated in the archaeological deposit.

SPIT	AVERAGE SPIT DEPTH (cm)	C14 AGES (years BP)/ DIAGNOSTIC TRAIT	D/A DATES (years BP)	DURATION (years)	NO. OF ARTEFACTS	NO. OF ARTEFACTS ACCUMULATED IN EACH MILLENNIUM IN EXCAVATED PIT	ESTIMATED TOTAL NUMBER OF ARTEFACTS ACCUMULATED IN THE ARCHAEOLOGICAL DEPOSIT
BC/T/S+1	5.0		0– 375	375	3		
BC/T/2	8.0		375– 650	275	7	10	350
BC/T/3	18.0		650–1450	800	0 (0/0)		
BC/T/4	22.5		1450–1800	350	1	2.5	50
BC/T/5	27.0		1800–2175	375	3 (1.5/1.5)		
BC/T/6	32.5	2370±60	2175–2600	425	6		
BC/T/7	34.0		2600–2755	155	1	8.5	100
BC/T/8	36.0				0		
				2755	21	21	500

Table A2/3 Boronia Shelter: number of artefacts accumulated in each millennium and estimated total number of artefacts accumulated in the archaeological deposit.

SPIT	AVERAGE SPIT DEPTH (cm)	C14 AGES (years BP)/ DIAGNOSTIC TRAIT	D/A DATES (years BP)	DURATION (years)	NO. OF ARTEFACTS	NO. OF ARTEFACTS ACCUMULATED IN EACH MILLENNIUM IN EXCAVATED PIT	ESTIMATED TOTAL NUMBER OF ARTEFACTS ACCUMULATED IN THE ARCHAEOLOGICAL DEPOSIT
BoS/T/S+1	2		0– 250	250	1		
BoS/T/2	8		250– 800	550	1	3	100
BoS/T/3	17		800–1550	750	2 (1/1)		
BoS/T/4	23	1880±60			0	1	50
BoS/T/5+6	33				0		
				1550	4	4	150

Table A2/4 Caramel Wave Shelter (Squares T1 and T2): number of artefacts accumulated in each millennium and estimated total number of artefacts accumulated in the archaeological deposit. [1] Depth/age dates based on square T1.

SPIT	AVERAGE SPIT DEPTH (cm)	C14 AGES (years BP)/ DIAGNOSTIC TRAIT	D/A DATES (years BP)	DURATION (years)	NO. OF ARTEFACTS	NO. OF ARTEFACTS ACCUMULATED IN EACH MILLENNIUM IN EXCAVATED PIT	ESTIMATED TOTAL NUMBER OF ARTEFACTS ACCUMULATED IN THE ARCHAEOLOGICAL DEPOSIT
CW/S+1	3.0		0– 275	275	0		
CW/2	5.5		275– 475	200	1		
CW/3-4	11.0		475– 900	425	12	13	450
CW/5-6	22.0	1430±60	900–1600	700			
					1		50
				1600	14	14	500

Table A2/5 Delight Shelter: number of artefacts accumulated in each millennium and estimated total number of artefacts accumulated in the archaeological deposit.

SPIT	AVERAGE SPIT DEPTH (cm)	C14 AGES (years BP)/ DIAGNOSTIC TRAIT	D/A DATES (years BP)	DURATION (years)	NO. OF ARTEFACTS	NO. OF ARTEFACTS ACCUMULATED IN EACH MILLENNIUM IN EXCAVATED PIT	ESTIMATED TOTAL NUMBER OF ARTEFACTS ACCUMULATED IN THE ARCHAEOLOGICAL DEPOSIT
DeS/T/Surf		)			55	79	1100
DeS/T/1	3.0	)	0–1600	1600	72 (24/48)		
DeS/T/2	6.0	Bondi points	1600–1775	175	82	185	2650
DeS/T/3	12.5	↓	1775–2175	400	97 (55/42)		
DeS/T/4	17.5		2175–2575	400	34		
DeS/T/5	22.5		2575–2650	75	11		
DeS/T/6	27.5	↑	2650–2730	80	1		
DeS/T/7	31.5	Qz predom	2730–2800	70	1	89	1250
				2800	353	353	5000

Table A2/6 Dingo Shelter (Square Tb only): number of artefacts accumulated in each millennium and estimated total number of artefacts accumulated in the archaeological deposit.

SPIT	AVERAGE SPIT DEPTH (cm)	C14 AGES (years BP)/ DIAGNOSTIC TRAIT	D/A DATES (years BP)	DURATION (years)	NO. OF ARTEFACTS	NO. OF ARTEFACTS ACCUMULATED IN EACH MILLENNIUM IN EXCAVATED PIT	ESTIMATED TOTAL NUMBER OF ARTEFACTS ACCUMULATED IN THE ARCHAEOLOGICAL DEPOSIT
DiS/Tb/I	3.0		0– 290	290	5		
DiS/Tb/II	11.0		290– 890	600	24	31	2000
DiS/Tb/IIIU	21.0		890–1600	710	8 (2/6)		
DiS/Tb/IIIL	26.0	1840±60	1600–2000	400	3	9	600
				2000	40	40	2600

Table A2/7 Elngarrah Shelter: number of artefacts accumulated in each millennium and estimated total number of artefacts accumulated in the archaeological deposit. [1] Estimated date of initial habitation based on depth of archaeological deposit.

SPIT	AVERAGE SPIT DEPTH (cm)	C14 AGES (years BP)/ DIAGNOSTIC TRAIT	D/A DATES (years BP)	DURATION (years)	NO. OF ARTEFACTS	NO. OF ARTEFACTS ACCUMULATED IN EACH MILLENNIUM IN EXCAVATED PIT	ESTIMATED TOTAL NUMBER OF ARTEFACTS ACCUMULATED IN THE ARCHAEOLOGICAL DEPOSIT
ES/T/S+1	5.0		0–1000	1000	2	2	50
ES/T/2	16.0		1000–<1300	<300	1	1	50
				1300	3	3	100

Table A2/8 Elongated Figure Shelter: number of artefacts accumulated in each millennium and estimated total number of artefacts accumulated in the archaeological deposit.

SPIT	AVERAGE SPIT DEPTH (cm)	C14 AGES (years BP)/ DIAGNOSTIC TRAIT	D/A DATES (years BP)	DURATION (years)	NO. OF ARTEFACTS	NO. OF ARTEFACTS ACCUMULATED IN EACH MILLENNIUM IN EXCAVATED PIT	ESTIMATED TOTAL NUMBER OF ARTEFACTS ACCUMULATED IN THE ARCHAEOLOGICAL DEPOSIT
EF/T/1	3.0		0– 125	125	0		
EF/T/2	10.0		125– 460	335	5		
EF/T/3	16.5		460– 800	340	0		
EF/T/4	21.5		800–1050	250	0	5	400
EF/T/5	25.5		1050–1250	200	2		
EF/T/6	31.5		1250–1600	350	2		
EF/T/7	37.0	1810±80	1600–2000	400	3	7	550
				2000	12	12	950

Table A2/9 Emu Tracks 2 Shelter (Squares T2a and T2b): number of artefacts accumulated in each millennium and estimated total number of artefacts accumulated in the archaeological deposit.

SPIT	AVERAGE SPIT DEPTH (cm)	C14 AGES (years BP)/ DIAGNOSTIC TRAIT	D/A DATES (years BP)	DURATION (years)	NO. OF ARTEFACTS	NO. OF ARTEFACTS ACCUMULATED IN EACH MILLENNIUM IN EXCAVATED PIT	ESTIMATED TOTAL NUMBER OF ARTEFACTS ACCUMULATED IN THE ARCHAEOLOGICAL DEPOSIT
ET2/T2/1	5.5		0– 400	400	97		
ET2/T2/2	10.0		400– 750	350	83	506	14,450
ET2/T2/3	15.0		750–1100	375	489 (326/163)		
ET2/T2/4	21.5		1100–1600	475	578		
ET2/T2/5	26.5	Bondi points	1600–1775	175	514		
ET2/T2/6	32.5	↓	1775–1975	200	883	2295	66,350
ET2/T2/7	37.0		1975–2100	125	777 (157/620)		
ET2/T2/8	42.0		2100–2300	200	900		
ET2/T2/9	47.0		2300–2475	150	1153		
ET2/T2/10	52.0	↑	2475–2650	200	827		
ET2/T2/11	56.5	Qz predom	2650–2800	150	633		
ET2/T2/12	62.0	FGS predom	2800–3000	200	257	4390	165,200
		↓					
ET2/T2/13	65.0		3000–3100	100	54		
ET2/T2/14	71.0		3100–3300	200	20		
ET2/T2/15	77.0		3300–3550	250	13	87	3650
				3550	7278	7278	249,650

Table A2/10 Emu Tracks 2 Shelter (Square T1): number of artefacts accumulated in each millennium and estimated total number of artefacts accumulated in the archaeological deposit.

SPIT	AVERAGE SPIT DEPTH (cm)	C14 AGES (years BP)/ DIAGNOSTIC TRAIT	D/A DATES (years BP)	DURATION (years)	NO. OF ARTEFACTS	NO. OF ARTEFACTS ACCUMULATED IN EACH MILLENNIUM IN EXCAVATED PIT	ESTIMATED TOTAL NUMBER OF ARTEFACTS ACCUMULATED IN THE ARCHAEOLOGICAL DEPOSIT
ET2/T1/S+1	5.5		0– 450	450	1		see Table A2/9
ET2/T1/2	11.0		450– 850	400	2	7	
ET2/T1/3	16.0		850–1250	400	8 (4/4)		
ET2/T1/4	20.5		1250–1600	350	25		
ET2/T1/5	25.5		1600–1750	150	7		
ET2/T1/6	31.0		1750–1975	225	25	63	
ET2/T1/7	36.0		1975–2175	200	16 (2/14)		
ET2/T1/8	40.5		2175–2475	300	35	49	
				2475	119	119	

Table A2/11   Harris Gully Shelter: number of artefacts accumulated in each millennium and estimated total number of artefacts accumulated in the archaeological deposit. [1] Estimated date of initial habitation based on depth of archaeological deposit, predominance of quartz throughout the sequence and presence of fragments of ground-edged implements.

SPIT	AVERAGE SPIT DEPTH (cm)	C14 AGES (years BP)/ DIAGNOSTIC TRAIT	D/A DATES (years BP)	DURATION (years)	NO. OF ARTEFACTS	NO. OF ARTEFACTS ACCUMULATED IN EACH MILLENNIUM IN EXCAVATED PIT	ESTIMATED TOTAL NUMBER OF ARTEFACTS ACCUMULATED IN THE ARCHAEOLOGICAL DEPOSIT
HG/T/S+1	1.0		0– 60	60	0		
HG/T/2	5.0		60– 200	140	1		
HG/T/2	10.0		200– 375	175	8		
HG/T/4	15.5		375– 575	200	4		
HG/T/5	20.5		575– 750	175	0		
HG/T/6	25.5		750– 900	150	4	21	1150
HG/T/7	30.0		900–1075	175	7 (4/3)		
HG/T/8	35.0		1075–1250	175	9		
HG/T/9	39.0	[1]	1250–1370	120	1	13	700
HG/T/10	43.0				0		
HG/T/11	47.5				0		
				1370	34	34	1850

Table A2/12   Kangaroo and Echidna Shelter (Squares T1 and T2): number of artefacts accumulated in each millennium and estimated total number of artefacts accumulated in the archaeological deposit. [1] D/a dates and duration based on Square T2; the number of artefacts retrieved from Square T1 is added in to the final two columns.

SPIT	AVERAGE SPIT DEPTH (cm)	C14 AGES (years BP)/ DIAGNOSTIC TRAIT	D/A DATES (years BP)	DURATION (years)	NO. OF ARTEFACTS	NO. OF ARTEFACTS ACCUMULATED IN EACH MILLENNIUM IN EXCAVATED PIT	ESTIMATED TOTAL NUMBER OF ARTEFACTS ACCUMULATED IN THE ARCHAEOLOGICAL DEPOSIT
						7	350
KE/T2/S+1	5.0		0–1600	1600	12 (7/5)		
						10 (+1 from T1)	1400
KE/T2/2	10.0		1600–2800	1200	11 (5/6)		
						9	450
KE/T2/3UP	16.0)		2800–			14	700
KE/T2/3LR	22.0)		–5000	2200	32 (3/14/15)	15	750
						0.5	50
						0.5	50
KE/T2/4ab	28.0	6700±150	5000–7300	2300	1 (0.5/0.5)		
						1 (+1 from T1)	950
						2	400
KE/T2/5b	41.5		7300–9790	2490	5 (1/2/2)	2	400
KE/T2/6b	51.0				0		
KE/T2/7b	58.5				0		
KE/T2/8b	68.0				0		
				9790	61 +2 = 63	61 +2 = 63	5500

Table A2/13   Loggers Shelter (Squares E/F): number of artefacts accumulated in each millennium and estimated total number of artefacts accumulated in the archaeological deposit.

SPIT	AVERAGE SPIT DEPTH (cm)	C14 AGES (years BP)/ DIAGNOSTIC TRAIT	D/A DATES (years BP)	DURATION (years)	NO. OF ARTEFACTS	NO. OF ARTEFACTS ACCUMULATED IN EACH MILLENNIUM IN EXCAVATED PIT	ESTIMATED TOTAL NUMBER OF ARTEFACTS ACCUMULATED IN THE ARCHAEOLOGICAL DEPOSIT
LS/EF/S+1	9		0– 200	200	678		
LS/EF/2	18	530± 90	200– 1000	800	690	1368	36,450
LS/EF/3	27		1000– 1950	950	429		
						442	11,800
LS/EF/4	38	2480± 60	1950– 3600	1650	432 (13/ 262/ 157)	262	7000
						219	5850
LS/EF/5	45		3600– 4950	1350	211 (62/149)	156	4150
LS/EF/6	55		4950– 6900	1950	262 (7/ 134/ 121)	134	3550
LS/EF/7	65	7950± 80	6900– 8050	1150	193 (16/ 161/ 16)	137	3650
						161	4300
LS/EF/8	73		8050– 8250	200	184		
LS/EF/9	82	8380±120	8250– 8550	300	206		
LS/EF/10	91		8550– 8800	250	278	870	23,200
LS/EF/11	103		8800– 9150	350	325 (186/139)		
LS/EF/12	109		9150– 9300	150	358		
LS/EF/13	120	9450±120	9300– 9600	300	333		
LS/EF/14	130		9600– 9800	200	36		
LS/EF/15	139		9800–10,000	200	38	904	24,100
LS/EF/16	150		10,000–10,200	200	42		
LS/EF/17	157		10,200–10,350	150	31		
LS/EF/18	169		10,350–10,600	250	32		
LS/EF/19	179		10,600–10,800	200	17		
LS/EF/20	189)		10,800–11,000	200	23	145	3850
LS/EF/21	206)	11,050±135	11,000–11,275	275	5	5	150
				11,275	4803	4803	128,050

Table A2/14 Sunny Shelter: number of artefacts accumulated in each millennium and estimated total number of artefacts accumulated in the archaeological deposit.

SPIT	AVERAGE SPIT DEPTH (cm)	C14 AGES (years BP)/ DIAGNOSTIC TRAIT	D/A DATES (years BP)	DURATION (years)	NO. OF ARTEFACTS	NO. OF ARTEFACTS ACCUMULATED IN EACH MILLENNIUM IN EXCAVATED PIT	ESTIMATED TOTAL NUMBER OF ARTEFACTS ACCUMULATED IN THE ARCHAEOLOGICAL DEPOSIT
SuS/T/S+1	5.5		0–350	350	26		
SuS/T/2	10.5		350–650	300	77		
SuS/T/3	15.0		650–920	270	97	231	16,150
SuS/T/4+5	22.5		920–1400	480	185 (31/154)		
SuS/T/6	26.0		1400–1600	200	274		
SuS/T/7	32.0	Bondi points	1600–1980	380	185	635	44,450
SuS/T/8	35.0		1980–2150	170	184 (22/162)		
SuS/T/9	39.5	↓	2150–2430	280	102		
SuS/T/10	45.0		2430–2800	370	80	361	25,250
SuS/T/11	50.0		2800–3150	350	29 (17/12)		
SuS/T/12	55.0)		3150–3500	350	8		
SuS/T/13	62.0)	3560±80	3500–3950	450	10	29	2150
SuS/T/14	69.0		3950–4400	450	3 (1/2)		
						2	150
				4440	1260	1260	88,150

Table A2/15 Uprooted Tree Shelter: number of artefacts accumulated in each millennium and estimated total number of artefacts accumulated in the archaeological deposit.

SPIT	AVERAGE SPIT DEPTH (cm)	C14 AGES (years BP)/ DIAGNOSTIC TRAIT	D/A DATES (years BP)	DURATION (years)	NO. OF ARTEFACTS	NO. OF ARTEFACTS ACCUMULATED IN EACH MILLENNIUM IN EXCAVATED PIT	ESTIMATED TOTAL NUMBER OF ARTEFACTS ACCUMULATED IN THE ARCHAEOLOGICAL DEPOSIT
UTS/T/S+1	4.0		0–200	200	52		
UTS/T/2	10.5		200–600	400	79		
UTS/T/3	17.0		600–1000	400	207	338	12,050
UTS/T/4	21.0		1000–1300	300	187		
UTS/T/5	26.5		1300–1600	300	107		
UTS/T/6	31.5		1600–2000	400	72	366	13,050
UTS/T/7	37.5	↑	2000–2400	400	40		
UTS/T/8	42.5	Qz predom	2400–2800	400	18	66	2,350
UTS/T/9	47.0	FGS predom	2800–3700	900	34 (8/26)		
		↓				36	1,300
UTS/T/10	53.0		3700–4650	950	30 (10/20)		
						32	1150
UTS/T/11	58.0		4650–5500	850	27 (12/15)		
						23	800
UTS/T/12	62.5		5500–6200	700	11 (8/3)		
						8	300
UTS/T/13	68.0		6200–7200	1000	7 (5/2)		
UTS/T/14	73.5		7200–8000	800	3	5	200
UTS/T/15	78.5	8430±130	8000–8800	800	1	1	50
UTS/T/16	83.0				0		
UTS/T/17	91.5				0		
UTS/T/18	110.5				0		
				8800	875	875	31,250

Table A2/16 White Figure Shelter: number of artefacts accumulated in each millennium and estimated total number of artefacts accumulated in the archaeological deposit. [1] +69 represents loading for artefacts that may have been overlooked in field retrieval — see comments in Chapter 5, Observer Bias, Excavation Results.

SPIT	AVERAGE SPIT DEPTH (cm)	C14 AGES (years BP)/ DIAGNOSTIC TRAIT	D/A DATES (years BP)	DURATION (years)	NO. OF ARTEFACTS	NO. OF ARTEFACTS ACCUMULATED IN EACH MILLENNIUM IN EXCAVATED PIT	ESTIMATED TOTAL NUMBER OF ARTEFACTS ACCUMULATED IN THE ARCHAEOLOGICAL DEPOSIT
WF/T/S+1	3.0		0– 375	375	35		
WF/T/2	6.0		375– 775	400	33	119 + 69[1] = 187	6000
WF/T/3	9.0		775–1150	375	83 (50/33)		
WF/T/4	12.5		1150–1600	450	254	537	17,200
WF/T/5	19.0	Bondi points	1600–2250	650	406 (250/156)		
WF/T/6	24.5	Qz predom	2250–2800	550	195	361	11,550
WF/T/7	30.0	FGS predom	2800–4150	1350	65 (10/		
					48/	48	1550
					7)		
WF/T/8	38.5)	5230±70	4150–6000	1850	13)	14	450
WF/T/9	52.0)				3) (7/9)		
						9	300
				6000	1087 +69	1156	37,050

Table A2/17 Excavated archaeological deposits where estimated duration is less than 1000 years: number of artefacts accumulated in each millennium/square and estimated total number accumulated in the archaeological deposits. [1] See notes at beginning of this appendix for basis of calculations.

SITE NAME	AV. BASAL DEPTH OF ARCH.DEP. (cm)	RADIO-CARBON AGE (years BP)	ESTIMATED DURATION OF HABITATION[1]	NO OF ARTEFACTS	NO OF ARTEFACTS ACCUMULATED IN EACH MILLENNIUM IN EXCAVATED PIT	ESTIMATED TOTAL NUMBER OF ARTEFACTS ACCUMULATED IN THE ARCHAEOLOGICAL DEPOSIT
Anadara Shelter	22.5		610	20	20	1850
Geebung Shelter	5.0		400	8	8	400
Low Frontage Shelter	16.0		900	6	6	300
McPherson Shelter	12.0		950	23	23	1600
Mangrove Mansions Shelter	12.0		300	13	13	3250
One Tooth Shelter	21.5	350±40	850	8	8	750
Ti-tree Shelter	15.0	490±50	750	11	11	500
Venus Shelter	21.0	560±50	830	21	21	700
Wolloby Gully Shelter	15.0	400±60	<400	9	9	2250

APPENDIX 3

The Upper Mangrove Creek catchment — random sampling units

Faunal remains

Part 1.   Upper Mangrove Creek catchment. Native animal taxa identified in faunal assemblages from the archaeological deposits.

Part 2.   Faunal remains from archaeological sites in the Mangrove Creek catchment — report no. 3 . The random sampling units. Ken Aplin, 1985.

Part 3.   Extracts from: Faunal remains from archaeological sites in the Mangrove Creek catchment. A report to NPWS of NSW. Ken Aplin, 1981.

Part 4.   Report on analysis of hair samples from four deposits in the Upper Mangrove Creek catchment. Barbara Triggs, 2002.

PART 1

Upper Mangrove Creek catchment. Native animal taxa identified in faunal assemblages from the archaeological deposits[1].

A: MAMMALS

ACROBATIDAE	*Acrobates pygmaeus*	Feathertail glider, pygmy glider
BURRAMYIDAE	*Cercartetus nanus*	Eastern pygmy-possum
CANIDAE	*Canis lupus dingo*	Dingo
DASYURIDAE	*Antechinus flavipes*	Yellow-footed antechinus
	Antechinus stuartii	Brown antechinus
	Antechinus swainsonii	Dusky antechinus
	Dasyurus maculatus	Spotted-tailed quoll, tiger cat
	Dasyurus sp.	Quoll, native cat, tiger cat
MACROPODIDAE	Large macropodid	Kangaroo or euro
	Macropus robustus	Euro / common wallaroo
	Macropus giganteus	Eastern grey kangaroo
	Medium macropodid	Wallaby
	Macropus rufogriseus	Red-necked wallaby
	Wallabia bicolor	Swamp wallaby
	Small macropodid	Wallaby or pademelon
	Petrogale penicillata	Brush-tailed rock wallaby
	Thylogale sp.	Pademelon
MICROCHIROPTERA	Microbats	
MURIDAE	*Pseudomys oralis*	Hastings River mouse
	Pseudomys novaehollandiae	New Holland mouse
	Rattus fuscipes	Bush rat
	Rattus lutreolus	Swamp rat
ORNITHORHYNCHIDAE	*Ornithorhynchus anatinus*	Platypus
PERAMELIDAE	*Isoodon* sp. (probably *I. obesulus*)	Bandicoot (southern bandicoot, short-nosed bandicoot)
	Perameles nasuta	Long-nosed bandicoot
PETAURIDAE	*Petaurus australis*	Yellow-bellied glider
	Petaurus breviceps	Sugar glider
	Petaurus sp.	Lesser gliding possum
PHALANGERIDAE	*Trichosurus vulpecula*	Common brushtail possum
PHASCOLARCTIDAE	*Phascolarctus cinereus*	Koala

---

[1] Includes species found in catchment sites outside the random sampling units, e.g., Mussel and Deep Creek Shelters. Scientific names for mammals according to Strahan 2000; and for reptiles according to Cogger 2000.

POTOROIDAE	*Bettongia gaimardi*	Eastern or Tasmanian bettong
	Potorous tridactylus	Long-nosed potoroo
	Potorous sp.	Potoroo
PSEUDOCHEIRIDAE	*Petauroides volans*	Greater glider
	Pseudocheirus peregrinus	Common ringtail possum
PTEROPODIDAE	*Pteropus scapulatus*	Little red flying-fox
TACHYGLOSSIDAE	*Tachyglossus aculeatus*	Short-beaked echidna
VOMBATIDAE	*Vombatus ursinus*	Common wombat

B: REPTILES
LACERTILIA

Varanidae	*Varanus* sp.	Goanna, monitor
Agamidae	Unidentified	Dragon
Scincidae	(e.g., *Egernia* sp.)	Skink
	Medium lizard	
	Unsized lizard	

OPHIDIA

Boidae	Unidentified	Python
Elapidae	Unidentified	Front-fanged snake (venomous)
	Medium snake	
	Small snake	
	Unsized snake	

C: BIRDS

Casuariidae	cf. *Dromaius novaehollandiae*	Emu
	Medium-sized bird	
	Unidentified bird	

D: FROGS AND FISH

ANURA	Frog	
TELEOST	Bony fish, unidentified	

E: INVERTEBRATES — Molluscs and Crustacea

HYRIIDAE	possibly *Velesunio ambiguus*, *Hyridella australis* and/or *H. depressa*	Freshwater mussel
ARCIDAE	*Anadara trapezia*	Sydney cockle
OSTREIDAE	*Saccostrea glomerata* (prev. *S.commercialis*)	Rock oyster
GASTROPODA	Unidentified terrestrial landsnail	
PARASTACIDAE	possibly *Euastacus australasiensis*, *E. nobilis* and/or *E. spinifer*	Yabby/freshwater crayfish

F: UNIDENTIFIED FAUNAL REMAINS
Bone fragments not assigned to specific faunal category due to small size and/or lack of diagnostic features.

PART 2

Faunal remains from archaeological sites in the Mangrove Creek catchment — report no. 3. The random sampling units.

by Ken Aplin 1985

General comments

Preservation

On average, this series of assemblages appears to be significantly better preserved than those from Upper Mangrove Creek sites previously analysed (Aplin 1981; Aplin and Gollan 1982). Three sites containing archaeological material, and one with purely non-archaeological bone, stand out as being especially well-preserved, and thus of particular promise for further work. These are:

Archaeological sites:	White Figure
	Dingo (upper levels)
	Caramel Wave
Non-archaeological sites:	Two Moths

In each of these sites, however, bone densities are relatively low compared with the major faunal assemblages in the catchment (Loggers, Mussel and Deep Creek Shelters). This is particularly noteworthy given the somewhat better preservation of the present series. Densities of invertebrate taxa, by contrast, appear to be somewhat higher on average; this presumably reflects the better preservation. Given the relatively low densities of bone in these sites, I estimate that, in order to obtain adequate faunal samples for detailed analysis, it would be necessary to excavate between 5 and 10 sq m of each deposit.

Origin of the remains

The fact that so many of the present series of sites contain non-archaeological faunal remains is probably partly explicable in terms of the generally good preservation. However, other factors, such as the probable lower levels of human activity in the sites, might also be at play.

Faunal composition

All of the taxa identified in the present series of sites are either:

(a)   known as living animals in the Mangrove Creek area; or

(b)   have previously been identified in the recent archaeological materials.

Two mammalian taxa new to the recorded prehistoric fauna are the microchiropteran bat (or bats), and the feathertail glider, *Acrobates pygmaeus*. As indicated in the 'comments' on Wolloby Gully Shelter, the recovery of a medium-sized bird from that site is of interest; I should be able to more clearly identify this specimen.

Among the invertebrate remains, features of interest are:

(1)   the regular occurrence of 'yabbies' in the faunas; and

(2)   the presence of *Anadara* shell fragments in many sites.

As indicated in the individual assemblage reports, the yabby remains, wherever they occur, appear to derive from human activities. Although their regular occurrence might be partly a reflection of the better preservation, I suspect that this is not the full story. However, without some basic information about the habitat preferences of these animals in the catchment, it is difficult to suggest any 'environmental' reason for their abundance. What I can say is that elsewhere in NSW (Capertee region) I have found these 'yabbies' (probably parastacid freshwater crayfish) occur primarily in fast-flowing, clear water. Could it be that the present series of sites are all located higher in the catchment than the previous ones?

With regard to the *Anadara* shell, it is my impression that the pieces recovered are derived mostly from large shells, and that these are almost always burnt. To me, at least, it would seem highly probable that the *Anadara* fragments represent bits of tools of some kind — the firing possibly used to harden the shell. Unfortunately for that theory, none of the pieces shows obvious 'use-damage'. But then, most pieces are either very small fragments only OR are too corroded to tell one way or the other. Certainly, *Anadara* would never have occurred locally in the Upper Mangrove Creek catchment and must have been brought up some distance from the estuarine regions.

Methods of analysis and data presentation

The assemblages have been analysed according to the methods developed during the earlier studies (Aplin 1981; Aplin and Gollan 1982); these should be consulted for further details. The tables presented below employ the following conventions:

Table *.1   Burning categories abbreviated as follows:
> U — unburnt bones
> B — burnt bones
> C — calcined bone

Shell types as follows:
> B — freshwater bivalve, possibly *Velesunio ambiguus*, *Hyridella australis* and/or *H. depressa*
> A — estuarine bivalve, *Anadara trapezia*, Sydney cockle
> T — terrestrial snail

All weights are presented in grams and to nearest 0.1g.

Table *.2   Burning status indicated in brackets and abbreviated as for Table *.1. Other abbreviations as follows:
> L   left side
> B   right side
> M (e.g. M4-5)   molar

Individual assemblage reports

Anadara (AS)
Several bone fragments from the surface of this deposit bear tooth-marks and other damage which suggest their introduction by a large carnivore, probably a dog. The excavated material, however, is typically archaeological in character (Tables A3-2/1 and A3-2/2).

Bird Tracks (BT)
This small but well-preserved assemblage appears to contain both archaeological and non-archaeological material (Tables A3-2/1 and A3-2/2). The non-archaeological component makes up the bulk of the assemblage, and probably accounts for all of the smaller mammal and lower vertebrate remains. This material is consistent in general character with an owl-pellet origin.

An archaeological component is inferred from the presence of two heavily burned specimens including the swamp wallaby tooth.

Table A3-2/1 Summary of faunal assemblage by excavation unit for small assemblages. See separate tables for Dingo, Two Moths and White Figure. Weights and counts exclude hairs and feathers listed in Table A3-2/2.

PROVENANCE	BONE		BURNING			SHELL		SHELL TYPE			YABBY	
	WT (g)	NO	U	B	C	WT (g)	NO.	B	A	T	WT (g)	NO.
Anadara												
AS/SurfGen	18.0	5	5									
AS/T1/2	2.2	2	2									
AS/T2/1	0.3	1		1								
Totals	20.5	8	7	1								
Bird Tracks												
BT/T/1	0.4	3	3									
BT/T/2	1.4	11	10	1								
BT/T/3	0.2	1	1									
Totals	2.0	15										
Boronia												
BoS/SurfGen						4.3	1	✻				
Caramel Wave												
CW/SurfGen						4.2	1	✻				
CW/T1/2	0.1	1	1									
CW/T1/30B	0.8	1		1								
CW/T1/3P	2.3	10	2	6	2						0.4	21
CW/T1/4	0.1	1			1						0.1	1
CW/T1/5	0.1	1		1								
CW/T2/1	0.5	1	1									
CW/T2/2	0.4	1		1								
CW/T2/3	0.5	4			4	0.1	2	✻				
Totals	4.8	20	4	9	7	4.3	3				0.5	22
Delight												
DeS/Tb/1	0.1	1	1									
Elngarrah												
ES/Tb/1	0.1	1	1									
ES/Td/1	0.1	1	1									
ES/Td/2						0.1	1	✻				
Totals	0.2	2	2			0.1	1					
Elongated Figure												
EF/T/2	0.3	5	5									
Emu Tracks 2												
ET2/T2a/WOB						0.1	5	✻				
ET2/T2a/1						0.1	1	✻				
ET2/T2b/1						0.7	1		✻			
Totals						0.9	7					
Harris Gully												
HG/SurfGen	0.3	1	1									
HG/T/1						0.1	1			✻		
HG/T/2	0.1	3			3							
Totals	0.4	4				0.1	1					
Kangaroo and Echidna												
KE/T2a/1	0.3	1		1								
KE/T2d/2						1.0	2	✻				
Totals	0.3	1		1		1.0	2	✻				

Table A3-2/1 (Continued)

PROVENANCE	BONE WT (g)	NO.	BURNING U	B	C	SHELL WT (g)	NO.	SHELL TYPE B	A	T	YABBY WT (g)	NO.
McPherson												
McP/SurfGen	1.1	1	1									
Mangrove Mansions												
MM/T1/1	0.2	2	2									
MM/T1/2	1.1	30	23	4		0.1	1	*				
MM/T1/3	4.0	19	8	11								
MM/T1/4	0.6	4	2	2								
Totals	5.9	55	35	17		0.1	1	*				
Moss Gully												
MG/T/3						0.1	1			*		
One Tooth												
SurfGen	0.3	1	1									
OT/T/1	12.7	6	3	2	1	2.2	7	*				
OT/T/2	0.9	20	3	4	13	0.1	3	*				
OT/T/3	0.2	3	2		2	0.1	2		*			
Totals	14.1	30	8	6	16	2.4	12					
Uprooted Tree												
UTS/Tb/1						0.2	1		*			
UTS/Tb/7	0.1	1?			1?							
Totals	0.1	1?			1?	0.2	1					
Wolloby Gully												
WoG/Ta/2	0.2	2	1		1						0.1	1
WoG/Ta/3	3.7	13	4	4	5	0.6	7	*				
WoG/Ta/4	0.1	3	1		2						0.1	1
Totals	4.0	18				0.6	7				0.2	2

Table A3-2/2 Taxonomically diagnostic faunal remains listed by site and excavation unit for small assemblages.

PROVENANCE	ANIMAL	SKELETAL ELEMENT	BURNING STATE
Anadara			
AS/SurfGen	medium-sized macropodid	R. maxilla/palatine/pterygoid fragments	U
		caudal vertebra; tooth-marked	U
		femur shaft fragment; tooth-marked	U
AS/T2/1	small macropodid	tibial shaft fragment	B
Bird Tracks			
BT/T/1	frog	sacral complex	U
	Perameles nasuta	R. maxilla with M2	U
		R. radius	U
BT/T/2	*Wallabia bicolor*	R. lower molar protolophid	B
	small macropodid	fibular shaft fragment (broken in two)	U
	murid	L. upper incisor	U
		ulna shaft fragment	U
		vertebra fragment	U
		calvarial fragment	U
	Rattus sp. cf. *fuscipes*	L. dentary	U
		R. dentary	U
	Cercartetus nanus	L. squamosal	U
BT/T/3	lizard	long bone fragment	U

Table A3–2/2 (Continued)

PROVENANCE	ANIMAL	SKELETAL ELEMENT	BURNING STATE
Caramel Wave			
CW/T1/3P	medium-sized macropodid	caudal vertebra fragment tooth-marked	U
CW/T1/5	small macropodid	R. mandibular condyle	B
Delight			
DeS/Tb/1	*Cercartetus nanus*	R. dentary	U
Elongated Figure			
EF/T/2	murid	tibial shaft fragment	U
		sacral fragment	U
	Isoodon sp.	R. squamosal + petrogal fragments	U
	bird	feather	
Kangaroo and Echidna			
KE/T2a/1	small macropodid	L. dentary fragment	B
Mangrove Mansions			
MM/T1/1	murid	humeral shaft fragment	U
	possum	pedal ungual	U
MMT1/2	medium-sized bird	distal tibiotarsal fragment	U
		2 x cervical vertebrae	U
	large possum	magnum	U
		metapodial	U
	possum?	manal ungual	U
	echidna	2 x quill	
	bird	feather	
MM/T1/3	peramelid	manal ungual and sheath	U
	small macropodid	tibial shaft fragment	B
		cuboid fragment	U
		L. lower molar (posterior; unerupted)	U
	medium-sized bird	distal tibiotarsus fragment	U
	bird	feather	
MM/T1/4	peramelid	tibial shaft fragment	U
One Tooth			
OT/SurfGen	medium-sized macropodid	R. lower incisor	U
	Petaurus sp. cf. *breviceps*	furred tail (not included in Table A3-2/1)	U
OT/T/1	small macropodid	femur shaft fragment	U
		fibular shaft fragment	C
	Isoodon sp.	R. lower molar 5	U
	murid	R. femur fragment	U
OT/T/2	small macropodid	pedal phalanx fragment	U
		L. upper molar fragment	B
Wolloby Gully			
WoG/Ta/3	snake	vertebra fragment	U
	large possum	R. maxilla fragment	B
	medium-sized bird	proximal humeral fragment	B
WoG/Ta/4	peramelid	distal femoral fragment	U

Boronia (BoS)

The single piece of freshwater bivalve from this site shows no sign of human modification, either through firing or use. However, the large size of the shell would seem to indicate human introduction (Table A3-2/1).

Caramel Wave (CW)

With the possible exception of the single, tooth-marked specimen from T1/3P, this assemblage appears to be of purely archaeological origin, including the abundant and uniformly burnt 'yabby' remains found in T1/3P and T1/4 (Tables A3-2/11 and A3-2/2). Preservation of the assemblage is relatively good throughout, though some deterioration with depth is evident. In the absence of strong evidence for differential preservation within the deposit, it seems likely that the concentration of faunal remains in T1/3P is due to a peak in human activity at that time.

As with the preceding site, the freshwater bivalve found on the surface, by virtue of its large size, is likely to be a human introduction.

Delight (DeS)

The solitary pygmy-possum jaw from this site displays a distinct tooth puncture on its lingual surface (Tables A3-2/1 and A3-2/2). The size of this puncture suggests a small species of Dasyurid or a brush-tailed phascogale (tuan), *Phascogale tapoatafa*, as the agent of introduction.

Dingo (DiS)

This assemblage also appears to be of dual origin, the two components in this case showing a spatial segregation in addition to distinct physical properties (Tables A3-2/3 and A3-2/4). The first component, concentrated in square Ta, comprises the unburnt and little fragmented remains of small mammals and frogs. This material most likely represents the remains of disaggregated owl pellets.

The second component, which is of probable archaeological origin, is spread more evenly between the two excavated squares. In contrast with the non-archaeological bone, this material is more thoroughly fragmented, is nearly always burnt to some degree, and is of larger prey species. Also of likely archaeological origin are the highly fragmented freshwater bivalve and *Anadara* materials, and the relatively abundant 'yabby' remains, virtually all of which show evidence of firing.

Preservation of both components is good throughout square Ta, and through spits 1 to 5 of square Tb. Material from Tb/6-7, by contrast, shows clear signs of post-depositional degradation; this probably accounts for the reduced quantities of shell and of 'yabby' in these spits. The sudden change in condition of the remains between Tb/5 and Tb/6 suggests some stratigraphic complexity at this level.

Table A3–2/3   Dingo Shelter: summary of faunal assemblage by excavation unit.

PROVENANCE	BONE		BURNING			SHELL		SHELL TYPE			YABBY	
	WT (g)	NO.	U	B	C	WT (g)	NO.	B	A	T	WT (g)	NO.
DiS/Ta/1	3.0	45	10	11	24	0.2	9	✳		✳	0.2	6
DiS/Ta/2	2.5	33	10	16	7	0.1	6	✳	✳	✳	0.1	7
DiS/Ta/3	4.7	45	9	19	17	0.9	6	✳		✳	0.4	14
DiS/Ta/4	0.1	10	3	4	3	0.1	5	✳			0.1	7
DiS/Ta/Swpgs	0.1	1		1		0.1	1			✳	0.1	2
DiS/Tb/Surf	2.4	5	5			1.5	2	✳		✳	0.1	2
DiS/Tb/1	0.6	8	1	4	3	0.1	3	✳		✳	0.1	3
DiS/Tb/2Upr	1.2	13	2	7	4	0.1	1	✳			0.1	1
DiS/Tb/2Upr(SWC)	0.6	6	2	4		0.1	3	✳		✳	0.1	3
DiS/Tb/2LwrPB	0.6	9		4	5	0.3	12	✳			0.1	13
DiS/Tb/3GB	1.1	10		8	2						0.1	11
DiS/Tb/3PB(Nth)	7.4	62	6	48	8	0.4	3	✳			0.4	15

Table A3–2/3 (Continued)

PROVENANCE	BONE		BURNING			SHELL		SHELL TYPE			YABBY	
	WT (g)	NO.	U	B	C	WT (g)	NO.	B	A	T	WT (g)	NO.
DiS/Tb/3LwrPB	1.4	21	2	14	5	0.6	4	*	*		0.8	30
DiS/Tb/4GB	2.2	17	1	11	5	0.1	5	*			0.1	2
DiS/Tb/4GBSth	4.0	61	19	28	14	0.4	15	*			0.3	13
DiS/Tb/5	3.7	8		7	1	0.5	21	*			0.1	2
DiS/Tb/6	0.9	17		13	4						0.5	20
DiS/Tb/7	1.4	9		3	6							
DiS/Tb/8	1.6	17		1	16							
DiS/Tb/Swpgs	0.1	2		2								
Totals	39.6	399				5.5	96				3.7	152

Table A3–2/4 Dingo Shelter: taxonomically diagnostic faunal remains listed by excavation unit.

PROVENANCE	ANIMAL	SKELETAL ELEMENT	BURNING STATE
DiS/Ta/1	medium-sized snake	rib fragment	B
	murid	cervical vertebra	U
		thoracic vertebra	U
		caudal vertebra	U
	bandicoot	scapular fragment	U
DiS/Ta/2	frog	cranial fragment	U
		long bone fragment	U
	murid	lumbar vertebra	U
	macropodid	caudal vertebra fragment	B
DiS/Ta/3	medium-sized macropodid	R. dentary fragment	B
	Petaurus australis/Petauroides volans	ulna shaft	U
DiS/Tb/Surf	murid	L. femur	U
	medium-sized macropodid	L. metatarsal V fragment	U
DiS/Tb/1	small macropodid	manal ungual	B
DiS/Tb/3PB(Nth)	large macropodid	L. lower incisor fragment	B
	medium-sized macropodid	metatarsal IV fragment	B
		astragalar fragment	B
		metatarsal IV distal epip.	B
DiS/Tb/3LwrPB	medium-sized/large macropodid	lower incisor fragment	B
DiS/Tb/4GB	pseudocheirine	R. dentary with teeth	B
DiS/Tb/4GB(Sth)	macropodid	lower incisor fragment	U
DiS/Tb/5	small/medium-sized macropodid	R. metatarsal V fragment	B
DiS/Tb/6	small macropodid	lower incisor fragment	B
DiS/Tb/7	peramelid	L. maxilla fragment	B
DiS/Tb/8	small macropodid	cuboid fragment	B

Elngarrah (ES)

Both bone fragments from this site display a type of surface polishing and rounding of fracture edge that is often seen in material derived from dog faeces. The small fragment of freshwater bivalve from Td/2 likewise shows no human modification, and could not by itself be regarded as evidence of human activity at the site (Table A3-2/1).

Elongated Figure (EF)
This small assemblage does not appear to contain any humanly derived material (Tables A3-2/1 and A3-2/2). Although the presence of small mammals might suggest an owl-pellet origin, the occurrence of one non-diagnostic fragment showing gastric corrosion suggests that at least some of the material derives from dog faeces.

Emu Tracks 2 (ET2)
All specimens from this site are unburnt and lack signs of human utilisation (Tables A3-2/1 and A3-2/2). The *Anadara* fragment in spit T2b/1, however, must presumably be a human introduction.

Harris Gully (HG)
The three calcined bone fragments from T/2 are all highly degraded, suggesting a high rate of faunal decay in this site (Table A3-2/1). This in turn makes it seem unlikely that either the unburnt bone from the surface of the site or the snail shell from T/1 are of archaeological vintage.

Kangaroo and Echidna (KE)
The solitary macropodid jaw recovered from this site is thoroughly burnt and hence presumably derives from human activity (Tables A3-2/1 and A3-2/2). Both shell fragments from T2d/2 are unburnt however, and are thus of equivocal status.

McPherson (McP)
The single non-diagnostic bone fragment from this site is not obviously derived from human activity (Table A3-2/1).

Mangrove Mansions (MM)
This assemblage is also of probable multiple origin, some fragments showing clear gastric corrosion, and others showing the thorough burning and fine fragmentation of archaeological remains (Tables A3-2/1 and A3-2/2). Because of the potentially large overlap in prey species between dog and human, it is not possible on present evidence to estimate the contribution of each component in this assemblage.

Preservation of both components is good throughout. Given this fact, the relative paucity of shell and the absence of 'yabby' are probably both 'original' features of the assemblage.

Moss Gully (MG)
The single unburnt terrestrial snail fragment from this site is almost certainly not of human derivation (Table A3-2/1).

One Tooth (OT)
This small assemblage most likely includes two components, a probable non-archaeological component confined to the surface and spit 1, and an archaeological component which extends through spits 1 to 3 (Tables A3-2/1 and A3-2/2). The recovery of a furred tail of a glider (*Petaurus* sp.) from the surface suggests the continued use of the site by a raptor, probably an owl.

Preservation of the archaeological material is relatively good in spit 1, but becomes progressively worse with depth. The small quantities of shell, and the absence of 'yabby' from the site, may thus both be due to post-depositional factors.

Two Moths (TMS)

With the possible exception of the large freshwater bivalve fragment in T/5, this assemblage appears to be entirely non-archaeological in origin (Tables A3-2/5 and A3-2/6). Even so, the assemblage appears complex, some material (e.g., the bats) being of likely pelletal origin, yet other specimens showing clear signs of gastric corrosion. These latter specimens occur at all levels in the site, but appear particularly common below spit T/5. Other material again (hairs and juvenile skeletal remains) would seem to derive from recent usage of the site by wombats.

Preservation is excellent throughout the deposit, suggesting very dry conditions. To date, Two Moths represents the only occurrence of a stratified and well-preserved micro-fauna in the Mangrove Creek area. As such, the site could well be of considerable value from a palaeo-ecological viewpoint. However, because of the relatively low density of remains, it would probably be necessary to excavate 5 sq m or more to ensure an adequate sample of diagnostic remains for detailed analysis.

Table A3-2/5   Two Moths: summary of faunal assemblage by excavation unit (totals exclude feathers and hairs).

PROVENANCE	BONE		BURNING STATE			SHELL		SHELL TYPE			YABBY	
	WT (g)	NO.	U	B	C	WT (g)	NO.	B	A	T	WT (g)	NO.
TMS/T/1	0.2	8	8			0.1	1			*		
TMS/T/2	1.4	14	14									
TMS/T/4	0.1	1	1									
TMS/T/5	0.9	18	18			7.1	1	*				
TMS/T/6	0.6	16	16									
TMS/T/7	0.6	15	15									
TMS/T/8	0.5	9	9									
TMS/T/9	0.1	3	3									
Totals	4.4	84				7.2	2					

Table A3-2/6   Two Moths: taxonomically diagnostic faunal remains listed by excavation unit.

PROVENANCE	ANIMAL	SKELETAL ELEMENTS	BURNING STATE
TMS/T/1	bird	feathers	
	large mammal (wombat?)	numerous hairs	
	murid	caudal vertebra	U
		2 x thoracic vertebrae	U
	peramelid	pubic symphysis	U
	lizard	long bone shaft	U
TMS/T/2	bird	feathers	
	large mammal (wombat?)	hair	
	microchiropteran bat	manal phalanx	U
	murid	thoracic vertebra	U
	Vombatus ursinus	distal radial epip.	U
		distal ulna epip.	U
TMS/T/4	murid	L. lower incisor fragment	U
TMS/T/5	*Potorous* sp.	L. lower incisor	U
	small dasyurid	L. dentary fragment	U
	Pseudomys oralis	L. maxilla with M1-3	U
	murid	L. ulna	U
	frog	tibial shaft	U

Table A3-2/6 (Continued)

PROVENANCE	ANIMAL	SKELETAL ELEMENTS	BURNING STATE
TMS/T/6	murid	L. premaxilla	U
		humeral prox. epip.	U
	microchiropteran bat	pelvic girdle	U
	small dasyurid	L. dentary fragment	U
		L. petrosal	U
		R. humeral shaft	U
		L. humeral shaft	U
	Acrobates pygmaeus	R. maxilla with P3-M3	U
TMS/T/7	small snake	vertebra	U
	murid	R. ulna	U
		axis vertebra	U
		atlas vertebra	U
	Pseudomys oralis	occipital complex	U
	small dasyurid	L. dentary with M1	U
		R. humerus	U
		R. ulna	U
	microchiropteran bat	tibial shaft fragment	U
		R. dentary with M2-3	U
TMS/T/8	small dasyurid	L. femur fragment	U
		lumbar vertebra	U
	murid	caudal vertebra	U
	Pseudomys oralis	R. dentary with M1-3	U

Uprooted Tree (UTS)

The single *Anadara* fragment from this site is presumably a human introduction; it is from a large, thick-shelled example, is highly burnt and poorly preserved (Table A3-2/1). The listed specimen from Tb/7 is likewise very highly degraded and is only tentatively identified as calcined bone.

White Figure (WF)

This assemblage, which represents a time period of some 5000 years, is the largest and most informative of the present series (Tables A3-2/7 and A3-2/8). The physical condition of the bone varies from moderately good in the upper four spits to badly corroded below this point. Shell and 'yabby' remains occur in reasonable quantities through the upper levels of the deposit, though much of this material is burnt or calcined, and poorly preserved.

Post-depositional degradation of the assemblage would thus appear to be advanced, even in the upper levels, and is markedly so in the lower levels of the deposit. This factor is probably sufficient to account for the low densities of bone and the virtual absence of shell or 'yabby' remains from the lower half of the deposit.

Comparison of the 'in field' versus 'laboratory' sorted samples for spits 3–6 indicates that approximately half of the bone, shell and 'yabby' remains, by weight, was overlooked during 'in field' sorting. All faunal quantities for Ta/1-2 and Tb/1-2 would thus need to be approximately doubled to bring them into line with data for the other spits. Not surprisingly, the 'in field' samples are also strongly biased toward the larger fragments of each faunal category.

Although the differences in sampling procedure make the evidence somewhat uncertain, it would appear from the available data that faunal densities were significantly lower in the surface context than at 10cm or so into the deposit. This does not appear to be due to preservational factors, but might conceivably reflect a continuation of sediment build-up over the 100 or more years since final abandonment of the sites by Aboriginal people.

In terms of taxonomic composition and general character, the White Figure assemblage is closely comparable with other 'archaeological' assemblages from the Mangrove Creek area. Special features of this assemblage include the relatively high abundance of *Potorous* sp. among the mammals, and the constant occurrence of the 'yabby' remains. Of these, the high abundance of *Potorous* sp. might suggest the proximity of the site to dense and relatively wet vegetation of the kind now found in the more sheltered portions of the upper catchment.

Wolloby Gully (WoG)

This small assemblage (Tables A3-2/1 and A3-2/2) probably derives solely from human occupation of the site. Preservation is relatively good throughout. The presence of a medium-sized bird in the assemblage is of interest in view of the poor representation of this group in the other Mangrove Creek sites. Further comparisons presently under way should result in a closer identification of this specimen.

Table A3–2/7 White Figure: summary of faunal assemblage by excavation unit (FS = field sort; LS = laboratory sort; Total = FS+LS; see Chapter 5).

PROVENANCE	BONE		BURNING STATE			SHELL		SHELL TYPE			YABBY	
	WT (g)	NO.	U	B	C	WT (g)	NO.	B	A	T	WT (g)	NO.
WF/Ta/1 FS = Total	0.4	8		1	7	0.4	4	*	*		0.1	2
WF/Ta/2 FS = Total	2.7	29	1	8	20	0.3	4	*	*		0.1	2
WF/Ta/3 FS	6.7	43	1	15	27	0.4	14	*	*	*		
WF/Ta/3 LS	6.7	188	8	45	135	0.5	24	*	*	*	0.2	24
WF/Ta/3 Total	13.4	231	9	60	162	0.9	38	*	*	*	0.2	24
WF/Ta/4 FS	6.9	55		24	31	0.4	5	*			0.1	2
WF/Ta/4 LS	7.2	218	12	38	168	0.2	13	*			0.1	11
WF/Ta/4 Total	14.1	273	12	62	199	0.6	18	*			0.2	13
WF/Ta/5 FS	4.7	17	1	7	9	0.8	4	*	*		0.1	2
WF/Ta/5 LS	2.1	58		5	53							
WF/Ta/5 Total	6.8	75	1	12	62	0.8	4	*	*		0.1	2
WF/Ta/6 FS	0.1	1			1							
WF/Ta/6 LS	0.2	8		3	5							
WF/Ta/6 Total	0.3	9		3	6							
WF/Tb/Surf	0.1	1			1							
WF/Tb/1 FS = Total	2.7	34		4	30	0.3	4	*	*		0.1	2
WF/Tb/2 FS = Total	5.9	57	4	13	40	1.2	10	*			0.1	3
WF/Tb/3 FS	2.8	27	2	8	17	0.2	10	*	*			
WF/Tb/3 LS	3.1	95	4	14	77	0.1	4	*			0.1	10
WF/Tb/3 Total	5.9	122	6	22	94	0.3	14	*			0.1	10
WF/Tb/4 FS	4.0	3+30	5	2+11	1+14	0.1	3	*				
WF/Tb/4 LS	3.9	126	5	19	102	0.1	3	*			0.1	2
WF/Tb/4 Total	7.9	159	10	32	117	0.2	6	*			0.1	2
WF/Tb/5 FS	0.4	2			2							
WF/Tb/5 LS	1.9	35		1	34						0.1	1
WF/Tb/5 Total	2.3	37		1	36						0.1	1
WF/Tb/6 FS = Total	0.2	5			5							
WF/Tb/7 FS = Total	0.1	1		1		0.1	1	*			0.1	1
Totals WF/Ta+Tb	62.8	1041				5.1	103				1.2	61

Table A3–2/8 White Figure: taxonomically diagnostic faunal remains listed by excavation unit.

PROVENANCE	ANIMAL	SKELETAL ELEMENT	BURNING STATE
WF/Ta/2	peramelid	L. tibial shaft	B
	small/medium-sized macropodid	petrosal fragment	B
		fibular shaft fragment	B
	possum?	clavicle fragment	B
WF/Ta/3	medium-sized/large macropodid	lower incisor fragment	B
	small macropodid	fibular shaft fragment	B
	pseudocheirine	L. dentary with M4-5	U
WF/Ta/3 FS	small/medium-sized macropodid	R. dentary fragment	C
	cf. *Potorous* sp.	L. petrosal fragment	C
		metatarsal IV fragment	C
	small macropodid	lower incisor fragment	B
		upper molar protoloph fragment	B
	peramelid	L. dentary fragment	B
	medium-sized snake	L. dentary fragment	B
WF/Ta/4	small/medium-sized macropodid	mandibular condyle	C
		lower incisor fragment	B
	small agamid	L. maxilla fragment	B
	medium-sized snake	R. dentary fragment	C
WF/Ta/4 FS	small/medium-sized macropodid	rib fragment	B
		lower molar fragment	U
	Potorous sp.	L. lower incisor fragment	C
		L. dentary fragment	C
	small dasyurid	R. dentary fragment	U
	medium-sized lizard	articular fragment	C
	medium-sized snake	vertebra fragment	C
WF/Ta/5 FS	small/medium-sized macropodid	metatarsal IV fragment	C
WF/Tb/2	medium-sized macropodid	L. metatarsal IV fragment	B
WF/Tb/3	small macropodid	fibular shaft fragment	C
WF/Tb/3 FS	medium-sized snake	vertebra fragment	C
WF/Tb/4 FS	*Potorous* sp.	posterior molar fragment	B
	peramelid	L. maxilla fragment	B
	small/medium-sized macropodid	L. upper molar fragment	B
		lower incisor fragment	B

References

Aplin, K. 1981. Faunal Remains from Archaeological Sites in Mangrove Creek Catchment. Appendix 4 in V. Attenbrow, Mangrove Creek Dam Salvage Excavation Project — Volume 2. Unpublished report to National Parks & Wildlife Service of NSW on behalf of Department of Public Works of NSW.

Aplin, K. and K. Gollan. 1982. Faunal Remains from Archaeological Sites in the Mangrove Creek Catchment 2: The Deep Creek Fauna. Appendix 3 in V. Attenbrow, Archaeological Investigation of Deep Creek Shelter, Mangrove Creek Dam. Unpublished report to National Parks & Wildlife Service of NSW on behalf of Department of Public Works of NSW.

PART 3

Extracts from:
Faunal remains from archaeological sites in the Mangrove Creek catchment. A report to National Parks & Wildlife Service of NSW.

Appendix 4 in V. Attenbrow 1981, Mangrove Creek Dam Salvage Excavation Project, Volume 2.

by Ken Aplin 1981

Details for Loggers, Black Hands and Geebung Shelters

Loggers (LS)

While faunal remains are preserved throughout the upper metre of the deposit, more than 95% by weight are derived from the first 50cm and thereby represent only a short part of the total sequence.

On the basis of changes within the stone artefact assemblage, Attenbrow divides the sequence into a total of six cultural levels. Only levels I-V produced faunal remains (Table A3-3/2).

Table A3–3/1 Loggers, Black Hands and Geebung: total number and weight of faunal remains (from Aplin 1981: Table 1).

| | BONE | | | SHELL – TOTAL | |
| | TOTAL | | IDENTIFIED | | |
SITE NAME	NO.	WT (g)	NO.	NO.	WT (g)
Loggers Shelter	9633	1317.7	395	211	20.1
Black Hands	451	55.0	12	1	0.1
Geebung Shelter	1	0.1	–	–	0.1

Fauna

Faunal remains were recovered from all squares excavated but did not extend below 90cm into the deposit (Tables A3-3/2 and A3-3/3). Figure A3–3/1 summarises variations in the density and physical condition of faunal materials found along the transect from square A inside the dripline, to square F near the outward limit of the deposit.

Table A3–3/2 Loggers Shelter: bone from all squares (from Aplin 1981: Table 2).

| ANALYTICAL UNIT | UNBURNT | | BURNT | | TOTAL | |
	NO.	WT (g)	NO.	WT (g)	NO.	WT (g)
LS/I	576	150.9	6641	903.4	7217	1054.3
LS/II	80	10.5	1920	199.4	2000	210.1
LS/III	5	0.3	218	19.6	223	19.9
LS/IV	-	-	50	4.7	50	4.7
LS/V	-	-	3	0.2	3	0.2

Table A3–3/3   Loggers Shelter: shell from all squares (from Aplin 1981: Table 3).

ANALYTICAL UNIT	HYRIIDAE		ANADARA TRAPEZIA		TERRESTRIAL GASTROPODS	
	NO.	WT (g)	NO.	WT (g)	NO.	WT (g)
LS/I	185	12.8	9	5.9	8	0.5
LS/II	8	0.8				
LS/III	1	0.1				

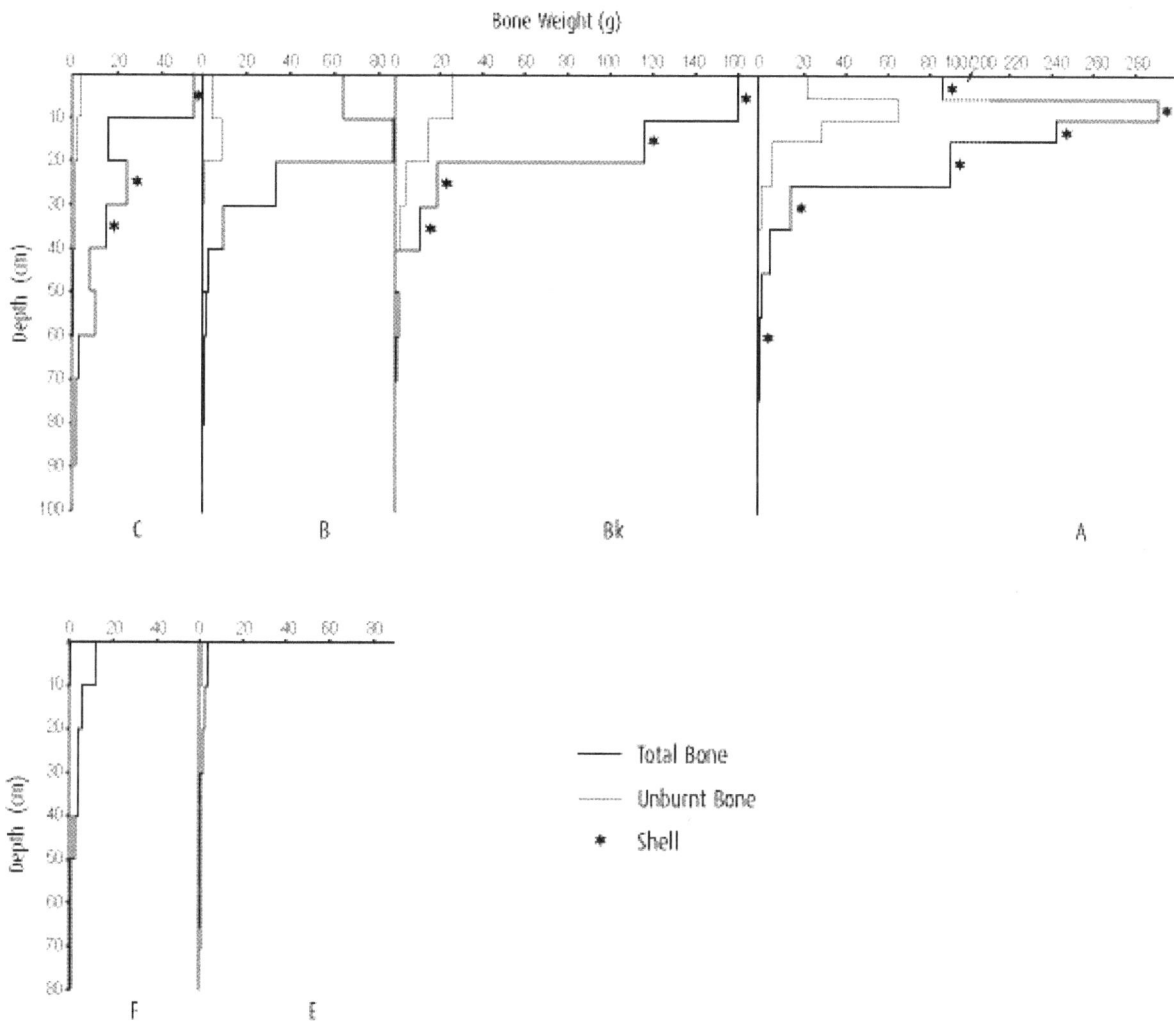

Figure A3–3/1 Loggers Shelter: distribution of bone and shell according to square and depth. Bone weights are adjusted to a standard volume (10cm spit) and are, therefore, relative density values.

Post-depositional history

A large part of the observed variation can be attributed to post-depositional alteration of the assemblage. This can be best described in terms of two components — the vertical decay profile and spatial variations of this profile.

The decay profile

The following series of changes in the composition of the assemblage with depth reflect the differential rate of decay of the component materials and, in combination, comprise the decay profile of the deposit.

1. Where preserved at all, shell and crustacean exoskeleton are confined to the upper levels of the profile.
2. Bone density decreases with depth, with unburnt bone disappearing more rapidly than burnt bone.

Additional features of the decay profile which are not represented in Figure A3–3/1, are:

3. lightly burnt bone decays and disappears more rapidly than calcined bone. As a result, calcined bone forms a progressively greater proportion of the total bone with depth.
4. the average weight of bone fragments shows a gradual decline with depth as remaining fragments are reduced in size by the decay process.

The overall regularity with which these changes take place in each square is suggestive evidence that, at least for the upper part of the deposit, the quantity of bone originally deposited in the site did not fluctuate markedly over time. Attenbrow describes a similar lack of change in the density of stone artefacts through the upper metre of the deposit.

Spatial variation

The faunal remains show as much variation in density and character along the spatial transect as down the decay profile. These variations clearly reflect the relative degree of exposure of the various squares.

Squares A and Bk

These squares lie wholly (A) or partly (Bk) inside the dripline of the shelter and have produced a large proportion of the total faunal assemblage. The greater part of this concentration is contained within the upper 25cm of the profile, where moderate quantities of shell and high densities of bone were encountered. The bone from these levels is relatively well preserved and includes a high proportion of unburnt and lightly burnt remains. Bone density decreases slightly through these levels but undergoes a dramatic decline about 20cm into the deposit. At this depth, the organic matter content also declines rapidly and the deposit takes on a mottled appearance. Below this point the surviving bone is virtually all calcined and bone densities fall more gradually.

Squares B and C

Squares B and C are positioned outside the dripline, but in the central, slightly mounded area of the deposit. Shell was not recovered from square B but a few fragments from square C attest to its former presence in this part of the site. Bone is considerably less abundant in the upper levels of these squares than at the same depth inside the dripline, but nevertheless, includes a reasonable proportion of unburnt and lightly burnt remains. As in squares A and Bk, these components have all but disappeared within 20cm of the surface, leaving only calcined remains to continue for a further 70cm into the deposit.

Squares E and F

These squares occupy a comparable position relative to the dripline as squares B and C. Shell is entirely absent from both squares and, while bone is preserved to similar depth as elsewhere in the site, it is present at uniformly low densities and contains a high proportion of calcined remains.

Discussion

The marked spatial variations within the faunal assemblage from Loggers Shelter provide a unique insight into the rate at which faunal remains may decay under different conditions.

Assuming the high density of remains found within the dripline to have once been continuous across the site, the difference between this quantity and the density of bone present at other points in the site constitutes a minimum estimate of the quantity of bone lost altogether over a time span of several centuries. In the case of squares E and F, the surviving bone would, by this reasoning, represent less than one-thirtieth of the postulated original quantity of remains. This represents an absolute decay rate in the order of 1kg of bone/cubic metre/100 years, which, given the exposed situation of these squares, must be near a maximum rate for a deposit of this kind.

Origin of the remains

Only the faunal remains from the upper levels of squares A and Bk are sufficiently well preserved to indicate their mode of accumulation. The following comments are based primarily on this material but apply equally to the entire assemblage.

The virtual absence of small vertebrate taxa from the assemblage excludes any likelihood that a raptorial predator has made a significant contribution. Furthermore, the few elements that do represent the smaller forms are fragmented and burnt, and do not stand out as an external element within the total fauna.

It is rather more difficult to exclude the possibility that the site was utilised by carnivores at various times during the past. Although no persuasive evidence of carnivore activity, such as tooth-marked bones, was noted within the assemblage, the general character of the material and, in particular, its thorough and even fragmentation, are reminiscent of some predator accumulations. The assemblage is also thoroughly burnt and, while this does not negate the presence of a secondarily burnt non-archaeological component, the degree of burning is probably sufficient to account for the fragmentation of the bone without the necessity of invoking other factors.

Faunal composition

Invertebrates

Three types of mollusc and two crustaceans are represented among the small quantity of invertebrate remains recovered (Table A3-3/1). A large proportion of the molluscan remains is contributed by the freshwater bivalve family Hyriidae, the more complete specimens of which appear to represent the genus *Hyridella*. Occasional fragments of at least two types of terrestrial gastropod, a large and a small form, are represented, but as these were all found at or near the surface of the deposit they are probably a recent addition.

In addition to these locally available forms, nine fragments of the estuarine bivalve *Anadara trapezia*, the Sydney cockle, were recovered from Level I of the deposit. The nearest populations of this species are probably found within the mangrove communities along Lower Mangrove Creek, approximately 20km downstream of Loggers Shelter. Although the robust shells of this species were quite possibly taken into the Upper Mangrove Creek area for use as implements, the specimens recovered thus far from Loggers Shelter and elsewhere in the catchment show no signs of any such function.

The two types of crustacean represented in the assemblage are a locally available freshwater yabby (family Parastacidae), and an as yet undetermined type of crab. The latter is almost certainly derived from the same estuarine reaches of Lower Mangrove Creek as the Sydney cockle.

Vertebrates

Vertebrates are represented by a total of 395 identified elements, most of which come from levels I (N = 319) and II (N = 66) of the deposit (Table A3-3/4). Analysis of the faunal sequence is thereby limited to a comparison of these samples.

Table A3–3/4 Loggers Shelter: number of identified taxon for each analytical unit in all squares and a site total (from Aplin 1981: Table 4).

IDENTIFIED TAXON	ANALYTICAL UNIT				SITE TOTAL
	I	II	III	IV	
Macropus robustus	3	-	-	-	3
Large macropodid	27	9	-	-	36
Macropus rufogriseus	2	1	-	-	3
Wallabia bicolor	7	-	1	-	8
Medium macropodid	83	20	2	3	108
Petrogale penicillata	3	1	-	-	4
Thylogale sp.	2	1	-	-	3
Small macropodid	123	21	2	-	146
Potorous sp.	3	-	-	-	3
Potoroidae	13	4	-	-	17
Trichosurus vulpecula	9	2	1	-	12
Pseudocheirus peregrinus	-	1	-	-	1
Pseudocheirine petaurid	8	1	1	-	10
Petaurus sp.	-	1	-	-	1
Isoodon sp.	2	-	-	-	2
Peramelidae	10	-	-	-	10
Vombatus ursinus	1	-	-	-	1
Pteropus scapulatus	1	-	-	-	1
Boidae	4	1	-	-	5
Elapidae	1	1	-	-	2
Ophidia	5	2	-	-	7
Agamidae	2	-	-	-	2
Egernia sp.	1	-	-	-	1
cf. *Dromaius novaehollandiae*	1	-	-	-	1
Teleost fish	8	-	-	-	8
Total number	319	66	7	3	395

The vertebrate faunas from levels I and II are extremely similar in virtually all respects. The main features in common are as follows:

1.   Mammals are dominant in both levels and contribute 93.4% of the total identified sample. Small numbers of reptiles (4.3%), fish (2%) and a bird (0.3%) account for the remainder of the material.

2.   Macropodids are by far the most commonly represented mammalian family, comprising between 71.5% and 100% of the identified remains. Size classes within this family maintain a constant order of abundance with the frequency of small/medium/large in both levels.

3.   There is an almost complete correspondence in the range of the mammal species present and their relative abundances. In particular, a number of macropodids (*Petrogale penicillata*, *Thylogale* sp. and *Macropus rufogriseus*) and several other small mammals (*Potorous* sp., *Trichosurus* sp. and pseudocheirines) are equally abundant in both levels.

Several aspects of the close similarity between the two levels may well be little more than an artefact of differential destruction of smaller or less compact elements during the early phases of post-depositional decay of the assemblage. This is probably true of the virtual absence of fish bone from the deposit and may also partly account for the general abundance of the macropodids.

Other stable features of the assemblage are, however, almost certainly not a product of differential decay. Most convincing in this regard is the predominance of the smaller and medium-sized macropodids over the larger forms (Table A3-3/5), an ordering contrary to that expected if differential decay alone was determining the faunal spectrum.

Table A3–3/5 Loggers Shelter: percentage composition of selected fauna (from Aplin 1981: Table 21).

IDENTIFIED TAXON	PERCENTAGE FREQUENCY
Large macropodid	9.9
Medium macropodid	30.1
Small macropodid	38.7
Potoroidae	5.1
Phalangeridae	3.0
Petaurinae	0.2
Pseudocheirinae	2.8
Paramelidae	3.0
Vombatidae	0.1
Chiroptera	0.1
Ophidia	3.5
Lacerilia	0.8
Teleost fish	2.0
Aves	0.2
Total (no.)	395
Total macropodid	78.7
Total macropodoid	83.8
Total phalangerid and petaurid	6.0

Despite this overall stability within the faunal sequence, a number of differences exist between levels I and II. These can be summarised as follows:

1. Large macropodids decrease in relative abundance from level II (13.6%) to level I (9.4%). This is compensated for partly by an increase in the abundance of small macropodids. The ecological significance of these changes is obscure.

2. *Wallabia bicolor* is present in low numbers in level I but absent from level II. This species appears to inhabit wet dense understorey in forested areas and its slight increase in abundance may indicate moister conditions during the later phase. It is, however, represented in the small assemblage from level III, suggesting that this sequence may be more complex than indicated through a study of levels I and II alone.

3. The remains of bandicoots are confined to level I, where they are relatively common. Within this class of remains, all diagnostic elements represent the short-nosed bandicoot, *Isoodon* sp., an inhabitant of dense understorey in drier communities. This indication of drier conditions during level I times is in contradiction to that suggested by the appearance at that time of *W. bicolor*.

4. A number of taxa were found only in level I. These include several mammals (*Vombatus ursinus* and *Pteropus scapulatus*) and reptiles (Agamidae, *Egernia* sp.), and the emu (*Dromaius novaehollandiae*). All of these occur infrequently, however, and their absence from level II is best attributed to the fivefold difference in sample size. Fish are also unrepresented in level II, but in this case, differential decay may be responsible.

In summary, the faunal sequence from Loggers Shelter displays a remarkable stability through time, both in overall composition and in the relative contributions of the various minor taxa. Species indicative of both 'wet' and 'dry' conditions are present in roughly even proportions, and this is taken to indicate the presence within the broad reaches of the main valley of a diverse mosaic of vegetation types from moist and dense to more open, dry communities. Evidence for change within the sequence is contradictory but weighs in favour of a slight areal reduction of wet communities between levels II and I.

Black Hands (BH)

This site is located in an isolated boulder near the foot of a long north-west-facing slope. The cavernous overhang has formed in the western face of the boulder, thereby leaving the floor area unprotected against the action of slopewash from the hillside above.

Due to recent disturbance within this site, the excavation (Square F) was conducted outside the dripline. At this point, more than one metre thickness of slopewashed sediments has accumulated over the last 3000 years. The deposit is sandy and possesses a low organic content throughout.

Fauna

Small quantities of poorly preserved shell were recovered from near the surface in the excavated area (Table A3-3/6). Larger quantities of better preserved shell were found in a disturbed context inside the dripline, thereby indicating that conditions may have been rather more conducive to preservation within the confines of the shelter overhang. Only freshwater shellfish are represented in these small samples.

Table A3-3/6 Black Hands and Geebung Shelters: bone and shell (from Aplin 1981: Table 8).

SITE NAME	SQUARE/SPIT	UNBURNT BONE		BURNT BONE		TOTAL BONE		HYRIIDAE		*ANADARA TRAPEZIA*		TERRESTRIAL GASTROPOD	
		NO.	WT (g)	NO.	WT (g)	NO.	WT (g)	NO.	WT (g)	NO.	WT (g)	NO.	WT (g)
Black Hands	F/1			26	3.3	26	3.3						
	F/2	2	0.2	110	15.0	112	15.2	1	0.1				
	F/3			127	16.0	127	16.0						
	F/4			49	4.8	49	4.8						
	F/5			51	4.5	51	4.5						
	F/6			10	0.4	10	0.4						
	F/7			1	0.1	1	0.1						
	Total	2	0.2	374	44.1	376	44.3	1	0.1				
Geebung	T/1			1	0.1	1	0.1	2	0.1				

Bone was recovered to a depth of 85cm in the excavation. Near the surface of the deposit, it was present in moderate quantities but is thoroughly degraded even here. Virtually no unburnt or lightly burnt bone has survived what must amount to a century or more of exposure in the surface context. Below this level, bone density decreases regularly with depth. Throughout the greater depth of its occurrence, the bone retains virtually none of its original morphology.

Due to the extremely poor condition of the remains, very few bone fragments proved diagnostic at even the broadest taxonomic level (Table A3-3/7). Macropodids of various sizes account for most of the identified sample and probably also comprise a large proportion of the unidentified remains. A single fragment of a pseudocheirine completes the assemblage.

Table A3–3/7   Black Hands Shelter, Square F: faunal composition (from Aplin 1981: Table 10).

IDENTIFIED TAXON			SPIT			
	SURFACE	F/1	F/2	F/3	F/4	F/5
Large macropodid				1		
Medium macropodid						1
Petrogale penicillata			1	2		
Small macropodid		1	2		1	
Pseudocheirine petaurid			1			

Geebung (GS)

A single piece of calcined bone and some fragments of freshwater bivalve were recovered from this shelter (Tables A3-3/1 and A3-3/6), which contains a shallow and very exposed deposit.

PART 4

Report on analysis of hair samples from four deposits in the Upper Mangrove Creek catchment.

by Barbara Triggs 2002

Sample No.	Site name	Provenance	Species identification Definite	Probable
1	Emu Tracks 2	ET2/T2a/4	Cat or fox	Fox, *Vulpes vulpes*
2	Mangrove Mansions	MM/T1/4	Common ringtail possum, *Pseudocheirus peregrinus* — hair in old predator scat	
3	Two Moths	TMS/T/1	Wombat, *Vombatus ursinus*	
4	Two Moths	TMS/T/2	Wombat, *Vombatus ursinus*	
5	Wolloby Gully	WoG/Ta/3	Common ringtail possum, *Pseudocheirus peregrinus*	

APPENDIX 4

Review of quantitative changes in other regions of eastern Australia: case studies

A: habitation indices
B: artefact accumulation rates in individual habitations

A: Habitation indices

NSW south coast and Sydney

Over the past 35 years, several researchers have based comments about population increase on numbers of sites in the NSW south coast-Sydney region.

Wade's (1967: 39) conclusion that increased site numbers in the Bondaian phase were 'indicative of changes in settlement pattern probably due to an increase in population', is based on a data set that, except for one site, consists of rockshelter sites from the Sydney area. The exception is Sassafras 1 in the hinterland of the NSW south coast. Curracurrang 1CU5/-, first occupied about 7500 years ago, is the only site with both pre-Bondaian and Bondaian evidence; other sites with Bondaian assemblages are Connels Point, Lapstone Creek, Smiths Creek, Marra Marra Creek, Gymea Bay and the minor Curracurrang sites.

Megaw and Roberts' (1974: 9) statement that Phase II (Bondaian) was 'a key period for maximum population expansion' was based on evidence from Royal National Park, where only one excavated site, Curracurrang 1CU5/-, has a Phase I (pre-Bondaian) assemblage compared with the more numerous sites with Bondaian and post-Bondaian (Phase III) assemblages. Based on his results from Curracurrang 1CU5/-, Megaw (1974: 35, Table 1) placed the beginning of the Bondaian phase in Sydney (and thus the increase in population) at between 3000±120 (Gak-394b) and 2360±90 (Gak-688), with transition to the most recent post-Bondaian phase at ca 840 BP.

Tracey (1974: 27) assigned sites to one of three phases: Early Bondaian (nine sites), Intermediate (three sites), and 'First occupied later' (seven sites) (the third period refers to 'the latest or post-Bondaian phase'). Tracey had a larger sample (19) than Wade, which included additional Sydney and south coast sites but excluded Connels Point. Tracey considered 'the numbers too even' to support Wade's comments. However, if the 'intermediate' sites (which all contain backed artefacts) are included with her earliest phase, her tabulated data suggest that there was a greater number of habitations established in the Bondaian phase than in the most recent period (12 and seven respectively).

Using data sets such as that on which Tracey calculated habitation establishment rates for different phases is, however, problematic. Tracey assigned sites to particular cultural phases according to whether or not their assemblages had backed artefacts, but her data set includes sites from areas where the timing of the transition from one phase to another differed from that of Curracurrang 1CU5/-. For example, at Lapstone Creek, backed artefacts were found in levels dated to 3650±100 BP (ANU-010) (McCarthy 1978: 55), which is earlier than the date Megaw assigned to the beginning of the Bondaian at Curracurrang 1CU5/-. At Currarong 1, backed artefacts were not found in levels dating later than ca 1600 BP, a much earlier date for their disappearance than the date given as the beginning of the post-Bondaian at Curracurrang 1CU5/- (ca 840 BP — see above). It is therefore not appropriate to calculate the habitation establishment rate for each cultural phase using samples such as Tracey's as there are no 'common' dates for the beginning and end of each cultural phase. Data sets need to consist of sites from geographic areas where it can be assumed that the timing for the transition from one phase to another was the same.

Hughes and Lampert (1982: Tables 1 to 3, Figs 6 and 7) analysed a larger and revised set of sites to show changes in the 'number of sites first occupied per 1000 years'. Their sample has 20 coastal sites from Sydney and the NSW south coast (but no hinterland sites). The earliest date for occupation at Burrill Lake, 20,830±810 BP (ANU-138) was extrapolated back to 25,000 BP (Hughes and Lampert 1982: Table 1). Hughes and Lampert (1982: 19) said that most excavated sites in the Sydney and south coast region 'apparently date from about the last 3000 years'. Their data (Hughes and Lampert 1982: Fig. 6) suggest *habitation establishment rates* fluctuated over the last 8000 years and that there were three periods in which the rate increased markedly — the seventh, third and first millennia BP — though in the eighth millennium BP, the rate increased such that habitations were established from thereafter in each millennium. Their data also indicate that the habitation establishment rate was highest in the last 1000 years. (In Hughes and Lampert's Fig. 6 and Table 3, data for the periods 8000 to 6000 BP, 6000 to 4000 BP and 4000 to 2000 BP have been averaged, which masks the fact that no sites in their sample were initially inhabited in the fourth and sixth millennia BP.) In terms of the *number of habitations used*, their data (1982: Tables 1 to 3, Fig. 7) show that the largest number used was in the last 1000 years.

I analysed data for the NSW south coast and Sydney (Fig. 7.3, Table A4/1) using only radiometrically dated sites given the large number now available. My data set (Table A4/2) thus excludes some sites used by Hughes and Lampert, but includes several more recently dated/excavated archaeological deposits as well as four south coast sites which they excluded. The 58 sites come from both coastal and hinterland zones in a region which extends from the Hawkesbury River in the north to Disaster Bay (Bay Cliff) in the south (ca 460km), and includes hinterland sites as far west as Lapstone Creek and Sassafras (65km and 30km from the coast respectively; that is, an area of ca 20,600 sq km). These 58 sites exclude shallow open, partially buried and/or deflated archaeological deposits (artefact scatters) and shell middens where it is not clear whether the site was occupied prior or subsequent to the radiometric age obtained (see Boot 1996b: Appendix 1 and Attenbrow 2002: Table 3.1 for other dated sites in the NSW south coast-Sydney region).

Table A4/1   NSW south coast and Sydney: rate of habitation establishment and number of habitations used in each millennium. N = 58, see Table A4/2 for sites included. [1] Figure excludes Yowie Bay, abandoned ca 2000 BP (Poiner 1974: 29); [2] figure excludes John Curtin Reserve, which has no deposit younger than 1500 BP (Attenbrow 1994), and PK20 Buckenboura, abandoned ca 1600 BP (Boot 1996a: 74).

PERIOD/ MILLENNIUM BP	NO. OF HABITATIONS ESTABLISHED IN EACH MILLENNIUM	RATE OF HABITATION ESTABLISHMENT (NO. PER MILLENNIUM)	NO. OF HABITATIONS USED IN EACH MILLENNIUM
25,000–24,000	1	)	1
24,000–23,000		)	1
23,000–22,000		)	1
22,000–21,000		) 0.2	1
21,000–20,000		)	1
20,000–19,000		)	1
19,000–18,000	1	)	2
18,000–17,000	1	)	3
17,000–16,000		) 0.5	3
16,000–15,000		)	3
15,000–14,000	1	)	4
14,000–13,000		)	4
13,000–12,000		) 0.3	4
12,000–11,000		)	4
11,000–10,000	2	)	6
10,000– 9000		) 0.7	6
9000– 8000		)	6
8000– 7000	2	2	8
7000– 6000	2	2	10
6000– 5000	3	3	13
5000– 4000	2	2	15
4000– 3000	9	9	24
3000– 2000	9	9	33
2000– 1000	17	17	49 [1]
1000–contact	8	8	55 [2]

Table A4/2   NSW south coast and Sydney: sites included in Table A4/1 and Figure 7.3, with millennium in which establishment is estimated to have occurred, radiometric age, geographic location and reference. [1] Ex. indicates that time of establishment has been extrapolated from the radiocarbon age. [2] Conventional radiocarbon ages are quoted, though sites are listed in millennium and in order as if corrected for marine reservoir effect. Sh indicates uncorrected shell date; correction factor for the NSW south and central coast is minus 450±35 years (Gillespie 1982: 21-2; 1990: 15); all other ages are from charcoal samples. [3] Coast includes ocean and estuarine locations.

MILLEN- NIUM BP	SITE NAME	EARLIEST RADIOMETRIC AGE [1] [2] YEARS BP	LAB. NO.	SOUTH COAST	SYDNEY	COAST[3]	HINTER -LAND	REFERENCE
25th	Burrill Lake	Ex 20,830±810	ANU-138	X		X		Lampert 1971a: 9
19th	Bulee Brook 2	18,810±160	ANU-9375	X			X	Boot 1996a: Table 1; 1996b: App. 1
18th	Bass Point	17,010±650	ANU-536	X		X		Hughes and Djohadze 1980: 15
15th	Shaws Creek K2	14,700±250	Beta-12423		X		X	Nanson et al. 1987: 76
11th	Bob's Cave	10,850±300	ANU-8313	X			X	Boot 1993b: 59; 1994: Table 2
11th	Darling Mills SF2	10,150±130	Wk-2511		X		X	Attenbrow 1994: 4, Table 10

Table A4/2　(Continued)

MILLEN-NIUM BP	SITE NAME		EARLIEST RADIOMETRIC AGE [1] [2] YEARS BP	LAB. NO.	SOUTH COAST	SYDNEY	COAST[3]	HINTER-LAND	REFERENCE
8th	Curracurrang 1CU5/-		7450±180	GaK-482		X	X		Megaw 1974: 35
8th	Jamisons Creek		7010±110	SUA-1233		X		X	Kohen et al. 1984: 57
7th	Currarong 1	Ex	3790±100	NSW-70	X		X		Hughes and Djohadze 1980: 10
7th	Currarong 2	ExSh	5990± 80	SUA-224	X		X		Hughes and Djohadze 1980: 6
6th	John Curtin Reserve		5640± 80	Wk-2085		X		X	Attenbrow 1992a: Table 1
6th	Cammeray	Sh	5840± 50	Wk-3219		X	X		Attenbrow 1994: Table 9
6th	Henry Lawson Drive		5240±100	SUA-60		X	X		White and Wieneke n.d. [ca 1975]
5th	Bantry Bay 3	Sh	4520±100	SUA-593		X	X		Ross and Specht 1976: 1
5th	Bourkes Road 2		4210± 50	ANU-9871	X			X	Boot 1996a: Table 1, 1996b: App. 1
4th	Sugarloaf	Sh	4170± 40	Wk-4196		X	X		Attenbrow 1995: Appendix 5
4th	PK 20 Buckenboura		4000±580	ANU-8762	X			X	Boot 1996a: Table 1
4th	Balmoral Beach BB2		3780±140	Beta-58864		X	X		Attenbrow 1993: Table 2
4th	Sassafras 1		3770±150	ANU-743	X			X	Flood 1980: 226, 328
4th	Great Mackerel		3670±150	ANU-6615		X	X		McDonald 1992b: 39
4th	Lapstone Creek		>3650±100	ANU-010		X		X	McCarthy 1978: 55
4th	Merimbula H. MHE-8		3610± 80	ANU-5000	X		X		Webb and Cane 1986: Table 13
4th	Burrill Shelter 2		3280± 70	ANU-8422	X		X		Boot 1994: Table 2
4th	Merimbula H. MHE-10	Sh	<3570± 90	ANU-5308	X		X		Webb and Cane 1986: Table 13
3rd	Pambula Lake B	Sh	<3150±170	ANU-2254	X		X		Sullivan 1982a: Table 8-1,1984: 4
3rd	Sassafras 2		>2780±115	ANU-744	X			X	Flood 1980: 233, 330
3rd	Mill Creek 11		2690± 50	SUA-2259		X		X	Koettig 1990: 24
3rd	Yowie Bay		2670± 85	ANU-175		X	X		Poiner 1974: 29
3rd	Bate Bay Site BHW		2402± 88	NZA-2323		X	X		Brayshaw pers. comm.
3rd	Bindea Street		2340±100	Beta-5787		X	X		Attenbrow and Conyers 1983: 23
3rd	Cherrybrook		2200± 60	Beta-11896		X		X	McDonald 1985: Addendum
3rd	Rock Pool		2140± 80	ANU-9376	X			X	Boot 1996a: Table 1, 1996b: App.1
3rd	Bardens Creek 9	Ex	1630± 90	SUA-1746		X		X	Attenbrow and Negerevich 1981,1984: 143
2nd	Bomaderry Creek		1930± 60	ANU-1021	X			X	Steele 1987: 68
2nd	Wattamolla (WL/-)		1900±115	ANU-178		X	X		Megaw and Roberts 1974: 4
2nd	Curracurrang 2CU5/-		1930± 80	Gak-898		X	X		Glover 1974: 17
2nd	Angophora Reserve		1890±130	ANU-6585		X	X		McDonald 1992a: 46-47, Table 1
2nd	Bull Cave		1820± 90	SUA-2106		X		X	Miller 1983: 25
2nd	Gnatilia Creek 3		1740± 60	ANU-8426	X			X	Boot 1993b: 59; 1994: Table 2
2nd	Abrahams Bosom		1630± 70	ANU-6446	X		X		Paton and Macfarlane 1989: 22
2nd	Boat Harbour BH1	Sh	1950±100	ANU-895		X	X		Dickson n.d. [ca 1973]: 47
2nd	Devlins Creek		1410± 50	Beta-76606		X		X	Haglund 1995: 13
2nd	McCue Midden		1840± 40	Beta-165771		X	X		Dallas 2002: Table 2.2
2nd	CC Landing Place (BB4/-)		1330±100	ANU-721		X	X		Megaw 1974: 36
2nd	Mt Trefle	Sh	1730± 50	Wk-2082		X	X		Attenbrow and Steele 1995: 51
2nd	Castle Cove	Sh	1650± 40	OZC-901		X	X		Attenbrow unpublished
2nd	Gymea (GY/-)		1220± 55	NSW-6		X	X		Megaw and Wright 1966: 28
2nd	Bowen Island		1180±260	ANU-2345	X		X		Blackwell 1982: 48
2nd	Hydrofoil	Sh	1630± 60	Wk-2510		X	X		Attenbrow 1994: 43
2nd	Curracurrang 7CU5/-		1050±100	ANU-179		X	X		Tracey 1974: 25
1st	North Head 15/67B	Sh	<1400± 70	ANU-3717	X		X		Hughes et al. 1984: Table 5
1st	Reef Beach	Sh	1150± 90	SUA-401		X	X		O'Donnell and Walker 1982: 3

Table A4/2 (Continued)

MILLEN-NIUM BP	SITE NAME		EARLIEST RADIOMETRIC AGE [1] [2] YEARS BP	LAB. NO.	SOUTH COAST	SYDNEY	COAST[3]	HINTER-LAND	REFERENCE
1st	Kangaroo Hill 4		550± 70	ANU-8438	x			x	Boot 1994: Table 2
1st	Durras North		480± 80	Gak-873	x		x		Lampert 1966: 94
1st	Greenglade		460±110	ANU-6934	x		x		Colley 1997: 7; Murray-Wallace and Colley 1997
1st	Cumberland Street	Sh	890± 60	Beta-47633		x	x		Attenbrow 1992b: 20
1st	Bay Cliff		330±110	ANU-6930	x		x		Colley 1997: 15
1st	Shellharbour		ca 140±100	Gak-337	x		x		Tindale 1964: 24

Trends based on this revised data set are similar to Hughes and Lampert's. The eighth millennium BP still appears as the period in which sites began to be established in each millennium (Fig. 7.3 and Table A4/1) and the highest number of habitations used was in the first millennium BP, though some sites have evidence of abandonment in either the second or first millennia BP. However, there are some differences in that:

- the greatest increases in the habitation establishment rate occurred in the fourth (+7) and second (+8) millennia BP and not the third and first millennia BP;
- the highest habitation establishment rate (17) and the most dramatic increase in the number of habitations used is in the second millennium BP rather than the third and first millennia BP; and,
- the habitation establishment rate decreased in the first millennium BP rather than continuing to increase.

Hughes and Lampert (1982: 20) quoted ca 5000 BP as the point after which substantial increases occurred in the number of sites showing evidence of occupation (i.e., in the number of habitations used), but the habitation establishment rate for the fifth millennium BP is low and, interestingly, remains low in the updated data set. It seems unlikely that this low figure is due entirely to coastal erosion as posited by Head (1987: 455–8), as the sample includes rockshelters as well as sites in the coastal hinterland.

A breakdown of the data set into sites from the south coast and Sydney, and the coast and hinterland (coded differently in Fig. 7.13A), suggests that late-Holocene habitation establishment rates may have varied in different geographic areas within the region. Alternatively, the patterns of site destruction, site recording and/or radiocarbon dating have varied in different parts of the region.

Hughes and Lampert concluded that 'over the last 5000 years the increase in the number of sites showing evidence of occupation was roughly two to three-fold' (1982: 20); that is, there was an increase in the number of habitations used from seven by 5000 BP to 20 by the time of contact. However, the growth rate in the first half of their data set (for example, in the 5000 years from 10,000 BP to 5000 BP when there was an increase in the number of habitations used from three to seven) could also be described as a two- to threefold increase ($\times 2.3$ versus $\times 2.9$). The average annual growth rate for a twofold increase over 5000 years is +0.01% p.a., and is +0.02% p.a. for a threefold increase over the same length of time.

Millennial growth rates for Hughes and Lampert's data set for the *number of habitations used* fluctuated, ranging from $\times 1$ to $\times 1.75$, with the highest in the seventh millennium BP. In my data set, millennial growth rates for the number of habitations used also fluctuated with a range from $\times 1$ to $\times 1.6$ (Table 7.5), though the highest growth rate was in the fourth millennium BP. Millennial growth rates for *habitation establishment rates*, which are calculated for only the last 7000 years, also fluctuated widely, ranging from $\times 0.5$ to $\times 4.5$ (Table 7.4), with the highest growth rate in the fourth millennium BP.

Average annual growth rates for the habitation establishment rates (Table 7.6) range from +0.04% to +0.15% for increases, and from -0.04% to -0.8% for decreases. For the numbers of habitations used in each millennium (Table 7.7), there are no decreases and the increases range between +0.01% and +0.05% (excluding increases from one to two sites).

South-western Victoria

Evidence for *habitation establishment rates* in south-western Victoria comes from Lourandos (1983a, 1985a) and Williams (1985, 1987, 1988). Basal habitation dates for all sites in these data sets were estimated by Lourandos or Williams, but no abandonment dates were given.

Lourandos (1985a: 393) said the archaeological sequence from south-western Victoria, which covers 12,500 years, 'indicates that the most intensive period of site establishment and use occurred **increasingly** during the last 4000 years or so'. Lourandos' evidence consisted of 19 dated sites (five excavated rockshelters, five coastal shell middens, five earth mounds, three open inland sites and Toolondo drainage system) (Lourandos 1983a: 86; Table 2). The earliest site (Lake Bolac) was established in the terminal Pleistocene (ca 12,500 BP), but Lourandos (1983a: 86) said most sites date to the last 4000 or 3000 years. Lourandos continued: 'During this final period sites appear to have been increasingly established, with the last 2000 years experiencing the most intensive phase.' As support for his argument, Lourandos added that a large number of surface sites have artefacts of the Small Tool Tradition, which generally date to the last 4000 years or so, but sites with earlier assemblages are quite rare. However, the graph presented by Lourandos to show that 'sites appear to have been increasingly established' (his Fig. 3 — a modified version is reproduced as my Fig. 7.4A), also indicates that fewer habitations were established in the final 1000 years than in the previous period.

Williams (1985, 1987, 1988) used a similar set of dated excavated sites to show the recent introduction of mound sites. William's (1985, 1988) Fig. 10.1 (1987: Fig. 4; a modified version is reproduced as my Fig. 7.4B) excluded some sites listed by Lourandos, but included other more recently excavated sites. Williams' sample of 25 sites is from the same geographic region as Lourandos' sample, but excludes Toolondo drainage system and several mound sites where she (1985: 311; 1988: 216) was not certain whether basal dates are dating the period of mound construction or an underlying occupation surface. Trends apparent in Williams' analysis are similar to those of Lourandos'. In Lourandos' (1983a) Figure 3, the habitation establishment rate increased to the stage where habitations were established in each millennium by the fourth millennium BP. In Williams' data set (1985, 1988: Fig. 10.1), this stage is reached in the sixth millennium BP — a difference probably attributable to the larger sample size in her study. In both studies, the most dramatic increase in the habitation establishment rate occurs in the second millennium BP and there is a marked decrease in the rate in the last 1000 years.

Williams (1985: 323–4) saw little if any change in the types or numbers of habitations used until after ca 2500 BP, especially after ca 2000 BP, when mounds were introduced and when there was an exponential increase in site numbers generally. She (see also 1988: 216–20) indicated that an increase in the habitation numbers is seen even when mounds are excluded; that is, there is an increase in previously existing habitation types such as shell middens and archaeological deposits in rockshelters. When Toolondo drainage system (210±120 BP, GX-4785) and Werribee burial site (7290±140, SUA-1085) are excluded, as they are not habitations (see Tables A4/3 and A4/4), the peak in the eighth millennium BP and the increase in the second half of the first millennium BP do not occur.

Millennial growth rates for the habitation establishment rates are calculated for the last 5000 years only (Table 7.4). The growth rate in the second millennium BP (×5.5) was much greater than at any other time in the preceding millennia (×2 to ×1) or in the first millennium BP (×0.5). *Average annual growth rates* (Table 7.6) are +0.07% and +0.17% for the third and second millennia BP, -0.08% for the decrease in the first millennium BP, while there was zero growth in the fifth and fourth millennia BP.

Table A4/3 South-western Victoria: number of habitations established in each millennium based on Lourandos 1983a: Table 2 and Williams 1988: Table 10.1, excluding Toolondo drainage system and Werribee burial site.

PERIOD/MILLENNIUM BP	LOURANDOS (1983a TABLE 2)	WILLIAMS (1988 TABLE 10.1)
13,000–12,000	1	1
12,000–11,000	1)	1)
11,000–10,000	) 0.25	) 0.25
10,000 – 9000	)	)
9000 – 8000	)	)
8000 – 7000	1)	1)
7000 – 6000	) 0.5	0) 0.50
6000 – 5000	1)	1
5000 – 4000	) 0.5	1
4000 – 3000	1	1
3000 – 2000	1	2
2000 – 1000	8	11
1000 – contact	4	5
Total sites	18	24

Table A4/4 South-western Victoria: sites included in Table A4/3 and Figure 7.4, with basal radiocarbon ages from Lourandos 1983a Table 2, N = 19; Williams 1988 Table 10.1, N = 25.

SITE NAME	RADIOCARBON AGE (BP) YEARS BP	LAB. NO.	SITE TRAIT	INCLUDED BY LOURANDOS (L) AND/OR WILLIAMS (W)
Lake Bolac lunette	ca 12,500		Arch. deposit (0)	L/W
Bridgewater South Cave	11,390±310	Beta-3923	Shell midden (Sh)	L/W
Tower Hill/Thunder Point	7300±150	Gak-2856	Shell midden (0)	L/W
Werribee burial site	7290±145	SUA-1085	Burial	W
Armstrong Bay/Tower Hill Beach	5120±120	Gak-610	Shell midden (0)	L/W
Thunder Point	4130±200	SUA-675	Shell midden (0)	W
Black Range 2 Grampians	3330±100	SUA-584	Arch. deposit (Sh)	L/W
FM/1	2350±110	SUA-574	Earth mound (0)	L/W
The Craigs	2265±100	SUA-774	Shell midden (0)	W
Drual DR/1 Grampians	1870±100	SUA-535	Arch. deposit (Sh)	L/W
MCC 6	1870±130	ANU-3888	Earth mound	W
Goose Lagoon (a)	1855± 85	Y-150-1	Shell midden (0)	L
Corra 3, C/3	1840±100	SUA-537	Earth mound (0)	L/W
Glenisla, GI/1 Grampians	1620±100	SUA-533	Arch. deposit (Sh)	L/W
KP/1	1420±100	SUA-672	Earth mound (0)	W
Seal Point	1420±130	SUA-522	Shell midden (0)	L/W
Corra 2, C/2	1320±100	SUA-571	Earth mound (0)	L/W
MMS	1270±100	ANU-3758	Earth mound	W
Goose Lagoon (b)	1177±175	C-600	Shell midden (0)	L/W
Berrambool	1090± 95	SUA-575	Arch. deposit (0)	L/W
Moonlight Head	1030±120	Gak-9010	Shell midden (Sh)	W

Table A4/4   (Continued)

SITE NAME	RADIOCARBON AGE (BP)		SITE TRAIT	INCLUDED BY LOURANDOS (L) AND/OR WILLIAMS (W)
	YEARS BP	LAB. NO.		
CH/1	995±100	SUA-778	Earth mound (O)	W
MK/1	820± 95	SUA-583	Earth mound (O)	L
MCC 5	790±190	ANU-3762	Earth mound (O)	W
Chatsworth	640± 95	SUA-572	Earth mound (O)	L
Gorrie Swamp Hut	380±150	ANU-3588	Arch. deposit (O)	W
Glen Aire Shelter	370± 45	NZ-367	Shell midden (Sh)	L/W
M 33	300± 60	ANU-4322	Earth mound (O)	W
Toolondo	210±120	GX-4785	Drainage system	L
Lake Bolac	105±1.8%	SUA-414	Arch. deposit (O)	L

Williams (1985: 324) commented that although differential preservation of sites could be responsible for the lack of **some** early sites, the increase in site numbers is so marked and abrupt that it appears the phenomenon is real. In addition, since distribution 'tails off' in the recent period, she contended that preservation factors alone are not responsible for the shape of the histogram. Williams acknowledged the lesser number of sites in the last 1000 years, but did not advance an explanation.

Bird and Frankel (1991a: Appendix) provided a more extensive list of radiometric ages for sites in western Victoria and south-eastern South Australia. These data confirm Williams' identification of the initial establishment of middens after 2500 years BP, indicate an increase in middens in the last 2000 years, and a more common use of rockshelters from ca 4000 years BP (Bird and Frankel 1991a: 9). However, of greater consequence for models proposed by Lourandos and Williams, as well as by Ross (1981), are the more recently obtained radiocarbon ages for previously dated rockshelters in the Grampians–Gariwerd region (Bird et al. 1998). Basal dates of 22,140±160 (Beta-88523) and 22,160±150 (Beta-98020) for Drual now extend occupation in the Grampians back to the time of the Last Glacial Maximum (Bird et al. 1998: 35, Table 1). Results for another shelter (Billimina/Glenisla 1) indicate use of the shelter began before the end of the Pleistocene rather than in the late-Holocene.

Central Queensland highlands

Morwood's 1984 synthesis of data for the central Queensland highlands included the results of archaeological investigations by Mulvaney and Joyce (1965), Beaton (1982) and his own fieldwork (Morwood 1979, 1981). These investigations provided a sample of 11 rockshelter sites for an area of some 21,000 sq km (Morwood 1984: 325). Basal habitation dates range from ca 22,000 BP at Kenniff Cave to ca 1280 BP at Goat Rock 2 (Morwood 1984: Table 6.2; my Table A4/5).

Beaton (1977: 185; 192 in Rowland 1983: 66) claimed there was a marked intensification of Aboriginal use of the south central Queensland uplands about 5000 BP to 4000 BP. The deposits he excavated are all younger than ca 4300 BP and are characterised by assemblages of the 'Small Tool Tradition'. To Beaton, this indicated that the increase was not gradual but occurred abruptly at the temporal boundary of the two major tool traditions.

Morwood (1984: 356–60) referred to the central Queensland highlands sequence of artefact assemblages as the 'Core Tool and Scraper Industry', the 'Small Tool Industry' and the 'Recent Industry'. He (1984: 358) divided the 'Small Tool Industry' into an early and late phase — the early phase, characterised by the restricted presence of pirri points, lasted from ca 4300

BP to ca 3560 BP. Morwood (1984: 358) argued that increased rates of sediment, artefact and pigment deposition indicated shelter use could have become more *intensive* about 3560 BP, and that the increased number of sites with late-phase assemblages (i.e., from five to nine sites) suggested Aboriginal use of the central highlands became more *extensive* after ca 3560 BP; that is, during the 'Small Tool Industry' late phase.

> *Habitation establishment rates.* Presenting the data as habitation establishment rates for each industry and phase (Table A4/5A, based on Morwood 1984: Table 6.2 and Fig. 6.8) indicates the rate was highest at the time of the 'Small Tool Industry', but also suggests the rate for both the early and late phases was similar (2.7 and 2.6). Since a relatively long time — ca 4000 years — elapsed before re-use of The Tombs (see below), it is included as a 'new' establishment in my analysis.

Table A4/5   Central Queensland highlands: rate of habitation establishment and number of habitations used in each millennium. N = 11, see Table A4/6 for sites included. -1/+1 indicates The Tombs abandoned then re-inhabited.

A. PHASED SEQUENCE

PHASE/INDUSTRY	DATES BP	DURATION (YEARS)	NO. OF HABITATIONS ESTABLISHED	RATE OF HABITATION ESTABLISHMENT (NO./MILLENNIUM)	NO. OF HABITATIONS USED IN EACH PHASE
Core Tool and Scraper	22,000/18,000 to 4300	17,700 or 13,700	4	0.3 – 0.2	4
Early Small Tool	4300 to 3560	740	1+1	2.7 (1.4)	5
Late Small Tool	3560 to 2000	1560	4	2.6	9
Recent	2000 to contact	1900	2	1.0	11

B. MILLENNIAL SEQUENCE

PERIOD/ MILLENNIUM	NO. OF HABITATIONS ESTABLISHED IN EACH MILLENNIUM	RATE OF HABITATION ESTABLISHMENT (NO./MILLENNIUM)	NO. OF HABITATIONS USED IN EACH MILLENNIUM
22,000–21,000	1	1	1
21,000–20,000			1
20,000–19,000			1
19,000–18,000			1
18,000–17,000			1
17,000–16,000			1
16,000–15,000			1
15,000–14,000			1
14,000–13,000			1
13,000–12,000	1	1	2
12,000–11,000			2
11,000–10,000	1	1	3
10,000– 9000	1	1	4
9000– 8000	-1		3
8000– 7000			3
7000– 6000			3
6000– 5000			3
5000– 4000	1+1	2	5
4000– 3000	2	2	7
3000– 2000	2	2	9
2000– 1000	2	2	11
1000–contact			11

Table A4/6 Central Queensland highlands: sites included in Table A4/5 and Figure 7.5, with radiocarbon ages from Morwood 1984: Table 6.2.

SITE NAME	RADIOCARBON AGE		COMMENTS
	YEARS BP	LAB. NO.	
Kenniff Cave	18,800±480	ANU-345	Extrapolated on d/a curve to 22,000 BP (Morwood 1984: 339)
Native Wells I	10,910±140	ANU-2034	Extrapolated on d/a curve to 13,000 BP (Morwood 1981: 27)
Native Wells II	10,770±135	ANU-2035	
The Tombs	9410±100	NPL-64	Gap of ca 5300 years between 9410 and 4100 BP
Wanderers Cave	4320± 80	ANU-1522	
The Tombs re-inhabited	4100		
Cathedral Cave	3560± 80	ANU-1762	
Rainbow Cave 1	3600±100	ANU-1521	
Rainbow Cave 2	2750± 80	ANU-2119	
Turtle Rock	2800±300	ANU-2202	
Ken's Cave	2000± 80	ANU-2090	To 530±80 (ANU-2118) then abandoned for past 500 years
Goat Rock 2	1280± 70	ANU-2004	

The habitation establishment rates, when calculated in millennial increments, suggest that although the highest rates occurred after ca 5000 BP, in each of the millennia between ca 5000 BP and ca 1000 BP the rate remained the same (two habitations/millennium) (Fig. 7.5A and Table A4/5B). However, the number of sites in this study is extremely small (11, see Table A4/6) and the addition of even one newly dated site between ca 5000 and ca 1000 BP could alter the trends presented here. In the last 1000 years no sites were established.

The *millennial and average annual growth rates* for the late-Holocene habitation establishment rates (Tables 7.4 and 7.6) suggest there was zero growth in the fourth, third and second millennia BP and a decrease in the first millennium BP.

Number of habitations used. All the archaeological deposits were in rockshelters and, apart from Ken's Cave and The Tombs, they appear to have been regularly inhabited at some stage in each millennium from the time of establishment to contact. Habitation ceased at ca 530 BP at Ken's Cave, and at The Tombs there was an apparent abandonment of the shelter between ca 9400 BP and ca 4100 BP.

The number of habitations used in each millennium fluctuated over time — there was an initial slow increase, then a decrease during the ninth millennium BP, when The Tombs was abandoned (Fig. 7.5B and Table A4/5B). The number did not increase again until the fifth millennium BP with one 'new' site and re-establishment of The Tombs. Between ca 5000 BP and ca 1000 BP, the increases were greatest, but they remained at the same level in the last 1000 years as in the second millennium BP. Abandonment of Ken's Cave in the first millennium BP is not reflected in the tables and graphs as it remained in use for the first part of the millennium.

The highest millennial growth rate and average annual growth rate occurred in the fifth millennium BP (x1.7 and +0.5% respectively). However, the *millennial growth rates* in the 11th and 10th millennia BP are similar to and/or higher than those in the fourth, third and second millennia BP (Table 7.5). *Average annual growth rates* for the *number of habitations used*, except for −0.03% in the ninth millennium BP, are increases ranging from +0.02% to +0.07% (Table 7.7).

South-eastern Queensland

Morwood (1987: 343, Fig. 4) used a sample of 25 sites excavated by several researchers to indicate that there was a mid-Holocene increase in site numbers, especially after ca 4000 BP, in south-eastern Queensland (an area of about 158,125 sq km). He pointed out that from 4500 BP, the growth of site numbers over time appeared to be logarithmic rather than linear. The earliest date of 20,560±250 BP (SUA-2341) is for Wallen Wallen Creek, a deeply stratified open shell midden/archaeological deposit on Stradbroke Island. The dated sample comes from 201cm to 207cm below the ground surface and, since archaeological materials extend to a depth of ca 310cm, initial habitation was probably much earlier than ca 20,000 BP (Neal and Stock 1986: 618–19).

Table A4/7   South-eastern Queensland: rate of habitation establishment and number of habitations used in each millennium from Morwood 1987: Fig 4. N = 23, see Table A4/8 for sites included. –1 in second millennium BP indicates Platypus abandoned; +1 1st mill. BP indicates Platypus reinhabited.

PERIOD/ MILLENNIUM BP	NO. OF HABITATIONS ESTABLISHED IN EACH MILLENNIUM	RATE OF HABITATION ESTABLISHMENT (NO./MILLENNIUM)	NO. OF HABITATIONS USED IN EACH MILLENNIUM
>21,000–20,000	1	1	1
20,000– 6000	0	0	1
6000– 5000	1	1	2
5000– 4000	4	4	6
4000– 3000	1	1	7
3000– 2000	3	3	10
2000– 1000	5 –1	5	14
1000–contact	8 +1	9	23

Table A4/8   South-eastern Queensland: sites included in Table A4/7 and Figure 7.6, with radiocarbon and estimated ages from Morwood 1987: Fig. 4. Except where noted, dated samples were charcoal.

SITE NAME	BASAL/EARLIEST AGE CORRECTED AGE		COMMENTS/MATERIAL DATED/CONVENTIONAL AGE
	YEARS BP	LAB. NO.	
Wallen Wallen Creek	20,560±250	SUA-2341	
Bushrangers Cave	5540±100	Beta-4852	Additional date 9270±100 (Beta-42847) (Ulm and Hall 1996: App. 1)
Platypus Shelter	4540± 80	Beta-3074	Gap in occupation between 2000 and 800 BP
Hope Island	4350±220	Beta-20799	
Maidenwell Shelter	4300± 70	Beta-6924	
Boonah Shelter	4300 BP	estimate	Additional date 3240±50 (Beta-25204) (Ulm and Hall 1996: App. 1)
Gatton Shelter	3820±120	Beta-15811	
Bishops Peak	2620± 90	Beta-16299	
Sandstone Point	2290±100	Beta-15810/B	
Browns Road	2030± 70	Beta-3077	
St Helena	1790± 80	Beta-6141	Shell: 2240± 70 BP
One Tree	1620± 60	Beta-3073	
Fraser Island 796/54	1515±105	Beta-1700	Shell: 1965±100 BP
Fraser Island 217/15	1510±115	Beta-1698	Shell: 1960±110 BP
Moon Point, Fraser Is	1020± 90	Beta-2609	Shell: 1470±80 BP
Fraser Island 799/54	820± 85	Beta-1699	Shell: 1270±80 BP
First Ridge	700± 60	Beta-1946	Shell: 1150±70 BP
Bribie Island 3	670± 95	SUA-481	Also known as White Patch Site 3
Deception Bay 1	550±105	LJ-949	Shell: 1000±140 BP
Minner Dint	520± 75	I-11095	
Toulkerrie	370± 75	I-11096	Additional date 2290±80 (Beta-32407) (Ulm and Hall 1996: App. 1)
Deception Bay 2	310±105	LJ-952	Shell: 760±140 BP
Little Sandhills	modern	Beta-1947	Shell: 102.1±0.7% BP

Morwood included the Talgai skull (12th millennium BP) and Broadbeach burial site (first and second millennia BP) in his sample but, as they are not habitations, they are excluded from my Figure 7.6 and Tables A4/8 and A4/7.

Habitation establishment rates. The largest increases in the habitation establishment rates occurred in the fifth and first millennia BP (+3 and +4 above the rate of the previous millennium respectively) (Fig. 7.6A and Table A4/7). A **decrease** occurs in the fourth millennium BP, when only one habitation was established. Although the highest habitation establishment rate (nine) is in the first millennium BP, the *millennial growth rate* for that period is not as high as in the fifth millennium BP, which has the highest millennial growth rate (x4) (Table 7.4). The *average annual growth rates* range between +0.05% and +0.14% for the increases, with -0.14% for the decrease in the fourth millennium BP (Table 7.6).

Number of habitations used. The largest number of habitations used was in the first millennium BP (23). Increases in the number of habitations used were relatively high in the fifth and second millennia BP, but were highest in the first millennium BP (Fig. 7.6B and Table A4/7). The highest *millennial growth rate in the number of habitations used* occurred in the fifth millennium BP (x3) (Table 7.5). In the last 4000 years, the growth rates were lower than those of the sixth and fifth millennia BP, fluctuating between x1.2 and x1.6. *Average annual growth rates* are all increases ranging between +0.02% and +0.11%, with the highest in the fifth millennium BP (Table 7.7).

Morwood's data set indicates an increase in both habitation indices in the first millennium BP, and the millennial and average annual growth rates for both of the indices indicate a slight increase in the first millennium BP, but not back to the much higher level of the fifth millennium BP. Most of the sites in his data set are open coastal shell middens (only six of the 23 are rockshelters). It is, in fact, a curious data set in that all sites <2000 BP are open coastal shell middens and all of the rockshelter sites are >2500 BP. If only rockshelter sites were used for the analysis, it would suggest no sites were established in the first or second millennium BP and no sites were occupied along the coastal strip — an obviously spurious suggestion.

Recently, Ulm and Hall (1996: Fig. 4, Appendix 1) produced an updated list of radiocarbon dates for this region which contained 57 sites (including burials, as well as rockshelters with deposit and open shell middens). As well as numerous additional sites, further dates have been obtained for Boonah, Bushrangers Cave and Toulkerrie, which increase the length of habitation at these sites. These revisions still show similar long-term trends over time to those illustrated in Figure 7.6, with increasing numbers of habitations being established and used in the last 2000 years. They concluded that 'the number of coastal sites increases gradually but consistently from about 6000 BP to ca 1200 BP after which a dramatic acceleration in site creation is apparent' (Ulm and Hall 1996: 52).

NSW–ACT–Victoria: southern uplands-tablelands

Flood's (1973, 1976, 1980) original search for Pleistocene occupation of the southern uplands-tablelands encompassed a wide geographic area, including the NSW coastal ranges (the sites of Sassafras 1 and 2) as well as the foothills in north-eastern Victoria (Cloggs Cave, Buchan). Flood recorded numerous sites, most of which are open archaeological deposits.

In the archaeological deposits which Flood excavated and/or dated for this study, evidence for Pleistocene and early Holocene habitation was absent (i.e., no sites were older than 4000 years) (Flood 1976: 32–3, 1980: 254) until the search was extended to the foothills near Buchan, Victoria, where habitation evidence at Cloggs Cave extends back to 17,720±840 BP (ANU-1044) (Flood 1980: 259, Table 24). In addition, in the 50 open archaeological deposits recorded, Flood (1976: 32) saw no artefacts which could be assigned to Pleistocene or early Holocene assemblages. It appeared as if the NSW–ACT–Victorian southern uplands-tablelands had not been occupied in the Pleistocene and early Holocene.

Subsequently, several dates between 21,000±220 BP (Beta-16886) and 10,160±160 (Beta-16653) came from artefact-bearing levels in a small rockshelter at Birrigai near Tidbinbilla, ACT, on the northern fringes of the south-eastern highlands (Flood et al. 1987: 9–16). At 730m above sea-level, the site is lower in elevation than other sites excavated by Flood, except for Sassafras 1 and 2 (also at 730m a.s.l.) and Cloggs Cave (<500m a.s.l.). Other recent research and consulting projects provide further dates for habitations in the southern uplands/tablelands (Tables A4/9 and A4/10). All new dates, except that for Nursery Swamp 2, are for open archaeological deposits. All radiocarbon dates fall within the last 4500 years, though one site (Butmaroo) has deep stratified deposits where initial habitation may be much older (Rhys Jones, pers. comm. 1996). Thus, although the presently available evidence shows that the NSW–ACT–Victorian southern uplands-tablelands (or at least their lower elevations) were occupied during the Pleistocene, most dates for initial occupation of habitations are within the latter half of the Holocene.

Table A4/9 NSW-ACT-Victorian southern uplands-tablelands: rate of habitation establishment and number of habitations used in each millennium. Rockshelter deposits N = 14, open deposits N = 11; see Table A4/10 for sites included. Sh indicates rockshelter; UndSh = undated rockshelter; OAD = open archaeological deposit.

PERIOD/ MILLENNIUM BP	NO. OF HABITATIONS ESTABLISHED IN EACH MILLENNIUM			RATE OF HABITATION ESTABLISHMENT (NO./MILLENNIUM)		NO. OF HABITATIONS USED IN EACH MILLENNIUM	
	Sh	UndSh	OAD	Sh	Sh+OAD	Sh	Sh+OAD
21,000–20,000	1			1		1	1
20,000–18,000						1	1
18,000–17,000	1			1		2	2
17,000–10,000						2	2
10,000–4000			1		1	2	3
5000–4000			1		1	2	4
4000–3000	2		1	2	3	4	7
3000–2000	1		1	1	2	5	9
2000–1000	2		1	2	3	7	12
1000–contact	2	5	6	7	13	14	25

Table A4/10 NSW-ACT-Victorian southern uplands-tablelands: sites included in Table A4/9 and Figure 7.7, with radiocarbon and estimated ages for rockshelters and time of known-use for open archaeological deposits, and references.

SITE NAME	RADIOCARBON OR ESTIMATED AGE YEARS BP	LAB. NO.	COMMENTS BY RESEARCHER	REFERENCE
Rockshelter sites (date of establishment)				
Birrigai	21,000±220	Beta-16886		Flood et al. 1987: 16, 22
Cloggs Cave	17,720±840	ANU-1044		Flood 1980: 259, Table 24
Sassafras I	3770±150	ANU-743		Flood 1980: 226, 328
Nursery Swamp 2	3700±110	ANU-3033		Rosenfeld et al. 1983: 54
Sassafras II	>2780±115	ANU-744		Flood 1980: 232-3, 330
Caddigat	1600± 60	ANU-1049		Flood 1980: 239
Yankee Hat 2	> 770±140	ANU-1051	Base of horizon above backed artefacts (assigned 2nd mill. BP)	Flood 1980: 239
Yankee Hat 1	<1000		Mainly Late Small Tool phase	Flood 1980: 239, 333

Table A4/10   (Continued)

SITE NAME	RADIOCARBON OR ESTIMATED AGE YEARS BP	LAB. NO.	COMMENTS BY RESEARCHER	REFERENCE
Bogong 1	<1000			Flood 1980: 342
Bogong 2	1000± 60	ANU-1050		Flood 1980: 246, 343S
Hanging Rock 1	370± 60	ANU-1047	Basal	Flood 1980: 239
Hanging Rock 2	<1000		Recent use	Flood 1980: 341
Rendezvous	<1000		Recent quartz industry	Flood 1980: 239, 334
Front Paddock	<1000		Last phase	Flood 1980: 335
Dated open archaeological deposits (date of known-use)				
Butmaroo	>4000 possibly back to 10,000 BP			Rhys Jones pers. comm. 1996
Little Thredbo 2	4390± 80	ANU-6867		Kamminga et al. 1989
SS2.4, nr Gundaroo	3300±100	ANU-3704		Packard 1984: 57–8, Fig.12
Little Thredbo 3	2460±120	ANU-6868		Kamminga et al. 1989
HCA.14, nr Berrima	1780± 60	SUA-2351		Koettig 1985a: 120
Nardoo	>760±110	ANU-1060	Above backed artefacts (assigned 2nd mill. BP)	Flood 1980: 347
Little Thredbo 1	940±150	ANU-6866		Kamminga et al. 1989
G17, Goulburn	330±100	SUA-2141		Koettig pers.comm.
ELG.1, nr L. George	<1000			Baker, Feary and Hughes 1984
GIL.1, nr L. Bathurst	<1000			Hughes, Barz and Hiscock 1984
GIL.2, nr L. Bathurst	<1000			Hughes, Barz and Hiscock 1984

There are only nine dated rockshelter habitations in this region and, to produce an analysable data set, I included several archaeological deposits which were not radiocarbon-dated but were assigned to specific millennia on the basis of their assemblages (Fig. 7.7, Tables A4/9 and A4/10). In the southern uplands-tablelands, Flood (1980: 341) records Bondaian artefacts (e.g., Bondi points) continuing into the first half of the first millennium BP. I thus assigned sites with assemblages referred to by Flood (1980) as 'Late Small Tool Phase' (pp. 221, 239, 250–1), 'recent quartz industry' (p. 239) or 'later quartz period' (p. 333) to the first millennium BP. Dated open archaeological deposits included in the analysis are listed separately in Table A4/9 and are coded differently in Figure 7.7.

Using only the dated rockshelters, the data suggest *habitation establishment rates* and the *number of habitations used* were very low until ca 4000 BP and relatively stable thereafter. If the undated rockshelters are included, the decreased habitation establishment rate in the third millennium BP remains, and a substantial increase and the most dramatic increase occurred in both habitation indices in the first millennium BP. If the open archaeological deposits are included, the trends remain essentially the same as that for all rockshelters.

The highest *millennial growth rate* for the habitation establishment rates, calculated for only the last 4000 years for all rockshelter deposits (both dated and undated), was in the first millennium BP (×3.5) (Table 7.4). For the number of habitations used, the highest millennial growth rate (×2) occurred in the fourth and first millennium BP (Table 7.5).

The *average annual growth rate* for the decrease in the habitation establishment rate in the third millennium BP was -0.07%; increases in the second and first millennia BP were +0.07% and +0.13% respectively (Table 7.6). For the number of habitations used in each millennium, the average annual growth rates were all increases ranging between +0.02% and +0.07%, the highest values being in the fourth millennium BP (Table 7.7).

The Mallee, north-western Victoria

The area of the Victorian Mallee studied by Ross is 30,000 sq km (1981: 146). The following discussion is based principally on data from Ross 1984, which provides greater detail than the 1981 article. The 141 open archaeological deposits in Ross' analyses are mostly stone artefact scatters but include some shell scatters. They occur on dune blow-outs, on lake-side sediments or on aeolian ridges around salinas where grass cover is thin (Ross 1984: 103). Some of the artefact or shell scatters recorded as individual sites may represent multiple exposures of a single partially buried site (Ross 1984: 106). However, the information presented does not indicate which scatters are likely to be part of the same site in order to work out 'minimum numbers', so site numbers quoted by Ross are used.

Nine archaeological deposits were dated by absolute methods (radiocarbon dating of freshwater mussel and charcoal, and thermoluminescent dating of burnt hearth materials) (Table A4/11). The earliest date for an archaeological deposit is 7650±110 BP (SUA-766) (Ross 1984: 178). Ross (1981: 149, 1982: 99–100, 1984: 116, 265) assigned undated sites to either an Early Phase (ca 12,000-10,000 BP to 6000 BP) or a Late Phase (<4500 BP to contact) on the presence or absence of geometric microliths and/or the size of artefacts. The date of 4500 BP was used on the assumption that geometric microliths entered the Victorian Mallee archaeological record about 4500–4000 BP. Ross assigned sites with assemblages predating 4500 BP to the period 12,000–10,000 BP to 6000 BP, since this was the period when the Mallee was wettest (Table A4/12).

Ross based her interpretations of the Victorian Mallee archaeological record on:

1. her calculations that there was a tenfold increase in the number of sites occupied after 4500–4000 BP in the southern Mallee (1984: 201, 235–8, 267); and,
2. the major period of use in the northern Mallee occurred during the early Holocene (i.e., between ca 12,000/10,000 BP and ca 6000 BP) rather than after ca 6000 BP (1984: 182–4, 265).

Table A4/11 The Mallee, north-western Victoria: sites included in Figure 7.8 with radiometric ages from Ross 1984: 178-80. Note: radiocarbon ages have not been corrected for environmental effects or calibrated; TL ages are in calendar years (Ross 1984: 178); ch indicates charcoal and sh = freshwater mussel shell.

SOUTHERN MALLEE SITE NAMES	RADIOMETRIC AGES			NORTHERN MALLEE SITE NAMES	RADIOMETRIC AGES		
Pine Plains (Pleasant Grove)	6200±600	Alpha-819	TL	Raak II	7650±100	SUA-766	C14-sh
Sunset Desert (Birthday Plain)	5780±100	Alpha-820 possibly younger	TL	HWH III	6390±700	Alpha-817	TL
Megaw 3	7030± 80	SUA-2103 below artefacts	C14-ch				
Pine Plains (Lake Bambruk 1)	1970± 90	SUA-1109	C14-sh	Eyesore	1015±100	Alpha-816	TL
Overall Hill (Pine Plains)	1200±1800	Alpha-818	TL				
Pine Plains (Lake Bambruk 2)	1170± 90	SUA-1110	C14-sh				

The northern Mallee

The northern Mallee sample consists of 20 sites at Raak Plains (Ross 1984: 134). Ross said these sites are distinguishable from the southern Mallee sites on the basis of artefact type, shape and size (1984: 159, 169), and are dominated by large core tools and large broad but thin implements which she considered belong to the 'Core Tool and Scraper Tradition' (1984: 123, 171). Of the 20 northern Mallee sites, Ross (1984: 120, 134) stated 60% contain artefacts most commonly associated with Pleistocene and early-Holocene technologies; only two contain stone artefacts in any quantity, and six (30%) are devoid of lithic remains consisting of only shell scatters or fireplaces; two (10%) have no clear diagnostic materials.

Table A4/12 The Mallee, north-western Victoria: rates of known-habitation use. N = 141. [1] One Rocket Lake site used in both phases; +3, −3 and bracketed totals in Late Phase represent figures if Rocket Lake sites were included in the northern Mallee. [2] Rate A is rate according to index used by Ross (1984: 198–9); Rate B is rate calculated as number of sites per millennium.

PERIOD	NORTHERN MALLEE				SOUTHERN MALLEE			
	NO. OF HABITATIONS [1]	RATE OF KNOWN HABITATION USE [2]		NO. OF DATED HABITATIONS	NO. OF HABITATIONS [1]	RATE OF KNOWN HABITATION USE [2]		NO. OF DATED HABITATIONS
		RATE A	RATE B			RATE A	RATE B	
Early Phase								
6000 years	12	1:500	2.0	2	11	1:545	1.8	3
4000 years		1:335	3.0			1:365	2.8	
Late Phase	8	1:565	1.8	1	111	1:41	24.0	3
+/- Rocket	+3 = 11	1:410	2.4		−3 = 108	1:42	23.8	
Totals	20[23]			3	121[118]			6

No northern Mallee site was said to contain any quantity of diagnostic artefacts of the 'Small Tool Tradition' (Ross 1984: 141); only Raak II was said (1984: 134, Tables 6.1) to have tools of the 'Small Tool Tradition' — four geometrics (out of a total of some 2500 artefacts). Ross (1984: 177) associated sites without stone artefacts with recent small-scale visitation; for example, Eyesore, a freshwater shell scatter with numerous hearths, one of which was TL dated to 1015±100 BP (Alpha-816) (Ross 1984: 179). She (1984: 180) argued that because larger sites on the southern part of Raak Plains are older than ca 5200 BP (TL = 4500 radiocarbon years BP), late-Holocene occupation of the plains was a much less substantial event.

Twelve of the northern Mallee sites were assigned to the Early Phase, and eight to the Late Phase (Table A4/12). If the rate of known-habitation use is calculated in the same way that Ross calculated the 'rate' for both the southern Mallee (see below), the figures suggest that the rates of known-habitation use for the Early and Late Phases are similar if the early period is taken as lasting from 12,000 BP to 6000 BP (6000 years); the rates are 1:500 for the Early Phase and 1: 560 years for the Late Phase. If the Early Phase is taken as 10,000 BP to 6000 BP (4000 years) then the rate for this period becomes 1:335 years, which is higher than the rate for the Late Phase. Ross (1984: 182, 198) based her statement that late-Holocene occupation in the northern Mallee was much less substantial than that of the early period on the lower number of artefacts in sites assigned to the late period.

Ross included Rocket Lake in the southern Mallee sample in her analyses, even though it is very close to Raak Plains (10km) and is shown in her 1984 Figure 3.3 as being within the area defined as northern Mallee. Three sites at Rocket Lake contain geometric microliths (Ross 1984: 335–6), which, at two sites, represent between 2% and 5% of the artefacts (1984: Fig. 6.5). If the Rocket Lake sites do belong in the northern Mallee, then,

1. geometrics are 'abundant' (>2%) at some northern Mallee sites, contrary to Ross' statement (1984: 141); and,

2. the rate of known-habitation use increased in the more recent period (1:410 years), though it may not alter the observation that there are fewer artefacts in Late Phase habitations.

The southern Mallee

Ross' southern Mallee sample includes 121 sites (1984: 120–30), which are described as having primarily tools characteristic of the 'Small Tool Tradition' (1984: 171). Artefacts diagnostic of the Small Tool Tradition ('backed blades, geometric microliths, bipolar implements and tulas') are present at 54 sites (42.3%) (1984: 134); backed artefacts represent <5% of the total assemblage in at least 16 sites (1984: 141), though this is less if Rocket Lake is included in the northern zone.

Large cores and flake tools were recorded at 10 of the 121 southern Mallee sites. Eight of the 10 were associated with quarries where large tools may be expected (Ross 1984: 134), but Ross believed her analysis showed that this did not negate their assignation to the Early Phase. In addition to these 10 sites, hearth materials at Pleasant Grove (Pine Plains) yielded a TL date of 6200±600 BP (Alpha-819). This date, along with the presence of numerous geometrics, suggests Pleasant Grove was visited during both the Early and Late Phases. Thus, artefact assemblages and/or radiometric dates at 11 southern Mallee sites indicated to Ross (1984: 198–9) that the southern Mallee was visited in the early Holocene wet period (from ca 12,000–10,000 BP to ca 6000 BP).

Ross calculated the *rate of known-habitation use* (referred to as the 'density of sites over time' [1984: 198–9]) for the Early Phase in the southern Mallee as 'approximately one site every 400 years' (1:400), and for the Late Phase as 'approximately one site every 40 years' (1: 40) ('at least 110 sites' in 4500 years). On this basis, there was a tenfold increase in the rate of known-habitation use in the later period as well as a tenfold increase in the number of habitations known to be used (11:111). Ross' 1:400 for the Early Phase is an averaged figure. If the Early Phase is taken as 6000 years (i.e., ca 12,000 BP to ca 6000 BP) the rate of known-habitation use is 1:545 years and the growth rate for this index is greater than tenfold (×13); but, if taken as 4000 years, then the growth rate is 1:365, which is less than tenfold (×9) (Table A4/12).

However, the increase in the rate of known-habitation use takes place over several millennia — that is, 11 sites between ca 12,000–10,000 BP and 6000 BP, and 111 sites between 4500 BP and contact. The establishment and/or use of these sites may have been spread out over these periods, or they may have been established/used within very restricted time periods. If the temporal distribution of known-habitation use was as set out in Table A4/13, then millennial growth rates were much lower than tenfold (×3 to ×1.5). That is, there could have been a gradual process of growth without any sudden increases, even if the number of sites used by the time of contact (111) was 10 times the number used by 6000 BP (11). The average annual growth rates based on the hypothetical figures range between 0.04% and 0.11% p.a.

Table A4/13   The southern Mallee, north-western Victoria: hypothetical distribution of number of known-habitations used in each millennium. N = 121.

MILLENNIUM BP	HYPOTHETICAL NUMBER OF KNOWN-HABITATIONS IN EACH MILLENNIUM		HYPOTHETICAL MILLENNIAL GROWTH RATE		HYPOTHETICAL AVERAGE ANNUAL GROWTH RATE
			X	%	%
10th	1)				
9th	2)		2	+100	0.07
8th	3)		1.5	+ 50	0.04
7th	5)	11	1.6	+ 60	0.05
6th	0		0		-100
5th	2)				–
4th	4)		2	+100	0.07
3rd	8)		2	+100	0.07
2nd	24)		3	+200	0.11
1st	44)	111	1.9	+ 88	0.06

Kefous (1982: 98) queried Ross' (1981) use of 4500 BP as the date for the appearance of the 'Small Tool Tradition' and her assumption that sites with geometric microliths postdate 4500 BP. Kefous argued that such sites could have formed any time after 5500 BP (see also Bird and Frankel 1991a: 3). If this was the case, then the rate of known-habitation use and growth rates for the Late Phase would be lower than those presented above.

Radiometric dates for the Victorian Mallee sites fall between ca 7750 BP (C14) and ca 5680 BP (TL), and between ca 2060 BP (C14) and ca 915 BP (TL), using 2-sigma ranges for uncorrected and uncalibrated radiocarbon and TL determinations (Table A4/11 and Fig. 7.8). When the radiocarbon dates are calibrated to make them comparable with the TL dates, which are in calendar years, the earlier time period begins possibly as early as ca 8600 BP and extends to ca 5680 BP, and the later period extends from ca 2130 to ca 925 BP. These dates could be taken to suggest that the Mallee was inhabited between ca 8600 BP and ca 5700 years BP and then again between or just before ca 2200 BP and 'contact'. It is therefore possible that the dates indicate re-occupation of the Mallee only after ca 2000 BP (Williams 1985: 326) when environmental conditions improved. Another possible interpretation is that there was a peak in occupation in the southern Mallee between ca 2000 and ca 1000 BP with a concomitant decrease in the last 1000 years, and that the increase in habitations may not have coincided with the introduction of the 'Small Tool Tradition' (cf. Ross 1984: 200).

The evidence presented by Ross for the *northern Mallee* suggests the rates of known-habitation use in both the early and late-Holocene were similar, or else higher in the earlier period. In the *southern Mallee*, the rate of known-habitation use appears to be much higher in the late-Holocene than in the early-Holocene (between ×9 and ×13), but this occurred within a 4500-year period and the millennial and average annual growth rates would be much lower. Whether the radiometric dates are indicative of regional trends and there was a late-Holocene peak habitation period in the second millennium BP, or whether there was a more even spread of occupation, will not be clear until more detailed work has been carried out and methods discovered which provide a finer scale of dating the establishment and length of occupation of open archaeological deposits.

NSW Hunter Valley

In the Hunter Valley, which is immediately to the north of the Upper Mangrove Creek catchment, Hiscock (Hiscock and Koettig 1985; Hiscock 1986: 45) undertook technological analyses of stone artefacts from 15 open archaeological deposits and Sandy Hollow, a rockshelter with a stratified archaeological deposit excavated by Moore (1970) in the 1960s. The open deposits were in the Mount Arthur North and South coal leases near Muswellbrook in the central lowlands.

On the basis of a sequence he identified at Sandy Hollow (SH/1), Hiscock (1986: 41) divided the Bondaian assemblages into an early phase (Bondaian-Phase I dated from ca 1300 BP to ca 800 BP) and a late phase (Bondaian-Phase II, ca 800 BP to ca 110 BP, i.e., 1840 AD [contact]). Assemblages of both phases were recognised at sites in Mount Arthur North and Mount Arthur South coal leases.

Of the 15 open archaeological deposits, three were identified as having only a Bondaian-Phase II assemblage, while 10 had Bondaian-Phase I assemblages, one site was classified as pre-Bondaian, and one contained elements of both Bondaian-Phases I and II (Table A4/14). Hiscock (1986: 45) discounted arguments for destruction of early sites. He pointed out that the pattern of high numbers during the Bondaian-Phase I and decreased numbers in Bondaian-Phase II parallels trends in accumulation rates at Sandy Hollow 1 (see following section on artefact accumulation rates in Hunter Valley sites). Hiscock (1986: 45) observed similar patterns in other areas of the central lowlands and he believed the Mount

Arthur North and South pattern probably accurately represent gross changes in site numbers near Muswellbrook during the Holocene. Hiscock (1986: 40) said his study indicates declines in site numbers and site use in this area during the last 800 years. His 1986 results also suggest a dramatic increase in the rate of known-habitation use in the period from ca 1300 BP to ca 800 BP. Hiscock (1993: 71) subsequently stated that he considered the date of ca 1300 BP for the appearance of Phase I a minimum.

Table A4/14 NSW Hunter Valley (central lowlands — Mt Arthur North and South): number of habitations known to be used and rates of known-habitation use in each phase. Hiscock's 1986 open archaeological deposits, N = 15.

HISCOCK'S PHASES	HISCOCK'S DATES (BP)	DURATION (YEARS)	NO. OF HABITATIONS KNOWN TO BE USED IN EACH PHASE	RATE OF KNOWN-HABITATION USE (NO./MILLENNIUM)
Pre-Bondaian	>1300	??	1	<1
Bondaian				
Phase 1	1300 – 800	500	11	22
Phase 2	800 – contact	700	4	5.7

Given the uncertainties about the timing and duration of the Bondaian Phase I and pre-Bondaian phases, millennial and average annual growth rates for the number of known-habitations used were calculated for only the last phase (Tables 7.5 and 7.7). Changes of these magnitudes (as decreases or increases) are not recorded for the number of habitations used/millennium in any other region.

Although Hiscock used a greater number of diagnostic features to assign assemblages to phases than Ross (1984), the same methodological predicament exists in that assemblages are assigned to phases on the basis of diagnostic attributes. The date at which each habitation was established or used may be **within** that phase, but not necessarily at the beginning of the phase. It may be that the trend was more gradual than data in Figure 7.9A and Table A4/14 suggest, or that there were dramatic increases and decreases but these changes occurred later or earlier than the dates given for the phase boundaries. In addition to the problems that Hiscock acknowledged (1986: 45), there are two other problems:

1. the 15 knapping floors on which Hiscock's model is based are only a small, purposefully selected sample of artefacts (Hiscock and Koettig 1985: 47–8) from a small number of all the recorded surface artefact scatters in both lease areas — a total of 228 sites (Hughes 1985: 7–8). Given the small percentage that the analysed sample represents, if the remaining sites could be assigned to the phases in which they were occupied, the trend may be quite different to that presented by Hiscock; and,

2. the sites are a series of artefact scatters in ground surface exposures along the relatively flat banks of small creeks; for example, in the Mount Arthur North samples, the 11 sites extend along both sides of a single creek. Some of the artefact scatters designated sites may be small areas of exposure within a single very large, partially buried scatter.

For many years, the earliest radiocarbon date from excavated archaeological deposits in the central lowlands of the Hunter Valley was 1410±90 BP (ANU-122) from Milbrodale (Moore 1970: 45). Further sites have been dated during salvage excavations and the earliest dates are now 3120±70 BP (Beta-62207) from Bulga (Koettig 1994, Vol. 5: 25) and 3600±300 (W-1417) from Warkworth, both near Singleton (Haglund 1992, Vol. 6: Appendix G). In other parts of the Hunter Valley, the earliest dates vary widely. In the southern sandstone rim, the earliest date is 2495±105 BP (ANU-756) (Big L, Moore 1981: 398). Further west, along the Goulburn River (a major tributary of the Hunter River), earliest dates are 3710±210 BP (SUA-1669) from KD/41 (Haglund 1981a: 32, 1984: 85) and 7750±120 BP (ANU-124) from Bobadeen (Moore 1970: 48). Moore (1981: 391) believed the latter date (ANU-124) pre-dates habitation in Bobadeen rockshelter and says other radiocarbon dates from the deposit indicate habitation began about 6000 BP. Along Fal Brook in the Hunter Valley's north-eastern mountains, stone artefacts were found at SGCD.16 in soils in which charcoal provided three dates: >20,020 BP (Beta-20056), 13,020±360 BP (Beta-17271) and 34,580±650 BP (Beta-17009); charcoal processed for the first of these dates came from a hearth. On the basis of these determinations, the artefacts were assigned a late Pleistocene age — sometime between 35,000 BP and 10,000 BP (Koettig 1987: 98–9).

Dates are now available for several open archaeological deposits excavated during salvage projects in the Singleton area of the Hunter Valley central lowlands (Table A4/15) (Koettig 1989: 8, 1992, Vol. 3: Table 1.1; Haglund 1992, Vol. 6: Appendix G; Rich 1992: 110; Koettig 1994, Vol. 5: 25; Haglund 2002: 28, Appendix D). Some of these sites have multiple dates which show they were inhabited during more than one century/millennium. For example, the 11 radiocarbon dates for Camberwell GCC 7/8 fall into three different millennia, with seven dates in the first millennium BP, one in the second millennium BP and three in the third millennium BP (Table A4/15). When these sites are assigned on the basis of the radiocarbon dates to a millennial sequence for the rate of known-habitation use (Table A4/16, Fig. 7.9B), the trends vary from Hiscock's 1986 model of a dramatic decrease in site numbers and site use in the last 800 or 1000 years. In contrast, they suggest a continual relatively steady increase in habitations, though with lower millennial and average annual growth rates in the last 2000 years (Tables 7.7 and A4/16 respectively).

Table A4/15 NSW Hunter Valley (central lowlands — Singleton area): sites included in Table A4/16 and Figure 7.9B with radiometric ages and references. All radiocarbon ages are from charcoal samples, except where TL noted after laboratory number.

PROJECT	SITE NAME	RADIOCARBON AGES		REFERENCE
		YEARS BP	LAB. NO.	
Bulga	Site B8, Area II	1730± 50	Beta-62206	Koettig 1994, Vol. 5: 25
	Site B8, Area IV	3120± 70	Beta-62207	ditto
	Site B58, Area I	2060± 50	Beta-62208	ditto
	Site B58, Area II	2620± 60	Beta-62209	ditto
Camberwell	GCC 7/8	200± 60	Beta-44524	Koettig 1992, Vol. 3: Table 1.1
		260± 60	Beta-39203	ditto
		270± 60	Beta-39206	ditto
		340± 60	Beta-44525	ditto
		450± 80	Beta-44523	ditto
		830± 50	Beta-39201	ditto
		970± 50	Beta-39207	ditto
		1200± 70	Beta-39205	ditto
		2210± 50	Beta-39200	ditto
		2460± 50	Beta-39204	ditto
		2750± 60	Beta-39202	ditto
	GCC 28/29	600± 60	Beta-39208	ditto
		660± 50	Beta-39210	ditto
		970± 50	Beta-39209	ditto

Table A4/15 (Continued)

PROJECT	SITE NAME		RADIOCARBON AGES		REFERENCE
			YEARS BP	LAB. NO.	
	GCC 33		960± 60	Beta-39212	ditto
			1020± 70	Beta-39213	ditto
			2370± 60	Beta-39211	ditto
	GCC 35		1890± 50	Beta-39214	ditto
Pokolbin	POK4		2820±50	Beta-32614	Koettig 1989: 8, Beta Analytic Lab. report
Narama	Site 30		260±60	Beta-48519	Rich 1992: 110
	Site 48		680±50	Beta-48521	ditto
			700±60	Beta-48520	ditto
Warkworth	Doctors Creek WL	(Sample 3)	800±60	Beta-54012	Haglund 1992, Vol. 6: Appendix G
		(Sample 2)	830±60	Beta-54011	ditto
	Doctors Creek WH (Upper)		3600±300	W-1417 [TL]	ditto
	Sandy Hollow Creek W6		300±100	W-1615 [TL]	Haglund 2002: 28, Appendix D
			600±100	W-1617 [TL]	ditto
			1800±200	W-1619 [TL]	ditto

Table A4/16 NSW Hunter Valley (central lowlands — Singleton area): rates of known-habitation use in each century/millennium. N = 12, see Table A4/15 for sites included.

CENTURY/MILLENNIUM	NO. OF HABITATIONS KNOWN TO BE USED IN EACH CENTURY	RATE OF KNOWN-HABITATION USE (NO./MILLENNIUM)	MILLENNIAL GROWTH RATE	
			X	%
4000–3000	2	2		
3000–2000	4	4	2	+100
2000–1900	0]			
1900–1800	1]			
1800–1700	2]			
1700–1200	0]	5	1.25	+30
1200–1100	1]			
1100–1000	1]			
1000– 900	3]			
900– 800	2]			
800– 700	1]			
700– 600	2]			
600– 500	2]	7	1.4	+40
500– 400	1]			
400– 300	1]			
300– 200	3]			
200–contact	1]			

More recent technological analyses of stone artefact assemblages in other parts of the central lowlands (e.g., Narama, Rich 1992: 23–5; Bulga, Koettig 1994; Baker 1994: 4) and the Goulburn River (Haglund 1989) have not found the same associations or chronological sequence of technological attributes identified by Hiscock at Sandy Hollow. It appears that spatial and temporal variations in the manufacture of stone artefacts in the Hunter Valley are more diverse than Hiscock originally envisaged. Dating open sites by Hiscock's methods may prove to be of advantage in some studies. However, using data sets such as those for Mount Arthur North and South to provide trends in the numbers of habitations established or used may be best applied as heuristic devices to set up hypotheses for testing with other evidence. As with the Victorian Mallee, whether the present radiometric dates are indicative of regional trends will not be clear until more detailed work has been carried out and methods discovered which provide a finer scale of dating for the establishment and length of occupation of open archaeological deposits.

B: Artefact accumulation rates in individual habitations

NSW south coast and Sydney

Implement accumulation rates for five sites on the NSW south coast have been presented by Lampert and Hughes (1974: Fig. 2) and Hughes and Lampert (1982: Figs 1 to 5). Each site was inhabited over a long period of time, that is, >/ = 7000 years, except for one where habitation extended back to ca 4000 BP. Hughes and Lampert's 1982 graphs are based on implement counts and not total numbers of artefacts.

Lampert and Hughes (1974: 232–3) presented evidence for Burrill Lake and Bass Point to show that increasing numbers of implements had accumulated at these sites, as well as at Curracurrang 1CU5/-, throughout their period of habitation. They believed that 'an increase in stone-working coincided with the arrival of the new small tool stone technology' and with an increase in the rate of humanly induced sedimentation. At Bass Point the dramatic increase is said to have occurred about 4000 BP, at Burrill Lake the increase was less dramatic, and at Curracurrang ICU5/- it occurred within the past 2000 or 3000 years.

In a later paper, Hughes and Lampert (1982) used evidence from five sites to describe increasing implement accumulation rates and sediment rates at sites on the NSW south coast (Burrill Lake, Bass Point, Currarong 1 and Currarong 2) and its hinterland (Sassafras 1) (1982: 16–20, Figs 1 to 5 reproduced as my Fig. 7.10 and Tables A4/17 to A4/21). They (1982: 19) argued that there was a 'marked intensification of site occupation during Holocene times' with the most dramatic increase (a six- to tenfold increase on average) occurring in the last 5000 years. They saw this increase continuing at least until 2000 BP, then 'after that time the trends diverged in that at some sites the increase in intensity of site occupation continued' (Burrill Lake and Currarong 2), 'but at others the intensity levelled off or there was a slight decline'. Hughes' (1977) data and Hughes and Lampert's (1982) graphs suggest:

- at Bass Point: the rate of implement accumulation ceased to increase sometime after ca 1800 BP and then levelled off or declined slightly; sediment accumulation continued to increase (Table A4/20 and Fig. 7.10E);
- at Currarong 1: the rate of implement accumulation increased substantially after ca 2000 BP and then declined after ca 780 BP (Table A4/18 and Fig. 7.10B); and,
- at Sassafras 1: the rate of implement accumulation increased dramatically between ca 3000 BP and ca 1700 BP then decreased (Table A4/21 and Fig. 7.10D); the sediment rate was stable in the last 3000 years.

Table A4/17 Burrill Lake, NSW south coast: rates of implement accumulation and average annual growth rates based on data from Hughes 1977: Table 2.13. *Italics* indicates highest number or rate, underline = greatest/most dramatic increase.

UNIT	PERIOD (years BP)	DURATION (years)	NO. OF IMPLEMENTS DISCARDED/100 YEARS	AVERAGE ANNUAL GROWTH RATE %
Shell midden	1550– 100	1450	*1.11*	*+0.10*
Top upper sand	7500– 550	5950	0.27	+0.02
Btm upper sand	20,500–7500	13,000	0.11	—

Table A4/18 Currarong 1, NSW south coast: rates of implement accumulation and average annual growth rates based on data from Hughes 1977: Table 3.10. *Italics* indicates highest number or rate, underline = greatest/most dramatic increase.

UNIT	PERIOD (years BP)	DURATION (years)	NO. OF IMPLEMENTS DISCARDED/100 YEARS	AVERAGE ANNUAL GROWTH RATE %
4	780– 100	680	54	-0.04
5	2040– 780	1260	*69*	*+0.18*
6	7000–2040	4960	7	—

Table A4/19 Currarong 2, NSW south coast: rates of implement accumulation and average annual growth rates based on data from Hughes 1977: Table 3.11. *Italics* indicates highest number or rate, underline = greatest/most dramatic increase.

UNIT	PERIOD (years BP)	DURATION (years)	NO. OF IMPLEMENTS DISCARDED/100 YEARS	AVERAGE ANNUAL GROWTH RATE %
1	1100– 100	1000	*15.6*	+0.04
2	2100–1100	1000	10.3	*+0.17*
3	3650–2100	1550	1.9	+0.05
4	7000–3650	3350	0.9	—

Table A4/20 Bass Point, NSW south coast: rates of implement accumulation and average annual growth rates based on data from Hughes 1977: Table 5.6. *Italics* indicates highest number or rate, underline = greatest/most dramatic increase.

UNIT	PERIOD (years BP)	DURATION (years)	NO. OF ARTEFACTS (EXCLUDING WASTE FLAKES) DISCARDED/ sq m/100 YEARS	AVERAGE ANNUAL GROWTH RATE %
Upper midden	740– 100	640	1.25	-0.003
Lower midden	1800– 740	1060	*1.27*	+0.03
Grey sand	3950–1800	2150	0.88	*+0.10*
Upper white sand	7700–3950	3750	0.11	+0.03
Lower white sand	17,500–7700	9800	0.03	—

Table 4/21 Sassafras 1, NSW south coast hinterland: rates of implement accumulation and average annual growth rates based on data from Hughes 1977: Table 4.3. *Italics* denotes highest number or rate; underline = greatest/most dramatic increase.

PERIOD (years BP)	DURATION (years)	NO. OF IMPLEMENTS DISCARDED IN EXCAVATED LEVELS/100 YEARS	AVERAGE ANNUAL GROWTH RATE %
1695– 100	1595	28	-0.04
3090–1695	1395	*43*	*+0.10*
3770–3090	680	9	—

Thus, of the five sites examined by Hughes and Lampert, only two show that implement accumulation rates continued to increase until contact — Burrill Lake and Currarong 2 (Figs 7.10A and 7.10C, Tables A4/17 and A4/19). However, very little of the upper deposits remained at Burrill Lake at the time Lampert excavated the site, and the figures for the most recent period for this site were extrapolated from Currarong 2 (Hughes 1977: 66–7). It is thus possible that the implement accumulation rates at Burrill Lake did not continue to increase until contact.

Average annual growth rates. Hughes and Lampert (1982: 19–20) postulated a six- to tenfold increase over the last 5000 years. Average annual growth rates based on Hughes' data (1977: Tables 2.13, 3.10, 3.11, 4.3 and 5.6) show that the highest average annual growth rate at each site falls between +0.1% and +0.18% (Tables A4/17 to A4/21). The period in which the highest growth rate occurred was not the same in each site, though it occurred after ca 4000 BP at each site. In all sites, the highest growth rate occurred in the same period as the most dramatic increase in the implement accumulation rates.

NSW Hunter Valley and adjacent areas

In the late 1960s, Moore (1970) excavated two rockshelter sites in the sandstone areas of the Hunter Valley (Sandy Hollow and Milbrodale) and a third (Bobadeen) on the upper reaches of the Goulburn River. He (Moore 1981) subsequently excavated two sandstone rockshelters on the southern rim of the Hunter Valley (Big L and Yango Creek) and another in the Macdonald River valley. Radiocarbon dates and extrapolations on the basis of depth/age curves suggest that initial habitation at these six sites began between ca 2000 BP and ca 6000 BP (Tables A4/22 to A4/27).

Table A4/22 Sandy Hollow, NSW Hunter Valley (Goulburn River): rates of artefact accumulation and average annual growth rates based on data from Moore 1970: 35-7, Table 2. *Italics* indicates highest number or rate; underline = period with greatest/most dramatic increase. [1] Excavation taken to 42 inches (107cm), but archaeological materials extend to only 38 inches (96.5cm).

LEVEL	DEPTH (cm)[1]	RADIOCARBON DATES Years BP Lab. No.	D/A DATES years BP	DURATION (years)	NO. OF ARTEFACTS	RATE OF ARTEFACT ACCUMULATION NO./MILLENNIUM	AVERAGE ANNUAL GROWTH RATE %
1	0–15	530±80 ANU-125	570– 100	470	698	1485	-0.11
2	15–31		820– 570	250	624	2500	-0.34
3	31–46		1080– 820	260	*1511*	*5810*	+0.24
4	46–61	1300±100 ANU-12	1320–1080	240	746	3110	+0.15
5	61–76		1580–1320	260	564	2170	*+0.92*
6	76–91		1830–1580	250	49	200	+0.65
7	91–96		1910–1830	80	3	40	

Table A4/23 Milbrodale, NSW Hunter Valley (central lowlands): rates of artefact accumulation and average annual growth rates based on data from Moore 1970: 41-45, Table 4. *Italics* indicates period with highest number or rate; underline = period with greatest/most dramatic increase.

LEVEL	DEPTH (cm)	RADIOCARBON DATES Years BP Lab. No.	D/A DATES years BP	DURATION (years)	NO. OF ARTEFACTS	RATE OF ARTEFACT ACCUMULATION No./millennium	AVERAGE ANNUAL GROWTH RATE %
1	0–15	630±60 ANU-121	990– 100	890	672	755	-0.07
2	15–31	1410±90 ANU-122	1830– 990	840	*1150*	*1370*	+0.21
3	31–46		2600–1830	770	189	245	*<+0.27*
4	46–<76		<3000–2600	<400	12	>30	

Table A4/24 Bobadeen, Ulan, NSW Hunter Valley (upper Goulburn River): rates of artefact accumulation and average annual growth rates based on data from Moore 1970: 45–9, Table 6. *Italics* indicates highest number or rate; underline = period with greatest/most dramatic increase. [1] Radiocarbon date 5150±170 BP (ANU-287) comes from between 63.5–66cm (25–26 inches) below the surface; 7750±120 BP (ANU-124) comes from between 63.5–76cm (25–30 inches) below the surface, but see comments by Moore (1981: 391).

LEVEL	DEPTH (cm)	RADIOCARBON DATES Years BP Lab. No. [1]	D/A DATES years BP	DURATION (years)	NO. OF ARTEFACTS	RATE OF ARTEFACT ACCUMULATION NO./MILLENNIUM	AVERAGE ANNUAL GROWTH RATE %
1	0–15	730±70 ANU-123	950– 100	850	3745	4406	-0.02
2	15–31		2100– 950	1150	*6011*	*5227*	+0.03
3	31–38		2700–2100	600	2216	3690	-0.03
4	38–46		3300–2700	600	2628	4380	+0.13
5	46–53		3900–3300	600	1193	1990	+0.18
6	53–61	4120±175 ANU-790	4650–3900	750	511	680	*+0.20*
7	61–76	5150±170 ANU-287 7750±120 ANU-124	4650– >6000?	>1850?	235	<130?	
8	76–91		?? –>6000		70		

Table A4/25 Big L, NSW Hunter Valley (southern rim): rates of artefact accumulation and average annual growth rates based on data from Moore 1981: 398, Table 2. *Italics* indicates highest number or rate; underline = period with greatest/most dramatic increase. [1] Moore (1981: 398) considered radiocarbon ages from spit 9 anomalous, and they were disregarded in calculating the depth/age curve.

LEVEL	DEPTH (cm)	RADIOCARBON DATES Years BP Lab. No. [1]	D/A DATES years BP	DURATION (years)	NO. OF ARTEFACTS	RATE OF ARTEFACT ACCUMULATION No./millennium	AVERAGE ANNUAL GROWTH RATE %
1	0– 8		324– 100	224	216	964	+0.14
2	8–15		648– 324	324	226	698	+0.20
3	15–23		972– 648	324	112	346	-0.37
4	23–31		1296– 972	324	364	1123	0.00
5	31–38		1620–1296	324	361	1114	-0.05
6	38–46		1944–1620	324	424	1309	-0.02
7	46–53		2268–1944	324	*445*	*1373*	+0.06
8	53–61	2495±105 SUA-756	2592–2268	324	372	1148	+0.33
9	61–69	480±75 ANU-648 930±50 ANU-648/2	2916–2592	324	127	392	+0.31
10	69–76		3240–2916	324	47	145	*+0.43*
11	76–96		4000–3240	864	31	36	

Table A4/26 Yango Creek, NSW Hunter Valley (southern rim): rates of artefact accumulation and average annual growth rates based on data from Moore 1981: 398–401, Table 4. *Italics* indicates highest number or rate; underline = period with greatest/most dramatic increase.

LEVEL	DEPTH (cm)	RADIOCARBON DATES Years BP Lab. No.	D/A DATES years BP	DURATION (years)	NO. OF ARTEFACTS	RATE OF ARTEFACT ACCUMULATION No./millennium	AVERAGE ANNUAL GROWTH RATE %
1	0–8		306–100	206	32	155	-0.11
2	8–15		612–306	306	59	193	-0.40
3	15–23		918–612	306	183	598	-0.44
4	23–31		1224–918	306	716	2340	-0.01
5	31–38		1530–1224	306	728	2379	-0.01
6	38–46		1836–1530	306	*735*	*2402*	+0.08
7	46–53		2142–1836	306	576	1882	+0.07
8	53–61	2350±85 ANU-648	2448–2142	306	<u>458</u>	<u>1497</u>	+0.29
9	61–69		2754–2448	306	191	624	+0.29
10	69–76		3060–2754	306	80	261	+0.24
11	76–84		3366–3060	306	38	124	*+0.83*
12	84–96		3366–3876	510	5	10	

Table A4/27 Macdonald River (Squares A–AA–BB–CC), NSW: rates of artefact accumulation and average annual growth rates based on data from Moore 1981: 401–15, Table 5 and Fig. 4. *Italics* indicates highest number or rate; underline = period with greatest/most dramatic increase.

LEVEL	DEPTH (cm)	RADIOCARBON DATES Years BP Lab. No.	D/A DATES years BP	DURATION (years)	NO. OF ARTEFACTS	RATE OF ARTEFACT ACCUMULATION No./millennium	AVERAGE ANNUAL GROWTH RATE %
1	0–13		515–100	415	106	225	-0.10
2	13–25		1030–515	515	198	384	-0.17
3	25–38		1545–1030	515	467	907	-0.10
4	38–51		2060–1545	515]	<u>*1529*</u>	*1484*	+0.02
5	51–54	2370±100 SUA-387	2575–2060	515]			
6	54–76		3294–2575	719	831	1156	+0.04
7	76–89		4013–3294	719	605	<u>841</u>	*+0.16*
8	89–101		4732–4013	719]			
9	101–114		5451–4732	719]	587	272	
10–11	114–127	5820±110 SUA-564	6170–5451	719]			

In each site, the highest number of artefacts does not occur in the uppermost level. For Big L, Yango Creek and Macdonald River, Moore (1981: 415) noted that the maximum occurrence of artefacts was in levels dating from ca 2300 BP to ca 1800 BP, ca 2000 BP to ca 1700 BP, and ca 2300 BP to ca 1800 BP respectively. My estimated dates for these levels, using depth/age curves based on information in Moore (1970, 1981), vary slightly from Moore's but indicate the same trends.

Artefact accumulation rates (Tables A4/22 to A4/27, Figs 7.11 to 7.16) indicate that at each of the six sites:

- levels with the highest number of artefacts also have the highest artefact accumulation rates. For Macdonald River (Table A4/27 and Fig. 7.16), figures are based on artefacts from squares A, AA, BB and CC and correlation of the levels as depicted in Moore's (1981) Figure 4, rather than the figures in Moore's (1981) Table 6, which were used in Attenbrow 1987: Fig. 9.18. For Sandy Hollow, Hiscock's (1986: Table 1) artefact accumulation rates (based on squares AA and BB only) differ slightly from mine in magnitude relative to each other, but level 3 still has the highest artefact accumulation rate and the overall trends are the same (Table A4/22).

- in each site, levels with the highest artefact accumulation rates began accumulating about or after 2600 BP. At Sandy Hollow and Milbrodale, the *most dramatic increase* in the artefact accumulation rate occurred in the level with the highest artefact accumulation rate. However, at the other sites the most dramatic increase occurred in levels earlier than those with the highest artefact accumulation rate — at Bobadeen, Big L, Yango Creek and Macdonald River.

- the artefact accumulation rates *decreased in the most recent levels*. The figures suggest that the decreases occurred within the last 1000 years BP at three sites (Sandy Hollow, Milbrodale, Bobadeen), after ca 1550 BP at two sites (Yango Creek, Macdonald River), and at Big L after 2000 BP. The magnitude of decreases at each site varied, and at Big L, where the decrease was earliest, the rate rose again in the last 600 or so years.

Average annual growth rates. The *highest* average annual growth rate occurred at different times in individual sites (Tables A4/22 to A4/27), though it was always between ca 4000 BP and ca 1250 BP. The highest average annual growth rate did not always occur in the same level as the greatest increase in the artefact accumulation rate or the highest artefact accumulation rate. At all sites except Macdonald River, it occurred in an earlier level. At Macdonald River, the highest growth rate (+0.16%) occurred in the same level as the greatest increase in the artefact accumulation rate (level 7).

Decreases in the average annual growth rates occurred in the upper levels of all sites. There are *substantial decreases* in the growth rates, associated with substantial decreases in the artefact accumulation rates, in three sites; for example, Sandy Hollow -0.34% in level 2; Big L -0.37% in level 3 and Yango Creek -0.44% in level 3. In each of these sites the substantial decrease occurs after 1000 BP.

NSW Blue Mountains and adjacent areas

Many (>27) sites have been excavated in the Blue Mountains and adjacent districts (Stockton 1970a, 1973, 1993; Stockton and Holland 1974; Johnson 1979). Only seven of these sites had information available on the artefact accumulation rates or artefact densities (number of artefacts per cubic metre) — Springwood Creek, Kings Tableland, Walls Cave, Capertee 1 and 3, Shaws Creek K1 and K2 (Tables A4/28 to A4/32). Revised radiocarbon dates for Springwood Creek and Kings Tableland published since Stockton and Holland (1974) (Gillespie and Temple 1976: 99; Stockton 1993) were used in estimating the age of deposits based on a depth/age curve.

Of the excavated Blue Mountains sites, three contain stratified deposits with more than one cultural assemblage — Walls Cave, Springwood Creek and Kings Tableland. Excavations at these sites indicate that habitation in the Blue Mountains dates back at least 22,000 years. The distribution of artefacts throughout the deposits and radiocarbon dates at these sites (in particular, Walls Cave and Springwood Creek) suggested to Stockton and Holland (1974: 46) that there was a hiatus in occupation of the Blue Mountains between ca 6000 and ca 3360 BP. They (1974: 60) believed this hiatus occurred between the Capertian and Bondaian assemblages, and they dated these two assemblages in the Blue Mountains from ca 12,000 BP to ca 6000 BP and from ca 3360 BP to contact respectively. Stockton and Holland divided the Bondaian period into Early, Middle and Late Bondaian.

Table A4/28 Springwood Creek, NSW Blue Mountains: rates of artefact accumulation and average annual growth rates based on data taken from Stockton and Holland 1974: Table 3 and Appendix, and revised radiocarbon ages from Stockton 1993: 38-9. *Italics* indicates highest number or rate; <u>underline</u> = period with greatest/most dramatic increase.

PHASE	LEVEL	DEPTH (cm)	RADIOCARBON AGES Years BP Lab. No.	D/A DATES years BP	DURATION (years)	ARTEFACTS No.	DENSITY No./m³	AREA EXCAVATED m²	RATE OF ARTEFACT ACCUM-ULATION No./mill.	AVERAGE ANNUAL GROWTH RATE %
Surf	1–2	0– 6		100– 0	<100					
I	3	6– 12		200– 100)						
	4	12– 20		600– 200)	500	*214*	888	1.5	<u>*285*</u>	*+0.15*
II	5	20– 28	595±85 SUA-204	1500– 600	900	158	*1319*	1.5	137	+0.05
III	6	28– 36		2500–1500	1000	139	<u>1111</u>	1.5	93	+0.09
IV	7	36– 44	2930±165 SUA-17	3300–2500)						
	8	44– 52		3950–3300)						
	9	52– 60		4600–3950)	2100	121	313	1.5	38	*
STERILE	10	60– 68		5300–4600	700	0	0	1.5	0	-100.00
V	11	68– 76	6050±170 SUA-18	6000–5300)						
	12	76– 86		6700–6000)	1400	85	181	2.0	30	+0.09
VI	13	86– 90		7000–6700)						
	(14	90– 95)		–7000						
	(15	95–100)	7420±140 SUA-205							
	16	100–120	7440±140 SUA-206	7700–						
	17	120–140	8565±430 SUA-285	9000–7700)	2300	56	15	3.0	8	

Table A4/29 Kings Tableland, NSW Blue Mountains: rates of artefact accumulation and average annual growth rates based on data from Stockton and Holland 1974: Table 3 and Appendix, Stockton n.d.; revised radiocarbon ages from Stockton 1977b: 49; 1993: 33. [1] SUA-157 and SUA-229 averaged for depth/age curve. *Italics* indicates highest number or rate; <u>underline</u> = period with greatest/most dramatic increase.

PHASE	LEVEL	DEPTH (cm)	RADIOCARBON AGES Years BP Lab. No.[1]	D/A DATES years BP	DURATION (years)	ARTEFACTS NO.	DENSITY No./m³	RATE OF ARTEFACT ACCUMULATION No./mill.	AVERAGE ANNUAL GROWTH RATE %
I	1	0– 8							
	2	8– 13							
	3	13– 18		750– 100	650	*869*	4333	1337	-0.04
II	4	18– 23							
	5	23– 25	965±75 SUA-155	1050– 750	300	515	*6449*	1717	-0.46
III	6	25– 29	)			)	)		
	7	29– 33	)			464)	<u>4988</u>)		
			)			)	)		

Table A4/29 (Continued)

PHASE	LEVEL	DEPTH (cm)	RADIOCARBON AGES Years BP Lab. No.[1]	D/A DATES years BP	DURATION (years)	ARTEFACTS NO.	DENSITY No./m³	RATE OF ARTEFACT ACCUMULATION No./mill.	AVERAGE ANNUAL GROWTH RATE %
IV	8	33– 39	)			)	)		
	9	39– 42	)			)	)		
	10	42– 47	)			482)	3014)		
			)	1250–1050	200	)	)	*9455*	☆
V	11	47– 53	)			)	)		
	12	53– 61	)			)	)		
	13	61– 66	)			)	)		
	14	67– 71	)			<u>793</u>)	1139)		
			)			)	)		
VI	15	71– 76	1100±80 SUA-229)			)	)		
	16	76– 84	1060±115 SUA-157)			)	)		
	17	84– 90	)			152)	445)		
10cm sterile zone — at bottom of level 17 and on top of level 18						0	0	0	-100.00
VII	18	90–100	)			28)			
	19	100–110	14,534± 300 SUA-194)	24,000–12,400	11,600	8)			
	20	110–120	)			10)			
	21	120–130	22,400±1000 SUA-158)			1)	86	4	☆
Sterile		130–220 taken to bedrock				0			

Table A4/30 Walls Cave (Site B), NSW Blue Mountains: rates of artefact accumulation and average annual growth rates based on depth/age curve for Levels 1 to 3, assuming constant rate of sediment accumulation using data from Stockton and Holland 1974: Table 3 and Appendix. *Italics* indicates highest number or rate; <u>underline</u> = period with greatest/most dramatic increase.

PHASE	LEVEL	DEPTH (cm)	RADIOCARBON AGES Years BP Lab. No.	D/A DATES years BP	DURATION (years)	NO. OF ARTEFACTS	RATE OF ARTEFACT ACCUMULATION No./millennium	AVERAGE ANNUAL GROWTH RATE %
Surf	1	0– 12	European					
II	2	12– 19		2600– 100	2500	*85*	34	*-0.005*
III	3	19– 30	3360±100 Gak-3446	4000–2600	1400	<u>53</u>	<u>*38*</u>	
STERILE	4	30– 37						
	5	37– 55						
	6	55– 82				0	0	-100.00
IV	7	82–106						
	8	106–122	12,000±350 Gak-3448			11	☆	
STERILE	9	122–146						

Stockton and Holland (1974: 56, 60, 64) stated that in the Bondaian period there was an increasing abundance of flaked material in rockshelters, with peak concentrations about 1000 BP (Stockton's Middle Bondaian). For example, at Springwood Creek the peak occurred in a level dating to ca 595±85 BP (SUA-204) and, consequently, the final Bondaian levels have a lower density of flaked material. Decreasing artefact densities in upper levels are documented for Kings Tableland as well (Stockton and Holland 1974: Table 3).

Springwood Creek

At Springwood Creek, initial habitation is dated by a radiocarbon date of 8563±430 BP (SUA-285) in the basal level (Stockton and Holland 1974: 64). The two habitation phases at the site are separated by a sterile sediment layer in level 10. The Capertian assemblage dates from initial occupation to about 6000 BP (6050±170 BP, SUA-18) and the Bondaian assemblage from sometime before 3000 BP (2930±165 BP, SUA-17) — ca 4600 BP based on depth/age curve — to contact.

Artefact accumulation rates. Reanalysis of the Springwood Creek data (Fig. 7.17 and Table A4/28) indicates that:

- decreasing artefact concentrations in the uppermost levels do not reflect decreasing artefact accumulation rates;
- the artefact accumulation rate was **higher** in the last 500 years of habitation than in the previous 8500 years (see also Johnson 1979: 24, 39);
- the artefact accumulation rate for the uppermost level of the Capertian phase (V) is similar to that for the lowest level of the Bondaian phase (IV).

The *highest average annual growth rate* (+0.15%) was in Phase I, which lasted from ca 600 BP to ca 100 BP (Table A4/28). The only decreases in the artefact accumulation rate and the average annual growth rates were those associated with the sterile layer between Phases IV and V.

Kings Tableland

Initial habitation associated with a radiocarbon date of 22,400±1000 BP (SUA-158) is represented by only a single artefact in level 21, but the three overlying levels, which together with Level 21 comprise Phase VII, have higher numbers (10, 8, 28) (Table A4/29). More than one artefact is thus present below Level 19, which was radiocarbon-dated to 14,534±300 BP (SUA-194). Evidence for earliest occupation at this site is scant, but in contrast to Johnson (1979: 28–9) and Bowdler (1981: 102), I do not discount occupation at about 22,000 BP. Two main cultural components were identified which, based on a depth/age curve, date from about 24,000 BP to 12,400 BP, and from 1250 BP to contact. The two assemblages were separated by a sterile zone about 10cm deep, partly in Level 17 and partly in Level 18 (Stockton and Holland 1974: 64). Stockton (1993: 34) attributes the gap between the two components to removal of deposits by storm water about 1000 years ago.

The upper component had a much greater sedimentation rate than the earlier component, particularly levels 6 to 17, where about 70cm of deposit accumulated in somewhere between one and possibly 300 years (see Johnson 1979: 29 for discussions and alternative interpretations).

Artefact accumulation rates. Assuming that a major disturbance did not occur (Johnson 1979: 29), the depth/age curve and artefact accumulation rates for the upper deposit (Fig. 7.18 and Table A4/29) suggest that for a short (but possibly up to 200 years long) period about 1100 BP, the artefact accumulation rate was very much higher than in either the final habitation phases (I and II) or the earliest phase (VII).

Average annual growth rates could be calculated for only the most recent phases (I and II). These both had negative values, that for Phase II between ca 1050 BP and ca 750 BP (-0.46%) indicating a dramatic decrease (Table 4/29).

Walls Cave

As at Kings Tableland, two habitation components were identified at Walls Cave. The earlier was a small assemblage associated with a radiocarbon date of 12,000±350 BP (Gak-3448) (Stockton and Holland 1974; Stockton 1993: 36–7). This was separated by some 50cm of sterile sediment from the later component, which dates from ca 4000 BP possibly to contact.

Artefact accumulation rates and *average annual growth rates* were calculated for only the upper unit, assuming a constant rate of sediment accumulation throughout the period (Fig. 7.19, Table A4/30). These figures suggest that in the most recent habitation phase there was a very slight decrease in the artefact accumulation rates, which is not considered significant and is assumed to represent stability in use.

Capertee 1 and 3

Capertee 1 and 3, on the western side of the Blue Mountains, were excavated in the 1960s by F. D. McCarthy (1964b) and re-excavated in the 1970s by Ian Johnson (1979). Initial habitation of Capertee 3 was dated to 7360±125 (V18) (Johnson 1979: Table 16), but no radiocarbon dates were obtained for Capertee 1.

McCarthy's distribution table (1964b: Table 3) includes 'only "tools" and a small selection of "waste"' (Johnson 1979: 41), and relevant information is not available on which to calculate artefact accumulation rates for each millennium for the materials he recovered (but see Hiscock and Attenbrow [in press, Table 76 and 81] for discard rates for retouched flakes and backed artefacts). McCarthy's artefact distribution table suggests, if it is accepted as indicative of the total assemblage size in each level, that there was a decrease in the number of artefacts recovered in the upper spits at Capertee 1 and 3 (see also Johnson 1979: 43).

Artefact densities. Johnson presented artefact densities (artefacts/kilo of deposit, implements/kilo of deposit) for his excavations at Capertee 3 (Johnson 1979: Figs 34 and 35; Fig. 35 is reproduced as my Fig. 7.20). If the variations in artefact densities reflect changes in artefact accumulation rates then these figures also indicate that in the last 1000 years BP there was a continuing *decrease* in artefacts accumulated at Capertee 3.

Shaws Creek K1 and K2

Shaws Creek K1 and K2 are near Emu Plains, adjacent to a tributary of the Nepean River at the base of the Blue Mountains eastern escarpment.

Shaws Creek K1 was excavated by Stockton (1973). No radiocarbon dates are available, but assemblages in the upper levels are typically Bondaian, and those in the lower levels (8 to 10) are described by Stockton (1973: 112) as 'archaic' and by Johnson (1979: 26) as having similarities with Capertian assemblages at Springwood Creek.

Artefact densities. In the absence of spit depths, I divided the estimated volumes for Phases IV, V and VI (0.15, 0.15 and 0.25 cu m) evenly to calculate artefact densities for the levels in each of these phases (Fig. 7.21 and Table A4/31). Variations in the artefact densities in the 10 levels suggest that there was an initial increase in artefacts accumulated (levels 10 to 5), and a subsequent decrease in the upper levels. Level 2 has a higher artefact density than Level 3, but it is still not as high as levels 4 and 5. Level 1 has a mixture of European and Aboriginal habitation debris, and Stockton (1973: 112) considered the flaked stone artefacts in this level to be displaced from lower deposits (see also discussions in Johnson 1979: 25–8, Fig. 6, Tables 2

Table A4/31   Shaws Creek K1, NSW: number and density of artefacts in each level based on data from Stockton 1973 and Johnson 1979: Tables 2 and 4. B indicates levels with backed artefacts; *italics* = highest number or rate; underline = period with greatest increase.

PHASE	LEVEL	DEPTH (cm)	ESTIMATED VOLUME m³	TOTAL NO. OF ARTEFACTS		NO. OF ARTEFACTS PER CUBIC METRE	
I	1	0–5	0.05	36	B	720	
II	2	5–15	0.10	872	B	8720	
III	3	15–25	0.10	492	B	4920	
IV	4)	25–40	0.15	988	B	13,173)	*17,920*
	5)			*1700*	B	22,667)	
V	6)	40–55	0.15	930	B	12,430)	11,040
	7)			726	B	9680)	
VI	8)	55–80	0.25	398	B	3980)	
	9)			255		2550)	2724
	10)			28		560)	

Table A4/32   Shaws Creek K2, NSW: density of artefacts in each unit based on data from Kohen et al. 1984: 67, Table 7. *Italics* indicates highest number or rate; underline = period with greatest/most dramatic increase.

SOIL UNIT	PHASE	SQUARES ABF NO./m³	SQUARE A ONLY NO./m³	KOHEN'S ESTIMATED DEPTH (cm)	DATES (YEARS BP)
6	I	5743	2240	0– 5	
			8420	5– 15	
5/6	II	*7820*	*9533*	15– 30	1700
5	III	3177	6242	30– 45	2200
4	IV	110	60	45– 60	4100
			160	60– 70	7900
3	V	1000	5529	70– 85	13,000
			60	85–105	
2	VI	865	910	105–125	
1			607	125–150	

and 4). The distribution of backed artefacts in Levels 1 to 8 (Stockton 1973: 113, Tables 1 and 2) suggests peak artefact densities were within the Bondaian phase, and that the decrease began in the latter part of this phase.

Shaws Creek K2 was excavated from 1979 to 1980 by Kohen, Stockton and Williams (1981, 1984). Evidence for occupation of this shelter goes back more than 15,000 years (14,700±250 BP [Beta-12423], Nanson et al. 1987: 76; Stockton 1993: 39). Charcoal for this date was associated with stone artefacts in the earliest part of Phase V in Soil Unit 3. Published information is not available on which artefact accumulation rates can be calculated (e.g., the actual number of artefacts in each square and spit, and the area excavated in each spit which appears to be unequal), and artefact densities calculated by Kohen are used below.

Artefact densities. The density or concentration of artefacts per cubic metre of deposit is provided for square A and for combined squares ABF, which are in undisturbed areas of the shelter deposits (Kohen et al. 1984: Table 7, reproduced in my Table A4/32). These figures show variations throughout the ca 15,000 years of habitation. Two peaks occur — one in Phase V in the Capertian levels and the other in Phase II in the Bondaian levels (Fig. 7.22). Phase II is placed at ca 1700 BP and Phase V at ca 13,000 BP by Kohen et al. (1981: 66; 1984: Table 7; Kohen 1986: Table 6.1).

Figures based only on Square A suggest that densities in the first part of Phase I were almost as high as Phase II (8420/cu m and 9533/cu m respectively) followed by a dramatic drop to 2240/cu m in the second part of Phase I. Even though there is obvious spatial variation in artefact densities across the shelter floor, and the figures for Square A and Squares ABF indicate the magnitude of the differences, both sets of data indicate similar trends over time and include a decrease in the uppermost levels.

Comment: Blue Mountains and adjacent areas

Human occupation of the Blue Mountains extends back at least 22,000 years, albeit its present late-Pleistocene/early-Holocene representation by small assemblages and periods of site abandonment. All sites indicate more substantial late-Holocene occupation.

Of the three sites in the Blue Mountains where artefact accumulation rates were calculated, one site had a substantial increase in the last 600 years (Springwood Creek), one site had a short period of massive accumulation about 1000 years BP and a subsequent decrease in the last 1000 years (Kings Tableland); and the third site (Walls Cave) shows a relatively steady rate over the last 4000 years. The Springwood Creek sequence suggested to Johnson (1979: 39) that 'use of the plateau area may only have reached its contact-period intensity during the recent past'. In making this statement on the basis of his recalculated figures from Springwood Creek, Johnson seemed to be assuming that the regional population size at contact was greater than in previous periods. Evidence from Kings Tableland suggests decreasing artefact accumulation rates occurred in the most recent period there, and it could be, for example, that events at Kings Tableland offset those at Springwood Creek. The number of excavated sites involved is too small, the artefact numbers are too low and the area too big for valid statements to be made about variations in the habitation levels on a regional scale. However, even if the evidence can be interpreted as a decrease in the 'intensity of use' of the plateau area in the most recent period, Johnson's statement 'that use of the plateau area may only have reached its contact-period intensity during the recent past' is still valid.

All sites where only artefact densities were available have decreased values in their uppermost levels (Capertee 1 and 3 to the west of the Blue Mountains, and Shaws Creek K1 and K2 at the base of the eastern escarpment). The sequences at Capertee 1 and Shaws Creek K1 were undated, but in Capertee 3 and Shaws Creek K2, the decreased artefact densities occurred within the last 1000 years and 2000 years respectively.

South-western Victoria

At the time of Lourandos' study, very few deep stratified archaeological deposits had been excavated in south-western Victoria and his evidence from this region came from two excavated sites — Seal Point and Bridgewater.

Bridgewater

At Bridgewater, two cultural units were distinguished in the archaeological deposit: an upper Unit C and a lower Unit A. Outside the rockshelter, these two units are separated by a zone of sterile rockfall (Unit B), which may be partial collapse of the overhang as it is not present inside the rockshelter (Lourandos 1983a: 83). A date of 11,390±310 BP (Beta-3923) comes from Unit A in the rockshelter at a depth of ca 65cm. Outside the shelter, cultural materials extend to a maximum depth of ca 3m, and it is probable that the rockshelter was first inhabited earlier than 11,400 years ago. Samples from the top of Unit A inside the shelter yielded dates of 10,900±90 (SUA-2175) and 10,760±110 BP (Beta-8465), and outside the shelter 8350±130 BP (Beta-8464) (Head 1985: 5; Bird and Frankel 1991a: 16). Lourandos (pers. comm. in Head 1985: 5) concluded that Phase A (Unit A) lasted from 12,000 BP to 8000 BP — a period of about 4000 years. Unit C, representing the most recent phase of habitation, dates from about 450 years ago (450±40 BP, Beta-3922).

Lourandos based his statement that there is 'an increased usage of the cave during the last 500 years' (1983a: 84) on the fact that stone artefacts, faunal remains and charcoal are more plentiful in the upper unit (Phase C) than in the lower unit (Phase A) (1980b: 348–9) — see Table A4/33.

Table A4/33   Bridgewater, SW Victoria: distribution of stone artefacts and faunal remains in Phase (Unit) A and Phase (Unit) C in Pits B, C, F and F. Rates of artefact accumulation and average annual growth rates, based on data from Lourandos 1980b: Tables 13.2, 13.3, 13.4 and 13.5.

PHASE	APPROXIMATE DURATION OF PHASE (YEARS)	NO. OF ARTEFACTS	FAUNAL REMAINS (MNI)	RATE OF ARTEFACT ACCUMULATION NO./MILLENNIUM	AVERAGE ANNUAL GROWTH RATE %
Phase C	450	1657	532	1064	0.72
Phase A	4000	593	140	35	*

Seal Point

Lourandos (1983a: 85) interpreted the sequence at Seal Point as two major periods of intensive occupation interspersed between less intensive phases of occupation. He (1980b: 286) said the second major habitation phase was less intense than the first. The radiocarbon date from the basal level indicates that Seal Point was first inhabited about 1500 years ago (1420±130 BP, SUA-552) (1983a: 84–5). There are two main zones of shelly midden accumulation — an upper, more loosely composed complex and a lower, more compacted humic horizon. The earliest phase, characterised by seal and a predominance of elephant seal over fur seal, has a greater number of stone artefacts than the second phase. In the second, more recent phase, the faunal remains diminish in quantity; the proportion of land mammal and fish increase and seal declines, with fur seal remains being more numerous than elephant seal. The upper and lower phases are separated in some pits by a horizon with a matrix of ashy hearths, sand and broken shell grit and an overall low frequency of shell, stone and bone (Lourandos 1980b: 221). Lourandos' interpretation is based on the distribution of both the faunal remains and the stone artefacts. Dates for the two phases were not suggested.

Comment: south-western Victoria

Lourandos (1983a: 85) stated that the evidence from Bridgewater and Seal Point suggests 'an intensity of site usage, and especially in the case of Seal Point, of economy, took place late in the Holocene, that is within the last 2000 years'. This may be true, but at Bridgewater it was not until very late in the sequence (ca 450 BP) and, at Seal Point, which was not established until ca 1500 BP, the concentration of archaeological materials varied throughout and in the most recent level was lower than in earlier levels. The evidence from these two sites provides minimal support for 'increased intensity of site use' for the whole of south-western Victoria.

Subsequent excavations at Koongine Cave, not far to the west in south-eastern South Australia, revealed a similar sequence to Bridgewater, with an initial period of occupation from ca 11,000 BP until ca 9000 BP, and then a gap of about 8000 years before reoccupation sometime within the last 1000 years (Bird and Frankel 2001: 74).

Lower Murray Valley, South Australia

Three published excavated sites with deep sequences and in relative proximity to each other occur in the lower Murray Valley: Devon Downs and Fromms Landing 2 and 6. Artefact accumulation rates for these sites are discussed below.

Devon Downs

Material from this site, originally excavated by Hale and Tindale (1930), was re-examined by Smith (1982), who presented data on the 'total numbers of artefacts' as well as other components of the assemblages in the six analytical units of Trench C.

Considerable variation in the distribution of stone artefacts occurs throughout the 6m depth of stratified deposit, which spans 6000–5000 years of habitation. Smith's (1982: 110, Fig. 3) analyses show that there were marked rises in the number of stone artefacts and in the total weight of stone in Units 5 and 4, and that the numbers drop dramatically in Unit 2 and remain similarly low in Unit 1. This trend is also seen in the retouched artefacts, unmodified flakes and cores. Ochre is markedly concentrated in Unit 4 and the faunal remains (according to counts of the minimum numbers of individuals [MNI]) are concentrated in Units 5, 4 and 3. Smith (1982: 114) argued that the idea of changes 'in the intensity of site use' is supported by the very similar distributions through time in the various types of archaeological remains. The period in which Smith (1982: 114–15) says 'the shelter was used more intensively', i.e., 4000 BP to 2000 years ago, is represented by Units 4 and 3, which contain the highest numbers of artefacts (both have twice the number of Unit 5).

Artefact accumulation rates are based on data provided by Smith (1982) and assume the area of each excavated unit was roughly equal (Fig. 7.23, Table A4/34). These rates follow the same trends as the figures presented by Smith. Units 4 and 3 had the highest artefact accumulation rates (Unit 4 had the highest). The artefact accumulation rate increased markedly in Unit 5, but more substantially in Unit 4. There is a dramatic decrease after Unit 3 to the lowest rates in Units 2 and 1.

The highest average annual growth rates were in Unit 5 (+0.11% p.a. between ca 4800 BP and ca 3800 BP) and in Unit 4 (+0.1% p.a. between 3800 BP and 2900 BP); that is, there were two successive periods in the sequence where the growth rates increased substantially (Table A4/34). The decrease in the artefact accumulation rate after 2000 BP (in Unit 2) also involved a dramatic decrease in the average annual growth rate (-0.3%).

Table A4/34 Devon Downs (Trench C), lower Murray Valley, South Australia: rates of artefact accumulation and average annual growth rates based on data from Smith 1982. Bracketed figures represent number of unifacial points retrieved in unit. *Italics* indicates highest number or rate; underline = period with greatest/most dramatic increase.

UNIT	RADIOCARBON AGES YEARS BP LAB. NO.	D/A DATES YEARS BP	DURATION (YEARS)	NO. OF ARTEFACTS	RATE OF ARTEFACT ACCUMULATION NO./MILLENNIUM	AVERAGE ANNUAL GROWTH RATE %
1		1200 100	1100	25	23	-0.08
2		1900–1200	700	38	54	-0.30
3		2900–1900	1000	500 (2)	500	-0.02
4	2980±90 Gak-1021					
	3460±100 Gak-1022	3800–2900	900	*538* (1)	*598*	+0.10
5	4360±110 Gak-1023					
	4290±140 L-217G	4800–3800	1000	250 (13)	250	*+0.11*
6	5180±100 Gak-1024	6300–4800	1500	130 (6)	87	*

Fromms Landing 2

Fromms Landing 2 (18km downstream from Devon Downs) has a near basal date of 4850±100 BP (R-456/1, NZ-364) (Mulvaney 1960: 70, 1975: 290). At this site, Smith (1982: 114) said there was a

> comparable increase in intensity of site use beginning about 4000 years BP, although the marked decline in the amount of occupational debris noted at Devon Downs in the recent levels is not matched.

The vertical distribution of artefacts at Fromms Landing 2 (Mulvaney 1960: Table 1; my Table A4/35) suggests a fluctuating increase in the number of artefacts accumulated over time, with the highest figure in Level 0 (the uppermost analytical level). However, the dimensions of the excavated trench varied in width and depth along its length. The width of the area excavated each season varied from 7 feet (215cm) in 1956 to 11 feet (335cm) in 1958, except for the first 2 feet (61cm) in depth, where it was 14 feet (427cm) wide (Mulvaney 1960: 59). The composite trench was 32 feet (975cm) long at the surface of the deposit but the back wall of the rockshelter (bedrock) sloped outwards so that with depth the trench decreased in length (Mulvaney 1960: Fig. 3). The area over which Levels 0, 1, 2 and 3 extended was about one-third greater than the area of Levels 4 to 6, which was greater again than the area of Levels 7 to 11. Estimated length measurements are given in Table A4/35. Each level also varied in depth, but the measurements were not given.

Table A4/35 Fromms Landing 2, lower Murray Valley, South Australia: number of artefacts in each level, radiocarbon dates and approximate length of pit, based on data from Mulvaney 1960: 65, 70, Table 1, Fig. 3; Mulvaney et al. 1964: Table 3; Roberts and Pate 1999: Table 1. *Italics* indicates highest number or rate; <u>underline</u> = period with greatest/most dramatic increase.

LEVEL	RADIOCARBON AGES		NO. OF	APPROXIMATE
	YEARS BP	LAB. NO.	ARTEFACTS	LENGTH OF PIT (cm)
0			*609*	975
1			201	975
2			601	975
3			<u>487</u>	700–760
4	3240±80	R-456/2 (NZ-365)	55	700–760
5			322	670
6	3750±85	P-308	508	670
7			279	550–610
8	3870±85	P-309	169	550–610
9	4050±85	P-311	112	550–610
10	4850±100	R-456/1 (NZ-364)	72	550–610
11			8	550

Since all dimensions for each level were not available and were so obviously variable, I did not calculate artefact accumulation rates. If allowance is made for the extra area in the upper levels, artefact densities and accumulation rates are unlikely to be as high in the upper levels (relative to the lower levels) as suggested by the raw figures in Mulvaney's Table 1 (1960). Whether there was a decline or increase in the artefact accumulation rates in the upper levels cannot be stated from the published information.

Fromms Landing 6

This rockshelter, ca 400m from Fromms Landing 2, has a near basal date of 3450±90 BP (NPL-63) (Mulvaney et al. 1964: 490). Level 11 has a date of 3170±94 BP (NPL-29) and Level 8 a date of 2950±91 BP (NPL-28). The depth of every level is not given and the section of the excavated deposit suggests the area of each level varied markedly (becoming smaller with depth) (Mulvaney et al. 1964: Fig. 2). However, the vertical distribution of artefacts and the radiocarbon dates (Mulvaney et al. 1964: Table 1) suggest that the upper levels (6–1) had a much lower number of artefacts than the middle levels (11–7).

Artefact accumulation rates and *average annual growth rates* based on the available data provide a rough substantiation of these conclusions (Table A4/36). They indicate a decrease in both the accumulation rate and the growth rate in the more recent period of the rockshelter's habitation; say, within the last 3000 years BP.

Table A4/36   Fromms Landing 6, lower Murray Valley, South Australia: rates of artefact accumulation and average annual growth rates based on data from Mulvaney et al. 1964: 490, Table 1. *Italics* indicates highest number or rate; underline = period with greatest/most dramatic increase.

LEVEL	RADIOCARBON AGES YEARS BP LAB. NO.	DEPTH (cm)	DURATION (YEARS)	'TOTAL FLAKES ETC'	RATE OF ARTEFACT ACCUMULATION NO./MILLENNIUM	AVERAGE ANNUAL GROWTH RATE %
1				15)		
2				19)		
3				3)		
4			2850	31) 208	73	-0.14
5				0)		
6				8)		
7				132)		
8	2950±91 NPL-28	137		*363*)		
9				249)		
10			220	279) *1052*	*4782*	*+0.94*
11	3170±94 NPL-29	214		161)		
12				65)		
13				24)		
14			280	42) 170	611	
15				3)		
16	3450±90 NPL-63	275		36)		
17				41		
18A				8		
18B				5		

Summary: Lower Murray Valley
In two sites in the lower Murray valley (Devon Downs and Fromms Landing 6), dramatic decreases occurred in the artefact accumulation rates of the uppermost levels — after ca 1900 BP at Devon Downs, and ca 3000 BP at Fromms Landing 6. These changes also involved substantial decreases in the average annual growth rate. At Fromms Landing 2, it was not possible to state whether there was a decrease or increase in the artefact accumulation rate.

At Devon Downs, there were also substantial increases in the growth rate during the periods ca 4800 BP to ca 3800 BP and ca 3800 BP to ca 1900 BP.

Central Queensland highlands
Of the 11 sites excavated in the central Queensland highlands, artefact accumulation rates (or the information from which they can be calculated) were available for four — Native Well 1 and 2, Kenniff Cave and The Tombs (Mulvaney and Joyce 1965; Morwood 1979, 1981, 1984).

Native Well 1

Native Well 1 has a near basal date of 10,910±140 BP (ANU-2034), from which Morwood (1981: 27) extrapolated an initial habitation date of ca 13,000 BP; deposition rates, however, were taken to ca 14,000 BP (1981: Fig. 23). Morwood (1981: 29–31) divided the stone artefact assemblages into three industries: the earliest, the Core and Scraper Industry (spits 16 to 8) lasting from ca 13,000 BP to ca 4300-4200 BP; the Small Tool Industry (spits 7 to 3) dating from ca 4300–4200 BP to ca 2300 BP; and the latest, the Recent Industry (spits 2 and 1) dating from ca 2300 BP to contact. Variation occurred throughout the depth of deposit in the number of implements (tools) and artefacts in each spit.

Implement accumulation rates. Morwood (1981: 32) briefly discussed implement deposition **rates** and variations in the rate of implement deposition in each 100 years are shown in Morwood's (1981) Figure 23 (see my Fig. A4/1). However, his discussions (1981: 28–31) about the stone assemblages refer principally to variations in the **number** of artefacts or implements per spit, noting the following changes throughout the depth of deposit:

1. in spits 16 to 8, in the lower half of the deposit: 'The number of tools/spit … peaks in Spit 12 … Above this spit there are very few artefacts until spit 7' (1981: 28);
2. from spit 7 to spit 4, 'the number of implements/spit increases rapidly… then declines' (1981: 28);
3. 'at 50–60cm depth there was a sudden increase in the number of artefacts per spit' (1981: 29–30) (spit 7 is at this depth);
4. spits 1 and 2, which accumulated during the last 2300 years, had 'a marked decrease in the number of artefacts and waste flakes/spit, the deletion of many implement types from the assemblage, and a minimum 48% decrease in the rate of sediment accumulation' (1981: 31; see also 1984: 354).

In terms of *total artefact numbers*, spits 7 and 8 have similar totals (456 and 410 respectively), and spit 6 rather than spit 7 has a substantial increase (Morwood 1981: Table 11, see my Table A4/37), with greater increases in spit 5 (after the gap in occupation) and spit 4. Morwood's implement accumulation rates, however, indicate that it is only in spit 5 that a dramatic increase occurred, though the trend towards increasing *implement accumulation rates* began much earlier — after spit 11 (1981: Fig. 23; see my Fig. A4/1).

Morwood's depth/age curve (1981: Fig. 19) indicates that spit 6 accumulated over the period ca 4500 BP to ca 4200 BP, spit 7 between ca 5000 BP to ca 4500 BP, and spit 2 began to accumulate about 2300 BP. Based on these dates, implement accumulation rates were relatively low and fluctuating until ca 4000 BP; the highest rate occurred in the latter part of the fourth millennium BP/first half of the third millennium BP, but the most dramatic increase was in the first half of the fourth millennium BP; and, in the latter half of the third millennium BP/second millennium BP, two dramatic *decreases of similar magnitude* occurred. Accumulation rates were very low in the last 2000 years.

Artefact accumulation rates were calculated using Morwood's data (1981: Table 11 and Fig. 23). Trends in the artefact accumulation rates (Fig. 7.24, Table A4/37) are similar to those in the implement accumulation rates, though there are some variations: rates in the lower spits (>4500 BP) increased gradually, with only one decrease (rather than fluctuating); spits 5 and 6 had similar rates (rather than spit 5 having a much higher rate); spit 4 still had the highest rate of accumulation; the most dramatic increase did not occur until spit 4 (rather than spit 5); and dramatic decreases in the last 2860 years are still apparent.

The highest average annual growth rate (+0.27%) occurred between ca 4500 BP and ca 4200 BP (spit 6), although there were also high growth rates between ca 6500 BP and ca 5935 BP (spit 10 with +0.21%) and between ca 3435 BP and ca 2865 BP (spit 4 with +0.13%) (Table A4/37). Substantial decreases (-0.1%) prevailed between ca 2865 BP and ca 1175 BP.

Table A4/37 Native Well 1, central Queensland highlands: rates of implement accumulation, rates of artefact accumulation and average annual growth rates based on data from Morwood 1979 and Morwood 1981: Figure 23 and Table 11. B indicates backed artefacts, P = pirri points recovered from these spits; *italics* = highest number or rate; <u>underline</u> = period with greatest/most dramatic increase.

SPIT	RADIOCARBON AGES YEARS BP LAB. NO.		D/A DATES YEARS BP	DURATION (YEARS)	IMPLEMENT ACCUMULATION RATE (NO./CENT.)	NO. OF ARTEFACTS		ARTEFACT ACCUMULATION RATE (NO./MILL.)	AVERAGE ANNUAL GROWTH RATE %
1			1175– 100	1075	1.2	492	B	458	-0.05
2	1270±70	ANU-2002	2300– 1175	1125	3.6	912	B	811	-0.10
3			2865– 2300	565	17.0	1357	B	2402	-0.10
4			3435– 2865	570	*33.0*	*2469*	*B*	<u>*4332*</u>	+0.13
5			4000– 3435	565	<u>24.0</u>	1192	BP	2110	*
STERILE			4200– 4000	200	0	0		0	-100.00
6	4230±90	ANU-2171	4520– 4200	320	5.1	729	BP	2278	*+0.27*
	4320±90	ANU-2003							
7			4990– 4520	470	2.2	456	BP	970	+0.02
8			5465– 4990	475	2.0	410		863	+0.03
9			5935– 5465	470	1.0	356		757	+0.04
10	6190±100	ANU-2001	6495– 5935	560	1.7	348		621	+0.21
11			7783– 6497	1286	0.9	244		190	-0.05
12			9070– 7783	1287	4.0	476		370	+0.04
13			10,295– 9070	1225	1.7	285		233	+0.07
14	10,910±140	ANU-2034	11,431–10,295	1136	0.9	109		96	+0.04
15			12,747–11,431	1316	1.6	84		64	+0.07
16			14,034–12,747	1287	0.7	29		23	

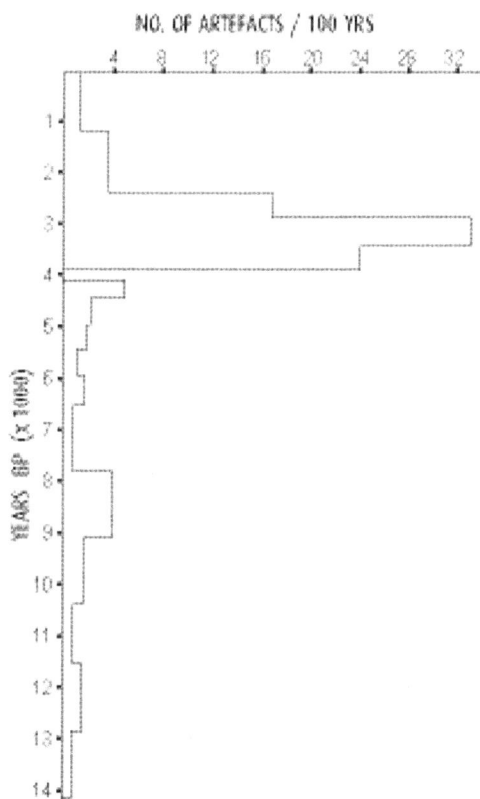

Figure A4/1 Native Well 1, central Queensland highlands: rates of implement accumulation. Redrawn from Morwood 1981:Fig 23.

Native Well 2

Morwood (1981: 38; 1984: 355) dated the initial habitation levels at Native Well 2 at about 11,000 BP (10,770±135 BP, ANU-2035), though data presented suggest the archaeological deposit extends down a further three spits (ca 20cm) beneath the dated level. Based on the distribution of formal implement categories, radiocarbon dates and use of a depth/age curve, Morwood (1981: 37–8) divided the deposit into a tripartite sequence: the earliest, Core and Scraper Industry (spits 21 to 12) lasting from 11,000 BP to ca 4150 BP; Small Tool Industry (spits 11 to 4) ranging from ca 4150 BP to ca 1450 BP; and Recent Industry (spits 3 to 1) dating from ca 1450 BP to contact. The Small Tool Industry was divided into the Early Stone Tool Industry (spits 11 to 9) and the Late Stone Tool Industry (spits 8 to 4).

Morwood (1981: 37) said a sudden increase in *artefact numbers* in spit 11 coincided with a number of technological innovations, and that there was a decrease in artefact numbers in the uppermost three spits. Morwood's artefact distribution data (1981: Table 15 — incorporated into my Table A4/38), however, suggests the increase in artefact numbers in spit 10 (a rise to 315 from 150 in spit 11) was of greater magnitude than that in spit 11 (a rise to 150 from 111 in spit 12). This is supported by the artefact accumulation rates.

Artefact accumulation rates were calculated using Morwood's (1979: Fig. 6.16) depth/age curve and assuming that all spits were ca 10cm in depth (an assumption supported by depths given by Morwood [1981: 37–8] for the spits in which radiocarbon samples were taken). Artefact accumulation rates (Fig. 7.25, Table A4/38) indicate there was:

1.   a very dramatic peak in artefact accumulation rates between ca 2450 BP and ca 2300 BP (spits 9 to 6), which was within the period from ca 3100 BP to ca 2000 BP, where the highest number of artefacts and the highest artefact accumulation rates occurred;

2.   a dramatic increase in artefact accumulation rates in spit 10; that is, between ca 3100 and ca 2450 BP (from 142 artefacts/millennium in spit 11 to 485 artefacts/millennium in spit 10);

3.   decreasing rates in the last 2300 years, with a dramatic decrease ca 2300 BP to 2000 BP (spit 5) and a subsequent substantial decrease between ca 2000 BP and ca 1450 BP (spit 4).

The highest average annual growth rate occurred between ca 2450 BP and ca 2300 BP — spits 9 to 6 with +1.97% (Table A4/38). This is one of the highest average annual growth rates calculated for the sites reviewed, but the time period involved is shorter than those calculated from depth/age curves for many other sites (Tables A4/17 to A4/42). There was also a high growth rate between ca 3100 BP and ca 2450 BP (spit 10 with +0.19%). The growth rate in spit 11 (where Morwood says artefact numbers suddenly increase and a number of technological innovations occur) is much lower than that of spit 10, and is the same as that in spit 12 (+0.02%). Substantial *decreases and negative values* (-0.66% and -0.65%) occurred in the growth rate in two periods — ca 2300 BP to ca 2000 BP (spit 5) and ca 500 BP to ca 100 BP (spit 1).

Kenniff Cave

The oldest radiocarbon date from Kenniff Cave is 18,800±480 BP (ANU-345) (Mulvaney 1975: 155, 288). From this date, Morwood (1984: 339) extrapolated initial occupation back to ca 22,000 BP on the basis of a depth/age curve. The archaeological record at this site is deep and complex. Reversals occur in some of the radiocarbon dates for the lower deposits (Mulvaney and Joyce 1965: Table 2, 169–70) and so the depth/age curve and artefact accumulation rates for layers earlier than ca 4000 BP are even more speculative than those for the later layers. Dates which were excluded in producing a depth/age curve appear in square brackets [] in Table A4/39.

Mulvaney and Joyce (1965: 166–7, 170) considered the shallow depth of deposit between 10,280 BP±180 BP (Gak-646) and 5370±140 BP (Gak-524) and an associated disconformity represented a hiatus in habitation or a period when deposition rates were very low or may have ceased. The number of finds over this length of time was described as 'meagre'. The

Table A4/38 Native Well 2, central Queensland highlands: rates of artefact accumulation and average annual growth rates based on data from Morwood 1979, 1981: Table 15. B indicates backed artefacts, P = pirri points recovered from these spits; *italics* indicates highest number or rate; underline = period with greatest/most dramatic increase.

SPIT	RADIOCARBON AGES YEARS BP LAB. NO.	D/A DATES YEARS BP	DURATION (YEARS)	NO. OF ARTEFACTS		RATE OF ARTEFACT ACCUMULATION (NO./MILLENNIUM)	AVERAGE ANNUAL GROWTH RATE %
1		500– 100	400	5		13	-0.66
2		1000– 500	500	92		184	-0.16
3		1450– 1000	450	182		404	-0.10
4		2000– 1450	550	349	B	635	-0.12
5	2170±80 ANU-2117	2300– 2000	300	375	B	1250	-0.65
6)		–2300)		358	B)		
7)		)		*471*	B)		
8)		)	150	204	B)	*9040*	*+1.97*
9)		2450–)		323	PB)		
10	2470±80 ANU-2091	3100– 2450	650	315	PB	485	+0.19
11		4150– 3100	1050	150	PB	142	+0.02
12		5100– 4150	950	111		117	+0.02
13		6100– 5100	1000	102		102	-0.02
14		7100– 6100	1000	125		125	+0.01
15		8100– 7100	1000	117		117	-0.04
16		9100– 8100	1000	172		172	-0.01
17		10,150– 9100	1050	195		186	-0.04
18	10,770±135 ANU-2035	11,300–10,150	1150	140		121	+0.16
19		12,400–11,300	1100	23		21	+0.05
20		13,500–12,400	1100	13		12	-0.07
21		14,500–13,500	1000	27		27	

Table A4/39 Kenniff Cave, central Queensland highlands: rates of artefact accumulation and average annual growth rates based on data from Mulvaney and Joyce 1965: Tables 2 and 3; Mulvaney 1975: 155, 288. B indicates backed artefacts; p = points; P = Pirri points; E = Elouera recovered in these layers; *italics* indicates highest number or rate; underline = period with greatest/most dramatic increase.

LAYER 1964	DEPTH (cm)	RADIOCARBON AGES YEARS BP LAB. NO.	D/AGE DATES YEARS BP	DURATION (YEARS)	NO. OF ARTEFACTS	RATE OF ARTEFACT ACCUMULATION NO./MILLENNIUM	AVERAGE ANNUAL GROWTH RATE %
1-6			1700– 100	1600	2181	1363	+0.02
1	0– 10		400– 100	300	515	1717	
2	10– 19		800– 400	400	767	1918	
3	19– 32		1050– 800	250	428	1712	
4	32– 36		1350– 1050	300	186	620	
5	36– 41		1550– 1350	200	89	445	
6	41– 43	1600±100 Gak-522	1700– 1550	150	196	1307	

Table A4/39 (Continued)

LAYER 1964	DEPTH (cm)	RADIOCARBON AGES YEARS BP	LAB. NO.	D/AGE DATES YEARS BP	DURATION (YEARS)	NO. OF ARTEFACTS		RATE OF ARTEFACT ACCUMULATION NO./MILLENNIUM	AVERAGE ANNUAL GROWTH RATE %
7-9				**3500- 1700**	**1800**	**1736**		**964**	**-0.004**
7	43- 48			1850- 1700	150	714		4760	
8	48- 61			2300- 1850	450	291	B	647	
9	61- 79	2550±90	NPL-32	3500- 2300	1200	731	pB	609	
10-11				**3900- 3500**	**400**	**415**		**1038**	**-0.25**
10	79- 81			3800- 3500	300	262	pB	873	
11	81- 84	3830±90	NPL-65	3900- 3800	100	153	pB	1530	
12-14				**4200- 3900**	**300**	**837**		**2790**	**+0.05**
12	84- 91			3950- 3900	50	489	pB	9780	
13	91- 95			4050- 3950	100	181	pE	1810	
14	95-105	4130± 90	Gak-523	4200- 4050	150	167	pE	668	
15-19				**5200- 4200**	**1000**	**2394**		**2394**	**+0.11**
15	105-109					592	pPE		
16	109-122					570	pE		
17	122-123					70			
18	123-126	5020±90	NPL-66			736)			
19	126-130	[4650±100	Gak-525]			426)			
				DISCONFORMITY					
20-23				**10,800- 5200**	**5600**	**4669**		**834**	**-0.02**
20	130-138	5370±140	Gak-524	6500- 5200	1300	658		505	
21	138-147			8000- 6500	1500	3002		2001	
22	147-156			9900- 8000	1900	637		335	
23	156-164	10,280±180	Gak-646	10,800- 9900	900	372		413	
24-26				**12,650-10,800**	**1850**	**3855**		**2084**	**+0.01**
24	164-174			11,800-10,800	1000	265		265	
25	174-180			12,250-11,800	450	1911		4247	
26	180-188	12,610±110	NPL-67	12,650-12,250	400	1679		4198	
27-29				**13,700-12,650**	**1050**	**1861**		**1772**	**+0.09**
27/28	188-197			12,850-12,650	200	1490		7450	
29	197-204	12,900±170	NPL-33	13,700-12,850	850	371		437	
30-32				**16,200-13,700**	**2500**	**1794**		**718**	**-0.10**
30	204-213			14,800-13,700	1100	1152		1047	
31	213-222			15,800-14,800	1000	279		279	
32	222-226	16,130±140	NPL-68	16,200-15,800	400	363		908	
33-42				**19,300-16,200**	**3100**	**2827**		**912**	*****
33	226-239			16,500-16,200	300	250		833	
34	239-244			16,675-16,500	175	477		2728	
35	244-249			16,850-16,675	175	277		1583	
36	249-257			17,070-16,850	220	138		627	
37	257-264			17,290-17,070	220	92		418	
38	264-272			17,510-17,290	220	77		350	
39	272-284	[13,200±300	Gak-526]	17,950-17,510	440	449		1020	
40	284-293			18,200-17,950	350	240		686	
41	293-305	[9650±100	Gak-645]	18,500-18,200	300	337		1123	
42	305-328	[9300±200	Gak-527]						
	'336'	18,800±480	ANU-345	19,300-18,500	800	490		613	

vertical distribution of artefacts suggests the deposit between these dates was not sterile. The artefact accumulation rate for this period (834/millennium, see Table A4/39) is slightly higher than the rate for layers 30–32, which is the lowest rate for the sequence. Layers 20–23 and 30–32 may be periods of very low sediment accumulation with lower artefact accumulation rates than other periods, the latter (if not both) being due to less frequent use of the rockshelter for habitation or stone-working activities rather than total human avoidance.

Richardson's (1992, 1996) conjoin analysis, which indicates vertical movements of artefacts up to 50cm and in one case possibly up to 90cm (1996: 85), also adds another dimension to the complexity of the site's archaeological record. However, the implications of Richardson's results for interpreting the overall distribution of artefacts and artefact accumulation rates are not yet clear. The wide fluctuations in the artefact accumulation rates for individual layers could partly reflect original deposition rates as well as subsequent site formation processes (Mulvaney and Joyce 1965: 164–7; Richardson 1992, 1996). Exceedingly high accumulation rates occurred in five individual layers — 7, 12, 25, 26 and 27/28. These rates may be due partially to the short durations assigned to them according to the depth/age curve. In light of the foregoing knowledge, I graphed artefact accumulation rates and calculated average annual growth rates for groups of layers between the radiocarbon dates only and not for individual layers (Fig. 7.26).

Artefact accumulation rates. High accumulation rates occurred in both the Holocene and Pleistocene levels. The highest artefact accumulation rate is in combined Layers 12–14 dating from ca 4200 BP to ca 3900 BP. Very high accumulation rates also occurred in the preceding period (Layers 15–19) and in combined Layers 24–26 dating from ca 12,650 BP to ca 10,800 BP.

Although accumulation rates calculated by Hiscock (1986: 46) for unretouched flakes declined in the last 1600 years relative to the preceding period (i.e., 117 flakes/100 years from ca 1600 BP to contact in contrast with 197 flakes/100 years for the period ca 2500 BP to ca 1600 BP), a slight increase is shown in artefact accumulation rates based on the total artefact numbers taken from Mulvaney and Joyce's (1965) Tables 2 and 3 (Fig. 7.26, Table A4/39). A substantial decreased accumulation rate is, however, seen in the period between ca 3900 BP and ca 3500 BP.

The highest average annual growth rate (+0.11%) was within a period with a high accumulation rate (between ca 5200 BP and ca 4200 BP), but not the highest (Table A4/39). There was also a relatively high growth rate (+0.09%) in the Pleistocene, ca 13,700 to ca 12,650 BP (Layers 29–27). A significant decline in the growth rate occurred between ca 3900 BP and ca 3500 BP (-0.25%), though it was not associated with the lowest accumulation rates.

The Tombs

This rockshelter was inhabited briefly about 9410 BP (Mulvaney and Joyce 1965) and not reoccupied until ca 4400 BP or ca 5000 BP (the latter dates are suggested by radiocarbon dates and a depth/age curve based on Mulvaney and Joyce 1965: Table 5).

Artefact accumulation rates. For a short period, between ca 3600 BP and ca 3400 BP, the highest artefact accumulation rate occurred, but then, over the next 1100 years, the rates decreased dramatically (Fig. 7.27, Table A4/40). The final 2200 years saw a continuing but minor decrease.

The area of each layer of excavated deposit was not equal as the back wall slopes backwards and is undercut, and large rocks were present (Mulvaney and Joyce 1965: 195–7, Fig. 24). Where the back wall is undercut, the deposit extends back further with depth and the area excavated in the middle layers (3 and 4) was greater than in the upper layers. This may account for the higher rates in Layer 3. However, Mulvaney and Joyce's section drawings

(1965, Fig. 24) suggest that the additional deposit excavated due to the undercut back wall was not of such magnitude to account fully for the decreasing trends in the upper levels. The difference between the artefact accumulation rates in Layers 3A and 2 is so great (i.e., a ninefold drop from 2050/millennium to 244/millennium) that a reduction in the artefact accumulation rate also must have been involved.

Average annual growth rates were highest in the period with the highest accumulation rates and the most dramatic increase in accumulation rates (Table A4/40).

Table A4/40   The Tombs (shelter), central Queensland highlands: rates of artefact accumulation and average annual growth rates, based on data from Mulvaney and Joyce 1965: Table 5, Shelter excavation. Bracketed figures represent alternative dates, duration and rates of artefact accumulation depending how depth/age curve is drawn. *Italics* indicates highest number or rate; underline = period with greatest/most dramatic increase.

LEVEL	DEPTH (cm)	RADIOCARBON AGES YEARS BP LAB. NO.	D/A DATES YEARS BP	DURATION (YEARS)	NO. OF ARTEFACTS	RATE OF ARTEFACT ACCUMULATION (NO./MILLENNIUM)	AVERAGE ANNUAL GROWTH RATE %
1	0 – 30.5		2300– 100	2200	345	157	-0.02
2	30.5– 58.5	3400±97 NPL-30	3400–2300	1100	268	244	-0.19
3A	58.5– 81.3		3600–3400	200	410	*2050*	*+0.74*
							(+0.33)
3B	81.3–119.4	3600±93 NPL-31	4500–3600	900	*426*	473	+0.21
			(4000–3600)	(400)		(1065)	(+0.62)
4A	119.4–129.5		5000–4500	500	36	72	*
			(4400–4000)	(400)		(90)	
4B	129.5–205.7				0	0	-100.00
5	205.7–213.4	9410±100 NPL-64			22		
6	213.4–228.6				0		

Comment: central Queensland highlands

In four of the central Queensland highland sites, a dramatic increase in the *artefact accumulation rate* is followed by a dramatic decrease in the uppermost layers. At Kenniff Cave, where habitation began much earlier than in the other sites, the figures suggest that substantial increases and decreases occurred in artefact accumulation rates in the late-Pleistocene/early-Holocene as well as in the late-Holocene.

At Kenniff Cave, the *greatest increase and decrease in the artefact accumulation rates* in the Holocene layers occurred earlier than at the other sites (i.e., between ca 5200 BP and ca 4200 BP for the increase, and between ca 3900 BP and ca 3500 BP for the decrease). There is an increase in the accumulation rates in the uppermost layers (1–6) at Kenniff Cave but they do not reach those of between ca 5200 BP and ca 3900 BP. At the other three sites, the timing of the dramatic increase varied, but always occurred within the period ca 3600 BP to ca 2300 BP.

At The Tombs, the *greatest decrease in the artefact accumulation rate* began in the fourth millennium BP (ca 3400 BP); at Native Wells 1 and 2 in the third millennium BP (ca 2900 BP and ca 2300 BP respectively). It therefore seems that major increases were occurring at some sites at the same time as major decreases were occurring at others.

At Native Well 2, Kenniff Cave and The Tombs, the highest *average annual growth rate* coincided in time with the most dramatic increase in the artefact accumulation rate; at Native Well 1, the highest growth rate occurred earlier. At Native Well 1 and 2 and The Tombs the growth rates declined in the uppermost levels. At Kenniff Cave, while there was a dramatic decrease in the last 3900 years, the final 1700 years had a minor increase in the growth rate.

South-eastern Queensland

At two of the sites excavated in south-eastern Queensland — Maidenwell and Gatton — Morwood (1986) considered the stone artefacts to be concentrated in their middle levels. Subsequent excavations at Platypus Rockshelter and Bushrangers Cave showed diverging trends in the last 2000 years (Hall and Hiscock 1988a, 1988b).

Maidenwell

At Maidenwell, the lowest date, 4300±70 BP (Beta-6924), comes from a depth of 38±4cm. Morwood (1986: 92, 98) concluded that use of the site began ca 4300 BP, though extrapolation from a depth/age curve using 55cm as the depth of the basal spit suggests it was earlier (Table A4/41 — based on Morwood's data [principally Table 1], and assuming a constant rate of sediment accumulation between radiocarbon dates; dates for various levels on my depth/age curve differ slightly from those on Morwood's).

Morwood (1986: 95–8) described the vertical distribution of artefacts in the site as follows: artefacts tended to be concentrated between 15cm and 30cm below the surface, or from about 3000 BP to 1000 BP 'on the basis of linear extrapolation'; at about 1000 BP the 'artefact deposition rate decreased significantly' and the use of backed artefacts may have ceased at this time. 'Backed blades, blade scrapers and axes are not definitely present until ca 2800 BP', when there is 'a significant increase in artefact density' (1986: 98).

The *artefact accumulation rates* which I calculated show similar trends (Fig. 7.28, Table A4/41), though there are two levels which could be said to show 'significant' or substantial increases:

- 'level' 25–30cm, in which the accumulation rate increased from 60 to 172 artefacts/millennium — this is the increase in 'artefact density' Morwood referred to as being about 2800 BP;
- 'level' 15–20cm, in which there was an increase from 245 to 380 artefacts/millennium.

The increase at the time the backed artefacts appeared is not as great as the later one, which is associated with the highest artefact accumulation rate.

The *average annual growth rate* associated with the earliest increase (0.11%) is not as great as that associated with the later increase (+0.18%) (Table A4/41), which occurred well after the backed artefacts appeared.

Gatton

At Gatton, the earliest radiocarbon date is 3820±120 BP (Beta-15811) from a depth of 122±4cm, immediately above bedrock (Morwood 1986: 104). Morwood (1986: 107) considered the majority of stone artefacts occurred in deposits dating between ca 3000 BP and ca 1000 BP. He (1986: 107, 117) believed that from about 3000 BP there were increases in the 'artefact deposition rates', the range of stone tool types and range of knapping debris. Greater numbers of backed artefacts occur in these levels, though they are also present in the earlier deposits.

About 1000 BP, there was a decrease in the quantity and range of knapping debris and the manufacture of backed blades and 'barbs' appears to have ceased. Those found in surface deposits derive from a fossicker's trench (Morwood 1986: 107, Table 5). Morwood (1986: 106, 177) pointed out that deposition rates for faunal remains increased significantly over the last 1000 years, with the upper levels having more than double the number of individuals per spit per 100 years. He (1986: 117) concluded that the increased rates of faunal, charcoal and sediment deposition in the last 1000 years indicate the site was being used more intensively, and that there were general changes in the technology of predation rather than a decrease in activity range and occupational intensity, which the stone artefact distribution pattern suggests.

Artefact accumulation rates were calculated for this site on the basis of the radiocarbon dates and data in Morwood's Table 5 (Table A4/42, Fig. 7.29). Though Morwood (1986: 92) commented that spits averaged between 3–5cm deep, I assumed an average spit depth of 4cm for the calculations on the basis of Table 5. This procedure will have produced rates which are slightly higher or lower than those resulting if the actual depths had been used.

The highest artefact accumulation rates are about 3000 BP. After 2900 BP the rates for individual spits fluctuate widely but all are relatively high. The average accumulation rates for spits between 0cm and 32cm and between 32cm and 68cm suggest the decrease in the artefact accumulation rate in the last 1000 years was not great (i.e., from 1753 artefacts/ millennium to 1576/millennium).

Average annual growth rates. The growth rates fluctuated markedly throughout the period of habitation (Table A4/42). Many spits have high growth rates (>0.1%). The highest growth rates occurred about 3500 BP and 3150 BP (+3.45% and +2.98% respectively; these are the highest rates recorded at any of the sites reviewed, but the artefact numbers are small and the periods of time are short).

Platypus Rockshelter

At Platypus Rockshelter, occupied for some 5000 years (4540±80, Beta-3074), there was an initial increase in the artefact accumulation rates (according to weight rather than number), followed by a decline in the upper two spits representing the last 2400 years (Hall and Hiscock 1988a: 57, Table 1). There was also a decline in the abundance of freshwater mussel shell and animal bone in the upper two spits. Hall and Hiscock (1988a: 59–60) argued, however, that trends in edge-damage and heat-shattering throughout the sequence make it plausible that the intensity of occupation continued to increase and did not decline in the last 2400 years.

Bushrangers Cave

At Bushrangers Cave, first occupied ca 6000 years ago (5540±100, Beta-4852), density figures display a clear bimodal pattern (Hall and Hiscock 1988b: 94, Tables 1 and 3). Artefact accumulation rates in the last 2350 years are generally higher than those of the previous 3350 years (Hall and Hiscock 1988b: 94, Table 2). Highest accumulation rates are in spits 2 and 3, with a much lower figure in Spit 1. Faunal remains have a similar vertical distribution to stone artefacts and, taken together, imply more intensive use of the shelter in the last 2500 years than previously (p. 102). Hall and Hiscock commented that the sharp decline in artefact and bone density in spit 1 is suggestive of the decreased discard rates seen at other eastern Australian sites (p. 103).

Summary: south-east Queensland

The trends in the artefact accumulation rates in Maidenwell, Gatton and Platypus rockshelters and Bushrangers Cave differ markedly with the highest rates and the dramatic increases occurring at different times, and the timing direction of trends varying in the uppermost levels of each site.

Highest artefact accumulation rates at Gatton were about 3300 BP, whereas at Maidenwell, Platypus and Bushrangers they were in the last 1000 years. Dramatic increases in the artefact accumulation rate at each site occurred in different millennia — between ca 4300 BP and ca 4800 BP and again between ca 1400 BP and ca 950 BP at Bushrangers; about 3100 BP at Gatton, between 2600 and 775 BP at Maidenwell, and in the last 1000 years at Platypus. Substantial decreases in the artefact accumulation rates in the final phases of occupation at Bushrangers Cave and Maidenwell occurred in the last 2000 and 1000 years respectively.

Average annual growth rates were calculated only for Maidenwell and Gatton. Gatton has widely fluctuating rates with both negative and positive values, with the highest values in the third millennium BP. Maidenwell's highest growth rate was at the beginning of the first millennium BP.

Table A4/41 Maidenwell, south-eastern Queensland: rates of artefact accumulation and average annual growth rates based on data from Morwood 1986: 92–3, Table 1. B indicates levels with backed artefacts; *italics* = highest number or rate; underline = period with greatest/most dramatic increase.

LEVEL/DEPTH (cm)	RADIOCARBON AGES YEARS BP	LAB. NO.	D/A DATES YEARS BP	DURATION (YEARS)	NO. OF ARTEFACTS		RATE OF ARTEFACT ACCUMULATION NO./MILLENNIUM	AVERAGE ANNUAL GROWTH RATE %
0–5			275– 100	175	12	B	69	-0.16
5–10			525– 275	250	23		92	-0.23
10–15			775– 525	250	41		164	-0.34
15–20			1025– 775	250	95	B	*380*	*+0.18*
20–25	1210±100	SUA-1915	1600–1025	575	141	B	245	+0.06
25–30			2600–1600	1000	*172*	B	172	+0.11
30–35			3650–2600	1050	63		60	+0.05
35–40	4300±70	Beta-6924	4700–3650	1050	36		34	+0.03
40–45			5750–4700	1050	26		25	+0.06
45–50			6750–5750	1000	13		13	*+0.26*
50–55			7750–6750	1000	1		1	

Table A4/42 Gatton, south-eastern Queensland: rates of artefact accumulation and average annual growth rates based on data from Morwood 1986: 104–7, Table 5. B indicates levels with backed artefacts; *italics* = highest number or rate; underline = period with greatest/most dramatic increase.

DEPTH (cm)	RADIOCARBON AGES YEARS BP	LAB. NO.	DEPTH (cm)	D/A DATES YEARS BP	DURATION (YEARS)	NO. OF ARTEFACTS		RATE OF ARTEFACT ACCUMULATION NO./MILLENNIUM	AVERAGE ANNUAL GROWTH RATE %
				180– 100	80	197	B	2463]	+0.28
				320– 180	140	276		1971]	+0.33
				460– 320	140	175		1250]	-0.06
				600– 460	140	191	B	1364]	+0.16
20				740– 600	140	152		1086] 1596	-0.35
				880– 740	140	248		1771]	+0.12
				1020– 880	140	211		1507]	-0.09
	1090±70	Beta-5897	31±2	1172–1020	152	261		1717]	+0.01
				1389–1172	217	367	B	1691]	+0.04
40				1606–1389	217	340	B	1567]	+0.21
				1823–1606	217	214	B	986]	-0.25
				2040–1823	217	366	B	1687] 1756	-0.18
				2257–2040	217	*545*	B	2512]	+0.09
				2474–2257	217	453	B	2088]	0.00
60				2691–2474	217	*453*	B	2088]	+0.25
				2908–2691	217	262	B	1207]	-0.25
	3030±90	Beta-5898	67±2	3050–2908	142	297	B	2902]	-0.45

Table A4/42 (Continued)

DEPTH (cm)	RADIOCARBON AGES YEARS BP LAB. NO.	DEPTH (cm)	D/A DATES YEARS BP	DURATION (YEARS)	NO. OF ARTEFACTS	RATE OF ARTEFACT ACCUMULATION NO./MILLENNIUM	AVERAGE ANNUAL GROWTH RATE %
			3105–3050	55	218 B	*3964*]	+0.61
			3160–3105	55	156 B	<u>2836</u>]	+2.98
80			3215–3160	55	31	564]	-1.44
			3270–3215	55	71	1291]	-0.53
			3325–3270	55	95	1727]	+1.07
			3380–3325	55	53 B	964]	+1.04
			3435–3380	55	30 B	546] 1033	-0.23
100			3490–3435	55	34	618]	-0.97
			3545–3490	55	58 B	1055]	*+3.45*
			3600–3545	55	9	164]	+1.07
			3655–3600	55	5	91]	+0.41
			3710–3655	55	4 B	73]	-1.25
120			3765–3710	55	8	146]	-1.98
	3820±120 Beta-15811	122±4	3820–3765	55	24 B	436]	+2.55
			3875–3820	55	6	109	-1.77
			3930–3875	55	16	291	

www.ingramcontent.com/pod-product-compliance
Lightning Source LLC
Chambersburg PA
CBHW061306270326
41935CB00028B/1846